WHOSE CANADA?

Whose Canada?
Continental Integration, Fortress North America, and the Corporate Agenda

EDITED BY
RICARDO GRINSPUN
AND
YASMINE SHAMSIE

Canadian Centre for Policy Alternatives

McGill-Queen's University Press
Montreal & Kingston · London · Ithaca

© McGill-Queen's University Press 2007
ISBN 978-0-7735-3191-8 (cloth)
ISBN 978-0-7735-3192-5 (paper)

Legal deposit second quarter 2007
Bibliothèque nationale du Québec

© Chapters 4 and 5, Stephen Clarkson and Maria Banda 2007
A section of chapter 8 draws on Andrew Jackson, *Work and Labour in Canada: Critical Issues*, Canadian Scholars Press Incorporated, Toronto, 2005. Reprinted by permission.

Printed in Canada on acid-free paper that is 100% ancient forest free (100% post-consumer recycled), processed chlorine free

This book has been published with the help of a grant from the Canadian Federation for the Humanities and Social Sciences, through the Aid to Scholarly Publications Programme, using funds provided by the Social Sciences and Humanities Research Council of Canada.

McGill-Queen's University Press acknowledges the support of the Canada Council for the Arts for our publishing program. We also acknowledge the financial support of the Government of Canada through the Book Publishing Industry Development Program (BPIDP) for our publishing activities.

Library and Archives Canada Cataloguing in Publication

Whose Canada? : continental integration, fortress North America, and the corporate agenda / edited by Ricardo Grinspun and Yasmine Shamsie.

Co-published by the Canadian Centre for Policy Alternatives.
Includes bibliographical references and index.
ISBN 978-0-7735-3191-8 (bnd)
ISBN 978-0-7735-3192-5 (pbk)

1. North America – Economic integration. 2. Free trade – Canada. 3. Free trade – North America. 4. Canada – Economic policy – 21st century. 5. Canada – Social policy. 6. Canada – Relations – United States. 7. United States – Relations – Canada. 8. National security – North America. 9. Political planning – Canada. I. Grinspun, Ricardo. II. Shamsie, Yasmine. III. Canadian Centre for Policy Alternatives.

HF3211.W48 2007   337.1'7   C2007–900686-8

Typeset in 10/12 Sabon with Frutiger display by True to Type

Contents

Contents

Tables and Figures

Acronyms

9/11	11 September 2001
ACN	Action Canada Network
AD/CVD	antidumping/countervailing duties
AFB	Alternative Federal Budget
AIDS	Acquired Immune Deficiency Syndrome
AIT	Agreement on Internal Trade
APEC	Asia Pacific Economic Cooperation
BC	British Columbia
BCNI	Business Council on National Issues (Canada)
BITS	Bilateral Investment Treaties
BPG	Canada-United States Bi-National Planning Group
BQ	*Bloc Québécois* (Quebec)
BTU	British thermal unit
CAA	*Compañía de Aguas del Aconquija* (Vivendi)
CAE	Canadian Electrical Association
CAF	Canadian Arab Federation
CANCOM	Canada Command
CANSIM	Statistics Canada's socio-economic database
CAP	Canada Assistance Plan
CBC	Canadian Broadcasting Corporation
CBSA	Canada Border Services Agency
CCC	Canadian Chamber of Commerce
CCCE	Canadian Council of Chief Executives
CCIB	Canadian Council for International Business
CCPA	Canadian Centre for Policy Alternatives
CCR	Canadian Council for Refugees
CDIC	Canadian Development and Investment Corporation
CDS	Chief of Defence Staff (Canada)
CEA	Canadian Exporters' Association

CEC	North American Commission for Environmental Cooperation
CEO	chief executive officer
CET	common external tariff
CFE	*Comisión Federal de Electricidad* (Mexican Federal Electricity Commission)
CFIB	Canadian Federation for Independent Business
CFR	Council on Foreign Relations (United States)
CGE	computable general equilibrium
CGE	*Compagnie Générale des Eaux* (Vivendi)
CHA	Canada Health Act
CHC	Canadian Health Coalition
CHST	Canada Health and Social Transfer
CIA	Central Intelligence Agency (United States)
CIPO	Canadian Intellectual Property Office
CLA	Canadian Library Association
CLSC	*Centres locaux de services communautaires* (local centres for community services – Quebec)
CME	Canadian Manufacturers and Exporters
CMEC	Council of Ministers of Education (Canada)
CMT	Country Music Television
COC	Council of Canadians
CPUC	California Public Utilities Commission
CRTC	Canadian Radio-Television and Telecommunications Commission
CSA	Customs Self-Assessment, Canada Customs and Revenue Agency
CSIS	Canadian Security Intelligence Services
CSTEB	Coalition for Secure and Trade-Efficient Borders
CMA	Canadian Manufacturers' Association
CPI	Consumer Price Index
C-TPAT	Customs-Trade Partnership against Terrorism
CUFTA	Canada-United States Free Trade Agreement
CUPE	Canadian Union of Public Employees
CUSP	Canada-United States Partnership
DFAIT	Department of Foreign Affairs and International Trade
DHS	Department of Homeland Security
DI	deep integration
DND	Department of National Defence (Canada)
DOE	Department of Energy (United States)
EI	Employment Insurance Programme
EIA	Energy Information Administration (US Department of Energy)

EMU	European Monetary Union
EPA	Environmental Protection Agency (United States)
EPF	Established Programme Funding
EU	European Union
FAST	Free and Secure Trade
FBI	Federal Bureau of Investigation (United States)
FCCC	UN Framework Convention on Climate Change
FCM	Federation of Canadian Municipalities
FDI	foreign direct investment
FERC	Federal Energy Regulatory Commission (United States)
FIFRA	Federal Insecticide, Fungicide, Rodenticide Act (United States)
FIRA	Foreign Investment Review Agency (Canada)
FTAA	Free Trade Area of the Americas
FTQ	*Fédération des travailleurs et travailleuses du Québec* (Quebec Federation of Labour)
G7–G8	Group of Seven/Group of Eight
GATS	General Agreement on Trade in Services
GATT	General Agreement on Tariffs and Trade
GDP	gross domestic product
GHG	greenhouse gas emissions
GMO	genetically modified organism
GVRD	Greater Vancouver Regional District
HGS	Human Genome Sciences, Inc
HIV	human immunodeficiency virus
IACHR	Inter-American Commission on Human Rights
ICBM	Inter-Continental Ballistic Missile
ICLMG	International Civil Liberties Monitoring Group
ICSID	International Center for Settlement of Investment Disputes
IEA	Initial Environmental Assessment
IJC	International Joint Commission
INS	Immigration and Naturalization Services (United States)
IPP	independent power producer
IRPA	Immigration and Refugee Protection Act (Canada)
IRPP	Institute for Research on Public Policy
ISO	independent systems operator
ITCAN	International Trade Canada
JPAC	Joint Public Advisory Committee
LEA	Local Education Authority
LFC	*Luz y Fuerza Centro* (Central Power and Light – Mexico)
LNG	liquefied natural gas
MASSH	Municipalities, Academic Institutions, Social Services and Health (Canada)

MAI	Multilateral Agreement on Investment
MFN	most favoured nation
MPAA	Motion Picture Association of America (United States)
MSP	Medical Service Plan (British Columbia)
NAAEC	North American Agreement on Environmental Cooperation
NACC	North American Competitiveness Council
NAEWG	North American Energy Working Group
NAFTA	North American Free Trade Agreement
NAM	National Association of Manufacturers (United States)
NAMU	North American Monetary Union
NASPI	North American Security and Prosperity Initiative
NATO	North Atlantic Treaty Organization
NAWAPA	North American Water and Power Authority
NCC	New Country Network
NDP	New Democratic Party (Canada)
NDPD	National Energy Policy Development Group (United States)
NEB	Canadian National Energy Board
NEP	National Energy Policy
NGO	non-governmental organization
NIH	National Institutes of Health (United States)
NMD	National Missile Defense (United States)
NORAD	North American Aerospace Defense Command
NORTHCOM	Northern Command (United States)
NSEERS	National Security Exit-Entry Registration System (United States)
OCP	Our Canada Project
OECD	Organization for Economic Cooperation and Development
OHRC	Ontario Human Rights Commission
OISE/UT	Ontario Institute for Studies in Education, University of Toronto
OPEC	Organization of Petroleum Exporting Countries
OSFI	Office of the Superintendent of Financial Institutions (Canada)
P3S	public-private partnerships
PAN	*Partido Acción Nacional* (National Action Party – Mexico)
PMRA	Pest Management Regulatory Agency
PPM	part per million
PQ	*Parti Québécois*
PRI	*Partido de la Revolución Institucional* (Party of the Institutional Revolution – Mexico)
PRI	Policy Research Initiative (Canada)
PTO	Participating Transmission Owner

PUC	Public Utility Commission
QLP	Quebec Liberal Party
R&D	research and development
RCMP	Royal Canadian Mounted Police
REA	*Régime Épargne-Actions* (Quebec Stock Saving Plan)
RTO	Regional Transmission Organization
SACU	South African Customs Union
SAGD	Steam Assisted Gravity Drainage
SAGIT	Sectoral Advisory Group on International Trade
SAP	structural adjustment program
SCC	Supreme Court of Canada
SCFAIT	Standing Committee on Foreign Affairs and International Trade (Canadian House of Commons)
SDI	*Société de développement industriel* (Industrial Development Society – Quebec)
SEA	strategic environmental assessment
SEN	*Sistema Eléctrico Nacional* (Mexican National Electricity System)
SGF	*Société générale de financement* (General Financing Society – Quebec)
SIRC	Security Intelligence Review Committee
SMD	Standard Market Design
SPP	Security and Prosperity Partnership of North America
STATSCAN	Statistics Canada
SUFA	Social Union Framework Agreement
TCF	trillion cubic feet
TINA	"there is no alternative"
TNC	trans-national corporation
TRIPS	Trade Related Aspects of Intellectual Property Rights
TRLS	Trade Remedy Laws
UI	unemployment insurance
UNCTAD	United Nations Conference on Trade and Development
UNEP	United Nations Environment Programme
UNESCO	United Nations Education, Scientific and Cultural Organization
UNHCR	United Nations High Commissioner for Refugees
UPS	United Parcel Services of America
US	United States
USAID	US Agency for International Development
USTR	US Trade Representative
VER	voluntary export restriction
WMD	weapons of mass destruction
WTO	World Trade Organization

Acknowledgments

Preparing *Whose Canada?* was a collective effort, and we gratefully acknowledge the contributions of a number of people and organizations. We were inspired by Aurèle Parisien, then at McGill-Queen's University Press (MQUP), who first raised the idea for this volume and who provided untiring support throughout the first stages of the journey.

Nearly all of the chapters in this volume were presented in draft form at a conference held at York University in Toronto, hosted jointly by York's Centre for Research on Latin America and the Caribbean (CERLAC) and the Canadian Centre for Policy Alternatives (CCPA) in Ottawa. Many individuals made the event a success, especially conference coordinator Phillip Stuart Courneyeur, with his passionate commitment and expertise. Equally committed and effective was Eduardo Sousa from the Council of Canadians, who, with a team of volunteers, coordinated a public teach-in on the evening prior to the conference. The conference and teach-in were co-sponsored by the Council of Canadians, the Centre for Social Justice, Common Frontiers-Canada, and the Making the Links Coalition. These events were made possible by generous financial contributions from the Social Sciences and Humanities Research Council of Canada (SSHRC), CCPA, CERLAC, the Canadian Auto Workers Union, the Canadian Labour Congress, and Leo Panitch (Canada Research Chair in Comparative Political Economy), as well as the support from various offices and departments at York University.

Our greatest debt is to the contributors to *Whose Canada?*, who shared their expertise in the many subjects they tackled. We have benefited immensely from their collaboration and would like to thank this stimulating and dedicated group of scholars, researchers, and social activists for their tremendous work and enthusiasm. The sponsorship of the CCPA and, in particular, the unwavering support of its executive director Bruce Campbell, deserve a special thanks. Bruce served as co-chair of the conference at York and contributed to making this book possible in more ways than can be said in words. Most of the book's contributors have been associated with the CCPA, and the CCPA, through a quarter century of progressive policy analysis, has contributed much to the intellectual foundation of this book. We hope that this book will, in turn, contribute to future work.

We extend our thanks as well to Nisreen Furniturewala, Timothy D. Clark, and Jon Lindemann for their editorial assistance, and especially to Ian T. MacDonald for preparing the conference report, for editorial assistance, and for preparing the list of acronyms. We are grateful to Ian T. MacDonald and Timothy D. Clark for compiling a thorough and comprehensive index. The comments on an earlier draft by two anonymous reviewers provided by MQUP were extremely helpful. At MQUP, we thank Jonathan Joseph Crago and Joan McGilvray for their professional and keen support, and Joanne Richardson, our copyeditor, for her assiduous editing and enthusiastic encouragement. CERLAC provided the ideal institutional home for the preparation of this volume. At every stage of this project, we received advice, encouragement, and help from Viviana Patroni, CERLAC's director, as well as Liisa North, Louis Lefeber, and other CERLAC colleagues. We are also deeply grateful to Benjamin Cornejo, Marshall Beck, Shana Yael Shubs, and John Carlaw for their terrific support. Further, a number of graduate assistants and volunteers provided invaluable support at various stages of the project.

We are thankful to Wilfrid Laurier University's Research Office and York's Sabbatical Leave Fellowship Fund for financially supporting this project. This book has been published with the help of a grant from the Canadian Federation for the Humanities and Social Sciences, through the Aid to Scholarly Publications Programme, using funds provided by the Social Sciences and Humanities Research Council of Canada.

Finally, we would like to acknowledge the support and encouragement of our colleagues, friends, and family. But, above all, our spouses, Doris Grinspun and Michael Colton, need to be singled out for their crucial contributions to this book as insightful readers, shrewd critics, and steadfast supporters.

Ricardo Grinspun and Yasmine Shamsie

Foreword

MAUDE BARLOW

This book addresses the most pressing issue facing Canadians today – our nation's future in Fortress North America. Not since 1984, when newly elected Prime Minister Brian Mulroney announced to a blue chip business audience in New York City that Canada was "open for business," has the groundwork been laid for such major structural change in Canada's relations with the United States.

The same economic and political elite that advanced the Canada-US Free Trade Agreement twenty years ago is back in full force advancing their ambitious agenda of deep continental integration. The grandiose plan includes a North American common market, trade bloc, passport, refugee and immigration systems, resource pact, public policy harmonization, and border regulations, all wrapped up in a North American security perimeter secured from Washington. The call for such a radical vision comes in the wake of September 11 and the growing fears in the US heartland about security – at home and abroad. Canada's big business community contends that, in order to salvage the cross-border trade advances made with the North American Free Trade Agreement (NAFTA), Canada must offer secured borders and whatever else it will take to satisfy the Washington administration that we are "safe" trading partners.

The Canadian Council of Chief Executives (CCCE), which has never stopped campaigning for lower standards for cross-border trade, calls this project the North American Security and Prosperity Initiative, and it must have been delighted when the heads of state of the three countries adopted the same slogan at their March 2005 summit in Waco, Texas, and launched the North American Security and Prosperity Partnership. To top it up, Prime Minister Stephen Harper named ten corporate executives to the new North American Competitiveness Council formed at the trilateral leaders' summit held in March 2006 in Cancun, Mexico. This development puts business leaders in the driver's seat and gives them the green light to advance a North American model for business security and prosperity.

Already, to satisfy US security concerns, significant changes have been made to a wide range of practices, including refugee and immigration procedures, anti-terrorism legislation, and regulatory policies. Canada's increasing entanglement in a counter-insurgency war in Afghanistan, initiated by a Liberal government and deepened under a Conservative one, signals that George W. Bush's "War on Terror" has become official policy in Ottawa. Greater strategic and defence integration under US command was the order of the day when the Harper government announced huge increases in military budgets and a shopping spree for new hardware. For the CCCE, however, and its allies in the C.D. Howe Institute as well as the Liberal and Conservative parties, these changes are just the beginning.

In *Whose Canada?* you will find the views and concerns of the most engaged thinkers and activists in our country. The social, cultural, environmental, and foreign policy legacy of NAFTA is brilliantly laid out, and this analysis stands in stark contrast to the daily dose of NAFTA cheerleading to be found in our mainstream media. Twenty years of neoliberal policies have profoundly changed Canada and these changes are documented here in detail, as are the myriad of forces that have come together to advance the agenda Brian Mulroney laid out in New York that fall day so long ago. In response to the question *Whose Canada?* the authors forcefully argue that Canada's future must be shaped by its citizens, not by its elites. In doing so, they present a citizen's agenda for Canada in North America and the world and leave us with great hope that another future is possible.

The issues dealt with in this remarkable book, beautifully crafted by editors Ricardo Grinspun and Yasmine Shamsie, are the core questions of our era. For Canadians, in essence, what is at stake is the kind of society in which we live, the legacy we will leave for our children, and Canada's role within a troubled world. Canada must play a role at home and abroad in seeking justice for all. In the end, justice is the only reliable security for the world.

PART ONE

Context and Overview

1

Canada, Free Trade, and "Deep Integration" in North America: Context, Problems, and Challenges

RICARDO GRINSPUN AND YASMINE SHAMSIE

Close to two decades have passed since the Canada-US Free Trade Agreement (CUFTA) and the North American Free Trade Agreement (NAFTA) went into effect (1/1/89 and 1/1/94, respectively), yet they remain central to Canadian public policy and the Canadian psyche. Questions and concerns regarding the scope and depth of our bilateral relationship with the US loom even larger since the 11 September 2001 attacks in New York and Washington. This volume spotlights these themes.

A central objective of this book is to reflect on almost two decades of free trade. Several authors assess progress or deterioration in such key areas as trade and economics, social policy, culture, environment, and natural resources within the current context of Canada-US relations, defined as they are by September 11 and the US policy transformations that followed. We also chronicle Canadian business responses to 9/11 and policy shifts enacted by the Bush administration by examining the corporate sector's proposals (both incremental and comprehensive) for Canadian alignment with US geostrategic goals and for strengthening security, resource, social, and economic integration. Contributors also explore the political drive towards that alignment, which has been strengthened significantly under the Stephen Harper-led Conservative government. We argue that the notion of a "slippery slope" (as raised by CUFTA and NAFTA opponents) was accurate – especially their belief that one step towards integration would generate pressure for further steps. We outline a number of possible scenarios for Canada's future and its ongoing relationship with Washington, and we suggest that another Canada is possible – one in which people resist integration and deepen their democracy.

Over the past two decades Canada has pursued numerous bilateral and regional free trade agreements, aggressively supported multilateral trade liberalization through the establishment of the World Trade Organization (WTO), and supported WTO expansion. A core theme in this volume is that trade and investment policies should not be examined and evaluated in isolation as they are part of a broader set of neoliberal policies aimed at economic restructuring and societal transformation. In Canada, such federal policies have included withdrawal from social services, distributing authority to provincial governments, privatizing state enterprises, deregulating markets, cutting government programs, downsizing civil services, and shifting tax burdens from corporations to citizens (Clarkson 2002b, 4–5).

While many governments in the North and South have adopted neoliberal policies, Canada's restructuring experience is unique in that reform adoption has been closely linked to continued integration with the United States. Canada's economic and political elites have simultaneously pushed for economic restructuring *and* for integration with the United States, using one as a tool to advance the other. A second major theme in this volume is that Canadian elites have exploited the September 11 crisis to pursue a new, broader phase of integration with Washington. This follows two decades during which transnational (particularly US-based) capital has secured a greater role in the Canadian economy. Some see this trend as effectively transforming Canada into the definitive US client state (Panitch 1994). Thus deeper North American integration has played a central role in defining the direction of our public policy by complementing and reinforcing the "structural adjustment" of our economy and society.

The objective of structural adjustment has always been to reshape the state. Some authors have described this as the "downsizing" of the state, but this term should be used with caution. While the nature of state intervention has changed, its role has not necessarily diminished (Panitch 1994, 63). True, the Canadian state has been withdrawing from some of its earlier functions: the 1995 federal budget of then finance minister Paul Martin included major cuts in areas related to economic equity, social services, regional development, and environmental and health regulations, among others (Dobbin 2003). While downsizing seems to fit this situation, the state has concurrently strengthened its role in other areas, such as securing and protecting the interests of transnational capital (e.g., corporate tax cuts), assisting Canadian capital in becoming more global (e.g., investment liberalization), fortifying investors' rights (e.g., stronger intellectual property rights), controlling counter-hegemonic groups (e.g., "anti-terrorist" bills), and supporting US strategic objectives (e.g., increased military integration). These actions suggest that the likely outcome of deeper integration in North America is not the downsizing or disappearance of the Canadian state but, rather, its transformation into an economic and strategic appendage of a North American corporate class and broader US global interests. Several authors explore this theme.

The debate over "free trade" polarized Canadian public opinion during the late 1980s and continues today to be a controversial subject. As is always the case where public policy is concerned, there is no "objective" academic analysis of this topic (Grinspun and Cameron 1993). This book is no exception. The contributors to this volume believe that differences in values, societal perspectives, and visions of the future are at the root of these debates. This is, therefore, not an analytical debate that can be resolved by simple recourse to factual evidence and logical deduction. Indeed, the authors are sceptical of the claims made, particularly by main-stream economists, that these questions can be resolved by an "objective" application of positive science. While we have insisted on rigorous schol-arly analysis and a careful consideration of the data and historical evi-dence, we also recognize that we owe the reader an honest account of the value-laden perspectives we bring to this debate. Our approach explicitly prioritizes a particular set of values (such as social justice and sustainabil-ity); a particular vision of Canada (as a socially advanced, democratic, and tolerant society at the northern tip of the Americas); and a view of human-kind as torn by conflict and inequities but clinging ardently to the belief that another world is possible.

Still, it is important to recognize major political and economic barriers to implementing such a vision in Canada – particularly the entrenched power of corporate capital, the acquiescent nature of our political class (both Liberal and Conservative), and the ever-powerful influence of our neighbour to the south. Those barriers have become more imposing since a right-wing Conservative government, with Stephen Harper as prime min-ister, assumed power in 2006.

The social and economic restructuring that has taken place in Canada under the aegis of free trade and increased alignment with US policies has already narrowed existing democratic spaces. In this volume we pay par-ticular attention to the loss of policy autonomy resulting from trade and investment agreements. These trade agreements serve as "conditioning frameworks" – that is, as institutional mechanisms that effectively restrict policy choices at the nation-state level (Grinspun and Kreklewich 1994). Conditioning frameworks become binding due to international constraints and obligations incurred to other countries or foreign investors. Particu-larly striking is the fact that domestic elites have used these international obligations to impose policies that would not otherwise meet with general domestic support. When applying a related concept, Stephen Clarkson warns of the "supraconstitutional" nature of these trade agreements and suggests that they create "a new mode of economic regulation with such broad scope and such unusual judicial authority" that they are capable of transforming the present political order. He explains that "the constitu-tional significance for Canada of the five major elements of NAFTA and the

WTO ... [are] their norms, limits on government, rights, adjudication procedures, and enforcement mechanisms" (Clarkson 2002b, 50).[1]

Although Canada can technically withdraw from these trade agreements, essentially they represent a one-way street. Because they lock in
reforms and diminish the democratic choices of Canadians, the growing
number of these conditioning frameworks is of significant concern. CUFTA
and NAFTA were the most important examples in the early 1990s; they have
since been joined by the WTO's multilateral framework. Governments currently face a more complex, layered, and restrictive mesh of external con-
stitutions in the form of numerous trade and investment agreements,[2]
future agreements related to ongoing WTO negotiations, a proposed (but
currently stalled) Free Trade Area of the Americas (FTAA), and the potential of new trade negotiations with the United States, with or without the
inclusion of Mexico.

The restrictions that these trade and investment agreements place on
domestic policy making would be less worrisome if they resulted in
favourable social and economic trends, but the opposite is the case.
Although mainstream economists and business representatives point to
positive macroeconomic performance and the tremendous expansion of
bilateral trade and investment exchange with the United States, the accumulation of wealth obscures the erosion of the social fabric and the ecological bases of life in Canada. In the views of our contributors, these
trends have worsened under free trade policies and deepening economic
integration with the United States – a country characterized by unchecked
capitalism, corporate rule, and rampant consumerism.

The contributing authors argue that conditioning frameworks have
allowed right-wing politicians to deploy the so-called "TINA argument"
("there is no alternative") to promote neoliberal reforms. Various governments have exploited this argument of inevitability to scale back their
responsibility in such areas as social policy, regional development, and
environmental protection. This approach has created a de facto "policy
chill" that is exerting a stronger impact than are the actual constraints
faced by policy makers.

The authors of this volume refuse to be cornered into inevitability: they
believe that there is a window of opportunity to present Canadians with a
fresh public policy vision. Despite policy constraints imposed by free trade
agreements, federal, provincial, and local governments in Canada still
control many policy levers that can be used to reverse these negative trends
and to take a different path. However, this opening will not last forever,
and progressive change will not come about without coordination and
strong effort. The authors recognize that a further slide down the integration slope is likely to reduce both the usefulness and effectiveness of policy
levers and, therefore, governments should focus on the dual objectives of

preventing further integration and preserving and enhancing existing policy-making space.

To achieve these objectives, Canadians must mobilize and assert their values and their vision of the future, and they must elect politicians and governments that reflect those values. We believe that a majority of Canadians share many of the values we espouse. In his book *Fire and Ice: The United States, Canada, and the Myth of Converging Values*, pollster Michael Adams uses extensive data on social values to counter the commonly held assumption that Canada has become Americanized. According to him, there is in fact a growing cultural divide between the two countries (Adams 2003).[3] It is therefore doubtful that Canadians would support further integration with the United States if they viewed the process as preventing their elected representatives from acting in accordance with their values in key areas. Results from other polls and studies support these findings (see Wolfe and Mendelsohn 2004). A March 2004 Ipsos-Reid poll conducted on behalf of the Council of Canadians and the Polaris Institute showed that a vast majority of Canadians (91 percent) agree with the statement "Canada should maintain the ability to set its own independent environmental health and safety standards and regulations, even if this might reduce cross-border trade opportunities with the United States." In addition, 90 percent of the respondents believe that "Canada should establish an energy policy that provides reliable supplies of oil, gas and electricity at stable prices and ... protection of the environment, even if this means placing restrictions on exports and foreign ownership of Canadian supplies" (Ipsos-Reid 2004).

Facing a disjuncture between core values (as expressed in polls) and the economic and political interests of elites, it appears that Canadians have arrived at a critical crossroads. They can continue to be dragged to the right, down a one-way road towards deeper integration with the United States and a continued loss of autonomy, or they can turn left and take on the arduous but worthwhile task of nurturing a democratic, tolerant, equitable, and sustainable society. The authors of this book reject the former and make a case for the latter, calling on governments at all levels to align their policies with the values of the Canadian majority.

A word needs to be said on the focus and research agenda of this volume. First, although a few chapters touch on Mexico, the book is about Canada and Canada-us integration. Furthermore, while we offer this as a comprehensive volume, some important gaps remain due to practical considerations such as author availability, time, and space limitations. The pursuit of any academic analysis oriented towards a progressive perspective of and agenda for North America is an ongoing process, of which this work is but one modest contribution. It is a challenge that others will no doubt take up, and we hope this book encourages such efforts. Furthermore, this work is a unique venture in that it brings together academics, researchers, and activists. As a result, the chapters vary in style, with some prepared as scholarly contributions and others having the form of political essays. The sum of these efforts provides a rich introduction to progressive perspectives on deep integration.

In this introductory chapter we present a summary of the context, problems, and challenges for Canada in light of deeper North American integration, drawing extensively, but not exclusively, on the chapters that follow. In an effort to present a comprehensive and self-contained overview, this chapter does not follow the parts and chapters in this book in a linear fashion but, rather, draws from them as it builds its argument. The chapter is divided into nine thematic sections. The first three sections focus on the economic record of free trade, its impact on essential services and public policy, and on the environment and natural resources. The middle three sections focus on various aspects of the "deep integration" agenda: September 11 and its aftermath as it concerns Canada, the merging of trade and security agendas, and the framing of the deep integration debate. In the final sections we offer an alternative policy vision and a description of the challenges associated with building a resistance movement.

ECONOMIC INTEGRATION: DUBIOUS BENEFITS, TROUBLING PROSPECTS

Canada's free trade debates of the 1980s and 1990s have evolved into debates on the benefits and drawbacks of globalization, North American integration, and US geo-strategic leadership. Both sides are reflecting upon how Canadian and North American economies and societies have changed since the early 1980s and the impacts of free trade. New data have become available, thus allowing analysts to develop more nuanced perspectives, yet their views can still be divided into two camps (Espinosa et al. 2002). Those who favoured free trade in the 1980s exaggerated the expected benefits and minimized the costs associated with proposed trade agreements, with some academic studies being instrumental in promoting bilateral negotiations. Richard Harris and David Cox's study (1983) (sponsored by the Macdonald Commission)[4] received wide public exposure in the mid-1980s. They predicted significant economic benefits for Canada from free trade, including a 9 percent gain in aggregate Canadian welfare, a 28 percent boost in real wages, an almost 30 percent increase in labour productivity, and a 100 percent increase in the volume of bilateral Canada-US trade. Furthermore, they predicted a 225 percent increase in average output per firm in the manufacturing sector (Harris and Cox 1983, 173). Although their methods and results were later challenged (Stanford 1993), the study had a strong political impact. In retrospect, projections of this type constituted a poor guide to understanding the consequences of free trade on the Canadian economy and society (see chapter 8 by Andrew Jackson).

Similar sanguine claims were made regarding access to the US market. In 1986 Alan Rugman (1986, 7) argued that "the emergence of US 'contingent protection,' as institutionalized in US trade laws establishing rules for the imposition of countervailing duties, anti-dumping measures and escape clause actions, implies that a US-Canadian comprehensive trade agreement is required to guarantee Canadian exporters access to US markets." Rugman and other academics insisted that such a comprehensive agreement would protect Canadian exporters from arbitrary and unilateral forms of US protectionism. However, as today's Canadian exporters of beef, lumber, potatoes, and various other products can attest, these promises have remained largely unrealized. The fact that current initiatives to advance deeper integration are premised upon achieving the same elusive security of access to the US market confirms the failure of earlier deals. As Jackson argues in his chapter, CUFTA and NAFTA ultimately failed to address these crucial forms of US protectionism; the much-touted dispute settlement mechanisms of NAFTA have been of little help.[5]

Those who supported CUFTA and NAFTA in the 1980s and 1990s are currently walking a fine line as they try to dampen previous expectations of huge gains while simultaneously asserting that the results of these trade agreements have been highly positive. On the occasion of the tenth anniversary of CUFTA, Richard Lipsey summarized the existing evidence on "real results versus unreal expectations" as follows:

The FTA was a far less dramatic policy initiative than its critics assumed. In trade policy, it continued, and nearly completed, the process of reducing trade barriers that began in the 1930s. In broader economic policy, it was part of a new package of reforms that increased the degree of openness of the Canadian economy to market forces. On both counts, it was a marked success – as well as making Canadian access to the US market more secure than ever before. (Lipsey 2000, 106)

This attempt to dampen expectations contrasts sharply with claims made by the Canadian government in 1987 that CUFTA was "the most important trade agreement Canada has ever concluded ... the culmination of almost one hundred years of Canadian efforts to secure open and stable markets."[6] Clearly, advocates have been adept at heightening expectations when trade deals are debated and negotiated, only to tone them down when the time comes to evaluate their impacts. One should be mindful of this fact as business lobbies again push for a "leap of faith" regarding the perceived benefits of deeper integration with the United States. It also provides food for thought when assessing claims that "this time" we will achieve the ever-elusive secure market access we seek (Jackson 2003).[7]

As in the past, current calls for a new phase of economic integration are being framed in terms of productivity and income gaps between Canada and the United States – an echo of the 1980s Macdonald Commission. When launching a government research initiative on North American link-ages in 2001, then deputy minister of industry Peter Harder (2001, 10) reminded participants that

Canada continues to lag behind the United States in productivity and income levels. If we do not want to fall further behind the benchmark US economy, we must focus more on innovation and productivity ... This is why Industry Canada, in partner-ship with other government departments, has embarked on an ambitious research program to look at North American linkage issues ... to ensure that Canadians are informed of the consequences, the possibilities and the realities of deeper integra-tion within the North American context.

The deputy minister failed to explain how new agreements would achieve such a convergence in productivity and income in light of earlier failures.

Assessing the impacts of free trade is strategically important since the logic that previous deals were beneficial for Canadians serves as the ration-ale for intensifying economic engagement. Thus, the effort to advance an optimistic evaluation of free trade (L.I. MacDonald 2000) should not be surprising. A primary goal of this volume is to provide some balance to that debate by introducing a measure of scepticism regarding benefits that have allegedly flowed from free trade and those that might flow from further integration.

Several chapters address the economic record of free trade. Andrew Jackson (chapter 8) provides a careful and detailed assessment of actual (as opposed to promised) impacts of increased economic integration with the United States on the Canadian economy. He argues that economic gains from CUFTA have been dismal, that manufacturing productivity has stag-nated, that a positive restructuring of Canadian industry has failed to take place, and that the Canadian economy's age-old problems (i.e., an exces-sive dependence on natural resources and an underdeveloped "knowledge-based" economy) have yet to be resolved.

In chapter 9 Mario Seccareccia addresses a poorly understood aspect of economic policy: the interaction between trade liberalization and macro-economic adjustment. He confirms that notable growth in Canada's export sector was brought about in part by CUFTA and NAFTA, which removed some institutional barriers to trade. However, he also identifies more impor-tant contributing factors in this growth spurt as the macroeconomic and monetarist policies leading to a lower exchange rate, depressed wages and prices, and restrained domestic growth. These policies resulted in greater growth in internationally traded goods production in Canada, largely at the expense of the domestic economy. As a result, the Canadian economy has become more crisis-prone and vulnerable to international shocks.

As for the impact of economic integration on wages, income distribution, and social programs, several contributors argue that these indicators have proven equally disappointing. For example, Jackson documents pressure for convergence in the areas of economic and social policy and suggests that concerns expressed by critics prior to CUFTA's implementation regarding the potential for "downward harmonization" to the US social model "were amply justified." Also worrisome, he suggests, is the fact that economic integration has "tilted the political scales against rebuilding and renewing the damaged but still intact Canadian social model" (chapter 8, 230).

In chapter 10 David Robinson focuses on the impacts of CUFTA and NAFTA on labour. He argues that both trade deals have had a devastating effect on unionized labour in Canada in that they have reduced bargaining power and worker benefits. He highlights the dismal performance of the Canadian labour market in the wake of trade liberalization over the past decade and considers the potential impact of further economic integration. A variety of factors were to blame for the deterioration of the labour market in the 1990s, including, centrally, the negative impact of high interest rates and fiscal retrenchment on the Canadian economy in the early part of the last decade. However, while restrictive monetary and fiscal policies were clearly the key drivers of the great slump of the 1990s, there are nevertheless strong links between these policies and Canada's deepening economic integration with the United States. Robinson argues that, while Ottawa retains considerable manoeuvring room when it comes to maintaining higher labour and social standards, deeper integration will nevertheless intensify the pressures to harmonize such standards downward.

In chapter 11 Marc Lee focuses on what is widely believed to be the next phase of greater economic integration between Canada and the United States – some form of a "customs union." But, as he points out, what is being proposed under that banner is not necessarily clear and consistent. Lee describes the various degrees of possible economic integration (from free trade areas to customs unions to single markets)[8] and how they relate to the proposals advanced so far. He then assesses the potential benefits of a customs union and examines the implications of a common trade policy with the United States. Lee also looks at the issue of trade remedy measures, considered a major irritant for Canada in its trade relations with the United States. He concludes that the likely benefits of a customs union are small and frequently overstated by its promoters. He identifies serious economic and political costs associated with this economic arrangement, including risks associated with the actual negotiation. For instance, expanding the

scope of a negotiation beyond a simple customs union could offer significant gains (e.g., exemptions from US trade remedy laws) but with costs and
risks that Canadians are unlikely to support.

Monetary integration is one of the most controversial issues addressed in
this book. At one level, such integration has been taking place for quite
some time, with the Bank of Canada increasingly coordinating its monetary policies with those of the US Federal Reserve. Seccareccia addresses
pressures for institutional change that could bring about greater monetary
integration in North America, including proposals for a monetary union.[9]
There has even been support in some quarters for the establishment of
"optimal currency" areas, the most spectacular example being the emergence of the European Economic and Monetary Union (EMU) with the
launching of the euro in 1999. However, given the existing power inequalities within North America, what is at stake here is the continued existence
of an independent monetary policy and the eventual transformation of the
Bank of Canada into a de facto branch of the US Federal Reserve. Seccareccia argues that the establishment of any monetary union would have
serious implications (especially for the role of the state) that few Canadians would deem desirable. Public unease explains why further monetary
integration has been rejected to date as an unviable political proposition,
with proposals from the assimilationist Fraser Institute standing out as
an exception. The proposal might re-emerge if and when other facets of
economic integration reach a level requiring greater monetary integration.

COSTING FREE TRADE:
IMPACTS ON ESSENTIAL SERVICES AND PUBLIC POLICY

The number of international trade agreements has expanded dramatically
in the past two decades. Steven Shrybman (chapter 12) argues that even
more remarkable than the increase in quantity is the extraordinary extension of the scope of these agreements to include areas of law, public policy,
and government services that have previously been considered strictly
domestic matters. Not unexpectedly, transnational corporations and Canadian trade negotiators have actively fought for provisions that eliminate or
strongly diminish trade and investment barriers. According to Kathy Corrigan (chapter 13), the main problem with this policy objective is that
almost any tax, subsidy, or regulation – practically any law made by any
government – has great potential to conflict with Canada's new international trade commitments. Jim Grieshaber-Otto, Scott Sinclair, and Ricardo
Grinspun make a similar point in chapter 14, arguing that new trade deals
are structured to give inordinately strong protections to private foreign
investors while limiting the ability of governments to pursue policies in the
public interest, including health care.

One of the most controversial areas of expansion has been the incorpo-ration of enforceable investor rights that supersede domestic law – the focus of Shrybman's chapter. These provisions have opened the door for investors – most often transnational corporations that are not signatories to trade agreements – to seek recourse via unaccountable and secretive trade tribunals for legislation deemed damaging to their interests, includ-ing in areas where they have yet to invest. Nowhere is the issue of investor rights more relevant than in North America. NAFTA's infamous Chapter 11 has already led to numerous lawsuits against member states, millions of dollars in damages, overturned laws, and aborted legislative proposals.

Grieshaber-Otto, Sinclair, and Grinspun focus on the Canadian health care system, which is currently being transformed by incremental commer-cialization, public-private partnerships, and outsourcing, and which has been the target of major reports arguing for larger structural changes, health accords, and a Supreme Court judgment that are all likely to facili-tate commercialization. While the commercial thrust of these reforms is worrisome in and of itself, the authors argue that specific features of Canada's trade commitments in NAFTA and the General Agreement on Trade in Services (GATS) threaten to make such reforms difficult to stop and costly to reverse. Accordingly, they believe that once foreign corporations acquire a greater role in health care insurance and delivery, Canadian federal and provincial governments will be hampered in their ability to reg-ulate the system and return services to the public sphere. Although those same governments argue that health care is protected by exemptions, the contributors note the inadequacy and fragility of these provisions once commercialization has been initiated. They also examine the potential of future trade deals (including an expanded GATS, new free trade agreements, and proposals for deeper integration with the United States) to further erode governmental capacity to maintain the public and universal nature of the Canadian health care system.

Kathy Corrigan (chapter 13) looks at the implications of trade treaties for public policy at the subnational level, particularly in the areas of edu-cation and municipal services. Although presently considered a service almost exclusively funded by public agencies, education has the potential to become a very profitable industry if privatized. Tentative steps in this direction are being taken in many provinces: proposals have been made to increase funding to private schools, and some pressure is being put on school boards to outsource services and to adopt corporate models of gov-ernance. If it becomes a marketable commodity, education will likely fall within the mandate of the GATS framework of rules that address govern-ment policies, laws, or regulations deemed inconsistent with trade liberal-ization provisions, thereby threatening a wide range of government statutes and services. Furthermore, GATS is being renegotiated to place more government services under its umbrella of provisions and to establish new obligations regarding domestic regulations, procurement, and subsidies. In response, some local governments are reconsidering policies aimed at privatizing municipal services – for example, deciding against public-private partnerships in the provision of water.

Canada's ability to develop and implement cultural policies is the focus of Garry Neil's chapter 15. This ability has eroded, and continues to erode, under CUFTA. He begins by tracing the history of Canadian cultural policies, including the country's long-standing commitment to supporting the arts, then examines the devastating impact that both CUFTA and NAFTA have had on the policy tools that Ottawa has traditionally used to support its cultural industries. He suggests that the slow erosion of Canadian cultural sovereignty can be traced directly to a report tabled with the United States Trade Representative (USTR) in 1984. In the report, US representatives from the motion picture and television, publishing, and advertising industries identified the major obstacles they encountered when exporting products and services, and pointed to Canada as a prominent problem country. Ever since, Washington has consistently sought to curb Canadian cultural policies, and CUFTA and NAFTA have proven to be effective tools in this mission. Although a cultural exemption was included in CUFTA (and duplicated in NAFTA), it has proven inadequate. Since the signing of these agreements, important Canadian content rules have been eroded, restrictions on foreign ownership lifted, support measures for magazines removed, and support to government-owned or government-subsidized distribution and production systems slashed.

Dorval Brunelle and Benoît Lévesque (chapter 16) offer an analysis of the effects of free trade on two development models implemented in Quebec since 1960. The first-generation model (arising from the "Quiet Revolution") envisioned a British-style welfare state within the context of a relatively self-sufficient provincial economy. It was developed and administered via a dialogue between the provincial government and its three main socioeconomic partners: the business sector, unions, and the cooperative movement. However, various social movements eventually questioned the model, its hierarchical approach, and its democratic credentials, and by the early 1980s there was a growing consensus that this first-generation model had become outdated. Inspired by a combination of 1980s neoliberalism and the Macdonald Commission, the second-generation model focused on markets, entrepreneurship, and regional dynamism rather than on any particular national plan or project. The model incorporated lessons learned from the Quiet Revolution and other social democratic experiences, notably in the European community. It therefore envisioned a pluralist economy in which civil society, the state, and the market play central roles.

Brunelle and Lévesque argue that Quebec is currently at a crossroads. On the one hand is the prospect of deepening free trade and neoliberal policies – the preference of the Jean Charest government; on the other are many social and economic actors who favour a new development paradigm with the potential for establishing another "second-generation" Quebec model, one that accepts shifts in provincial institutions to a market-oriented economy but insists on the need to address social, community, and cooperative imperatives.

COSTING FREE TRADE: IMPACTS ON THE ENVIRONMENT AND NATURAL RESOURCES

Although Canada is a trustee of an enormous environmental responsibility, its natural wealth is in decline and its citizens are not living in a sustainable manner. Despite considerable environmental concerns, especially among young Canadians, our economy continues to be driven by corporate capital and to be oriented to unfettered growth and consumerism. Moreover, it is built around false and dangerous assumptions promoted by the global trade regime that tie destruction of our life support systems with economic growth. These core themes are addressed in Elizabeth May and Sarah Dover's overview of the environmental landscape (chapter 17), Marjorie Griffin Cohen's analysis of continental electricity markets (chapter 18), Larry Pratt's discussion of the oil and gas sectors (chapter 19), and Michelle Swenarchuk's exploration of how American influences have driven changes in the Canadian legal regime, thus allowing for patenting of life forms and expanding intellectual property rights (chapter 20).

CUFTA and NAFTA opponents voiced their concerns about the threat that both agreements posed for Canada's environment, but rather than incorporate these concerns directly into the NAFTA agreement, the three participating governments signed an environmental side agreement that established the North American Commission for Environmental Cooperation (CEC), which has evolved into a mechanism for investigating, coordinating, and reporting on continental environmental concerns. According to May and Dover (and against all odds), the CEC has managed to resist political pressures from the three governments and report on levels of toxic pollution, expose the negative impacts of the NAFTA regime, and maintain an independent watchdog role. Despite these achievements, the authors argue that the CEC has been a complete failure with regard to its main purpose: curbing NAFTA's impact on the environment, specifically the devastating impact of the agreement's Chapter 11 on domestic environmental regulation.

The lessons in terms of further integration with the United States are clear. Several contributors point out that a likely US demand in new negotiations will be access to Canadian fresh water resources. May and Dover add that the proposal for "deeper" integration in natural resource sectors is actually an attempt to decouple a wide range of Canadian resources (including water) from the minimal protections offered by our domestic regulatory regime. Further, they argue that any purported benefit from this integration will be a Trojan horse that leaves Canadian environmental law exposed to US corporate interests. They go on to examine how the Bush administration's energy agenda affects global environmental concerns, with Washington's ongoing objectives being to further develop continental energy markets that respond to its almost insatiable energy needs and to aggressively exploit all remaining coal, oil, and gas deposits. The authors also argue that the most dangerous feature of Washington's plans in this area lies in its efforts to sabotage global action on climate change through the Kyoto Protocol. They note that an important trigger of Canada's own rapid increase in greenhouse emissions was its decision to develop the Athabasca tar sands – an energy-intensive and ecologically damaging operation oriented to serve US demand. With Stephen Harper as prime minister, we in Canada now have a full-blown anti-Kyoto government.

Marjorie Griffin Cohen looks at Washington's push to create an integrated continental energy market under the control of its own Federal Energy Regulatory Commission (FERC). She asserts that the main issue for Canada and Mexico is deciding whether their electric energy systems should remain independent and controlled by their own public regulatory agencies or be subsumed within a larger US-controlled system. Griffin Cohen looks at FERC's attempts to move towards a fully integrated North American electricity market, describes how the Mexican and Canadian governments are responding, and outlines the options that both countries have for dealing with FERC's efforts in this direction. Her assessment is that integrating North American electricity markets will result in prices being established by the United States and in regulations that further the energy objectives of Washington and private US energy companies. She also points out that neither Canada nor Mexico need to adopt the US strategy for continental electricity integration since NAFTA allows for trade and investment across borders without requiring such integration. The question is not whether the Canadian government and its National Energy Board (NEB) can adopt an independent set of policies aimed at protecting the country's interests in this strategic sector, but whether they choose to do so.

In his chapter Larry Pratt assesses the prospects and implications of further continental integration for Canada's oil and gas industry. Historically, technical barriers have limited the extent of energy trade between Canada and the United States, particularly for natural gas. The abandonment of national development strategies in favour of a free trade regime initiated a shift in Canadian production towards the US market and promoted US investment in Canadian energy markets. Major infrastructure projects (e.g., the construction of north-south pipelines) and innovations in exploration and processing have further advanced the potential of a continental integration agenda.

Pratt notes that Canada has become the number one foreign supplier of oil and gas to the United States. The associated financial benefits have come at the cost of reducing Canadian ownership and passing up an opportunity to use the country's oil resources to encourage the development of upstream industries and thus insulate the industry from an erratic world market. Moreover, the financial benefits are tenuous: the Alberta oil patch is showing signs of depletion, with exploration moving into the much heavier oil deposits of the tar sands, whose development is significantly more expensive than are foreign sources due to increased energy requirements for processing – all accompanied by heavy environmental costs. Pratt concludes that, although the United States has encouraged the continental integration of the Canadian oil and gas industry for security and other reasons, it has no real interest in creating a "Fortress North America" in terms of energy; rather, the US strategy is to diversify its supply sources around the world, thereby keeping costs down and ensuring continuity in the face of political upheavals. As a relatively high-cost supplier to the US market, the future of the Canadian oil and gas industry may lie further afield rather than across the border.

Michelle Swenarchuk addresses a particular aspect of US-Canada cross-border harmonization. Her chapter sheds light on one of the most controversial aspects of the Canadian intellectual property rights debate – patents on life – and how it has been influenced from south of the border. While corporate sponsors argue that the patenting of individual cells and higher life forms is essential to spurring innovative research and making critical breakthroughs in areas such as medicine and agriculture, Swenarchuk counters that such a position defies logic. The original purpose of patent law was to protect inventors while ensuring the full and public disclosure of new inventions. However, as she rightly asks, is life a human invention? Humans may discover essential life properties and processes, but that does not mean we invented them or that life forms should be the property of any one individual or firm. Furthermore, evidence from the academic, medical, and health sectors shows that patents on life often inhibit advancements and disclosure, with serious implications for scientific freedom, medical research, and health care.

In this area, Canada also finds itself at a crossroads. While the Canadian Intellectual Property Office (CIPO) has followed the US legal precedent to grant patents on single-cell life forms, the Supreme Court of Canada has made two confusing and contradictory rulings in this area, rejecting a Harvard application for a patent on a genetically modified mouse but conferring property rights for a genetically modified seed. Given the social, moral, and ethical stakes at hand, Swenarchuk argues that decisions regarding the patenting of life cannot be left to unaccountable bureaucrats or the courts. Canadians must insist upon a full and public debate on the issue of life patents and press for legislation that protects the original social purpose of patent law and reflects Canadian values.

SEPTEMBER 11
AND THE DEEP INTEGRATION AGENDA

The events of 11 September 2001 put security and global geopolitical concerns at the top of Washington's agenda. As Stephen Clarkson and Maria Banda argue in chapter 4, September 11 produced an unforeseen paradigm shift, from the "economic liberalization paradigm" that prevailed during the Clinton administration to a "national security paradigm." This shift entailed not only a reordering of basic priorities but also the establishment of new institutions, such as the massive Department of Homeland Security. During its initial phase Washington was able to assemble a broad coalition of states (including Canada) to implement "anti-terrorist" and retaliatory measures aimed at regime change in Afghanistan. Before long, the neoconservatives in the Bush White House used September 11 to twist the new national security paradigm into a series of unsettling and contentious projects, the most controversial being a pre-emptive attack on Iraq. This "paradigm twist" shattered the multilateral consensus that prevailed during the Afghanistan operation, thus estranging the European Union as well as Canada and Mexico.

Post-September 11 policy shifts in Washington severely disrupted the terms and framework of Canada-US relations. The US decision to temporarily close the border to transborder shipments, coupled with assertions that Canada was a "haven for terrorists," thoroughly unnerved Canadian government officials and the country's corporate class. In their second contribution to this volume, Clarkson and Banda (chapter 5) argue that the new security context threatened Canada's status as an attractive site for US investment (a benefit it had gained through CUFTA and NAFTA) by fusing the previously separate issues of economic and territorial security into one indivisible problem. Ottawa quickly took steps to address border security and the free flow of cross-border trade. These actions have had broad implications, and these are explored by various contributors. Clarkson and Banda argue that September 11 galvanized the desire of Canada's corporate sector and some academics to dramatically alter Canada-US relations to match the new policy context. Business associations, in collaboration with right-wing foundations and think tanks, developed and launched a round of proposals aimed at achieving stronger relations with Washington across a number of policy areas. Before long, this coalition was well on its way to articulating, organizing, and promoting a more aggressive, "deeper" phase of integration.

Integrationist proposals fell into two broad categories, with the first advancing a "big idea," "strategic deal," or "grand bargain" with the Bush administration. Wendy Dobson's (2002) proposal for comprehensive negotiations leading to economic and institutional integration stands out here, as does the North American Security and Prosperity Initiative advanced by Thomas d'Aquino (2003) of the Canadian Council of Chief Executives (CCCE). The underlying assumption of both proposals was that, if Canada responded favourably to Washington's heightened defence, security, and energy concerns, then the Bush White House would respond by rewarding Canadians with economic and trade security. The second category of proposals was much narrower in scope, focusing specifically on security matters by suggesting greater homeland security integration (e.g., a common security perimeter and harmonized immigration controls) and military integration (e.g., Northern Command and National Missile Defence). According to Clarkson and Banda, both sets of proposals were deficient in one sense: while they envisioned increased coordination across a number of functional areas, they failed to specify the institutional structures for governing the new interactions. In their view, the integrationist vision remained vague (beyond the basic goal of keeping trade flowing) and largely divorced from the realities of power politics.[10]

All that started to change in 2004. The recognition that integration proposals were deficient and that NAFTA was institutionally weak and static fuelled efforts to develop institutions that would include Mexico. Indeed, proposals for building a "North American Community" inspired by the European experience of integration had been available for some time (Pastor 2001).[11] Elite sectors in Canada re-assessed their exclusive focus post-9/11 on the bilateral Canada-US relationship and altered their position on Mexican inclusion. The Canadian business lobby decided to seek Mexican involvement, having recognized that it is unlikely to lure Washington into serious talks without Mexico's presence.

Pursuing this trilateral approach, the Council on Foreign Relations (CFR) in Washington summoned, in 2004, an influential group of politicians and corporate leaders from the three countries to "develop a roadmap for the future of the North American community," indicating discussion of a possible "NAFTA-plus" agreement. The result was the establishment of the Task Force on the Future of North America, which was charged with addressing issues of "deepening economic integration; reducing the development gap; harmonizing regulatory policy; enhancing security; and devising better institutions to manage conflicts that inevitably arise from integration and exploit opportunities for collaboration" (CFR 2004). Prominent Canadians such as former deputy prime minister John Manley and the CCCE's Tom d'Aquino co-chaired the task force. A confidential leaked document suggested a far-reaching vision that includes long-term integration:[12]

Task Force members favored articulating a bold vision for regional integration, even if elements of that vision could not immediately be put into practice ... [P]articipants divided their suggestions ... into those that are politically feasible today and those that, while desirable, must be considered long-term goals. One implication of this approach is that no item – not Canadian water, not Mexican oil, not American anti-dumping laws – is "off the table"; rather, contentious or intractable issues will simply require more time to ripen politically. (CFR 2005a, 1)

The task force agenda strongly resembles the CCCE's Security and Prosperity Initiative (COC 2005a). According to Maude Barlow of the Council of Canadians, this suggests a strong need for vigilance:

It's clear that what this task force has in mind is a North American common market with common security policies, common immigration and refugee systems, a harmonized border system so that we will not be able to have independent health and safety standards and a common resource policy that includes trade in Canada's water at a future time when we have been softened up to accept it. (COC 2005a)

Indeed, in their March 2005 official statement, the task force chairs proposed "the creation by 2010 of a community to enhance security, prosperity, and opportunity for all North Americans," where "the boundaries of the community would be defined by a common external tariff and an outer security perimeter" (CFR 2005b, 6). This would entail "the creation of a single economic space [encompassing Canada, the United States, and Mexico] that expands the economic opportunities for all people in the region, and the establishment of a security zone that protects the region from external threats while facilitating the legitimate passage of goods, people, and capital" (9).

In chapter 3 Tony Clarke focuses on the architects of these proposals: Canada's corporate class, or what he refers to as "Washington's empire loyalists." Similar to Clarkson and Banda, he argues that Canada's now unambiguously continental capitalist class has a strong stake in preventing any reduction in Canada-US trade and investment. The central objective of commercial lobbies is to ensure that Canada remains attractive as a centre for new investments in a more uncertain security climate. Clarke notes that CUFTA and NAFTA have led to a far-reaching restructuring of North American industry, and he argues that US corporations have not only furthered their penetration of the Canadian market but have also taken advantage of the low Canadian dollar to acquire Canadian assets. The fact that Canada's leading corporations now operate in key sectors of the US economy (including, most notably, finance) and depend on the US market to an unparalleled degree has profound implications for Canadian public policy.

Clarke concludes that Canada's capitalist class – now substantially integrated into US capital circuits and thus subservient to Washington – is willing to dissolve all that is distinctive about the northernmost section of North America. Cognizant that this will most likely meet with stiff opposition in Canada, the federal government and Tom d'Aquino's CCCE are proceeding by stealth whenever possible. The Paul Martin government, which assumed power in December 2003, discreetly adopted much of the CCCE agenda, a position later openly embraced by Prime Minister Stephen Harper when he formed a government in 2006.

The influence of the CCCE and the CFR task force recommendations was apparent when Prime Minister Paul Martin, President George Bush, and President Vicente Fox announced the Security and Prosperity Partnership of North America (SPP) in March 2005 at their summit in Waco, Texas. The SPP resembles the CCCE's North American Security and Prosperity Initiative in more than name as it established "the principle that our prosperity is dependent on our security" (White House 2005). "Through the SPP, the United States, Canada, and Mexico ... seek to establish a cooperative approach to advance our common security and prosperity," to "develop a common security strategy to further secure North America," and to "promote economic growth, competitiveness, and quality of life" (White House 2005). According to Bruce Campbell (chapter 22), the Martin government played the lead role in creating the SPP. The SPP effectively replaced NAFTA as the organizational framework under which various deep integration initiatives are advancing, and ten ministerial working groups were established with concrete implementation targets. In June 2005 the first SPP implementation report released work plans for nearly 100 initiatives covering a wide range of economic and security issues – to be implemented by trilateral working groups on an ongoing basis with regular progress updates (SPP 2005).

The minority Conservative government that assumed power in February 2006 signalled a new stage in consolidating the CCCE's agenda. One of Stephen Harper's first steps was to renew the Canadian commitment to the SPP in the March 2006 summit in Cancun, Mexico, with George Bush and Vicente Fox. The three leaders went on to announce the creation of the North American Competitiveness Council (NACC), which will "provide recommendations and priorities on promoting North American competitiveness globally" (Industry Canada 2006). Of the ten Canadians appointed by Prime Minister Harper to the NACC, nine are CCCE members, which makes it clear who is going to give advice to the prime minister when it comes to shaping Canada's North American agenda. The NACC has already begun meeting to prepare a list of suggestions to be delivered to politicians in fall 2006. Among the other profiled items at the Cancun summit were a North American energy security initiative (to assure the flow of oil and gas from

Canada and Mexico to meet US demand) and a framework agreement on regulatory cooperation, to be finalized in 2007. Thus, the deep integration agenda continues to move forward under the mantle of the SPP.

Sovereignty is a delicate issue for the business lobbyists promoting such an agenda in Canada, and they have attempted to move Canadians away from what they call "defensive postures on sovereignty" (Foster 2002a, 4). The present debate seems to revolve around whether "Canadian sovereignty with respect to the United States can best be exercised by getting closer to the Americans or staying farther away" (Kitchen 2004, 701). Hugh Segal (2003, 6), of the Institute for Research on Public Policy, clearly supports getting closer when he describes sovereignty as a tool "to expand freedom and opportunity" and to "build a North American Community." Thomas d'Aquino (2003, 3) concurs, and he cautions that "leaders in both countries ... [should not] allow outdated concerns about sovereignty to cloud their vision." The peculiar contention here seems to be that if Canada *willingly* initiates further permanent cuts to its policy-making space in essential areas, then it is asserting its sovereignty. One scholar has nicely captured the tenor of this idea with the observation that integrationists would like "to get us to use our sovereignty in order to participate more consciously in the act of giving it up" (Foster 2002a, 4). The traditional notion of sovereignty as an expression of democratic control is clearly lost here. From the perspective of the contributors to this volume, this is an altogether undesirable view of sovereignty. We discuss popular notions of sovereignty in a later section of this chapter.

On the political front, Duncan Cameron (chapter 2) traces the origins of the current drive towards deep integration to earlier Canadian debates between economic nationalists and continentalist elites,[13] and then evaluates the prospects of a "new continentalism." In his overview of the 1980s debates, Cameron discusses how the Liberal and Conservative parties approached closer economic integration with the United States in response to pressure from the business sector and in the face of public and popular opposition. According to Cameron, the business lobby was successful because it recognized the need for its own centralized political organizations and think tanks to make direct appeals to Canadians. Of course, a significant segment of today's Liberal Party has been supportive of deeper integration with Washington. Key figures such as John Manley and Frank McKenna have enthusiastically driven this agenda forward, while a weaker left-leaning faction appears both ambivalent and subdued. In many ways, Paul Martin and these Liberal leaders paved the way for the Conservative government that came after them.

As several contributors observe, while business has been largely satisfied with the outcomes of trade liberalization, it has set its sights on furthering Canada's dependence on the US economy. Even more so than in the past, business groups and right-wing think tanks have aggressively mobilized their resources to promote the continentalist agenda. Furthermore, the Liberal Party has continued to shift the basis of its support towards the upper-income bracket and has strengthened its commitment to the interests of corporate Canada, in the image of the corporate-driven Conservative Party. However, the ultimate goal has changed little. As Cameron notes, the integration agenda remains driven by the desire to secure access to the US market and to dismantle Canada's welfare state. Still, the new continental-ism does have several unique features, including an attempt to link trade and security, as we discuss in the following section.

The means by which this new continentalism will be advanced are slowly taking shape. As Clarkson and Banda observe, Dobson's notion of a "big idea" has failed to gain acceptance (at least for the moment), largely due to political reasons. The business lobby has adopted a strategy, which is now reflected in the trilateral Security and Prosperity Partnership, that focuses on advancing policy in a number of areas of interest to the Bush adminis-tration. The Liberal government was comfortable with this gradualist approach, which aims at policy harmonization across key areas, and it is likely to be the preferred approach of Prime Minister Stephen Harper while heading a minority government. It is a method that allows for the building of closer economic ties with Washington while avoiding the pitfalls associ-ated with a more comprehensive renegotiation of a NAFTA-plus agreement.

Bruce Campbell notes that this incremental integration strategy has the advantage of being less harmful to Canadian sovereignty since it does not entail the kinds of broad trade-offs across sectors that characterize more comprehensive negotiations. Nevertheless, there are drawbacks to this instalment approach. Big idea schemes stand out in the policy arena, making mobilization and resistance easier to organize. Individual agree-ments across numerous and varied issue areas are more difficult to spot, while their cumulative effect can be extremely damaging. While the policy alignments that have taken place in recent years indicate that the inte-grationists are adopting an incremental approach, the CFR's task force reports signal that the big idea is not dead. As noted earlier, their confi-dential report outlines a broad integrationist vision that does not ex-clude any policy from discussion; the only constraint appears to be public acceptance.

UNHOLY ALLIANCE:
THE COMING TOGETHER OF TRADE AND SECURITY

As already stated, "security" is the one word that epitomizes the North American policy context following September 11.[14] Those who favour deep integration are well aware of this matter: the CCCE's five-point

Security and Prosperity Initiative, presented to senior members of the Bush administration in April of 2003, acknowledged and reflected the fusing of trade and security matters, and appeared to be the blueprint for the Security and Prosperity Partnership of North America launched in 2005 by the three governments. For the Canadian advocates, the plan is for Canada to increase military spending and to harmonize its immigration and security policies with those of its neighbour in return for secure access to the US market. As several contributors suggest, the barely concealed intent of these proposals is to integrate Canadian and US defence policies. Steven Staples, in particular, chronicles in chapter 6 a number of developments pointing to deeper defence and security integration.[15]

As cited by Staples, C.D. Howe Institute scholar Wendy Dobson (2003, 3) argues that "Canadian concerns about economic security must be linked with US domestic priorities to attract US notice. And homeland security is the single overriding US goal. What's needed is a strategic framework that links security and defence with economic goals." This comprehensive approach to transforming the Canada-US relationship differs fundamentally from the strictly economic arrangements that defined CUFTA and NAFTA. Clearly, and perhaps necessarily, business leaders have abandoned past claims that free trade deals are strictly about economics and now admit that long-standing Canadian positions on a variety of issues might have to be reconsidered in order to achieve economic objectives. They are promoting the need for Canada to discard or rethink its traditional positions on numerous issues where US interests are concerned. In the words of trade scholars Bill Dymond and Michael Hart, Canada's foreign policy should shed "outdated orthodoxies" and recognize "the central role of the United States in our future" (Dymond and Hart 2003, abstract).

Due to intense public and political pressure, Paul Martin's Liberal government decided to opt out of a controversial US-led "missile defence" program in February 2005. However, Ottawa quietly agreed to expand the mission of the North American Aerospace Defense Command (NORAD) – a joint organization of the United States and Canada – in order to allow the transmission of satellite and radar data on incoming missiles to the US Northern Command (NORTHCOM), which will operate and manage the program. According to Steven Staples, this change leaves a back door open for further Canadian involvement in missile defence and even space weapons. In May 2006 the Harper government quietly renewed the NORAD agreement, albeit with significant changes. This revised agreement no longer needs to be renewed every five years (but can be amended at any time upon agreement of both governments). According to Ernie Regehr from Project Ploughshares, in a context of deepening military and security integration, the indefinite extension of NORAD without public consultation on current and proposed changes in North American security raises grave security and sovereignty concerns (Regehr 2006).

Paul Martin's missile defence decision ended a chapter of the Canadian missile defence issue but by no means closed the book on it. In fact, even prior to the 2006 federal election Stephen Harper indicated his intention to revisit the issue. With Washington continuing to deploy the system in stages over the next few decades, direct Canadian participation will remain a goal of the defence lobby and those seeking closer ties to the United States. In May 2006 the North Atlantic Treaty Organization (NATO) opened a new front in this debate as it announced that it, too, was considering a missile defence shield to protect continental Europe from long-range missile threats (Blanchfield 2006). Canada, as a member of the twenty-six-nation alliance, fully endorsed the decision.

Before the September 11 attacks, a single unified command of all US forces for the defence of North America did not exist. The attacks, however, shocked the US government into reorganizing its military to focus more intensely on the defence of its territory. On 1 October 2002 the United States created Northern Command (NORTHCOM), with responsibility for US military operations in the United States, Mexico, Canada, and the northern Caribbean. Northern Command is the military equivalent of the civilian Department of Homeland Security. While Northern Command is a US-only military command, its four-star general is also the commander of NORAD. In effect, the general and his staff are "dual hatted," responsible for both NORTHCOM and NORAD.

In December 2002 the Canadian government instructed its military to enter into talks with its US counterparts to explore how Canadian military forces might "cooperate" more closely with Northern Command, thus satisfying NORTHCOM's requirement that Canada be incorporated into its area of responsibility. A Bi-National Planning Group (BPG) was subsequently established within NORAD, and Canada decided to create a new arrangement mirroring the US Northern Command: Canada Command (CANCOM). The establishment of Canada Command was made public in June 2005. It was announced as a unified and integrated chain of command at the national and regional levels, with the immediate authority to deploy maritime, land, and air assets in support of domestic operations (CBC 2005).

The creation of a CANCOM independent of a joint Canada-US continental command may be merely a temporary compromise, responding to Canadian sovereignty concerns. This is clear from the Bi-National Planning Group's final report, released in May 2006 (BPG 2006). Michael Byers, from the University of British Columbia, argues that, although the professed goal of the report is to improve cooperation between the Canadian and US militaries, the real intent is "nothing less than the complete

integration of Canada's military, security and foreign policy into the decision-making and operating systems of the US" (Byers 2006).

Ottawa's recent review of defence policies appears to legitimize the ever
closer military relationship with Washington. The Canadian government's
2005 *International Policy Statement on Defence* builds on previous security and defence measures that include the Smart Border Declaration
(Canada 2001), the creation of the Bi-National Planning Group (Canada
2002), the *National Security Policy* (Canada 2004b), and the *Joint Statement on Common Security, Common Prosperity* (Canada 2004a). This
most recent statement pledges to "renew our commitment to continental
defence, including through enhancing our domestic capabilities and establishing a single national command structure" (Canada 2005, 22). It
commits the government to "improving our ability to operate alongside
American forces ... and cooperate even more closely with the US Navy and
Coast Guard" (23). With military and security integration advancing
quickly, the nature of the Canadian armed forces and their international
role (centred in part on peacekeeping and peace building) is changing.[16]
Difficult questions are being raised, among others, about the legalities
associated with Canadian soldiers answering to a US commander and of US
soldiers operating on Canadian soil (Sallot 2004).

Although nominally committed to peace building, facts confirm where
the real priorities of the government lie. Afghanistan and related military
operations accounted for 68 percent of the about $6 billion spent on inter-
national missions between the fall of 2001 and the end of March 2006.
During the same time period, Canada devoted only $214 million, or 3
percent of its spending on international military operations, to United
Nations operations. By 31 March 2006, Canada contributed only fifty-
nine military personnel to UN missions around the world, while approximately 2,300 troops were stationed in Afghanistan (Robinson 2006, 1). As
W. Andy Knight (2006) from the University of Alberta concludes, "Canadians will realize that we are no longer a peacekeeping nation."

Steven Staples also explores the political context within which military
and security integration is proceeding – the so-called "Bush Doctrine,"
which is characterized by unilateralism, military build-up, pre-emptive
warfare, the restriction and suspension of basic civil liberties, and the
explicit fusion of security, military, and economic objectives to advance US
interests. As Staples and several other contributors observe, the linking of
security, military, and economic goals has strongly influenced the strategy
of Canada's corporate leaders. Fear that foreign policy and security disputes between Ottawa and Washington could jeopardize hard-won economic gains during the 1980s and 1990s is at the root of their support for
a "big idea." These business leaders now view the integration of foreign
policy instruments as the inevitable price to be paid for Canada's privileged

access to the lucrative US market, and they have fashioned an agenda that combines their desire for economic security with Washington's demands for increased military security. This has led to the formation of a strategic alliance between corporate Canada and the country's defence lobby that is encouraging Ottawa to support US military, security, and foreign policy objectives. The Canadian government has responded positively to these demands, as is reflected in the words of Canada's former ambassador to the United States, Frank McKenna: "Trade is our issue, security is theirs, which means our interest has become security and trade" (Campion-Smith 2005b).

One agenda item that has been affected by this new posture is immigration and refugees. Sharryn Aiken (chapter 7) details how Canadian security and immigration policy responses to September 11 have threatened to curtail the rights and liberties of many Canadians, especially ethnic minorities and refugee claimants. Aiken argues that much of the impetus behind policy reviews and legal and institutional changes has come from a perception that Canada is overly lax on security (i.e., a "haven for terrorists") and, therefore, in need of tighter border restrictions, which could lead to reduced access to the US market. Integrationist proposals have been explicit on this question: policy autonomy in the areas of security, privacy, immigration, and refugees have been identified as concessions to be offered in exchange for secure market access. Aiken outlines the legal and institutional changes that have taken place, which include an increase in the surveillance powers of the state, acknowledging an association between immigration and crime, the raising of barriers to refugee claimants, and the condoning (and in some instances, encouragement) of racial profiling. She makes a compelling case that such changes signify a move towards a system of dualistic citizenship, where certain people and communities are singled out for arbitrary attention and differential treatment by state authorities. She concludes that public debate on security policy in a post-September 11 environment must continue and that civil society must persist in challenging the construction of what is beginning to resemble a "Panopticon" state.[17]

There is little doubt that momentum is building for closer political and economic ties with Washington, a trend that emerged under the Liberal government and was dramatically enhanced by the 2006 Conservative victory. What remains to be seen is whether the corporate and defence lobbies, the corporate media, and their allies in government who openly champion the Bush Doctrine will be able to persuade the Canadian public to accept their vision. Missile defence, a unilateral foreign policy, and pre-emptive military aggression do not reflect Canadian values and enjoy little popular support. In the aforementioned March 2004 poll, 77 percent of the respondents agreed with the statement that "Canada's limited military spending should be used to enhance our abilities in peacekeeping and conflict resolution rather than trying to maintain multi-purpose forces intended for heavy combat alongside us military forces" (Ipsos-Reid 2004).

As public opinion on Iraq suggests, Canadians are more likely to support the reinvigoration of the country's traditional international role as peacekeeper, peace builder, and independent arbiter of international relations rather than a closer alignment with a us administration that has attempted to weaken multilateral institutions and international law. Canada's shifting role in Afghanistan from reconstruction and development to fighting a counter-insurgency war under us command has been a divisive issue. As more and more fallen Canadian soldiers are brought home from the battlegrounds in Afghanistan, an Ipsos Reid survey reports support for Canada's military mission there has been sinking over the first half of 2006 (Ipsos 2006).

The alignment with Washington's policies has been accompanied by a shift in worldview. Some of the most passionate integrationists have suggested that Canada should abandon its "idealistic" approach to foreign policy in favour of a more "realist-inspired" strategy (Burney 2005; Gotlieb 2005). Allan Gotlieb (2005, 16), Canada's former ambassador to Washington, describes the idealist approach (which he finds objectionable) as based on "a mission to create a more just world, promote democracy, reduce inequities among nations, protect victims of injustice and alleviate the conditions of the poor and oppressed." He instead calls for a "reality-based" foreign policy (24) that makes "deeper and wider integration" with Washington the principal long-term goal (26).[18] According to Gotlieb, this us-centred vision is premised on the notion that "our potential for influencing the world's greatest power is our comparative advantage in the world. It gives us credibility in other capitals. As us power grows, so does Canada's opportunity" (24).

These positions have elicited strong responses from prominent Canadians, including former foreign affairs minister Lloyd Axworthy (2005), who argues:

Anyone who thinks that neighbourly proximity brings favours or privileges is living in a dream world. In the changing landscape of us politics and policies, Canada lacks the necessary traction ... [the] reality is that we are dealing with an American political system currently steeped in the ideology of "empire." It recognizes few rules, adheres only to those treaties that are expedient to basic interests, and believes that the only political currency that counts is the exercise of raw power.[19]

The contributors to this volume reject Gotlieb's worldview and Canada's place in it; instead, they support both Roméo Dallaire's (2003) call for a greater focus on humanity and Axworthy's (1999) notion of human security, which focuses on protecting people from acts of violence and creating a greater sense of security for individuals within individual nation-states. This values- and humanitarian-centred approach to Canada's relations with other countries emphasizes pluralism, democracy, human rights, and the rule of law, and it acknowledges a role for ordinary citizens in the development of foreign policy goals. Derek Burney (2005, 2), one of the architects of CUFTA, argues today[20] that when it comes to foreign policy, "the purpose of government is to lead, not follow, public opinion." We disagree. We believe, instead, that a country's foreign policy should be a reflection of its people and their values. Accordingly, public participation should be central to defining Canadian foreign and defence policies.

FRAMING THE DEBATE: INTEGRATION, DEEPER INTEGRATION, AND EVEN DEEPER INTEGRATION

Calls for new forms of governance in North America and the negotiation of NAFTA-plus agreements have come from both inside and outside of Canada, with former president Fox of Mexico and American academics and think tanks pushing the integrationist agenda. But the most extraordinary activity on this issue has taken place in Canada, where a large number of well funded academic conferences, publications, and media events have been organized since 9/11 by governments, think tanks, business associations, and private foundations to explore and advance North American integration. Such is the case with the C.D. Howe Institute's "Border Papers" series "on Canada's choices regarding North American integration," produced with financial support from the Donner Canadian Foundation (Dobson 2002, copyright page). Parliamentary committees have also been very active on this issue. The Standing Committee on Foreign Affairs and International Trade (SCFAIT) has called for "intensified public debate and parliamentary engagement in regard to closer relations among North American partners" (SCFAIT 2002). The Senate Foreign Affairs Committee has held hearings on trade and security relations with the United States and Mexico (Senate 2003), and the Standing Senate Committee on National Security and Defence produced a document entitled *Defence of North America: A Canadian Responsibility* (Senate 2002). Academic publications have joined the fray, arguing that the negative effects of free trade have been exaggerated, that Canada has retained significant "capacity for choice" (Hoberg 2001), and that NAFTA has been a success (Weintraub 2004; Hufbauer and Schott 2005). An earlier volume chronicled the proceedings of a conference whose starting point was a Royal Bank impact study entitled *Two Cheers for the FTA* (L.I. MacDonald 2000, x), while another study entitled *Deeper, Broader: A Roadmap for a Treaty of North America* (Schwanen 2004) laid out a blueprint for the "big idea."

There is a common thread running through these initiatives. Although several have included healthy debates and even dissent, a dominant discourse has taken hold, its purpose being to frame public discussion of Canadian options. The May 2002 conference organized by the federal government's Policy Research Initiative (PRI) at Carleton University illustrates this point. The organizers presented for discussion three possible scenarios for the future of North America:

The first scenario, *Bilateral, Asymmetric North America*, described a relationship based on incremental increases in cooperation and coordination ... Political leaders in all three countries are strongly committed to realizing the full potential of NAFTA and its two side accords, but they show little inclination to tighten or broaden linkages. To the degree there is a sense of a distinct North America, it is only in terms of relations between sovereign states. In this scenario, the continued protection of distinct identity and policy autonomy is a growing concern ... [T]his scenario in many ways represents a continuation of the current situation. (PRI 2002, 3)

The second scenario, *Confederation North America*,

envisioned a future where citizens, firms, non-governmental organizations and government policy-makers identify first and foremost with North America. Human, social, environmental, institutional and economic linkages are tight and intense. A rich panoply of continental institutions, including an elected North American Parliament and North American system of courts, penetrate deeply into social, political and economic life. There is a North American currency. Interdependence is the norm. (PRI 2002, 6)

The third scenario, *Consortium North America*, and the one clearly favoured by the organizers of the conference,

set forth a middle ground between the "bilateral" and the "confederation" views of North America. In this future, three national states with clear identities work together on a range of functional tasks. Political leaders publicly support a deepened awareness of North America and contemplate shared policy- and decision-making in some areas. Systemic policy emulation between the three countries is standard. The NAFTA regime provides the basis for stronger ties at the level of business, non-governmental organizations, schools, professional associations, and national and sub-national governments. New trilateral institutions have been created and the effectiveness of existing ones significantly increased. On the economic front, a customs union is formed. A North American central bank has been established to handle monetary policy and support regional economic development. Nonetheless, political leaders continue to put the highest priority on advancing national interests and achieving net benefits for the citizens in their respective countries. (PRI 2002, 8)

These scenarios reveal how promoters of deeper integration are working to frame public discourse. It is especially telling that all three envision deepening integration to one degree or another. John Foster (2002b), a conference participant, described the three scenarios as "integration," "deeper integration," and "even deeper integration." All of them make a number of assumptions: that NAFTA constitutes a first step towards integration, that pressures for deepening integration will grow, and that the role of policy makers is to move forward while mitigating harmful effects. They also assume that economic integration is irreversible, that closer commercial relations with the United States will bring widespread economic benefits, and that deeper integration will not lead to an "Americanization" of Canadian life. This language of inevitability is reminiscent of the Thatcherite TINA ("there is no alternative") dictum.

However, North American democratic forces with visions of a different future are challenging this language, reframing the discussion, dispelling false assumptions, and clarifying the real nature of these proposals. Towards this end, the task of deconstructing the meaning of the three scenarios is crucial. We suggest the following interpretation:

- The first scenario, *Bilateral Asymmetric North America,* should be renamed the *Slippery Slope* scenario. It continues down the road of almost two decades of bilateral free trade in Canada. As the contributors to this volume show, this "slippery slope" has become even steeper following the tragic events of September 11. The prime ministerial transition from Jean Chrétien to Paul Martin and then to Stephen Harper, coupled with George W. Bush's re-election in 2004, have made matters worse. This scenario represents an accentuation of the serious and detrimental social, economic, cultural, and ecological trends of the last two decades.
- The second scenario, *Confederation North America*, is a euphemism for *Assimilation North America*. It has been advanced as a straw man in order to make the real proposals of the business lobby appear moderate. It essentially suggests that Canada will eventually be absorbed by the United States. Not surprisingly, few Canadian business and political leaders openly advocate this scenario, which is politically indefensible. The reference to "North American" institutions (e.g., common currency and judicial systems) is a convenient fiction since the United States is unlikely to abandon its dollar, its Constitution, and its political institutions. If North American institutions were ever to materialize, surely they would be a façade for assimilating Canada (and perhaps Mexico) into US institutions. The implication of this scenario is rule without representation: Canadians would be ruled from Washington but lose their rights of citizenship and political representation. Some have argued that outright political annexation would be preferable since it would at least provide the benefits of US citizenship and suffrage.

• The third scenario is *Consortium North America*. Although promoted as the "moderate" option, it represents the *Big Idea* scenario, one that demands an even greater leap of faith than did CUFTA. It embodies ambitious proposals for comprehensive new deals with the United States, including "shared policy and decision-making, in some areas"; "stronger ties at the level of business, non-governmental organizations, schools, professional associations, and national and sub-national governments"; "new trilateral institutions"; "a customs union"; and a "North American central bank ... to handle monetary policy" (PRI 2002). These proposals are anything but moderate. What they represent is a dramatic alteration of Canadian democratic governance, the long-term outcome of which is likely to be nothing less than *Assimilation North America*.

What is clearly absent from this "debate" among political and business elites is a fourth scenario – an option involving a lesser degree of integration and an entirely different set of policy goals. A frequent criticism of campaigners for social change is that they tend to hold an "underdeveloped vision of the alternative worlds that they desire" (Scholte 2000, 120). That such campaigners are rarely supported by elites or invited to participate in the debate (and here the federal government's Policy Research Initiative conference is no exception) explains in part the difficulties associated with moving from protest to proposal. This volume, therefore, seeks to articulate not only what its contributors are against but also what they are for – their visions for the future. The contributors agree that a fourth scenario is essential not only in order to preserve the democratic gains achieved by Canadians through the social struggles of the twentieth century but also to project and pursue *The Canada We Want*[21] for the twenty-first century. Such a scenario, which might be called *Revitalizing Democracy and Upholding the Public Good,* is the shared vision put forth by the authors of this volume in an effort to forge a citizens' alternative to deep integration.

REVITALIZING DEMOCRACY, UPHOLDING THE PUBLIC GOOD

In believing that Canada can pursue a sovereign and democratic destiny, the contributors reject the defeatism implied in the deep integration agenda. Although the policy constraints imposed by NAFTA, the WTO, and other conditioning frameworks are serious, and the erosion of our social fabric and environment are painfully real, a great deal of policy space remains reasonably intact for governments at all levels. In chapter 22 Bruce Campbell argues that, while significant, the loss of policy space has been overstated, and any government willing to act creatively and assertively still has room to manoeuvre. Still, policy spaces must be reclaimed and their boundaries challenged and extended by governments at all levels so that their policies reflect Canadian values regarding social justice, ecological sustainability, and the country's peaceful role in world politics.

Campbell proposes a three-pronged strategy to halt the erosion of Canadian sovereignty and to reclaim national policy freedom. The orientation of his strategy is not new: it is an approach inspired by social democratic values and goals that we believe remain both relevant and valuable. The contributors acknowledge that participation in the international economic system imposes constraints on governments but argue that those constraints should not be exaggerated. While it is currently fashionable to argue that aspects of economic globalization are forcing governments in the North to abandon their traditional social safety net and redistributive functions, we reject the inevitability of that trend, preferring to promote the idea that the depth, pace, and form of integration and globalization are and will be shaped by governments at all levels. In sum, it is choice rather than destiny that must determine our future development and our relations with Washington and the rest of the world.

According to Campbell, the first and most important point is that *government must reassert and rebuild its capacity to actively manage the economy* using a variety of macroeconomic, labour market, industrial policy, and public investment tools. Government should also be more active and aggressive in regulating foreign investment and domestic resources, strengthening the cultural sector, and rebuilding public infrastructure. For example, Campbell urges that the environmental regulatory capacity that has been gutted over the last decade and a half should be rebuilt. NAFTA does not require Canadian governments to weaken rules in this area, nor does it prevent government from restoring effective environmental regulations.

Campbell's second point emphasises *wise management of the relationship with the United States* – that is, Canada should conduct its economic business with the United States in a spirit of cooperation and mutual respect, as befits neighbours with deep interlocking interests and an unparalleled history of friendly co-existence. But Campbell also signals a cautionary note in calling upon federal policy makers to resist, reshape, and reverse further integration. He argues that Canada's distinctiveness stems primarily from the fact that we have accepted the role of the state as guarantor of social safety nets and as a mechanism to redistribute resources and entitlements when the market fails. In short, our distinctiveness lies in the public sphere, shaped by government actions and institutions. For this reason, Campbell stresses that it is essential for further negotiations with

Washington to be carried out prudently and vigilantly in order to ensure that the Canadian state's ability to maintain our distinct identity is not compromised or weakened.

This means dealing with Canada-US issues and irritants as they arise and, where possible, developing strategies for dealing with them before they reach crisis proportions. According to Campbell, agreements should be sought in areas where the impact of the current power imbalance is minimized. He makes a convincing case for ensuring that integration agreements are of limited scope and are negotiated along terms that minimize the loss of policy flexibility.[22] Because of the power imbalance, the Canadian government should avoid linking issues when negotiating bilateral agreements since most agreements are (as they should be) compartmentalized and of limited scope. Where bilateral agreements are not necessary, Canada should favour multilateral forums. In all cases, he argues, the core national interests of identity and autonomy must be given precedence over considerations of market efficiency.

In terms of addressing US security demands, Campbell believes that the crucial consideration is to respond without compromising fundamental civil liberties or policy autonomy. It is important for the Canadian government to acknowledge that secure market access is unattainable since the US Congress will never surrender power over its trade protection laws; hence, like Canadian winters, US harassment of Canadian resource exports will remain an unpleasant fact. Since there is no permanent solution short of political union, this goal should be abandoned. Rather than push for deeper integration, Canada must lower its expectations, exercise patience, and refuse to be driven by improbable scenarios. Where trade is concerned, Canada must allow existing dispute resolution processes – trilateral and multilateral – to play themselves out. Ottawa must also work with political allies in Mexico and the United States to prune back the most egregious aspects of NAFTA, to strengthen social services and cultural exemptions, and to neuter the investor-state dispute mechanism.

Campbell's third strategy calls for Canada to *focus on maintaining and strengthening multilateral institutions*. Our government should use multilateral forums to forge agreements in the area of human rights, the environment, health, culture, and taxation that are enforceable and that supersede and circumscribe such trade agreements as the WTO and NAFTA. At the same time, we should revisit measures to expand and diversify economic, security, development, and cultural relationships with other countries.

Marc Lee (chapter 11) underscores this point when he argues that gains for Canada from trade are more likely to be found in enhancing trade with Europe and the global South. Thus, he suggests that trade policy should focus on a multilateral rather than a narrow bilateral approach. The current global political and economic context is markedly different from that of a decade ago, thus enhancing the potential of such an alternative path. The chronic US trade imbalance and declining US hegemony in terms of production, coupled with the rise of new economic powerhouses such as China and India, make the option of diversifying our economic ties (rather than limiting them to economic integration with the United States) both reasonable and appealing. Lee believes that Canadian concerns would be better addressed via multilateral institutions and international cooperation with other countries that share common concerns. In his opinion, this is the best way to gain the leverage necessary with Washington to extract meaningful compromises on issues of real substance, such as the current set of punitive trade remedy laws.

There is general support for Campbell's approach among the book's contributors, with several developing specific policy proposals that fall within the broad parameters of Campbell's strategy. According to these authors, one area where change is required is in Canadian trade and investment policy. In chapter 12 Steven Shrybman asserts that Canadian governments must rethink their support for international investor-state arbitral regimes, such as the one established by NAFTA's Chapter 11. Instead of promoting binding investor rights that undermine basic human, environmental, and social rights, Shrybman argues that governments should pursue the establishment of meaningful international protections. Furthermore, investment provisions in international treaties should respect Canadian constitutional guarantees and uphold Canada's solemn commitments to international human rights and to environmental and labour conventions.

Jim Grieshaber-Otto, Scott Sinclair, and Ricardo Grinspun (chapter 14) also call on the federal government to change its current approach to trade treaties – both existing ones and ones currently being negotiated, which, they argue, have led to persistent pressure to commercialize Canada's health care system. The federal government must begin by acknowledging existing threats to public service systems and public interest regulation, and then alter its trade negotiating objectives and existing treaty commitments to secure the strong, fully effective protection for medicare that Canadians have been promised but never given. Kathy Corrigan (chapter 13) makes a similar case regarding the commercialization of public education and the privatization of municipal services. She states that municipalities must ensure that they do not lose their ability to make policy because of trade treaty provisions. For instance, under current arrangements, provincial governments can set conditions regarding investment aimed at spurring local development, and it is important that future trade accords preserve that power. Finally, Corrigan argues that, rather than diligently search for advice on how best to comply with trade agreements once they are in place, jurisdictions at all levels should dedicate their resources towards advancing public policy positions during the course of trade negotiations. By ensuring that trade agreements comply with their needs and mandates rather than vice versa, this would go a long way to safeguarding their respective missions.

Two contributors advance specific proposals in the area of "meaningful protections" for human rights. In chapter 15 Garry Neil outlines some steps that Canada can take to retain a strong sense of cultural sovereignty, and he describes a plan that governments and civil organizations developed to address the threat that cultural industries are facing. These actors collaborated in order to establish a global charter of cultural rights that would permit countries to support their own artists and cultural producers and that would require multinational media conglomerates to support local and diverse cultures. From a Canadian perspective, the intent in establishing the UNESCO *Convention on the Protection and Promotion of the Diversity of Cultural Expressions* in 2005 was to resist US pressure on Canadian cultural policies.

David Robinson (chapter 10) focuses on the future of labour rights, describing the negative impact of deeper integration on labour's bargaining power, wages, benefits, and employment standards. He argues that an appropriate course of action would be to develop an alternative international agreement in which labour rights and standards take precedence over trade agreements. Such a project would involve generating new continental regulatory instruments and institutions that raise and promote labour standards rather than harmonize them downwards (as is the case with CUFTA and NAFTA). Robinson also notes that to halt and eventually reverse negative trends in labour rights, Canadian and US labour movements must work to increase union membership in order to restore a more equitable balance of power between capital and labour. To achieve this, Robinson believes that organized labour must rethink its strategies on how best to respond to deepening economic integration.

Several authors emphasize the idea that Canada should focus on deepening democratic participation and respect for human rights rather than deepening integration with the United States. Sharryn Aiken (chapter 7) challenges the Canadian government to ensure that the fight against terrorism remains consistent with broader commitments to human rights and the rule of law – for instance, making sure that Canada's immigration and refugee laws, border security policies, and racial profiling practices conform to and meet existing commitments. In her view, Canadians need to carefully scrutinize the impact of the complex web of new laws and policies adopted in the aftermath of September 11. She believes that civil society groups have an important role in promoting "a vision of a Canada in which a two-tiered citizenship is not tolerated, a country that refuses to succumb to siren calls for deeper integration or to compromise on its principled differences" (chapter 7, 202). In chapter 6 Steve Staples calls for a redefinition of Canadian foreign and defence policies that is consistent with Canadian values of international activism and that is designed to achieve independent and progressive positions. He outlines a preference for a non-combat military force that would match the needs of a defence policy focused on territorial surveillance and peacekeeping missions under UN auspices. Staples also calls on Canada to promote multilateralism as the foundation of its foreign policy, particularly in the face of the current Washington preference for unilateralism.

A cross-cutting concern of many contributors is the need to steward natural resources and to convert to a sustainable society. Elizabeth May and Sarah Dover (chapter 17) call on the government to substantially reform and increase funding for Canada's natural resource and environmental regulatory regimes, arguing that environmental assessments of trade agreements need to be effective and open to greater public participation. In addition, the authors call on the federal government to establish environmental protocols to protect Canada's bulk water from export and to ensure that they are not nullified by integration proposals. Regarding NAFTA, May and Dover suggest that the definition of "environment" be expanded since the NAFTA definition is so narrow that it makes the bulk of environmental concerns external to the agreement. Marjorie Griffin Cohen (chapter 18) argues that neither Canada nor Mexico needs to accept the US strategy for continental electricity integration, and she calls on the Canadian government and National Energy Board to adopt a vigorous set of policies aimed at protecting the country's interests in this strategic sector.

Larry Pratt (chapter 19) similarly argues that Canada should reconsider its abandonment of national oil and gas development strategies in favour of a free trade regime built around CUFTA and NAFTA. According to Pratt, the government should adopt a more critical stance with regard to the shift of Canadian energy production towards the US market and the predominance of US investment in the Canadian energy sector. Finally, Michelle Swenarchuk (chapter 20) calls on Canadians to insist upon a full and public debate on the issue of life patents and to press for legislation that would both protect the original social purpose of patent law and reflect Canadian values in this key area.

Combined, the contributors to this volume offer an alternative (although far from comprehensive) vision of Canada – a vision of an economy and society based upon a different set of values and principles than those of free trade and neoliberalism. The contributors agree that Canadians should challenge the "no alternative" spin and analyses emanating from business think tanks and mainstream academics and, instead, insist that the problem is not the lack of alternatives but the lack of political will to pursue them. We turn now to the question of political will.

MOVING FORWARD:
RESISTING ASSIMILATION, DEEPENING DEMOCRACY

Murray Dobbin (chapter 21) posits that devising a strategy for resisting "deep integration" is no different from developing a strategy to resist the harmful effects of a broader neoliberal agenda (i.e., the Washington Consensus model). Developing such a strategy requires examining the material, social, political, and economic realities of Canada after twenty years of structural adjustment by Tory and Liberal, federal and provincial governments, as well as understanding the neoliberal ideology that has framed and produced those realities. Dobbin argues that a strong and united elite not only introduced neoliberal ideas to public discourse but also marginalized opposing viewpoints in the process. Simply stated, neoliberal ideas have become accepted as "natural" and are rarely questioned by Canadian politicians or citizens. And deep integration is simply the latest stage of this corporate agenda – one that requires what Dobbin calls "a counter-hegemonic response."

Dobbin places democracy at the centre of his analysis, in which he contends that the right has skilfully seized control of almost all of Canada's major democratic institutions. For instance, he notes that the right owns the majority of media outlets (aside from our national broadcasting corporation) and is consciously using them to establish its hegemony. Dobbin dubs this ideological project "a counter-revolution of lowered expectations," whose success is evidenced by the ways that Canadians have accepted fewer government responsibilities, lower levels of economic growth, smaller wage increases, and the view that a social democratic alternative is unfeasible. He goes on to show how this "counter-revolution of lowered expectations" has allowed the right to address one of its long-standing irritants: an "excess of democracy," which was identified as a problem by Samuel Huntington as far back as 1975 (Huntington, Crozier, and Watanuki 1975, 113). According to Dobbin, it is the left that is now decrying a crisis constituted by a declining quality of democracy and manifested in declining expectations and a hesitant acceptance of an eroding social democratic role for the Canadian state. Dobbin describes the right's twenty-year effort to lower people's expectations as a series of campaigns built around five key ideas: the inevitability of corporate globalization, deficit "terrorism," an assault on public employment and government in general, the promotion of the private sector as the repository of the public interest, and a drive to cut taxes for the wealthy and corporations. According to Dobbin, these campaigns have led to a shift in Canadian political culture, a shift that must be addressed and countered if "systemic Americanization" (perhaps a more accurate term than "deep integration") and its consequences are to be effectively challenged.

While Canada's current political state of mind is problematic, Canadian values are not. Dobbin suggests that a bright spot in this ideological battle can be found in the progressive social and cultural values of Canadians, which have persisted and grown stronger over the last decade even though the political expectations of a significant percentage of Canadians may have changed. But if these progressive values remain strong, then how has the right succeeded in bringing about such a dramatic shift in political expectations? Dobbin suggests that Canadians gravitated towards the right's neoliberal ideology in part because progressive forces failed to launch an ideological campaign of their own, largely due to their failure to understand that the battle was over ideas rather than policies. So while progressives succeeded in winning the hearts and minds of Canadians on CUFTA, they did less well with subsequent assaults on democracy and equality. In sum, business elites won the ideological contest while progressive forces focused on defending specific public policies and programs such as medicare, education, the environment, poverty, workers rights, and corporate regulation.

In short, progressive forces failed to frame and fight the neoliberal battle as a counter-hegemonic struggle. The absence of a formal national coalition that could devise a coherent counter-hegemonic vision certainly made matters more difficult. Progressive forces have spent the past twenty years fighting each new battle largely as a discrete engagement without adequately linking them to past conflicts. Moreover, the left has been forced to adopt a posture of "defending" education, "defending" environmental laws, and "defending" public ownership, workers rights, democracy, and government. Of course, some will argue that "discrete engagements" have produced significant victories at times – for instance, the national mobilizations to prevent Canadian involvement in the Iraq invasion and to keep Canada from joining missile defence.[23] But Dobbin argues that the "fight back strategy" lacks one element that has been at the core of every successful campaign for social progress in Canadian history – the promise of hope: "What is needed, then, is a good offence, a visionary response that ultimately posits a coherent strategy for rebuilding and reconceiving the Canadian nation within the context of a socially just and economically equitable hemisphere and an evolving challenge to corporate globalization" (chapter 21, 519).

Even though Dobbin offers a valuable prescription for moving forward, he admits that fighting deep integration as a single initiative is much more problematic than was the free trade fight of the mid-1980s because CUFTA was viewed as containing a multitude of threats to cherished Canadian institutions and social programs (also, there was a clearly defined implementation date around which to organize). Conversely, deep integration consists of multiple initiatives that will likely be pursued via an incremental strategy determined by what its promoters perceive to be politically achievable at any given moment. While contesting deep integration requires exposing the overall initiative and its corporate backers, much of the opposition that emerges will have to mobilize on multiple fronts. For progressives, these fronts are united by two common guiding principles under which all individual and strategic issues fit: sovereignty and democracy. In Dobbin's view, these two themes should not be treated independently when developing a counter-hegemonic response to neoliberalism.

The contested concept of "sovereignty" presents a unique challenge for progressive forces wanting to respond to deep integration in Canada. Many who fought against free trade in the 1980s saw themselves as Canadian nationalists defending their country's sovereignty, Canada's status as a social-democratic state, and a half-century of domestic social achievements. Their position evolved as they joined forces with progressive Americans, Mexicans, and other Latin Americans also resisting free trade and neoliberalism on the continent. They developed a more nuanced view of the international role of the Canadian state and adopted sharper internationalist positions on many issues.

The shift in the way that resistance forces framed their struggle reflected the increasing transnationalization of Canadian corporate capital and transformation of the Canadian state. Tony Clarke observes that continental integration is part of a business-driven, corporate restructuring process led by Canadian elites with more financial interests in the United States than in Canada. He argues that the interests of big capital in this country have become increasingly North American, to the point where the concept of a national business class has become almost meaningless.

Addressing the issue of sovereignty, Maude Barlow argues that Canadians must recognize that

the Canadian government does not play a progressive role at home or abroad. Internationally, Canada is not a victim – it is much of the problem ... this acknowledgement requires us to re-examine the language that we employ in opposition to deeper integration. We should move away ... from the old language of nationalism. We should not demand the re-assertion of a Canadian sovereignty that plays such an injurious role in the world. We should relate, on the contrary, in solidarity with progressive Americans who feel colonized, as we do, by Hollywood and Lockheed-Martin. We must fight not only for ourselves ... but so that everyone may share in the global commons. (I.T. MacDonald 2004, 1-1)

At the same time, it is difficult for those Canadian coalitions centred on cross-border alliances and issues of hemispheric integration to reorient their struggles to focus on the Canada-US relationship. Moreover, structuring such a struggle in a way that is not perceived as a replay of earlier

nationalist efforts requires a nuanced approach.[24] Some progressive thinkers have insisted that the concept of sovereignty remains highly relevant
but that the emphasis should be placed on "popular sovereignty." In the
words of political economist Gordon Laxer (2005): "Deep democracy is
the ultimate goal for all peoples. Popular national sovereignties, whether
national or regional, are necessary means. There is no real democracy if the
people do not have the sovereign power to decide their own collective and
individual lives."[25]

Duncan Cameron concludes that if greater integration with the United
States is to become a major political issue for public debate, then progressive civil society groups will have to lead the battle. The prospects of this
occurring are propitious, given the rise of new social movements in opposition to corporate globalization in Canada, the United States, and beyond.
In practice, resistance to deeper integration has been real and significant.
Things have not always worked as planned for the sponsors of deep integration: the ratification of the Kyoto Protocol, the tabling of the Romanow
Report on the future of health care, and opposition to joining the Iraq invasion prove that resistance can be effective. Various groups have also
defended civil, minority, immigrant, and refugee rights against the "anti-
terrorist" onslaught, and the Liberal government's temporary shift to the
left in the last year of Prime Minister Chrétien's tenure was due in great
part to his reading of the Canadian public's mood and its aversion to Bush
administration policies in the wake of the invasion.

Similarly, deep integration supporters failed to convince Ottawa to openly
participate in a Bush-sponsored missile defence program in 2005. Prior to
this, President Bush had cancelled his planned visit to Ottawa in May 2003
as an expression of displeasure with Canada's position on Iraq. Between
2003 and 2005, former us ambassador to Canada Paul Cellucci, in his
assumed role of colonial governor, intervened regularly in Canadian domestic affairs. Ottawa was eventually given an opportunity for reconciliation:
joining the ballistic missile defence program. When the government
responded to Washington's demands to initiate talks on this issue, it felt pressure from Canadians who oppose the militarization of space and the further
undermining of global stability. In the context of a minority Liberal government and a very effective public campaign led by the Polaris Institute and
others, the Martin government was forced to announce that Canada would
not participate in the missile defence program.

Canada's approach to missile defence and deeper integration in general
is likely to change with the arrival of a hawkish minority Conservative
government in February 2006. Stephen Harper's win can be attributed to
a Liberal party mired in corruption allegations in the wake of the Gomery
Inquiry, increased public scepticism about "politicians" in general and a
desire for "change," and a corporate-controlled media that increasingly

displays a right-wing bias. The fact that the Conservative Party is dominated by factions from the earlier extreme right-wing Reform and Canadian Alliance parties, and that Stephen Harper was once president of the
National Citizens Coalition – a lobby group established to fight public
health care in Canada – are grounds for intense concern.

Economic and political elites have seized the moment in order to push
for integrationist initiatives, both above and below the radar screen, mitigated only by the realities of the political conjuncture. The Harper government's rapid embrace of a business-led integration agenda under the
SPP, its announcement of large increases in defence spending aimed primarily at equipment purchases rather than conflict prevention through development assistance, its decision to extend and deepen Canada's counter-
insurgency mission in Afghanistan and to alter the NORAD agreement, its
capitulation to US demands on softwood lumber, and its steadfast support
for the Bush administration's Middle East and United Nations policies[26] –
these are just some of the ways in which the Conservative government has
moved to harmonize Canadian policies with those of Washington during
its first half year in power. As the new government announced large
increases in military expenditures, Canada's entanglement (initiated by the
Liberals) in low-intensity conflict in Afghanistan under US command[27]
became headline news. Urging Canada to go after the "scumbags" (Campion-
Smith 2005a), Chief of the Defence Staff Rick Hillier had already signalled
during the Martin government that the Bush administration's geo-strategic
interests – and its worldview – are now driving military and foreign policy,
while Canada's traditional UN-driven peacekeeping role appears to be
waning. The actions of the Harper government thus far are reinforcing this
trend.

The Conservative economic program builds on earlier structural adjustment measures initiated by then finance minister Paul Martin in the mid-
1990s, further bringing into line Canada's socioeconomic model with
Washington's. The Harper government's commitment to address the "fiscal
imbalance" between federal fiscal surpluses and provincial deficits as well
as to enact new tax cuts may be used as the excuse to reduce Ottawa's
ability to enforce national standards and sustain social programs. Actions
to increase private for-profit initiatives within Medicare, to dismantle an
incipient national childcare program (initiated by the Liberals in response
to popular demand), and to abandon the implementation of the Kyoto Protocol are all contributing to such restructuring.

Harper's agenda will be tempered by the limited manoeuvrability of a
minority government and his determination to appear moderate to an electorate that he hopes will give him a majority in the next federal election. If
the Conservatives do win such a majority and those restraints disappear,

the integrationist agenda will likely be advanced aggressively and some of the worst-case scenarios analyzed in this book could become a reality.

The struggle continues, and progressive forces are promoting various counter-proposals to integration. Both the New Democratic Party (NDP) and the Bloc Quebecois (BQ) have challenged specific parts of the deep integration agenda; both parties were vocal opponents of Washington's space-based missile system, of Canadian participation in the invasion of Iraq, of Canada's growing counter-insurgency role in Afghanistan, and, more recently, of Harper's blind allegiance to Bush's policies in the Middle East. The NDP's progressive engagement on this front has been far more sustained and comprehensive than has the BQ's. While it may be true that the BQ has supported numerous progressive causes, such as benefits for the unemployed, anti-scab legislation, and industrial development policy, the party remains an ideological mish-mash with an important and influential right wing. In fact, it may be the ideological contradictions at the heart of the party that have prevented it from developing a coherent policy on relations with the United States (Graefe and Mayo 2004).

Progressive policy work is also being performed by think tanks such as the Canadian Centre for Policy Alternatives,[28] the Parkland Institute,[29] and the Polaris Institute,[30] as well as by magazines such as *Canadian Dimension*[31] and websites such as rabble.ca. The Council of Canadians has taken a leadership role in mobilizing civil society responses to deep integration, organizing a national tour, a citizens' inquiry, and a number of publications.[32] Mel Hurtig (2002, 2004) and others are calling for action before it is "too late to save Canada." Maude Barlow cautions that "many of the values we hold dear and that tie us together as a nation would be undone" by Fortress North America. She argues that the challenge is to "recast the notion of security to include the fundamental right to health and education, clean air and water, and peace and justice" (Barlow 2005, cover, 256). Clearly, much work remains to be done.[33] Progressive forces will need to continue to expose deep integration policies for what they are: agendas for Americanization and for further undermining Canadian democracy.

Duncan Cameron points out that, since integration supporters have powerful allies in the corporate-owned media and institutional defenders on both sides of the border, the current campaign of disinformation is likely to continue. One of their objectives is to discredit the concerns raised by free trade critics since the 1980s that agreements such as NAFTA and CUFTA "would lead to a downward harmonization of Canadian standards in social policy to levels prevailing in the US" (Cameron 1993, xvii). For example, integrationists claim that Canada's gradual move towards the legalization of marijuana and the recognition of gay marriage are but two of many examples that demonstrate Canada's continued political and social autonomy. This assessment by integrationists is highly selective, however. The contributors to this volume provide many examples that show that the identified threats were indeed accurate and that damage resulting from the overall direction of change continues to occur under free trade and neoliberal restructuring.

What has tempered the shift towards Americanization (and what has brought about important victories such as the recognition of gay marriage) has been the broad resistance by wide sectors of Canadian society and organized political mobilization against specific policies related to neoliberal restructuring. In sum, Canadians have shown a willingness to assert their values and rights through the democratic spaces available to them. There are also indications that postwar achievements – strong democratic institutions, public services, tolerance and multiculturalism, a charter of rights, an active labour movement, social democratic parties, and an increasingly organized civil society – have created an imprint deep enough to withstand two decades of neoliberal policies and propaganda.

Still, Canadians cannot be complacent in light of real threats and considerable challenges. The Canadian Council of Chief Executives and its allies in the Conservative government are mounting a major push for the ultimate corporate agenda – assimilation with the United States – because from their perspective, their earlier efforts to move Canada down the road of neoliberal restructuring have been only partially successful. Their assessment of limited gains is correct. Although earlier trade agreements have removed significant control over our energy policies, we still have levers to control water resources. Although labour contracts have been eroded, we still have very strong public-sector services. And although democratic spaces have narrowed, there is still a vibrant yearning for a better future.

NOTES

The authors wish to express gratitude for comments on an earlier draft from Louis Lefeber, Liisa North, several of the contributors to this volume, and two anonymous reviewers. We acknowledge editorial assistance from Ian T. Macdonald, Timothy D. Clark, and Jon Lindemann.

1 See also (Clarkson 2002a) and McBride (2001, 2003).
2 Since NAFTA, Canada has entered into a number of other trade and investments deals, including three free trade agreements (Israel, Chile, and Costa Rica), twenty-one bilateral investment agreements (or foreign investment protection and promotion agreements [FIPAs]), and other less ambitious trade agreements with various countries and regions. Other agreements are being negotiated, including the

Canada-Central America Free Trade Agreement (CA4FTA) and the Canada-Korea Free Trade Agreement.

3 Rima Berns-McGown (2005, 9) compellingly argues that it is not Canadian and US values that are different but, rather, our political cultures, or how those values are expressed "both collectively and in the public sphere."

4 The 1982–85 Royal Commission on the Economic Union and Development Prospects for Canada (the Macdonald Commission) examined Canada's economy and called for bilateral free trade negotiations with the United States.

5 The perception of "little help" was reinforced by the August 2005 ruling of an extraordinary challenge committee (a panel of last resort under the NAFTA dispute resolution mechanism) and Washington's refusal to respect the ruling (Brennan 2005). This ruling upheld earlier NAFTA rulings that countervailing duties applied by the United States on Canadian softwood lumber since 2002 were illegal. Despite Washington's disregard of the rulings, in July 2006 the Stephen Harper government signed an agreement on softwood lumber with the United States, which, according to critics, constitutes "a huge sellout of Canadian sovereignty, jobs and commercial interests" (Piatkowski 2006).

6 Department of External Affairs (DEA 1987, 5), cited in Winham (1988, 53).

7 The myth of a "secure market access" has been debunked by the Harper government's softwood lumber agreement. It effectively capitulates to US demands that trade be regimented by "managed trade" rules driven by domestic US interests. See note 5 above.

8 These concepts are defined in Marc Lee's chapter 11.

9 This and other related concepts are defined and explained in Seccareccia's chapter 9.

10 The proposals were unrealistic in a number of respects. For example, according to Clarkson and Banda, "[o]n the one hand, the panic-infused business proposals underestimated Canada's bargaining leverage, which would make most of the big and small ideas pointless. On the other hand, in a 'leap of logic,' Canadian businesses and think tanks overestimated the attractiveness to the United States of any strategic deals with Canada, making most of their proposals unrealistic" (chapter 5, 148).

11 It is worth noting that the term "community" in this instance obscures the stark power disparities that characterize any North American agreement.

12 The task force was a joint project of the Council of Foreign Relations (CFR) in the United States, the Mexican Council of Foreign Relations (MCFR), and the Canadian Council of Chief Executives (CCCE). The leaked document, made available through the Council of Canadian's website, is a confidential summary of the task force's first meeting, which took place in Toronto in October 2004 (COC 2005a; CFR 2005a). The official task force recommendations came out in 2005 (CFR 2005b, 2005c).

13 Contributors to this volume refer in various ways to the promoters of deeper integration, depending on historical perspectives and the nuances of their analysis:

continentalists, integrationists, free traders, assimilationists, empire loyalists, and so forth.

14 Leo Panitch and Sam Gindin (2003, 30) point to the important change in the structure of the Washington administration in the transition from Clinton to Bush II: "The branches of the American state that control and dispense the means of violence are now in the driver's seat; in an Administration representing a Republican Party that has always been made up of a coalition of free marketers, social conservatives and military hawks, the balance has been tilted decisively by September 11th towards the latter."

15 The next few paragraphs are adapted from Staples' chapter 6.

16 Even though there is a clear focus on North American defence and security in the defence portion of the document, it also confirms the role of the military "in delivering humanitarian assistance to those in desperate need, and in rebuilding shattered communities and societies" (Canada 2005, 2). According to some critics, however, in Afghanistan (since 2001) and Haiti (since 2004) Canada's role has been defined primarily by US strategic interests, not humanitarian need (Fenton 2005).

17 This is a term applied by Michel Foucault as a metaphor for modern "disciplinary" societies and the surveillance that characterizes them.

18 Gotlieb's realist-based approach advances a number of other prescriptions, including the need to recognize that US power is the dominant feature of the current world order, that Canada will never regain its status as a middle power, that Canadians must "liberate themselves from the belief that the UN is the sacred foundation of our foreign policy," and that we must abandon our focus on international rule making or norm making (Gotlieb 2005, 24–5).

19 Axworthy (2005) believes we should be "seriously considering an end to NAFTA and [rely] instead upon the World Trade Organization to regulate the terms and provisions of free trade." He suggests that Canada should strengthen its multilateral approach linking up with new economic powers such as China, India, Brazil and South Africa. He also calls for activist national policies on issues such as freshwater resources and energy policy. He believes "the bottom line is that [we require] the essentials of a vibrant public domain, capable of taking greater control of our own decisions and pursuing global economic and security initiatives in a forceful, made-in-Canada way" (Axworthy 2005).

20 Derek Burney was until 2004 president and chief executive officer of CAE Inc., a major Canadian defence contractor with direct ties to the Pentagon.

21 This is the title of a report by the Council of Canadians (Barlow 2004).

22 The 2006 softwood lumber agreement is of limited scope but fails Campbell's criteria of minimizing the loss of policy flexibility. See notes 5 and 7 above.

23 We are grateful to one of the anonymous reviewers for raising this point.

24 To the extent that comprehensive North American negotiations will take the form of a NAFTA-plus agreement that fully incorporates Mexico into the negotiations,

the Canadian coalitions will find, again, a natural partner in like-minded Mexican coalitions.

25 See the valuable discussion on the question of popular sovereignty begun in *Canadian Dimension* magazine (vol. 36, no. 4, July/August 2002).

26 The reaction of the Harper government to the Israel-Hezbollah conflict in mid-2006 raised much criticism in Canada (Albo 2006).

27 In July 2006 NATO assumed command from the United States of the counter-insurgency effort in southern Afghanistan, where most Canadian forces are active.

28 This volume and the conference that initiated it were co-sponsored by the CCPA. Three of the chapters appeared earlier as CCPA reports, and one is an updated and abridged version of a CCPA book. Other work includes Campbell (2005), Robinson (2005), and Campbell and Finn (2006).

29 Various articles in the *Parkland Post* have dealt with the "deep integration" agenda as well as conferences such as one in fall 2003 entitled Challenging Empire and another in fall 2005 entitled Resisting the Empire: Challenges to US Power.

30 The Polaris Institute has placed a spotlight on the "corporate security state" and specific issues such as national missile defence. See Staples and Robinson (2005), Robinson (2006), and Staples (2006).

31 See note 25.

32 *Colony or Country? The Future of Canada-US Relations* was a public forum tour in seven cities across the country (COC 2004). *Crossing the Line: A Citizens' Inquiry on Canada-US Relations* included public hearings in ten cities across Canada (Caron 2005). In addition, the council has been responsible for a number of publications (Barlow 2004, 2005; COC 2004, 2005b; Dobbin 2002).

33 Important critical work addressing various aspects of Canada-US relations, the post 9/11 context, and deepening continental integration is already available. See, for example, in addition to the works cited above, Axworthy (2003), CBC (2004), Clarkson (2002a, 2002b, 2003), Cox (2005), Drache (2004), Gabriel and Macdonald (2003), Griffin-Cohen and Clarkson (2004), Helleiner (2004, 2006), J. Laxer (2004), McCullum (2006), McDougall (2006), Roach (2003), and Seccareccia (2004).

REFERENCES

Adams, Michael. 2003. *Fire and Ice: The United States, Canada and the Myth of Converging Values*. Toronto: Penguin Canada.

Albo, Greg. 2006. Israel and the Crises in Lebanon and Canada. July 17. *rabble.ca*. Available at <http://www.rabble.ca/news_full_story.shtml?x'51330>.

Axworthy, Lloyd. 1999. *Human Security: Safety for People in a Changing World*. Ottawa: Department of Foreign Affairs and International Trade.

– 2003. *Navigating a New World: Canada's Global Future*. Toronto: Knopf Canada.

– 2005. Time to Redefine Ties with US. *Toronto Star*, 22 August, A17.
Barlow, Maude. 2004. *The Canada We Want: A Citizens' Alternative to Deep Integration*. Ottawa: Council of Canadians.
– 2005. *Too Close for Comfort: Canada's Future within Fortress North America*. Toronto: McClelland and Stewart.
Berns-McGown, Rima. 2005. Political Culture, Not Values. *International Journal* 60 (2): 341-9.
Blanchfield, Mike. 2006. Missile Defence Returns: Canada Part of NATO Study of European Shield. *National Post*, 12 May, A1.
BPG. 2006. *The Final Report on Canada and the United States (CANUS) Enhanced Military Cooperation*. Peterson Air Force Base, CO: Bi-National Planning Group.
Brennan, Richard. 2005. Goodale Warns US on Lumber. *Toronto Star*, 16 August, A6.
Burney, Derek. 2005. *Foreign Policy: More Coherence, Less Pretence*. The Simon Reisman Lecture in International Trade Policy. Ottawa: Centre for Trade Policy and Law.
Byers, Michael. 2006. Continental Integration by Stealth. *Toronto Star*, 28 April, A17.
Cameron, Duncan. 1993. Introduction. In *Canada under Free Trade*, ed. D. Cameron and M. Watkins, ix-xxiii. Toronto: Lorimer.
Campbell, Bruce. 2005. *Of Independence and Faustian Bargains: Going down the Deep Integration Road with Uncle Sam*. Ottawa: Canadian Centre for Policy Alternatives.
Campbell, Bruce, and Ed Finn, eds. 2006. *Living with Uncle: Canada-US Relations in an Age of Empire*. Toronto: Lorimer.
Campion-Smith, Bruce. 2005a. Canada Urged to Go after "Scumbags": General Talks Tough as Mission Looms. *Toronto Star*, 15 July, A1.
– 2005b. Canada Won't Join US Missile Defence Plan. *Toronto Star*, 23 February, A9.
Canada. 2001. *Canada and the United States Sign a Smart Border Declaration*. Ottawa: Department of Foreign Affairs and International Trade.
– 2002. *Enhanced Canada-US Security Cooperation*. Ottawa: Department of National Defence.
– 2004a. *Joint Statement by Canada and the United States on Common Security, Common Prosperity: A New Partnership in North America*. Ottawa: Office of the Prime Minister, Government of Canada.
– 2004b. *Securing an Open Society: Canada's National Security Policy*. Ottawa: Privy Council Office, Government of Canada.
– 2005. *Canada's International Policy Statement: A Role of Pride and Influence in the World – Defence*. Ottawa: Government of Canada.
Caron, Guy. 2005. *Crossing the Line: A Citizens' Inquiry on Canada-US Relations*. Ottawa: Council of Canadians.
CBC. 2004. *Canada and the New American Empire – Briefing Notes*. Canadian

Broadcasting Corporation and the Centre for Global Studies, University of Victoria. Available at <http://www.globalcentres.org/can-us/bn.html>.

– 2005. Indepth: Canada's Military. Canadian Forces in the 21st Century. CBC News Online, 26 July. Available at <http://www.cbc.ca/news/background/ cdn-military/>.

CFR. 2004. Council Joins Leading Canadians and Mexicans to Launch Independent Task Force on the Future of North America. Press release. Washington: Council on Foreign Relations.

– 2005a. Task Force on the Future of North America: Summary of the Toronto Meeting. Washington: Council on Foreign Relations. Available at <http://www.canadians.org/documents/TF_ReportFeb05.pdf>.

– 2005b. Creating a North American Community: Chairmen's Statement – Independent Task Force on the Future of North America. Washington: Council on Foreign Relations.

– 2005c. Building a North American Community: Report of an Independent Task Force. Washington: Council on Foreign Relations.

Clarkson, Stephen. 2002a. Canada's Secret Constitution: NAFTA, WTO and the End of Sovereignty. Ottawa: Canadian Centre for Policy Alternatives.

– 2002b. Uncle Sam and Us: Globalization, Neoconservatism, and the Canadian State. Toronto: University of Toronto Press.

– 2003. The View from the Attic: Towards a Gated Continental Community? In The Rebordering North America: Integration and Exclusion in a New Security Context, ed. P. Andreas and T. J. Bierstecker, 68–89. New York: Routledge Press.

COC. 2004. Colony or Country: The Future of Canada – US Relations Strategy Sessions Report. Ottawa: Council of Canadians.

– 2005a. Confidential Task Force Document Reveals True Business Agenda for Canada. Press release. Ottawa: Council of Canadians.

– 2005b. A Citizen's Guide to Fighting Deep Integration. Ottawa: Council of Canadians.

Cox, Robert W. 2005. A Canadian Dilemma: The United States or the World. International Journal 60 (3): 667–84.

d'Aquino, Thomas. 2003. Security and Prosperity: The Dynamics of a New Canada-United States Partnership in North America. Toronto: Canadian Council of Chief Executives.

Dallaire, Roméo A. 2003. Shake Hands with the Devil: The Failure of Humanity in Rwanda. Toronto: Random House Canada.

DEA. 1987. The Canadian-US Free Trade Agreement: Synopsis. Ottawa: Department of External Affairs.

Dobbin, Murray. 2002. Ziplocking North America: Can Canada Survive Continental Integration? Ottawa: Council of Canadians.

– 2003. Paul Martin: CEO for Canada. Toronto: James Lorimer.

Dobson, Wendy. 2002. Shaping the Future of the North American Economic Space:

A Framework for Action. In *C.D. Howe Commentary – The Border Papers*, no. 162. Toronto: C.D. Howe Institute.

– 2003. Trade Can Brush In a New Border. *Galt Global Review* <http://www.galt-globalreview.com>, 4 February.

Drache, Daniel. 2004. *Borders Matter: Homeland Security, Borders and the Search for North America*. Halifax: Fernwood Publishing.

Dymond, Bill, and Michael Hart. 2003. Canada and the Global Challenge: Finding a Place to Stand. In *C.D. Howe Commentary – The Border Papers*, no. 180. Toronto: C.D. Howe Institute.

Espinosa, J. Enrique, Jaime Serra, John Cavanagh, and Sarah Anderson. 2002. Happily Ever NAFTA? *Foreign Policy* (September/October): 58–65.

Fenton, Anthony. 2005. Canada's Growing Role in Haitian Affairs. Part 1. *Z-Net*, 21 March.

Foster, John W. 2002a. "The Big Idea": Conference Report for NSI. Ottawa: North-South Institute.

– 2002b. Personal communication.

Gabriel, Christina, and Laura Macdonald. 2003. Beyond the Continentalist / Nationalist Divide: Politics in a North America "Without Borders". In *Changing Canada: Political Economy as Transformation*, ed. W. Clement and L.F. Vosko, 213–40. Montreal and Kingston: McGill-Queen's University Press.

Gotlieb, Allan. 2005. Romanticism and Realism in Canada's Foreign Policy. *Policy Options/Options Politiques* 26 (2): 16–27.

Graefe, Peter, and Sara Mayo. 2004. Road Bloc or Building Bloc? Social Democratic Futures in Québec. *Canadian Dimension* 38 (3). Available at <http://canadiandimension.com/articles/2004/05/01/140/>.

Griffin Cohen, Marjorie, and Stephen Clarkson, eds. 2004. *Governing Under Stress: Middle Powers and the Challenge of Globalization*. London: Zed Books.

Grinspun, Ricardo, and Maxwell A. Cameron. 1993. The Political Economy of North American Integration: Diverse Perspectives, Converging Criticisms. In *The Political Economy of North American Free Trade*, ed. R. Grinspun and M.A. Cameron, 3–25. New York: St. Martin's Press.

Grinspun, Ricardo, and Robert Kreklewich. 1994. Consolidating Neoliberal Reforms: "Free Trade" as a Conditioning Framework. *Studies in Political Economy* 43 (Spring): 33–61.

Harder, V. Peter. 2001. Address to Ottawa Roundtable on North American Linkages. *Micro-Economic Policy Analysis Branch Bulletin (Industry Canada)* 8 (2): 10.

Harris, Richard G., and David Cox. 1983. *Trade, Industrial Policy, and Canadian Manufacturing: Report from the Ontario Economic Council*. Toronto: University of Toronto Press.

Helleiner, Eric. 2004. Canada as a 13th Reserve District? Federalism and the Governance of North American Monetary Union. *Canadian Foreign Policy* 11 (2): 91-109.

– 2006. *Towards North American Monetary Union? The Politics and History of Canada's Exchange Rate Regime*. Montreal and Kingston: McGill-Queen's University Press.

Hoberg, George, ed. 2001. *Capacity for Choice: Canada in a New North America*. Toronto: University of Toronto Press.

Hufbauer, Gary Clyde, and Jeffrey J. Schott with Paul L.E. Grieco and Yee Wong. 2005. NAFTA *Revisited: Achievements and Challenges*. Washington: Institute for International Economics.

Huntington, Samuel, Michel Crozier, and Joji Watanuki. 1975. *The Crisis of Democracy: Report on the Governability of Democracies to the Trilateral Commission*. New York: New York University Press.

Hurtig, Mel. 2002. *The Vanishing Country: Is It Too Late to Save Canada?* Toronto: McClelland and Stewart.

– 2004. *Rushing to Armageddon: The Shocking Truth about Canada, Missile Defence, and Star Wars*. Toronto: McClelland and Stewart.

Industry Canada. 2006. *United States, Canada, and Mexico Launch North American Competitiveness Council*, 15 June. Ottawa: Industry Canada.

Ipsos-Reid. 2004. *Canadians' Views on Future Canada-*US *Relations: Canadians Support Policy Independence from* US. Toronto: Ipsos-Reid.

– 2006. *As Canadian War Casualties Mount, Support for Afghanistan Mission Sinks*. 29 July. Toronto: Ipsos News Center.

Jackson, Andrew. 2003. *Why the "Big Idea" Is a Bad Idea: A Critical Perspective on Deeper Economic Integration with the United States*. Ottawa: Canadian Centre for Policy Alternatives.

Kitchen, Veronica. 2004. Smarter Cooperation in Canada-US Relations? *International Journal* 59 (3): 693–710.

Knight, W. Andy. 2006. Canada Abandons Its Role as UN Peacekeeper. *Edmonton Journal*, 12 April, A19.

Laxer, Gordon. 2005. *The* US *Empire and Popular Sovereignty*. Edmonton: Parkland Institute. Available at <http://www.ualberta.ca/~parkland/research/perspectives/LaxerWSFJ ano5.htm>.

Laxer, James. 2003. *The Border: Canada, the* US *and Adventures along the 49th Parallel*. Toronto: Doubleday Canada.

Lipsey, Richard G. 2000. The Canada-US FTA: Real Results versus Unreal Expectations. In *Free Trade: Risks and Rewards*, ed. L.I. MacDonald, 99–106. Montreal and Kingston: McGill-Queen's University Press.

McBride, Stephen. 2001. *Paradigm Shift: Globalization and the Canadian State*. Halifax: Fernwood Publishing.

– 2003. Quiet Constitutionalism in Canada: The International Political Economy of Domestic Institutional Change. *Canadian Journal of Political Science* 36 (2): 251–73.

MacDonald, Ian T. 2004. *Canada, Free Trade and Deep Integration in North America: Revitalizing Democracy, Upholding the Public Good*. Conference

Report. Toronto: Centre for Research on Latin America and the Caribbean, York University.

MacDonald, L. Ian, ed. 2000. *Free Trade: Risks and Rewards*. Montreal and Kingston: McGill-Queen's University Press.

McDougall, John. 2006. *Drifting Together: The Political Economy of Canada-US Integration*. Calgary: Broadview Press.

McCullum, Hugh. 2006. *Fuelling Fortress America: A Report on the Athabasca Tar Sands and US Demands for Canada's Energy*. Ottawa: Canadian Centre for Policy Alternatives, Parkland Institute, and Polaris Institute.

Panitch, Leo. 1994. Globalisation and the State. In *Between Globalism and Nationalism: The Socialist Register 1994*, ed. R. Milliband and L. Panitch, 60–93. London: Merlin Press.

Panitch, Leo, and Sam Gindin. 2003. Global Capitalism and American Empire. In *Socialist Register 2004: The New Imperial Challenge*, ed. L. Panitch and C. Leys, 1-42. London: Merlin Press.

Pastor, Robert A. 2001. *Toward a North American Community: Lessons from the Old World for the New*. Washington, DC: Institute for International Economics.

Piatkowski, Scott. 2006. Checking the Fine Print on Softwood Deal. 13 July. *Rabble.ca*. Available at <http://www.rabble.ca/columnists_full.shtml?x'51253>.

PRI. 2002. *Strengthening the North American Partnership: Scenarios for the Future*. Conference Summary, Ottawa, Ontario, 12–13 May. Ottawa: Policy Research Initiative, Government of Canada.

Regehr, Ernie. 2006. NORAD *Renewal: Considerations for the Parliamentary Debate*. Ottawa: Project Ploughshares.

Roach, Kent. 2003. *September 11: Consequences for Canada*. Montreal and Kingston: McGill-Queen's University Press.

Robinson, Bill. 2005. *Let's Not Go Ballistic: The Case against Canadian Participation in the US Missile Defence System*. Ottawa: Canadian Centre for Policy Alternatives.

– 2006. *Boots on the Ground: Canadian Military Operations in Afghanistan and UN Peacekeeping Missions*. Ottawa: Polaris Institute.

Rugman, Alan R. 1986. US Protectionism and Canadian Trade Policy. In *Canada/US Free Trade Agreement: An Assessment*, ed. E.H. Fry and L.H. Radebaugh, 4–24. Provo, UT: Brigham Young University.

Sallot, Jeff. 2004. Deadline Looms on Continental Defence Project. *Globe and Mail*, 10 November, A4.

SCFAIT. 2002. *Foreign Affairs Committee Calls for Canada to Advance Strategic North American Vision*. News release. Ottawa: Standing Committee on Foreign Affairs and International Trade.

Scholte, Jan Aart. 2000. Cautionary Reflections on Seattle. *Millennium: Journal of International Studies* 29 (1): 115–21.

Schwanen, Daniel. 2004. Deeper, Broader: A Roadmap for a Treaty of North America. In *The Art of the State II: Thinking North America*, ed. T.J. Courchene, D.J. Savoie, and D. Schwanen, 3–60. Montreal: Institute for Research on Public Policy.

Seccareccia, Mario. 2004. Is Dollarization a Desirable Alternative to the Monetary Status Quo? A Critical Evaluation of Competing Currency Arrangements for Canada. *Studies in Political Economy* 71/72 (Autumn/Winter): 91–108.

Segal, Hugh. 2003. North American Community: A Prospect to Excite and Inspire. *Inroads* 13 (Summer-Fall): 2–9.

Senate. 2002. *Defence of North America: A Canadian Responsibility.* Ottawa: Standing Senate Committee on National Security and Defence.

– 2003. *Uncertain Access: The Consequences of US Security and Trade Actions for Canadian Trade Policy*, vol. 1. Ottawa: Standing Senate Committee on Foreign Affairs.

SPP. 2005. *Security and Prosperity Partnership of North America: Report to Leaders.* 27 June. Washington: US Department of Commerce.

Stanford, James O. 1993. Continental Economic Integration: Modeling the Impact on Labor. *Annals of the American Academy of Political and Social Science* 526 (March): 92–110.

Staples, Steven. 2006. *Missile Defence: Round One.* Toronto: Lorimer.

Staples, Steven, and Bill Robinson. 2005. *It's Never Enough: Canada's Alarming Rise in Military Spending.* Ottawa: Polaris Institute.

Weintraub, Sidney. 2004. NAFTA's *Impact On North America: The First Decade.* Washington: Center for Strategic and International Studies.

White House. 2005. *Fact Sheet: Security and Prosperity Partnership of North America*, 23 March. Washington: Office of the Press Secretary, White House.

Winham, Gilbert R. 1988. Why Canada Acted. In *Bilateralism, Multilateralism and Canada in US Trade Policy*, ed. W.J. Diebold, 37–54. New York: Ballinger Publishing Co.

Wolfe, Robert, and Matthew Mendelsohn. 2004. Embedded Liberalism in the Global Era: Would Citizens Support a New Grand Compromise? *International Journal* 59 (2): 261.

2

Free Trade Allies: The Making of a New Continentalism

DUNCAN CAMERON

Free trade with the United States has been a recurring theme in Canadian politics since prior to Confederation, and it has always generated considerable political controversy. In establishing the terms of debate, free trade advocates and foes alike look to economics and political economy to help guide their arguments. Appeals are made to national identity, historical destiny, and conceptions of Canadian foreign policy as well as to how free trade affects wealth creation and distribution, and its impact on structural economic weaknesses and regional disparities.

The debates have pitted diverse social forces against one another, and they use whatever strategies and tactics they can call upon to defeat each other in their political struggles. The links between political parties and other actors in the free trade battle lead to the formation of free trade alliances and counter-alliances. The purposes and workings of these alliances merit further attention, and this chapter examines the forces centred in corporate Canada that have campaigned in favour of free trade in contemporary Canada.

The chapter is divided into four main sections. Section one examines the issue of partisan politics and business policy development, and provides the context of business efforts to promote free trade. Section two looks at traditional continentalism and how business has worked to foster a new continentalism. The corporate trade and investment agenda for North America includes the important debate over the US economic model and its implications for Canada. To explore what this debate is about, section three places the "United States question" in recent historical perspective. Section four examines the issues that arise in Canada due to Washington's political and economic dominance. A separate conclusion evaluates the prospects for the corporate continental agenda in Canada.

As Canada moved into the first decade of the new millennium, the issue of further economic integration in North America became a priority for

Canadian business lobby groups. What is being proposed is properly described as a "deep integration" agenda, and it is closely examined in other contributions to this volume. This chapter, instead, focuses on the political relationships that have made free trade agreements a contemporary reality and that continue to drive the ongoing debates, discussions, and negotiations: primarily, the links between partisan politics and corporate lobbies and how they affect policy development. Setting the agenda and framing the issues, working out a public relations strategy, and seizing the initiative with government are all key components of the business strategy to influence governments and to guide public policy formation. Past success is a tribute to skilfull political manoeuvring. But it is no guarantee that the policy victories of the past will be repeated in the future. In order to succeed with their plans to promote further economic integration in North America, Canadian business needs to ensure the continued support of the government of the day and to neutralize opposition from both the partisan political world and civil society.

This chapter argues that both the federal Liberal Party and the Conservative government that took power in February 2006, have broken with the position of pursuing counterweights to US power – a position set out in an important 1972 policy statement that focused on enhancing Canadian independence as a "third option" (Sharp 1972). Indeed, perhaps the principal effect of the North American integration ushered in by Brian Mulroney was to prefigure even deeper continentalist initiatives on the part of the Liberals, who responded, as did Mulroney, to business policy development initiatives. Under the initial stewardship of Paul Martin, and now of Stephen Harper, the federal government is prepared to pursue a "new continentalism" that goes well beyond the North American integration agenda it inherited in 1993, demonstrating the effectiveness of the political strategies used by corporate Canada to consolidate an alliance with governments, irrespective of partisan stripes.

POLITICS, BUSINESS, AND THE FREE TRADE AGENDA

The bilateral Canada-US Free Trade Agreement (CUFTA) came into force on 1 January 1989, and the North American Free Trade Agreement (NAFTA) replaced it five years later. These two agreements were the result of considerable corporate efforts deployed on both sides of the border and in Mexico. While governments played the lead role in negotiations, the corporate sector was the key player in securing support for government negotiations. Without a commitment from business, no Canadian government would have been able to proceed with talks. And now business forces are actively pushing Canada to adopt even closer economic relations with the

United States. Obviously, though pleased with the direction of Canadian policy, corporate leaders are not satisfied with what has been achieved to date.

The issue of bilateral trade with the United States is a priority for the federal government at any time. Statements about trade disputes with the United States are staples of daily news reporting. All political leaders are judged by their ability to "manage the relationship" with their US counterparts. Political fortunes can rise or fall based on policy towards the United States. The March 2003 decision of the Chrétien government not to send Canadian ground forces to Iraq won wide support from the public, despite opposition to the prime minister's stance from the business elite and the Anglophone press, fearful of what Canada's non-participation would do to economic relations with its southern neighbour. Yet while politicians may take their lead from business leaders, they must also respond to the electorate. Knowing this, business groups have made managing public opinion a high priority.

Although the business push for a continental project of deep integration includes measures in the areas of defence, foreign policy, immigration, human rights, and social policy – as well as trade, investment, and industrial and economic policy – for Canada, the deep integration agenda is primarily about adopting the US economic model and accepting that other policies must either fit into the constraints imposed by the free market conditions of competition and laissez-faire or be set aside. Policy areas affected include all forms of government ownership, legislation, regulation, and administration covering a host of subjects for all levels of government.

As a significant departure from current policies, the new continentalism would normally be brought forward within a climate of extensive partisan political debate. But the most important debate took place away from the public eye, within the Liberal Party itself, in the post-11 September 2001 period: behind the scenes, the party of government at that time had been persistently pressured by business coalitions into implementing and supporting further continental integration. Since the then main opposition party, the Conservatives, already supported integration, the partisan political debate was muted. As the ruling party, it had been up to the Liberals to decide internally whether or not they agreed with the Conservatives on the need for deeper continental integration and, if so, how this should be pursued. Rather than the Canadian public, it was the Liberal cabinet that decided how much more Canadian constitutional authority should be given up in order to secure further cross-border deals. That this happened without public debate is a significant victory for Canadian business because the "new continental" agenda goes well beyond the "old continentalism."

Policy shifts routinely take place within political parties and can sometimes be worked out internally and away from the public eye, through a give-and-take resulting in compromise. But on other occasions the issues are carried outside the party and into the public debate, where one side wins and the other loses. For instance, dissent within the Liberal Party and opposition to continentalism by Canadian civil society groups could eventually lead to the debate spilling into the public realm. Both members of the government and its free trade allies in business are well aware of this threat to the deep integration project, and efforts to control public debate in the post-9/11 period were extensive and continuous.

Control of the debate is facilitated by the full support given to the deep integration agenda by the CanWest Global/Southam media empire and their rivals at Bell/CTV/Globe and Mail. The Canadian Broadcasting Corporation (CBC), moreover, seems to have abandoned its role as an independent broadcaster serving the public interest, rejecting the vision of one of its two founders, Graham Spry, who argued that public broadcasting in Canada is crucial since the choice is between "the state or the United States" (*Canadian Encyclopedia* 2005). Despite its mandate to serve the public, the current CBC shows little desire to oppose a policy its main advertisers and government masters support.[1]

A wide-open public debate on Canada's future role in North America is exactly what business groups have been working to avoid – and to great effect. What they prefer is a controlled dialogue, behind the scenes, with spokespeople emerging to make reassuring comments. They had an important success when they joined forces with allies in the United States and Mexico to put North American integration back on the US agenda, to be taken up by President George W. Bush during his second mandate. In the fall of 2004 the very prestigious and influential New York-based Council on Foreign Relations announced that a task force had been created to develop policies on the next steps to be taken in furthering North American integration (CFR 2004). Council task forces were designed to provide the incoming US president with policy choices that have the support of US business and establishment figures. The task force included a significant number of Canadian members, including former deputy prime minister John Manley, who was named a co-chair. In its final report, the task force claimed it had "developed a roadmap to promote North American security and advance the well-being of citizens of all three countries" (CFR 2005).

What characterizes the deep integration agenda is the attempt by Canadian business to fuse the security agenda (so important in post-September 11 Washington) to the economic agenda (so important to Canadian business). Positions on issues such as border security measures, immigration, and continental defence are being set out by the powerful forces within Canadian society that favour deeper integration with the United States.[2] Canadian business groups work continuously to develop coherent policies and to affect government legislation. Efforts to establish an elite consensus are necessary so that the issues of sovereignty, independence, economic control, and Canadian citizenship can be kept from emerging as public issues, which could make the government nervous about acting on the continental integration project.

Evidence of the business effort to establish a new continental agenda is widely available. Over recent years, when one adds together research projects under way at the Fraser Institute, the C.D. Howe Institute, the Institute for Research on Public Policy (IRPP), and the Public Policy Forum, such efforts amount to the equivalent of a private-sector Royal Commission. In addition, the Donner Canada Foundation, Dominion Institute, BorderLines, and Maytree Foundation have sponsored a series of conferences and consultations (BorderLines 2005). A major business alliance on "secure and trade-efficient borders" has already scored its first policy successes (CSTEB 2001, 2005), and more projects are under way, with a customs union the leading candidate for winning support from the Canadian continentalist elite. Within the federal public service the Policy Research Initiative, a group housed within the Privy Council Office and able to draw on resources across government, is undertaking its own studies on deeper integration with the United States, the direct outcome of the private-sector efforts to make a new relationship with the United States a public policy priority (PRI 2005).

CONTINENTALISM: OLD AND NEW

Canadian business has always maintained privileged relations with both the Conservative and Liberal parties, and each in turn has promoted business interests. But the two main political parties have traditionally had differences in their foreign policy outlooks that were critical to their self-definition as parties. Partisan identities, particularly until the post-1945 period, were linked to attitudes towards the United States. Historically, the Conservative Party favoured continued close ties to Great Britain, while the Liberals expressed more openness to the United States. Indeed, the tendency among political scientists and historians was to see the Conservatives as the nationalist party and the Liberals as the continentalist party (Thornburn and Whitehorn 2001).

After 1945, however, the usefulness of this way of distinguishing between the parties was diminished as the Liberals presented themselves as internationalists who were sometimes nationalists and frequently, but not exclusively, continentalists. The Conservative Diefenbaker regime, first elected in 1957, wanted to restore the traditional pattern (without much success). Under Brian Mulroney the Progressive Conservatives soundly rejected their heritage as the party of the British connection, taking important steps towards deepening continental integration by signing CUFTA and then negotiating NAFTA (Martin 1993; McDonald 1995; McQuaig 1991).

Prior to the corporate push for free trade, the Canadian government position on Canada-US relations had been defined in the famous "options" paper, authored by Mitchell Sharp (1972), which called for building counterweights to the United States and its dominant position in Canada's international relations. This represented a departure from the usual Liberal Party position in favour of close economic relations with the United States, and it reflected over a decade of internal party and national debate about the issue of foreign ownership and its effect on Canadian economic development.

The emergence of nationalist political and economic policies in the 1970s caused business to re-evaluate its way of doing politics. Rather than simply lobbying political parties and supporting them behind the scenes as well as financially, Canadian business leaders decided to become full actors in the process of public policy development. As well as supporting research groups such as the C.D. Howe Institute and the Fraser Institute, Canadian business created the Business Council on National Issues (BCNI), which is made up of 150 chief executive officers from major corporations. The BCNI, which was later on rebranded as the Council of Canadian Chief Executives (CCCE), has played the leading role in pushing free trade agreements and calling for deeper integration.

With the economic arguments rehearsed and the issues examined, the case for free trade was made in a 1975 report by the Economic Council of Canada (1975), whose basic ideas were presented more publicly in the Macdonald Commission report (Macdonald Report 1985). Both these reports, though sponsored by the government, clearly reflected the views of business leaders, as did the 1982 report of the Canadian Senate committee chaired by George Von Rogen (Standing Committee on Foreign Affairs 1982). Canadian business was indeed mastering the art of public policy formulation, using research reports to put issues on the public agenda, policy statements to have views reported in the press and the electronic media, and opinion polls to track public reaction to their campaigns.

On the issue of relations with the United States, companies worked together through the BCNI to keep government and opposition parties abreast of their thinking as well as of the public and media approval they were able to marshal for their policy options. The parties knew in advance where support for continentalism was coming from and what opposition to business-led policies such as free trade would mean in terms of electoral financing and media coverage. In the early 1980s the Liberal government published its own study of trade relations (Department of External Affairs 1983). Authored by trade bureaucrats, it argued for a sectoral approach to free trade with the United States, while stopping short of adopting the pro-free trade position being developed by business groups.

With the elections of the Conservative governments of Brian Mulroney in 1984 and 1988 the business agenda assumed full control in Ottawa. Returned to power in 1993, the Liberals clearly recognized the altered political landscape, moving ahead with NAFTA and becoming enthusiastic proponents of the Free Trade Area of the Americas (FTAA) and the World Trade Organization (WTO). The importance of the corporate perspective was reflected in the House of Commons report *Partners in North America: Advancing Canada's Relations with the United States and Mexico* (SCFAIT 2002), which addressed a wide range of key corporate issues, including the formation of a North American monetary and customs union and talks on the "smart border" initiatives. What is clear is that for the twenty years following the election of Brian Mulroney, the government agenda of both Liberals and Conservatives on trade and investment with the United States has been that favoured by Canadian business groups.

Ironically, it was business groups, including the Canadian Manufacturers Association, who most strongly opposed the continental integration championed by the Liberal government of Sir Wilfrid Laurier in the free trade election of 1911. When business lobby groups changed sides following the efforts of the BCNI, however, the issue came to life again. Since the 1980s, with neoclassical economists cheering them on, led by the BCNI (now CCCE) corporate groups have developed strategies to win not just government support but support from the media and the Canadian public as well. Indeed, it was the combination of traditional lobbying efforts and public diplomacy that secured support for CUFTA in 1988. Free trade has been further assisted by those provincial governments with substantial natural resource revenues from sales to the United States. Yet while pro-free trade voices are heard from within the federal government and public service, as well as in the provincial legislatures, business groups have remained the most persistent, vocal, and influential voice.

The case for free trade has been made and amended over more than two decades of serious political campaigning by its proponents, and the Canadian experience with free trade since 1989 has been interpreted through that lens. Given the dismal economic results (see Jackson, this volume), business is not emphasizing the economic evidence of how Canada has fared; rather, the new continentalism is always about the future, about how new benefits can be reaped by going ahead with further negotiations. What has become increasingly clear is that neither CUFTA and NAFTA nor the proposed FTAA and the WTO are sufficient. Corporations want to enlist their free trade allies in government for new undertakings; they want to negotiate a new "grand bargain," to cite Alan Gotlieb (2004), or a "big idea," as Wendy Dobson (2002) has called it.

With a new push under way by business to integrate security and economic questions, it matters greatly where the federal government stands on the issue of further continental integration. The traditional answer during the Liberal governments had been that they saw the question of Canada-US relations as allowing for a split agenda, where issues could be addressed separately. Economic issues could be dealt with on their own terms, with military and political issues bringing together other players and responding to different circumstances. In Liberal policy circles there had traditionally been little coordination between, for example, Canadian immigration and human rights policies, on the one hand, and trade or investment questions on the other. Such policy areas were thought to be separate until September 11 created a new reality where, for instance, immigration policy had become part of the trade agenda. This shift cast doubt on the notion of policy autonomy and demonstrated how, in trade talks, both foreign and domestic policies became subject to the American security imperative.[3]

The business approach of linking support for the US security agenda on anti-terrorism to economic integration would force the Liberals to abandon their issue-by-issue approach to Canada-US relations. The new continentalism that arose after 11 September 2001 makes explicit that closer economic relations between Canada and the United States necessitate eliminating policy independence and differences around security, border, and immigration issues.

Since 1945 the Canadian debate over whether to promote or resist continentalism has passed through several stages (Clarkson 1984). Generally speaking, the debate has revolved around the role of the democratic state in promoting economic growth and regulating private business. The "interventionist" state has been seen as the instrument of Canadian independence by the Walter Gordon wing of the Liberal party, by the Diefenbaker and George Drew Conservatives, and by the Waffle faction of the New Democratic Party (NDP).

However, since the public controversy over CUFTA in the run-up to the 1988 election, and the subsequent introduction of NAFTA, the terms of the public debate have changed somewhat. Rather than seeing the issue as being mostly about the appropriate balance between the private market and the state, it is now more apparent (if not more generally understood) that it is about the nature of the economy itself. Specifically, those debating economic issues are clearly divided over the question of whether or not the US economic model is the appropriate one for Canada (Cameron 1986a, 1986b; Cameron and Watkins 1993).

The new continentalism means accepting the US economic model and paying the price of public policy subservience. The US economic model rests on the assumption that the market for labour is like any other market: lower the price and the market "clears." This contrasts with the robust system of income support available to European workers, including minimum wages, active labour market policies with job training funds, and generous basic incomes. For opponents of the US model it also means accepting its social consequences. As Canada becomes more like the United States in income and wealth distribution, it would develop a similar profile on social issues, from public housing and education to homelessness and drug use. Citizen movements no longer take for granted the presence of a benign state dedicated to serving democratic aims; rather, they recognize that the Canadian state has become subservient to corporations. The very existence of movements to counter corporate power is evidence of a crisis of legitimacy. People are losing trust in government, even as they mobilize in defence of an imagined "social contract" between government and its citizens (Cameron and Smith 1992).

For the large corporations that have financed and supported the Liberal and Conservative parties, the positive values of the corporate-driven free market model are taken for granted. For the popular-sector groups that have emerged to fight the corporate agenda, the question of what can be done to resist US economic domination around the world is at the centre of their concerns. These "anti-globalization" activists are following in a tradition initiated by economic nationalists who struggled against Canadian dependence on the United States.

The issue of foreign ownership in Canada was first raised by the Gordon Royal Commission (Canada 1958) and then in the 1963 budget of Walter Gordon himself. The subsequent Watkins (Task Force on the Structure of Canadian Industry 1968) and Grey (Department of Trade and Commerce 1972) reports confirmed the trends identified by Gordon: rising US ownership of the Canadian economy was a threat to Canadian political independence. As the levels of foreign control over natural resources and manufacturing increased, the government's capacity to further employment and income goals diminished. For instance, it was seen as difficult to encourage US companies to undertake research and development in Canada or to further process natural resources (rather than to simply export the raw materials). The US-dominated Canadian business climate did not create opportunities to ensure quality head office employment contracts for legal, accounting, advertising and other services within Canada or to promote exports outside corporate walls. As these foreign actors ended up with more economic clout in Canada, they could use their power to play an increasingly dominant role in Canadian politics, influencing political parties and even entire parliaments and provincial legislatures (Azzi 1999). This was why continentalism had to be resisted.

Gordon argued that, since Canadian branches of foreign-owned corporations did not make share-holdings available to Canadian investors, it was impossible for Canadians to participate in the payout of dividends from profitable Canadian holdings, except through the purchase of shares in the parent corporation. This meant a significant drain of Canadian investment capital to New York. It also meant the continued underdevelopment of capital investment markets within Canada.

According to economic nationalists, the financial dependence of the branch-plant economy would undermine the Canadian standard of living. Foreign-owned Canadian companies operated through borrowing Canadian funds. When they needed to make investments for expansion, or to take over independent Canadian firms, they could finance their activities from retained earnings or Canadian bank loans. Profits could be remitted to the head office directly, or through payments of dividends on preferred shares of wholly owned subsidiaries, or through elaborate "transfer pricing" arrangements designed to report profits in low-tax jurisdictions. In short, the takeover of Canadian business by foreign interests was largely financed in Canada, and the outflow of profits far exceeded the puny amounts of foreign capital actually invested in Canada.

Under pressure from the NDP, the minority Trudeau government of 1972–74 created a Foreign Investment Review Agency (FIRA) to screen new investments for their "potential benefit" to Canada. But, as critics such as Mel Hurtig pointed out, the issue of how to deal with US companies that already controlled over 50 percent of the key manufacturing industry was not dealt with under FIRA. One of the first acts of the Mulroney government, moreover, was to withdraw the FIRA legislation and to replace it with Investment Canada, a new agency mandated to promote foreign investment only (Hurtig 1991).

The debate over trade policy and foreign investment culminated in CUFTA and NAFTA. As discussed in other chapters, these agreements enshrined investor rights to national treatment in each country. They provided for restrictions on state action to influence investment. In effect, both trade deals represented the adoption by Canada of continental economic integration as its principal economic strategy. Politically, free trade was championed by the Tories as signifying the coming-of-age of Canada, showing our ability to compete head to head with the United States on a level playing field. In this way the Conservatives, like those who opposed free trade, shrouded themselves in the cloak of economic nationalism.

What the trade agreements in fact represented, however, was the enshrinement of US corporate objectives for investment policy, intellectual property rights, and trade in goods and services as Canadian state policy. Moreover, they discriminated against those corporations based outside North America, such as Japanese auto companies. Politically, Canada shifted its allegiance from multilateral economic diplomacy as a forum for dealing with the United States to head-to-head bilateralism, or the "hub-and-spoke" arrangement of NAFTA. Canada downplayed the postwar

policy of seeking to deal with the United States through creating alliances
with others to set rules multilaterally, choosing instead the path of bilateral
and subregional trade negotiations, where there were few allies to offset US
power. Predictably, the United States was able to gain more through bilateral talks than was Canada.

CANADA AND US HEGEMONY

One of the unforeseen consequences of multilateral trade liberalization
after 1945 was that Canadian vulnerability to a more aggressive US foreign
economic policy actually increased rather than decreased. To illustrate, in
eight rounds of the General Agreement on Tariffs and Trade (GATT) trade
talks, the customs tariff established to protect Canadian industry was pro-
gressively reduced so that, prior to the 1989 CUFTA, the average tariff on
Canadian imports from the United States was already minimal. Industrial
protection, a part of the old National Policy first introduced in 1879 by the
Macdonald Conservatives, and defended by the Tories and the Canadian
Manufacturers Association in the celebrated 1911 free trade election, had
largely been eliminated through multilateral trade talks prior to CUFTA.

The withdrawal of tariff protection meant that government policies were
mainly limited to macroeconomic measures with uneven regional effects.
This led to regional development efforts beginning in the 1960s. Reducing
regional disparities was even enshrined as a national goal in the 1982 constitutional package. But the "great inflation" of the 1970s called Keynesian
economic stimulation policies into question, and the subsequent "great
recession" of 1982 left Canada searching for a new economic direction
(Campbell 1987). In 1985 this new direction was publicly pronounced
when the Macdonald Royal Commission proposed free trade, deregulation, and privatization. In effect, Macdonald was saying it was time to end
the social contract of the postwar welfare state. This was well understood
at the time by the groups that contributed their dissenting views to *The
Other Macdonald Report* (Drache and Cameron 1985).

Of course, as Canadian companies saw tariff protection negotiated away
through the multilateral trade agreements under the GATT, they gained
reciprocal access to the US market. The average tariff on Canadian exports
to the United States was negligible at the time of CUFTA – 1 percent on all
goods and 4 percent on dutiable goods (Clark 1993, 45) – and the vast
majority of Canadian exports entered duty free to the US market (Cameron
1986b, xxiv). The insignificant tariffs in place before CUFTA signalled the
already considerable level of economic integration in North America.
Those Canadian companies that were successful exporters were shipping
upwards of 60 percent of all production south of the border, and fully 80

percent of all Canadian exports were destined for the US market. Similarly, Canadians were purchasing 60 percent of all their imports from the United States, and Canada had one of the highest levels of import penetration of any industrialized country (Montcalm 1988, 178).

The high concentration of Canadian exports to the US market, however, made Canada extremely vulnerable to US protectionist measures. Because the percentage of Canadian production being exported to the United States was much higher than was the percentage of US production being exported to Canada, retaliation against Washington's protectionist initiatives would not get Canada very far. For this very reason, Canada had traditionally looked for allies in the GATT who shared the same distrust of US protectionism and who desired enhanced access to the US market.

Though it described its principal policy option – free trade – as a "leap of faith," what the Macdonald Commission recommendations amounted to were more a *loss* of faith in the GATT and the multilateral policy framework of the postwar era. The commission suggested that Canada should adopt a new national policy, whereby the benefits of economic expansion are trade-driven, and it called for a bilateral pact with our southern neighbour as the best way to secure productivity and income gains. But the consequences of bilateralism went far beyond questions of productivity and income, placing Canadian public policy under constant pressure to harmonize its policies along US standards. What Macdonald was proposing was more than economic integration with the United States, which had already been largely attained. Understanding this, Canadian popular-sector groups mobilized against so-called free trade and for the preservation of the Canadian social contract, defined by public ownership, social programs, redistributive taxation, public support for arts and recreation, and regulation of private business.

For Canada, trade liberalization in the postwar era had meant increased dependence on the US export market. When the United States introduced an across-the-board tariff of 10 percent in 1971, it was Canada that got hit the hardest. Following tough protectionist talk in the US Congress after the collapse of the GATT ministerial meetings on trade in 1985, it was the Canadians who were panicked into accepting the US strategy of bilateralism, abandoning the multilateral approach. In office from 1968 until 1984 (except for a short period in 1979), the Trudeau Liberals failed to produce an industrial strategy to replace the tariff. Stephen Clarkson and Christina McCall have argued persuasively that Canada was therefore left vulnerable to the claim that further liberalization through free trade was the only viable policy option (McCall and Clarkson 1991, 1994).

With free trade and continental integration presented as the only viable solution to the economic slowdown of the 1970s, the Liberals under Jean

Chrétien – despite opposing free trade in the 1988 election and calling for the renegotiation of NAFTA in 1993 – aggressively supported the expansion of free trade to include all of Latin America (except Cuba) through the FTAA and to include Asia through the Asia–Pacific Economic Cooperation (APEC) agreement, which included corporations as members (Dobbin 1998). Support for multilateral free trade rules was a focus of the Liberal government, which advocated at the Organization for Economic Co-operation and Development (OECD) in the 1990s for the ill-fated Multilateral Agreement on Investment (MAI) and strongly supported the WTO before and after it came into being in 1995.

Canadian policies have thus shifted to become increasingly aligned with those of our southern neighbour (McBride and Shields 1997), with the Harper government radically moving in that direction. As such, they are not so much the policies of the US government as they are the policies of the US corporate elite. These institutional and individual actors occupy a privileged position within the United States, and drive much of the country's foreign policy. Their favoured policies have been aptly described by John Williamson of the influential Institute of International Economics as the "Washington Consensus" (McQuaig 2001).

The consensus enforcers include the US Treasury and the Federal Reserve Banks as well as the International Monetary Fund (IMF) and the World Bank. Critics in Latin America and Europe describe this approach as neoliberalism. A wide network of establishment think tanks and their in-house intellectuals work to promote this ideology. The dominant media treat neoliberalism favourably. In substance it can be summarized, unsurprisingly, as the view that state policies should be subordinated to the workings of the market, which, in practice, means the interests of large corporate actors. A particularly influential group in translating neoliberalism into policy has been the New York-based Business Roundtable, which brings together the chief executives of major US transnationals.

Canadian policy discussions that arise within the context of how to pursue further integration within the North American economy are closely tied to the dominant US discourse of neoliberalism. That is why "deep integration" is really about pushing the neoliberal agenda forward in Canada. The question that needs to be brought forward in Canada, however, is who benefits and who pays the costs of renewed continentalism? Will Canada become wealthier through closer relations with the United States, or will Canada become more exploited economically by the dominant partner? And the new continentalism brings in other perspectives as well. The viability of the "made-in-Canada" social contract will depend on whether a Canadian economic development model – other than continentalism – is considered undesirable, impossible, or worth even working towards (see Campbell, this volume).

CONTESTING THE NEW CONTINENTALISM

The Canadian economy is usually characterized as being made up of two sectors: a market sector under private ownership and a public sector financed by taxes and public borrowing. However, it is important to note the increasing importance of a third sector, or social economy, comprised of not-for-profit and non-governmental organizations (NGOs) of all sorts. Whereas the traditional private sector operates on the profit principle, and the public sector is traditionally concerned with security (defined in the broadest sense), third-sector activities arise to meet needs that go unfulfilled in both the private and public realms. NGOs operate on a cost-recovery basis, some receiving state support, others soliciting membership dues or donations or selling services. Within this popular sector much valuable new thinking about economics and politics is taking place.

For example, in recent years popular-sector groups have produced an alternative federal budget (AFB), spelling out in detail measures to improve employment prospects, reduce poverty, enhance social protection, and strengthen public finances. Although small in scale, the AFB process has been consciously democratic. It is open to any group that accepts its basic priorities, such as employment creation. For example, over 150 political economists endorsed the 1997 AFB, and it was discussed on CBC's *The National*. Budget workshops and consultations have taken place across Canada. The AFB is released simultaneously with the federal budget in cities and communities all over the country. Originally coordinated by CHOICES and the Canadian Centre for Policy Alternatives, it has had the support of labour, women's groups, churches, and various social organizations representing seniors, students, farmers, and anti-poverty activists. It sets out a program for enhancing the Canadian social contract through re-regulating capital, and it offers a coherent alternative to continentalism and Americanization (CCPA 1997).

Washington Consensus policy options, on the other hand, are championed by Canadian business lobby groups, which are greatly influenced by their US-based counterparts, which hold significant sway because Canadian corporate capital is so highly integrated with US-based transnational capital. For those who oppose further assimilation with the United States, confronting the new continentalism entails identifying and criticizing the impact of Washington Consensus policies on Canada. It also requires a broader approach centred on international civil society and the network of non-governmental organizations that operates as a sort of "open conspiracy" against the dominant economic order (Murphy 1999).

Popular-sector groups, moreover, have "set the bar higher" in taking on the task of not just influencing Canadian government policies but of joining with others around the world to influence international public opinion. Canadian groups are reaching out to others in a postcolonial world that has failed to realize much of the promised gains of political independence. Indeed, many of the concerns about the neoliberal economic order in Canada are widely shared across the developing world.

For the popular sector, thinking globally means controlling short-term speculative movements of money in and out of the currency market through a Tobin tax on foreign exchange transactions, as proposed in the AFB. It means adopting a social clause in the WTO that would ban exploitation of child labour and uphold worker rights. It means global accords on environmental protection, gender equality, and human rights. In general, it means using international law and international institutions to constrain the freedom of corporations to exploit, pollute, and drive down wages and taxation levels, and to stop the race to the bottom. In short, resisting the new continentalism and Uncle Sam's economic domination means recapturing some of the internationalist idealism of the postwar period.

For recent Canadian governments, thinking and acting globally has meant promoting great power policies at G7/8 economic summits. It has meant supporting structural adjustment policies (SAPs) imposed by the IMF, primarily upon Third World nations but also upon developed nations such as Canada.[4] As discussed elsewhere in this volume, it has meant championing the corporate agenda on intellectual property rights, investment, and services at the OECD and the WTO. It has also meant using international treaties to limit the ability of national assemblies, parliaments, and legislatures to act in the public interest. In short, it has meant supporting Washington on every major issue facing the world economy and abandoning Mitchell Sharp's "third option."

During the last decade the Liberal Party shifted its social base of support, reaching out to the upper-income bracket and, especially, to aspiring upper-income earners. Evidence of the new strategy was clear in then finance minister Paul Martin's budgets, which cut social spending while providing tax breaks to this social group (Dobbin 2003).[5] It is no coincidence that the social group that benefited most from Martin's policies was precisely the group that is most prepared to follow the corporate political lead and the least likely to ask too many questions about continental integration (Jackson and Robinson 2000). When the Martin government faltered, upper-income Canadians were quick to shift their support to Stephen Harper, who became prime minister in 2006.

The same business lobby groups that have pushed for these budgetary measures also favour some form of customs union with the United States (see Lee, this volume). A common external tariff would in turn require a common trade policy at the WTO. Since trade policy is a major part of foreign economic policy, Canada would in effect be limiting its ability to express differences with the United States publicly on international economic issues of importance. In effect, the business lobby is trying to get what Canada failed to obtain in CUFTA and NAFTA: the elimination of US trade remedy law. But there is no reason to believe that the demand would be met. A common tariff, however, might be of interest to the United States if it were presented as a package deal along with increased US influence over Canadian immigration and refugee policy and border security.

In its public pronouncements and electoral campaigns, the Liberal government duplicitously invoked images of the Canadian social contract that its own policies were busily undermining. From 1993 on, with both the former Reform Party and the Progressive Conservatives attacking it from the political right, the Liberal government gave up much of the centre, shifting sharply to the right in order to maintain business support (Dobbin 2003). The social liberalism of the party became overwhelmed by business liberalism; however, the party never dared openly to tout the superiority of the US economic model. The actions of popular-sector groups may be one reason why it did not do so. Resisting economic domination from the south provides a basis for organizing common action in Canada and gives Canadians a way of acting in concert with others abroad, including segments of US society where corporate rule has its share of home-grown critics. As the extreme right rose to power in early 2006 under Stephen Harper's leadership, the stakes for such resistance have become even larger.

CONCLUSION

By the turn of the new millennium the Liberal Party had adopted the new continentalist agenda proposed by business, without regard for the loss in national independence. As this book goes to print, a minority Conservative government intends to advance an extreme version of that same agenda. And yet there were certainly economic grounds for questioning the move towards more integration. Moreover, there was no evidence to suggest that this was something most Canadians wanted to pursue. Integration resulted in a Gross Domestic Product (GDP) per capita ranking in the World Bank Atlas that fell from eighth before free trade to twenty-first by 1997. Overall, the 1990s produced the second worst economic results for Canadians of the twentieth century, exceeded only by the disastrous 1930s (Jackson and Robinson 2000, 75–94, 195). Beyond that, a sense of national belonging is very prevalent in Canada. That may be the reason why, in his successful election campaign, Harper relied on this sentiment, calling on his supporters to "stand up for Canada" and ending his speeches with "God Bless Canada."

Nonetheless, left unchecked, the push towards a further stage of continental integration, initiated by the Liberal government, is likely to become the Canadian reality under a Conservative government. Since the 2003

merger of the Canadian Alliance with the Progressive Conservative Party
or, more accurately, the takeover of the latter by the former, the Conservatives under Stephen Harper have defended earlier trade agreements and
championed new ones, despite the historical position of the party and the
challenge by erstwhile leadership candidate David Orchard. While the NDP
is likely to stake out an economic nationalist position, it has yet to show an
ability to ignite widespread public support.

Deep integration can proceed without emerging as a partisan issue
between the government and the official opposition since both the Liberals
and the Conservatives support it. Conservative support is open and forth-
right, and another Liberal government would be likely to continue in the
same direction. The Westminster model of parliamentary government suggests that a government anxious to maintain support in the country act in
accordance with opposition policy, thus denying the opposition issues
around which to raise money and build support. In fact, the opposition
Liberals remember all too well being outspent by the Conservatives, awash
with corporate money in the 1988 election. It is unlikely they would allow
a schism with corporate Canada to arise again, allowing political investments and economic resources to flow to the revitalized Conservative
Party.

As this book goes to print in mid-2006, the Liberal adherence to continentalism has yet to be affirmed by a new leader. But, since the departure
of Pierre Trudeau in 1984, the decisive victory of the business Liberals over
the social Liberals augurs poorly for internal party resistance to the continental project. The new continentalism has political repercussions for
Canadian identity and serious implications for the nature of Canadian citizenship. These issues may yet surface within the Liberal Party, but this is
unlikely unless a social liberal leader emerges to challenge the dominant
business faction. The presidency of George W. Bush and the strength of US
Republicans ensures that an important part of civil society will continue to
be wary of the United States and, moreover, will continue to seek points of
difference between the two countries in political and social outlook. It is to
these civil society groups that we must now look to defend Canada against
the corporate-led deep integration agenda.

NOTES

1 See Raboy and Bruck (1989) for the political implications of media power.
2 The classic study of the Canadian corporate elite remains Clement (1975).
3 In fact, in the past free traders within the party argued that having commercial
   questions dealt with under a CUFTA or NAFTA process would mean *more* room for
   Canadian manoeuvring in foreign policy because the United States could not link

market access to foreign policy complicity. Now, in the hope of winning commercial concessions from the United States, free traders are negotiating on issues that
have little to do with commercial policy.

4 In 1995 then Finance Minister Paul Martin bowed to IMF pressure and implemented a severe austerity package (Dobbin 2003, 54–5).

5 For instance, in 1995 Martin cut spending to education and health by about $25
billion over five years and reduced unemployment insurance benefits by about
$10 billion per year, ostensibly to eliminate the deficit (Finance Canada 1995). In
2000, however, Martin allocated the hard-earned federal surplus to tax breaks
worth $100 billion, which primarily benefited upper-income earners. Martin went
on to provide further relief for upper-income earners through the elimination of
the 5 percent surtax, the expansion of capital gains exemptions from a 75 percent
inclusion rate down to 50 percent, and the creation of special benefits for holders
of stock options (Finance Canada 2000).

REFERENCES

Azzi, Stephen. 1999. *Walter Gordon and the Rise of Canadian Nationalism*. Montreal: McGill-Queen's University Press.

BorderLines. 2005. *BorderLines: Canada in North America*. BorderLines. Available
at <http://www.borderlines.ca/>, cited 31 July 2005.

Cameron, Duncan. 1986a. *The Free Trade Papers*. Toronto: Lorimer.

– 1986b. Preface. In *The Free Trade Papers*, ed. D. Cameron, xi–xix. Toronto:
Lorimer.

Cameron, Duncan, and Miriam Smith. 1992. *Constitutional Politics*. Toronto:
Lorimer.

Cameron, Duncan, and Mel Watkins. 1993. *Canada under Free Trade*. Toronto:
Lorimer.

Campbell, Robert M. 1987. *Grand Illusions: The Politics of the Keynesian Experience in Canada, 1945–1975*. Peterborough: Broadview.

Canada. 1958. *Final Report of the Royal Commission on Canada's Economic
Prospects*. The Gordon Report. Ottawa: Government of Canada.

Canadian Encyclopedia. 2005. *Graham Spry*. Historica Foundation of Canada.
Available from <www.thecanadianencyclopedia.com/>, cited 19 September 2005.

CCPA. 1997. *The Alternative Federal Budget*. Ottawa: Canadian Centre for Policy
Alternatives.

CFR. 2004. *Council Joins Leading Canadians and Mexicans to Launch Independent
Task Force on the Future of North America*. Press release. Washington: Council
on Foreign Relations.

– 2005. *Task Force Urges Measures to Strengthen North American Competitiveness, Expand Trade, Ensure Border Security*. Press Release, 17 May. Washington:
Council on Foreign Relations.

Clark, Mel. 1993. Canadian State Powers: Comparing the FTA and the GATT. In *Canada under Free Trade*, ed. D. Cameron and M. Watkins, 41-91. Toronto: Lorimer.

Clarkson, Stephen. 1984. *Canada and the Reagan Challenge*. Toronto: Lorimer.

Clement, Wallace. 1975. *The Canadian Corporate Elite: An Analysis of Economic Power*. Toronto: McClelland and Stewart.

CSTEB. 2001. *Coalition for Secure and Trade-Efficient Borders: About the Coalition*. Coalition for Secure and Trade-Efficient Borders 2001. Available at <http://www.cme-mec.ca/national/template_na.asp?p'104>, cited 31 July 2005.

– 2005. *Rethinking Our Borders: A New North American Partnership*. Ottawa: Coalition for Secure and Trade-Efficient Borders.

Department of External Affairs. 1983. *Canadian Trade Policy for the 1980s: A Discussion Paper*. Ottawa: Department of External Affairs.

Department of Trade and Commerce. 1972. *Foreign Direct Investment in Canada*. The Grey Report. Ottawa: Government of Canada.

Dobbin, Murray. 1998. *The Myth of the Good Corporate Citizen*. Toronto: Stoddart.

– 2003. *Paul Martin: CEO for Canada*. Toronto: James Lorimer.

Dobson, Wendy. 2002. What's the Big Idea, Canada? Globe and Mail, 16 April, A17.

Drache, Daniel, and Duncan Cameron. 1985. *The Other Macdonald Report*. Toronto: Lorimer.

Economic Council of Canada. 1975. *Looking Outward: A New Trade Strategy for Canada*. Ottawa: Economic Council of Canada.

Finance Canada. 1995. *Canadian Federal Budget 1995*. Budget Speech February 27. Ottawa: Finance Canada.

– 2000. *Canadian Federal Budget 2000*. Budget Speech February 28. Ottawa: Finance Canada.

Gotlieb, Allan. 2004. Protecting Canada's Eggs in the US Basket. In *Policy Options*, October, 5–9.

Hurtig, Mel. 1991. *The Betrayal of Canada*. Toronto: Stoddard.

Jackson, Andrew, and David Robinson. 2000. *Falling Behind: The State of Working Canada*. Ottawa: Canadian Centre for Policy Alternatives.

McBride, Stephen, and John Shields. 1997. *Dismantling a Nation: The Transition to Corporate Rule in Canada*. Halifax: Fernwood.

McCall, Christina, and Stephen Clarkson. 1991. *Trudeau and Our Times*. Vol. 1. Toronto: McClelland and Stewart.

– 1994. *Trudeau and Our Times*. Vol. 2. Toronto: McClelland and Stewart.

Macdonald Commission. 1985. *Report of the Royal Commission on the Economic Union and Development Prospects for Canada*. The Macdonald Report. Ottawa: Minister of Supply and Services.

McDonald, Marci. 1995. *Yankee Doodle Dandy*. Toronto: Stoddart.

McQuaig, Linda. 1991. *The Quick and the Dead: Brian Mulroney, Big Business and the Seduction of Canada*. Toronto: Penguin.

- 2001. *All You Can Eat*. Toronto: Penguin.

Martin, Lawrence. 1993. *Pledge of Allegiance: The Americanization of Canada in the Mulroney Years*. Toronto: McClelland and Stewart.

Montcalm, Mary Beth. 1988. Free Trade and Continental Integration. In *The Free Trade Deal*, ed. D. Cameron, 176–83. Toronto: James Lorimer and Co.

Murphy, Brian K. 1999. *Transforming Ourselves Transforming the World: An Open Conspiracy for Social Change*. London: Zed Books.

PRI. 2005. *North American Linkages*. Policy Research Initiative, Government of Canada. Available at <http://policyresearch.gc.ca/page.asp?pagenm'rp_ nal_ index>, cited 31 July 2005.

Raboy, Marc, and Peter A. Bruck. 1989. *Communication For and Against Democracy*. Montreal: Black Rose Books.

SCFAIT. 2002. *Partners in North America: Advancing Canada's Relations with the United States and Mexico*. Ottawa: Standing Committee on Foreign Affairs and International Trade.

Sharp, Mitchell. 1972. Canada-US Relations: Options for the Future. *International Perspectives* (Autumn issue).

Standing Committee on Foreign Affairs. 1982. *Canada-United States Relations*. Ottawa: Parliament of Canada.

Task Force on the Structure of Canadian Industry. 1968. *Foreign Ownership and the Structure of Canadian Industry*. The Watkins Report. Ottawa: Government of Canada.

Thornburn, Hugh G., and Alan Whitehorn. 2001. *Politics in Canada*. 8th ed. Toronto: Prentice Hall.

3

Corporate Canada: Washington's Empire Loyalists

TONY CLARKE

Behind the scenes in Ottawa, since the late 1990s Canada's big business leaders have been quietly mapping out a blueprint for a new deal with the United States. Arguing that "everything has changed" in the wake of 11 September 2001 and the subsequent wars in Afghanistan and Iraq, they started lobbying to achieve new forms of economic union and strategic alignment with Washington. Plans crystallized during 2002 and 2003 as the C.D. Howe Institute called for a "Big Idea" and others for a "Grand Bargain."

The strongest political muscle was flexed by the Canadian Council of Chief Executives (CCCE), representing the country's largest 150 corporations. During the second week of April 2003, CCCE head Thomas d'Aquino led a delegation of this country's corporate leaders to Washington, DC, where they held a series of meetings with their counterparts in the United States, the Business Roundtable, and high-level figures in the Bush administration (Francis 2003, 7). The CCCE had just undergone a facelift. Formerly known as the Business Council on National Issues (BCNI), the group suddenly announced in January 2003 that, after twenty-five years, it was changing its name. But the change of name was more than mere public relations. In launching the CCCE, d'Aquino also unveiled the next phase of the big business agenda for continental assimilation into the United States post 9/11. Canada's business leaders had begun working on a five-point plan of action called the North American Security and Prosperity Initiative, or NASPI (Bertin 2003). The prime objective of the April meetings in Washington was to promote their new plan as effectively as possible.

The political moment, however, was particularly sensitive. In Ottawa, Jean Chrétien's government had recently declared Canada's intention not to join Washington in its invasion of Iraq, while anti-US sentiments had been publicly expressed by some cabinet ministers and back bench members of Parliament. In an effort to mend fences, d'Aquino and his delegation of one hundred business leaders from the CCCE shifted their meeting from Montreal to Washington. Briefings were scheduled with Tom Ridge, Homeland Security Secretary; Spencer Abraham, Energy Secretary; Andrew Card, White House Chief of Staff; and Richard Perle, former chair of the White House Defence Policy Board.

By all accounts, it was Richard Perle's lecture that sharpened the agenda for the Washington summit. An influential advisor to President Bush and an associate with the American Enterprise Institute, a conservative think tank, Perle is known to be the chief architect of the Bush Doctrine on National Security. According to reports, Perle told the Canadian business elite that Ottawa had to come clean as an unquestioning US ally and beef up its commitments to military and security priorities (Morton 2003). The terms of engagement for a new deal with the United States were thus laid on the table.

Canada's chief executive officers (CEOs) got the message. Ottawa would have to change its priorities dramatically, building up its military and strengthening its security commitments. In short, these were the price tags to be paid for round three of free trade with the United States. The message was even more urgently received by business leaders like Derek Burney, former Canadian ambassador in Washington during the Mulroney government and now CEO of aerospace and defence contractor, CAE. Having contracts with the US Department of Defence, CAE was in danger of facing a backlash from Bush administration officials. Arguing that "Canada's place in the world is defined by our relationship with the US," Burney called on Canada to "play a strong role" in helping Washington rebuild Iraq after the invasion, thereby setting the stage for Canadian corporations to cash in on lucrative postwar construction contracts (Morton 2003, 6).

In retrospect, the April 2003 meeting in Washington may turn out to have been a defining moment in US-Canada relations. The Paul Martin government, which assumed power in December 2003, discreetly adopted much of the CCCE agenda, a position later aggressively embraced by Prime Minister Stephen Harper when he formed a government in February 2006. At a time when the rest of the world looks openly upon the United States as an imperial power, we are now seeing the emergence of a new breed of "empire loyalists." Historically, Canada's empire loyalists were those who sided with the British during the American Revolution in 1776 and later fled to Nova Scotia, Quebec, and southern Ontario. In the War of 1812 they and their descendants defended the interests of the British Empire in North America by fighting against the US expansionists. Today, more than two centuries later, Canada's corporate elite, heavily dependent upon the US market, have become Washington's new empire loyalists.

This chapter advances two arguments: first, that continental integration is a business-driven process of corporate restructuring and integration led by Canadian elites with more interests in the United States than in Canada; second, that, while the first two rounds of integration had high costs for Canadians, the costs of a third round will likely be much, much higher. To better understand how corporate Canada has come to play the role of Washington's new empire loyalists and to comprehend the broader institutional processes of which it forms a part, we need to briefly review some key strategic lessons from the last time a "grand bargain" was struck between Canada and the United States.

STRATEGIC LESSONS

In the early 1970s corporate Canada concluded that a new political lobby machine was needed to promote its interests in Ottawa more effectively. Beginning in 1975 the country's top business leaders held a series of meetings behind closed doors to map out their plan of action, establishing the Business Council on National Issues (BCNI). In developing their new lobby group, Canadian corporations took their cues from their counterparts south of the border who, in 1972, had formed the Business Roundtable, which is composed of the chief executive officers from the largest US corporations and banks (Clarke 1997).

From the outset the BCNI was designed to be a powerful alliance. Its membership list included the presidents or CEOs of the country's eight leading chartered banks, ten top insurance companies, and eighteen oil and pipeline corporations. Brand-name oil and gas companies like Shell, Imperial Oil, Gulf, and Texaco were represented by their CEOs, along with their counterparts from big manufacturing firms such as Ford, Kodak and CIL. Canadian transnational firms like Inco, Alcan, Stelco, and Trizec worked side by side with US giants like IBM, Xerox, Bechtel, and ITT. Indeed, the BCNI was largely composed of corporations that followed the dictates of US capital. While US ownership of business remained high in Canada, there was now the added complication of an increasing number of Canadian-owned companies becoming transnational enterprises in the emerging global economy. As a result, the distinction between foreign and domestic corporations became increasingly blurred.

To advance their agenda of building a liberalized continental economy, members of the BCNI met every six months. Between these bi-annual plenary sessions an inner circle of twenty-one members made up of representatives from each of the major economic sectors on the council (e.g., agriculture, automobiles, finance, petroleum, steel manufacturing, and food processing) met to devise detailed strategies. Task forces were set up around a wide range of policy concerns, including national finances, international trade, corporate taxation, energy policy, social programs, natural resources, and foreign policy. Studies were commissioned from business

consultant firms like Touche-Ross Associates and business research institutes like the C.D. Howe Institute to develop policies on a range of economic and social issues that were of special interest to big business.

Almost immediately, the BCNI emerged as the single most important and
effective voice of corporate Canada in Ottawa. The country's top CEOs
made their views known in meetings with the Prime Minister's Office and
the Privy Council Office as well as in provincial capitals and in numerous
business forums across the country. As a former Trudeau advisor and international law specialist, d'Aquino proved a particularly effective leader. He
knew the inner workings of the Ottawa bureaucracy as well as the strategic interests and priorities of big business. In this way, the BCNI positioned
itself to re-engineer the country's economic governance and to advance a
comprehensive free trade deal with the United States.

Following the 1980 election the BCNI had to tackle a new set of obstacles posed by the return to power of the Liberal Party and Pierre Trudeau
on a nationalist economic platform. In particular, two controversial programs had to be defanged: the National Energy Program (NEP) and the
Foreign Investment Review Agency (FIRA). NEP was designed to increase
Canadian ownership of the petroleum industry from 30 percent to 50
percent by 1990, while FIRA aimed at reversing the high levels of foreign
ownership in the Canadian economy more generally. In response, US petroleum giants, aided by the newly elected administration of Ronald Reagan,
organized a fierce campaign of economic retaliation, demanding that NEP
be "buried" and that FIRA be "de-clawed" (Clarkson 1984).

Perceiving the threat posed to their interests by NEP and FIRA, the BCNI
set up an energy policy task force chaired by the CEO of Imperial Oil. The
task force conducted a series of one-on-one meetings in 1983 with the premiers of Alberta and Ontario, followed by two major summit meetings
with the CEOs of major corporations in the energy sector. The initiative
proved successful, and provincial and federal officials agreed on the terms
of a new energy policy that, in effect, followed much of the blueprint initially proposed by the BCNI task force, including the virtual elimination of
the NEP, the adoption of world energy prices, and the overhaul of corporate taxation. Ottawa's plans to strengthen FIRA were also shelved (Clarkson 1984).

Brian Mulroney's landslide victory in 1984 opened the doors further for
corporate Canada, setting the stage for the BCNI to promote a comprehensive free trade deal with the United States. The primacy of securing access
to the US market was hardly surprising, given that 200 Canadian corporations, most of which were members of the BCNI, accounted for 90 percent
of all Canadian trade with the United States and more than 95 percent of
Canada's foreign direct investment in that country (Robinson 1997).
Indeed, the BCNI had mapped out a plan for a rules-based free trade regime

even before Mulroney's election. In 1983 d'Aquino visited Washington to aggressively promote the idea with the US Business Roundtable and the Reagan administration, which had already raised the idea of a North American free market. Immediately following the 1984 election the BCNI set up a forty-five-member business task force "to coordinate a responsible Canadian business approach to the Canada-US trade issue" (Langille 1987, 67).

Shortly after being sworn into office, the new Tory cabinet was invited by the BCNI to an extensive briefing at a secluded retreat in the Gatineau Hills. Although Mulroney had campaigned against free trade during the 1983 Tory leadership race, he was singing a different tune only two years later at the so-called Shamrock Summit in Quebec City, where he and Ronald Reagan formally announced the launching of free trade negotiations. Mulroney's commitment to free trade negotiations was vindicated by the release of the Macdonald Commission's findings, which made free trade with the United States the centrepiece of its three-volume report on Canada's economic future (Macdonald Commission 1985). It is noteworthy that the Macdonald Commission's recipe of taking a "leap of faith" with free trade was essentially the same message that the BCNI had presented during the commission's cross country hearings.

The battle for free trade quickly became a full-time preoccupation for d'Aquino and the BCNI. To generate public support and offset the growing Canadian opposition to a free trade deal, the BCNI established the Alliance for Trade and Job Opportunities in April 1987, co-chaired by former Alberta premier Peter Lougheed and Donald Macdonald, head of the Royal Commission. Not surprisingly, the alliance's membership was formed of corporations and banks, which were also members of the BCNI, reflecting the considerable economic weight behind the initiative. The alliance also worked closely with its US counterpart, the American Coalition for Trade Expansion with Canada, representing some 600 corporations and business associations. Through their Canadian subsidiaries, a significant number of US corporations also became directly involved in the Canadian alliance.

On 1 January 1988 Brian Mulroney and Ronald Reagan signed the Canada-US Free Trade Agreement (CUFTA), scheduled to come into force exactly one year to the day, pending parliamentary approval. It was passed by the House of Commons that year, at which point Liberal Party leader John Turner asked Liberal senators to delay passage of the bill in the Senate until the Canadian public had the opportunity to weigh in on the divisive issue via a national election. The stage was thus set for an intense confrontation when Prime Minister Mulroney called the federal election for the fall of 1988, pitting the ruling Conservative Party against their Liberal and New Democratic challengers, both of whom publicly opposed the signed agreement. Backed by an intense corporate media campaign and the promise of the BCNI's leading corporations to create "more and better jobs" if CUFTA were to be ratified, the Conservative Party won a plurality of votes and a majority of seats in the House of Commons. The corporate agenda had won the day, and CUFTA came into law on 1 January 1989.

The 1988 election proved to be a watershed moment for corporate Canada. Not only had the pro-business Tories squeezed out a crucial victory at the polls, but the country's continental free trade destiny was deepened as the Conservatives went on to negotiate the North American Free Trade Agreement (NAFTA), which was implemented in 1994. While the core of NAFTA was to be the original CUFTA, the new agreement involving Mexico would include some additional, even more disturbing features. By this point, however, the BCNI and its allies had clearly won the public relations battle. Public opposition to free trade had dwindled and NAFTA did not become a major issue in the 1993 federal election campaign. Recognizing that by 1993 public confidence in the Conservative Party had been severely damaged, the BCNI quickly switched horses. Behind the scenes, consultations and briefings began in earnest with Jean Chrétien and the Liberal Party.

By the time Brian Mulroney announced his resignation in the spring of 1993, the political repercussions of the 1988 election had become strikingly clear: that a fundamental shift in power had taken place in the country. The BCNI had emerged as the unified face of corporate Canada in Ottawa, representing 160 of the largest corporations and banks in the country with assets totalling over $1.5 trillion, and had established itself as a permanent and formidable political force. As one earlier observer had put it, the BCNI functioned as "a virtual shadow cabinet" (Langille 1987, 55). Its twenty-eight-member policy council was comprised of the most powerful CEOs in the country. By this time, the council had six policy task forces in operation, covering the national economy, social policy, political reform, environmental policy, international economy, and foreign affairs. All of these task forces (including previous ones that could still be reactivated, if needed) were chaired by the CEOs of member corporations, backed up by advisory committees and a battery of policy research personnel from institutes like the C.D. Howe and other corporate think tanks (Clarke 1997).

The promised economic results of CUFTA for Canadian workers never materialized. In spite of the pledge of the BCNI to create "more and better jobs," its constituent companies promptly turned around and chopped hundreds of thousands of jobs in the years that followed. Between 1988 and 1994 thirty-seven BCNI companies, employing a total of 765,338 workers, "downsized" their workforces to a combined total of 549,924, representing a loss of 215,414 jobs (CCPA 1995, 9). Nor did the BCNI's free trade deal generate job opportunities through greater foreign investment. Shortly after coming to power, the Mulroney government killed FIRA and replaced it with Investment Canada, ostensibly to attract foreign investment and to generate new jobs. What Investment Canada ended up promoting, however, was little more than the sale of Canadian firms to foreign interests, which swallowed up more than 6,000 Canadian companies worth over than $64 billion (Robinson 1997). And in almost every case, these foreign takeovers resulted in job losses as production was shifted abroad.

CORPORATE RESTRUCTURING

The BCNI's free trade agenda accelerated the economic integration and assimilation of Canada into the United States (for detailed accounts, see Jackson, chapter 8, this volume; and Robinson, chapter 10, this volume). Twelve and seventeen years after the passage of CUFTA and NAFTA, respectively, the structure of the Canadian economy has been fundamentally redirected from a largely east-west-mid-north axis within the country to an increasingly north-south axis between Canada and the United States. Between 1989, when CUFTA took force, and 2001, Canada's imports from the United States grew from 25 percent to 40 percent of our GDP (Campbell 2001, 21). And with the depreciation of the Canadian dollar until the early 2000s, Canada's exports to the United States increased dramatically, to the point that, by 2001, 85 percent of the country's total exports went to the US market (ibid.).

Canada's increasing economic assimilation by the United States can be measured in other ways. By 2001 more than half of Canada's manufacturing output flew to the United States, while Canadian producers accounted for less than half of domestic demand in this country. During the 1990s Canadian foreign direct investment and portfolio flows to the US grew much faster than did US flows to Canada (Campbell 2001, 21). It is also worth noting how corporations have restructured their operations to consolidate continental economic integration. Many of the BCNI's leading corporations, for instance, have not only been branch plants of major US corporations but they have also been increasingly run by CEOs who are US citizens.

What is important here is to take a closer look at how both Canadian and US corporations from diverse economic sectors have restructured their operations over the past two decades in order to understand the nature and objectives of the process of continental restructuring and integration. Upon closer examination, two key trends appear. First, through cross-border mergers and acquisitions, Canadian companies have been steadily expanding into the United States while US corporations have been swallowing up

Canadian companies; second, production itself has been reorganized on a continental basis, often being outsourced to cheap labour regions in the South.

Although these trends differ from sector to sector, two clear conclusions emerge: first, Canadian companies are becoming increasingly intertwined with, and dependent upon, the US market; second, corporate restructuring in key sectors of the economy has not simply followed some invisible process of continental integration – rather, corporate restructuring and continental integration are, in fact, one and the same.[1]

Finance

Canada's big-five chartered banks – Royal Bank of Canada (RBC), Canadian Imperial Bank of Commerce (CIBC), Bank of Montreal, Toronto-Dominion, and Bank of Nova Scotia – are all active members of the CCCE. Traditionally, they have held a monopoly over banking in Canada, with few or no operations in the United States. Yet since NAFTA and the World Trade Organization (WTO) financial services agreement in 1997, this has changed. By 2002 all five banks were among the top twenty foreign banks operating in the United States (O'Neill 2002). The RBC in particular has pursued an aggressive marketing strategy in the southeastern states, opening more than 250 retail and business centres. Further, through a series of acquisitions, the RBC Mortgage Company has become one of the top ten retail mortgage businesses south of the border, with 200 offices in 32 states. Meanwhile, nine US banks – Citibank, Bank of America, State Street, Amex, J.P. Morgan, Bank One, MBNA, Capital One, and UBS – are now among the top twenty foreign-owned banks in Canada. Citibank, for example, is now the second-largest foreign bank operating in Canada, behind the UK-based Hong Kong and Shanghai Banking Corporation (HSBC) (O'Neill 2002).

Agriculture

Since CUFTA and NAFTA came into effect, the various components of Canada's agricultural industry have become concentrated in the hands of a few corporations, largely US owned. A prime example is US agribusiness giant Cargill (Qualman 2001). In 1988 Cargill purchased Maple Leaf Mills grain division in Ontario and a year later acquired the retail fertilizer distribution network of Cyanamid Canada. With these two businesses forming the core of its grain-handling operations in Canada, Cargill entered a joint venture in 1990 with the Saskatchewan government to form Saskferco Products, the world's largest nitrogen fertilizer manufacturing plant. A year later Cargill purchased three inland grain terminals in Alberta. In

1996 it built the country's largest canola-crushing plant and expanded its beef processing plant in High River, Alberta. Then, in 1997, Cargill acquired a 51 percent interest in Prairie Malt Ltd. and went on in 1998 to buy out the Alberta Wheat Pool's 50 percent ownership of Cascadia Terminal, a major grain export terminal located in the Port of Vancouver. These acquisitions have allowed Cargill to gain a stranglehold over key components of Canada's agricultural production and distribution networks.

Forestry

In recent years Canadian and US logging and paper product industries have become increasingly integrated through cross-border acquisitions. Two of the largest US timber companies, Weyerhauser and Louisiana Pacific, managed to secure significant takeovers in Canada in 1999–2000 (Draffan 1999). Weyerhauser bought out one of Canada's premier forestry companies, BC-based MacMillan Bloedel, while Louisiana Pacific purchased Evans Forest Products, a BC-based producer of engineered wood and lumber products. Both US takeovers included logging licences providing the timber giants access to thousands of acres of British Columbia's forests (Louisiana-Pacific Corporation 1999). Similarly, two Canadian forest companies, Norbord (formerly Nexfor) and West Fraser Timber, purchased mills in the United States. Norbord, for example, opened plants in Mississippi in 1995, in North Carolina in 2000, and in Alabama in 2001, and it acquired mills in Georgia and Texas in 2002. For its part, West Fraser Timber acquired mills in Arkansas and Louisiana in 2000 (Norbord Corporation 2004; West Fraser Timber Company 2000).

Textiles

Textiles and clothing were among the industries hardest hit by CUFTA, forcing US and Canadian companies to reorganize on a continental basis. According to a 1996 study there were fifty-four US textile and clothing retailers operating in Canada, more than five times the number operating in 1985. Walmart increased its share of the total Canadian department store market in Canada from 16 percent in 1994 to 40 percent in 2000, thereby giving the US giant a substantial lead over The Bay (15 percent), Sears Canada (25 percent), and Zellers (25 percent) (Maquila Solidarity Network 2000). The trend continues; by 2004 Wal-Mart had reached half of all department store sales in Canada (Maquila Solidarity Network 2004, 11). With the purchase of the iconic Hudson's Bay Company by major US retailer Target, US investors now control most of the Canadian department store market (Hamilton Spectator 2006). Meanwhile, Canadian-based textile companies like Gildan of Montreal, one of North America's largest T-shirt manufacturers, have taken advantage of NAFTA rules to expand their market operations. Gildan has positioned itself to compete with US apparel companies in the United States by outsourcing its production to low-wage sites in Mexico and Central America. By moving its production offshore, Gildan has, under NAFTA, been able to sell its products duty- and quota-free directly to its US customers, which include Nike, Fortune Fashion, and Walt Disney.

Auto

The big-three automakers – General Motors (GM), Ford, and Daimler-Chrysler – have also made major geographical shifts in their production as a result of the free trade regimes, particularly NAFTA (Allen 2004; Quintero Ramírez 2001). CUFTA changed the original 1965 Auto Pact requirement that vehicles produced in Canada have 60 percent Canadian content to a 50 percent North American content requirement. NAFTA then raised this content requirement to 62.5 percent but redefined "North America" to include Mexico as well as Canada and the United States. As a result the big-three were given an unprecedented degree of capital mobility. For example, under NAFTA rules, GM can relocate any amount of its Canadian production to the United States or Mexico without being penalized with tariffs on vehicles imported into Canada. Since NAFTA came into effect all three automakers have returned some production from Canada to their traditional US plants, while establishing new production plants in the southern United States and northern Mexico. In 1991, for example, GM-Canada began to restructure their plant in St. Catharines, which employed 8,800 and included an engine plant, a components plant, and a foundry. By 1992, however, GM decided it would be more profitable to consolidate the production of rear axles in Buffalo and Detroit and, two years later, closed the foundry, thereby putting almost 3,000 Canadians out of work (Allen 2004; Quintero Ramírez 2001:9). The downsizing continues. On November 2005, GM-Canada announced cuts to thirty thousand jobs in North America as part of a restructuring plan. The detail included the closure of the Oshawa and St Catharines plants by 2008. The two plants employ 3,900 people, about 20 per cent of Canada's automotive workforce (CBC 2005).

Energy

The oil, natural gas, and electricity industries in Canada and the United States are also well on their way to becoming fully integrated (see in this volume Pratt, chapter 19; Griffin Cohen, chapter 18). Not only does

Canada supply 94 percent of US natural gas imports, it is now the largest foreign supplier of oil products to the United States, providing 17 percent of its crude and refined oil products. With Canada's Imperial Oil as its major subsidiary, the US energy giant Exxon-Mobil has been able to maintain a strong presence in Canada's oil patch, including its 25 percent interest in the Athabasca tar sands project, the most promising new source of oil on the continent. Similarly, Canadian gas companies, such as Suncor, have been expanding their operations in the United States. Suncor, also a major player in the Athabasca tar sands, alone has purchased refineries (e.g., in Denver, Colorado), the Rocky Mountain and Centennial pipeline systems, plus Phillips retail outlets and an assortment of storage, pipeline, and distribution facilities in the United States (Suncor Corporation 2004). In terms of electricity, Canada provides 100 percent of all US imports. Canadian-based electricity distribution companies have recently become "NAFTA focused." Transalta, for example, has transformed itself from an exclusively Alberta-based company into one with extensive operations in both the United States and Mexico.

Military

Canada's military operations have also become assimilated by the massive US military machine. Through the Defence Production Sharing Agreement between the two countries, Canadian defence and aerospace companies have been able to take advantage of certain contracts issued by the Pentagon. Canadian companies like General Dynamics Canada, CAE Inc., CMC Electronics, Bombardier, Litton Systems Canada, and Raytheon Systems Canada, among others, have benefited significantly from such contracts. More recently, however, Washington has demanded more "interoperability," so that Canadian armed forces will eventually fit seamlessly into US military operations (see Staples, chapter 6, this volume). But interoperability would require Canada to purchase its military weapons and equipment from US corporations like Boeing, Lockheed Martin, and Raytheon. Canada's Department of National Defence, for example, is arming its CF-18 planes with Paveway II laser-guided bombs made by Raytheon in the United States, while SM-2 surface-to-air missiles are being purchased from US manufacturers for Canadian naval ships (Staples 2002).

In short, these trends in corporate restructuring are indicative of the degree to which the Canadian economy is now integrated with, and dependent upon, the US economy, largely as a result of the CUFTA and NAFTA regimes. Canada's leading corporations now operate in key sectors of the US economy, while US corporations have not only set up shop in Canada but have also taken advantage of the low value of the Canadian dollar until 2003 to buy up Canadian companies, purchasing close to

6,500 Canadian companies between 1985 and 2002 (Barlow 2004, 5). Meanwhile, Canadian corporations have become highly dependent on the US market for the accumulation and expansion of their wealth. Driven by expansion into the colossal US market, the collective assets of the CCCE's 150 corporations rose from $1 trillion in 1988 to $2.1 trillion in 2003 (Barlow 2004, 7). What all this means is that Canada's big business class, represented by the CCCE, has a powerful vested interest in protecting both sides of the border.

SECURITY PARADIGM

The dramatic events of 11 September 2001 posed a serious threat to the continental free trade regime. The attacks on New York and Washington sent shock waves through the Canadian and US corporate communities. Suddenly, the border was closed to the free movement of capital, goods, and services, which amount to over a billion dollars a day in business for corporations in both countries. For d'Aquino and Canada's big business leaders, this kind of political and economic instability required urgent attention. They recognized, as did their US counterparts, that terrorist activities would likely disrupt economic flows between the two countries again. In order to avoid future economic disruptions, the CCCE realized that a new kind of deal was needed between the United States and Canada.

After September 11 "security" was no longer simply a buzzword in policy-making circles. It became, instead, the defining metaphor of a "new era," both in Washington and in capitals around the world. For the Bush administration the war on terrorism became the unquestioned number one priority. Even before the Bush Doctrine was pronounced in September 2002, it had become clear that, for the foreseeable future, security issues would trump trade matters in Washington, and securing the US-Canada border against terrorist activity would take precedence over the free movement of goods, services, and capital. If this meant slowing cross-border business to a crawl, then so be it. Alarm bells quickly sounded off for big business in both countries.

For its part, Ottawa moved swiftly with a series of measures designed to tighten border security in the wake of September 11. The Chrétien government proposed an omnibus package of anti-terrorist legislation (bills C-35, C-36, C-42) containing various elements consistent with anti-terrorist laws enacted by the United States (Clarke 2002). The definition of "terrorist activity" was expanded to include activities of protest and dissent, while "new terrorist offences" were defined broadly in terms of "participating, facilitating, instructing, [and] harbouring" activities (Clarke 2002, 49). Under the new laws, "internationally protected persons" included government and business personnel involved in international events. New investigative powers were also granted to the police for search and seizure, while the government itself was given the legal powers to declare and create a "military security zone" or armed encampment, if necessary, in order to thwart terrorism.

In addition, Ottawa signed a "Smart Border" accord with Washington in December 2001, which gave the United States new rights of inspection at Canadian border crossings, along with the merging of US and Canadian immigration and customs databases. As a result, US customs agents now have direct access to the personal files of Canadians crossing the US border, including their work records, the property they own, and their investments. Although the CCCE had certainly applauded and encouraged the Chrétien government's initiatives to tighten border security along these lines, they also recognized that these measures did not, in and of themselves, guarantee an uninterrupted flow of goods, services, and capital across the border. Bolder and more imaginative initiatives would have to be taken by big business to ensure "trade security" on the continent and, thereby, to protect the gains that had been made under the two free trade regimes.

In January 2003 the CCCE announced the North American Security and Prosperity Initiative (NASPI). Whereas the free trade deals (CUFTA and NAFTA) constituted the first phase of the big business agenda to transform the relationship between the two countries, NASPI constituted, in d'Aquino's words, "the second chapter of that transforming initiative" (Curry 2003). Based on the assumption that Canada and the United States share "core values, history and institutional roots," the CCCE developed common ways for the two countries to tackle new global challenges as one North American community.[2] Building on the framework established by NAFTA, the NASPI plan contains the following components (CCCE 2003a, 2003b, 2004).

Reinventing National Borders

While the Smart Border plan focuses exclusively on providing security against terrorism at the Canada-US border, the CCCE calls for nothing less than the reinvention of our national borders to secure an "integrated economic space" on the continent (CCCE 2003a, 4). Here, the NASPI plan emphasizes a twofold approach: (1) refocusing security efforts to protect the air and sea entry points to North America while (2) eliminating obstacles at our internal borders, such as regulatory, procedural, and infrastructural barriers that hinder the flow of goods and services. In other words, "the demands of security," according to the CCCE, must "respect the imperative of free North/South flows" (CCCE 2003b, 8). In order to do this, the border between Canada and the United States should be transformed into "an effective but shared checkpoint within an integrated economic space"

(CCCE 2003a, 4). Shared approaches are to be developed between the two countries with regard to commercial processing, infrastructure, intelligence, and policing, including a North American identity card that would allow business personnel and other frequent travelers to cross borders with greater ease.

Harmonizing Economic Regulations

According to the CCCE, an integrated continental economy would make many of the current domestic economic regulations that exist in each country redundant. In particular, NASPI cites rules regulating standards, inspection, and certification procedures. Instead of applying regulations in both countries, a common set of standards would mean that products, for example, would only have to be "tested once," in the country in which they originated (CCCE 2003a, 4). NASPI goes on to target several national economic policy-making tools for elimination, including the application of trade remedy laws in key sectors of the economy, restrictions on foreign access and ownership in major industries, and regulations on the mobility of skilled labour. While historically, governments in both countries have used such policy tools to build their national economies, the CCCE argues that they become redundant within an integrated continental economy and must be eliminated in order to "maximize economic efficiencies" (CCCE 2003a, 4).

Guaranteeing Resource Security

The CCCE also wants to create a "resource security pact" between Canada and the United States that would guarantee a constant flow of "oil, natural gas, electricity, coal, uranium, primary metals, forest products and agriculture" within the continental market (CCCE 2003a, 1, 5). "The security of our countries," asserts the CCCE, "depends on the assurance of uninterrupted flows among us" (CCCE 2003a, 5). In part, this demand is already met by the "proportional sharing clause" in CUFTA and NAFTA, which states that Canada must continue to export its natural resources to the United States at levels equal to the average amount exported over the previous three years. Now, the CCCE argues, it is time to go beyond this to create "a zone of resource confidence in North America" (CCCE 2003b, 13). This would ensure "unrestricted flows of ... oil, gas, electricity, minerals, agricultural products and construction materials" at a moment when the United States faces the prospect of a "disruption in global supply chains" (CCCE 2003b, 12–13). In return, NASPI calls for the removal of trade dispute threats between the two countries and the resolution of such controversial issues as resource pricing and subsidies.

Defending North America

The CCCE contends that Canada does not pull its weight when it comes to continental defence and the global war on terror. Building on the North American Aerospace Defence Command's (NORAD) record of cooperation, NASPI calls for the creation of "a North American defence community of sovereign nations" (CCCE 2003a, 5). Continental defence would protect against missile attacks and airborne threats; share naval protection against seaway invasions; and protect critical infrastructure like pipelines, railways, bridges, and hydroelectric and transmission lines from potential terrorist attacks. To carry its share of the burden, the CCCE insists, Ottawa must make two major commitments: first, reinvest public dollars in the build-up of Canada's defence and military capability; and second, ensure the interoperability of Canadian and US equipment on land, at sea, and in the air.

Developing Binational Institutions

In order to manage this stage of continental integration, declares the CCCE, new binational institutions (or trinational if Mexico is involved) would have to be created. These new institutions would be designed to govern the four areas of continental integration outlined above on a bi- or tri-national basis. The supranational institutions developed by the European Union, says the CCCE, would not work within the North American context, given the major divergences in size among the three countries and their economies; instead, NASPI proposes that specialized joint commissions be developed for the purpose of overseeing the four areas targeted for action. As a viable model, NASPI points to the International Joint Commission for Transboundary Waters, with its history of over one hundred years of working as a binational agency on common issues in a flexible and non-bureaucratic manner.

STRATEGIC BARGAIN?

With its blueprint for a new Canada-US partnership in place, the CCCE began the task of bringing the political elite onboard. The first step was preparing for the transfer of power within the Liberal Party, from Jean Chrétien to Paul Martin. Just as the BCNI had prepared the way for the Mulroney regime two decades ago by promoting the free trade agenda, so the CCCE started to set the stage with a new political agenda to further continental integration. When the Martin government took over in December 2003 all the signs indicated that from now on a top priority was to be given to developing "better relations" with our neighbour to the south. During the summer of 2003 Martin's election team took part in ongoing briefings and discussions with the Bush administration. When forming his cabinet, Martin was careful to award key posts to pro-US ministers. Martin's formal meetings with Bush, during the January 2004 Summit of the Americas in Mexico, and later at the White House, were orchestrated to convey the message that a new era of cooperation was at hand. While the grand debacle surrounding the sponsorship scandal certainly threw the Martin government off its agenda leading up to a minority status after the federal election of 2004 as well as to its defeat in the 2006 election, there was little doubt that US-Canada relations would remain a defining feature of the Canadian political landscape for the foreseeable future.

Meanwhile, the CCCE had come to the realization that there could be no new deal with Washington unless Ottawa prioritized military build-up and homeland security. Thomas d'Aquino as much as confirmed this at a conference on US-Canada relations in December 2003, when he replayed his conversations with George Bush Sr about the need for a new trade deal between the two countries during a three-day fishing trip in Labrador (d'Aquino 2003). It was only when d'Aquino spoke about our common "security" concerns, the certainty of facing further attacks in North America, and the need for both countries to "build an island of security and prosperity" together that the former president, who had presided over the NAFTA negotiations, responded with enthusiasm, indicating that these matters were of real interest to the United States (d'Aquino 2003). Post-September 11, the "security paradigm" continues to dominate US politics, setting the terms for any new deal with Canada.

These ideas nurtured the recommendations coming out of the trinational Task Force on the Future of North America sponsored by the Council on Foreign Relations (CFR) in Washington in association with the *Consejo Mexicano de Asuntos Internacionales* and the CCCE, with former deputy minister John Manley and Thomas d'Aquino serving as the Canadian chairs. The CCCE's central role in this task force signalled its recognition that Canada would be unable to elicit Washington's interest in strategic negotiations without Mexican participation. In its March 2005 statement, the task force proposed "the creation by 2010 of a community to enhance security, prosperity, and opportunity for all North Americans," where "the boundaries of the community would be defined by a common external tariff and an outer security perimeter" (CFR 2005a, 6). This would entail "the creation of a single economic space [encompassing Canada, the US, and Mexico] that expands the economic opportunities for all people in the region, and the establishment of a security zone that protects the region from external threats while facilitating the legitimate passage of goods, people, and capital" (9).

The influence of these recommendations was clear when Paul Martin, George Bush, and Vicente Fox announced the Security and Prosperity Partnership (SPP) of North America later in the same month, March 2005, in their summit in Waco, Texas. The SPP resembles the CCCE's NASPI (North American Security and Prosperity Initiative) in more than name as it established "the principle that our prosperity is dependent on our security" (White House 2005a). "Through the SPP, the United States, Canada, and Mexico ... seek to establish a cooperative approach to advance our common security and prosperity," to "develop a common security strategy to further secure North America," and to "promote economic growth, competitiveness, and quality of life" (ibid.).

The Stephen Harper-led minority Conservative government that assumed power in February 2006 signalled a new stage in consolidating the CCCE's agenda. One of Harper's first steps was to renew Canada's commitment to the SPP in his March 2006 summit meeting with George Bush and Vicente Fox in Cancun, Mexico. The three leaders went on to announce the creation of the North American Competitiveness Council (NACC), which will "provide recommendations and priorities on promoting North American competitiveness globally" (Industry Canada 2006). Of the ten Canadians appointed by Prime Minister Harper to NACC, nine are CCCE members and, of those, seven are either on the CCCE board of directors or its executive committee.[3] It could not be more clear who is going to give advice to the prime minister with regard to shaping Canada's North American agenda.

Despite these advances, the CCCE has not yet obtained what it ultimately wants: a comprehensive new arrangement in North America that will dramatically change the nature of Canadian society. The vague tenor of various recommendations in the CCCE's NASPI, in the CFR task force report, and in the three leaders' SPP suggest that these are guiding principles and efforts to engage a process rather than detailed and comprehensive implementation plans. The central question that Canadians must now ask is what price must they pay for the CCCE to achieve its vision. What will it take to interest Washington in a "strategic bargain" this time around? This is the question that the Harper government will have to answer if it is serious about advancing Canada's integration with the United States to the next stage.

The Harper government will most certainly have to recast the various proposals into a comprehensive plan for deeper continental integration based on the post-September 11 security paradigm. Rather than a single comprehensive negotiation, this process is more likely to proceed as a series of interconnected agendas that move in parallel and, where possible, under the radar screen. Many of these agendas have already been in motion, several of them aggressively, since 9/11. But what are those key agendas involved in this assimilation plan? The following represents an attempt to outline the main areas involved in the new security-focused strategic bargain that is already shaping up with the United States.

Military Security

From the Bush administration's standpoint, Canada's non-cooperation on military priorities such as the invasion of Iraq will no longer be tolerated. During his official visit to Canada on 1 December 2004 President Bush made it clear that he expected the Martin government to come onside by politically supporting his plan to build a North American missile defence system. Although subsequently Martin grudgingly bowed to public pressure, declaring his minority government could not formally join Bush's missile defence program, Ottawa had already given Washington what it needed in August 2004 – namely, an amendment to the NORAD accord allowing missile launch information to be made directly to the US Northern Command. In addition, Martin committed Canada, without any public discussion, to fighting a civil war in Afghanistan as a US proxy, and later on, very soon after assuming power, Harper won a Commons vote to extend that commitment for another two years.

Yet, what the Bush administration has repeatedly demanded of the Canadian government, through the representations of US ambassador Paul Cellucci (2003) and his successor David Wilkins, is for Canada to "pull its own weight" through substantial increases in military spending. Finally, in its February 2005 federal budget, the Martin government confirmed this policy shift, committing Canada to an additional $12.8 billion in cash for military operations over the next five years (Canada 2005), while in June 2006 Harper announced plans for $15 billion in new military spending, including money for planes, ships, trucks, and helicopters (Galloway 2006). Even before these latest budget boosts, Canada was ranked sixth among the nineteen nations that comprise NATO in terms of defence spending based on actual dollars (Canada 2002, 42).

As well, Washington expects Ottawa to cooperate in the expansion of NORAD's role and responsibilities for North American defence, including, if necessary, the patrol and protection of Canada's immense coastline and Arctic regions. To do its part, Canada will have to make correspondingly large increases in current levels of military spending for high-tech equipment just to keep pace with US commitments (now more than US$500 billion annually) and to ensure the interoperability of Canadian and US armed forces on land, sea, and in the air.[4] Achieving technological interoperability, which means purchasing military equipment from the United States, is imperative for Bush's vision of a continental defence system. Taken together, these new military security measures, and Canada's increasing entanglement in a counter-insurgency war in Afghanistan, would further lock Canada into a war-based economy with no choice but to support America's future pre-emptive strikes. As the United States shifts the focus of its war on terrorism from Iraq to the nuclear armaments of Iran and North Korea, Canada will undoubtedly be drawn into a spiral of aggressive foreign policy and expanding militarization.

Homeland Security

Following the September 11 attacks, US demands for "military security" have been increasingly reinforced by demands for "homeland security" measures. Washington has repeatedly insisted that Canada join in creating a common security perimeter in North America. The Martin government had already moved in this direction by establishing the powerful new Ministry for Public Safety and Emergency Preparedness in Ottawa, modelled after the US Homeland Security Agency. In addition, as noted above, Canada has enacted its own anti-terrorism legislation (C-36) patterned after the US Patriot Acts; set up a data bank to track foreign air travel by all Canadians (C-23); implemented the Smart Border Accord, which coordinates Canadian and US intelligence operations while overseeing the harmonization of visa, immigration, and refugee practices between the two countries; and signed the Safe Third Country agreement, whereby Canada and the United States recognize each other's rules on refugee claims to the point where refugees denied status by the latter cannot go on to claim refugee status with the former.

Collectively, these "homeland security" measures not only pose a serious threat to the civil liberties of Canadians accorded under the Charter of Rights and Freedoms but also provide mechanisms for the criminalization of legitimate dissent and the proliferation of racial profiling (see Aiken, chapter 7, this volume). The public inquiry into the Maher Arar case – involving the detainment, deportation, imprisonment, and torture of a Canadian citizen of Arab origin – showed just how vulnerable people have become under the new "homeland security" regime. The Bush administration now wants to ensure that Canada contributes to the creation of a continental security perimeter, one of the goals of the SPP (White House 2005b). Here, provisions would be made to secure fast-track clearance of cross-border goods and services (including biometric identity cards for fast tracking business and frequent travellers) while security intelligence operations and police-state tactics would be accelerated to track the movement of other peoples. With its body of anti-terrorism legislation in place, the

Canadian government can proceed to do its part in creating and strengthening a common security perimeter largely through administrative actions under the new Ministry of Public Safety and Emergency Preparedness.

Energy Security

In order for Washington to build and expand its economic and military power, it must have access to a stable supply of oil, gas, and electricity. While Canada has traditionally been a major supplier of natural gas to the United States, it has also recently become its number one source for imported oil. Given the insecurity of oil supplies from Venezuela, Saudi Arabia, and Iraq, US energy secretary Spencer Abraham declared that Washington will decrease its dependence on Middle East sources in favour of Canadian sources (Lakely 2003). In particular, the United States has set its sites on the Athabasca tar sands in northern Alberta, where proven reserves are second in size only to Saudi Arabia and roughly equal to those of Kuwait. With reserve estimates between 176 and 311 billion barrels that could be extracted using current "rip-and-tear" technologies (up to a high of 2.5 trillion barrels from the deeper tar sands sources requiring still new technologies) (EIA 2001), Canada would be able to supply the United States and its military with a safe, reliable, and consistent supply of oil (McCullum 2006).

What is more, the new Mackenzie Valley pipeline project (scheduled for completion in 2009), designed to bring Arctic natural gas south to Fort McMurray, will allow Canada to maintain export commitments to the United States as well as fuel oil extraction and refinement processes from the Athabasca tar sands. This, along with a more integrated electricity grid and more harmonious regulatory mechanisms for energy security between the two countries, will put Canada in a position to provide the United States with ironclad guarantees of uninterrupted supplies of oil and natural gas. In short, Canada would be nothing less than the US's next door gas pump. Meanwhile, such a massive increase in energy production would have untold environmental consequences and would most certainly put in jeopardy our commitments to reduce greenhouse gas emissions under the Kyoto Accord. It will certainly not help things that Stephen Harper has all but abandoned Canada's Kyoto commitments and is undertaking to find a "made-in-Canada" solution to emissions – borrowing a page from Bush's policy book. Continued mass exports of oil and gas will also jeopardize our own energy security in this country, given the rapid depletion of our conventional supplies and the fact we no longer have a made-in-Canada energy policy. In assessing the progress of the SPP, Harper, Bush, and Fox list "North American energy security" as one of their areas of collaboration (White House 2006a).

Social Security

This is an area the Canadian government would prefer to keep beneath the radar screen. At the same time, it is a priority for Washington to seek greater harmonization of social as well as economic regulations between the two countries. The Bush administration has made inroads in its effort to privatize the US social security system. Increasingly, the management of state social assistance programs is being handed over to for-profit corporations, with hundreds of billions of dollars in federal social security funds now earmarked for investment in Wall Street. In addition, the same corporations that are taking over social security in the United States – like Cigna or HCA Columbia in health care, EDS in education, and Lockheed-Martin in social assistance – want to expand their market reach into Canada's public system through public-private partnerships (P3s). A continental social security regime with the private sector playing a more dominant role would certainly aid in facilitating these plans for corporate expansion. And harmonizing the Canadian and US social security systems would go a long way towards reducing "barriers" to competitiveness and creating a level playing field between the two countries. In announcing the creation of a North American Competitiveness Council, Harper, Bush, and Fox stated that it would "provide us recommendations on North American competitiveness, including, among others, areas such as ... services" and affirmed their "commitment to strengthen regulatory cooperation" (White House 2006a).

Will Canadian governments go along despite the reluctance of the Canadian public? A disturbing indicator is the creation, during the Martin government, of a new cabinet portfolio charged with developing "public-private partnerships," or P3s, through which governments contract out some if not all aspects of public facilities and services to for-profit private "partners." More pro-privatization pressure is also looming from the World Trade Organization, which is planning to open up cross-border trade in services in its current GATS (General Agreement on Trade in Services) negotiations. If these new rules are adopted by WTO members, they will greatly facilitate the privatization and deregulation of publicly delivered social security programs in Canada. Canadian governments, until now, have insisted they will never allow foreign-based companies to have access to Canada's health care, education, or social assistance programs, but the Harper government has promised to dismantle an incipient national childcare program and instead provide tax credits so families can purchase services from private providers. Furthermore, if Canada signs the new GATS, it will become even more vulnerable to US demands to open up these sectors to US corporations (see in this volume Corrigan, chapter 13; Grieshaber-Otto, Sinclair and Grinspun, chapter 14).

Canada's top business leaders, through their NASPI agenda, also favour the privatization of parts of Canada's social programs – the potentially most profitable parts – and can be expected to add their powerful lobbying pressure for this "reform" to the pro-privatization demands coming from Washington.

Water Security[5]

Certainly, one of the most provocative issues in Canada-US relations these days is the prospect of bulk water transfers. The United States needs an adequate supply of water as much as it needs a reliable source of energy – and it is rapidly running out of the water it can derive from its domestic lakes, rivers, and aquifers (underground reservoirs). Indeed, several states and regions of the US – Arizona, New Mexico, and California, among them – are close to drying up. One of the world's largest freshwater sources, the Ogallala aquifer, which is used to irrigate the farm belt of the US Midwest, is now being drained at a rate of fourteen times its ability to replenish itself (Barlow and Clarke 2003, 16). Unless new sources of fresh water can be tapped, this region of the US could be stricken by a severe and prolonged drought. No wonder, then, that Washington's eyes have been turned enviously upon Canada, which is seen as a land blessed by bountiful lakes, rivers, and streams – and thus the nearest and best source for quenching the prodigious US thirst.

Although the governors of states bordering the great lakes are opposed to bulk water diversions from the lakes, they have opened the door by allowing water takings on the part of bottled water companies. Indeed, this move could well set the stage for US schemes to further tap Canada's freshwater sources. Meanwhile, millions of bottles of water from various Canadian springs and streams are already being shipped to US consumers by private bottling companies licensed by some provinces (Clarke 2005). This trans-shipment, of course, falls far short of meeting future overall US water requirements. Washington will not remain satisfied with just our bottled water: it will be looking for and demanding much greater access to our lakes and rivers.

During the 1980s, two megaprojects for bulk water transfers were proposed (Barlow and Clarke 2003). One, called the Grand Canal scheme, was designed to redirect the flow of northern Quebec rivers to bring water downstream through an elaborate canal system into the Great Lakes, where it would then be flushed into the US Midwest through canals and pipelines. The other, called NAWAPA (North American Power and Water Authority), was designed to redirect water from northern British Columbia and Yukon rivers into a huge crater within the Rocky Mountains, where it would then be transported by pipelines through the western US states into the Midwest. Neither of these megaprojects was developed at the time, due to lack of capital and sufficient demand. But the blueprints for both are still in place. If the current "security" talks between the US and Canadian governments were to be held a few years from now, it's safe to assume that the US demand for bulk water exports from Canada would be front and centre. Until then, "water security" will not be as high on the priority list as energy – but, as the United States gets thirstier and thirstier, it is bound to become a major flash-point in Canada-US relations.

Global Security

Washington is exerting pressure on Canada – as well as other nations – to realign its foreign affairs policy to conform to the imperatives of the US "war on terrorism." What the Bush administration wants is for its "allies" to accept and follow the unilateralist foreign policies of the United States rather than the multilateral policies of the United Nations as outlined in the UN's Millennium Development Goals.

A prime example is Canada's overseas development aid, most of which used to go to poor countries in the global South to help them alleviate the crippling scourges of poverty, hunger, and disease. Now, under US pressure, much of this foreign aid – $916 million to be disbursed between 2002 and 2008 – has been redirected to Afghanistan and Iraq, which have been devastated by US-led military attacks (Simpson and Tomlinson 2006, 258). Since 2002, the phrase "to support international efforts to reduce threats to international and Canadian security" has been added to the CIDA's mandate (ibid.).

Canada has also bowed to US demands to cancel much of Iraq's debt. At the Paris Club meeting in November 2004, the Martin government committed to cancelling 80 percent of Iraq's US$590 million debt to Canada, and a bilateral agreement with Iraq was signed soon after (Portal Iraq 2005). In effect, Canada managed to offer more debt relief to Iraq in one meeting than it has done for the poorest countries over the past few years. Meanwhile, Canadian aid commitments to sub-Saharan Africa have been substantially scaled back.

The United States is also pressuring Canada to allocate some of its overseas aid funds to train police and military forces in developing nations so they can more effectively join in the US war on terrorism. If Canada continues to succumb to such US-driven changes in its overseas assistance policy, this money will increasingly be used to mop up after US military operations instead of fulfilling its proper function of helping to alleviate poverty and disease. Indeed, humanitarian and peacemaking activities on the part of Canadian governmental and nongovernmental organizations in

Afghanistan have been seriously compromised by Canada's growing involvement in the NATO-led counter-insurgency war in that country. Ironically, neglecting the plight of the world's poor will further erode US security – and Canada's too – since poverty and misery breed anger and desperation, which in turn provide the main breeding ground for terrorism.

Trade Security

Reducing the barriers to competitiveness, of course, is the ultimate objective of the CCCE and its counterparts in the United States and Mexico. The NASPI proposals advance an "integrated economic space" designed to secure cross-border flows of goods and services, a goal reasserted by the CFR task force, which called for "a single economic space" that would also include Mexico (CCCE 2003a, 4; CFR 2005a, 9). The NASPI proposals stopped short, however, of calling for a customs union (as advocated by the C.D. Howe Institute). A customs union would represent an even greater loss of sovereignty as it would lock partner countries into a common trade policy with external countries (see Lee, chapter 11, this volume).

The CFR task force does call for the implementation of a common external tariff on a sector-by-sector basis (CFR 2005a, 11).[6] These and other measures suggest that the task force also prefers a gradual approach to the establishment of a customs union. It recommends the formation, by 2010, of "a common economic zone through the elimination of remaining tariff and non-tariff barriers to trade within North America. The three countries must also expand cooperation on trade-related areas, including border and transportation infrastructure ... [and promote] a concerted effort to reduce the many regulatory gaps and inconsistencies that hamper the flow of trade in North America" (CFR 2005b, 19). Various administrative means to achieve such ends have already been engaged and incorporated within the SPP. The measures being advanced range from building more cross-border infrastructure to providing common oversight on matters like food safety and energy regulation to a full Open Skies aviation agreement between Canada and the United States (White House 2006b). In this way, a de facto customs union could be established without either country having formally to cede political sovereignty.

NASPI also calls for joint binational commissions that would provide the infrastructure required for ongoing governance and oversight. The CFR task force, aware of Washington's reluctance to support institutions that may hamper US sovereignty, presents modest institutional recommendations (which also include Mexico), calling for an annual North American summit meeting, trinational minister-led working groups, a North American Advisory Council, and a North American Inter-Parliamentary Group. The first three CFR recommendations were implemented by the leaders in their March 2005 and March 2006 SPP initiatives (changing the name of the council to North American Competitiveness Council). Together, both elements – reducing barriers to competitiveness and new governance mechanisms – go some distance towards setting the stage for greater trade security between the two countries (or the three, where Mexico is included).

Altogether, these seven security areas (military, homeland, energy, social, water, global, and trade) constitute the kind of business-friendly agenda that the federal government, whether led by Conservatives or by Liberals, is likely to continue to advance. Unlike its predecessors, this new phase of continental integration is likely to proceed incrementally, and away from the public eye, building upon the infrastructure already laid down in NAFTA. Occasions such as the three leaders' summits provide fodder for the corporate media while keeping the public blissfully ignorant of the profound transformations that are in the offing.

Of the seven areas, the first six are the price that Canadians would have to pay in order to achieve the prime objective of the CCCE, the seventh plank of trade security. As far as Washington is concerned, the first three (military, homeland, and energy) are absolutely essential conditions that would have to be met by Ottawa before Washington would even consider new commitments. The CCCE and Washington may well tread slowly on social security, aware of the sensitivities of the Canadian public in this area. Under the Martin and Harper leaderships, the shift in Canadian positions on global security has, to a large extent, already happened.

Water security has not been in the spotlight as yet. It is worthwhile recalling that, when CUFTA negotiations reached a stalemate in 1988, Ottawa was compelled to sweeten the pot by putting our energy resources on the table, which, in the end, proved to be the "deal maker." The "deal maker" this time around could very well be Canada's freshwater resources.

CONCLUSION

The stakes for Canadian sovereignty have never been higher (Barlow 2005). The political forces pressing the new agenda of continental integration in Canada are clearly the big business elites. But these business elites are Canadian in name only. Over the past twenty years Canadian and US corporations have become so intertwined on a sector-by-sector basis that there is little left to distinguish one from the other. Corporate interests on both sides of the border are now virtually identical, posing enormous challenges to the maintenance of national sovereignty. Moreover, the new push for integration is happening at a time when we are witnessing the resurgence of the United States as the single, unchallenged superpower on the planet. Under the Bush administration the United States has reasserted its hegemonic power on the world stage, with Canada as one of its key strategic satellites. Recognizing a post-September 11 paradigm shift, Canada's big business leaders have championed US national security interests in order to strike a "new deal" that would consolidate the gains they have made through continental economic integration under the free trade regimes.

In effect, corporate Canada has become Washington's "empire loyalists." To achieve their main goal of securing cross-border trade and investment, Canada's big business leaders now see their mission in terms of ensuring that Ottawa fulfills its proper role as a satellite of the US empire by substantially increasing its commitment to military, energy, homeland, and global security on a continental basis, and, if need be, even with regard to social and water security. It would be inaccurate, however, to imply that Canadian capital has simply become a lackey of Washington and US business. Canada's big business class stands to benefit considerably from increased continental integration. Indeed, the interests of big capital in this country have become increasingly North American, to the point where the concept of a national business class has become almost redundant.

Furthermore, Canada's major corporations are better positioned now than they were two decades ago to carry out their new mission as Washington's empire loyalists. In Ottawa, as in Washington, the collusion between big business and government in the realm of policy making is unquestionable. As the premier corporate lobby machine in Ottawa, the CCCE works quietly, often crafting the country's key laws and policies affecting the economy. Armed with policy think tanks like the C.D. Howe Institute, public relations firms like Earnscliffe, and a battery of law firms, the CCCE and its member corporations are able to direct, if not dictate, a considerable portion of Canadian public policy.

Despite the Chrétien government's elimination of big business financing of elections and political parties, the collusion continues, aided by a "revolving-door" process that allows senior government and big business officials to move seamlessly between the private and public sectors. What this collusion amounts to, in effect, is a "corporate security state." In both Ottawa and Washington the prime role of government has been to reorganize the national economy in order to facilitate the investment and competitiveness of transnational corporations. Under these conditions, the security of capital takes precedence over the security of citizens. Indeed, this is precisely what the CCCE's NASPI is designed to accomplish.

It remains to be seen whether the Canadian people, in this historical moment, will have a real opportunity to discuss and debate the plans for a new deal with the United States, let alone whether they wish to be a satellite of the US empire. Unlike in 1988 there is no draft treaty that can serve as the lightning rod for energizing public discussion and debate; instead, much of the agenda for continental security is likely to be implemented quietly by Washington and Ottawa, well below the public radar. In effect, this has been the main outcome of the trilateral summit meetings in March 2005 and in March 2006, where at least ten trinational policy committees were set up to advance pieces of this agenda, all operating below the radar screen. That is why civil society groups, along with allied members of Parliament, need to seize the moment by coming together and mounting a public challenge to this new political agenda. In doing so, the stage could be set for Canadians to engage in a full-scale democratic debate on the agenda for continental security and our destiny as a country and our relation to the US empire.

The stakes for Canada are high indeed. If this new political agenda is fully implemented, Canadians will pay a very high price in terms of their sovereignty and democracy. We know where the CCCE wants to lead the country. Now is the time for Canadians to prepare for a full-scale debate on whether to accept this view of our destiny and the political, economic, and social sacrifices it entails. Has the historic 200-year struggle over our relationship with the United States finally come to an end? Will Canada become a mere satellite of the US hegemon?

NOTES

Some segments of this chapter appear in Clarke with Dobbin and Finn (2005). The author wishes to acknowledge and appreciate the timely editorial assistance of Ricardo Grinspun on this chapter.

1 The following analysis of sector-by-sector corporate restructuring is based on research conducted by Richard Girard at the Polaris Institute.
2 The CCCE's agenda for North American "security" and "prosperity" has been further supported by the C.D. Howe Institute. The majority of the institute's members belong to the CCCE. In its series entitled *The Border Papers*, the institute outlines proposals for the next stage of continental integration. For further detail, see Clarkson and Banda's chapters 4 and 5, this volume.
3 The Harper appointees are listed in Canada (2006). The CCCE members and their roles can be found in CCCE (2006).
4 For a discussion on "interoperability," see Staples (2002) and his chapter 6, this volume.
5 The sections on water security and global security are adapted from Clarke with Dobbin and Finn (2005).
6 This falls short of a customs union, since as long as one sector remains without an external tariff, NAFTA rules of origin must remain in place.

REFERENCES

Allen, Bruce. 2004. NAFTA: *Auto Restructuring and Mexico's Maquila Zone*. Black Flag. Available at <http://flag.blackened.net/blackflag/210/210nafta.htm>, cited 31 July 2004.
Barlow, Maude. 2004. *The Canada We Want*. Ottawa: The Council of Canadians.
– 2005. *Too Close for Comfort: Canada's Future within Fortress North America*. Toronto: McClelland and Stewart.
Barlow, Maude, and Tony Clarke. 2003. *Blue Gold: The Battle against the Corporate Theft of the World's Water*. Toronto: McClelland and Stewart.
Bertin, Oliver. 2003. CEOs Urging Stronger Ties to US. *Globe and Mail*, 15 January, B3.
Campbell, Bruce. 2001. False Promise: Canada in the Free Trade Era. In *NAFTA at Seven: Its Impact on Workers in All Three Nations*, ed. Jeff Faux, 21–9. Washington, DC: Economic Policy Institute.
Canada. 2002. *The Defence Portfolio 2002*. Ottawa: Department of National Defence.
– 2005. *Budget 2005: Overview – Delivering on Commitments*. Ottawa: Department of Finance, Government of Canada.
– 2006. *Prime Minister Announces Canadian Membership of North American Competitiveness Council*, 13 June. Ottawa: Office of the Prime Minister, Government of Canada.
CBC. 2005. Indepth: Auto Industry. Introduction. CBC *News Online*, 21 November. Available at <http://www.cbc.ca/news/background/autos/ index.html>.
CCCE. 2003a. *Security and Prosperity: Toward a New Canada-United States Partnership in North America: Profile of the North American Security and Prosperity Initiative (NASPI)*. Ottawa: Canadian Council of Chief Executives.
– 2003b. *Security and Prosperity: Toward a New Canada-United States Partnership in North America: Background, Questions and Answers*. Ottawa: Canadian Council of Chief Executives.
– 2004. *New Frontiers: Building a Twenty-First Century Canada-United States Partnership in North America*. Ottawa: Canadian Council of Chief Executives.
– 2006. *Members*. Ottawa: Canadian Council of Chief Executives. Available at <http://www.ceocouncil.ca/en/about/members.php>, cited 21 June 2006.
CCPA. 1995. CCPA *Monitor, October*. Ottawa: Canadian Centre for Policy Alternatives.
Cellucci, Paul. 2003. Remarks by Ambassador Paul Cellucci to Canadian Institute of International Affairs: Current Issues in the United States-Canada Relationship, 28 October. Ottawa: Embassy of the United States of America.
CFR. 2005a. *Creating a North American Community: Chairmen's Statement – Independent Task Force on the Future of North America*. Washington: Council on Foreign Relations.

- 2005b. *Building a North American Community: Report of an Independent Task Force*. Washington: Council on Foreign Relations.
Clarke, Tony. 1997. *Silent Coup: Confronting the Big Business Takeover of Canada*. Toronto: Lorimer.
- 2002. The Re-Criminalization of Dissent: Canada's Anti-Terrorism Legislation and the Threat to Freedom, Justice and Democracy. *Policy Options* (September): 49–50.
- 2005. *Inside the Bottle: An Exposé of the Bottled Water Industry*. Ottawa: Polaris Institute.
Clarke, Tony, with Murray Dobbin and Ed Finn. 2005. *National Insecurity: Bowing to US "Security" Demands Will Make Canadians Less Secure*. Ottawa: Canadian Centre for Policy Alternatives.
Clarkson, Stephen. 1984. *Canada and the Reagan Challenge*. Toronto: Lorimer.
Curry, Bill. 2003. Business to Push Manley, Ridge for Joint Perimeter. *National Post*, 1 April, A9.
d'Aquino, Thomas. 2003. Concluding remarks at a conference hosted by the Summit Institute on Canada's options for dealing with today's top bilateral challenges (as recorded by the Polaris Institute), Ottawa, 4–5 December.
Draffan, George. 1999. *A Profile of the Weyerhaeuser Corporation*. Seattle: Public Information Network.
EIA. 2001. *Canada Energy Oil Information*. Washington: US Energy Information Administration, Department of Energy.
Francis, Diane. 2003. Canada Deserves the Stern Rebuke: Liberals Have Grossly Mishandled the Iraqi File. *National Post*, 10 April, FP3.
Galloway, Gloria. 2003. Martin, Business Discuss Border Issues. *Toronto Star*, 14 January, A6.
- 2006. Ottawa to Spend $15 Billion to Boost Military. *Globe and Mail*, 23 June, A4.
Hamilton Spectator. 2006. Canadian Icon The Bay in American Hands. 11 March, A18.
Industry Canada. 2006. *United States, Canada, and Mexico Launch North American Competitiveness Council*, 15 June. Ottawa: Industry Canada.
Lakely, James G. 2003. Abraham Outlines Plans for Hydrogen Fuel, Canadian Oil. *Washington Times*, 17 November. Available at <http://www.washingtontimes.com/archive/long_term.php>.
Langille, David. 1987. The Business Council on National Issues and the Canadian State. *Studies in Political Economy* 24 (Autumn): 41–85.
Louisiana-Pacific Corporation. 1999. *Louisiana-Pacific Corporation Acquires Evans Forest Products*. Press release. Nashville: Louisiana-Pacific Corporation.
Macdonald Commission. 1985. *Report of the Royal Commission on the Economic Union and Development Prospects for Canada*. Ottawa: Minister of Supply and Services.

Maquila Solidarity Network. 2000. *A Needle in a Haystack: Tracing Canadian Garment Connections to Mexico and Central America.* Toronto: Maquila Solidarity Network.

– 2004. *Mapping the Canadian Retail Apparel Industry.* Toronto: Maquila Solidarity Network.

McCullum, Hugh. 2006. *Fuelling Fortress America: A Report on the Athabasca Tar Sands and US Demands for Canada's Energy.* Ottawa: Canadian Centre for Policy Alternatives, Polaris Institute, and Parkland Institute.

Morton, Peter. 2003. CEOs Seek Role beyond Postwar Iraq: Border Security, Defence Will Shape Business Decisions. *National Post*, 9 April, FP6.

Norbord Corporation. 2004. *Mills: North America.* Norbord Corporation. Available at <http://www.norbord.com/mills_na.htm>, cited 17 December 2004.

O'Neill, Tim. 2002. *North American Economic Integration.* Toronto: Bank of Montreal Economics Department.

Portal Iraq. 2005. *Canada: Eighty Percent of Iraq's Debt Cancelled.* 21 June. Portal Iraq Online. Available at <http://www.portaliraq.com/news/Eighty+percent+of+Iraq%27s+debt+cancel led__.html>.

Qualman, Darrin. 2001. *The Farm Crisis and Corporate Power.* Ottawa: Canadian Centre for Policy Alternatives.

Quintero Ramírez, Cirila. 2001. Unions and the North American Free Trade Agreement (NAFTA): The Canadian and Mexican Experiences, CERLAC Working Papers, Centre for Research on Latin America and the Caribbean, Toronto.

Robinson, David. 1997. *Who Owns Canada: Foreign Ownership and Corporate Power.* Ottawa: Council of Canadians.

Simpson, Erin, and Brian Tomlinson. 2006. Canada: Is Anyone Listening? In *The Reality of Aid 2006: Focus on Conflict, Security and Development*, ed. Reality of Aid Management Committee, 257–60. London: Zed Books.

Staples, Steve. 2002. *Breaking Rank: A Citizens' Review of Canada's Military Spending.* Ottawa: Polaris Institute.

Suncor Corporation. 2004. *About Suncor: Straight Forward.* Suncor Corporation. Available at <http://www.suncor.com/default.aspx? ID=1>, cited 17 December 2004.

West Fraser Timber Company. 2000. *West Fraser to Acquire Plum Creek's Southern US Manufacturing.* Press release. Vancouver: West Fraser Timber Company.

White House. 2005a. *Fact Sheet: Security and Prosperity Partnership of North America*, 23 March. Washington: Office of the Press Secretary, White House.

– 2005b. *Security and Prosperity Partnership of North America: Security Agenda*, 23 March. Washington: Office of the Press Secretary, White House.

– 2006a. *The Security and Prosperity Partnership of North America: Progress.* 31 March. Washington: Office of the Press Secretary, White House.

– 2006b. *Security and Prosperity Partnership of North America: Next Steps*, 31 March. Washington: Office of the Press Secretary, White House.

PART TWO

September 11
and the Deep Integration Agenda

4

Paradigm Shift or Paradigm Twist? The Impact of the Bush Doctrine on Canada's International Position

STEPHEN CLARKSON AND MARIA BANDA

Many aspects of the catastrophe that struck the United States on 11 September 2001 were not novel. Local terrorism was as old as the perception of political oppression by the militantly aggrieved, and global terrorism had been a reality for two decades. Even global terrorism directed at US targets was well established. What was new about the attacks was the United States' humiliation at having its own civilian airplanes used as missiles guided by Osama Bin Laden's adepts, who had been legally admitted to the country by the Immigration and Naturalization Service (INS), having slipped through the fingers of the Central Intelligence Agency (CIA) and then trained at free-enterprise flying schools without the Federal Bureau of Investigation (FBI) managing to understand what they were perpetrating.

The incineration of New York's World Trade Center (site of US global financial power), the destruction at the Pentagon (headquarters for US global military might), and the near miss on Congress or the White House (control centres of US global hegemony) were not just a feat whose symbolism reverberated in all corners of the earth. More important for our concerns in this chapter, the attacks had a transformative impact on the American public, who finally realized that even the United States was vulnerable to the darker sides of globalization.

The resulting seismic shift in the nation's consciousness presented the Bush administration with the opportunity radically to shift the government's policy priorities. Having spent eight months in office without a clear plan for implementing his conservative beliefs, US president George W. Bush was suddenly handed a rationale for bolstering the state's coercive and police power at home while remilitarizing US policy abroad. With national security legitimating its unilateralist proclivities under the slogan of a war against terrorism, a fervently neoconservative White House "found a threat and built a world order around it."[1] The Bush administration's move from economic liberalization to national security was shrewdly conceived, deftly executed, masterfully marketed, overwhelmingly popular, and so transformative that it is best described as a "paradigm shift."

For our purposes, a paradigm is a prioritized set of policy objectives demonstrating a number of features:

- It has its own specialized network of players who are mobilized within their national state but often develop transnational linkages and epistemic communities (Coleman and Skogstad 1990);
- Because government policies create winners as well as losers, struggles among competing interests can be observed in every policy area;
- This continuing contest is typically expressed along ideological spectra formulated between polarities such as left versus right, Protestant versus Roman Catholic, local versus central, national autonomy versus international convergence; and
- Over the decades, battles over particular sets of issues typically result in the creation of institutions dedicated to producing policies on behalf of the clientele that has successfully voiced demands for government action.

Domestic political actors first struggle over the development of a policy paradigm and then compete for control of its contents. At any particular historical moment, the popular political discourse and the government's budgetary allocations reveal which policies are dominant and which are secondary in this hierarchy. The priorities defining a nation's policy paradigm are determined by political choices expressing societal values at any particular historical moment.

If the relationship between a country's policies within a given paradigm is more congruent than conflictual, it will persist over a long period of time, as was the case in the Keynesian welfare state. This stability may then be shattered if conflicts among policy communities become too intense. A period of instability may then ensue; later a new policy paradigm may emerge. We understand such a paradigm change to be a more monumental shift of societal priorities than the simpler micro-alterations of the political agenda that characterize most political change.

Unlike previous paradigm shifts, such as the move from free market liberalism to Keynesianism half a century ago, the Bush transformation was far from stable. The new US national security paradigm rapidly passed through three variants:

- Counter-terrorist prevention focused on building up domestic police powers (homeland security measures taken after 11 September 2001) and pressing the international community to collaborate in strengthening its intelligence capacities;

• Anti-terrorist retribution relied on diplomatically sanctioned military force (intervention in Afghanistan to destroy Al Qaeda along with its host, the Taliban government);

• Account-settling pre-emption implemented the unilateralist Bush Doctrine (a controversial war to achieve regime change in Iraq).

Before assessing the impact on Canadian autonomy of the interactions between Washington and Ottawa at each of these phases of the new US policy order, we need to understand the preceding economic liberalization paradigm that prevailed on the eve of the catastrophe.

ECONOMIC LIBERALIZATION

In the year 2000 general elections in all three countries belonging to the North American Free Trade Agreement (NAFTA) heralded what seemed to be a new stage in a clear trend towards more institutionalized continental governance.

Least surprising was the re-election in October of Jean Chrétien's Liberal Party. His third consecutive majority in the House of Commons suggested that Canada would be able to move quickly on any change to deepen or broaden continental, hemispheric, or global liberalization that the three-term prime minister endorsed. For the most part, Canada-US relations were functioning according to what a former US ambassador had called "the wheel that didn't squeak" theory: a seamlessly interdependent relationship between two similar countries equally committed to market integration (Griffin 2002). Although the paradigms in the two developed North American neighbours were congruent, reflecting not just deep integration but considerable ideological compatibility, Ottawa became concerned towards the end of 2000 that the "specialness" of its US relationship was being pre-empted by Mexico.

At issue was right-wing Vicente Fox's dramatic electoral victory in July. In his campaign to oust the Institutional Revolutionary Party (PRI) after seventy-one years in power, the governor of Guanajuato had vowed to set Mexico more firmly on the path to neoconservative liberalization, which included ambitious proposals for further continental integration (Pastor 2001).[2] It seemed that President Fox's "Vision 20/20" to build European-Union-like institutions in NAFTA might capture the Mexico-US, if not the continental, agenda once the US Supreme Court declared George W. Bush president of the United States.

The new US president and his foreign policy advisers, who had vowed to proceed "from the firm ground of the national interest and not from the interest of an illusory international community" (Hirsh 2002, 32), soon announced their opposition to the Kyoto Accord on climate change, abrogated the Anti-Ballistic Missile Treaty, and unsigned the United States' accession to the International Criminal Court. But this retreat into unilateralism at the multilateral level was tempered by the interdependence practised by their own transnational corporations (TNCs), which required access to energy, raw materials, and cheap labour both abroad for their globalized production networks and at home. Since Mexico provided the bulk of this low-cost personpower in the form of some four million undocumented workers who had slipped across the border, the United States had "firmground" interest in addressing the labour situation.

Fox managed to change Mexico's relationship with Washington because former Texas governor Bush, with his affinity for Mexico, was a continentalization president as opposed to Clinton, the "globalization president" (Hirsh 2002, 30). The enthusiastic reception of Fox in the White House and in Congress seemed to signal the United States' acceptance of his migration and labour agenda as well as Canada's definitive eclipse. But the date of this triumph was 6 September 2001, and Osama bin Laden had already set in motion a scheme so traumatizing that it would replace the US commitment to trade liberalization within a rules-based multilateral trading system with a policy paradigm far less palatable to its two neighbours.

PREVENTION: NATIONAL SECURITY AT HOME

The Bush administration's conception of "homeland security" initially focused on the domestic front, first buttressing the resources of first responders and then strengthening intelligence, immigration, and police services – or, more specifically, the CIA, the INS, and the FBI, the agencies that had allowed the martyrs of jihad to execute their mission in the first place. The counter-terrorism variant of the new national security paradigm had two facets affecting Canada – continental security and continental defence.

North America: Continental Security

The rise of counter-terrorism to paradigmatic status was confirmed by the creation in Washington of a new set of security institutions. The US attorney general set up the Foreign Terrorist Tracking Task Force. The Department of Justice established another 150 terrorism task forces. The colour-coded Homeland Security Advisory System was put in place for public consumption (Stevenson 2003, 78).[3] Ultimate institutional evidence of the new policy paradigm was the creation of a megaministry, the Department of Homeland Security (DHS), which merged twenty-two separate existing agencies in March 2003 to give counter-terrorism its physical base within the Washington Beltway.

Since "security" to the United States is territorially based, the actions of an obsessive US government unconstrained – at least temporarily – by economic concerns,[4] threatened the commercial essence of continental integration. To the dismay of their own business community, members of Congress refused to entertain "economic security" as one of the DHS's objectives. It was only after a major lobbying effort by the US Chamber of Commerce that the token position of "Special Assistant to the Secretary (Private Sector)" was established in the new department.

Economic liberalization could be downgraded, but it could not be entirely jettisoned. Washington soon relaxed its border security measures in the interest of its own corporate sector, whose entire system of just-in-time production was being jeopardized by bottlenecks at the country's land borders, seaports, and airports. Fifty percent of the one million containers arriving yearly at the port of Montreal, for instance, were destined for US locations.[5]

Washington's response to the terrorist attacks put its reconfigured national security paradigm in conflict with its allies' views about how to combat terrorism while promoting the multilateral world order they had constructed after the Second World War. While no country trading with the United States was unaffected, nowhere was the impact of the US paradigm shift more direct than on its immediate neighbours since the new approach, in which "security trumps trade," directly jeopardized the goal of an integrated North American market. NAFTA's two peripheral states had already reconfigured their own policy priorities in response to Washington's demands that they deregulate and further open their already highly exposed economies to US investment. Since close to 90 percent of Canada's exports were going to the United States, the temporary shutdown of the US border after September 11 stunned Canadian firms whose very survival now depended on maintaining uninterrupted transcontinental trade and personnel flows.

For Canada, the shock of September 11 was not the loss of twenty-three fellow citizens in the World Trade Center's wreckage. The spectre that haunted Ottawa was another shutdown of its territorial borders, which would jeopardize the interconnected objectives of securing access to the US market, making Canada an attractive site for foreign direct investment, and closing its chronic productivity gap with the United States. Since terrorists could be lurking within its multiracial communities, the government of Canada knew it was seen as a potential haven for terrorists. Not surprisingly, Ottawa had a different assessment of the situation. It viewed Washington's rapid elevation of the national security paradigm as producing a "Mexicanization" (read: militarization) of the world's longest undefended border[6] – a far more serious threat to its short- and long-term stability than Al Qaeda. So Ottawa's tough new counter-terrorism policies were less about fear of Al Qaeda than about rescuing its neoconservative economic paradigm.[7]

If it was to restore unhindered commerce, the United States had to be satisfied that the border with Canada was secure enough to meet its homeland security concerns. Ottawa thus quickly elevated counter-terrorism to the top of its policy hierarchy, which meant tightening immigration policy, passing extensive anti-terrorism legislation, enhancing border controls, and stepping up law enforcement and intelligence cooperation with Washington (see Aiken, chapter 7, this volume). The Prime Minister's Office created the ad hoc Cabinet Committee on Public Security and Anti-Terrorism in October 2001 to ensure these measures were effectively implemented. Chaired by Foreign Affairs Minister John Manley, the committee coordinated significant improvements to border infrastructure, introduced high-tech programs to speed the cross-border flow of low-risk vehicles and people, and buttressed other existing security measures.

In subsequent weeks, intense negotiations between Washington and Ottawa came to grips with a host of specific questions, many of which had been promised in a series of border agreements signed between 1997 and 1999 but subsequently ignored – such as the Canada-US Border Vision Initiative, which focused on immigration and smuggling, a cross-border crime forum on law enforcement cooperation, and a Canada-US partnership (CUSP) to promote high-level dialogue among governments, border communities, and stakeholders on border management. Business associations lobbied desperately for the implementation of these previously proposed measures in the hope that they would preserve their project of economic liberalization by simultaneously speeding up border traffic and enhancing surveillance. Canadian diplomats in Washington claimed that the bulk of the proposals forming the 30-Point Smart Border Plan signed by Homeland Security Advisor Tom Ridge and John Manley in Ottawa on 12 December 2001 had been made in Canada (DFAIT 2001). Ottawa also established a border task force at this time. A favourable half-year progress report was released on 28 June 2002, followed by a one-year status report on the Smart Border Action Plan on 6 December 2002.

In addition to US government measures implementing the established Customs-Trade Partnership Against Terrorism (C-TPAT), Canadian trade-facilitating initiatives included such programs as the Canada Customs and Revenue Agency's Customs Self-Assessment (CSA) to reduce border pressure through pre-approval of low-risk traders, which was implemented on 6 December 2001 after several years of planning. At the Bush-Chrétien meeting in September 2002, the two leaders jointly announced the launch of Free and Secure Trade (FAST) – a program whose purpose was to facilitate commercial flows and that was built on the two earlier initiatives, CSA and C-TPAT. Under another program, NEXUS, fast lanes for low-risk pre-cleared travellers were opened in June 2002 at two border crossings.

Ottawa's fiscal commitment to US counter-terrorism efforts was reflected in the $7.7 billion that Finance Minister Paul Martin allocated over the next five years to counter-terrorism, border infrastructure, and security – a commitment that he announced in a special December budget (SCFAIT 2002, 90).

Although Ottawa's responses to US security concerns had been initially motivated by its perceived economic vulnerability, a consensus also developed on the danger that terrorism posed. In fact, Canadian officials, who shared the business community's integrationist agenda, were relieved that Washington was finally considering the linked proposals they had been making for nearly a decade to accelerate economic flows while improving their security. For their part, Canadians generally supported their government's actions, although human rights advocates expressed serious alarm about the impact the counter-measures might have on civil liberties and on refugees and immigrants who would likely suffer from more stringent scrutiny and tougher entry requirements. Beyond the hypothetical issue of would-be citizens' rights, actual Canadian citizens of Middle Eastern provenance soon found themselves profiled for harsh treatment at the border.

Fears that Washington would insist on the creation of a continental zone to ensure US security seemed overblown. In practice, it became clear that its concerns about its northern neighbour had been exaggerated. Far from being the "Club Med for terrorists," Canada had been the transit point for none of September's deadly hijackers. Indeed, during his visit to Ottawa in December 2001, Attorney-General John Ashcroft acknowledged the efficacy of the Canadian intelligence that had contributed to the capture in December 1999 of the terrorist Ahmed Ressam as he crossed the border en route to bomb the Los Angeles airport.

Canada's swift reordering of its domestic policy priorities in congruence with the new US paradigm was also facilitated by historical attitudes. As in the Cold War, Ottawa found itself on the familiar terrain of having to coordinate, if not harmonize, its policies with an enemy-obsessed Washington. With the disappearance of the Soviet Union, the threat, the players, the ideologies, and the theatre of war had all changed, but the old patterns of asymmetrical cooperation reappeared once the United States declared its new security agenda. Security assurances through border and immigration controls, such as the Safe Third Country Agreement (see Aiken, chapter 7, this volume), were still the sine qua non for good bilateral relations, but there were limits to how far Canada would go to satisfy its demanding neighbour. Ottawa may have rushed to strengthen its counter-terrorism capacities, but it was not Pavlovian enough to conform immediately to US plans for beefing up its continental military security.

North America: Continental Defence[8]

The real Pavlovians were in the Pentagon, which insisted upon defining anti-terrorist security in military terms through a sweeping reorganization of its internal defences initiated by Secretary of Defence Donald Rumsfeld. The decision announced on 17 April 2002 to create Northern Command (NORTHCOM)[9] – a defence megastructure integrating all four US forces in the United States and with responsibility for the geographic area stretching from the North Pole to Guatemala and part of the Caribbean – placed Canada in a quandary because of its discomfort with using the military to deal with what it considered to be an essentially non-military threat.

Chrétien was publicly reluctant and officially non-committal about deeper continental military integration. Commentators were dubious about NORTHCOM's implications for the existing structure of bilateral defence cooperation,[10] and Ottawa initially resisted endorsing either an extension of the North American Aerospace Defence Command (NORAD) or the US National Missile Defence (NMD) program understood by many as a step towards weaponizing space (SCFAIT 2002, 106).

Within Canada's Department of National Defence (DND), however, there was strong support for any further integration that would increase the interoperability of Canadian with US forces. For over a decade, the federal government had cashed in on the so-called peace dividend. Prime Minister Brian Mulroney's Conservatives encountered little resistance when they cut military spending since there seemed to be little need for the armed forces. As for Canada's peacekeeping responsibilities, which did require well armed, well equipped, and well trained forces, these budget cuts seriously reduced the country's capacity in that regard as well. Without the capability to engage in military operations on its own, the Canadian military leaned to increased cooperation with Washington, knowing that this would force thrifty-minded politicians to increase its budget. Given the threat implicit in President Bush's "you're-with-us-or-against-us" rhetoric, DND had good reason to fear it would be excluded from planning North American defence if Canada did not wholeheartedly buy into all the Pentagon's prescriptions.

Following 11 September 2001, Canadian and US military personnel at NORAD cooperated more closely. Canada's elaborate structure of reciprocal defence obligations with the United States, which included over eighty treaty-level defence agreements, 250 memoranda of understanding, and 145 bilateral defence discussion forums,[11] enabled it to re-engage with its neighbour without public deliberation or notice.

As a result, the two countries agreed on 5 December 2002 to create the Binational Planning Group (BPG) – located at the NORAD/NORTHCOM headquarters in Colorado Springs – to proceed unobtrusively with operationalizing the new phase of the old partnership.[12] The new group had no forces at its disposal, since it was intended to prepare contingency plans for maritime and land threats and for military assistance to civilian authorities in emergencies. Although it was created outside NORAD's formal structure, there was notable personnel overlap: NORAD's deputy commander – a Canadian – was named the director of the BPG. As a result, within the continental theatre Canadian and US policy priorities remained similar.

Although the commander of NORTHCOM (and NORAD), General Ralph E. Eberhart, expressed an interest in defence cooperation with Mexico by expanding NORAD or even forming a bilateral defence alliance, historic public suspicions and his military's reluctance[13] forced the Mexican defence secretary immediately to deny any intent to change the distant bilateral military relationship (Alegre 2002). For the time being, North American military integration remained a bilateral, Canada-US enterprise based on the Cold War principle of "defence against help," which admonished Canadians to cooperate in defending against Uncle Sam's enemy lest he defend Canada himself but on his own terms.

While a defence-against-help arrangement put the hegemon in the driver's seat, it still left the junior partner some autonomy to decide how many resources to devote to defence and where to allocate them. It also presumed that Washington's enemy was Canada's as well. When the Bush administration moved from retribution to pre-emption, it became clear that not every imagined enemy of the United States would be considered a valid foe by the government of Canada.

RETRIBUTION AND PRE-EMPTION: MILITARY FORCE FOR REGIME CHANGE

Whereas Europeans viewed the September 11 attacks as sabotage requiring a defensive stance and transnational cooperation among intelligence agencies, immigration services, and police forces, the Bush administration viewed them as acts of war requiring first retribution and then pre-emption through armed intervention. Moving immediately to assert its institutional primacy, the Pentagon insisted that military force prevail over undercover intelligence operations as Washington's prime agent of coercion. The ascent of the military could be seen from its budgetary allocations, which stood at US$390 billion in 2001, exceeding the combined expenditures of the next fourteen largest military spenders on the planet (Hirsh 2002, 37).[14] This reaffirmed military might was to be directed against two Muslim countries – Afghanistan and Iraq – but only the first intervention was perceived in Canada as legitimate.

Afghanistan: The Global Defence Paradigm

Within a month of the September 11 attacks Bush linked his rhetorical "war on terrorism" to an actual battleground. With Secretary of State Colin Powell promising a clear mission and credibly tying the barbaric and globally ostracized Taliban regime to Al Qaeda, the White House assembled a multilateral "coalition of the willing" to topple the Muslim fundamentalist government. As a result, 136 countries offered a range of military assistance to Operation Enduring Freedom, which began on 7 October 2001.

Canadian troops have a history of fighting alongside US troops (Clarkson 2003). In both Bosnia and Kosovo they formed part of multilateral forces under UN and NATO mandates. Ottawa accepted Washington's military rationale for Afghanistan and, in early 2002, sent 750 soldiers from Princess Patricia's Canadian Light Infantry Regiment to Kandahar, where it became part of a US Army task force. There were serious implications to fighting *for* rather than *alongside* the United States, particularly since Washington had decided not to honour the Geneva Convention on the treatment of prisoners of war. From first handing over its captured Taliban fighters to the United States in contravention of international law, to covertly deploying the elite JTF-2 military unit, to losing troops in a US "friendly fire" incident for which President Bush issued an offensively belated apology, Canadian participation was controversial. The operation of naval units in the Arabian Gulf region under the command of Canadian ships was less contentious and, in the end, more critical to the coalition's success.[15]

As with the Bush administration's homeland security policy, Canadian policies remained congruent with those of the United States in this second phase of Washington's new security paradigm, although Ottawa's meagre military financial allocations revealed its reluctance to make the military a priority. In sum, Canada's intervention in Afghanistan was part of a long tradition of subservient defence cooperation characterized by Ottawa spending as little as possible on defence while still expecting economic favours from Washington in return. This time, economic favours were not forthcoming. On the contrary, the Canadian contribution to the US war on terror in Afghanistan was met with higher US duties on British Columbia's lumber and Prairie wheat. Expecting brownie points for offering victims to friendly fire, Canada received instead a punch in the face.

Iraq: The Pre-emptive Defence Variant

The war in Afghanistan was the first application of the Bush Doctrine, articulated at West Point in June 2002. Formalized in the National Security

Strategy issued the following September, it confirmed that a hard-line, military-weighted approach centred in the Pentagon had won out over a softer diplomacy-led variant championed by the Department of State. The unilateralist, anti-détente policy network from the old Reagan administration (Donald Rumsfeld, Deputy-Secretary Paul Wolfowitz, Vice-President Dick Cheney, and the arch-hawks Richard Perle and John Bolton of the American Enterprise Institute) elbowed aside the moderate multilateralist community led by Colin Powell and his director of policy planning, Richard Haass.

The outcome of this Beltway struggle made a world of difference to Canada. The official commitment of the Bush White House to the pre-emptive use of military power was at odds with Canada's own foreign policy doctrine. Canada's "voice opportunities"[16] closed down as US liberal internationalism was silenced. Unlike the diplomatic and economic arenas where its influence corresponded to its considerable size, Canada was perceived to be a pygmy in the realm of military power.[17] As long as the United States was seeking the international community's support at the United Nations, it subordinated its military to its diplomacy-led approach under Colin Powell's guidance. But the third variant of the new national security paradigm made pre-emption Washington's policy of choice for countering terrorism (notwithstanding that there was no evidence linking Saddam Hussein's regime to the September 11 attacks). Once it became obvious that US diplomacy at the UN was merely aimed at securing cover for a war that Canadian diplomacy was trying to avert, the discrepancy between the American and Canadian policy agendas became apparent. The gap between the hegemon and its neighbour's policy hierarchy became too difficult to bridge once the Bush administration elevated the alleged threat of Iraq's weapons of mass destruction (WMD) to the top of its security agenda (Ikenberry 2002, 56). The White House's goal in Iraq of ousting Saddam Hussein was at odds with the Canadian government's non-interventionist approach to containing proliferation. When the Bush administration announced it would proceed even if Iraq voluntarily disarmed, nothing could make the two policy orders congruent. The world got "marching orders from Bush and not a common vision," so it was disinclined to stay in step (Hirsh 2002, 28).

As the United States committed itself to regime change, Canada intensified its diplomatic activity. Rooted in traditional soft-power doctrines of multilateralism, respect for international organizations, and primacy of international law, trade, and aid, Canadian ambassadors made concerted efforts in global forums to avert the looming crisis – first by preventing an irreparable schism in NATO and then by putting forward a compromise resolution at the United Nations.

Reverting to its instinctive helpful fixer role, Canada allied itself with its other NAFTA partner, whose seat on the Security Council placed it uncomfortably in the limelight. Ottawa's position converged with Mexico City's, so the two peripheries coordinated their efforts to find a diplomatic alternative to war. During an official visit to Mexico in late February 2003, the Canadian prime minister discussed with President Fox his proposal for a more precisely detailed and extended ultimatum. Chrétien then followed up with a telephone call to President Ricardo Lagos in Santiago since Chile was also serving on the Security Council. Mexican foreign minister Luis Ernesto Derbez raised the Canadian proposal with Powell the next week in a meeting in Washington.[18] But the Bush administration interpreted its northern neighbour's goodwill in trying to bridge the transatlantic divide as unhelpful meddling. Ambassador Cellucci said Canada's proposal for a new UN resolution that would give the Iraqi dictator a 28 March deadline was "not particularly helpful" because it would allow Iraq to hold out longer: "We can't let this go on for ever" (Perkel 2003). The United States rejected Canada's compromise resolution even though elements of it made their way into British prime minister Tony Blair's own last-minute effort to salvage peace. After much wavering, Chrétien's decision not to participate in the US-led military coalition for "Iraqi freedom" drew the withering scorn of the neoconservative establishment in Washington and its mouthpieces in the media.

For the first time since the early 1980s, Ottawa did not align its policies with Washington, whose view of the world it had generally shared. The Liberal budget announced on 18 February 2003 indicated that its spending priorities were more socioeconomic than military. When the Department of National Defence decided in February 2003 to deploy 1,200 peace-building troops to Afghanistan, it sought the help of NATO and a *European* partner. Canadians would not be in Kabul under US command, in marked contrast to its military deployment the year before. The Canadian government then openly defied a White House committed to an uncompromisingly militarized position on Iraq. Bush's goal of disarmament and regime change drew an uncharacteristically sharp, public response from the Canadian prime minister who warned that US unilateralism would undermine the United Nations (Laghi and Koring 2003).[19]

Still, Canada's own position vis-à-vis the war was in flux. Business leaders who feared US retaliation in the form of border blockages clamoured for Canada's military participation in the conflict or, at the very least, rhetorical support for the US war[20] (Sanders 2003). Such pro-war sentiment was strongest in the west but clashed with significant grassroots mobilization across central Canada and especially staunch opposition in Quebec. US ambassador Paul Cellucci's rebuke that Washington was "disappointed" with Canada unsettled the Canadian domestic political order, strengthening right-wing critics in the House of Commons and emboldening the premiers of Ontario and Alberta to voice their support for Washington's war with Iraq. Following Cellucci's rebuke, approval of the prime minister's handling of the situation "declined a significant 10 points" since the previous week's polling (Ipsos News Center 2003b).

The ambassador's disappointment was actually misplaced, considering Canada's already significant contribution to the multilateral forces in the Gulf region. As Cellucci himself pointed out, "Ironically, the Canadians indirectly provide more support for us in Iraq than most of those 46 countries that are fully supporting us" (Sanders 2003). Canada's military contribution put it right after Britain and Australia in the coalition. Nevertheless, because President Bush had made it clear that countries were either "with us or against us" in his war on terror, many took Cellucci's disappointment with Ottawa for a veiled threat of retaliation. The cancellation of President Bush's first official trip to Canada scheduled for May 2003 was perceived as an initial punishment. It is worth noting that the United States had delivered the same stern message to a number of other unwilling capitals from Brasília to Berlin. In fact, the United States was far more annoyed with Mexico, whose diplomatic support in the Security Council it had taken for granted (Weintraub 2003).

While other countries' US relations might have suffered a greater setback than Canada's, whose policy priorities had been more congruent until Washington broke the global consensus with its venture in Iraq, Jean Chrétien's decision was initially contested since 48 percent of Canadians supported Bush's war. Going into the third week of the war, Canadians were split evenly between those who supported (48 percent) and those who opposed (48 percent) the US-led military action. However, an Ipsos-Reid/CTV/*Globe and Mail* poll revealed that "a division is clearly developing between the two solitudes:" a slight majority (54 percent) of Canadians outside Quebec expressed approval of the war, compared to (29 percent) in Quebec. Two weeks earlier, 52 percent of all Canadians opposed the military action, with English Canada again split evenly (49 percent in favour, 48 percent against). This division between Quebec and the rest of Canada also emerged on the question of whether Canada should offer help to the US coalition after the military action had begun: 51 percent of Canadians supported such a move (58 percent in English Canada and 28 percent in Quebec). The prime minister's approval rating on the handling of the Iraq situation remained steady at 55 percent (down one point from the previous week) – with a major difference between Quebec (75 percent) and the rest of Canada (48 percent). In fact, 50 percent of Canadians outside of Quebec then disapproved of his handling of the crisis (compared to the 50 percent of English Canada that had expressed approval one week earlier) (Ipsos News Center 2003a). Beyond the poll data, Chrétien's decision resonated strongly with the left-of-centre public in Canada, much of which thought this was "Jean Chrétien's finest hour" (Morris 2003).

CONCLUSION

Our analysis of the impact on Canada of the most far-reaching US security reconfiguration since 1945 leads us to draw inferences on four issues: Canada's unique characteristic as neighbour to the world's only superpower, its capacity for autonomy, the nature of continental governance, and the future of Canada–US relations.

The Unique Interdependence
of the North American Periphery

Analyzing only one country during a specific historical moment incurs the risk of ascribing uniqueness to phenomena that exist in other states or at other times. Canada was not alone in having to respond to three consecutive shifts in the paradigm hierarchy of the global hyperpower following September 2001. Many of its responses resembled those of Mexico or European states, which also tightened their airport security, scoured their underground for terrorists, and cooperated with US counter-terrorism efforts. Cooperation was extended when the United States militarized its homeland security paradigm with its intervention in Afghanistan. The UN Security Council debates on Iraq from October 2002 to March 2003, which alienated Canada from the United States, also estranged Mexico and created a schism in the Atlantic alliance that ultimately fragmented the European Union (EU).

Notwithstanding the fact that, as "the key recruitment, planning, and logistics base for the attacks," Europe posed the greater security threat to the United States, it was Canada that felt compelled to reorder its domestic policy agenda in the immediate aftermath of the attacks (Stevenson 2003, 80). Even by early 2003 the EU was only beginning to implement substantial changes. In the end, the Iraq crisis may have harmed France's and Germany's relations with Washington much more than it did Canada's, but the fear of US retribution was felt more acutely in Ottawa than in Paris or Berlin.

What makes Canada-US teamwork in Afghanistan different from that of the Korean War, and what makes the squabble over Iraq different from the disagreements about Vietnam, is the existence of NAFTA, which acts as a common external constitution (Clarkson 2002). NAFTA ties the two countries into a formalized interdependent relationship that places definite limits on the weaker player's ability to define its policies independently as well as definite constraints on the hegemon's freedom to punish what it considers deviant behaviour with economic sanctions.

Complex interdependence in North America seemed to oblige Washington to tolerate Ottawa's policies, even when they clashed with its own security priorities. In 2001 US exports to Ontario alone were worth twice as much as were those to Japan. Canadians imported $5,254 worth of US products per capita, and thirty-seven states had Canada as their largest single trading partner. Seventeen percent of US crude oil imports came from Canada. Clearly, prolonged border congestion could wreak disaster in many key border states and "make Mr. Bush a one-term wonder" (Tandt 2003).

Convergence versus Autonomy

Implicit in tracking the metamorphoses of US policy priorities since September 11 has been the question of whether Canada, the weaker partner in a deeply interdependent relationship with the global hegemon, can pursue an independent set of domestic and foreign policies. "Free trade" was designed, after all, to accelerate Canada's convergence to the deregulatory US model. Furthermore, Washington's increased assertiveness in the aftermath of September 11 might have been expected to intensify this process, making incongruent paradigms in the peripheries untenable.

The hypothesis is persuasive. "Hegemony sits in tension with the principle of equality," and the shift after September 11 ended the NAFTA-generated illusion that all three countries had an equal voice in the construction of the continent's dominant paradigm (Glennon 2003, 29). The progression of the three variants of the US national security paradigm (counter-terrorist prevention and homeland security, anti-terrorist retribution in Afghanistan, and diversionary pre-emptive war in Iraq) forced Canada to respond immediately in order to forestall damaging actions by an aroused Uncle Sam. A perverse dynamic developed in which allegedly poor security in the peripheries made the United States feel more vulnerable, while Washington's strong homeland security measures made its neighbours more vulnerable, compelling them to align themselves with the US paradigm despite their disagreement with it.

The actual outcome was counter-intuitive, demonstrating the paradoxical power of the weak. Despite all these pressures to converge, Mexico, though weaker and poorer, showed more autonomy than did Canada, which followed in lockstep every shift in the US paradigm variant until late 2002.

For Ottawa, divergence from the US paradigm manifested itself in a bout of short-lived diplomatic activism, which coincided with and responded to the high point of US unilateralism. Soon after Washington declared the Iraq war won, this brief assertion of a separate Canadian way was followed by announcements signalling a desire to re-establish close relations with the United States. The Chrétien government moved towards endorsing National Missile Defence, and hurriedly announced a $100 million contribution to the reconstruction of Iraq, which, when thought too picayune to impress the White House, was soon followed by another $200 million. Whether these fence-mending efforts were prompted by exaggerated fears of US economic retaliation is immaterial. The point for our analysis is this: Ottawa was under such political and corporate pressure that, after its declaration of temporary independence, it hurriedly reordered its policy mix to re-establish congruence with that of its continental leader.

It is equally important to remember that the Canadian prime minister's efforts at rapprochement were rather half-hearted. He pushed ahead with his domestic program, which included one item to which the Bush administration openly objected – the decriminalization of possessing small amounts of marijuana. He added insult to injury by signalling that the federal government would support the Ontario court ruling that sanctioned the marriage of same-sex partners, a prospect deeply offensive to social conservatives in Washington. And to make it clear that, unlike Tony Blair, he was in no way George Bush's poodle, he went out of his way before the Evian, France, G8 Summit in June 2003 to criticize the huge US budget deficit.

Such observations about the emperor's scant clothing came to a temporary end with Paul Martin's long-delayed assumption of the prime ministership in December 2003. The change in tone was immediate, if not longlasting. Martin patched things up with Bush at the personal level and appointed as minister of national defence a strong proponent of close military integration with the Pentagon. Finding himself in electoral difficulties during his prematurely called campaign later in 2004, Martin strove to put some distance between himself and Washington by attacking Conservative Party leader Stephen Harper for wanting to send troops to Iraq, maintaining Canada would never participate in the Americans' weaponization of space, and pointedly asserting the superiority of Canadian over American social policies.

Continental Governance or Government by States?

The United States' reconstitution of its policy paradigm around homeland security in the aftermath of September 11 also confirmed the continent's failed institutionalization and continuing dual bilateralism. For instance, Washington chose to deal with Mexico and Canada separately on issues of border security. While the thirty points in the Canada-US border

plan were conveyed through Canadian diplomatic channels to the Mexican
government as a courtesy, they were formally put forward as a template by
Washington for the Mexico-US border. The border plans were neither discussed nor adopted through a trilateral process. President Fox's November
2001 suggestion of a common "North American Security Policy" was
ignored (Serrano 2003). Whether the hegemon refused to deal with both
neighbours at the same table or whether the two peripheries preferred to
deal separately with Uncle Sam, North American governance in the age of
counter-terrorism still consisted of bilateral, divide-and-rule relations with
little significant interaction along the still-weak axis between Ottawa and
Mexico City. The intense collaboration between the two peripheries in the
Security Council during the winter of 2003 was a notable exception.

NAFTA had served as the conduit to increase awareness in Ottawa and
Mexico City of their shared vulnerabilities as well as their common
interest in containing their common neighbour. The Iraq crisis triggered
a genuine attempt at cooperation between the two peripheries as their
foreign policies converged, while an equally strong and shared opposition to Washington's Indochina quagmire some thirty years earlier had
not.

The Mexican-Canadian relationship could become increasingly important as a complement to each periphery's vital US relationship. Real solidarity of the weak could diffuse US preponderance, but this potentiality
remains unrealized. The trilateral relationship, which developed due to
NAFTA, remained in place while the three domestic paradigms were congruent under economic liberalization. But without EU-style structures,
North American governance could not mature through institutional means.
Conceived "as a simple, narrow, stand-alone agreement on foreign trade"
(Faux 2003) and empowered with rules rather than institutions, NAFTA
accelerated market integration in the short term without the constitutional
substance to cope with emerging problems in the long term. When the
World Trade Center attacks ended the continent-wide agreement on a
policy paradigm, US-driven bilateralism displaced NAFTA's embryonic tri-
lateralism. The re-emergence of an assertive, militarized hegemon forced
continental governance into retreat. North American economic integration
– and the whole project of continental governance – remained a creature of
its constituent states.

For NAFTA to recover any coherence as a governance regime, its three
states would have to replace the revived bilateralism that followed in the
fallout from Ground Zero with some consensus on their respective policy
agendas. Paradigm congruence could occur if Washington realigned its
policy priorities with Ottawa's and Mexico City's, a scenario that was
doomed by George W. Bush's re-election. With the Bush Doctrine providing the script for his second administration's continuingly aggressive global

unilateralism, persistent paradigm conflict among the three countries ensued until the election of Stephen Harper's new Conservative government shifted Canada into line with his American counterpart. Felipe Calderon's success in maintaining the National Action Party's (*Partido Acción Nacional*) business-friendly and pro-American hold on the Mexican presidency should guarantee smooth – though not necessarily productive – relations between Mexico City and Washington.

If the price for achieving further integration is satisfying Washington's need for increased security, the Canadian business community will likely accept whatever schemes are deemed necessary by Washington. The Canadian public, however, may not be as acquiescent. The integrationist Canadian business community may want to enact every type of continental accommodation from customs and currency unions to a continental security perimeter and armed services' integration. But as the values and attitudes of the Canadian public are diverging from those of their southern neighbours, Harper's integrationist proclivities had to be contained lest they jeopardize his party's electoral chances following the dissolution of his minority government.

With such dim prospects for continental convergence, the likelihood of a new dawning of continental paradigm stability is even dimmer. The source of turbulence has been the radicalism of the Republican Party's Washington leadership and the institutional primacy of a bellicose White House and a militant Pentagon. The domestically polarizing effects of the Bush agenda have prevented the kind of paradigm entrenchment that requires a bipartisan consensus about its basic assumptions. The combination of paradigm instability at the centre and dissonance with its periphery suggests that the post-September 11 future of continental governance for North America is far from rosy except at the administrative level. For this reason, the Security and Prosperity Partnership of North America, signed by the three heads of government in March 2005 and beefed up in March of the next year with a big-business-led North American Competitiveness Council, is exploiting the considerable potential for Mexico and Canada to achieve executive-led regulatory harmonization without requiring controversial legislative action.

Prospects for Canadian-us Relations

Even if this dissonance of views had seriously negative implications for those hoping to move North America towards a European model of governance, it did not threaten Canada's basic relationship with the United States. Ottawa responded expeditiously and effectively when Washington's paradigm shift redefined the agenda for border control. The Canadian government then balked when the zealots driving the Bush administration turned paradigm shift to counter-terrorism to paradigm twist in an effort to settle old scores with Saddam Hussein and to impose their formula for "freedom" on the Middle East. Chrétien's decision to oppose the US objective of regime change in Iraq certainly caused the already frosty relations between the two countries' leaders to deteriorate further, but this personal tension in Canadian-US relations did not outlast the Liberal Party's hold on power.

The misunderstanding and ideological disconnect, which was manifested in Canada's immediate isolation by a frosty Washington, have been smoothed over by Harper's commitment to military engagement against the Taliban in Afghanistan and by President Bush's evident satisfaction with his newfound ideological soulmate, expressed at the North American summit in Cancún in March 2006. But the president's persistent championing of his disastrous Iraq policy does not bode well for new bliss in the Canadian-US relationship – a relationship that continues to be disturbed by commercial disputes. It is to the business community's ambitious agenda for redesigning Canada's US relationship that we turn in chapter 5.

NOTES

The research for this chapter was accomplished in large part thanks to the support of the Dean of Arts and Science, University of Toronto, the Woodrow Wilson Center, and the Social Sciences and Humanities Research Council of Canada. It is based on twenty-six interviews in Washington, DC, and twelve in Mexico City, carried out in April 2003. A version of this chapter was presented at the annual meeting of the Canadian Political Science Association at the Learned Societies Conference in Halifax, NS, on 1 June 2003.

1 John Ikenberry, cited in Althaus (2002).
2 Fox and his foreign minister, the political scientist Jorge Castañeda, endorsed Robert Pastor's proposals to correct NAFTA's institutional deficit while fostering Mexico's development with capital, trade, and aid. The plan included a customs union, considerable policy coordination, transborder labour mobility, and supranational institutions that could transfer funds to Mexico from its richer partners for renovating its generally rudimentary infrastructure.
3 Other institutional changes took the form of US Senate and House of Representatives committee reorganizations.
4 Confidential interview.
5 Stephen Flynn (2002), cited in Fry and Bybee (2002, 33).
6 For an overview of the two plans and their differences, see Gabriel, Jimenez, and Macdonald (2003).
7 The most wide-reaching proposals came from the right-wing think tanks and

business associations that proselytized for measures that went so far as proposing
a continental security perimeter and defence integration. See Dobson (2002),
Granatstein (2002), as well as our chapter 5 in this volume.

8 For further discussion of Canada-US defence integration, see Steven Staples
(chapter 6, this volume).

9 NORTHCOM became operational on 1 October 2002.

10 SCFAIT and a number of other observers were sceptical about this opaque process,
whose broader implications were not understood even by the government's poli-
cymakers (SCFAIT 2002, Recommendation 11).

11 Desmond Morton (1985, 182), cited in *Partners in North America* (SCFAIT 2002,
100).

12 Confidential interview.

13 Ibid.

14 US defence spending makes up 36 percent of the world total (Sepúlveda 2002).

15 Confidential interview.

16 John Ikenberry, cited in Thomas Risse (2003, 8).

17 NATO secretary-general George Robertson, cited in Hirsh (2002, 38).

18 Fox had also "styled himself in the role of broker, trying to bridge the differences
between the Anglo-American perspective and the others: 'We have to convince the
United States that we have alternatives to attain the objective of disarming Iraq ...
What we believe is that we still have time in formulas and proposals to do what
we have to do without a war'" (Laghi 2003).

19 However, even Chrétien's own foreign minister then exclaimed that Canada
backed regime change.

20 It was mainly political symbolism and moral support that the White House was
expecting from its "close friend and ally."

REFERENCES

Alegre, Luis. 2002. Bajo la sombra militar de EU. *El Norte*, 29 September, 7.
Althaus, Dudley. 2002. Our Changed World: Terror Shifts Diplomatic Priorities.
Houston Chronicle, 8 September, 24.
Clarkson, Stephen. 2002. *Canada's Secret Constitution: NAFTA, WTO and the End of
Sovereignty.* Ottawa: Canadian Centre for Policy Alternatives.
– 2003. The View from the Attic: Towards a Gated Continental Community? In
*The Rebordering of North America: Integration and Exclusion in a New Secu-
rity Context*, ed. P. Andreas and T.J. Biersteker. New York: Routledge Press.
Coleman, William D., and Grace Skogstad, eds. 1990. *Policy Communities and
Public Policy in Canada: A Structural Approach, University of Toronto.* Missis-
sauga, ON: Copp Clark Pitman.
DFAIT (Department of Foreign Affairs and International Trade). 2001. *Canada and
the United States Sign Smart Border Declaration.* News release 162. Ottawa.

Dobson, Wendy. 2002. Shaping the Future of the North American Economic Space: A Framework for Action. In *The Border Papers*. Toronto: C.D. Howe Institute.

Faux, Jeff. 2003. Corporate Control of North America: And How to Bring NAFTA under Popular Governance. *The American Prospect* vol. 13, no. 24, January. Available at <www.prospect.org>.

Flynn, Stephen. 2002. America the Vulnerable. *Foreign Affairs* 81 (1): 64–5.

Fry, Earl H., and Jared Bybee. 2002. NAFTA 2002: A Cost/Benefit Analysis for the United States, Canada, and Mexico. In *Canadian-American Public Policy*, ed. R. Babcock, no. 49. Orono: University of Maine.

Gabriel, Christina, Jimena Jimenez, and Laura Macdonald. 2003. *The Politics of the North American Security Perimeter: Convergence or Divergence in Border Control Politics*. Ottawa: Carleton University.

Glennon, Michael J. 2003. Why the Security Council Failed. *Foreign Affairs* 82 (3): 29.

Granatstein, Jack L. 2002. A Friendly Agreement in Advance: Canada-US Defence Relations Past, Present, and Future. In *Commentary: Border Papers*. Toronto: C.D. Howe Institute.

Griffin, Gordon. 2002. *Remarks to the Canadian-American Business Council*. Washington, DC: The Canadian American Business Council.

Hirsh, Michael. 2002. Bush and the World. *Foreign Affairs* 81 (5): 30.

Ikenberry, G. John. 2002. America's Imperial Ambition. *Foreign Affairs* 81 (5): 41–61.

Ipsos News Center. 2003a. *Canada and the Iraq War: Two Solitudes Emerge*. Toronto: Ipsos Reid.

– 2003b. *A Country Divided on War in Iraq*. Toronto: Ipsos Reid.

Laghi, Brian. 2003. Fox Warns of Economic Costs of War on Terrorism. *Globe and Mail*, 28 February, A11.

Laghi, Brian, and Paul Koring. 2003. Chrétien and Bush Clash over Regime Change. *Globe and Mail*, 1 March, online edition. Available at <www.theglobeandmail.com>.

Morris, Cy. 2003. Kudos to Chrétien for Stance on War. *Straight Goods*, 22 March 2003. Available at <http://www.straightgoods.com>, cited 11 November 2003.

Morton, Desmond. 1985. *A Military History of Canada*. Toronto: McClelland and Stewart.

Pastor, Robert. 2001. *Towards a North American Community: Lessons from the Old World for the New*. Washington, DC: The Institute for International Economics.

Perkel, Colin. 2003. US-Canada Relationship Could Suffer, Cellucci Says. *Globe and Mail*, 1 March, A9.

Risse, Thomas. 2003. *Beyond Iraq: Challenges to the Transatlantic Security Community*. Washington, DC: American Institute for Contemporary German Studies, Johns Hopkins University.

Sanders, Richard. 2003. Who Says We're Not at War? *Globe and Mail*, 31 March, A15.

SCFAIT. 2002. *Partners in North America: Advancing Canada's Relations with the United States and Mexico.* Ottawa: Standing Committee on Foreign Affairs and International Trade, House of Commons, Canada.

Sepúlveda, Bernardo. 2002. Terrorismo transnacional y seguridad colectiva. In *México en el Mundo: Cambio y Continuidad en la Política Exterior de México,* ed. Rafael Fernández de Castro, 23–44. México: Editorial Ariel.

Serrano, Mónica. 2003. Bordering on the Impossible: US-Mexico Security Relations after 9–11. In *The Rebordering of North America: Integration and Exclusion in a New Security Context,* ed. P. Andreas and T.J. Bierstecker, 46–67. New York: Routledge Press.

Stevenson, Jonathan. 2003. How Europe and America Defend Themselves. *Foreign Affairs* 82 (2): 75.

Tandt, Michael Den. 2003. Trade as Crucial to the US as to Canada. *Globe and Mail,* 27 March, B2.

Weintraub, Sidney. 2003. Interview, April 9.

5

"Community of Law:" Proposals for a Strategic Deal with the United States

STEPHEN CLARKSON AND MARIA BANDA

As we saw in chapter 4, Al Qaeda's attack shocked the United States into a complete reordering of the policy priorities that had been in place up to 10 September 2001. For its part, Ottawa felt threatened less by Osama Bin Laden's jihad than by the Bush administration's concern about possible incursions of terrorists across its northern boundary. Consequently, the federal government responded with short- and medium-term measures designed to reassure Washington that the transborder flow of goods and people was as secure as public policies and technological wizardry could make possible.

But alleviating Uncle Sam's anxieties did not ipso facto calm the nerves of the Canadian business community. The spectre haunting its boardrooms was not just the possibility of another blockade following a future coup. The worry – voiced explicitly by business spokespersons – was that new investment would now pre-emptively locate in the United States rather than in Canada for fear that another terrorist exploit, in which Canada was indirectly implicated, would provoke further border constrictions.

Because vulnerability to US security reflexes was thought already to have made Canada unattractive for new investment, some advocates proposed a radical change in Canada's relationship to the United States in order to eliminate the final economic barriers still separating the two countries. This chapter reviews the origins, content, and logic of the various proposals made to achieve fuller economic integration as the definitive solution to Canada's vulnerability in the context of the US "war on terror." Since business organizations and business-funded think tanks took the lead in generating these proposals, our study looks at the role they played in setting the public policy agenda in Canada.

CONTEXT: THE POLITICAL
AND ECONOMIC CONJUNCTURE SINCE 1994

Although the Canadian business community had pressed for the bilateral Canada-United States Free Trade Agreement (CUFTA) in 1989 and had supported Mexico's inclusion in the North American Free Trade Agreement (NAFTA) in 1994, during the late 1990s it grew increasingly uneasy about the outcomes of these two accords, driven by disappointments in policy as well as in implementation. On the policy side, "free" trade had not abolished US harassment of Canadian export via anti-dumping and countervailing duties (AD/CVD), so genuinely secure access to the US market remained a mirage. On the implementation side, while truck volumes had increased 10 percent per annum since 1989, the same transportation infrastructure and, nominally, the same number of customs and immigration officials serviced the Canada-US border in 2001 as in 1980 – although in fact one-third of US border enforcement agents had been seconded to the Mexican border in the 1990s (Beatty 2002c). By July 2001 the cost of transportation delays at the Fort Erie crossing had reached an estimated $2.5 million a day (Beatty 2002b). As a result of these concerns, business on both sides of the border organized to propose both immediate solutions to the security-versus-trade conundrum as well as longer-term ideas to achieve a much more radical agenda.

   Having already established country-wide industry associations and interest groups, Canadian businesses had long lobbied the federal government for trade-facilitating measures. The most prominent players in the post-September 11 policy debates included:

- the Canadian Chamber of Commerce (CCC);
- the Canadian Council of Chief Executives (CCCE) – the former Business Council on National Issues (BCNI), still led by Thomas d'Aquino;
- the Canadian Council for International Business (CCIB);
- the Canadian Federation of Independent Business (CFIB);
- the Canadian Manufacturers and Exporters (CME), known as the Alliance of Manufacturers and Exporters Canada until October 2000, which had been formed from a merger of the Canadian Manufacturers' Association (CMA) and the Canadian Exporters' Association (CEA) in 1996 and was presided over by the former Mulroney government minister of defence, Perrin Beatty; and
- the Coalition for Secure and Trade-Efficient Borders (CSTEB).

Business-funded think tanks such as the C.D. Howe Institute (Dobson 2002; Granatstein 2002), the Conference Board of Canada (Barrett and Williams 2003), and the Public Policy Forum (Hulley and Poisson 2003) advocated one version or another of the integrationist agenda and supplied the analytical details that were largely absent from the business proposals, adding policy substance to the Canadian corporate vision. The House of Commons Standing Committee on Foreign Affairs and International Trade (SCFAIT 2002) presented its own recommendations after extensive public hearings with business and such participants in the public policy debate as the government-supported Foundation for the Americas (FOCAL) (Wilson-Forsberg 2002).

Perceived governmental inaction in the face of a growing need for accelerating border procedures prompted an effort to transcend immediate border issues and "update" the Canada-US partnership. As the CME president described it, leadership on issues of continental integration since the implementation of NAFTA had shifted to the private sector (Beatty 2001b). For instance, the CCCE launched the Canada Global Leadership Initiative in 2000 because the "bilateral trade, investment, regulatory, security and institutional relationship did not reflect the advanced level of integration between the two countries" (d'Aquino 2003b). It argued that "visionary leadership on both sides of the border was needed to move the partnership to a 21st century footing" (ibid.), although most of the CCCE's specific recommendations were couched almost exclusively in terms of such economic indicators as fiscal and monetary policy, human capital, productivity, internal barriers to trade, and research and development, without any overarching political or integrative vision (d'Aquino 2000).

The CME linked with other business groups in Canada and the United States through the CAN/AM Border Trade Alliance to raise awareness in customs agencies and governments about the problems caused by complex regulations and resulting border congestion. A joint working group on border issues was struck with the American National Association of Manufacturers (NAM) in August 2001 to press for trade facilitation and border management improvements (Beatty 2002c) and to urge the two governments to strengthen their commitment to a shared border agreement, which would lead to the development of a "common perimeter approach to customs, immigration, and security at first points of entry for goods and people in North America" (Beatty 2001c).

Pre-dating these developments, the two capitals had created a series of bilateral forums on the common border in the late 1990s. Between 1997 and 1999 Canada and the United States established a border vision initiative to address immigration and smuggling, a cross-border crime forum to focus on law enforcement cooperation, and a broader Canada-US Partnership (CUSP) to examine the future of Canada-US border management (SCFAIT 2002). Early success of the CME's active lobbying of the federal and provincial governments for improvements in customs administration and transportation infrastructure through its Standing Committee on Customs and Market Access could be seen in Ottawa's unilateral decisions to set up the CANPASS and NEXUS systems as well as the Customs Self-Assessment Program, which it helped design (Beatty 2001c).

Although these business forces had brought the continent to an economic integration agreement early in the 1990s, their subsequent efforts failed to produce further significant change. Whether visionary or simply practical, most of the border-improvement ideas they raised were never translated into action. Moreover, Canadian business groups did not get much support from their US counterparts to address these issues. Given already high levels of integration and similarity in corporate structures and legal systems, US groups had little incentive to expend their energies on Canada or to engage in lobbying their local politicians in the northern border states. They paid far more attention to other countries, such as Brazil, where US firms faced constant harassment. The bilateral US-Canadian business council of the US Chamber of Commerce shut its doors in the early 1990s, due to a lack of interest.[1]

The impact of government measures on the practical issue of border management was negligible and Canadian business groups expressed their frustration. By mid-2001 no headway had been made on an agenda that seemed too radical, unnecessary, and politically costly, leaving policy initiatives at the border in what Canadian business complained was a state of benign neglect. Washington's lack of interest was explained by the US focus on its southern border, where concerns about illegal immigration and narco-trafficking made the infrastructural inadequacies along the forty-ninth parallel pale in comparison (Haynal 2002). "Overburdened and congested highways, lengthy delays at border inspection stations, deteriorating and inadequate infrastructure, and the looming threat of gridlock in our major trade corridors" (Beatty 2001c) proved to the CME not just that the system was "broken long before 9/11, but [that Canada and the US] lacked the political will ... to fix it" (Beatty 2002b).

On one level, this corporate hyperbole could be taken as a cry for rescue from a situation of its own creating – heightened transborder integration. On another level, such public condemnation of a "gridlocked" border that nevertheless facilitated the largest flow of unimpeded trade in the world was disingenuous, a rhetorical bombardment serving to soften up any political defences that might impede further moves to erase the economic boundary completely.

AFTER THE SHOCK: FALL 2001

The shock of September 11 galvanized Canada's corporate and academic community into launching a new round of long-term proposals for "fixing" Canada-US relations. Because September 11 scrambled together the previously separate questions of economic and territorial security into one indivisible omelette, it revealed the hidden potential for continental governance by triggering transnational corporate cooperation faster than governments could coordinate their policies. Provoked by the crisis, business lobbies immediately moved into action, rapidly presenting government with proposals, many of which were implemented. When, in the aftermath of the attacks, an organized corporate community worked together within and across boundaries, governments heeded their pressure. BC lumber exporters may have had little in common with Ontario's automobile producers, but they concurred on the fundamental need to keep the border open. For the first time in decades, import- and export-based Canadian businesses "came together in ... immediate solidarity on a critical issue" (Beatty 2002b).

While all of the major business associations in Canada released statements on the trade-security problematic, some also took concrete steps to lobby the decision makers in Ottawa. The CME formed a policy/strategy task force of its members, re-established a joint working group on key border issues with the National Association of Manufacturers, and combined senior representatives of business associations and firms into an umbrella conglomeration of some forty business associations and businesses – the Coalition for Secure and Trade-Efficient Borders (CSTEB) – to address these issues (Beatty 2001a).

Business activism in Canada was also seen in a limited mobilization of Canadian companies in the United States, where a few Canadian groups had made the necessary political investment to develop a standing presence in Washington's corridors of power.[2] A number of these participants in the US market, such as the Canadian-American Business Council, the Canadian-American Border Trade Alliance, and the Chamber of Commerce of Canada, joined their US counterparts in the Americans for Better Borders to lobby Washington on security-trade issues (US Chamber 2004). The hurriedly mobilized business associations also responded to the two federal governments' new set of costly user fees (Beatty 2002b). Rejecting the neo-conservative idea of running the government on business principles when applied to its own dealings with the government, the corporate community demanded that costs be "shared equitably [read: offloaded on the public] rather than downloaded onto business" (Beatty 2002c).

Beyond the immediate measures it proposed to prevent illegal entry of people and goods and to facilitate the passage of low-risk goods and people across Canada's borders (Beatty 2001a), the CSTEB recommended ways to strengthen Canadian security and intelligence, immigration and refugee determination, border processing, and civil emergency preparedness. It also explored a continental perimeter approach to security and raised the longer-term question of the role of Canada's military.

At the same time, various schemes loosely referred to as "NAFTA-Plus" were advocated at numerous business-oriented studies and conferences. These proposals sought to establish a regulatory framework for the continent-wide regime of capital accumulation that had emerged from integrated supply chains, cross-border intra-industry trade, US corporate investment in Canada, Canadian corporate investment in the United States, and transnational border alliances. Several recurring, if contestable, themes ran through the integrationist proposals:

- Canada-US economic integration is as irreversible as it is desirable;
- As a vital membrane for the Canadian economy, the Canada-US border must enable low-risk people and goods to pass unimpeded;
- Under the proposed border management, security resources must focus on high-risk travellers and cargo; and
- The Canadian government must take the lead in redefining Canada's place in North America's institutional structures.

It is impossible to determine with any certainty to what extent the business community's mobilization in the aftermath of the fateful September 11 was motivated solely by the need to maintain an open border. This is because the crisis had provided an unequalled opportunity for reactivating an ambitious integrationist agenda for transcending border management that had been in gestation for years and that could now be dressed up for political expediency as a response to the threat of global terrorism. Whatever the mix may have been between long-term schemes and short-term solutions, most measures for immediate improvement in border management had been set in motion by 2004. We now proceed to review the ideas advanced to achieve a fundamental transformation of the still real economic border.

PROPOSALS FOR
A NEW CONTINENTAL ARCHITECTURE

Following the common assumption that "NAFTA set us down a road, but it did not give us a map" (Faux 2002, 27), the integrationist proposals fell into two broad categories. On the one hand were the various schemes for a NAFTA-Plus economic and institutional integration, such as Wendy Dobson's proposal for "big idea" negotiations with the United States (Dobson 2002); on the other hand, two bolder thrusts related to the enhanced threat of terrorist attacks were articulated: homeland security integration (a common security perimeter and harmonized immigration controls) and military integration (Northern Command and national missile defence – NMD).

Economic and Institutional Integration

Most proposals focused on one or more aspects of the vision for an integrated North America. If fully implemented, the NAFTA-Plus vision would include the following five elements: a trade tribunal, an energy pact, a common external tariff, monetary union, and a single labour market. Below, we appraise each one.

TRADE TRIBUNAL

Because of North America's vast power asymmetries, Canada was at a distinct disadvantage whenever it dealt with the United States outside a rules-based infrastructure, so the country's best protection arguably lay in "continental, rules-based solutions and institutions"(SCFAIT 2002, Recommendation 15). CUFTA and NAFTA had provided Canada with a dispute settlement system that was "only partly rules-based. Some of the rules [left] open the possibility of political intervention, such that Canada [and Mexico were] still susceptible to the adverse effects of US political decisions and power" (SCFAIT 2002, Chapter 4). By maintaining national systems of anti-dumping and countervail, NAFTA also failed to develop a common North American competition regime.

Since over 80 percent of NAFTA disputes involved anti-dumping and countervailing duties (AD/CVD), they fell under the provisions of Chapter 19's *binational* panel processes. As a result, the *three* sets of domestic AD/CVD jurisprudence made the panel rulings opaque and inconsistent and the process unpredictable even to government trade experts. Moreover, the panels were susceptible to political manipulation. The procedure under Chapter 20 for resolving general disputes was equally subject to a power-based resolution of conflicts. Chapter 11's international tribunals for arbitrating the claims of transnational corporations (TNCs) against governments were a still more contentious feature of NAFTA's dispute settlement procedure (see Shrybman, this volume).

Notwithstanding the unresolved debates about the rules they were to adjudicate, the manifest inadequacy of these judicial mechanisms (Kerr 2001) made a permanent NAFTA arbitration court a common element among a number of proposals and the most feasible candidate for a future Canada-US agreement (Herman 2003; Pastor 2001; SCFAIT 2002, Recommendation 15). Given the difficulty experienced in finding panellists with the necessary expertise but without conflicts of interests, a court with permanently sitting judges would be able to function more effectively. Moreover, full-time judges would be more likely to render rulings that did not conflict with earlier panel determinations. In sum, the attractiveness of a permanent panel system and uniform NAFTA jurisprudence in lieu of the present ad hocery, in addition to widespread support in Canada for an improved adjudication mechanism, make a permanent court the most politically feasible of the proposed measures.

A CONTINENTAL ENERGY DEAL

Striking a trilateral deal on energy was the primary goal of several proposals, as integrationists who were dissatisfied with the continental market in oil, natural gas, and electricity pushed for a formal North American energy pact. FOCAL, for instance, proposed that energy cooperation be the first sector explored. The CCCE suggested the creation of a resource security pact as a key element in a new North American partnership, based on the two principles of open markets and regulatory framework compatibility (d'Aquino 2003b).

That a partial continental market already existed in electricity on a north-south and not an east-west basis became obvious on 14 August 2003, when a massive blackout hit the northeastern US states and Ontario, sparing the neighbouring provinces (see Griffin Cohen, this volume). Formalizing or intensifying integration in some energy markets is easier said than done, though. Petroleum can hardly be integrated much more as long as Mexico defends its constitution's Article 27, which keeps oil, natural gas, and electricity in the public domain. Electricity can be further integrated across national boundaries, but, as Quebeckers were reminded on 14 August 2003, there are considerable advantages to sovereignty association when it comes to a semi-autonomous provincial hydro system. Following the California brownouts, Enron's collapse, and Ontario's failed deregulation, the attractiveness of the CCCE's proposed energy pact has dimmed.

Supporting movement towards a continental energy accord, the North American Energy Working Group (NAEWG) had been established by the three governments at the April 2001 Summit of the Americas in Quebec City. Reinforcing the thrust of business thinking on the issue, the NAEWG has no mandate to examine the environmental implications of further continentalizing the market. Nor does it appear prepared to consider either the risk for Canada of accelerating the depletion of its remaining low-cost petroleum reserves or the conflict between enhancing unsustainable energy consumption and achieving Canada's Kyoto Protocol commitments or whatever lower targets the Stephen Harper government may ultimately be induced to accept (see May and Dover, chapter 17, this volume).

CUSTOMS UNION

Rules of origin that specify in excruciating detail how much value must be added domestically or regionally to qualify for tariff-free treatment at the border have exposed Canadian producers to occasional bullying. A Honda assembly plant in Oshawa was a case in point. Because its finished cars destined for the US market employed Japanese parts that entered Canada under low barriers, US customs authorities rejected Honda's claim that it complied with the CUFTA's 50 percent value-added requirement. Costly and cumbersome, this rules-of-origin process could be replaced by a common external tariff (CET) that would, in theory, erase the Canada-US border as a trade boundary.

As advocated by the C.D. Howe Institute and a number of business associations, the CET was the basic prerequisite for a limited or full-fledged customs union that would finally achieve a North America without borders for the movement of goods (see Lee, this volume). Its negotiation would involve harmonization of tariffs, customs procedures, and such unrelated issues as sanitary and phyto-sanitary standards for products crossing the border.

The most powerful argument, however, was economic. While Canadian and US external tariffs generally fell within the same range, even slight differences required complex rules of origin detailing what kind of local content was necessary for goods produced in one NAFTA country to pass duty-free to another (Goldfarb 2003, 31). The cost of administering the certificates of origin was estimated at 2 percent to 3 percent of the total NAFTA GDP. With a more than trillion-dollar economy in Canada, this alone could save up to $30 billion a year for Canadians (Barrett and Williams 2003). However, Marc Lee (this volume) argues that this particular estimate is unreliable since it comes from a study with "shortcomings that tend to bias results in favour of free trade."

While an intermediate customs union would involve the establishment of a CET and policy harmonization, a full customs union would necessitate the development of common trade remedies against non-member states. In such an arrangement, however, the United States Congress would have to abandon its cherished trade remedy laws (TRLs) against its customs-union partners. Otherwise, there would be little incentive for Canadians to move beyond a more limited model. A more feasible option for the short run suggested by a number of observers was a sectoral customs union for certain highly integrated sectors, such as the steel industry.[3]

But even an intermediate solution was contentious. As Daniel Schwanen, then of the Institute for Research on Public Policy (IRPP), pointed out, while harmonized tariffs would eliminate the need for complicated rules of origin, the hard questions of whether "we would be exempt from US antidumping and countervailing duty, whether we would be able to access procurement opportunities in the States" would not necessarily be answered to Canada's satisfaction (SCFAIT 2002, 178).

The downside of a customs union for Canada would be the abdication of its sovereignty over external tariffs, which would make a mockery of the CCCE's commitment to closer cooperation and/or trade deals with Mexico,

Japan, China, and India (d'Aquino 2003a). The flexibility that member countries have over trade policy is characteristic of free trade areas (but not of customs unions), and it exposed the inconsistency of the CCCE's proposals. The loss of autonomy over economic policy would also have foreign policy implications. Whereas Canada and the United States have in the past taken a common position against the European Union and aggressively promoted their hormone-fed beef exports, their interests on other trade issues have often diverged. Under a CET Canada could no longer freely trade with countries such as Cuba, Iran, or any other targets of US trade embargoes. As a simple illustration, the CET would require either that Ottawa suddenly comply with the provisions of the Helms-Burton Act or that Washington rescind it.

Quite apart from what decisions are made, there is the far more intractable issue of how these decisions would be made. Since no set of rules is ever final, how subsequent tariff changes would be made would also need to be established. If there were to be a common tariff-setting body, would each member have one vote or would voting muscle be proportional to population or economic strength? In future trade negotiations, members of a US-Canada (and Mexico) customs union would have to speak with a single voice; it does not require much imagination to guess whose voice it would be.

NORTH AMERICAN MONETARY UNION

A monetary union with a common currency was no less controversial than a customs union (see Seccareccia, this volume). After September 11 few new theoretical or practical reasons were added to the arguments that had been in circulation since the early 1990s. The business community, for its part, remained distinctly uninterested in replacing the Canadian dollar that had been on a steady course of recovery, along with the entire Canadian economy, ever since the year 2000.

As soon as proposals for monetary integration were rearticulated, the old counter-arguments resurfaced. Currency floaters insist that exchange-rate flexibility gives Canada a shock absorber that allows the Bank of Canada – within very real constraints – to fine-tune an economy, which, with its still excessive dependence on staple exports, responds to changes in the terms-of-trade at a different rhythm and with different needs from that of the United States. Even though it may have the eighth-largest economy in the world, Canada is a midget relative to the United States, with a mere 7 percent of total US GDP. Its influence on the monetary policy of a North American Monetary Union (NAMU) would be correspondingly minuscule. But, outside a limited segment of the academic community, there was little interest in abandoning the flexible exchange-rate system. Simply put, the "vital preconditions to North American monetary integration (e.g., similarity in the economic structures of NAFTA participants, existence of labour mobility across borders, availability of a fiscal transfer system)" (SCFAIT 2002, 209) were absent.

A LABOUR MARKET DEAL

It is telling that the barriers to the movement of citizens or permanent residents and the free exchange of human resources between Canada and the United States have been consistently overlooked in corporate and think tank proposals since September 11. Yet such a free movement of people is an essential feature of a common market, advocated by Fred McMahon of the Fraser Institute, who suggested it include a common perimeter (McMahon 2001). Europe's Single European Act is based on the "Four Freedoms" – free movement of capital, goods, services, and people. While a bilateral US-Mexico labour and migration deal seemed feasible in the days just before 11 September 2001, when Vicente Fox seemed to be George Bush's favourite foreign president, it subsequently disappeared from the US administration's agenda. A US-Canada labour agreement was never even contemplated. Although Mexico and Canada have long operated a temporary agricultural workers agreement, which Fox offered Bush as a model for resolving the problem of illegal immigration, prospects for US-Mexico labour peace seem bleak.

Homeland Security and Military Integration

"Security" is a multidimensional concept, alternately signifying carefully guarded territorial borders that keep out undesirable individuals or military defences against outside aggression.

CONTINENTAL SECURITY PERIMETER

Growing flows of goods and people among the three countries of North America had already shown that deepening economic integration facilitates the movement of narcotics, guns, and criminals. The challenge at the northern and southern US borders to encourage benign crossings of goods and people while blocking the malign ones was dramatized by Al Qaeda's appalling achievement. The comprehensive government actions to strengthen security at airports, seaports, and along the forty-ninth parallel (described by us in chapter 4, this volume) nonetheless left some Canadians unconvinced that Uncle Sam's homeland security anxieties had been assuaged. In the CCCE's view, nothing less would suffice than a continental "security perimeter" for Canada and the United States, and possibly Mexico.

The apparently simple concept of a common security perimeter would need to address a whole host of questions, both geographical and functional. Would it encompass North America from the Arctic to Panama or only Canada and the mainland United States? Would Washington insist that US officials replace Canadian officials in airports and seaports? And would these US officials be monitoring the application of Canadian visa requirements before passengers boarded an Air Canada flight from Paris or Tokyo? Would Canadians really feel more secure if their safety depended on the US security systems that had already let nineteen terrorists highjack those four civilian aircraft on September 11? Would a security perimeter require policy harmonization of a vast array of practices demanding far more integration than a customs union and tolerating the torture of suspects denied access to domestic courts?

If a continental security perimeter were to consist of more than closer Canada-US cooperation on intelligence, law enforcement, and enhanced border control it would likely signify a high degree of policy harmonization and implementation in the areas of immigration, refugee policy, and coastal control. Only this would reassure the United States enough to disband its monitoring of the Canadian border. According to Sidney Weintraub (2003b, 1):

The notion of perimeter screening to speed up the movement of goods and residents of the two countries is logical on the surface, but there are inherent problems that must be considered. Without any border screening, the two countries would need identical immigration laws to permit the free movement of people from one country to the other and a common tariff and other trade restrictions so that the transshipment of goods from one country to the other would not matter. These steps smack of sharing sovereignty rather than "mutual respect for sovereignty," which is an essential element of the CCCE proposal.

The security perimeter discussion evoked the provisions of the Schengen Agreement, which implemented a "Europe without borders," one of the last steps in a long process of the EU's economic and political integration. Requiring centralized decision making on security and immigration policies, the deep integration necessary for a North American security perimeter would require a degree of sovereignty sharing that seems singularly ambitious and unworkable, given the embryonic shape of North American governance. Because it could all too readily embrace *all* aspects of Canadian-US cooperation, "very few sectors are excluded from the pretext of security."[4]

DEFENCE INTEGRATION

If counter-terrorism were considered a matter for police and counter-intelligence, our many queries could be left here. But the global hegemon defines security more in military than in police terms, and the Canadian private sector decided that alleviating US defence concerns was a price worth paying for its economic security. Here the most inventive integrationists applied the old Cold War doctrines to their current trade liberalization philosophy: if the Canadian government handled the security issues to the Pentagon's satisfaction, so the thinking went, Washington would permit business to continue operating in the framework it had developed over the previous forty years (see Staples, this volume). Profits could be maintained only by "fireproofing the border from political uncertainty" (d'Aquino 2003b).

Beyond criticizing Ottawa's indecisiveness in the fall of 2001, urging closer cooperation with the US military in Afghanistan, and sponsoring pro-US, pro-Iraq-war rallies, the corporate sector actively advocated complete integration of an expanded Canadian military under the Pentagon's aegis. Echoing the arguments raised by J.L. Granatstein and the Council for Canadian Security in the 21st Century, business groups effectively resorted to the old logic of "Defence against Help," which had governed Canada's military planning during the Cold War when Canadian policy makers knew that they could either defend their territory to meet the United States' requirements for its security or Washington would do so unilaterally (CCS21 2001; Granatstein 2002). Shortly after the terrorist attacks, Granatstein (2002, 1) reintroduced the argument that Canada had "no choice" but to agree to the US demands on security and military cooperation. Noncompliance was not an option – unless Canada was willing to let its longstanding partnership unravel or allow the Pentagon completely to take over its national defence.

Washington's April 2002 decision to establish a Northern Command (NORTHCOM) – the Pentagon's homeland defence agency – was thus seen with alarm not only by a Canadian government wanting to preserve existing Canada-US defence arrangements but also by Canadian integrationists fearing its implications. For future cooperation under the North American Aerospace Defence Command (NORAD), Granatstein recommended that Canada restructure its military forces in order to integrate with their US counterparts even further. In addition, he suggested that Ottawa support the US national missile defence (NMD) project whether or not it would lead to weaponizing space. And, of course, it had to increase defence spending to be taken seriously by Washington in the first place (Granatstein 2002).

But the old Cold War equation of "contribution equals influence" did not apply in 2003. Promoters of greater military spending expected Canada would regain its alleged influence in the Pentagon and asserted that this would reverberate favourably on other bilateral issues. However, the expected payoff for Canadian defence contributions to the US war in Afghanistan in the form of concessions on the softwood lumber issue had never materialized (Weintraub 2003a).

THE BIG IDEA:
INSTITUTIONAL DILEMMAS AND POLITICAL REALITIES

Beyond the ambitious listing of *what* items Canada should peddle to Uncle Sam, the integrationist manuals diverged greatly on *how* to sell reform to the United States. The C.D. Howe Institute went farthest in advocating the "big idea" – a comprehensive intergovernmental strategic bargain that would set up a series of institutions leading towards deeper union (Dobson 2002).

The various proposals for redesigning North America's architecture were more imaginative when it came to identifying the already-reviewed functions that needed to be filled at the continental level than it was when specifying the nature of the structures that would be needed to make them work. The scenarios for North American integration remained curiously silent on its political implications, providing little explanation of how policies would be made or administered. Firmly resisting the bureaucratization and democratization inherent in any EU-styled structure, the corporate vision simply omitted any description of the institutional and legal structures that would be needed to remodel North America. The CCCE recognized new institutions would be needed but offered platitudes that obfuscated instead of clarifying:

What is needed ... is commitment to a new partnership, the cornerstone of which would be cooperation based on mutual respect for the sovereignty of each country ... The institutional framework that would govern the process will require careful consideration. Beyond [the direct involvement of the president and the prime minister at the political level], it should be guided by creativity and flexibility. (d'Aquino 2003b, 11)

As for the prototype of institutions that would be needed, the council offered the International Joint Commission (IJC), which had managed contentious water management issues along the Canadian-US border since 1909 (d'Aquino 2003b). But the IJC was not just binational: it was supranational and based on parity – characteristics that Washington is unlikely ever to accept for managing major issues, whether with one neighbour or two.

It is worth noting that none of the proposed institutions addressed the question of North America's power asymmetries. No checks-and-balances were proposed for any institutional framework that could place the weaker partners on a more equal footing with the hegemon in a common regulatory or decision-making system. The integrationists' failure to deal with this fundamental conundrum undermined much of their rationale for a more integrated North America that might conceivably work in Canada's interests.

While the big idea did help to shape a dynamic debate on the direction of Canadian policies, in corporate circles at least it focused on "NAFTA plus, trade dispute settlements, or some form of deeper economic and political union" (Beatty 2002a) to the neglect of assessing what might be possible in the prevailing political climate. Beyond the basic goal of keeping trade flowing, the business groups' vision remained vague and largely divorced from the realities of power. A constellation of political factors in North America – from the United States and Mexico to Canada – combined to thwart their plans.

US *Politics*

Washington's focus on security after the terrorist attacks meant that a comprehensive trade and security deal would be attractive only if it would clearly enhance homeland security. US ambassador Cellucci bluntly reminded Canadian integration enthusiasts of Washington's priorities: Canada and the United States should focus on building "smart borders" and not debating a "more formal economic union like Europe." He added, "I'm not saying the debate should not take place. I'm just saying it should take place at a later date" (Persichilli 2002, 1). As long as the Pentagon remained bogged down in Iraq and the Middle East demanded the White House's full attention, a bilateral deal with Canada that required major legislation being passed through Congress remained a political non-starter.

While a historic deal would have been unthinkable with Prime Minister Jean Chrétien, given his antagonistic relations with the Bush administration, such a deal would still have been difficult to strike with Prime Minister Paul Martin – unless he had been willing to take a huge political gamble. Even when Mr Harper ousted "Mr Dithers" from the Prime Minister's Office in 2006, the continuingly fragile realities of governing with a minority only made such a risk acceptable if further terrorist attacks involving, for example, nuclear, biological, or chemical weapons were found to be the result of Canadian security failures.

Even outside Republican neoconservative circles, US politicians showed little interest in deepening economic (let alone political) ties with their neighbours. Many in the United States believed they had not come out of NAFTA as a winner, and much of the economic slowdown in the United States was blamed on free trade with Mexico. In 2003, Democratic presidential candidate Dennis Kucinich argued for cancelling NAFTA and closing down the WTO. Washington's "national security preoccupations and the ever-present domestic political calculations that prevail within America's complex federal system" (SCFAIT 2002, 15) made progress on Canadian integrationists' project doubly unlikely.

The Mexican Factor

Critical to the success of any plan for further Canadian-US integration was the thorny question of whether to include Mexico, integrated into North America's market governance since 1994. If North America were defined to include Mexico, would Washington be more likely to take notice?

There may well be as many Canadians living in the United States, or US citizens with Canadian family connections, as there are Mexican Americans; but they are not visible, they do not identify themselves as Canadian, and they do not vote as such within the US political system. By contrast, Mexican Americans amount to eight million out of about twenty million Hispanic Americans – now greater in number than all black Americans combined. Furthermore, they have a voice, a vote, and a growing consciousness of their split identity. All this means that Congress is extremely unlikely to accept changes affecting Canada without requiring that the same changes apply to Mexico. Ottawa might decide unilaterally to replace its separate currency with the US dollar, but a Canadian-US monetary union would hardly be worth pitching to Washington without Mexico's participation.

If Mexican support is needed to tip the balance in Washington towards a NAFTA-Plus, then the exclusion of Mexico from the bilateral consultations by Canadian business groups was not helpful in raising support. Most associations effectively ignored their Mexican counterparts, whom they saw more as competitors than as allies for gaining Washington's ear. The CCCE claimed to have conducted studies with its counterparts in the United States, but its assertion to have consulted Mexico (d'Aquino 2003b) was rhetorical at best. The CCCE's Action Group on Canada-United States Cooperation, for example, did not include Mexican partners (d'Aquino 2001). Its proposals had been drafted in its rich members' boardrooms with little to no Mexican participation. When it did admit that the southern periphery could not be ignored, the Canadian corporate community still preferred dreaming of a North America *à deux vitesses* – with Canada taking the lead and Mexico joining in to the extent it was able. Given the temporary political estrangement between the United States and Mexico after September 11, a "two-speed" North America appeared possible[5] – but only on questions of local, strictly Canadian-US relevance.

The CCCE maintained that "building ever-closer economic and political relations with Mexico must be a strategic priority," and it urged the government to "engage more fully in exploring how the three countries can act together to advance our common goals."[6] Yet, because "the Mexico-United States relationship is profoundly different from that of Canada and the United States," the envisaged long-term blueprint for trilateral continental integration was designed for the "attainment of common goals in different ways and at varying speeds." This was to become embedded in an all-encompassing proposal that Tom d'Aquino dubbed the "Treaty of North America."

Notwithstanding the "consultations" undertaken with their Spanish-speaking colleagues, Canadian continentalists were in a state of deep denial about Mexico. In reality, the CCCE's call for Canadian leadership was premised on resuscitating the special relationship of the 1960s: Canada should articulate "a vision for closer North American security and economic co-operation," and "then propose to the United States Administration the elements of a strategy for a new Canada-United States partnership within a common North American vision." The absence of Mexico surely doomed this plan. Their 2003 proposals essentially rehashed Canadian-US business ideas from the summer of 2001, reducing the prospect of Vicente Fox endorsing the idea.

Still, a greater corporate willingness to include Mexico in the proposed governance structures would not have guaranteed their adoption. For instance, Mexico's many free trade agreements would have made their incorporation into a customs union and a CET difficult to negotiate. The Fox government would have been unwilling to re-erect tariff barriers against the EU, effectively nullifying a much-prized free trade deal that continued to evade Canada. The military proposals would likewise have been difficult. The institutional fragmentation of Mexico's military would have made continental defence integration impossible without dramatic internal, even constitutional, changes. While domestic reforms were a focal point of Vicente Fox's administration, they focused on social and labour policies. These areas, in turn, were entirely overlooked in Canadian business proposals. The Canadian corporate ideas, big or small, could not be easily translated into "Mexican."

Having transnationalized the concept of homeland security, September 11 had made a reversion to a pre-NAFTA bilateralism less, not more, feasible.

Canada's Political Realities

Before Washington could be presented with a big strategic deal, the integrationists had first to get the Liberal government on board. Even ignoring Jean Chrétien's personal discomfort with his counterpart in the White House, a formal commitment to deep integration would have provoked a rebellion within his own party and, possibly, a popular backlash.

Even though opinion polls indicated that Canadians remained well disposed to further continental economic integration, the corporate agenda failed to address NAFTA's main shortcoming, as identified by public interest groups – its focus on corporate rights, its democratic deficit, and its lack of transparency. Nor had long-standing concerns about NAFTA's effects on environmental degradation, societal inequalities, and restricted employment opportunities been addressed. Canadian and US governments and business alike remained distinctly disinclined to add a "social dimension" to the trade agreement. Change was contemplated only in so far as it solidified firmer economic rules or a deeper union – or added security and defence pillars to Canada-US economic cooperation. Widespread enthusiasm for a NAFTA-Plus was therefore unlikely.

Even if it were true that only a big idea could bring Uncle Sam to the negotiating table,[7] the Canadian government's experience with US trade negotiators showed them to be far less interested in debating grand schemes than in resolving existing bilateral "irritants." From the perspective of the US Trade Representative's Office, if Canada wanted a customs union or a trade court, it would first have to pay for it by addressing the grievances of the US business community.

The unasked question was just how high would be the price. Having already surrendered most of its bargaining chips in the CUFTA/NAFTA negotiations, Canada – as the *demandeur* – would have to accept many *quids* for its *quo*: abolishing the Prairie farmers' Canada Wheat Board and central Canada's supply management systems; terminating cultural policies favouring Canadian artistic expressions; opening the public health and education sectors to US investment; privatizing public energy and water systems and guaranteeing Washington higher flows; and expanding military budgets and integrating the armed services. While some government officials, such as Peter Harder of Industry Canada, expressed interest in the big idea, most took a more cautious approach. Big, one-time deals connect too many areas, and Canada learned during the CUFTA negotiations that putting too many unrelated issues on the table can tie its hands and cost far too much.

More tellingly, Canadian business groups were also not united on the question of deeper integration with the United States, which – contrary to the assertion of the C.D. Howe Institute – would have created greater and not lesser dependence on the US market (Goldfarb 2003). The economic slowdown in the United States in the first term of the George W. Bush presidency validated fears in Canada about "the risks associated with the current concentration of Canada's trade and investment" in the United States (Beatty 2002a). Speaking for the Canadian Manufacturers and Exporters (CME), Perrin Beatty argued: "To simply hitch your caboose to someone else's train is risky – it can be great when there is a powerful engine pulling you up the mountain, but it provides little protection if things start to go off the rails" (Beatty 2002a). In the view of the Canadian manufacturing community, trade expansion into the European market would "increase our wealth when times are good and ... protect ourselves when the American economy starts to slow."[8]

The CME's concern about excessive dependence on the global giant was natural given the composition of its membership. Unlike those businesses engaged in the highly integrated automotive and parts industry, many CME members were an easy target for US trade remedy laws and other instruments of regulatory harassment. Ultimately vulnerable to the whims of the US Congress – as well as to competition from Mexico – the CME advocated not a customs union but, rather, another typically Canadian idea: "Rules and obligations established on a multilateral level, within the FTAA, or in NAFTA, continue to be Canada's best safeguard against unilateral actions on the part of the United States that may have a negative impact on Canada" (Beatty 2002a). Even the CCCE advocated both a bilateral customs union and multilateralism. As a relatively small economy, Canada had a "vital interest in strengthening the international rule of law and multilateral institutions such as the World Trade Organization" (d'Aquino 2003a). The council expressed its commitment to multilateral and regional discussions aimed at continued trade liberalization and to cooperating with other business organizations and governments in developing countries (d'Aquino 2003a).

The higher the price of the big idea, however, the lower the chances of selling it to the Canadian public. Given Canadian concerns over the loss of sovereignty, the integrationists espoused highly contradictory positions on the question of independence. On the one hand, the business community argued that integrating Canada into the US system by adopting its policy orientations was the way to "affirm our sovereignty effectively, or ... run the risk of losing it" (d'Aquino 2003b); on the other hand, the CCCE turned around and rejected this positive evaluation of sovereignty, arguing that Canada and the United States faced a historic opportunity "that could be squandered if leaders in both countries fail to grasp the real potential that closer co-operation offers, or allow outdated concerns about sovereignty to cloud their vision" (d'Aquino 2003b). What such contradictory positions reflected was the cold reality that business ideas on sovereignty did not coincide with those of the Canadian government or of a public concerned about sustaining a viable Canadian state. They understood that, no matter how you cut it, a strategic deal seemed to imply the loss of Canada's primary jurisdiction over any matters of concern to US security interests.

Deep asymmetries of power and dependence in the Canada-US relationship notwithstanding, even the Bush White House could not ignore its own large national interest in keeping the borders open. The American Data Management Improvement Act task force on security issues on the northern border "firmly believes that there are two security elements ... First, the public must be protected from terrorist acts and injuries. Second, the economic security of the US *and its trading partners* must be preserved. The latter depends on the efficient and facilitated movement of individuals and

legal trade activity."[9] On the one hand, the panic-infused business proposals underestimated Canada's bargaining leverage, which would make most
of the big and small ideas pointless. On the other hand, in a "leap of logic,"
Canadian businesses and think tanks overestimated the attractiveness to
the United States of any strategic deals with Canada, making most of their
proposals unrealistic.

TOWARDS THE BIG IDEA IN SMALL INSTALMENTS

The difficulties inherent in each element of the big idea were considerable.
Lumping them together and labelling the product a new "community of
law" that would make North America look like the European Union
without having supranational institutions raised more questions than it
answered (Gotlieb 2003). But just because the big idea is politically imprac-
tical in the present does not mean that the bulk of its components could not
be implemented. The alternative to a mega-deal was gradual change. A
second generation of institution building was feasible, "not by offering
politically unrealistic suggestions such as moving to a full customs union ...
but by carefully building on existing NAFTA institutions" (Herman 2003).
Canada was more likely to come out of negotiations having achieved its
objective if it operated case-by-case because it could then focus its resources
and so offset the inherent asymmetry in the power relationship, though
much would depend on what was being negotiated.

The Conference Board published a counter-argument to Wendy
Dobson's "big idea fallacy" by proposing that Canada proceed incrementally (Barrett and Williams 2003). FOCAL presented a similar plan in a
series of studies, arguing that, because there was neither an overwhelming
common interest to further North American integration beyond trade and
investment nor any well articulated plans from which all three countries
would reap significant political, economic, or social benefits, North American integration should proceed in increments (Wilson-Forsberg 2002).
This incrementalism would take place sectorally in those areas where there
was a perceived net national benefit – such as energy, border management,
public security, and environmental issues – and which were capable of
grabbing Washington's attention.

One option for accelerating cross-border movements was to harmonize
rules, standards, and regulations that inhibited the free flow of goods, services, and investment. The Conference Board distinguished between maintaining different regulatory regimes for compelling public policy reasons
(standards for product labelling, health, and safety concerns) and maintaining them for "other" – presumably protectionist – reasons. The CCCE
proposed eliminating regulatory differences in key industries through harmonization or mutual recognition agreements (d'Aquino 2003b).

Seemingly non-contentious and technical, in reality this proposal had vast implications for the smaller partners' autonomy over their public policy. Any talk of "harmonization" really meant unilateral adjustment of laws and regulations by Canada or Mexico to parallel the hegemon's standards. Given the preponderance of the United States, even such proponents of trade liberalization as Minister of National Defence John McCallum (2001) admitted that "Canada can achieve 'North American policy harmonization' only by copying existing US policies, whether we're talking about taxes, regulations, external tariffs, immigration policy, or social policies." As an alternative to developing common policies, mutual recognition of each country's regulations was the preferred alternative among many members of the Canadian government (Pettigrew 2002). Complete policy harmonization was inconceivable in the short run, the new federal gun registry being the least of the obstacles to an unobstructed flow of goods from the United States.

Harmonization in transportation, telecommunications, financial services, oil, gas, and electricity sectors would mean constructing a one-way street completely to align the Canadian transportation grid with that of the United States; dismantling Bell Canada's market power; abandoning the Canadian banks; and integrating the provincial governments' electricity grids. It would also necessitate adopting US anti-trust laws to complement or supplant the Canadian competition regime. And ultimately, it could require opening up a number of semi-protected public sectors – such as health care and education – to competition from US companies.

Theoretically speaking, then, one type of incrementalism could drive forward a variable-speed North America by keeping issues below the radar screen and keeping Mexico away from the Canadian negotiating table. In fact, it was a trilaterally incrementalist approach to managing the forces of integration that prevailed as the Mexican and Canadian governments, vulnerable businesses, and their anxious publics continued to engage with a crusading hegemon wanting to trump trade with security.

Many months of back-channel negotiations between the three executives culminated in March 2005, when the three heads of government recognized and responded to the blow to North American economic development that had resulted from the post-11 September 2001 shift by the United States to a security paradigm. In their North American Security and Prosperity Partnership (SPP) signed in Waco, Texas, the three leaders reaffirmed their commitment to the continent's economic integration. In Ottawa three months later, a trilateral ministerial SPP meeting published a slick trilingual *Report to Leaders* of some three hundred measures that had been cobbled together by working groups of bureaucrats from the three governments to constitute an agenda for intergovernmental cooperation.

This very general wish list spoke to the SPP's diplomatic strategy of enhancing continental integration through the three executives' sponsoring incremental bureaucratic actions, given that political paralysis in the Mexican legislature prevented a major move towards further energy deregulation or any privatization of Pemex that might divest it of its dominion over the country's petroleum industry (SPP 2005, 28–33).

Meeting in Cancún in March 2006, Presidents Fox and Bush along with the newly elected Conservative prime minister of Canada, Stephen Harper, declared the SPP successful after its first year in operation and announced the creation of a North American Competitiveness Council by big business to advise the three governments about how to promote further integration.

CONCLUSION

We can only speculate about what content and form further integration will take. Regardless of how they were pitched, all of the integrationist policy proposals agreed on one point: the status quo was not tolerable. The Canadian-US relationship, NAFTA, and broader continental relations were in need of mending, revising, and redefining. In this context, September 11 had presented both a challenge and an opportunity for corporate Canada to set clear goals for the future direction of its most important foreign relationship.

Ever since they subscribed to Canada-US free trade, Canadian business groups have been staunch believers in economic determinism, making silent integration a self-fulfilling prophecy. At their most basic level, the integrationists shared a sense of manifest North American destiny – taking for granted that long-run integration was not just desirable but inevitable. In FOCAL's words, it "is important to now focus on specifics over generalities and begin to gather the building blocks of integration" (Wilson-Forsberg 2002). Seeing a positive-sum game (a win-win situation) between sovereignty and security, integrationists believed Canadian political independence would not be compromised by further absorption into the United States because deepening NAFTA would protect Canada against US unilateralism. Indeed, if sovereignty only meant having a seat at the United Nations and a distinctive flag, then the big idea would not be problematic.

But if sovereignty meant policy-making autonomy, then the big idea implied complete subordination and a virtual annexation of North America's kinder, gentler alternative. Incrementalism under Stephen Harper may proceed along this path, gradually leading to extensive integration across a variety of policy areas. Progressive Canadians concerned about preserving their social programs need to take seriously this ambitious business agenda for the continent. It is a road map heralding many more battles ahead.

NOTES

The research for this chapter was accomplished in large part thanks to the support of the dean of arts and science, University of Toronto; the Woodrow Wilson Center; and the Social Sciences and Humanities Research Council of Canada. It is based on twenty-six interviews in Washington, DC, and twelve in Mexico City, carried out in April 2003.

1 Confidential interview.
2 Confidential interview.
3 See for instance Sean Cooper of the Atlantic Provinces Chamber of Commerce, in his submission to SCFAIT (SCFAIT 2002, 176).
4 Stéphane Roussel as reported in SCFAIT (2002, 29).
5 Confidential interview.
6 All the quotes in this paragraph are from d'Aquino (2003b).
7 Confidential interview.
8 According to DFAIT's analysis, a free trade agreement between Canada and the European Union would lead to a net economic gain for Canada of at least 200 million dollars. See Beatty (2002a).
9 It went on to recommend strongly that Canada be included as a full partner in securing the common border. Quoted in Barrett and Williams (2003), emphasis added.

REFERENCES

Barrett, Charles, and Hugh Williams. 2003. *Renewing the Relationship: Canada and the United States in the 21st Century.* Ottawa: Conference Board of Canada.

Beatty, Perrin. 2001a. CME Presentation by the Hon. Perrin Beatty to the Sub-Committee on International Trade, Trade Disputes and Investment of the Standing Committee on Foreign Affairs and International Trade, 18 October, Ottawa.

– 2001b. Isolation or Integration: Canada in North America – Notes for a Presentation to the Brookings Institution, 6 December, Washington, DC.

– 2001c. Perspective for Different Trade-Related Organizations on the Various Challenges That NAFTA Has Presented. Paper presented at the Border Trade Alliance Conference on "Canada and Key NAFTA Issues," 30 July, Toronto.

– 2002a. Canada's Prosperity: The Business Case for Trade Diversification. Presentation at the Canada-Europe Roundtable (CERT/FORCCE) Annual General Meeting and CEO Roundtable on "International Trade and Business Competitiveness," 29 October, Montreal.

– 2002b. Panel Presentation at the Global Business Forum, 26 September, Banff, Alberta.

– 2002c. Presentation at the Ontario-Michigan Economic Summit, 14 June, Detroit.

CCS21. 2001. *Canadian Defence and Security in the 21st Century: To Secure a Nation – The Case for a New Defence White Paper.* Calgary: Council for Canadian Security in the 21st Century.

d'Aquino, Thomas. 2000. Global Champion or Falling Star? The Choice Canada Must Make. Remarks made at CEO Summit 2000. Toronto: Canadian Council of Chief Executives.

– 2001. Canadian Council of Chief Executives Launches CEO Action Group on Canada-United States Cooperation, December 13. Toronto: Canadian Council of Chief Executives.

– 2003a. The National and Global Policy Agenda: Priorities for Canadian Business Leadership. Notes for an Address to the Annual General Meeting of the CCCE, January 14. Toronto: Canadian Council of Chief Executives.

– 2003b. Security and Prosperity: The Dynamics of a New Canada-United States Partnership in North America. Presentation to the Annual General Meeting of the CCCE, January 14. Toronto: Canadian Council of Chief Executives.

Dobson, Wendy. 2002. Shaping the Future of the North American Economic Space: A Framework for Action. In *The Border Papers.* Toronto: C.D. Howe Institute.

Faux, Jeff. 2002. *Toward a North American Community.* Washington: Woodrow Wilson International Center for Scholars.

Goldfarb, Danielle. 2003. The Road to a Canada-US Customs Union: Step-by-Step or in a Single Bound? C.D. Howe Institute Commentary No. 184, C.D. Howe Institute, Toronto.

Gotlieb, Allan. 2003. A Grand Bargain with the US. *National Post,* 5 March, A16.

Granatstein, Jack L. 2002. A Friendly Agreement in Advance: Canada-US Defence Relations Past, Present, and Future. In *Commentary: Border Papers.* Toronto: C.D. Howe Institute.

Haynal, George. 2002. Interdependence, Globalization and North American Border, *Policy Options,* September, 20–26.

Herman, Lawrence. 2003. *Thoughts on Market Access and Resolving Disputes in Canada-US Relations.* Brief submitted to the Standing Senate Committee on Foreign Affairs. Toronto: Cassels Brock and Blackwell LLP.

Hulley, Crystal, and Yves Poisson. 2003. *Rethinking North American Integration.* Conference Report, 29–30 October, Ottawa: Public Policy Forum.

Kerr, William A. 2001. Greener Multilateral Pastures for Canada and Mexico: Dispute Settlement in North American Trade Agreements. *Journal of World Trade* 35 (6): 1169–80.

McCallum, John. 2001. Adopt the Greenback? Never! Keep the Change, Uncle Sam. *Globe and Mail,* 14 May, online edition. Available at <www.theglobeandmail.com>.

McMahon, Fred. 2001. Perimeter Puzzle. In *Fraser Forum.* Vancouver: Fraser Institute.

Pastor, Robert. 2001. *Towards a North American Community: Lessons from the Old World for the New.* Washington, DC: Institute for International Economics.

Persichilli, Angelo. 2002. Cellucci Says Canada-US Relationship a Role Model for the World. *Hill Times*, 7 October, 1.

Pettigrew, Pierre. 2002. The Canada We Want in the North America We Are Building. Notes for an Address by the Honourable Pierre Pettigrew, Minister for International Trade, at the 8th Annual Canadian-American Business Achievement Award and International Business Partnership Forum, Toronto, 16 October, Canadian-American Business Council.

SCFAIT. 2002. *Partners in North America: Advancing Canada's Relations with the United States and Mexico*. Ottawa: Standing Committee on Foreign Affairs and International Trade, House of Commons, Canada.

SPP. 2005. *Security and Prosperity Partnership of North America: Report to Leaders*. 27 June. Washington: US Department of Commerce.

US Chamber. 2004. *Americans for Better Borders*. US Chamber of Commerce. Available at <http://www.uschamber.com/coalitions/abb/abbissue.htm>, cited 22 July 2004.

Weintraub, Sidney. 2003a. Interview, April 9.

– 2003b. Strains in the Canada-US Relationship. *Issues in International Political Economy* 40 (15 April).

Wilson-Forsberg, Stacey. 2002. *North American Integration: Back to Basics*. Ottawa: Canadian Foundation for the Americas.

6

Fortress North America: The Drive towards Military and Security Integration and Its Impact on Canadian Democratic Sovereignty

STEVEN STAPLES

"This is our time," President George W. Bush told his war council when they assembled in the White House's underground bunker just twelve hours after the 11 September 2001 terrorist attacks. "Get the troops ready" (Fournier 2002). Days later, as the war plans were being laid for the attack on Afghanistan, Bush used his 20 September speech to the special Joint Session of Congress to issue his challenge to governments around the world: "Every nation, in every region, now has a decision to make. Either you are with us, or you are with the terrorists" (Bush 2001). The stark choice put before old enemies and current allies alike, including Canada, made it clear that Washington expected not just support for, but active participation in, the looming "War on Terrorism."[1] Unable to sit on the sidelines any longer, Canada is being forced to stake a clear position, to reply to the question: what is your response to the US-led War on Terrorism?

Two views have emerged on this fundamental question. One view is that the United States is our closest neighbour, largest trading partner, and most powerful defender and that we therefore have no choice but to join with it in its War on Terrorism, subordinating whatever discomfort or concerns we have to the greater goal of maintaining good relations with our southern neighbour. The other view is that the War on Terrorism as it is being carried out is fundamentally incompatible with Canadian values and diplomatic traditions and that Canada needs to maintain its own independent foreign and defence policies if it is to continue to play a role on the international stage. This is the dilemma. Our response will determine the degree to which Canada integrates its foreign and defence policies with those of the United States.

AFTER SEPTEMBER 11: A WORLD REDRAWN

At the time of the 11 September 2001 attacks, the policy group of Canada's Department of National Defence (DND) was going to press with its annual global security survey, *Strategic Assessment 2001* (Canada 2001b). Analysts quickly wrote a two-page assessment of the global changes that the terrorist attacks against the United States would precipitate and attached it to the end of the main report as an epilogue. The assessment was chilling. It predicted a dramatic global military build-up, large-scale conventional military operations, and the abandonment of international cooperation in favour of achieving military objectives.

The DND analysts concluded that transnational terrorism would be regarded as the primary threat to international security and that "the balance between the notion of 'human security' and traditional concepts of security will likely shift in the direction of defending national territory and populations and away from championing poverty eradication and human rights." The result would be that "previous concerns to avoid combat casualties in military operations and to minimize collateral damage will be of less importance than achieving military objectives" (Canada 2001b, 166).

For the United States, DND analysts predicted the establishment of the US Department of Homeland Security, a Northern Command, and a missile defence system. "Americans' heightened sense of territorial vulnerability will intensify homeland defence initiatives including those relating to ballistic missile defence" (Canada 2001b, 166). Further, the DND saw that international law would be cast aside in order to effectively hunt down terrorists. "The standards of proof for complicity in or responsibility for terrorist attacks before undertaking counter-terrorist actions will likely be relaxed in favour of results" (ibid.). "The international system will be re-ordered into allies or enemies in the fight against terror," wrote the analysts. "Countries that try to adopt a neutral stance will find themselves under pressure to take sides. Traditional US allies will find that calls for military, diplomatic and other support from Washington will be regarded as a test of their loyalty" (167).

THE ASSAULT ON "HUMAN SECURITY"

The defence department's *Strategic Assessment 2001* reads like a death knell for Canada's foreign policy achievements over the past decades. Given impending changes within the United States and in that nation's relationship with Canada and the rest of the world, were this path to be followed, little political space would remain for Canada's traditional reliance upon multilateralism to project the country's role as a middle power.

During the 1990s Canada tried to help shape the post-Cold War security environment by promoting various international initiatives that sought to strengthen international law. Canada's support for the creation of the International Criminal Court, for example, was an attempt to put the conduct of war within the constraints of law. Similarly, post-Cold War disarmament initiatives, including reviews of the North Atlantic Treaty Organization's (NATO) reliance upon nuclear weapons and the establishment of the Land Mines Treaty, were used to reverse the proliferation of weapons.

At the initiative of then foreign affairs minister Lloyd Axworthy, the government attempted to redefine security by promoting peacekeeping skills in the Canadian Forces and developing the controversial doctrine of human security. The notion of human security, as defined by Axworthy, is best understood as a shift in perspective – a shift that makes people rather than states the focus of security (ICISS 2001). In sum, supporting a human security agenda means addressing the sources of people's insecurity, which can often mean overriding respect for national sovereignty in favour of defending citizens' human rights. None of these initiatives was accepted by the US government. The Clinton administration supported neither the International Criminal Court nor the Land Mines Treaty. US control within NATO, moreover, quashed any notion of NATO giving up its reliance upon the nuclear umbrella. Peacekeeping and human security remained alien concepts to the Pentagon's war-fighting imperatives.

The distinctiveness of Canadian security policies within North America has been the source of great national pride and identity. A new national monument was built in Ottawa celebrating Canada's peacekeeping heritage, and the so-called Ottawa Process (ICBL 2004) that led to the creation of the Nobel Prize-winning Land Mines Treaty is a source of national pride and international admiration. But President Bush's challenge to Canada and other allies to join the War on Terrorism could spell the end of independent Canadian foreign and defence policies. The Bush administration is visibly less tolerant of criticism than was the previous administration, and it is more willing to exercise its influence over Canada to ensure that its views prevail in any debate.

THE BUSH DOCTRINE
AND THE NEXT PHASE OF GLOBALIZATION

It is possible that the DND was able to predict so accurately how the War on Terrorism would unfold because it knew first-hand the ideas that emanate from the hawk-dominated US Republican Party. The presidency of George H.W. Bush (1988–92) was marked by much triumphalism and boldness in the use of military power and by the use of such terms as "New World Order." Paul Wolfowitz's *Defense Planning Guidance*, which was leaked to the *New York Times*, exposed the plans of the Bush administration to move towards unilateralism and pre-emptive warfare (Tyler 1992). The defeat of George Bush Sr by the Clinton Democrats in 1992, however, effectively prevented these wide-eyed plans to promote US unilateralism and hegemony from becoming overt policy, although many components, such as a less restrained nuclear weapons policy and the development of missile defences, took shape during the Clinton years.

The George W. Bush administration's landmark 2002 National Security Strategy (United States 2002), with its focus on unilateralism and the unrestrained use of military power to project US interests, can thus be viewed as an extension of the post-Cold War strategic planning of the earlier Republican administration. What makes the so-called Bush Doctrine unique is its explicit fusion of military and economic objectives in order to achieve the national interest.

The day following the announcement of the Bush Doctrine, US Trade Representative Robert Zoellick announced a new orientation for his office (Davis 2002). Trade agreements would henceforth be used as leverage to achieve reforms in countries that want to deal with the United States. Zoellick argued that bilateral agreements between the United States and other countries, smaller regional agreements, and the lure of membership in the World Trade Organization (WTO) were more effective in achieving US-friendly reforms than were traditional means. The new strategy moved away from multilateral trade and financial bodies, such as the International Monetary Fund (IMF) and even the WTO, towards country-to-country bilateral agreements.

The new strategy places the US government as the central arbiter of the global economy, marginalizing the WTO, the IMF, and other multilateral bodies. The patience and restraint required in multilateral venues such as the WTO was seen as unable to deliver both the required economic rewards and punishments.

Trade unilateralism represented a major departure from the trade strategies of the Clinton administration. Indeed, the creation of the WTO was possible only because the United States was willing, in principle, to agree to abide by international trade rules forged through an international consensus (or, at least, a consensus among the United States, Europe, and Japan). The establishment of the WTO in 1995 was a great victory for international business interests that sought a global regime to impose a free-market discipline on member governments. Because the trade rules favoured the powerful countries, their governments were willing to cede, in principle, certain powers to the WTO.

Critics of globalization argued that the proliferation of free trade agreements signified the establishment of "corporate rule," where trade agreements heavily favoured the interests of business, and the WTO acted as a sort of governing body for transnational corporations. Governments were shirking their responsibilities and giving up too many of their powers to organizations that acted in the interests of only one group – transnational corporations. But the September 11 attacks and the subsequent political and economic shock waves pushed globalization into a new phase. In this vein, economist Walden Bello argues that the game plan for globalization has shifted significantly. "For the Bush people, strategic power is the ultimate modality of power. Economic power is a means to achieve strategic power. This is related to the fact that under Bush, the dominant faction of the ruling elite is the military-industrial establishment that won the Cold War" (Bello 2003, 3–4).

The Bush Doctrine does not pre-empt economic globalization but, rather, fuses it with US security and military objectives. "The Bush administration has supplanted the globalist political economy of the Clinton period with a unilateralist, nationalist political economy that intends to shore up the global dominance of the US corporate elite economically [in a way] that parallels the aggressive military policy ... meant to ensure the military supremacy of the United States" (Bello 2003, 3). The "global capitalist elites," as described by Bello, who had benefited from the global political economy of the Clinton years, are now being forced to accept the Bush Doctrine. "In the WTO, it's always been understood that security trumps trade," said Joseph G. Gavin, vice-president for trade policy with the powerful corporate lobby group the US Council for International Business (Edmonson 2003). For Bush, free trade can progress in so far as it furthers US national security interests or at least does not interfere with them.

In this new phase of globalization, all tools, including free trade agreements, are being used by the Bush administration to bring nations on board in the War on Terrorism. Since September 2001 new trade agreements have been made or promised to important wartime allies such as Indonesia, Jordan, Russia, China, Taiwan, Pakistan, India, Chile, Australia, and Singapore. For instance, in October 2003 President Bush stunned many Asian leaders when he used the annual Asia-Pacific Economic Co-operation (APEC) forum to urge nations to join the fight against terrorism, focusing upon issues that many nations felt did not belong at a forum for economic liberalization. Later, during his visit to Thailand, Bush told hundreds of Thai troops that they were fighting on the front lines in the war against terrorism and then rewarded his close ally by announcing that Washington would launch negotiations with Thailand on a comprehensive free trade agreement (WTD 2003).

Economic ties have been used to punish reluctant allies as well. A multibillion-dollar loan from the United States to Turkey was taken off the table when Turkey refused to join the invasion of Iraq and allow US troops to use Turkey as a staging base (BBC 2003). A long-time dispute between the

United States and New Zealand over the latter's refusal to allow visits by US nuclear-powered or armed warships has unofficially delayed a long-sought free trade agreement between the two countries (O'Sullivan 2003). The prospect of another closure of the Canada-US border like that which occurred on September 11 has sent Canada's corporate elite scrambling in fear that foreign policy divergences, such as Canada's refusal to endorse the invasion of Iraq, could bring economic retaliation. Having worked so hard to achieve the Canada-United States Free Trade Agreement (CUFTA), corporate Canada believes that Ottawa must sign on to Washington's war efforts in order to protect Canadian access to the US market.

CORPORATE CANADA RALLIES FOR A "BIG IDEA"

Clearly demonstrating the Bush administration's union of security and economic objectives, then US ambassador to Canada Paul Cellucci used a speech to the Economic Club of Toronto in March 2003 to express his country's displeasure with the Chrétien government's decision not to join the US-led invasion of Iraq. "There is a lot of disappointment in Washington and a lot of people are upset," said Ambassador Cellucci (Galloway 2003). The speech to the Canadian corporate elite kicked off a series of public engagements and media appearances that the ambassador used to lambaste the Chrétien government. The rumour was that Cellucci got his instructions for the very public display of displeasure directly from the White House, and even from the president personally. "Security will trump trade," Ambassador Cellucci warned, raising the spectre of increased frustrations at the border (ibid.). It was a carefully crafted message designed to agitate resistance to the Chrétien government and to energize pro-US elements within the Canadian body politic. Indeed, the ambassador openly appealed to the Canadian business class, the then Canadian Alliance and Progressive Conservative parties, conservative elements of the Liberal Party, and especially the military.

The US government's direct interference in Canadian domestic politics split the Chrétien Liberals. Some members could barely contain their anger with the prime minister's decision not to join the war, while others, including some cabinet members, wanted to send Cellucci packing back to Washington. But with public opinion polls showing a majority of Canadians, especially in Quebec, opposed to the war, the prime minister chose to side with the Canadian public over the country's corporate CEOs.

Concern over how Washington's new security measures would affect Canadian access to the US market remained a priority issue for Canadian business well after the attacks of 11 September 2001. Incorrect reports that the terrorist hijackers came from Canada stoked unsubstantiated fears in

the United States that the long, undefended border between the two countries was a prime security risk. The fact that the Canada-US border was
closed by US officials during the September crisis, causing a huge disruption
in cross-border trade, promoted a series of discussions between the two
governments over how to help facilitate trade in a more security-conscious
environment. Canadian business urged the government to satisfy US security concerns to avoid onerous and profit-dampening security measures at
the border.

Discussions between then foreign affairs minister John Manley and the
future director of the US Department of Homeland Security, Tom Ridge,
resulted in several government initiatives. Ottawa brought in new anti-terrorism legislation, increased security-related and military spending, formed
a new bilateral military preparedness planning committee, and negotiated
the 30-point Smart Border Action Plan, which introduced new computer
surveillance systems and harmonized immigration policies. The federal
budget of 2001 committed $7.7 billion dollars to multi-year military and
security-related programs (Canada 2001a).

Yet despite this slate of impressive and expensive measures, the corporate
lobby and its related think–tanks argued that the government was pursuing an incremental approach to Canada-US relations when what was
needed was a comprehensive approach. Some have called this the "big
idea," others the "grand bargain": On the first anniversary of the terrorist
attacks against the United States, Canada's former ambassador to the
United States, Allan Gotlieb, used the pages of the *National Post* to call for
a grand bargain with the United States. "The Canadian political agenda is
economic security; for Americans it is homeland security. Therein lay the
potential elements of a grand negotiation," Gotlieb (2003) wrote. A succession of reports, op-ed pieces, speeches, and conferences have emanated
from conservative think–tanks and foundations to argue for a comprehensive agreement with the United States in order to ensure Canada's economic
security (see in this volume Clarke, chapter 3, and Clarkson and Banda,
chapters 4 and 5). All of these proposals contain an admission, explicit or
implicit, that the gains achieved towards greater economic integration with
the United States by CUFTA in 1989 and the subsequent North American
Free Trade Agreement (NAFTA) in 1994 risked being undermined by US
security measures at the border.

Bill Dymond, a former Canadian trade negotiator and current director
of a free trade think–tank at Carleton University, argues that, "just as the
NAFTA and the WTO could not prevent the closure of the border in September 2001, so are they ... unable to move beyond trade rules and deal with
security, immigration and cooperation on geopolitical issues which [are]
becoming increasingly the touchstone of US foreign policy, including trade
policy" (Dymond 2003). And many others agree. "NAFTA has largely out-

lived its usefulness," wrote Wendy Dobson of the corporate-funded C.D. Howe Institute. "Canadian concerns about economic security must be linked with US domestic priorities to attract US notice. And homeland security is the single overriding US goal. What's needed is a strategic framework that links security and defence with economic goals" (Dobson 2003).

BUILDING FORTRESS NORTH AMERICA

This new, comprehensive approach to transforming the Canada-US relationship is fundamentally different from the strictly economic arrangements that defined CUFTA and NAFTA. This next phase of deeper integration reaches beyond the economic sphere into the security and military realms. Deeper integration proposals envision a defence perimeter that surrounds North America, with Canada firmly ensconced within the new "Fortress North America."[2] While having Canada within the US homeland security perimeter will hopefully do away with the Canada-US border as far as the US security apparatus is concerned, building Fortress North America will necessitate the harmonization of Canada's defence and security policies with those of the United States. As Dobson points out, the new comprehensive relationship between Canada and the United States will link economic goals to security and defence goals. This will require falling into line behind the Pentagon and the newly formed US Department of Homeland Security to ensure that Canada's security policies in no way deviate from US priorities.

The Bush administration has made it clear that there can be no ambivalence towards the US-led War on Terrorism. It's all or nothing; you're either with us or you're against us. Standing aside or tending one's own backyard is not sufficient. The US government clearly expects its allies to participate actively and to contribute to the global war. Acceding to US security concerns therefore requires much more than defending North America territorially: it requires the acceptance of the Bush Doctrine of pre-emptive war, unilateralism, the globalization of free markets, and the militarization of foreign and economic policies. These policies, however, directly contradict many Canadian values and institutions. The Bush Doctrine is anathema to Canadians who cherish multilateralism, who see the United Nations as a great force for peace, and who think Canadian military forces should be mostly concerned with UN peacekeeping, not pre-emptive warfare.

So what is driving this radical new agenda? The answer is simple: the same corporate forces and institutions that managed the integration of the Canada-US economy through CUFTA, and then the restructuring of the role of government with the debt- and deficit-inspired budget cuts of the mid-1990s, have returned to push the next phase of integration. For example, the *Globe and Mail* used its editorial on New Year's Day 2004 to advise the newly anointed prime minister, Paul Martin, to challenge peace-seeking Canadian values. Its editors urged Martin to use the same persuasive tactics that he used in the 1990s to convince Canadians to fight the federal budget deficit to advocate military spending: "Does Mr. Martin have the strength of conviction to slash budgets in less essential government departments while dramatically boosting military spending, even though polls show that Canadians have a limited appetite for defence spending? Or can he lead Canadians to appreciate new priorities, as he once helped mould a public aversion to budget deficits?" (*Globe and Mail* 2004). The Stephen Harper-led Conservative government that took power in February 2006 did not require advice from the *Globe and Mail* to embrace the Bush view of the world. Gordon O'Connor, the new defence minister, said terrorists threaten the "security and prosperity" of Canadians (Campion-Smith 2006). Arguing in favour of Canada's counter-insurgency role in Afghanistan, he asked: "Must we wait for terrorists to appear in Vancouver, Montreal or here in Ottawa before we recognize the very real threat that they represent to our security?" (ibid).

THE STRATEGIC ALLIANCE
BETWEEN THE CORPORATE AND DEFENCE LOBBIES

The focus of Canadian business on security and military matters has resulted in a new strategic alliance between the corporate and defence lobbies. The corporate lobby's support for dramatic increases in military spending and greater government attention to defence issues gives a boost to the defence lobby's long-standing demand for more military spending. The defence lobby comprises many defence associations, retired military officers, university-based military and strategic studies programs, foreign policy institutes, defence industry associations, and hawkish parliamentarians whose ridings often include large military bases or industries that support the military. Many of the organizations whose spokespersons comment on defence issues in the Canadian media receive funding from the Department of National Defence or depend upon military contracts. Since members of the Canadian Armed Forces are not allowed to comment publicly on public policy, the military brass depends upon these associations to "educate" the public about the department's viewpoint.

The Conference of Defence Associations is one such organization. Headed by retired military officers, it receives funding from the Department of National Defence and bills itself as "the voice of Defence since 1932" (CDA 2004). This organization uses lobbying and media appearances to advocate increases to Canada's military spending. Another influential body is the $2-million DND-funded Security and Defence Forum that supports strategic studies and related institutes in a dozen universities across Canada (Canada 2002b). The DND fund is intended to promote informed public discussion about security matters; instead, it pays for a steady stream of hawkish opinions in the national media.

Defence industry organizations play a similarly influential, though less public, role. The Canadian Defence Industry Association and the more powerful Aerospace Industries Association of Canada draw on the deep political connections and resources of corporate heavyweights such as Bombardier, General Motors Canada, General Dynamics Canada, CAE, Bell Helicopter Textron, Pratt and Whitney Canada, and SNC-Lavalin. These industry organizations have been lobbying for closer Canada-US military ties to better secure their access to lucrative missile defence, fighter aircraft, and Iraqi reconstruction contracts. Ron Kane of the Aerospace Industries Association of Canada has lobbied the government on behalf of corporations seeking missile defence contracts. "If we don't commit over the next couple of months [to the missile defence initiative], we'll be shut out [of contracts]," Kane told the *Globe and Mail* following a personal conversation with then US Ambassador Paul Cellucci (Tuck 2003).

The corporate and defence lobbies in both countries came together in September 2002, under the auspices of the Center for the Study of the Presidency in Washington, for a seminar that resulted in an influential report entitled *The US-Canada Strategic Partnership in the War on Terror* (CSP 2002). The report advocated increased Canadian military spending and an expansion of NORAD's current air-defence function to include sea and land forces as well. Seminar participants included high-level Canadian military and political advisors, academics, and members of the corporate and military lobbies. Notably present were representatives from Canada's Department of National Defence, the Department of Foreign Affairs, the Privy Council Office, the Conference of Defence Associations, and the Canadian Council of Chief Executives.

Traditionally, the corporate and defence lobbies have worked in separate policy circles. The defence lobby has traditionally commanded much less influence, focusing almost exclusively on increasing levels of military spending. By contrast, the corporate lobby, through its broad and influential membership, can deliver significant corporate donations and influence in exchange for policies that favour deregulation, privatization, and free trade. The new security paradigm in the United States, however, has interwoven economic and military interests. As Canada's then top soldier, Chief of Defence Staff (CDS) General Ray Henault, explained to Parliament in the CDS's 2004 annual report, Canada-US economic and military integration go hand in hand:

Both countries' economies rely on our free trade relationship. And, while neither country wants to restrict trade, security considerations are increasingly driving

concern for American decision-makers following September 11th. In this environment, it is in Canada's national interest to work collaboratively with the US to
strengthen continental security. (CDS 2004, 26)

The Stephen Harper government elected in 2006 embodies the coming
together of these two lobbies, and Gordon O'Connor, the defence minister,
personifies one of them. He was, until 2004, a lobbyist for the defence
industry, representing, among others, BAE Systems, United Defense,
General Dynamics, Atlas Elektronic GmbH, Raytheon Canada, and Airbus
Military (Gray 2006). Today, closer relations with the United States
through greater military cooperation on homeland security and the War on
Terrorism satisfy both lobbies' objectives, and increased military spending
and endorsement (even behind doors) of programs such as national missile
defence are seen as essential to preserving the economic integration
achieved through NAFTA. Ironically, greater military integration is needed
not to defend Canada but to defend NAFTA.[3]

BACKGROUND TO CANADA-US
CONTINENTAL MILITARY COOPERATION

Cooperation between Canadian and US military forces is not new. There
exist any number of agreements governing such cooperation, including
more than eighty treaty-level defence agreements, more than 250 memoranda of understanding, and approximately 145 bilateral forums covering
defence matters. In fact, Canada-US cooperation is a fundamental principle
of Canadian defence policy. For example, the three main objectives outlined in the 1994 *White Paper on Defence* are: the protection of Canada,
Canada-United States defence cooperation, and contributing to international security (Canada 1994).

The 1994 White Paper charges the Canadian Forces with the territorial
defence and maintenance of Canadian sovereignty. However, even the most
cautious military planners do not envision a territorial attack against
Canada; instead, the role of Canadian Forces is to provide aid to civil
authorities in times of natural disasters or terrorist attacks, conduct coastal
patrols, and monitor for illegal activities such as smuggling and overfish-
ing. The White Paper directs Canadian Forces to "maintain the ability to
operate effectively at sea, on land, and in the air with the military forces of
the United States in defending the northern half of the western hemisphere"
(Canada 1994). This requirement provides the policy underpinning of joint
military cooperation and integration.

Formal country-to-country joint military planning was established in
1940, following the Ogdensburg Declaration between Prime Minister
William Lyon Mackenzie King and President Franklin Delano Roosevelt,

with the creation of the Canada-United States Permanent Joint Board of Defence. This board is the highest-level bilateral defence forum and comprises senior military and diplomatic staff. Its theme for the October 2001 meeting in Ottawa was continental defence, and in 2002 the board met in Washington, DC, to discuss "transformation." The latter term describes the new military doctrine, force structures, and military technologies adopted by the Pentagon to wage the War on Terrorism.[4]

In the years following 1940 other binational military bodies were established to address more specific joint planning functions. In 1946 the Canada-US Military Cooperation Committee was formed to manage cooperation at the military planning level, including such tasks as mapping, oceanography, and communications. Recently, this body has been entrusted with the task of developing joint space endeavours, and it could assume functions required for national missile defence. The committee doubles as the Canada-US Regional Planning Group reporting to NATO.

During the 1950s the Cold War was at its height, with the United States and the USSR engaged in a nuclear arms race. As intercontinental ballistic missiles had yet to be invented, to reach targets inside the United States Soviet nuclear bombers would have had to fly over the polar ice cap and, hence, over Canada. To counter the threat from Soviet bombers, the North American Aerospace Defence Command (NORAD) was created in 1957. It was, and remains, the most significant binational military agreement governing Canada-US military relations. NORAD established lines of radar stations high in the Canadian north and along the coasts to watch for surprise attacks by Soviet bombers. Its headquarters was built deep inside Cheyenne Mountain in Colorado; a smaller centre was established in North Bay, Ontario, to feed information from Canadian radar stations to Colorado. The NORAD command structure was significantly different from previous binational defence bodies because it placed Canadian military forces under US command for the first time. The NORAD commander has always been a US general, with a Canadian counterpart assigned as his second-in-command. Canadian jet fighters and Bomarc air defence missiles, armed with nuclear weapons provided by the United States, could therefore be launched under US authority.

But as is the case with many military technologies and systems, NORAD's air defence role was already growing obsolete by the time it was created. Just as NORAD was getting under way, the Soviet threat began to shift from manned bombers towards intercontinental ballistic missiles (ICBMs) launched from Soviet territory or from submarines. US radar (based on US territory, in Greenland, and in the United Kingdom) and satellite systems capable of watching for missile launches slowly replaced the role of Canadian-based ground radar. Despite its declining importance in defending North America, Canada continued to dedicate fighters to NORAD and even accepted US nuclear weapons as part of NORAD's air defence role. Dozens of nuclear-armed Bomarc missiles were deployed in North Bay, Ontario, and La Macaza, Quebec, and nuclear-armed Genie missiles for launch by Canadian fighter aircraft were deployed across Canada at air-defence bases devoted to NORAD. By the 1980s US nuclear weapons were returned to the United States, but NORAD continued to play cat-and-mouse games with Soviet bombers in the High Arctic, scrambling fighters to meet the Soviets in the air and forcing them to turn back to Soviet-controlled airspace.

While its actual defensive purpose waned, NORAD became a focal point for Canada-US military cooperation. It represented a prized relationship for Canadian military leaders, who enjoyed the special role Canada had with its much more powerful ally – a relationship like no other in NATO. With the end of the Cold War in 1990 and the decline of the nuclear threat, NORAD's purpose was put in doubt. That uncertainty continued until one sunny day in September 2001, when NORAD was handed a new lease on life. Immediately following the attacks on the World Trade Center, NORAD dispatched jet fighters, though belatedly, to protect US cities and coordinated surveillance with domestic air traffic control authorities. In the period following September 11 and the restructuring of all US government agencies responsible for the defence of North America, NORAD was given enhanced capability to look inward and not just outward to its approaches. For instance, NORAD now works with domestic air traffic control agencies to monitor commercial air traffic in North American airspace.

While the public debate raged over Canada's participation in national missile defence, in August 2004 the Canadian government quietly agreed to amend the NORAD agreement. The change allowed NORAD to provide missile warning information to US commands responsible for missile defence. This change leaves a back door open for further Canadian involvement not only in missile defence but also the weaponization of space.

In May 2006 the two governments signed a renewal of the NORAD agreement. This new agreement makes two significant changes: Maritime warning for North America is added to NORAD's missions, and the agreement is no longer renewed every five years but, rather, can be amended at any time (assuming both governments wish to do so). With this change the governments want NORAD to warn of possible threats from ships along coastlines, in the Arctic, or on internal waters such as the Great Lakes. National commands, such as the new Canada Command, retain control of sovereign waters and can then decide to intercept and board suspicious ships.

Although it may sound reasonable to add maritime warning to NORAD, there are a number of unresolved issues. Most important, adding maritime responsibilities does nothing to resolve, and, indeed, can only complicate, sovereignty and territorial disputes between Canada and the United States, especially in the Arctic, where the latter considers the thawing Northwest Passage to be international, not Canadian, waters. Second, this NORAD deal ignores another major security and sovereignty concern for Canada: nuclear submarines. Why should NORAD's maritime role stop at the water's surface? Why not continue underwater? Third, the August 2004 amendment that allows NORAD to have a role in missile defence remains in place in the renewed agreement.

In a context of deepening military and security integration, the indefinite extension of NORAD without public consultation on current and proposed changes in North American security is of grave concern. Ernie Regehr (2006, 1) from Project Ploughshares argues that the government should have renewed the agreement only for two years and committed to carry out "a thoroughgoing and public review of continental security" that would have provided "opportunity to reassess changing security needs in light of two important recent developments: changes to Canada's national command structure, in which Canada Command (CANCOM) is to coordinate all Canadian defence roles and missions; and the report of the Bi-National Planning Group (BPG), which proposes major changes in Canada-US security arrangements."

NEW COMMANDS
AND THE BI-NATIONAL PLANNING GROUP

Before the September 11 attacks, the US military did not have a single unified command for North America. The attacks, however, shocked the US government into reorganizing its military to focus on the defence of its territory. On 1 October 2002 the United States created a new area of responsibility: NORTHCOM (Northern Command), for the first time putting the continental United States under a joint command. Northern Command is the military equivalent of the civilian Department of Homeland Security. It has a staff of about 500 but no standing military forces; instead, it coordinates the military activities of the army, navy, air force, and marines to defend the territorial United States and to provide assistance to civilian agencies. While Northern Command is a US-only military command, its four-star general is also the commander of NORAD. In effect, the general and his staff are "dual hatted," responsible for both NORTHCOM and NORAD. Both commands are headquartered at Peterson Air Force Base in Colorado, near Cheyenne Mountain (which acts as the nerve centre for NORAD's satellites and radar).

The close connection between the US-only NORTHCOM and the Canada-US NORAD is not an uncommon arrangement. In fact, since its creation NORAD has been twinned with US-only commands in various forms. Such was the case with NORAD and the US Space Command, which was later combined with the US nuclear forces command, known as the Strategic Command. But the creation of a US military command responsible for continental defence from air, sea, and land threats nevertheless put pressure on Canada to expand its military cooperation with the United States. Since NORAD was intended only for air threats, this clearly left the door open for US pressure to create an expanded agreement with Canada for integrated defence against land and sea attacks. Indeed, then US ambassador Cellucci made Washington's intent clear on the day following the announcement of the creation of NORTHCOM and the expression of Canadian concern: "This has got nothing to do with sovereignty. This has everything to do with ... security and protecting our people" (Granatstein 2002, 11).

Consequently, in December 2002 the Canadian government instructed the military to enter into talks with its US counterparts to discuss the means by which Canadian military forces could more closely "cooperate" with Northern Command, thus satisfying NORTHCOM's requirement to incorporate Canada into its area of responsibility. A Bi-National Planning Group (BPG) was subsequently established within NORAD. According to the arrangement, each country was to be represented by twenty-five members, and Canada's delegation was to be led by the highest-ranking Canadian in NORAD. The group was given a two-year mandate (later on extended to 2006) to review existing Canada-US cooperation agreements and to draft plans detailing how each country's military could assist the other in times of domestic emergencies, such as a terrorist attack near the Canada-US border.

The prospect of an agreement that would allow US troops to cross the border into Canada raised concerns about Canadian sovereignty (Thompson 2002). Canadian officials were quick to argue that Canadian or US troops would only cross the border if "invited" and that foreign troops would be put under the command of the host nation's military leadership. Critics pointed out, however, that the United States rarely allows its military personnel to be put under foreign command and that Congress had recently almost passed a law outlawing the practice altogether.

Despite sovereignty concerns, the BPG laboured away at NORAD headquarters in Colorado. Both nations' militaries and related civilian agencies were involved in the discussions, including the Department of Homeland Security and Canada's equivalent, the Department of Public Safety and Emergency Preparedness. One of the results of this process was the decision to create a new arrangement mirroring the US Northern Command: Canada Command. In fact, when the planning group was created it was suggested that the BPG was a means for Canada to avoid being put under NORTHCOM without our consent. It is no surprise, therefore, that the talks led to the creation of a new command with NORTHCOM's responsibilities but without requiring Canada to join Northern Command outright.

The establishment of Canada Command (CANCOM) was made public in June 2005. It was announced as a unified and integrated chain of command at the national and regional levels with the immediate authority to deploy maritime, land, and air assets in support of domestic operations (CBC 2005). The goal was to respond more quickly to domestic disasters and terrorist threats, and to improve coordination between the military and Canada's security and border control agencies. In particular, it "will be responsible for the conduct of all domestic operations – routine and contingency – and will be the national operational authority for the defence of Canada and North America" (Canada 2005a). The headquarters was to be in the Ottawa region, and six regional headquarters were planned across the country. It became operational in February 2006.

The creation of a CANCOM independent of a joint Canada-US continental command may be merely a temporary compromise, responding to sovereignty concerns in Canada. This is clear from the Bi-National Planning Group's final report, released in May 2006 (BPG 2006). Michael Byers (2006), from the University of British Columbia, argues that, although the professed goal of the report is to improve cooperation between the Canadian and US militaries, the real intent is "nothing less than the complete integration of Canada's military, security and foreign policy into the decision-making and operating systems of the US." It is worthwhile quoting him at length:[5]

The BPG recommendations are far-reaching. They aim at "enhanced co-ordination and co-operation among our foreign policy, defence and security organizations" [i] at "the level (although not necessarily the form) of co-operation that now exists in NORAD." [i] In NORAD, the defence of Canadian and US airspace is assigned to a single command which, while supposedly based on the equality of the two countries, is always headed by a senior US officer. The BPG is, in actuality, advocating co-operation at the level of a single, US-dominated command for all of Canada's territory and our surrounding seas. Under this plan, the entire Canadian Forces, unless deployed overseas in operations not led by the US, could find themselves under American "operational control" with Americans making all key day-to-day decisions ...

The BPG also recommends closer co-operation in security and foreign policy: "Canada and the US must continue to act as partners; indeed ... the partnership must be expanded, to shape the future of North American defence and security, using all of the instruments of diplomatic, economic, informational and military power." [7]

... [The BPG] calls the [May 2006] NORAD agreement renewal "an important step toward enhancing the defence and security of our continent. To continue this momentum a 'Comprehensive Defence and Security Agreement' is the logical next step ..." [42] The BPG presents four alternatives for the new agreement [having to

do with the roles of and relationships among NORAD, US, NORTHCOM, and CANCOM]
... The fourth, most ambitious alternative involves "a truly integrated approach to
continental defence and security through a deliberate melding of defence and security functions." [40] This would be achieved by "establishing a single organization
responsible for all-domain, bi-national warning and execution in the realms of
defence and security." [40]

This fourth alternative – full integration – is presented as the ultimate goal of
improved co-operation. The BPG report thus reveals that expanding NORAD to
include maritime surveillance sharing [as mentioned in an earlier section] is
intended to create momentum toward complete military, security and foreign policy
integration. (Byers 2006).

NATIONAL MISSILE DEFENCE

The debate in Canada over missile defence in many ways epitomizes the
debate over greater Canada-US military and security integration. Since
negotiations for Canada's participation in the US missile defence system
were initiated in June 2003, the debate has revolved around our obligations
to defend North America versus our traditional international role as an
independent peacekeeper and advocate for disarmament.

Even before the attacks of 11 September 2001, during the presidential
election campaign of 2000, George W. Bush made the deployment of a
weapons system capable of shooting down missiles launched by "rogue
nations" against the United States a key commitment for his first term in
office. In fact, missile defence and the invasion of Iraq so dominated the
administration's agenda that a former White House insider criticized the
administration for allowing these issues to blind it to the more real threat
posed by Al-Qaeda (Clarke 2004).

In 2004 a crude system of radar stations and satellite tracking systems
linked to interceptor missiles in Alaska and California was set up. But some
experts have described the system as being more of a scarecrow than a real
mechanism for defence. Report after report from independent scientists,
retired generals, and even the US General Accounting Office, have pointed
out that the technology is not ready despite the system's more than $50
billion price tag and that missile defence will consume more than $10 billion
per year until the end of the decade, with no performance guarantees. Some
estimates are the amount could double by 2013 to about $19 billion per
year (Coyle 2006, 2).

In Canada the issue of missile defence became deeply divisive. Within the
Liberal Party there were strong opponents to missile defence, though some
of the more vocal opponents were neutralized when Paul Martin took over
the party leadership in late 2003. Even so, more than thirty Liberal MPs
sided with the NDP and the Bloc Québécois to vote in favour of an anti-

missile defence motion sponsored by the Bloc in that year. In addition, former Liberal foreign affairs minister Lloyd Axworthy became one of the most vocal opponents of Canada's joining the missile defence plan. Outside Parliament, a broad spectrum of civil society organizations and cultural figures joined the call for Canada to stay out of missile defence, and letters to the government demanding the same were signed by Canadian church leaders, scientists, labour and citizen-group leaders, and some of Canada's best known international figures (CCOMD 2004).

The missile defence issue strikes a chord with Canadians because it typifies the very different approaches to security taken by Canada and the United States. The Bush administration – and much of the Democratic Party – has endorsed missile defence as a key requirement for US national security, despite the system's risks, inherent fallibility, and tremendous cost. Canadians, on the other hand, worry that missile defence, perhaps even more than the question of Canada's participation in the Iraq war, will have long-lasting implications that will undermine Canada's international reputation as a peacekeeper and neutral arbiter while tying us and our military more tightly to an increasingly belligerent and unilateralist US national security establishment.

Concerns about the military integration issue and Canada's involvement in missile defence are well founded. For the departments of foreign affairs and national defence, Canada's participation in missile defence had little to do with protecting Canada from missile attack and a great deal to do with protecting the crown jewel of Canada-US military integration: NORAD. James Wright (2004), then assistant deputy minister for global and security policy in the foreign affairs department, warned a Senate committee in February 2004 that "we need to ask ourselves what the consequences would be for NORAD if, by not participating in [the program], we pushed the US to develop its own, US-only missile warning system." In fact, the Canadian security establishment was worried that keeping Canada out of missile defence will impede the process of making the Canadian Forces more deeply interoperable and integrated with US forces. In short, missile defence was seen as the lynchpin for future interoperability.

The defence lobby's concern originated when the United States had not yet decided which command system should house the missile defence system. That is why including NORAD in missile defence became central to Canada's negotiation strategy – because it would effectively prevent the missile shield from becoming a US-only system. Missile defence proponents worried that if the United States decided to keep their missile defence system exclusively under US command, Canada's role in NORAD would be limited to air defence against hijacked airliners and the unlikely threat of bombers attacking North America. All missile attack detection and space monitoring roles would be assigned to the US command responsible for launching the interceptor missiles from their bases in Alaska or California or from US warships.

Facing stiff opposition from the electorate and from within his own party, on 24 February 2005 Prime Minister Martin announced that Canada would not join the US missile defence program. The decision essentially meant that the system did not receive Canada's political endorsement. But, as mentioned earlier, the fact that the Canadian government agreed in August 2004 to allow missile warning and tracking data from NORAD to be used by US Northern Command, the military command responsible for operating the missile defence system, left a back door open for indirect Canadian participation in the system.

Negative reaction from the defence and corporate lobby was swift. The *National Post* published a poll on its front page claiming that 85 percent of CEOs felt that the government's missile shield decision would be bad for Canadian business (Tait 2005). The Canadian Chamber of Commerce vowed to work to reverse the decision, and Conservative Party leader Stephen Harper pledged to go back to the negotiating table if the Conservatives were to form the next government.

Paul Martin's missile defence decision ended a chapter of the Canadian missile defence issue but by no means closed the book on it. In fact, prior to the 2006 federal election Stephen Harper indicated he wanted to revisit the issue. With the United States continuing to deploy the system in stages over the next few decades, Canadian participation will remain a goal of the defence lobby and those seeking closer ties to the United States. In May 2006 NATO opened a new front in this debate when it announced that it was considering a missile defence shield to protect continental Europe from long-range missile threats (Blanchfield 2006). Canada, as a member of the twenty-six-nation alliance, fully endorsed the decision. Clearly, Canadians who oppose these initiatives will need to remain vigilant.

CONFRONTING THE MILITARY-CORPORATE LOBBY

In a 2002 background paper on Canada-US relations, the Department of National Defence (DND) argued that Canada will continue to modify its defence relationship with the United States consistent with the "priorities of the new era," presumably a reference to the post-September 11 context and the Bush Doctrine. According to the DND, Canada-US cooperation continues to serve our fundamental interests, and Canadian forces must work closely with the US armed forces and remain interoperable. If Canada were to significantly reduce the level of defence cooperation, it would be forced to rely on the United States to help protect Canadian territory and approaches, with such assistance being provided strictly on US terms (Canada 2002a).

These principles were fleshed out in the 2005 *International Policy Statement* on defence (Canada 2005b), which "presents a vital new vision for the Canadian Forces that is firmly grounded in the realities of the post-Cold War, post-September 11th world" (Canada 2005c). The new policy statement "sets out a plan to make Canadian security the first priority for the Canadian Forces" so as "to more effectively and quickly respond to domestic crises" … and "we will seek to develop new, innovative approaches to defence co-operation with the United States to better meet the threats to both countries" (ibid.). In terms of their international role, the Canadian forces will contribute both to "global security" and to "peace building" (ibid.).

Although nominally committed to peace building, facts confirm where the real priorities lie. Canada has spent $4.146 billion on military operations in, or on issues related to, Afghanistan since 9/11 (Robinson 2006, 1). Afghanistan and related operations accounted for 68 percent of the $6.132 billion spent on international missions between the fall of 2001 and the end of March 2006. During the same time period, Canada devoted only $214.2 million, or 3 per cent of spending on international military operations, to United Nations operations. By 31 March 2006, Canada contributed only fifty-nine military personnel to UN missions around the world, while approximately 2,300 troops were stationed in Afghanistan. Once a top-ten contributor, Canada ranked fiftieth out of ninety-five countries contributing military personnel to UN missions (Robinson 2006, 1). As W. Andy Knight (2006), from the University of Alberta, concludes, "Canadians will realize that we are no longer a peacekeeping nation."

Achieving "interoperability" with the US military has been a central objective for Canada's war planners for many years. For them, success is measured by the ability of Canada's military to operate seamlessly with US forces by using similar equipment and strategies and acting under US command. The navy boasts of its ability to have its ships integrate easily into US naval battle groups. In 2001 the HMCS *Vancouver*, one of Canada's frigates, joined the armada of ships and submarines led by the aircraft carrier USS *John C. Stennis*, which launched more than 10,000 bombing runs against Afghanistan.

Achieving interoperability with US forces is an expensive objective. The main driver of extremely high levels of military spending is the perceived need to make our forces more interoperable with US forces, to assist in the US-led War on Terrorism. The 2005 Liberal budget announced major increases in defence spending, and Stephen Harper ran his 2006 federal election campaign on a commitment to increase them even further – a commitment he has kept.

By Fall 2005, Canada's level of military spending was already very high by NATO standards. In real dollars, Canada was the seventh highest within the twenty-six-member NATO alliance, and the fifteenth highest globally (Staples 2006, 2). In the coming few years, the 2005 and 2006 federal budgets have set Canada's military spending to rise at a precipitous rate. Spending in 2005–06, which is about $15 billion, is already just 5 percent below spending at the end of the Cold War. Within two years, we will exceed what we were spending then, having clawed back the entire post–Cold War peace dividend. With the increases announced in the Liberals' 2005 budget of $12.8 billion over five years, combined with the additional topping up $5.3 billion provided by the Conservatives in the 2006 budget, Canada's military spending will reach $21.5 billion by 2010–11. This is an increase of 43.3 percent over 2006 spending (Staples 2006, 2). This will put Canadian military spending at a higher level than any amount of spending in adjusted dollars since the Second World War.

As though this were not enough, Defence Minister Gordon O'Connor announced in June 2006, just prior to Stephen Harper's planned visit to the White House, a massive shopping spree over the next few years for new military hardware. The spending, valued at $17 billion, will include "new trucks, aircraft, ships and helicopters [and] will extend the reach of Canada's military around the globe" (Campion-Smith 2006). O'Connor dismissed suggestions he has major conflicts of interest on a number of spending announcements – conflicts stemming from his days as a lobbyist for the defence industry (CTV 2006).

Of even greater importance than the budgetary implications will be the impact of further security integration on Canada's ability to set an independent foreign policy that reflects the fundamental values of its citizens. The government's decision to not endorse the 2003 invasion of Iraq, for example, was the result of a groundswell of public opposition measured in poll after poll and demonstrated by the hundreds of thousands of people who filled the streets to show their opposition to the war. It was arguably the single greatest Canadian policy victory for "people power" in decades. The Canadian Forces' de facto support for the US-led war, however, provided evidence of just how military integration with the United States could undermine Canada's ability to pursue an independent foreign policy.

For instance, confusion arose about the role of Canada's ships and planes in the Persian Gulf region. While Canada had not officially joined the war, our patrol aircraft were feeding surveillance data to the US regional military command responsible for the Iraq war and our ships were escorting US warships and supply ships all the way to Kuwait. It was further revealed that dozens of military exchange personnel were operating alongside US and British troops in Iraq. Moreover, during the invasion, then Ambassador Cellucci remarked that Canadian forces were making a greater contribution to the war than most of the forty-five countries of the "coalition of the willing." Spain, an ardent supporter of the war, had committed only a medical ship and no combat troops whatsoever; Denmark sent a single submarine.

Yet in spite of this contribution, the truth remains that Canadian forces made little military difference to the massive US war machine; rather, what interested the Bush administration was political support from Canada to provide legitimacy to its war – support that Jean Chrétien denied them. But the contradiction between our publicly anti-war foreign policy and the supportive role our military played in the war against Iraq left many Canadians rightly asking why the Canadian military, the very institution charged with ensuring our sovereignty, had become one of the greatest obstacles to its exercise.

Paul Martin, and, with more decisiveness, Stephen Harper set out to repair the damage done by Jean Chrétien's decision on the Iraq invasion and Martin's reluctant decision to not join Bush's missile defence initiative. The decisive turn towards greater defence and security integration with the United States presaged in the March 2006 final report of the Bi-National Planning Group (BPG 2006) is clearly part of the "repair." For one observer, this is part of a "trend that includes Canada's involvement in the US-led counterinsurgency in southern Afghanistan, the instantaneous sharing of NORAD aerospace surveillance for US missile defence, and the Harper government's support for Bush administration foreign policies on climate change, nuclear proliferation, and the Middle East" (Byers 2006).

A REINVIGORATED MOVEMENT IS NEEDED

The corporate and defence lobbies have successfully seized the political agenda, and the so-called security and prosperity agenda is working its way into government policy. The fact that this subtle but important shift has occurred without any public debate, or even acknowledgment, is alarming. Citizen organizations and progressive research institutes need to assume responsibility for increasing public awareness of the push for greater economic and military integration with the United States and the implications of such integration for Canada.

Much of the integration agenda has been discussed behind closed doors without public debate, and for good reason: most Canadians are at least sceptical and many are outright opposed to many aspects of the proposed Fortress North America. While this widely held sentiment is unorganized and absent in the mainstream media, a reinvigorated citizens' movement created to confront the corporate and defence lobbies could expose and ultimately push back the agenda. The following is a list of potential strategies that could be employed to contest the next phase of corporate-driven integration:

- Build on Canadian values of international activism to achieve an independent progressive Canadian foreign policy.
- Use Canadians' preference for a peacekeeping, non-combat military force to promote a defence policy and budget focused on territorial surveillance and peacekeeping missions under UN auspices.
- Redefine the concept of security from simply military and police matters to a broader human concept encompassing environmental safety, social security, and international development.
- Counter the economic costs argument of pro-integration groups by demonstrating the social, political, and economic benefits of pursuing independent foreign and economic policies.
- Promote multilateralism as the foundation of Canada's foreign policy, in contrast to the Bush Doctrine's preference for unilateralism.

The assertion of Canadian sovereignty means reaffirming the ability of its citizens to exercise their democratic rights. As Canadians we must demand that our foreign and defence policies be open to public participation. We must ensure that the government is not easily captured by the corporate and defence lobbies but, rather, is guided by traditional Canadian values as expressed through an open and democratic process.

NOTES

1 The term "War on Terrorism" is used to describe the Bush administration's response to the attacks of 11 September 2001. It includes the invasions of Afghanistan and Iraq, the adoption of increased homeland security measures, and a doctrine of pre-emptive warfare as described in the US National Security Strategy (United States 2002). It is worth pointing out that the War on Terrorism has thus far had little to do with combating terrorism and much to do with advancing US geo-strategic interests, particularly in the Middle East, and imposing a repressive and right-wing domestic agenda.
2 Canadian proposals have wavered on whether Mexico should be included in the North American security perimeter (see Clarkson and Banda, chapter 5, this volume).
3 A major official Canada-US report confirms this: "The increasing integration of the Canadian and United States (as well as the Mexican) economies stands as a model of mutually beneficial trade ... To preserve that economic freedom, our defense and security initiatives should be planned and coordinated continentally" (BPG 2006, 4).
4 The Pentagon defines it this way: "Transformation is meant to create new competitive areas and new competencies. It is meant to identify, leverage and even create new underlying principles for the way things are done. Transformation

is meant to identify and leverage new sources of power. The overall objective of these changes is simply – sustained American competitive advantage in warfare" (DOD 2006).

5 The quotes in Michael Byer's text are all from BPG (2006). Page numbers have been indicated in squared brackets.

REFERENCES

BBC. 2003. Turkey Gets IMF Extension. BBC *News Online*. 3 August. Available at <http://news.bbc.co.uk/2/hi/business/3118351.stm>.

Bello, Walden. 2003. *The Stalemate in the WTO and the Crisis of the Globalist Project: Update on the World Trade Organization and Global Trends*. Bangkok: Focus on the Global South.

Blanchfield, Mike. 2006. Missile Defence Returns: Canada Part of NATO Study of European Shield. *National Post*. 12 May, A1.

BPG. 2006. *The Final Report on Canada and the United States (CANUS) Enhanced Military Cooperation*. Peterson Air Force Base, Colorado: Bi-National Planning Group.

Bush, George W. 2001. *Address to a Joint Session of Congress and the American People*. Washington: White House.

Byers, Michael. 2006. Continental Integration by Stealth. *Toronto Star*, 28 April, A17.

Campion-Smith, Bruce. Commitment Is "long term," PM says: MPs Debate Deployment of Canadians. *Toronto Star*, 11 April, A11.

Canada. 1994. *White Paper on Defence*. Ottawa: Department of National Defence. Available at <http://www.forces.gc.ca/admpol/eng/doc/white_e.htm>.

– 2001a. *Budget 2001*. Ottawa: Department of Finance.

– 2001b. *Strategic Assessment 2001*. Ottawa: Department of National Defence.

– 2002a. *Canada-United States Security Relations*. Ottawa: Department of National Defence.

– 2002b. *Security and Defence Forum: Annual Report 2002–2003*. Ottawa: Department of Defence.

– 2005a. *Backgrounder: Canada Command*. Ottawa: Department of National Defence.

– 2005b. *Canada's International Policy Statement: A Role of Pride and Influence in the World – Defence*. Ottawa: Department of National Defence.

– 2005c. *Defence Policy Statement*. Ottawa: Department of National Defence. Available at <http://www.forces.gc.ca/site/Reports/dps/index_e.asp>.

CBC. 2005. Indepth: Canada's Military – Canadian Forces in the 21st Century. CBC *News Online*, July 26. Available at <http://www.cbc.ca/news/background/cdn-military/>.

CCOMD. 2004. *Canada's Stars Urge Paul Martin to "Keep Canada out of Star Wars."* Ottawa: Canadian Campaign to Oppose Missile Defence.

CDA. 2004. *About* CDA. Conference of Defence Associations. Available at <http://www.cda-cdai.ca/english-frame.htm>, cited 17 January 2005.

CDS. 2004. *Annual Report 2002–2003 Highlights: A Time for Transformation.* Ottawa: Chief of the Defence Staff, Department of National Defence.

Clarke, Richard. 2004. *Against All Enemies: Inside America's War on Terror.* New York: Free Press.

Coyle, Philip E. 2006. Missile Defence and Space Weapons: Challenges for the New Canadian Government. Remarks to the National Press Club, Ottawa. 24 February 24. Available at <http://www.ceasefire.ca/>.

CSP. 2002. *The* US-*Canada Strategic Partnership in the War on Terrorism.* Washington: Center for the Study of the Presidency.

CTV. 2006. Military Spending Plan Has Many Benefits, 25 June. Available at <http://www.ctv.ca>.

Davis, Bob. 2002. US Pushing Trade Pacts as Best Route to Reforms. *Globe and Mail*, 22 September, B8.

DOD. 2006. *Transformation Overview.* Washington: Department of Defence. Available at: <http://www.defenselink.mil/transformation/about_transformation.html>, cited 29 June 2006.

Dobson, Wendy. 2003. Trade Can Brush in a New Border. *Galt Global Review*, 4 February. Available at <http://www.galtglobalreview.com>.

Dymond, William A. 2003. *Memorandum to the New Prime Minister Re: Canada-United States Trade Relations.* Remarks to Canadian Centre for Management Development, 17 June. Ottawa: Canadian Centre for Management Development.

Edmonson, R.G. 2003. Next Stop: Cancun. *Journal of Commerce*, 19 May, 34.

Fournier, Ron. 2002. Attack Matures Bush. *Chicago Sun-Times Online*, 8 September. Available at <http://suntimes.com/special_sections/sept11/nation/ bush.html>.

Galloway, Gloria. 2003. US Rebukes Canada. *Globe and Mail*, 26 March, A1.

Globe and Mail. 2004. Martin's Juggling Act: The Budget and Defence. Editorial, 1 January, A16.

Gotlieb, Allan. 2003. A Grand Bargain with the US. *National Post*, 5 March, A16.

Granatstein, Jack L. 2002. A Friendly Agreement in Advance: Canada-US Defence Relations Past, Present, and Future. In *Commentary – Border Papers.* Toronto: C.D. Howe Institute.

Gray, John. 2006. The New Defence Minister and Caesar's Wife. CBC *News Online*, 8 February. Available at <http://www.cbc.ca/news/background/reality-check/20060208.html>.

ICBL. 2004. *What Is Significant about the Ottawa Process?* Ottawa: International Campaign to Ban Landmines.

ICISS. 2001. *The Responsibility to Protect.* Ottawa: International Commission on Intervention and State Sovereignty, Foreign Affairs Canada.

Knight, W. Andy. 2006. Canada Abandons Its Role as UN Peacekeeper. *Edmonton Journal*, 12 April, A19.

O'Sullivan, Fran. 2003. Ship Ban Hits War on Terror Says US. *New Zealand Herald*, 12 August, Available at <http://www.nzherald.co.nz>.

Regehr, Ernie. 2006. NORAD *Renewal: Considerations for the Parliamentary Debate*. Ottawa: Project Ploughshares.

Robinson, Bill. 2006. *Boots on the Ground: Canadian Military Operations in Afghanistan and* UN *Peacekeeping Missions*. Ottawa: Polaris Institute.

Staples, Steven. 2006. *Presentation to the Standing Committee on National Defence*. 8 June. Ottawa: Polaris Institute.

Tait, Carrie. 2005. 85% of CEOs Say Shield Refusal Bad for Business: 52% Say Canada Is Freeloading: Poll. *National Post*, 7 March, A1.

Thompson, Allan. 2002. Pact Lets US Patrol Canada. *Toronto Star*, 9 December, A1.

Tuck, Simon. 2003. Missile Defence Decision Urged Soon. *Globe and Mail*. 12 May, B3.

Tyler, Patrick E. 1992. US Strategy Plan Calls for Insuring No Rivals Develop. *New York Times*, 8 March, 1.

United States. 2002. *The National Security Strategy of the United States*. Washington: White House.

Wright, James R. 2004. Presentation to the Standing Senate Committee on National Security and Defence, 23 February, Ottawa, Parliament of Canada.

WTD. 2003. Untitled. *Washington Trade Daily*, 20 October. Available at <http://www.washingtontradedaily.com/>.

7

Risking Rights: An Assessment of Canadian Border Security Policies

SHARRYN J. AIKEN

Both historically and today, times of real or perceived crisis have often exacerbated social conflicts, producing a backlash against "outsiders." Well before the emergence of the modern nation-state, the Romans rounded up and killed defenceless aliens as a stark warning to the barbarians pressing against the border of their empire. From the past century alone, the mass deportations of "foreign-born agitators" in the wake of the Winnipeg General Strike of 1919, the 1918–21 Palmer raids and anti-immigrant legislation enacted following a series of explosions in US cities due to the mounting "red scare," and the internment of over 100,000 US and Canadian citizens of Japanese descent in response to the bombing of Pearl Harbor in 1941 are tragic illustrations of the extent to which governments have been willing to cast non-citizens and naturalized citizens alike as dangerous outsiders. The current backlash against Arabs, Muslims, and refugees more generally in Canada and the United States in the aftermath of the attacks of 11 September 2001 fits comfortably into a familiar pattern of moral panic over immigration (Akram and Johnson 2004, 22). Numerous studies confirm that the overall impact of immigration on the crime rate and internal security of receiving countries tends to be misjudged and overestimated. In Canada and the United States refugees and immigrants are actually less likely to commit violent crimes than are the native-born, and they are underrepresented in the national prison populations (Simon 2004, 5; Thomas 1993). Nevertheless, instead of seeking genuine solutions for legitimate security concerns, governments have all too often resorted to the quick fix of restrictive laws and policies (Stuart 2002, 185–86). While the government's anti-terrorism agenda has had a corrosive effect on the rights of everyone living in Canada, the primary victims have been immigrants, refugees, and citizens of Arab and Muslim descent.

Canada's economy is highly integrated with, and dependent upon, the United States (see Jackson, chapter 8, this volume). Pressure from the US government and Canadian business interests anxious to safeguard trade and capital flows between the two countries has been an increasingly important factor shaping Canadian policy responses. In this regard, the airplane hijackings and deliberate attacks on the World Trade Center and the Pentagon in 2001 have provided a potent narrative for Canadian proponents of greater integration with the United States. The "deep integration" agenda includes the elimination of customs and immigration controls at the Canada–US border and a deal with the United States to harmonize immigration, refugee, and security policies. As James Laxer (2003, 18) explains, deep integrationists "insist that since, in the aftermath of September 11, the US is constructing a security fortress, Canada must do whatever is necessary to be *inside* the perimeter of that fortress – regardless of the effect on Canada's nationhood." Consistent with this vision, the Canadian Council of Chief Executives (CCCE) has urged the creation of a zone of cooperation encompassing the continent "rather than focusing security efforts on the line that separates us" (CCCE 2003, 4). Thomas d'Aquino, president of the CCCE, has called for borders to be reinvented in a new "North American Security and Prosperity Initiative." He suggests that "we need to emphasize protection of the approaches to North America while eliminating regulatory, procedural and infrastructure barriers at our internal border" (ibid.).

In the weeks following September 11 a chorus of insistent voices on both sides of the border was pressing for a common North American security perimeter and suggesting that Canada should bring its immigration laws into line with those of the United States to help combat terrorism. The federal government responded with the swift adoption of a complex array of anti-terrorism laws, policies, and technologies in an effort to protect cross-border trade flows and to address perceptions that Canada had been asleep at the switch on terrorism. Despite these efforts, a recent study by the US Library of Congress on the risks posed by individual states to global security asserted that Canada's immigration laws were still the foremost factor in making Canada hospitable to terrorists and international criminals. The study warns that the "economic necessity of expedient movement across the US-Canadian border and Canada's liberal democratic identity" may continue to limit the adoption of security measures necessary to halt the operations of terrorist groups using Canada as a safe haven or as a venue to raise funds (US Library of Congress 2003, 154). Responding to the report's assessment, a Canadian intelligence analyst with the MacKenzie Institute suggested that "the problem is that we have a political culture that reflects public opinion (Woods 2004, 7).[1]

Kent Roach has compared the challenges presented to Canadian law by September 11 to Canada's acceptance of nuclear arms in the wake of the Cuban missile crisis of 1962 – an event that caused George Grant to predict the death of Canadian sovereignty (Roach 2003). Grant warned that

Canada's "social and economic blending into empire will continue apace" and that political union would be accelerated by an international catastrophe or great shift of power (Grant 1965, 86). As Roach notes, Grant's prediction of the eclipse of a distinctive Canadian nation still seems premature. In the perpetual push and pull between integration with and separation from Washington, the deep integrationists have not prevailed (Roach 2003, 167). Indeed, "globalization has made the border more, not less important for security and immigration, for all countries" (Drache 2004, 110).

Contrary to the predictions of both free trade advocates and pessimistic nationalists, the border has persisted with a vengeance. Among other reasons, concerns about the entry of drugs and guns into this country kept Canadian regulators distinctly cool to the "perimeter" concept and the phasing out of border controls (SCFAIT 2002, 93). On the plus side of the ledger, Canada has maintained distinctive social welfare policies (albeit at diminished levels), supported multilateralism in the international arena, and stood up to the United States on Iraq (Drache 2004; Whitaker 2004). However, the September 11 attacks have posed significant challenges to Canadian democracy as the border has become a renewed focal point of Canada-US relations (Roach 2003). This chapter offers an analysis of recent Canadian immigration and border policy developments. National security provisions in immigration law before and after September 11, the "smart border" initiative, and racial profiling practices are the primary focus. Developments after September 11 do not represent a sea change in attitudes towards non-citizens but merely the latest chapter in a fitful history of grand gestures of humanitarianism, political expedience, and racist exclusion (Akram and Johnson 2004; Dauvergne 2003, 743; Richmond 2001; Simmons 1998). While the "big idea" of policy convergence in immigration and security has not been embraced by the Canadian government, a series of coercive, incremental measures has led to a serious erosion of human rights, particularly for non-citizens. The chapter concludes by underscoring the importance of efforts by civil society to resist this erosion through grassroots organizing, public education, and test case litigation.

SECURING THE NATION WITH IMMIGRATION LAW

Terrorism and the Former Immigration Act

An established means of immigration control, security provisions have been included in federal immigration law since 1872. For the purposes of this chapter, however, my starting point is the early 1990s. It was a time when Cold War security considerations were giving way to a preoccupation with deterring "spontaneous arrivals," transnational crime, and terrorism.

Over the following decade in Europe, the United States, and Australia, immigration laws would be enacted aimed at "cracking down" on "illegal" migration (Dauvergne 2003, 735). Responding to Canadians' worries about their personal safety came to be seen as a key priority by the federal Conservative government. The notion that more effective legal tools were needed to improve "system integrity" swiftly acquired currency in the Canadian policy arena. Promulgated in 1992 and featuring a series of new deterrents, Bill C-86 added "terrorism" to the Immigration Act's pre-existing list of security-related exclusions. Refugees and prospective immigrants would be "inadmissible" where there were reasonable grounds to believe they would "engage in terrorism" or were "members of an organization that there [were] reasonable grounds to believe [would] ... engage in terrorism." An additional subsection provided that persons were inadmissible if they had engaged in terrorism in the past or were "members of an organization that was engaged in terrorism" unless they could satisfy the minister that their admission would not be detrimental to the national interest. As "terrorism" and "membership" were undefined in law, these largely indeterminate concepts afforded both immigration officers and the judges who reviewed their decisions the broadest possible discretion.[2]

Less than six months after Bill C-86 came into effect, a defiantly "law-and-order" federal government moved the entire immigration bureaucracy to a newly created Department of Public Security, reinforcing negative stereotypes of refugees and immigrants as dangerous outlaws intent on abusing Canadian generosity.[3] At the same time, efforts were stepped up to prevent undocumented migrants as well as terrorists and criminals from reaching Canada. A coordinated, global interdiction strategy was implemented with no safeguards to ensure that genuine refugees were afforded access to protection (CCR 1998). Some 33,000 people were "successfully" intercepted far beyond Canada's borders between 1996 and 2001 (Thompson 2001). Little is known about their circumstances, but reports surfaced very occasionally of refugees who suffered serious human rights violations upon return to their countries of origin.

One such case that became public in 1998 involved the interception of a boat carrying 192 Sri Lankan Tamils in the territorial waters of Senegal. With the assistance of Canadian authorities, all the passengers were returned to Sri Lanka. No one was interviewed prior to boarding a specially chartered flight in order to ascertain whether any had valid reasons to fear going home in the face of an ongoing civil war and the country's poor human rights record. Upon arrival in the Colombo airport, all the men were arrested and detained and, subsequently, one individual was rearrested and tortured (AI 1998; Aiken 2001b, 47–8). While no state has an absolute obligation to grant asylum to persons seeking admission to their territory, as a signatory to the 1951 Refugee Convention Canada is supposed to ensure that refugees are not returned to a country where their life or freedom would be threatened.

Meanwhile, within Canada certain refugee communities found themselves increasingly subject to surveillance by Canadian Security Intelligence Services (CSIS). Many of the criticisms that had been levelled against the RCMP during the 1970s began to surface with regard to the security intelligence agency and the practices and conduct of its officers. Complaints were made to the Security Intelligence Review Committee (SIRC), the civilian oversight agency, documenting the extent to which CSIS had deployed the mantle of counter-terrorism not just to monitor national security threats but, like the RCMP before it with regard to "subversives," to intrude into the lives and futures of those involved in legitimate forms of expression and dissent (Leddy 1997, 76–82; SIRC 2000, 82). Media reports exposed how, in some cases, refugees were overtly or implicitly induced to become informers on fellow community members – with promises of prompt resolution of their own residence applications (Thompson 1996, 1998a, 1998b; Thompson and MacCharles 1998).

In a study completed in March 2001, *Refugees and Security*, the Canadian Council for Refugees (CCR) documented the extent to which certain refugee communities seemed to be particularly targeted, including Iranians associated with the Mujahedin-E-Khalq movement, Kurds, Sri Lankan Tamils, Sikhs, Algerians, and Palestinians, while other groups were not subjected to the same levels of security scrutiny (CCR 2001b). In public reports produced by CSIS itself, it was easy to discern that the agency's views were informed by a highly partisan analysis of global politics that placed disproportionate reliance on state-based sources of information as opposed to information obtained from human rights NGOs or even the United Nations.

Political activism that was lawful for citizens had become a basis for expelling non-citizens. Federal Court judges applying terrorism provisions tended to consistently endorse a generalized bias in favour of designating the acts of non-state agents as terrorist but not similar acts carried out by a state (Aiken 2001a). In Canada, organizations formed to defend the interests of particular refugee populations can play a key role in the community, offering newcomer settlement services, representing the community's political aspirations, and providing a venue for cultural events. Typically a wide cross-section of the community is involved in these organizations – from active supporters of violent homeland struggles to those who merely express sympathy for a political cause but reject violence. The organizations bring together large numbers of people who may have little in common apart from a shared ethnicity and an experience of persecution (CCR 2001b). Yet any degree of participation in these groups risked the prospect of being identified as a security threat should CSIS suspect links between the diaspora community and the country of origin. The same treatment was accorded to the mastermind of a hijacking as to the person who raised money in Canada to support an orphanage in a war-ravaged homeland. The result was that individuals were forced to choose between either abandoning their associational life or living in constant fear that their involvement in the local community centre might lead to their expulsion from the country.

Further, refugee claimants seeking asylum as well as prospective immigrants applying for permanent residence were subjected to security interviews that all too frequently resembled interrogations and for which the individuals arrived unprepared, having been given no notice of the purpose of the interview or their entitlement to be represented by counsel (Leddy 1997, 76–82). Most of the adverse information that CSIS collected would be classified on national security grounds and therefore not disclosed to the person concerned. Proceedings very often left individuals in a legal limbo while their files awaited review by department analysts. The long delays associated with security clearance procedures meant that some individuals could expect to wait more than eight years before being able to sponsor and reunite with family members, enrol in post secondary education, start a business, or travel outside the country. Once a "security certificate" was issued, the decision of a single "designated" judge was considered conclusive proof of the allegations against the individual and could not be appealed. The certificate process allowed the government to arrest, detain, and deport non-citizens on security grounds, without ever showing them, or their lawyers, the evidence against them.

In 1999 the case of failed refugee claimant Ahmed Ressam became a flashpoint for concern on the part of media and government alike. Ressam was caught at the border with a Canadian passport, explosives hidden in his car, and a plan to bomb the Los Angeles airport. His capture sparked renewed criticism that the refugee program was to blame for Canada becoming a "safe haven" for terrorists to plan and carry out attacks against the United States. In fact CSIS had knowledge of Ressam prior to his arrest in 1999 but didn't consider him a threat. Ressam's continued presence in Canada was a result of Canada Immigration's failure to enforce a deportation order against him and weaknesses in the Canadian passport application process, which were subsequently addressed (SIRC 2003, 3–6). Nevertheless, the Ressam case appeared to give the federal government new impetus for a long-awaited overhaul of the Immigration Act. After the first bill died on the order paper with announcement of the 2000 federal election, a new Immigration and Refugee Protection Act (IRPA) was finally proposed in 2001. Then immigration minister Elinor Caplan suggested that the reform was necessary to reflect the dual mandate of her department – namely, "to close the back door to those who would abuse our rules, in order to open the front door wider to those who would come to us from around the world to help us build our country" (CIC 2002, 2).

Law Reform Post September 11:
The Immigration and Refugee Protection Act

Within days of the September 11 attacks, reports surfaced from various US sources that as many as five of the hijackers or their associates had entered the United States from Canada. Senior US officials speculated about a "Canadian connection" to the attacks that had produced some 3,000 fatalities (UNHCR 2001). While the reports were quickly proven to be false, Canadian policy makers scrambled to address lingering concerns that Canada had become a terrorist staging ground and that a flawed refugee policy was to blame (Roach 2003, 5; Sallot 2001a). Prime Minister Jean Chrétien indicated that tougher requirements for would-be refugee claimants would be part of a package of reforms to respond to the new global realities (Harper 2001). A Liberal senator expressed concern that "a series of governments have been lax" concerning terrorism and immigration and signalled that proposed changes to the refugee scheme would receive "tougher scrutiny" in the Senate (*Toronto Star* 2001a).[4] In fact, no changes were made before the bill was hurriedly proclaimed on 1 November 2001 – new enforcement measures had already been included in earlier versions of the bill, well before September 11.

The new act maintained the category of inadmissibility on the grounds of "membership" in a "terrorist" organization and added further grounds for security inadmissibility. Persons found inadmissible for reasons of national security or serious criminality lost all appeal rights. IRPA expanded the powers of immigration officers to provide for the examination of non-Canadians not only on entering Canada but also at any time while they are living in Canada. As noted by the CCR (2001a), "this change means that the border is brought into Canadian society" – all non-citizens are treated as if they are eternally at the border, subject to examination at any time by immigration officers. For the purposes of security certificate procedures, IRPA stripped SIRC of its former review mandate for permanent residents. Both refugees and permanent residents are now accorded an "informal and expeditious" Federal Court review of the reasonableness, but not the merits, of ministerial security opinions with no possibility of further review or appeal. Although fewer than thirty security certificates have been issued since 1991, the inadequacies of the procedure and related preventive detention provisions drew special mention in a 2000 report on Canada by the Inter-American Commission on Human Rights (IACHR 2000). IRPA not only failed to address existing shortcomings on these issues but also further eroded an essential safeguard.

The act barred persons found inadmissible on grounds of security, human, or "international rights" violations from making a refugee claim in direct contravention of advice from the United Nations High Commissioner for Refugees (UNHCR 2001). Although compliance with Canada's international human rights commitments is identified as a new requirement in IRPA, the explicit exemption authorizing the minister to deport people regardless of the consequences remained in place for designated security cases. While UN resolutions consistently urge states to ensure that refugee status is "not used for the purpose of preparing or organizing terrorist acts," the Convention against Torture and related international jurisprudence firmly support an absolute prohibition against deporting anyone to a country where they are at risk of torture.[5] The security provisions in IRPA, however, expressly permit immigrants and refugees to be deported to countries where they will be at risk of torture and other forms of persecution.

IRPA also expanded the powers of immigration officers to arrest and detain non-citizens on entry to Canada, affording an increased scope for detention without warrant where an officer is not satisfied with a person's identity. Regulations create an explicit link between mode of arrival and likelihood of detention, targeting persons who have arrived as part of a criminally organized smuggling or trafficking operation. While detention may be justified under certain circumstances, international law stipulates that detention of asylum seekers should ordinarily be avoided. The decision to detain should be an individuated decision, based on the particular facts of an individual's case and not on generalizations. Indeed, the UNHCR has cautioned against establishing a policy based solely on the mode of arrival, as "many asylum seekers are forced to resort to the services of smugglers in order to reach safety" (UNHCR 1999).

After September 11 the federal government's budget allocation for immigration detention was increased. While it remains to be seen whether the government will make routine use of its expanded powers of arrest and detention, since implementation of IRPA in June 2002 and the availability of greater revenue there has been an increase in the overall numbers of people subject to preventive immigration detention. In 2001–02 there was an average of 455 people detained at any one time across the country, while a more recent report for the six-month period from June to December 2003 indicates that an average of 683 persons were subjected to immigration detention each week. Reports through the 1990s suggest that relatively few refugee claimants were subject to detention, but by 2003 an average of 45 percent of immigration detainees were refugee claimants (Dench 2004).

More alarming, however, was the arrest and detention on security grounds of a group of twenty-three South Asian men in August 2003 pursuant to "Operation Thread," a joint investigation by the RCMP and Citizenship and Immigration Canada. Twenty-two of the young men were from Pakistan, and one was from India. Initial reports splashed in Canadian newspapers identified the group as an Al-Qaeda sleeper cell. The incriminating allegations, which department officials were unable to substantiate, included a plot to destroy the CN Tower, a student pilot with a flight course over the Pickering Nuclear Plant, several young men living together in sparsely furnished apartments, the setting off of a smoke alarm in the kitchen (supposedly a sign of testing explosives), and one man who knew someone with an Al-Qaeda connection (CCR 2004a, 4; Jimenez, Freeze, and Burnett 2003; Khan 2004). Officials very quickly backed away from their initial claim that the men posed a threat to national security as the cases devolved into simple immigration fraud with an illegitimate Scarborough business college at the centre. The aftershocks of the investigation, however, cast a long shadow over the men's lives. Marked as terrorists, many of the men continue to face harassment and unemployment back in Pakistan (Shepard and Verma 2003; Verma 2004). Department officials may have had a reasonable basis for pursuing investigations in at least some of the "Operation Thread" cases – namely, the visa violations – but the decision to detain the men as security risks appears to have been a blatant example of racial profiling (a practice that is discussed in greater detail below).

Interestingly, the change in refugee eligibility procedures and adoption of "front-end screening" has not resulted in the detection of an increased number of people representing a threat to security. In 2003, of 31,837 applications, only two were found ineligible to proceed with their refugee claims based on the very broad security inadmissibility criteria (CCR 2004a). In November 2001 the government reported that three persons were in detention across Canada pursuant to security certificate procedures (CCR 2004b). Two years later the number had increased to six – five of whom were Arabs.

Hassan Almrei, one of the five jailed on a security certificate, is a refugee who fears being returned to his native Syria. Government lawyers, arguing against a stay of his deportation order, suggested in Federal Court that Almrei was at no risk of torture if returned to Syria, just when human rights monitors and even the US Department of State had documented that torture in detention was routine in Syria and that members and associates of the Muslim Brotherhood (such as Almrei) were at particular risk (Abbate and Freeze 2003; CBC 2003). At the time of writing, Almrei was still detained but the Supreme Court had agreed to review the constitutionality of the security certificate procedures that resulted in his detention.[6]

BORDER (IN)SECURITY

In mid-October 2001 the federal government announced a multipronged "Anti-Terrorism Plan." A $646 million investment would ensure, among other things, that the Canada–US border would be prevented from "being held hostage by terrorists and impacting on the Canadian economy" (CIC 2001b). By the late fall of 2001, Citizenship and Immigration Minister Elinor Caplan disclosed that her department was in visa convergence talks with Washington and that the idea of a "safe third country" agreement concerning the allocation of asylum claims between the United States and Canada was being resurrected (Clark 2001; Greenspon 2001). In December 2001 the government gave concrete expression to its security strategy, signing two important declarations with the United States and pursuing a series of initiatives that would culminate, in the spring of 2004, with the release of an integrated national policy on security. In contrast to the measures described in the preceding section, these initiatives were premised on administrative and policy reform rather than on any significant changes to federal laws.

The "Smart Border"

On 3 December 2001 US attorney general John Ashcroft, Canadian immigration minister Elinor Caplan, and Solicitor General Laurence MacCaulay initialled a Joint Statement on Border Security and Regional Migration Issues. The joint statement focused on "deterrence, detection and prosecution of security threats, the disruption of illegal migration and the efficient management of legitimate travel." It outlined a series of new measures, including joint border patrols, a policy review on visitor visas and information sharing on high-risk visa applications, an increase in the number of Immigration Control Officers overseas, and the development of common biometric identifiers for documents (CIC 2001a).

For refugee advocates the most controversial part of the announcement was the proposed "safe third country agreement," which requires, with limited exceptions, all refugee claimants arriving at a Canadian land border from the United States to pursue their asylum claim in the United States. A similar agreement was aborted in the mid-1990s after a successful lobbying campaign by US public interest groups with support from their Canadian counterparts. Although justified by Canadian officials as a measure aimed at "burden sharing" for international refugee flows, the agreement's greatest impact likely will be to encourage asylum seekers to put themselves at risk by crossing Canadian land borders illegally and then pursuing their claims inland.7 Refugees have every reason to assume those risks given the lower standards of due process protection available in the United States with respect to refugee hearings, the greater prospect of detention and deportation in expedited removal procedures, as well as differing (and detrimental) US interpretations of international refugee law.

In late 2005 a constitutional challenge of the safe third country agreement was launched by a coalition of groups, including the Canadian Council for Refugees, the Canadian Council of Churches, and Amnesty International. Arguably, however, the significance of the agreement has waned as increasing resources are being allocated to interceptions overseas – far from any North American land border. In support of this contention is the fact that the numbers of refugee claimants arriving at Canadian ports of entry (land or air) have plummeted in the past several years with overall numbers at their lowest point since 1994. Also in December 2001, soon after the Joint Statement on Border Security had been signed, Deputy Prime Minister John Manley and US homeland security director Tom Ridge announced the Smart Border Declaration with an accompanying thirty-point Action Plan (Canada 2001). The accord spelled out in detail the commitments expressed in the joint statement. Meanwhile, the immigration minister had announced that citizens from eight additional countries would require Canadian visitor visas before travel to Canada, matching requirements in the United States. Among the countries subject to the new rules was Zimbabwe, just as increasing numbers of genuine refugees were fleeing serious human rights violations there. The minister suggested that the new rules reflected the government's "concern with improperly documented travelers to Canada" (CIC 2001c). However, despite the immigration minister's initial enthusiasm for policy harmonization with Washington, the new visa requirements fell short of full visa convergence. Two and a half years after the issuance of the joint statement, Canadian and US visa policies continued to diverge with respect to more than forty countries.

Furthermore, Canada refrained from adopting the selective rules embodied in Washington's National Security Exit-Entry Registration System (NSEERS). In addition to a call-in registration program that applied to some 82,000 men and boys residing in the United States on temporary visas, NSEERS required visitors to the United States "with ties" to twenty-five predominantly Muslim countries to be digitally fingerprinted, photographed, and registered. In response to NSEERS, the Canadian government actually issued a travel advisory warning Canadian citizens who were born in Iran, Iraq, Libya, Sudan, Syria, Pakistan, Saudi Arabia, and Yemen "to consider carefully whether they should attempt to enter the United States for any reason, including transit to or from third countries." A government spokesperson indicated that Canada considered the regulations discriminatory and unfriendly (Labott 2002). A direct appeal to the Bush administration succeeded in achieving an exemption for Canadian citizens from NSEERS, but by the end of 2002 a parliamentary committee was endorsing the concept of effectively similar, though not identical, policies (SCFAIT 2002, 93). Inside government, greater emphasis was being placed on the importance of coordination and consultation with Washington to address any negative impact felt at the border as a result of policy incongruities (CIC 2002, 4).

In the fall of 2003, Canadian citizen Maher Arar's compelling, first-hand account of being detained by US authorities during a stopover in New York and then deported to Syria, where he was jailed and tortured for over a year, succeeded in dampening the public's appetite for a blanket adoption of US-style immigration enforcement practices.[8] However, in a nod to a similar reorganization in the United States (and resonant of the short-lived reorganization attempted by the former Conservative government in 1992), then Prime Minister Paul Martin quietly introduced structural changes to the federal civil service in December 2003. With no advance notice or public consultation, a cabinet directive created the new portfolio of Public Safety and Emergency Preparedness, lumping under its umbrella immigration enforcement activities together with emergency preparedness, crisis management, national security, corrections, policing, and crime prevention. A newly established Canada Border Services Agency (CBSA) would be reporting directly to the minister of public safety and assume responsibility for a number of core immigration functions, not all of which were strictly enforcement related. While some aspects of the reorganization may be viewed as a sensible, positive step towards more effective coordination of national policing and security functions, the immigration-related changes were sharply criticized by refugee and immigrant advocates. Primary concerns include a potential conflict of interest arising from the agency's security mandate and certain protection functions being housed under one roof as well as the diminished priority that will likely be afforded to human rights in an agency dedicated exclusively to law enforcement. Somewhat less tangibly, the move further reinforces the construction of non-citizens as a safety threat in the public imagination. The cabinet directive also eliminated the requirement for two ministers to sign a security certificate, concentrating the authority to decide who should be deemed a security threat in the hands of the minister of public safety.[9] Non-citizens subject to adverse security reports would be afforded one less safeguard in a procedure that already fails to comply with minimal due process guarantees.

A National Security Policy

Released in the spring of 2004 in the lead-up to a federal election, *Securing an Open Society: Canada's National Security Policy* was a wide-ranging status report and action plan addressing intelligence, emergency planning and management, public health, transport security, border security, and international security. Among the report's constructive commitments were proposals to establish an arm's-length review mechanism for RCMP national security activities and a cross-cultural roundtable on security, which will engage in "a long-term dialogue to improve understanding on how to manage security interests in a diverse society" as well as the promise to undertake a legislative review to ensure that the measures adopted in the wake of September 11 "struck the appropriate balance" (Privy Council Office 2004, 2).

Less positively, the chapter on border security signalled an intention to reform the refugee system. Without any elaboration, there was an oblique reference to new measures being tabled to "better provide protection to those genuinely in need and to more efficiently identify and remove those individuals who may be attempting to abuse our refugee and immigration system" (Privy Council Office 2004, 45). The plan to revisit the subject of admissions and removals and the implicit identification of refugees and immigrants as the source of Canada's security problems could be viewed as a cynical re-election bid on the part of Paul Martin's administration. It could also be an indicator that long-standing interests pushing for the resource-intensive, quasi-judicial system of refugee status determination to be dismantled were gaining ground. In light of the five-year process of public consultations and the parliamentary review leading up to the passage of the IRPA, the measures already implemented to address a perceived security deficit in Canada's refugee and immigration programs (including the new legislative tools to screen newcomers arriving at Canadian ports of entry as well as controversial new procedures adopted by the Immigration and Refugee Board to streamline its decision making), the call for further reform was puzzling at best. At worst, it raised concerns that the Canadian government was on the brink of caving in to ongoing pressure from Washington to restrict the refugee program in a manner that will threaten the integrity and fairness of the entire system. After charting the "progress" achieved through the Smart Border agreement with the United States, the chapter on border security concluded by suggesting that the "way forward" will be to apply the smart border principles around the world, a further indication of the increasing importance of interdiction in controlling and managing border flows far from any actual border or public scrutiny (Privy Council Office 2004, 44–6).

In the first throne speech of the new Conservative government immigration and refugee issues were not included in the short-list of key policy priorities. Nevertheless, an express commitment to foster a closer relationship with Washington is likely to reinforce and probably extend many of the basic directions of the previous government. Indeed, Immigration Minister Monte Solberg has suggested that the only genuine refugees in need of Canada's protection were overseas, while the continued allocation of significant resources to claimants within Canada was an "inefficiency" his government intended to address (CIMM 2006).

RACIAL PROFILING

Before September 11 public discourse in Canada about racial profiling focused primarily on African Canadians, usually within the context of policing and the conduct of customs and immigration officials at ports of entry (James 1998; Wortley 1996). As a strategy of law enforcement, racial profiling has proven to be both ineffective and offensive to constitutional equality protections (Bahdi 2003; Choudhry 2001; Davies 2003; OHRC 2003; Smith 2003). In the United States a number of state and local legislatures had either passed laws requiring their police forces to collect racial and ethnic data in connection with traffic stops or had adopted an outright ban on racial profiling in law enforcement. However, just days after September 11, the debate about racial profiling turned an abrupt corner (Davies 2003, 46). In Ontario the premier announced the formation of an elite police unit to track down illegal immigrants and to see that they are deported, suggesting that Ontario residents want protection from these immigrants – and their potential crimes – in the wake of the September 11 attacks (Aiken 2001b). The premier's newly appointed security advisor was more explicit, indicating that ethnic profiling of certain communities would have to be part of new security measures (OLA 2001). After September 11 the legitimizing of racial profiling and a sharp increase in hate crimes against Arabs and Muslims were the concrete expressions of everyday racism in North America (Grewal 2001; Sallot 2001b; *Toronto Star* 2001b).

While various definitions of racial profiling have been advanced by scholars and policy makers over the years, the Ontario Human Rights Commission has offered a useful starting point. The commission defines racial profiling broadly to include "any action undertaken for reasons of safety, security or public protection that relies on stereotypes about race, colour, ethnicity, ancestry, religion, or place of origin rather than on reasonable suspicion, to single out an individual for greater scrutiny or different treatment" (OHRC 2003, 6). The report notes that profiling can occur because of a combination of the above factors and that age and/or gender can influence the experience of profiling. Racial profiling, the report explains, differs from criminal profiling, which is not based on stereotypes but, rather, relies on actual behaviour or on information about suspected activity on the part of someone who meets the description of a specific individual. In other words, criminal profiling is not the same as racial profiling since the former is based on objective evidence of wrongful behaviour while racial profiling is based on stereotypical assumptions. As the commission suggests, "while it may be somewhat natural for humans to engage in stereotyping, it is nevertheless wrong. And, it is a particular concern when people act on their stereotypical views in a way that affects others. This is what leads to profiling" (ibid.).

Drawing on the criminological literature, Scot Wortley and Julian Tanner (2004, 369) address racial profiling in the context of law enforcement, suggesting that racial profiling is said to exist when the members of certain racial or ethnic groups become subject to greater levels of criminal justice surveillance than others. Racial profiling, therefore, is typically defined as a racial disparity in police stop and search practices, in Customs searches at airports and border-crossings, in police patrols in minority neighbourhoods and in undercover activities or sting operations which target particular ethnic groups.

Under certain circumstances, racial profiling may also be the impetus for discriminatory exercises of investigative detention powers (Tanovich 2002, 145). Within the context of Canada's war on terrorism, legal scholars have emphasized that racial profiling entails the use of race as a proxy for the risk of committing terrorist acts, either in whole or in part (Bahdi 2003, 295; Choudhry 2001, 372).

Adopted on the heels of new anti-terrorism legislation in the United States (the Patriot Act), Canada's Anti-Terrorism Act, proclaimed in December 2001, amends nineteen other laws in addition to the Criminal Code. A discussion of the wide-ranging nature and impact of these reforms is beyond the scope of this chapter. Key features, however, include a legal definition of terrorism, provisions for the listing of terrorist individuals and organizations and the freezing of their assets, as well as a series of new offences. The amendments abolish a number of due process safeguards and make it easier to use electronic surveillance against suspected terrorist groups. Scheduled to sunset after five years, and among the most controversial of the act's new measures, are those relating to preventative arrest and investigative hearing. A companion piece of legislation amending twenty-three federal laws, the Public Safety Act was first introduced in November 2001 as an important plank in the government's Anti-Terrorism Plan and was finally adopted in May 2004 after four rewrites. Among other reforms, the new law permits designated federal officials to have access to airline passenger lists and reservations information for a full week – without a warrant – for the purposes of national security and transportation security, broadly defined; expands the government's ability to share personal information pertaining to all individuals with a designated list of government agencies; and eliminates the need for cabinet authorization or a formal agreement as a condition precedent to sharing personal information pertaining to immigrants and refugees with foreign governments. Plans have also been announced to grant police, regulatory, and national security agencies access to telecommunications and Internet service provider subscriber and "traffic data" under a lower threshold than that now required for search warrants (Justice Canada 2002b).

None of the measures described above has anything to say about racial profiling. They neither explicitly condone nor prohibit racial profiling. However, as Reem Bahdi (2003, 297) notes, "the lack of explicit endorsement of racial profiling in the anti-terrorism legislation does not mean that it does not take place in Canada ... the silence of the legislature regarding the practice, at best, fails to effectively check racial profiling and, at worst, creates opportunities for racial profiling." As in other manifestations of systemic discrimination, racial profiling is embodied in the exercise of discretionary powers by officials acting pursuant to apparently neutral laws. While Canadian regulators have not adopted explicitly selective policies as in the United States, there is ample anecdotal evidence to suggest that Canadian Arabs and Muslims have been the targets of increased surveillance and security scrutiny by a range of public and private actors.

A few of the cases cited by the Ontario Human Rights Commission are illustrative: an employer wanting stricter security clearance for a Muslim employee after September 11; law enforcement officials going to the workplaces of community leaders and questioning them in front of colleagues; a money transfer agency refusing to transfer money to a man's parents without first conducting a security clearance because his first name is "Muhammad"; a Palestinian child being exposed to a guest speaker in her classroom whose presentation implied that Palestinian persons should not be trusted as they are raised to be hateful and to perpetrate terrorist attacks; children and youth being subjected to comments by teachers and other students linking them to terrorism; being terminated from employment and/or having trouble finding a new job due to a perception of being a security threat; being questioned by law enforcement authorities due to membership in a Muslim religious organization; and being searched more often or scrutinized differently from others when flying or crossing the Canada-US border (OHRC 2003, 32).

Many of the more draconian provisions in the package of laws implemented in response to September 11 have yet to be invoked. To date there has been just one set of charges laid pursuant to the anti-terrorism amendments to the Criminal Code. The Department of Justice has not made use of its new powers of preventative arrest or investigative hearing (Justice Canada 2002a). To a significant degree it has been business as usual: for all new security cases involving non-citizens, government officials have opted for immigration remedies, which are less costly and easier to prosecute than are criminal charges. There is little doubt, however, that as security consciousness continues to grip many Canadians, racialized individuals and communities have been feeling increasingly under attack. Post-September 11 law reform has contributed to a climate in which many people feel less, rather than more, secure. The very definition of terrorism and proscribed terrorist activities that are now incorporated into the Criminal Code, the expanded role for financial institutions with respect to the freezing of terrorist assets, and the growing role of new surveillance technologies constitute a non-exhaustive list of particularly problematic provisions and are considered in turn below.

Manufacturing Terrorists

As the Criminal Code's new definition of terrorist activity is the threshold for the application of all the expanded powers and penalties in the remainder of the anti-terrorism amendments, a closer look at the definition is warranted. It begins by incorporating offences from the twelve United Nations anti-terrorism treaties to which Canada is a signatory. These treaties adopt an objective, functional approach by defining terrorism through a series of proscribed acts – ranging from hijackings and international abductions to crimes in relation to nuclear materials, terrorist bombings, and the financing of terrorism. If it had ended there, as a number of advocates had urged, there would be little cause for concern. However, the code goes on to identify a complex list of supplementary circumstances that can constitute terrorist activity. Acts of domestic and international terrorism as well as threats to commit acts are now criminalized. Such acts must be motivated in whole or in part by "a political, religious or ideological purpose, objective or cause" and be committed "in whole or in part with the intention of intimidating the public ... with regard to its security, including its economic security, or compelling a person, a government or a domestic or an international organization to do or to refrain from doing any act ... and intentionally ... cause death or serious bodily harm to a person." A further subsection indicates that "every one who knowingly facilitates a terrorist activity is guilty of an indictable offence ... regardless of whether the facilitator knew that a particular terrorist activity was facilitated; any particular terrorist activity was foreseen or planned at the time it was facilitated; or any terrorist activity was actually carried out."

While the field of terrorism studies has generated a proliferation of definitions, the consensus among many authors is that there is no universally or even generally accepted definition. As Levitt (1986, 97) once quipped, the "search for a definition of terrorism in some ways resembles the quest for the Holy Grail." Proposals by India, Sri Lanka, Algeria, and Turkey to include an aggregate crime of terrorism within the International Criminal Court's jurisdiction were rejected, and the international community has so far failed to agree on a definition of terrorism for a proposed comprehensive terrorism convention. The Supreme Court of Canada has recognized that "the absence of an authoritative definition means that at least at the margins, 'the term is open to politicized manipulation, conjecture and polemical interpretation'" (SCC 2002, 53). A series of pre-existing offences in the Criminal Code already criminalized the full range of violent acts that characterize contemporary terrorism; provisions relating to conspiracy, as well as aiding and abetting, ensured that those who planned or financed the commission of such offences were within the law's reach. Nevertheless, consistent with the growing trend of "governing through crime," the quick and symbolic fix of new laws would enhance the optic of a government intent on doing its fair share for the us-led war on terrorism (Roach 2003, 23–5).

In this regard, Canada's new definition of terrorism casts an exceedingly wide net. Special exemptions are provided for acts committed in the course of armed conflicts conducted in accordance with rules of international law and official duties undertaken by military forces, but international law was not marshalled to draw the requisite distinctions between acts directed against severely repressive dictatorships *versus* democracies. The new provisions do not criminalize membership in political movements per se as in the case of IRPA: but it is clear that anyone who provides any kind of assistance or indirect support to groups that include violent resistance within their activities, other than within the context of an armed conflict, will run the risk of being caught by the definition and the facilitation provisions. As in the case of IRPA's membership provisions, the likely victims will be members of diasporic communities who are merely associated with, but not actual members of, organizations in their homelands. Further, the unnecessary inclusion of religious or political motives risks the prospect that police may blur the lines between terrorism and radical political or religious dissent, that stereotypes equating religious orthodoxy with violence will inform the administration of the law, and that terrorism trials in Canada will be political and religious trials (Roach 2003, 25–8). Aside from an array of evidentiary, constitutional, and general rule of law concerns that the definition of terrorist activity and facilitation engage, these provisions afford wide scope for racial profiling on the part of the broad range of actors charged with responsibility for applying the new law. The Criminal Code also affords power to the federal cabinet, upon the solicitor general's recommendation, to bypass the regular criminal process and simply designate terrorist groups without any sort of hearing. Shortly after the bill was tabled in the House of Commons, a *Globe and Mail* columnist observed that "most people will not be terribly inconvenienced by Ms. McLellan's proposals. Instead the costs will be borne by people who find themselves targets of police suspicion because of their ethnic background, radical political views or association with immigrant communities that have ties with groups deemed to be terrorist fronts" (McCarthy 2001).

Frozen Assets and Mistaken Identities

Measures relating to the freezing of terrorist assets provide a concrete example of how new discretionary powers may give rise to instances of racial profiling. Pursuant to regulations issued by the federal cabinet in October 2001 and specific provisions in the Anti-Terrorism Act, the Office of the Superintendent of Financial Institutions (OSFI) is responsible for distributing a consolidated list of named terrorists to financial institutions. These institutions, including banks, federally regulated trust and loan companies, and life insurance companies, are then required to freeze the assets of anyone whose name is on that list. Few would contest the desirability of curtailing terrorism by cutting off its money supply, but the system the government enacted is problematic because the lists and instructions issued to financial institutions by the OSFI encourage racial profiling (Bahdi 2003, 302). According to a government document, financial institutions themselves must make the determination as to whether they are in possession or control of any property owned or controlled by a listed entity (PSEP 2002). OSFI advises financial institutions to regard with suspicion not only people whose names are on the list but also anyone whose name *resembles* the name of a listed person: " if you have grounds for suspicion do not rely on different (but similar) spelling as grounds for deciding that a person is not intended to be covered by the list" (Bahdi 2003, 302; OSFI 2004). Commenting on this guideline, Bahdi (2003, 302) states: "bank managers and employees, working under the shadow of risk of financial and criminal sanction, are thus implicitly encouraged to regard Arabs and Muslims as especially suspect. In short, race and religion, through the use of names, becomes a proxy for risk."

The case of Liban Hussein illustrates the flaws in the listing mechanisms and the serious consequences that may arise for individuals placed on these lists. Hussein is a Canadian citizen who ran a money transfer business to help Somalis send money home to a country where there are few banks. In November 2001 US authorities placed Hussein on a list of sixty-two people who allegedly supported terrorism. On the same day the UN Security Council and the Canadian government adopted that list. Hussein's bank accounts were frozen for seven months, his business was shut down, and it became a crime for anyone to have any financial dealings with him. Although he was ultimately "delisted" when the Canadian justice department found no evidence to link him with terrorist activities, by then Hussein's personal reputation had been ruined (Dosman 2004). Although financial institutions are permitted to release assets in the case of mistaken identity if the matter cannot be resolved at that level, the mechanisms for individuals to have their names cleared and assets released are burdensome and afford inadequate procedural protections.

The Panoptic State

The image of the Panopticon, an architectural design for a model prison, permeates all contemporary discussions of surveillance (Whitaker 1999, 32). Originally conceived by Jeremy Bentham in 1787, it featured a circular tower pierced by windows that permitted the prison inspector to see into all the cells without being seen himself. Having no way of discerning when or if they were actually being watched, the prisoners would assume that they were and would conduct themselves accordingly. For Michel Foucault, panopticism was a coercive "political technology," inducing in the subject "a state of conscious and permanent visibility that assures the automatic functioning of power" (Foucault 1978, 201, 207; Whitaker 1999, 32–3).

While empirical evidence on police surveillance practices after September 11 remains limited, there are growing concerns that the new definition of terrorist activity, combined with the loosening of rules by which federal officers may intercept private communications, may be moving Canada closer to a panoptic state in which certain communities, including Muslim Canadians, are targeted for enhanced surveillance (Young 2003, 6). As Cockfield (2003, 338) suggests, "pervasive and unseen scrutiny by state agents could inhibit freedom of expression, as individuals fear that the police *could* monitor their speech and actions." Another commentator adds that "diluted judicial oversight in the context of cybercrime investigations expands law enforcement and third party discretion to discriminate and could lead to the *de facto* offences of, for example, 'surfing while Muslim,' or belonging to any negatively-stereotyped group in cyberspace" (Young 2003, 2–3). Even Reid Morden (2002, 7), a former CSIS director, has expressed concerns about the new police powers. Arguably, the chill that immigrant and refugee communities have already experienced as a result of the application of security measures under the former Immigration Act is likely to be further reinforced with the threat of penal sanctions. Surveillance practices and the threat of surveillance will disproportionately affect certain communities, including Canadian Arabs and Muslims. Indeed, by 2003 representatives of the Canadian Muslim Lawyer's Association and the Canadian Arab Federation were reporting a widespread reluctance to participate in community and youth groups for fear that the authorities would learn of their involvement and perceive it as a reason to interrogate them or worse.

Racial profiling has profound consequences for individuals, communities, and society. In the words of one criminologist, "to argue that racial profiling is harmless, that it only hurts those who break the law, is to totally ignore the psychological and social damage that can result from always being considered one of the 'usual suspects'" (Wortley 1997).[10] Research psychologists have found that "victim effects" of racial profiling include post-traumatic stress disorder and other forms of stress-related disorders as well as failure to use available community resources. Racial profiling promotes a two-tiered sense of citizenship in which many individuals do not feel like equal members of society. Exclusion and alienation readily produce diminished levels of civic participation and mistrust of institutions

(OHRC 2003, 53). Ultimately, society pays the price for racial profiling as the social consensus necessary for both security and the preservation of rights is undermined.

CONCLUSION

In the international arena, Canada has often asserted that the fight against terrorism must be consistent with broader commitments to human rights and the rule of law. The institutions entrusted to fight terrorism would attract public support by respecting those principles (Fowler 1999). Nevertheless, an assessment of developments in immigration and refugee law, border security policies, and racial profiling practices indicates that Canada's current record falls far below its expressed commitments. Since the early 1990s the increasingly intertwined objectives of counter-terrorism and bilateral cooperation have supported a web of incremental legal and policy measures that have led to a significant erosion of immigrant and refugee rights. Business leaders have failed so far to persuade either Washington or Ottawa to pursue a North American perimeter strategy to eliminate the border-induced costs associated with bilateral trade. However, Canadian policy makers have appeared willing to join the United States in a race to the bottom on the human rights dimension of immigration and border issues.

The Uruguayan writer Eduardo Galeano once observed that no system falls without being pushed. He suggested that the decisive blows of change are dealt "in a thousand and one ways" through the denunciation of what is occurring, finding out what happened, and encouraging what will happen "when these evil winds change" (Galeano 1992, 147). In Canada, one positive outcome of the tragic events of September 11 has been the organization and mobilization of a diverse range of public interest groups dedicated to monitoring and resisting the onslaught of regressive laws, policies, and practices. Well before September 11 national advocacy groups like the Canadian Council for Refugees, the Canadian Bar Association, and Amnesty International played an important role in providing an informed critique of national security policies and in lobbying for change. The political climate of the past three years, however, has served as a catalyst for the formation of new civil society organizations. A Toronto-based coalition, Project Threadbare, formed in response to "Operation Thread," organizing community meetings, supporting the detainees' legal defence, and producing a documentary film. The International Civil Liberties Monitoring Group (ICLMG) coalesced around opposition to the government's anti-terrorism agenda. An exceptionally broad based coalition made up of development NGOs, faith organizations, unions, environmental advocates, and civil rights advocates as well as groups representing immigrant and refugee communities in Canada, the ICLMG has prepared two comprehensive reports and issued a series of press releases in efforts to educate the public on the negative impacts of post-September 11 anti-terrorism measures (ICLMG 2004).

Existing, smaller groups from particular ethno-racial communities have developed websites and media savvy, appeared before parliamentary committees, and gained both strength and broader constituencies. Members of the Canadian Arab Federation (CAF), for example, have prepared action alerts to facilitate grassroots organizing, implemented a sophisticated national media and communications strategy, and launched a legal defence fund to protect the civil rights of Arab Canadians. In its annual report for 2003, CAF president Raja Khouri reported that the organization's membership had increased by more than 60 percent and that "the silver lining to these difficult times" was that "our communities have come together like never before. We have organized like we never thought we could. We have reached out to Canadians like we never thought we would. Our response to September 11th has become a response to our chronic fragmentation, and has created a will for developing a space and a voice for Canadian Arabs that we never thought we could achieve" (CAF 2003, 1). Faculty and students in universities across the country have organized teach-ins and conferences, frequently drawing in members of the broader public. Particularly significant has been the inclusion of immigrant and refugee interests in advocacy agendas that had frequently overlooked these issues in the past. The Council of Canadians, for example, has submitted a brief to the Arar Inquiry and has included a special focus on immigration and refugee issues in its current campaign against deep integration. Homes Not Bombs, an Ontario-wide direct action group, has launched a "Stop Secret Trials in Canada" campaign and is supporting the efforts of activists in Québec to protest the detention and proposed deportation of Montreal resident Adil Charkaoui on a security certificate.

In terms of legal advocacy, community groups have conducted consultations to plan litigation strategies that will overturn at least some of the new anti-terrorism laws. Maher Arar has launched a suit against the Canadian government for its role in his deportation to Syria while test case litigation is proceeding in the form of some thirty suits launched by refugees and other non-citizens who have had their applications for permanent residence delayed or denied on security grounds. In addition to challenging the security related provisions of IRPA as an infringement of equality and associational rights, the lawsuits are seeking general and punitive damages against the federal government for the psychological damage and economic hardship the plaintiffs have suffered after spending years in limbo. While the federal government has yet to repeal any of its new laws or policies in response to any of these initiatives, the Canadian public has become better informed and the necessary groundwork for change is in progress.

Managing security is a complex task. In acknowledging that reality, this chapter has not attempted to design a blueprint which resolves all the concomitant dilemmas. Thoughtful essays by a range of journalists and scholars as well as the recent findings of the September 11 Commission in the United States have underscored the need for better coordination and information sharing among domestic intelligence agencies in order to more effectively protect against and prepare for future terrorist attacks. More fundamentally, we must all accept that genuine, global security will not be attained in the short or even the medium term. For the present and in the Canadian context, it remains to be seen whether the limited government restructuring (which left the security agencies themselves intact) has actually addressed existing deficits or whether the creation of the public security portfolio amounts to little more than window dressing, leaving in place entrenched problems. There should be little doubt, however, that the impact of the complex web of new laws and policies adopted in the aftermath of 11 September 2001 has been far reaching. In this regard, the parliamentary review of the Anti-Terrorism Act, which is slated to produce a report in the fall of 2006, may provide an important opportunity for some sober second thoughts. In the meantime, it is hoped that civil society groups will continue their efforts to monitor and denounce security related abuses and promote a vision of a Canada in which a two-tiered citizenship is not tolerated, a Canada that refuses to succumb to siren calls for deeper integration or to compromise on its principled differences.

NOTES

I am grateful to Janet Dench, Don Galloway, Kent Roach, and Don Stuart for helpful comments and suggestions on a draft of this chapter. A version with extensive notes and referencing is available from the author.

1 According to an Ipsos-Reid poll released in March 2004, when told that "the Federal Government wishes to repair the relationship between Canada and the US that has been hurt by differences of opinion on measures to deal with terrorism and the War in Iraq," a vast majority of Canadians (91 percent) believed that Canada should maintain the ability to set its own independent standards and regulations, even if this might reduce cross-border trade opportunities with the United States (Ipsos-Reid 2004).
2 In *Suresh v. Canada* (SCC 2002) the Supreme Court of Canada found that the Immigration Act's failure to define any of these terms was not unconstitutional.
3 Later in the same year, the newly elected Liberal government transferred the immigration department to Citizenship and Immigration Canada.

4 Refugee acceptance rates had already declined dramatically from a high of 89 percent in 1989 to less than 50 percent in 2001.

5 However, in *Suresh v. Canada* the Canadian Supreme Court ruled that "exceptional circumstances" could justify deporting a non-citizen to torture (SCC 2002, 78).

6 By early 2006, one of the six detainees had been deported (Ernst Zundel) while Adil Charkaoui, a permanent resident from Morocco, had secured temporary release on stringent conditions. The Supreme Court will rule on the constitutionality of security certificate procedures in three cases: *Almrei v. Canada* (Court File No. 30929), *Charkaoui v. Canada* (Court File No. 30762), and *Harkat v. Canada* (Court File No. 31178).

7 In testimony before a parliamentary committee in 2002, Judith Kumin, former representative of the United Nations high commissioner for refugees in Canada, cited the example of Germany. When refugee claims became illegal at German land borders after adoption of a safe third country rule in 1993, the claims received at land borders dropped from 100,000 annually to zero almost overnight. Since then, the overall numbers have shot back up to previous levels, with all claims being pursued inland. See also Harvard (2006).

8 As a result of the Arar incident, the federal government established a protocol with the United States stipulating that Canada "would be notified and consulted before a Canadian is deported to a third country" (Chossudovsky 2004). Information sharing between the two countries appears to have been what led to Arar's detention in the United States in the first place (ibid.). In February 2004, a public inquiry led by Justice Dennis R. O'Connor was convened to investigate and report on the actions of Canadian officials in relation to the Arar affair and to conduct a broader policy review. The O'Connor Commission received testimony from eighty-five witnesses in both open and closed sessions (Arar Commission 2005a). The US government, however, declined to directly cooperate with the commission – either through the production of documents or witness testimony (Arar Commission 2004). A fact finder appointed by the commission confirmed that the treatment Maher Arar received at the hands of Syrian security personnel "constituted torture as understood in international law" (Arar Commission 2005b). Justice O'Connor's reports are expected to be released by late summer 2006.

9 After this chapter was completed, and in the wake of concerted advocacy by civil society groups, the requirement for two ministerial signatures was reinstated in 2005.

10 Wortley (2002) as quoted in OHRC (2003, 17).

REFERENCES

Abbate, Gay, and Colin Freeze. 2003. Ottawa Plans to Deport Terror Suspect Soon. *Globe and Mail*, 25 November, A4.

AI. 1998. Amnesty International Index, ASA 37/19/1998; ASA 37/21/98, Amnesty International.

Aiken, Sharryn J. 2001a. Manufacturing "Terrorists": Refugees, National Security and Canadian Law, Part 2. *Refuge* 19 (4): 116–33.

– 2001b. Of Gods and Monsters: National Security and Canadian Refugee Policy. *Revue Québécoise de Droit International* 14 (2): 1–51.

Akram, Susan, and Kevin Johnson. 2004. Race and Civil Rights Pre-September 11: The Targeting of Arabs and Muslims. *International Socialist Review* 36: 22–3.

Arar Commission. 2004. US Declines to Directly Cooperate with Arar Commission of Inquiry. Press release. 21 September. Ottawa: Commission of Inquiry into the Actions of Canadian Officials in Relation to Maher Arar.

– 2005a. The Arar Commission Has Completed 127 Days of Testimony and Made Public Thousands of Formerly Secret Government Documents Relating to the Arar Affair. Press release. 14 September. Ottawa: Commission of Inquiry into the Actions of Canadian Officials in Relation to Maher Arar.

– 2005b. Commissioner Dennis O'Connor Releases the Fact Finder's Report on Maher Arar's Treatment in Jordan and Syria. Press release. 27 October. Ottawa: Commission of Inquiry into the Actions of Canadian Officials in Relation to Maher Arar.

Bahdi, Reem. 2003. No Exit: Racial Profiling and Canada's War against Terrorism. *Osgoode Hall Law Journal* 41 (2/3): 293–317.

CAF. 2003. *Annual Activity Report, April 2002–March 2003.* Toronto: Canadian Arab Federation.

Canada. 2001. *Canada and the United States Sign a Smart Border Declaration.* Ottawa: Department of Foreign Affairs and International Trade.

CBC. 2003. *Almrei Can Stay in Canada during Review.* CBC News Online. Available at <http://www.cbc.ca/story/canada/national/2003/11/27/almrei.html>, cited 28 November 2003.

CCCE. 2003. *Security and Prosperity: Toward a New Canada-United States Partnership in North America.* Ottawa: Canadian Council of Chief Executives.

CCR. 1998. *Interdicting Refugees.* Montreal: Canadian Council for Refugees.

– 2001a. Bill C-11 Brief: Canadian Council for Refugees.

– 2001b. *Refugees and Security.* Montreal: Canadian Council for Refugees.

– 2004a. *Anti-Terrorism and the Security Agenda: Impacts on Rights, Freedoms and Democracy.* Forum of the International Civil Liberties Monitoring Group. Montreal: Canadian Council for Refugees.

– 2004b. *Key Issues: Immigration and Refugee Protection.* Montreal: Canadian Council for Refugees.

Chossudovsky, Michel. 2004. Canada's New "Homeland Department" of Public Safety and Emergency Preparedness (PSEP) Complicit in Deportation of Maher Arar. *GlobalResearch.ca.* Available at <www.globalresearch.ca/ articles/ CHO401D.html>.

Choudhry, Sujit. 2001. Protecting Equality in the Face of Terror: Ethnic and Racial

Profiling and s. 15 of the Charter. In *The Security of Freedom*, ed. R. Daniels, P. Macklem, and K. Roach, 163–78. Toronto: University of Toronto Press.

CIC. 2001a. Canada-United States Issue Statement on Common Security Issues, *Citizenship and Immigration Canada*. News release. 3 December.

– 2001b. Strengthened Immigration Measures to Counter Terrorism. *Citizenship and Immigration Canada*, News Release. 12 October.

– 2001c. Visitor Visas. *Citizenship and Immigration Canada*. News release. 4 December.

– 2002. *Government Response to the Report of the Standing Committee on Citizenship and Immigration, "Hands across the Border: Working Together at our Shared Border and Abroad to Ensure Safety, Security and Efficiency."* Ottawa: Citizenship and Immigration, Canada.

CIMM. 2006. Presentation by Hon. Monte Solberg, Minister of Citizenship and Immigration. Evidence, 39th Parliament, 1st Session, No. 3, House of Commons Standing Committee on Citizenship and Immigration, 10 May, 1530.

Clark, Campbell. 2001. Canada in Talks with US on Pact Dealing with Refugees, Visitor Visas. *Globe and Mail*, 26 October, A6.

Cockfield, Arthur. 2003. The State of Privacy Laws and Privacy Encroaching Technologies after September 11: A Two Year Report Card on the Canadian Government. *University of Ottawa Law and Technology Journal* 1: 325–44.

Dauvergne, Catherine. 2003. Evaluating Canada's New Immigration and Refugee Protection Act in Its Global Context. *Alberta Law Review* 41: 725–44.

Davies, Sharon L. 2003. Profiling Terror. *Ohio State Journal of Criminal Law* 1: 45–101.

Dench, Janet. 2004. Detention Statistics. Ottawa: E-mail communication to the Canadian Council for Refugees distribution list (CCRLIST), 23 March.

Dosman, E. Alexandra. 2004. For the Record: Designating "Listed Entities" for the Purposes of Terrorist Financing Offences at Canadian Law. *University of Toronto Faculty of Law Review* 62 (2): 1.

Drache, Daniel. 2004. *Borders Matter: Homeland Security, Borders and the Search for North America*. Halifax: Fernwood Publishing.

Foucault, Michel. 1978. *Discipline and Punish: The Birth of the Prison*. Trans. A. Sheridan. New York: Pantheon.

Fowler, Robert R. 1999. United Nations Security Council. Press release. In *SC/6741*, 19 October.

Galeano, Eduardo. 1992. *We Say No*. Trans. M. Fried. New York: W.W. Norton and Company.

Grant, George. 1965. *Lament for a Nation: The Defeat of Canadian Nationalism*. Toronto: McClelland and Stewart.

Greenspon, Ed. 2001. Seizing the Day on Canada-US Border Flows. *Globe and Mail*, 13 November, A21.

Grewal, San. 2001. Prejudice, Yes, but Fear? *Toronto Star*, 17 September, B2.

Harper, Tim. 2001. Chrétien Pledges Battle over Global Terror Threat. *Toronto Star*, 18 September, A1.

Harvard. 2006. *Bordering on Failure: The US-Canada Safe Third Country Agreement Fifteen Months after Implementation.* Cambridge, MA: Harvard Law School. Available at <http://www.law.harvard.edu/academics/clinical/ asylum_law/Harvard_STCA _Report.pdf>.

IACHR. 2000. *Report on the Situation of Human Rights of Asylum Seekers within the Canadian Refugee Determination System*, OEA/Ser.L./V/II.106/ Doc.40 rev., paras. 143–57, Inter-American Commission on Human Rights, Washington, DC.

ICLMG. 2004. *Anti-Terrorism and the Security Agenda: Impacts on Rights, Freedoms and Democracy.* Ottawa: International Civil Liberties Monitoring Group.

Ipsos-Reid. 2004. *Canadians' Views on Future Canada-US Relations: Canadians Support Policy Independence from US.* Toronto: Ipsos-Reid.

James, Royson. 1998. Black Passengers Targeted in Pearson Searches? *Toronto Star*, 29 November, A1.

Jimenez, Marina, Colin Freeze, and Victoria Burnett. 2003. Case of 19 Terrorists Unraveling. *Globe and Mail*, 30 August, A5.

Justice Canada. 2002a. *Annual Report Concerning Investigative Hearings and Recognizance with Conditions.* Ottawa: Department of Justice Canada.

– 2002b. *Lawful Access: Consultation Document.* Ottawa: Department of Justice Canada.

Khan, Sami. 2004. Shattering the Fantasy of Multiculturalism: "Project Thread" and Canada's Secret War on Immigrants. *Samar* 17 (Summer). Online article available at <www.samarmagazine.org>.

Labott, Elise. 2002. Canada Issues US Travel Warning. 30 October. *CNN.com*. Available at <http://archives.cnn.com/2002/TRAVEL/10/30/canada.us.travel/>.

Laxer, James. 2003. *The Border.* Toronto: Doubleday Canada.

Leddy, Mary Jo. 1997. *At the Border Called Hope.* New York: Harper Collins.

Levitt, Geoffrey. 1986. Is "Terrorism" Worth Defining? *Ohio Northern University Law Review* 17: 97.

McCarthy, Shawn. 2001. Sweeping Curbs on Freedom in Antiterrorism Legislation Likely to Go to Top Court. *Globe and Mail*, 16 October, A5.

Morden, Reid. 2002. Domestic Security: Finding the Balance. Paper read at a Symposium jointly sponsored by the Robarts Centre for Canadian Studies and the Centre for Public Law and Public Policy, 17 June, York University, Toronto.

OHRC. 2003. Paying the Price: The Human Cost of Racial Profiling, Inquiry Report. Toronto: Ontario Human Rights Commission.

OLA. 2001. Debates: P. Kormos on "Ethnic Profiling," Legislative Assembly of Ontario, 3 October, Toronto.

OSFI. 2004. *Consolidated List of Names Subject to the Regulations Establishing a List of Entities Made under Subsection 83.05(1) of the Criminal Code or the United Nations Suppression of Terrorism Regulations: Part A – Individuals.* Ottawa: Office of the Superintendent of Financial Institutions.

Privy Council Office. 2004. *Securing an Open Society: Canada's National Security Policy.* Ottawa: Government of Canada.

PSEP. 2002. *Frequently Asked Questions.* Ottawa: Public Safety and Emergency Preparedness Canada.

Richmond, Anthony. 2001. Refugees and Racism in Canada. *Refuge* 19 (6): 12–20.

Roach, Kent. 2003. *September 11: Consequences for Canada.* Montreal and Kingston: McGill-Queen's University Press.

Sallot, Jeff. 2001a. Canadian Connection Suspected in Hijackings. *Globe and Mail,* 13 September, A1, A13.

– 2001b. PM "Shamed" by Hate Crimes against Muslims in Canada. *Globe and Mail,* 22 September, A9.

SCC. 2002. *Suresh v. Canada* (Minister of Citizenship and Immigration), SCC 1. Ottawa: Supreme Court of Canada.

SCFAIT. 2002. *Partners in North America: Advancing Canada's Relations with the United States and Mexico.* Ottawa: Standing Committee on Foreign Affairs and International Trade, House of Commons, Canada.

Shepard, Michelle, and Sonia Verma. 2003. They Only Arrested the Muhammads. *Toronto Star,* 30 November, A6.

Simmons, Alan. 1998. Racism and Immigration Policy. In *Racism and Social Inequality in Canada: Concepts, Controversies and Strategies of Resistance,* ed. V. Satzewich, 87–114. Toronto: Thompson Educational Publishing.

Simon, Rita. 2004. Immigration and Crime across Seven Nations. Paper read at IZA Annual Migration Meeting, 25 June, Bonn, Germany.

SIRC. 2000. *SIRC Report 1999–2000.* Ottawa: Security Intelligence Review Committee.

– 2003. *SIRC Report 2002–2003.* Ottawa: Security Intelligence Review Committee.

Smith, Charles. 2003. Borders and Exclusions: Racial Profiling and Canada's Immigration, Refugee and Security Laws. Paper read at Court Challenges Program AGM, 25 October, Winnipeg, Manitoba.

Stuart, Donald. 2002. The Anti-Terrorism Bill (Bill C-36): An Unnecessary Law and Order Quick Fix that Permanently Stains the Canadian Criminal Justice System. In *Terrorism, Law and Democracy: How Is Canada Changing Following September 11?* ed. D. Daubney, 175–191. Montréal: Éditions Thémis.

Tanovich, David M. 2002. Using the Charter to Stop Racial Profiling: The Development of an Equality Based Conception of Arbitrary Detention. *Osgoode Hall Law Journal* 40: 145–87.

Thomas, Derrick. 1993. *The Foreign Born in the Federal Prison Population.* Ottawa: Strategic Planning and Research, Employment and Immigration.

Thompson, Allan. 1996. How a Spy Is Hired, Case of Tamil Refugee Claimant Shines Light on How CSIS Operates. *Toronto Star,* 20 January, A2.

– 1998a. Not Our Policy to Coerce Refugees. *Toronto Star,* 1 May, A7.

– 1998b. Spy Agency Tactic under Fire. *Toronto Star,* 4 April, A2.

– 2001. Is Canada Really the Weak Link? *Toronto Star,* 6 October, A1.

Thompson, Allan and MacCharles, Tonda. 1998. Watchdog Slams Spy Agency for Recruiting Refuge Seekers. *Toronto Star,* 29 October, A1.

Toronto Star. 2001a. Immigration Act to Face Tough Review: Senator Jerry Grafstein. *Toronto Star*, 14 September, A23.

– 2001b. Indian Immigrant Shot Dead at US Gas Station. *Toronto Star*, 17 September.

US Library of Congress. 2003. Nations Hospitable to Organized Crime and Terrorism, Report prepared by the Federal Research Division, Library of Congress, Washington, DC.

UNHCR. 1999. Detention of Asylum Seekers and Refugees: The Framework, the Problem and Recommended Practice. Paper read at UNHCR Executive Committee, 15th Meeting, EC/49/SC/CRP.13, 4 June, Geneva.

– 2001. Comments on Bill C-11, Submission to the House of Commons, Standing Committee on Citizenship and Immigration. Canada: United Nations High Commissioner for Refugees.

Verma, Sonia. 2004. Our Dreams Are Now Dust. *Toronto Star*, 8 February, A8.

Whitaker, Reg. 1999. *The End of Privacy: How Total Surveillance Is Becoming a Reality*. New York: The New Press.

– 2004. Jean Chrétien's Surprise: A Canadian Nationalist Legacy. *Canada Watch* 3/4: 10–11.

Woods, Allan. 2004. Liberalism Makes Canada Soft on Terror. *National Post*, 16 February, A1, A7.

Wortley, Scot. 1996. Justice for All? Race and Perceptions of Bias in the Ontario Criminal Justice System – A Toronto Survey. *Canadian Journal of Criminology* 38 (4): 439–467.

– 2002. *Racial Differences in Customs Searches at Pearson International Airport: Results from a Pilot Survey*. Report prepared for the African Canadian Legal Clinic, Toronto.

Wortley, Scot, and Julian Tanner. 2004. Data, Denials and Confusion: The Racial Profiling Debate in Toronto. *Canadian Journal of Criminology and Criminal Justice* 45 (3): 367–89.

Young, Jason. 2003. Surfing While Muslim: Privacy, Freedom of Speech and the Unintended Consequences of Cybercrime Legislation. Paper read at University of Waterloo's Centre for Applied Cryptographic Research Privacy and Security Workshop "Privacy: The Next Wave," 6–7 November, University of Toronto, Toronto.

PART THREE

Free Trade:
Economic and Labour Impacts

8

From Leaps of Faith to Hard Landings: Fifteen Years of "Free Trade"

ANDREW JACKSON

This chapter evaluates the impacts of increased economic integration with the United States in the wake of the Canada-US Free Trade Agreement (CUFTA) and the North American Free Trade Agreement (NAFTA) and against the backdrop of the "great free trade debate" of the late 1980s. The first part briefly summarizes the key issues raised in the debate, when proponents claimed that the CUFTA would boost long-term economic growth with minimal impacts on the Canadian social model, while critics expressed concerns about the loss of needed economic policy levers and the dangers of "downward harmonization" to the US social model. The second part considers the economic record of the past fifteen years and argues that the promises of a significant boost to productivity growth and positive restructuring of Canadian industry have been largely unrealized. The Canadian economy has changed, but long-standing structural problems such as excessive resource dependency and the underdevelopment of a sophisticated "knowledge-based" economy remain very much with us. The final part looks at the impacts of closer economic integration on wages, income distribution, and social programs, and argues that fears of "downward harmonization" were amply justified. The chapter does not address the impacts on Canada of the addition of Mexico to the original CUFTA but, rather, concentrates on the much more important impacts of Canada-US integration. For reasons of space, little is said about pressures for policy convergence outside of economic and social policy, though environmental and cultural policies are clearly important. In many ways, NAFTA has worked to perpetuate an environmentally unsustainable development path.

It is worth underscoring at the outset that Canada-US economic integration was already well advanced before CUFTA and that it has not been the only factor shaping Canadian economic and social performance over the past decade and a half. As argued in the successive Alternative Federal Budgets of the Canadian Centre for Policy Alternatives (CCPA), restrictive fiscal and monetary policies were the major factor behind Canada's dismal record from the late 1980s to the latter part of the 1990s. And, as argued by Stephen Clarkson (2002), the "new constitution" of trade deals has interacted in complex ways with other elements of the neoconservative agenda, which have a life of their own. While it is true that economic integration has given the right a stronger political hand, the left falls into a trap if it believes that politics has been made irrelevant by trade deals. Our history under "free trade" could have been different, and this chapter attempts to separate out what can be reasonably attributed to deepening economic integration as opposed to other factors. Moreover, a critical assessment of CUFTA should not be read as a call to return to the status quo ante. The real challenge is to construct an alternative policy agenda for a profoundly changed Canada.

THE GREAT FREE TRADE DEBATE

In line with the neoclassical argument for gains from trade based upon comparative advantage and increased competition, proponents of bilateral free trade forecast a boost to long-term economic performance. The central case for further reduction of tariff and regulatory barriers to trade and investment in the mid to late 1980s was that it would help close the long-standing productivity gap between Canadian and US manufacturing. Tariff elimination was expected to lead to gains from increased specialization and economies of scale, as manufacturing production shifted from short, diversified product runs for national markets to longer runs of more specialized products for continental markets. The official forecast of the Department of Finance was that there would be a long-term increase to real GDP of about 3 percent, a modest one-time boost reflecting the rather low level of remaining "barriers" to trade with our neighbour to the south (Finance Canada 1988). There was also expected to be a boost to long-term productivity growth arising from greater exposure to a more dynamic US economy. This was the famous "leap of faith" of the Macdonald Commission (Macdonald Report 1985). Labour adjustment was seen as a small, manageable problem because it was assumed that there would be a small net job gain as both capital and labour flowed from shrinking to expanding sectors and firms. CUFTA was also advocated for purely defensive reasons ("protection from US protectionism") and because it complemented and "locked in" the key policy reforms of the mid to late 1980s: privatization, deregulation, and dismantlement of Trudeau-era cultural and economic nationalism. With respect to distributive issues, the explicit assumption was that the gains from trade would be shared with workers in the form of higher wages in better jobs and that higher growth would support and sustain social programs.

For their part, left critics of free trade argued that CUFTA deprived Canada of the interventionist economic policy tools needed to deal with excessive resource dependency and an underdeveloped manufacturing sector (Cameron 1988; CLC 1987). Both sides of the debate accepted that Canadian manufacturing was less efficient and less innovative than was US manufacturing. Proponents said that the free market would help solve the problem, while critics argued that Canada needed to use policy tools that were undercut by the trade deals (foreign investment review, use of government procurement, resource processing requirements, etc.). The Canadian Labour Congress (CLC 1987) argued that CUFTA risked "freezing the status quo" of excessive resource dependency and a weak capital goods sector. The difference was not so much over whether trade with the United States was good or bad as over how much policy space was needed to "shape comparative advantage" in the interests of Canadian workers and communities. Critics also argued that greater liberalization of trade and investment would increase the bargaining power of mobile capital compared to workers and governments, and that threats to move investment, production, and jobs to the United States would work towards "downward harmonization" of wages (in relation to productivity) and of social standards (which add to business costs). Free trade was seen not only as a threat to the more progressive Canadian social model of stronger unions, higher levels of income protection, and broader access to public and social services but also to our environment and culture. It was also feared that adjustment costs in terms of lost jobs would be much greater than forecast. Underpinning the debate were very different assumptions about the relationship between economic space and policy space. The fundamental fear of CUFTA opponents was that greater economic integration would undermine, if not ultimately destroy, the capacity of Canadians to maintain a distinctive society.

Structural Economic Change

Canada-US economic integration in terms of two-way trade flows proceeded extremely rapidly in the wake of CUFTA – far faster than anyone envisaged. Exports rose from 25.7 percent of (nominal) GDP in 1989 to 45.5 percent in 2000, while imports rose from 25.7 percent in 1989 to 40.3 percent in 2000. (Except as otherwise indicated, statistical calculated data are from the Canadian Economic Observer Historical Statistical Supplement.) Trade has since fallen back as a share of GDP. The extremely rapid growth of Canadian exports, entirely accounted for by trade with the United States, was not, however, mainly due to CUFTA but, rather, to the strong growth of the US domestic market, a rising US trade deficit with all countries, and the significant depreciation of the Canadian dollar after

1992. Industry Canada estimates that 90 percent of export growth is explained by non-NAFTA factors (Acharya, Sharma, and Rao 2001). It is notable that the US share of Canadian merchandise exports (85 percent in 2001 compared to 73 percent in 1989) has risen much more rapidly than has the US share of Canadian imports (73 percent in 2001 compared to 70 percent in 1989).

The resource and auto sectors were already very heavily export-oriented before CUFTA, and most manufacturing industries have now also become strongly oriented towards the North American rather than towards the domestic market. Supply chains in manufacturing have become more deeply integrated on a continental basis, as is shown by the fact that the share of imported inputs in goods production has risen from 29 percent in 1990 to 37 percent in 1997 (Acharya, Sharma, and Rao 2001, 33). While two-way trade flows of intermediate goods have increased in most manufacturing subsectors, the metaphor of a single production chain spanning both sides of the border is most true of two major industries – auto and "high-tech" electrical machinery and equipment – which have very tightly integrated North American production chains.

While tariff changes played only a modest role in deepened trade and investment links, CUFTA cemented the *strategic* integration of most large Canadian manufacturers to a North American economic space. In 1988 exports were a bit over one-third of manufacturing output, and imports served just one-third of the Canadian market for manufactured goods (Dion 2000, table 1). The great majority of large Canadian and transnational corporations with major operations in Canada are now strongly oriented towards the North American market rather than towards the domestic Canadian market. The United States is now a larger market for Canadian manufacturers than is Canada (exports account for about 53 percent of manufacturing production), and almost one-half of the Canadian market for manufactured goods is now met from imports.

CUFTA and NAFTA have had some impact on direct investment flows as transnational corporations have restructured production chains and invested across the border. The level of US foreign direct investment (FDI) in Canada climbed from 12 percent to 20 percent of Canadian GDP between 1989 and 2001, but it fell from 70 percent to 65 percent as a share of the total stock of FDI in Canada (O'Neill 2002). FDI flowing into Canada can come in the form of new "real" investments or in the form of takeovers. The latter seem to have predominated, and the relative failure of Canada to attract large new "greenfield" investment by US and non-US transnationals serving the North American market has been a source of disappointment to proponents who had expected inward investment to increase (McCallum 2000). Large foreign-owned plants tend to be the most productive and technologically advanced, but the ratio of new entries to exits has changed for the worse in the post-CUFTA era (Baldwin and Gu 2003). On the other side of the ledger, the stock of Canadian FDI in the United States has risen from 10 percent to 18 percent of Canadian GDP between 1989 and 2001, and it is less likely than is inward investment to be financed from retained earnings. Canadian corporations have made major investments in US financial services and, to a lesser extent, in manufacturing (e.g., Nortel, Magna, and Bombardier). Changes in FDI flows and stocks between Canada and the United States have been roughly balanced, though there has probably been more real Canadian investment in the United States than real US investment in Canada. These flows probably help explain why real investment in industrial machinery and equipment was much weaker in Canada than in the United States through most of the 1990s.

Despite the reality of close economic integration with the United States in terms of trade and direct investment, its extent can be exaggerated. First, Canadian capitalism has "globalized" to an astonishing extent outside North America. Between 1990 and 2001, despite roughly balanced FDI flows with the United States, the ratio of Canadian FDI abroad to FDI in Canada jumped from 0.75 to 1.2. The US share of very rapidly rising Canadian FDI abroad has fallen from a high of 70 percent in the mid-1980s to about half today (O'Neill 2002). Second, the growth of Canadian exports to the United States, while significant, is highly overstated if not adjusted for growing imports of intermediate goods. In 1997 exports represented 40.2 percent of GDP, but net exports (exports minus imported inputs) were a significantly smaller though still substantial 27.7 percent of GDP. Third, Helliwell (2002) has detailed a very strong "border effect" on Canada-US trade. The Canada-US border is still at least 10,000 miles wide in terms of its impact on goods trade flows thought of as a function of distance alone. National networks and tastes continue to favour domestic production despite advanced "comparative advantage" specialization. Finally, CUFTA and NAFTA do not extend to many services. Domestic regulation remains important in many services industries (finance, communications, culture, social services); services trade remains small relative to the size of the domestic market; and the US share of Canadian services trade (58 percent of exports and 63 percent of imports) is surprisingly low. In sum, it is an exaggeration to speak of a single North American economy. What we have instead is a Canadian economy that is tightly integrated with its southern neighbour in some industries (e.g., auto, energy, high tech) but that also has strong investment links with the rest of the world and a domestic services economy that remains national in many respects, despite high levels of foreign ownership.

As noted, CUFTA was expected to boost weak manufacturing productivity and help close the long-standing Canada-US productivity gap. Given that increased trade was much greater than anticipated, the productivity gains should have been substantially greater as well, but this has not been the case. Analysis suggests that there were, indeed, small average productivity gains in previously heavily protected sectors attributable to the tariff changes (Trefler 1999). While widely seen as proof of the success of free trade, this is misleading. Average sector productivity rose in tariff protected sectors as weak firms went out of business and the survivors shed workers. The productivity change due to tariff changes was the result of the increased failure of uncompetitive plants rather than the increased economies of scale expected by CUFTA proponents (Gu, Swachuk, and Whewell 2003). Huge layoffs in 1989–91, amounting to more than one in five manufacturing workers, were probably driven more by the high dollar than by CUFTA itself, but they were relatively concentrated in the previously most protected sectors. These huge adjustment costs for workers and communities were far greater than either proponents or critics had imagined, and there was little in the way of compensation for the "losers."

The jobs lost between 1989 and 1991 were, over time, more than offset by gains in the firms and sectors that survived restructuring and began to grow as the dollar started depreciating in 1992. The extent of total restructuring in manufacturing is underlined by the fact that 47 percent of all the plants in existence in 1988 (accounting for 28 percent of all jobs) had closed by 1997, while 39 percent of all plants in 1997 (accounting for 21 percent of all jobs) did not exist in 1988 (Baldwin and Gu 2003). Many of the new plants were, however, small and not highly productive. Depreciation of the dollar gave a major boost to Canadian goods exporters and set the stage for a major recovery in manufacturing output and employment. This has been good news for Canadian workers and the Canadian economy. However, closer North American integration has done nothing to close the long-standing Canada-US productivity gap in manufacturing, making CUFTA pretty much a bust in terms of its key goal of improving the relative long-term efficiency of Canadian manufacturing.

As shown in table 8.1, both output and employment in manufacturing grew rapidly in the economic recovery between 1992 and 2002. Real output rose by 47.6 percent (more than in the United States), and employment rose by 21.5 percent (compared to a job loss of 10 percent in the United States). However, manufacturing productivity growth between 1992 and 2002 was much lower than it was in the United States. Output per hour rose by just 17.9 percent over the decade compared to 51.9 percent south of the border. Between 1995 and 2002 labour productivity growth in Canadian manufacturing averaged just 0.7 percent per year compared to 4.2 percent in the United States.

Even though wage growth was even slower in Canada than in the United States, cost competitiveness would have deteriorated very seriously had not

Table 8.1   Productivity and competitiveness in manufacturing
Key comparisons in 2002 (1992 = 100)

	US	Canada
Output per Hour	151.9	117.9
Output	135.9	147.6
Employment	90.4	121.5
Real Hourly Compensation	112.3	103.3
Unit Labour Costs		
National Currency	92.8	104.6
$US	92.8	80.5
Average Annual Rate of Change, Output per Hour		
1990–95	3.3	3.8
1995–02	4.2	0.7
Nominal Hourly Labour Compensation		
1990–95	3.5	3.7
1995–02	3.9	2.2
Unit Labour Costs – National Currency		
1990–95	0.2	–0.1
1995–02	–0.3	1.5
Unit Labour Costs – $US		
1990–95	0.2	–3.3
1995–02	–0.3	–0.5

Source: US Bureau of Labor Statistics. Release USDL 03-469. September 9, 2003 (revisions to 2002 report).

the dollar depreciated. While the dollar fell slightly more than was necessary to preserve cost competitiveness, our healthy export position in the US market until 2003 was almost entirely due to the continuing fall of the dollar after 1992. This resulted in falling relative unit labour costs despite much slower productivity growth. This was great while it lasted, but constant dollar depreciation is hardly a formula for building a successful industrial economy.

Our poor relative productivity performance is due to the long-standing structural problems of the Canadian industry: too many small, undercapitalized plants; relatively low firm investment in machinery and equipment, research and development (R&D), and in training; over-dependence on resources and low value-added industrial materials; and an underdeveloped advanced capital goods sector. Canadian industries in the same sector are often just about as productive as are US industries, but our industrial structure is less heavily weighted towards those sectors that are highly productive. We are more productive in primary metals, the forest industry, and the auto industry, and we are very close to US productivity levels in food processing and furniture. The key problem is a much smaller and less productive advanced industrial sector. In 1997 the two major capital goods industries – electrical and electronic equipment (e.g., computers and telecommunications equipment) and industrial machinery and equipment (which includes aerospace) – accounted for 34.8 percent of US manufacturing production compared to just 13.5 percent in Canada (Nadeau and Rao 2002). Between 1989 and 1997 the production share of the capital goods sector in US manufacturing almost doubled (from 18.5 percent to 34.8 percent), far, far ahead of the modest increase in Canada from 11.9 percent to 13.5 percent. US productivity gains in the second half of the 1990s came from very rapid productivity gains in the high productivity information-based technology sectors. Our productivity performance was depressed by a much smaller capital equipment sector and by much slower productivity growth in that particular sector (Nadeau and Rao 2002). The fact that the manufacturing productivity gap is a product of industrial structure is shown by the fact that Canada has not done nearly as badly compared to its neighbour in terms of productivity growth in the business sector as a whole. Business sector labour productivity growth averaged 1.5 percent per year in Canada over the whole period, 1988–2001, just a little below the US rate of 1.9 percent, and the gap began to close after 1997 (Statistics Canada 2002).

Deeper integration of the manufacturing sector in the North American economy has done little to decisively shift the structure of our industrial economy away from natural resources and relatively unsophisticated manufacturing towards the more dynamic and faster growing "knowledge-based" industries. Machinery and equipment exports did grow somewhat more rapidly than total exports between 1990 and 2001, mainly because of the growth of the telecom and aerospace sectors. As a share of Canadian goods exports, machinery and equipment increased modestly from 19 percent in 1990 to 22 percent in 2001. Meanwhile, the export share of the large and highly productive auto sector (largely unaffected directly by CUFTA and NAFTA but totally integrated into the North American market) has remained unchanged at about 23 percent over this period. One big change has been the increased energy share of exports, up from 9 percent to 13 percent of the total since 1990, an increase which is driven mainly by a huge growth in natural gas exports and rising energy prices. This has hardly been a long-term gain for Canada given that conventional oil and natural gas resources are rapidly depleting. Resources, resource-based manufacturing, and crude industrial material production combined (i.e., agriculture and fish products, energy products, forest products, and basic industrial goods, including iron and steel and smelted minerals) still make up about 45 percent of all exports, down a little from 1990 but still a hugely important part of the economy.

Table 8.2   Structure of traded goods sectors of GDP: 1988 and 2001

	% Total Real GDP ($1997)	
	1988	2001
PRIMARY		
Agriculture, Fishing, Hunting, Forestry	2.7%	2.2%
Primary Oil and Gas	2.4%	2.4%
Mining (excluding Oil and Gas)	1.7%	1.5%
Total Primary	6.8%	6.1%
MANUFACTURING		
Total Manufacturing	17.5%	17.0%
Sub-sector (as % real manufacturing GDP)		
Resources/Industrial Goods and Materials:		
Wood and Paper	15.5%	13.0%
Petroleum and Coal	1.1%	1.1%
Primary Metals	7.1%	6.7%
Non-Metallic Mineral Products	3.6%	2.6%
Chemicals	9.0%	8.6%
(including Pharmaceuticals)	1.4%	1.9%
Sub-total: Resources/Industrial Goods and Materials	37.7%	33.9%
Food	10.8%	10.1%
Beverages and Tobacco	4.3%	3.1%
Textiles and Clothing	4.9%	3.0%
Furniture	2.4%	3.0%
Printing	4.4%	2.7%
Plastics and Rubber	3.9%	5.3%
(approximately one-third auto-related)		
Fabricated Metal Products	6.3%	6.9%
Motor Vehicles and Parts	9.0%	11.0%
Other Transport Equipment	4.5%	5.5%
(including Aerospace)	3.1%	4.1%
Capital Goods:		
Machinery	5.6%	6.0%
Computer and Electronic Products	3.6%	7.4%
Sub-total: Capital Goods	12.3%	17.5%
(Machinery, Information and Communications		
Technology, Aerospace)		
Miscellaneous	1.8%	1.3%

Source: Statistics Canada National Accounts Data provided by Informetrica Ltd.

As shown in table 8.2, production of resource-based commodities and basic industrial materials, such as wood and paper, minerals and primary metal products (but not including food), still account for over one-third of manufacturing sector value-added, while machinery production (machinery plus aerospace) accounts for just 17.5 percent. Despite increased trade, there have been only very modest shifts in the overall sectoral structure of the traded goods sector of GDP, with resources and resource-based manufacturing shrinking a bit and advanced industrial goods sectors expanding very modestly. Canada is unlikely to experience a shift to a more sophisticated industrial economy given the continuing low levels of investment in R&D, particularly by the private sector. Despite a modest increase in the 1990s, private-sector financing of R&D amounts to 0.83 percent of GDP, less than half the US rate of 1.88 percent (CBOC 2002). Moreover, a huge share of private-sector R&D is undertaken by just a handful of companies, such as Nortel and Bombardier. Reflecting resource dependency, the Canadian dollar is still mainly driven by the trend in commodity prices.

Despite the collapse of the high-tech bubble of the 1990s, the capital goods sector remains hugely important to the long-term economic future of advanced industrial countries given the ongoing shift of consumer goods production to lower wage developing countries. A strong resource-based and commodity production sector is no bad thing to the extent that it is an important source of wealth and jobs and helps sustain regional economies. The distinction between a resource-based economy and a knowledge-based economy glosses over the fact that the resource industries are increasingly technologically sophisticated. Canada, however, has not benefited as much as has the United States from this trend. There is still a long-standing Canadian structural bias to production of relatively low value-added commodities in capital-intensive industries, such as smelting, pulp and paper, oil and gas production, and petrochemical production. Commodity and raw material prices, energy aside, have tended to increase only very slowly, explaining why Canadian personal incomes, adjusted for consumer price inflation, have grown at a much slower pace than has real GDP in the 1990s. (Between 1989 and 2001, real GDP per capita grew by a total of 18.1 percent, while real personal income per capita grew by a cumulative total of just 7.2 percent.) It will be very hard to raise Canadian living standards over the long term and create well paid jobs if we do not shift production towards goods and services that command rising rather than falling prices in world markets. That means producing more unique or sophisticated goods and services. Our dependence on large-scale crude energy exports is particularly unwise in a world of finite conventional resources, and it is environmentally unsustainable from a global perspective.

Overall, CUFTA has not closed the gap between Canadian and US living standards, as crudely measured by GDP per person. Canadian GDP per person, measured to equalize purchasing power, fell relative to the United States in the sharp recession of the late 1980s and then converged a little from 1993 onwards. But GDP tells us nothing about economic and social security, poverty and inequality, environmental sustainability, or the quality of life at work and in the community, all of which have been influenced by the economic model embodied in CUFTA.

The striking fact of the matter is that getting the so-called "fundamentals" right – free trade, balanced budgets, low interest rates, lower corporate and personal taxes – has failed to build a much more sophisticated industrial economy. CUFTA has also helped lock in an environmentally unsustainable path of energy exports. Leaving it all to the market has not worked, and debate over appropriate industrial and energy policies to actively shape comparative advantage should resume.[1] This does not necessarily mean a return to pre-CUFTA policies, though there is a role for the state in leading the transition to a knowledge-based and environmentally sustainable economy through public investment, regulation, and subsidies.

CUFTA was also, of course, expected to deliver the holy grail of secure access to the US market and protection from US protectionism. However, even the most fervent fans of "free trade" must acknowledge that Washington still actively uses its countervail and anti-dumping trade laws to selectively harass and penalize Canadian exports (see Lee, this volume). Binational dispute settlement panels can only decide if US trade law was fairly applied, and procedures can take years making the notion of a "win" a hollow victory. Our few "wins" have, in any case, been eclipsed by continuing US management of trade in politically sensitive sectors such as lumber and agriculture. Some Canadian FDI in the United States – for example, by the steel industry and Bombardier – has been prompted by protectionist US border measures and the political need for transnational corporations to establish a US production base. Many large Canadian companies, from Nova to Nortel, have shifted their real head offices across the border, giving rise to acute concern about the "hollowing out" of corporate Canada even on the part of CUFTA proponents like the Canadian Council of Chief Executives (CCCE). Ironically, the defenders of free trade now argue that still deeper integration is needed to secure the original key goal of market access for which so much policy space was surrendered.

DOWNWARD HARMONIZATION: SOCIAL DIMENSIONS OF THE INTEGRATED ECONOMIC SPACE[2]

In the great free trade debate of the late 1980s, advocates argued that a stronger economy would support higher wages and better social programs. However, after the deal was signed, business representatives increasingly argued that decent wages and high social expenditures, financed from progressive taxes, make Canada uncompetitive in a shared economic space. "Competitiveness" came to be defined as lower taxes, lower social spending, and more "flexible" labour markets. Experience has shown that there are, indeed, downward pressures from North American economic integra-

Table 8.3   Indicators of social development

	Canada	US
INCOME AND POVERTY		
Poverty Rate	10.3%	17.0%
Child Poverty Rate	15.5%	22.4%
JOBS		
Low Paid Jobs	20.9%	24.5%
Earnings Gap	3.7	4.6
SOCIAL SUPPORTS		
Health Care (Public Share as % GDP)	69.6%	44.7%
Tertiary Education (Public Share)	60.6%	51.0%
Private Social Spending (as % GDP)	4.5%	8.6%
HEALTH		
Life-Expectancy (Men)	75.3	72.5
Life-Expectancy (Women)	81.3	79.2
Infant Mortality/100,000	5.5	7.2
CRIME		
Homicides per 100,000	1.8	5.5
Assault/Threat per 100,000	4	5.7
Prisoners per 100,000	118	546
EDUCATION		
Adults with Post Secondary Education	38.8%	34.9%
High Literacy (% Adults)	25.1%	19.0%
Low Literacy (% Adults)	42.9%	49.6%

Notes and Sources:
Data are from the OECD Social Indicators Database.
Poverty defined as less than half the mean income of an equivalent household.
Low pay is employed in a full-time job and earning less than 2/3 the median hourly wage.
Earnings gap is ratio of bottom of top decile to top of bottom decile.

tion on progressive, redistributive social policy that arise mainly from the tax side

Canada has a very different social model than its neighbour – a model that is highly valued by most Canadians. Among the enduring elements of difference, Canada has a significantly more equal distribution of both earnings and disposable (after-tax and after-transfer) income. Our more narrow distribution of earnings reflects higher unionization rates, somewhat higher minimum wages, and a smaller pay gap between the middle and the top of the earnings spectrum. More equal after-tax incomes and lower rates of after-tax poverty than in the United States reflect the impacts of a more generous system of transfers acting upon a somewhat more equal distribution of market (pre-tax) income. Until its reform in the mid-1990s the Canadian Unemployment Insurance system was notably more generous than the US insurance system, and Canadian welfare programs benefited a much larger share of the non-elderly poor. All Canadian provinces, but very few US states, provide welfare to individuals and families without children, and benefits, while low and falling in real terms, are generally higher in Canada than in the United States. In the mid-1990s the Canadian poverty rate for all persons was 10 percent compared to 17 percent in the United States, using a common definition of less than half of median income, and the minimum distance between the top and bottom deciles of the family income distribution was 4 to 1 compared to almost 6.5 to 1. Comparing Canadian and US after-tax income distributions in real purchasing power terms, the bottom one-third of Canadians are much better off than are the bottom one-third of US citizens, and the US average income advantage of about 15 percent goes overwhelmingly to the top one-third or so of the income distribution. In other words, affluent Americans have significantly more disposable income than do affluent Canadians, but the gap is very small for middle-income families (particularly if adjusted for out-of-pocket health care costs) and does not exist at all for lower income families (Wolfson and Murphy 1998). The level of public provision of services on a citizen entitlement basis is also higher in Canada, reducing dependence on market income for some basic needs. Medicare is the key example, but Canada also provides a somewhat higher level of community services, such as not-for-profit child care, home care, and elder care services. Greater equality has sustained better social outcomes in terms of health, crime, and educational attainment (see table 8.3).

It is far beyond the scope of this chapter to detail changes in income distribution and social outcomes during the 1990s. Still, one clear trend is a significant increase in income inequality among working-age Canadian families. Table 8.4 shows the distribution of both market (wage and investment) income and after-tax and government transfer income among families of two persons or more. The population of families is divided into five groups of equal size (quintiles). The 1989 to 2001 change in the post-CUFTA era is what economists would term "structural" since the start and end years both came at the end of a period of strong job growth and economic recovery. Real family incomes from the market grew most in both dollar and percentage terms for higher income families. The inflation-adjusted market incomes of the top 20 percent rose by 16.5 percent compared to a loss of almost 7 percent for the bottom 20 percent. The share of market income of the top 20 percent rose from 42.4 percent in 1989 to 45.6 percent in 2001, while the share of all other income groups fell. The after-tax/transfer share of the top 20 percent of families also rose, from 36.9 percent to 39.2 percent, and the share of all other income groups fell. Poverty rates rose between 1989 and 2001 for Canadians aged eighteen to sixty-four but fell among the elderly.

Table 8.4   Family income trends in the 1990s

	1989	2000	2001	% Change 1989-2001
MARKET INCOME				
Bottom Quintile	$8,969	$8,781	$8,362	–6.8%
Second Quintile	$33,729	$32,688	$32,362	–4.1%
Middle Quintile	$53,144	$54,115	$54,127	1.8%
Fourth Quintile	$73,844	$78,039	$78,389	6.2%
Top Quintile	$124,953	$142,451	$145,580	16.5%
SHARES OF MARKET INCOME				
Bottom Quintile	3.0%	2.8%	2.6%	
Second Quintile	11.5%	10.3%	10.2%	
Middle Quintile	18.0%	17.1%	17.0%	
Fourth Quintile	25.1%	24.7%	24.6%	
Top Quintile	42.4%	45.1%	45.6%	
POST-TAX/TRANSFER INCOME SHARES				
Bottom Quintile	7.7%	7.3%	7.1%	
Next Quintile	13.6%	12.8%	12.7%	
Middle Quintile	18.2%	17.6%	17.6%	
Next Quintile	23.6%	23.5%	23.4%	
Top Quintile	36.9%	38.8%	39.2%	

Data are for Economic Families of Two Persons or More. Statistics Canada. Income in Canada CD-ROM 2001.)
(Constant $ 2001)

POVERTY (POST-TAX LICO)				
All Persons	10.0%	10.9%	10.4%	
Children	11.5%	12.5%	11.4%	
18–64	9.3%	11.0%	10.6%	
65 plus	10.9%	7.3%	7.3%	

Statistics Canada: Income in Canada CD-ROM. Table T802.

Rising income inequality has been driven primarily by stronger wage growth for high-income earners and by cuts in social transfers that have reduced the income equalizing effects of social programs. Neither can be blamed directly upon North American economic integration, and, undoubtedly, a complex range of factors have been at play. However, there is a link between continental integration and the increased market incomes of the most affluent. The (still limited) labour mobility measures of NAFTA and closer trade and investment links have almost certainly fed competitive pressures to raise salaries and stock options for highly mobile professionals and managers in the corporate sector to US levels. CUFTA and NAFTA can also be plausibly associated in a direct way with downward pressures on wages in sectors most exposed to the threat of relocation of production or new investment to the United States and Mexico. Increased competitive pressures help explain the very sharp decline in the unionization rate in Canadian manufacturing, which has fallen from 45.5 percent in 1988 to just 32.4 percent in 2002, and the more modest decline in the private sector as a whole (Jackson and Schetagne 2003). Union decline reflects disproportionate closures of unionized plants, and the disproportionate concentration of new hiring in non-union plants, not to mention legislative assaults on union organizing capacity. Real manufacturing wage growth has lagged consistently behind manufacturing sector productivity in both Canada and the United States, as is indicated in table 8.1, which shows that Canadian real hourly wages in manufacturing rose by just 3.3 percent over the decade between 1992 and 2002, while productivity rose by 17.9 percent. Within manufacturing, the wages of less skilled and hourly paid workers have eroded compared to those of technical workers and managers. The post-CUFTA era has been generally a period in which real wages have lagged behind productivity, and corporate profitability has increased. The 1980s peak for corporate profits as a share of GDP was in 1988 (10.6 percent), but the high point of the recent expansion was 12.2 percent in 2000, and pre-tax corporate profits, including in most of manufacturing and the resource sector, have remained above 1988 levels. In short, it is hard to sustain the argument that workers have fully shared in the relatively modest productivity gains that some have attributed to CUFTA, and it is hard to deny that integration has tended to tilt the bargaining scales against workers.

Closer integration can also be linked to the erosion of income transfers to the working-age population. Most observers would argue that the Employment Insurance (EI) cuts imposed by the Liberal government in 1995, the cuts in federal transfers to the provinces for social programs, and the provincial welfare cuts were all driven by fiscal and political/ideological rather than competitive considerations. There is no doubt that the drive to eliminate federal and provincial deficits played a major role in cuts to income transfers and that some provincial governments, such as those of Ontario and Alberta, were ideologically hostile to "hand-outs" to so-called "employable" recipients. However, the Department of Finance, the Organization for Economic Co-operation and Development (OECD), and the International Monetary Fund (IMF) have long argued that welfare state "generosity" in Canada contributes to higher unemployment rates[3] than in the United States because income benefits strengthen the bargaining power of workers and thus raise the wage floor. Cuts to transfers, particularly EI, were consciously intended to promote greater labour market and wage flexibility, and this has been seen as particularly desirable given the closer bilateral economic integration. In short, integration made the US model of a more minimalist welfare state attractive to those who worried about the relative strength of Canadian workers (Jackson 2000a).

The argument that closer economic integration also requires convergence in social policies should be critically assessed. In particular, this argument ignores the fact that progressive and redistributive social models have significant economic pluses and, thus, may actually enhance competitiveness (Jackson 2000a, 2000b). In fact, the experience in other advanced capitalist countries shows that economic integration does not eclipse the space for national choice in social policy, and there is no universal trend towards decreased social expenditures and lower taxes. Some high-equality countries with high levels of spending on public and social services, high taxes, and very high levels of collective bargaining coverage did well in the 1990s in terms of productivity and job creation (e.g., Denmark, the Netherlands, and Sweden from the mid-1990s). The lack of a demonstrable link between egalitarian policies and poor economic performance even under conditions of increased global competition is not surprising if one takes account of the positive impacts of relative equality on "human capital" and "social capital" and the greater efficiency of public over market delivery of many key services, such as health and education. In short, a good economic argument can be made that integration per se does not mean that Canada has to harmonize down to US levels of social spending and public services in order to build a productive economy.

Yet the operative, endlessly repeated proposition of business think tanks and the policy mainstream has been that economic success will go to countries that most closely emulate the US model of deregulated labour markets, low taxes, and low social spending. Over the 1990s, particularly after the elimination of the federal deficit in 1997, the political argument was constantly advanced that taxes had to be harmonized down to US levels to maintain competitiveness and fuel growth and job creation. The argument has been that Canadian business taxes (corporate income taxes and capital taxes) and personal income taxes on higher earners are too high relative to our neighbour, helping to make the latter a more attractive locale in which to invest and produce for mobile corporations. While many advocates of tax cuts would also argue that lower taxes per se boost economic efficiency, a great deal of stress has been placed on Canada-US tax differences as a factor in weaker Canadian economic performance through much of the past decade. The major advocates of the "tax cuts for competitiveness" argument have been business lobby groups, such as the CCCE and the Chamber of Commerce, and conservative think tanks, such as the C.D. Howe Institute. The November 2002 Pre-Budget Report of the Standing Committee on Finance of the House of Commons reported that submissions from business organizations continued to stress that Canadian tax rates – particularly personal income tax rates on high income groups and business taxes – should be "competitive" with those of our neighbour and biggest trading partner. The report underlined that "tax competitiveness is a key component of the federal government's strategy to become a magnet for investment and skilled labour," and it heeded calls from business for the elimination of capital taxes and ensuring that corporate income tax rates are kept at or below us levels.

Arguments for tax cuts for competitiveness are suspect since foregone expenditures have positive impacts on productivity. Canada-us corporate tax differences in the mid-1990s were very small and were offset by other cost factors, such as lower energy prices and lower health costs for workers. On the personal income tax side, high-income earners did tend to pay somewhat more than did those in the United States, but the gap was quite modest in the aftermath of the Clinton administration's tax hikes, and the alleged "brain drain" was hugely exaggerated (Helliwell 2002). Nonetheless, the ideological and self-serving argument for tax cuts won the day after deficits were eliminated. Driven by personal and corporate income tax cuts, the federal revenue share of GDP has fallen from 17.2 percent in 1997–98 to 15.4 percent in 2002–03 (Finance Canada 2003, table 2). The reduced fiscal capacity of the federal government amounted to foregone potential expenditures in 2002–03 of $21 billion. By 2004–05 the five-year federal tax reduction program will have cut federal tax revenues by 18.6 percent, or 2.4 percent of GDP (OECD 2003, table 29). Provincial tax revenues have also fallen since 1997–98, by a bit under 1 percent of GDP.

The major beneficiaries of the changes to personal income tax rates and brackets were those making more than $70,000 who will pay about 5 percent less of their taxable income in income tax. The lower paid got a smaller proportional tax cut, ranging from almost nothing at the bottom to about 3 percent of taxable income for an average worker. The very affluent also won the elimination of the 5 percent high-income surtax and a major reduction (from 75 percent to 50 percent) in the proportion of capital gains income that is liable to tax – a measure that has cost the federal government about $1 billion in foregone revenues, with about half of the benefit going to very high-income persons earning more than $250,000 per year. Reduction of capital gains taxes, which apply to profits earned on stocks and stock options, was top on the business agenda in 2000, with Canada-us tax competition arguments featuring heavily in the debate. The federal government tax plan also featured a phased-in reduction of the corporate income tax rate from 28 percent to 21 percent, with the explicit objective of cutting the rate to levels that are lower than those in the United States. The key point is that, after the deficit was eliminated, the growing federal surplus went to personal income and corporate tax cuts rather than to a renewal of social spending. The tax cuts were tilted to

Table 8.5   Canada-US fiscal comparisons: Change in government spending as % GDP

	1992			2001		
	US	Canada	Gap	US	Canada	Gap
Function						
Income Security	7.9	14.3	6.4	7.1	11	3.9
Housing and Community						
Services	0.7	1.9	1.2	0.5	1.4	0.9
Economic Affairs	3.2	5.8	2.5	3.2	3.5	0.3
Recreation and Culture	0.3	1.3	1	0.3	1	0.7
Education	5.7	7.7	2	6.2	5.9	-0.3
Health	6	7.3	1.2	6.7	7	0.4
General Public Services	2	2.4	0.4	1.9	1.9	0
Public Order and Safety	1.9	2.3	0.5	2.2	1.9	-0.2
National Defence	6	1.7	-4.3	4	1.2	-2.8
Total Program Spending	33.7	44.6	10.9	31.9	34.8	2.9
Non-Defence Program Spending	27.7	42.9	15.2	27.9	33.6	5.7

Source: "Government Spending in Canada and the US." Department of Finance Working Paper 2003- 05.

the more affluent and business despite the fact that lower income groups had been hit hardest by the earlier federal program spending cuts.

While Canadian governments still spend significantly more on social programs and public services than do US governments, the difference has been shrinking dramatically. Table 8.5, based on Department of Finance data, details program spending differences between the two countries in 1992 and 2001 for all levels of government expressed as a share of GDP. The bottom line is that Canadian governments collectively spent 34.8 percent of Canadian GDP on spending programs in 2001, while US governments spent 31.9 percent of GDP. The difference fell from 10.9 percentage points of GDP in 1992 to just 2.9 percentage points in 2001 as Canadian government spending fell by almost 10 percentage points. The spending gap between the two countries is greater for non-defence spending, at a still significant 5.7 percentage points of GDP, but this is down dramatically from a much greater difference of 15.2 percentage points in 1992. Non-defence program spending actually increased under President Clinton, while falling by almost 10 percentage points of GDP in Canada. The main differences between Canada and the United States are in national defence (where we spend much less) and in income security programs. In the latter, we still spend 11.0 percent of GDP compared to the 7.1 percent that Washington spends, but the gap has shrunk greatly since 1992, reflecting cuts to welfare and EI benefits as well as falling unemployment. Canada now spends relatively less than its neighbour on public education, the result of recent cuts in Canada and of increases in the United States, and we spend only a bit more on health (though we spend much more efficiently because of public delivery and a single-payer Medicare system).

It is important to spend money wisely and efficiently, but the size of spending clearly matters as well. The Canada-US gap has shrunk dramatically in the 1990s because of deep cuts to Canadian spending on social programs and public services, and this was clearly driven in significant part by the campaign of the right for downward harmonization of taxes, financed through social spending cuts. Competitive pressures trumped the desire of most Canadians to renew social spending once deficits had been eliminated. Public opinion survey evidence shows that there was a deep class cleavage over the key issue of tax cuts or social reinvestment after the federal budget was balanced. Polling in 1998 for the Department of Finance by the Earnscliffe Group found that all broad income groups placed a greater priority on social investment than on tax cuts and rejected harmonization of Canadian and US tax policies, albeit with a clear difference by income level. However, an EKOS survey ("Reinventing Government") that regularly charts differences between elite and non-elite opinion has found that the former very strongly favoured corporate and personal tax cuts as the best use of the emerging federal surplus.[4] In the final analysis, corporate elite views were clearly the most influential in policy terms, and the desire of middle- and lower-income Canadians for significant social reinvestment went largely unheeded until the Chrétien "legacy budget" of 2003.

The cleavage between elite and non-elite views on the tax cuts versus social spending debate has probably been influenced more by class positions than by the economic implications of North American integration. In an ever more closely integrated economic space, corporate elites increasingly see their personal prospects and future in continental terms, and they compare their personal well-being to that of their US peers rather than to that of other Canadians. Career prospects have been continentalized to some extent at this level given the increasing linkages between the Canadian and US economies mediated through transnational corporations operating on both sides of the border. The Canadian trade-off of higher taxes for better services and greater security is also less relevant to high-income groups who can afford to buy what they need on the market. By contrast, for middle-class and lower-income families, the trade-off of higher taxes for social programs is still relevant, and comparisons to US disposable income are not relevant. Public opinion evidence shows no loss of support for the Canadian social model and, indeed, increasing divergence between Canadian and US values (Mendelson 2002).

To summarize, there continues to be space for autonomy in social policy, and the Canadian social model is not doomed to extinction because of closer trade and investment ties with the United States per se. But, there are strong downward pressures on our capacity to finance social spending, which arise mainly from pressures to lower business taxes and taxes on high-income earners to US levels. Canadian expenditures on public and social services have been severely constrained and are financed to a great degree from relatively less progressive forms of taxation. Privatization of public services, such as health and education, has been aided by the erosion of quality public programs. Economic integration has thus been a factor in the pronounced erosion and downward harmonization of the Canadian social model in the 1990s. Moreover, it should be noted that CUFTA and NAFTA do place serious constraints on the establishment of new programs such as pharmacare or a national childcare program. The "investor's rights" provisions of NAFTA also make it extremely difficult to bring public and social services back into the public sector once they have been privatized or commercialized (see Shrybman, this volume).

MOVING FORWARD

CUFTA has significantly increased Canada-US economic integration, but it has left us with a weak "knowledge-based" economy. Furthermore, economic integration has tilted the political scales against rebuilding and renewing the damaged but still intact Canadian social model. The champions of deeper economic integration in North America are (almost) all champions of deregulation of economic space and admirers of the US social model. For them, still deeper integration is desirable because it involves the prospect of limited gains – a more seamless border – at no real cost in terms of valued economic, social, or environmental policies. If free trade has not worked out as well as expected in terms of growth and productivity, as many will concede, their answer is to say that we have not done enough to break down remaining "barriers" and that "there is no alternative" to continue pushing for more integration. For those of us of who want to maintain Canadian distinctiveness, the path forward is not so clear.

The left, which opposed CUFTA in the late 1980s, has changed, just as Canada has changed. In the wake of the shift from CUFTA to NAFTA to the proposed Free Trade Area of the Americas (FTAA), the transformation of GATT into the WTO, and the emergence of the so-called "anti-globalization" movement there has been a partial shift from economic nationalism to progressive internationalism. The argument has been increasingly heard that the way forward is not so much to reconnect economic and political space at the national level as to build a different kind of global economic order. Key issues, such as environmental sustainability, global inequality, and justice for the developing world – not to mention the instability of global capitalism – have to be addressed at a supranational level, and this task has been taken up by new social movements. In Europe, the social democratic left has attempted to reconnect political and economic space through the explicit "social dimension" of the European Union. While instructive, the European lessons for progressive North Americans seem limited given the huge political weight of the United States in the Americas and the weakness of potential political allies in that country.

The way forward for Canada is to retain as much room for policy manoeuvre as we can vis-à-vis the United States, while advancing a progressive agenda at the national and international levels (see Campbell, this volume). There can, realistically, be no return to the somewhat more insulated economic space of the late 1980s given the realities of globalized capitalism and close continental integration in terms of trade in goods, mobility of capital, and, to a much lesser but growing extent, services. But there is reason and space to exercise sovereignty in key domains: to maintain regulation of the cultural sector; to more actively review foreign investment; to actively shape comparative advantage though public investment in positive industrial restructuring, innovation, education, and training; to rebuild and renew social programs and public services; and to take environmental sustainability seriously (see Campbell, this volume). Small, open economies still retain considerable capacity for political choice at the national level, and they can help shape a different international agenda. CUFTA may have led to a hard landing, but the future is still open.

AFTERNOTE

This chapter is based on data available at the end of 2004. Since that time, there has been a pronounced further shift in the composition of Canadian exports to resource-based commodities, which now make up 60 percent of value-added embodied in exported goods (Cross and Ghanem 2005, 3.1). This mainly reflects increased Asian demand for commodities and the impacts of a much higher Canada-US exchange rate upon Canadian exports of non-resource-based manufactured goods. Meanwhile, there has been a marked shift in the origin of Canadian manufactured imports, from the Unites States to China and other parts of developing Asia. In short, the pattern of Canada-US economic integration is now being increasingly affected by the shift of global production to Asia. This in itself makes deepening integration with the United States highly problematic from the point of view of positive Canadian participation within a rapidly changing global economic framework.

On the social side, the harmonization of social spending down to US levels went into temporary reverse during the final years of the Chrétien-Martin Liberal regime, when reinvestment in social programs and public services moved temporarily to the fore, albeit modestly and in tandem with continued downward harmonization of corporate taxes. However, the election of the Harper minority government in early 2006 likely signals a further round of policy harmonization with the US social model.

NOTES

This chapter was available earlier as a report from the Canadian Centre for Policy Alternatives and the Canadian Labour Congress (Jackson 2003a, 2003b).

1 The extreme reliance on one major export market has also increased the macroeconomic vulnerability to external shocks (see Seccareccia's chapter 9, this volume).
2 This part of the chapter draws on earlier work (Jackson 2005, chap. 10).
3 In technical terms, it is associated with a higher non-accelerating inflation rate of unemployment (NAIRU).
4 Mendelson (2002). See Charts 56, 118, 119, 123, 124, 149, and 152.

REFERENCES

Acharya, Ram C., Prakesh Sharma, and Someshwar Rao. 2001. Canada's Trade and Foreign Direct Investment Patterns with the United States. Paper presented at Industry Canada Conference on North American Linkages: Opportunities and Challenges for Canada, 20–22 June, Calgary, AL.

Baldwin, John, and Wulong Gu. 2003. *Plant Turnover and Productivity in Canadian Manufacturing*. Ottawa: Statistics Canada.

Cameron, Duncan, ed. 1988. *The Free Trade Deal*. Toronto: Lorimer.

CBOC. 2002. *Performance and Potential 2002–2003: Canada 2010 – Challenges and Choices at Home and Abroad*. Ottawa: Conference Board of Canada.

Clarkson, Stephen. 2002. *Uncle Sam and Us: Globalization, Neoconservatism and the Canadian State*. Toronto: University of Toronto Press.

CLC. 1987. *Submission to the House of Commons Standing Committee on External Affairs and International Trade*. Ottawa: Canadian Labour Congress.

Cross, Philip, and Ziad Ghanem. 2005. Canada's Natural Resource Exports. *Canadian Economic Observer*, Statistics Canada. 18, 5: 3.1–3.7.

Dion, Richard. 2000. Trends in Canada's Merchandise Trade. *Bank of Canada Review* (Winter): 29–41.

Finance Canada. 1988. *The Canada-US Free Trade Agreement: An Economic Assessment*. Ottawa: Department of Finance.

– 2003. *Fiscal Reference Tables*. Ottawa: Department of Finance.

Gu, Wulong, Gary Swachuk, and Lori Whewell. 2003. *The Effect of Tariff Reductions on Firm Size and Firm Turnover in Canadian Manufacturing*. Ottawa: Statistics Canada.

Helliwell, John. 2002. *Globalization and Well-Being.* Vancouver: UBC Press.

Jackson, Andrew. 2000a. The Perverse Circularity of NAIRU Driven Economic Policy. *Canadian Business Economics* 8 (2): 66–81.

– 2000b. *Why We Don't Have to Choose between Social Justice and Economic Growth: The Myth of the Equity-Efficiency Trade-Off.* Ottawa: Canadian Council on Social Development.

– 2003a. *From Leaps of Faith to Hard Landings: Fifteen Years of "Free Trade."* Research Paper No. 28. Ottawa: Canadian Labour Congress.

– 2003b. *From Leaps of Faith to Hard Landings: Fifteen Years of "Free Trade."* Ottawa: Canadian Centre for Policy Alternatives.

– 2005. *Work and Labour in Canada: Critical Issues.* Toronto: Canadian Scholars Press.

Jackson, Andrew, and Sylvain Schetagne. 2003. *Solidarity Forever? An Analysis of Changes in Union Density.* Research Paper No. 25. Ottawa: Canadian Labour Congress.

McCallum, John. 2000. Appendix A. Two Cheers for the FTA: Ten-Year Review of the Canada-US Free Trade Agreement. In *Free Trade: Risks and Rewards,* ed. L.I. MacDonald, 259–74. Montreal and Kingston: McGill-Queen's University Press.

Macdonald Report. 1985. *Report of the Royal Commission on the Economic Union and Development Prospects for Canada.* Ottawa: Minister of Supply and Services.

Mendelson, Matthew. 2002. *Canada's Social Contract: Evidence from Public Opinion.* Discussion Paper No. 1. Ottawa: Canadian Policy Research Networks.

Nadeau, Serge, and Someshwar Rao. 2002. The Role of Industrial Structure in Canada's Productivity Performance. In *Productivity Issues in Canada,* ed. S. Rao and A. Sharpe, 137–64. Calgary: University of Calgary Press.

OECD. 2003. *Economic Survey: Canada 2003.* Paris: Organisation for Economic Co-operation and Development.

O'Neill, Tim. 2002. *North American Economic Integration.* Toronto: Bank of Montreal Economics Department.

Statistics Canada. 2002. *The Daily,* September 13. Available at <http://www.statcan.ca/english/dai-quo/>.

Trefler, Daniel. 1999. *The Long and the Short of the Canada-US Free Trade Agreement.* Industry Canada Research Paper No. 6. Ottawa: Industry Canada.

Wolfson, Michael, and Brian Murphy. 1998. New Views on Income Equality Trends in Canada and the United States. *Monthly Labour Review* 121 (4): 1–21.

9

Critical Macroeconomic Aspects of Deepening North American Economic Integration

MARIO SECCARECCIA

A number of economists, especially those who have been influenced by the work of Robert Mundell and his followers, view the process of economic integration, both commercial and monetary, as a natural and irreversible tendency in the world economy today. The pattern of post-Bretton Woods trade "liberalization" has, indeed, entailed a revamping of trade relations in favour of large international trading blocs such as the European Union (EU) and the North American free trade zone. At the same time, deepening trade links have generated strong pressures within these commercial trading blocs in support of greater monetary integration and the establishment of so-called "optimal currency" areas,[1] the most spectacular example being the emergence of the European Economic and Monetary Union (EMU) with the launching of the euro in 1999.

Earlier empires of the eighteenth and nineteenth centuries asserted state control over world commerce by enforcing mercantilist trade restrictions to ensure massive gold inflows from both their colonies and the rest of the world. In contrast, the emerging international blocs of the late twentieth and early twenty-first centuries have been founded primarily on the principle of greater trade liberalization and monetary penetration, commonly described as "dollarization" in this hemisphere and as "euroization" in the European continent.[2] This has resulted in the retreat of the Keynesian interventionist state and the abandonment of national macroeconomic stabilization policy. Late twentieth-century "globalization" has entailed, therefore, the reconfiguration of world markets into large trading blocs, within which mega-corporations are given free reign, and outside of which these corporations can tie the hands of governments and enforce control over the international flow of goods and services based on the trade liberalization-cum-"structural adjustment" model. The latter model has been marketed extensively over the last decade by international agencies, such as the International Monetary Fund (IMF) and World Bank, to those countries in the developing world and the so-called emerging markets that had succumbed to the pressures arising from economic misalignment and peripheral growth.

The forces of globalization and greater integration have, indeed, promoted large economic blocs as well as increased the volume of world trade and related commercial activities. However, contrary to what some mainstream economists would tell us, there is nothing inevitable about this pattern of geo-political alignment, which favours wider trading and monetary blocs. Under pressures from business and financial interests, this international reconfiguration of commercial trading has resulted primarily from a conscious attempt on the part of governments to promote exports via the removal of obstacles to international trade and the application of strong doses of macroeconomic austerity, even at the expense of lower domestic growth. Consequently, those same forces of globalization that were unleashed with the breakdown of the Bretton Woods system in the early 1970s have imparted a recessionary bias on the contemporary world economy. Except for the United States and some of the countries of the European Union that are at the top end of the trading food-chain, the current international economy is now merely a constellation of export-dependent national economies facing economic stagnation, mass unemployment, and unsustainable household debt as well as a growing disparity of income and wealth both within and among these economies. As pointed out by a recent report (Pettifor 2003), instead of a global tide of rising living standards that would supposedly lift all boats, the legacy of globalization has been different. Above all, it has been one of overhanging debt, deflation, and greater despair for the vast majority of the world's population as countries have been drawn more and more into a competitive race to the bottom.

The object of this chapter is to situate Canada within the context of the post-Bretton Woods system and evaluate the macroeconomic aspects of deepening economic integration, especially since the adoption of the Canada-US Free Trade Agreement (CUFTA) in 1989 and the North American Free Trade Agreement (NAFTA) in 1994. Such integration has, indeed, meant greater growth in internationally traded goods production in Canada. However, much like in a textbook zero-sum game, this has occurred largely at the expense of the domestic economy by unleashing forces that slow down the growth of domestic markets and have made the Canadian economy more crisis-prone and vulnerable to international shocks. The first portion of the chapter looks, therefore, at the Canadian record of commercial integration by highlighting the spectacular shift of resources away from production for domestic demand in favour of exports. This is followed by an analysis of the changing role of monetary and fiscal

Figure 9.1   Canada's vulnerability to foreign trade (Exports plus imports as a
percentage of GDP, 1926–2002)

—— Percentage share of exports + imports/GDP

Source: Statistics Canada, CANSIM I, Series D14442, D14464, AND D14468; and
CANSIM II, Series V646937, V646954, AND V646957.

policy in sustaining this process of trade liberalization and export promotion. Finally, I seek to explain, within this context, the pressures for greater
monetary integration.

NORTH AMERICAN COMMERCIAL INTEGRATION: SOME STYLIZED FACTS

As noted early on by Harold A. Innis (1930), the Canadian economy has
always found itself in a core-periphery relationship, which made its macroeconomic performance highly susceptible to the whims of the international
economy. This has been primarily due to its colonial past, relative openness, and reliance on foreign trade as an important source of growth. During the eighteenth and nineteenth centuries, Canada's principal export
markets were its colonial masters – France and Great Britain, respectively.
This changed over the course of the last century, with the United States
becoming Canada's principal trading partner. Despite the structural differ-

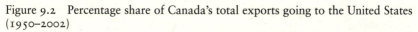

Figure 9.2   Percentage share of Canada's total exports going to the United States (1950–2002)

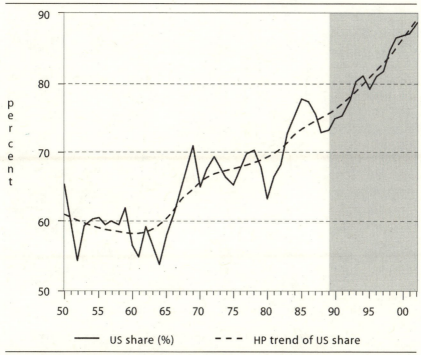

Source: Statistics Canada, CANSIM I, Series D400000 and D400465.

ences in the two economies, the strong linkages between the two neigh-bours have long been recognized as the principal reason for their highly correlated business cycles (Bryce 1939; White 1967).

Undoubtedly, the benefits of foreign trade have been felt by Canadians, particularly during times of high growth in the world economy. At the same time, such dependence on trade has made Canada highly vulnerable to external shocks. This vulnerability became painful during periods of economic retrenchment internationally, such as during the 1930s. One measure of vulnerability, which is sometimes used to highlight a country's exposure to international fluctuations, is the sum of exports and imports as a proportion of gross domestic product (GDP). Given its relative size, Canada's exposure to the rest of the world has always been high, especially when compared to other industrialized countries. However, as shown in figure 9.1, this index of exposure actually declined during the early postwar "golden age" as expansionary Keynesian policies were adopted to support domestic demand. On the other hand, Canada's vulnerability rose

Figure 9.3   Percentage share of Canada's total exports going to Mexico
(1950–2002)

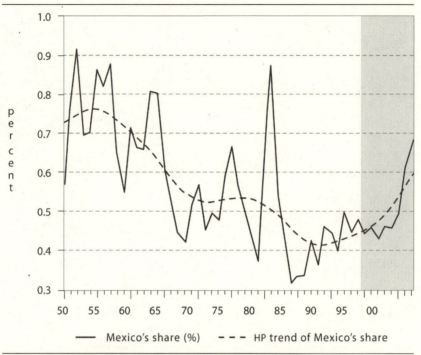

p
e
r
c
e
n
t

——— Mexico's share (%)   – – – HP trend of Mexico's share

Source: Statistics Canada, CANSIM I, Series D400027 and D400465.

by leaps and bounds during the post-Bretton Woods "leaden age"[3] of
increased trade liberalization and persistent economic austerity. The index
of international exposure in figure 9.1 has gone from a mere 30 percent
during the 1960s to as high as 85 percent of GDP at the beginning of the
new millennium.

While Canada's vulnerability to foreign shocks has recently attained
unprecedented historical levels, figure 9.2 demonstrates an ominous pattern
relating to Canada's increasing dependence on trade with its southern
neighbour. Over the last century the United States replaced Britain as the
principal importer of Canadian products. By the 1950s and 1960s US
shores became the destination of approximately 60 percent of Canada's
total exports. This level rose significantly during the 1970s and 1980s, an
era of increasing trade liberalization, and even more sharply during the
post-1989 free trade era, with almost 90 percent of Canada's total exports
destined for the United States.[4]

Figure 9.4   Share of non-traditional exports of manufactured products out of Canada's total merchandise exports, 1971–2001

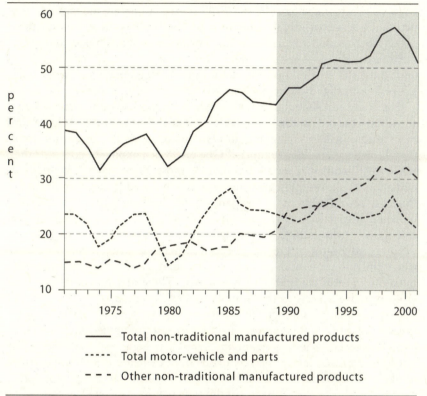

Source: Statistics Canada, CANSIM I, Series B1050, B1080, and B1083.

Even with Mexico's entrance into NAFTA in 1994, there was little change in the US share of Canada's exports of goods and services. Mexico's share remains quite insignificant, absorbing less than 1 percent of Canada's total exports. Indeed, as can be inferred from figure 9.3, under NAFTA, Mexico's share of Canadian exports has not even reached the levels that it had attained during the early postwar years. Hence, greater trade liberalization has meant unprecedented levels of economic integration with the United States. At no time since its decolonization from Great Britain in the mid-nineteenth century has Canada been so dependent on *one* foreign market for its major source of external demand.

During the nineteenth century Canada essentially exported primary products, which were later complemented by some manufactured goods. The post-1970s trend towards greater trade liberalization has led to an increase in the export of manufactured products, especially products that have not traditionally constituted a significant component of Canada's exports. Figure 9.4 shows the share of non-traditional manufactured products (such as motor vehicle and auto parts) as well as other manufactured goods (such as electronic, industrial, and agricultural machinery and equipment) as a share of total merchandise exports since 1971. During this period the share of non-traditional products, especially equipment goods, jumped from slightly over one-third to over half of our total exports.

One could conclude that trade liberalization has had an unexpected consequence – the increase in value-added in our export sector, meaning a shift from traditional (primary and low value-added products) to non-traditional (high value-added) exports.[5] One might be tempted to conclude that, while the Canadian economy has become more vulnerable to outside (particularly US) shocks, this growing exposure has had positive employment impacts, resulting from the expansion of the high value-added export industry. In particular, we can expect to achieve a higher "employment multiplier" – the change in employment resulting from a given change in exports. Advocates of greater integration may view this relation between trade liberalization and greater value-added as an important positive outcome of freer trade in North America. There are, however, some obvious negative aspects to this admittedly positive trend.

First, a higher employment multiplier from export demand[6] means greater volatility in total employment to any given fluctuation of Canada's exports. Hence, when US economic growth is high, we might be seeing stronger effects on labour market demand; but when it is low, employment is likely to fluctuate downward even more violently than during earlier decades. In short, employment instability may have worsened. Second, high export multipliers may not necessarily imply greater net employment effects. This is because higher exports tend to be associated with higher import coefficients, especially capital goods imports, which have grown concomitantly with exports in Canada. Third, under the financial pressures of "structural adjustment," just about every newly industrialized or developing economy in the world is promoting an export-led growth strategy, spearheaded by the manufacturing sector. One has only to observe the economic policies of our NAFTA partner further to the south. But, in order to keep and further attract such manufacturing jobs, Canada will have to compete with countries such as Mexico and China on the basis of lower unit labour costs.[7] Hence, as the following section argues, Canada's international competitiveness has been preserved, and could be maintained, only by capping the growth of domestic incomes (i.e., keeping wage growth relatively low). In turn, depressing wages implies placing a lid on domestic growth not related to the export sector.

MACROECONOMIC POLICIES: THE RECORD

As argued in the previous section, the post-Bretton Woods era of greater trade liberalization has been associated with a historically unprecedented sharp and massive exposure to foreign trade. Much of this strategy, especially since the Macdonald Report (1985) (which recommended bilateral free trade with the United States), has been a conscious one on the part of our political leaders to deepen economic integration institutionally via CUFTA and NAFTA. Its success, however, has been made possible primarily by the macroeconomic policies that were embraced during the 1970s. The deflationary role that monetary policy played during the years prior to and immediately following CUFTA and the supportive role of fiscal policy in maintaining these recessionary pressures is discussed below.

An Era of High Real Interest Rates and Monetary Austerity

Canadian monetary policy has played a central role in the post-Bretton Woods competitiveness strategy of promoting trade at the expense of domestic growth. Indeed, one could argue that such recessionary monetary policy effectively laid the foundations for the economic restructuring that would follow during the free trade era with its low labour cost competitiveness strategy. Following the spikes in oil prices in 1973 and 1979, pressure from both industry (because of growing wage demands) and finance (because of declining real interest rates) persuaded the government to tackle inflation, regardless of the consequences on output and employment.

Numerous observers during the 1970s and 1980s believed that double-digit inflation was the result of expansionary monetary policy by the Bank of Canada. They urged Canada's monetary authorities to abandon so-called misguided Keynesian policies and to adopt a monetarist strategy of high interest rates and monetary austerity. The Bank of Canada complied in 1975 when it began to target the growth of what was viewed at the time as a key monetary indicator (Courchene 1976).[8] This monetarist strategy was then further refined starting in 1987 by John Crow, the new governor of the Bank of Canada. The strategy rested on the questionable principle that the single focus of monetary policy ought to be price stability and that a persistent policy of "zero inflation"[9] would ultimately bring about growth in living standards and in aggregate productivity.

Even though the theoretical and empirical underpinnings for this orthodox hypothesis were highly questionable or non-existent (Seccareccia and Lavoie 1996), the Bank of Canada continued to prescribe massive doses of monetary austerity in the form of high real interest rates. As is evident from figure 9.5, not since the 1930s had the Canadian economy experienced

Figure 9.5   Evolution of real interest rates: Bank rate and prime lending rate, Canada, 1935–2002

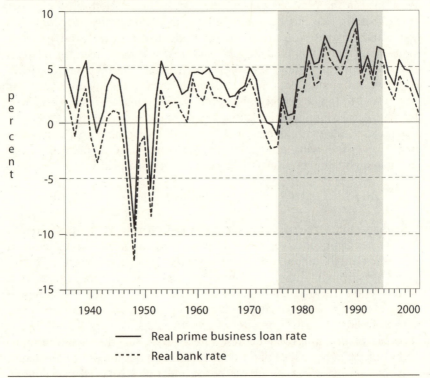

      ———— Real prime business loan rate

      - - - - - Real bank rate

Source: Statistics Canada, CANSIM I, Series B14006, B14020, and P100000; and CANSIM II, Series V122495, V122530, and V735319.

such high rates. Real interest rates, as measured by the nominal rate (either the prime lending rate or the central bank administered bank rate) less the rate of change in the Consumer Price Index (CPI), began to rise sharply during the late 1970s as Canada's central bank adopted the monetarist policy framework (see shaded area). These rates remained targeted at historically high levels throughout the 1980s and peaked towards the end of the 1987–93 Crow governorship (Seccareccia 1998).

Such policies brought about a massive transfer of income in favour of financial capital, a phenomenon dubbed by Smithin (1996) as "the revenge of the rentiers." The effect was to reduce inflation significantly but at the cost of two deep recessions (during 1981–82 and 1990–91) and long-term mass unemployment. Again, this was a scenario that had not been observed since the 1930s. Indeed, as figure 9.6 shows, for the first time in the postwar era, Canada's unemployment rate rose substantially over that of

Figure 9.6   Pattern of Canadian and US unemployment rates, 1948–2002 (annual averages)

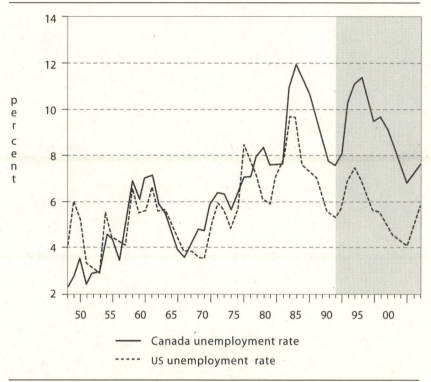

Source: Statistics Canada, CANSIM II, Series V122076, V159398, and Statistics Canada, *Historical Statistics of Canada* (Second Edition, 1983).

the United States, and it remained higher for over two decades (Seccareccia and Parguez 1998).

The perversity of this type of concealed incomes policy – high real interest rates that favour interest income earners – would have been politically unacceptable if it were not for its presumed positive effects. Such effects derived from the greater international competitiveness that a low-inflation environment was supposed to bring about. The idea was that monetarist austerity would contribute to Canada's competitiveness by increasing aggregate labour productivity. In practice, however, this mechanism never materialized in a low-growth economy (Seccareccia and Lavoie 1996). As Stanford (1999) points out, Canada's competitiveness did improve, but it was achieved mostly by bringing down relative labour costs in relation to those of Canada's prime export market, the United States.[10]

Figure 9.7a   Evolution of Canada-us hourly compensation, total business sector, 1975=1.00, 1975–2001

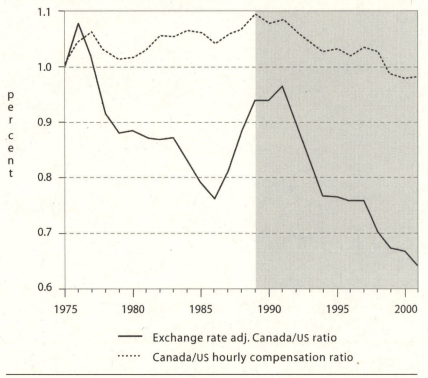

── Exchange rate adj. Canada/US ratio

······ Canada/US hourly compensation ratio

Source: Statistics Canada, CANSIM II, Series V720734 and V37426, and US Bureau of Labor Statistics, Series PRS84006103.

Figure 9.7a and figure 9.7b reveal the magnitude of the impact of high real interest rates beginning in the late 1980s. Specifically, the figures highlight the labour cost effects of restrictive monetary policy in Canada. As the figures are somewhat technical, the details are provided in endnotes.[11] The figures show that, between 1975 and the late 1980s, most of Canada's labour cost competitiveness advantage was realized primarily via exchange rate adjustment. On the other hand, for the zero-inflation, post-CUFTA period, the competitiveness advantage for Canadian industry was the result of both a falling exchange rate and declining relative hourly compensation in Canada vis-à-vis the United States.[12]

In short, the decline of the foreign exchange rate, which started in 1992, led to a dramatic growth of the export sector, despite the recessionary monetary policy. Indeed, as was shown earlier in figure 9.2, the post-1987 period was associated with an unprecedented growth of exports to the

Figure 9.7b   Evolution of Canada-US unit labour cost, total business sector, 1975=1.00, 1975–2001

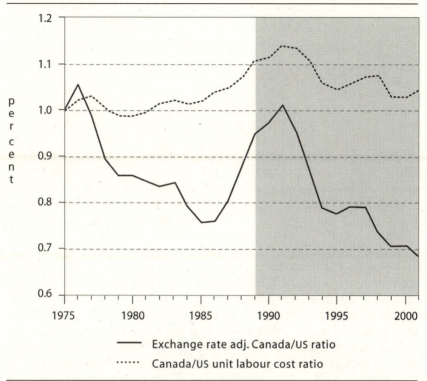

Source: Statistics Canada, CANSIM II, Series V720956 and V37426, and US Bureau of Labor Statistics, Series PRS84006113.

United States. When measured by the jobs being created in the export sector, especially since the late 1980s, the competitiveness strategy did, at first glance, succeed, even though the net effect is less obvious given that imports were also growing. Thus, the shock therapy of the low inflation strategy, which largely guaranteed the success of the export drive, simultaneously paralyzed domestic growth unrelated to the export sector.

The data in table 9.1 clearly substantiate the dramatic slowdown in real (constant dollar) GDP growth between the early postwar period (1951–74) and the last quarter century (1975–2001). From an average growth rate of 5.5 percent per annum for the postwar Keynesian era of low real interest rates, it fell to approximately one-half that growth in real GDP (2.8 percent) for the subsequent era of monetary austerity, with the lowest growth taking place primarily during the first half of the 1990s.

However, by the mid-1990s the Canadian monetary authorities began to

Table 9.1   GDP growth rates, Canada, 1951–2001 and selected sub-periods

Time period	Average percentage real GDP growth
1951–2001	3.9
1951–74	5.5
1975–2001	2.8
1975–89	3.1
1990–2001	2.5

Source: Statistics Canada, CANSIM I, series D102198, and CANSIM II, series V716152.

moderate their previous stance in support of high real interest rates. In its place the government increasingly relied on tight fiscal policy to quell the growth of domestic aggregate demand, wages, and prices. In part, this major shift in monetary policy was the result of too rigorous an application of the Crow doctrine of price stability. Indeed, by 1994 the monetary shock treatment that had so energetically been implemented since the late 1980s had brought about a serious downward price spiral in the Canadian economy for the first time in almost half a century (see figure 9.8), with the total CPI actually declining for a few months during mid- to late 1994. Also throughout a significant portion of the 1990s "core inflation"[13] remained stubbornly at (if not below) the low-end threshold of the Bank of Canada's target range of 1-to-3 percent. As can be seen from figure 9.8, as early as 1992 the heavy doses of monetary austerity that had vigorously been applied during the previous years had already attained the low inflation objective of a core inflation of less than 2 percent – a rate of inflation that was to be sustained throughout most of the 1990s and during the early years of the twenty-first century. It may be ascertained that the monetary authorities had indeed been successful in bringing down the rate of inflation from its peak rates of the 1970s and 1980s and, accompanying it, the rate of change of unit labour costs in Canada. However, this process of "disinflation" was achieved only at the terrible cost of persistently high long-term unemployment rates not seen since the Great Depression.

The Deflationary Nature of Fiscal Austerity

The Mulroney government had marketed the view that wasteful social programs put in place during the Trudeau era had caused the explosive public deficits and debt of the 1980s and early 1990s. In reality, the true cause of the growing fiscal imbalance was the high interest rate policy of the Bank of Canada. Rising interest charges on the public debt of all levels of government increased public spending, while government revenues went down

Figure 9.8   Percentage change in monthly CPI and core inflation calculated on annual basis, Canada, 1975–2002, and 1984–2002, respectively

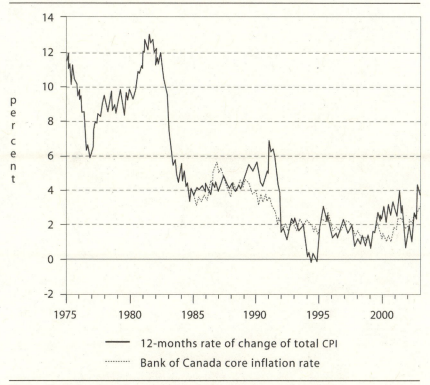

Source: Statistics Canada, CANSIM II, Series V735319 and V36398.

as unemployment rose. The compounding effect of these two factors was an explosive public debt (McCraken 1998).

Figure 9.9 presents the evolution of the actual, the primary, and the cyclically adjusted (or structural) fiscal budget balances[14] of all levels of government as a percentage of GDP, calculated on a national accounting basis.[15] The figure reveals that actual fiscal deficits began to explode when real interest rates started to rise in the mid-1970s, even though primary balances continued to remain in surplus territory, with the exception of the early 1980s recession. Faced with these growing actual deficits, and under pressure from both business and finance to pursue a policy of "sound finance," governments reacted by raising taxes and/or cutting program spending or, in some cases, by selling off public assets (commonly referred to as "privatization"). Hence, except for the few years following the recession of 1981–82, where some form of discretionary spending was still pursued, after the mid-1980s both Conservative and Liberal governments

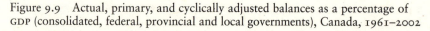

Figure 9.9   Actual, primary, and cyclically adjusted balances as a percentage of
GDP (consolidated, federal, provincial and local governments), Canada, 1961–2002

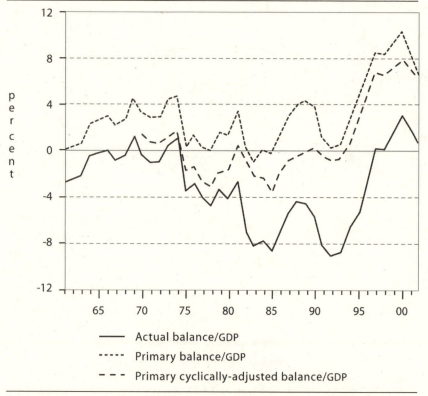

―――   Actual balance/GDP

-----   Primary balance/GDP

‒ ‒ ‒   Primary cyclically-adjusted balance/GDP

Source: Statistics Canada, CANSIM II, Series V498332, V498333, V498906, and
Federal Department of Finance.

in Ottawa began to target structural primary surpluses. Indeed, by the late
1980s the Conservatives had achieved significant primary surpluses, only
to be frustrated by John Crow's high real interest rate policy that pushed
the Canadian economy into a serious recession in 1990–91.

It was under the Chrétien government, however, that the targeting of
both primary and actual fiscal surpluses reached its peak. After 1994 the
Liberals learned that they could stimulate the economy somewhat by lowering interest rates while still keeping a considerable lid on inflation and
growth of domestic output by adopting a very restrictive fiscal policy (i.e.,
high structural primary surpluses). Hence, instead of relying on the less
predictable effects of restrictive *monetary* policy, during the last decade the
focus has shifted to restrictive *fiscal* policy. Governments have cut budgets
and created fiscal surpluses and, thus, have contributed to persistent high

Figure 9.10   Consumer debt to GDP and personal savings rate, Canada, 1961–2002

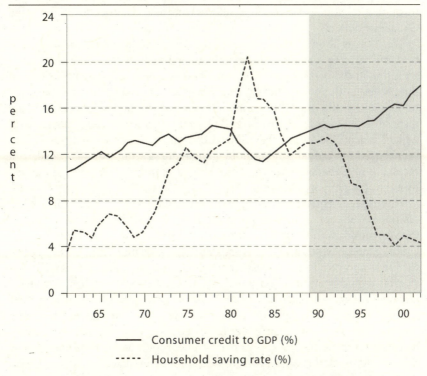

```
Consumer credit to GDP (%)
Household saving rate (%)
```

Source: Statistics Canada, CANSIM II, Series V122689, V498906,V508766, and V691783.

levels of unemployment. Instead of promoting growth and high employment, budget surpluses have served as enormous vacuums that have sucked money out of the economy[16] rather than as instruments for injecting money back in. Moreover, Canadian surpluses have been remarkable. They have been larger than those of our neighbours to the south and those of practically every other G7 country.

The strategy of deflation through fiscal austerity, accompanied by a loose monetary policy, did succeed in achieving record trade surpluses with the United States during the late 1990s. However, there are signs that this macroeconomic strategy may no longer be viable. First, the recession in the United States since 2001 has slowed US imports down somewhat, thereby presaging problems with Canada's export-led strategy. Second, the relatively slow growth in the United States has meant a declining US dollar vis-à-vis most major currencies, including the Canadian dollar. The latter phenomenon can quickly erode Canada's competitive advantage, which, as was discussed earlier, had been achieved during the late 1980s and 1990s through a combination of falling relative unit labour costs *and* a declining Canadian dollar.

Third, as is shown in figure 9.10, the huge rise in public surpluses has been mirrored by a tremendous expansion in household consumer debt and a decline in the personal savings rate. This is a new phenomenon since, in the 1960s and 1970s, the two variables (consumer debt and personal savings) generally moved together, in tandem with the rise in real personal disposable income (Seccareccia 2002a). The fragility of Canada's growth, which, much like during the Clinton expansion in the United States, has been based on growing household indebtedness, could quickly lead to a recession in Canada, as it did in the United States, unless saved somehow by expanding export demand.

There is currently renewed pressure in some policy circles for greater continental monetary integration with the United States. The reasons vary. One is the likelihood of a prolonged or "double dip" recession[17] in the United States (Arestis and Karakitsos 2003), which may further weaken the us dollar and put upward pressure on the Canadian dollar. Monetary integration would prevent a continued rise in the Canadian dollar from frustrating our export-led growth strategy. Another reason for the current push towards monetary integration is fear among conservatives that a future, more progressive Canadian government could revert to "interventionist" Keynesian policies. They see monetary integration as an insurance policy that would block this option. Moreover, these economists argue that Canada and the United States have become so closely integrated commercially since the adoption of CUFTA and NAFTA, why not go a step further and adopt a single currency that would reduce transactions costs and free producers and consumers in both countries from exchange rate risk?

GREATER NORTH AMERICAN MONETARY INTEGRATION?

Certain economists and policy analysts in Canada who support the logic of deeper continental integration, such as Courchene and Harris (1999) and Grubel (1999), view monetary union as the next stage in the integration process. The Europeans, who have recently established the European Economic and Monetary Union (EMU), have been quite clear that monetary integration is just one more step on the long road to the political unification of the European continent (Parguez, Seccareccia, and Gnos 2003). Although supporters of North American monetary integration have never made clear what should be the final *political* outcome for the North American continent, the possible *economic* outcomes are usually stated upfront.

First, it is argued that monetary integration would both consolidate and enhance cross-border trade, thereby transforming the two countries into an optimum currency area – that is, a common transactions space in which trade is carried out more efficiently and intensively than under the previous separate currencies (Rose 2000). Since the share of Canadian trade with the United States has already reached close to 90 percent, such a percentage share could only increase further under greater monetary integration. However, while there may be some economic benefits from greater trade, putting still more of our eggs in a single export basket would make Canada even more vulnerable to economic fluctuations in the United States. Hence, while eliminating exchange rate risk, greater monetary integration would certainly increase the macroeconomic risk of being tied to a single trading partner.

Second, a monetary union is seen as a way of tying the hands of the nation-state by taking away both its monetary and fiscal policy instruments. This is disconcerting for those who believe that there is a positive macroeconomic role for national governments in achieving greater welfare for their citizens. For instance, in dollarized regimes in Latin America, as well as in countries that joined the EMU, there is not only a loss of important instruments of monetary policy but also an effective loss of control over fiscal policy. This can be de facto, as in a dollarized regime, or de jure, as under the Maastricht Treaty and the Growth and Stability Pact in Europe. Either way, the country becomes more susceptible to the vagaries of the international economy since it can no longer engage in macroeconomic stabilization policies.

Third, monetary integration imparts a deflationary bias domestically whether it happens through a hard fix, currency boards, or dollarization (Bougrine and Seccareccia 2004).[18] It prevents governments from engaging in Keynesian policies to stabilize domestic incomes. It also inhibits the ability to respond to a negative export demand shock[19] (such as a US recession) by not allowing the Canadian dollar to depreciate – an action that mitigates the negative effect on domestic incomes. Without such a shock-absorbing capacity, the full impact of the shock would be transmitted directly to the domestic economy, much like under the gold standard (meaning that, rather than exchange rate depreciation, employment and output would fall). Hence, once again, what has happened is the substitution of exchange rate risk for a much worse risk – namely, the instability of the domestic economy.

If these negative deflationary effects are significant and they increase the vulnerability to international fluctuations, one wonders at the wisdom of greater monetary integration. Advocates claim there are many benefits to greater monetary integration that would more than offset these negative implications. In particular, they mention lower transactions costs, greater productivity growth, and lower long-term interest rates. However, when one seriously analyzes these supposed benefits, they turn out to be as fictitious and vacuous as are the supposed benefits of zero inflation, which were so strongly defended by the same advocates over a decade ago (Seccareccia 2002b).

CONCLUSION

This chapter describes how Canada has raced along the path of deep commercial integration during the post-Bretton Woods era, and especially over the last fifteen years of "free trade." The inordinate growth of the country's export sector was brought about in part by CUFTA and NAFTA, which removed some of the institutional barriers to trade. However, a more important contributor was macroeconomic policies that produced a lower exchange rate, depressed wages and prices, and restrained domestic growth. While this strategy succeeded in generating export growth, primarily to the United States, some advocates of deeper integration are now calling for institutional change that will bring about greater monetary integration. As argued earlier, such a jump towards monetary union would have serious implications, especially for the role of the state, which few Canadians would deem desirable.

Why then, one could ask, is there such support for an extreme export-led growth strategy among our political and business leaders, and even some trade unions? The answer is essentially ideological. It is premised on the principle that jobs are scarce in a capitalist economy and that the role of government should be limited to promoting the growth of private-sector jobs. If the private sector is incapable of providing such jobs when serving the domestic market, we should look to foreign trade as the mechanism for further job creation. Under this view, many high- and low-wage jobs in manufacturing and in services have become a scarce, internationally mobile resource, and thus countries have no choice but to compete for them. And to do that, one should deflate the domestic economy, in order to increase competitiveness and free up the resources required by export industries.

What if, instead, we stood this reasoning on its head and started from the premise that jobs are *not*, in fact, scarce because ultimately they *can* be created by the state to achieve effective full employment along Keynesian lines (Wray 1998)? It follows from this that exports can no longer be considered as a strategic source of scarce jobs. Much as in pre-capitalistic societies historically, a country would now want to export only because its citizens would wish to import goods that they cannot themselves produce. In this case, the prime motive for exports is the need to import scarce commodities and *not* the need to "import" scarce jobs (an action that requires deflating domestic incomes via a competitive race to the bottom).[20]

If the public sector plays the stabilizing role of creating jobs whenever the private sector is incapable of providing them, foreign trade need no longer be entrusted with the crucial role of job creation. Perhaps, much like Keynes (1933) suggested, it is only by breaking away from this ideological straitjacket regarding the negative role of government in creating jobs that current discourse and present trends in search of an elusive deeper integration can be reversed. This would entail a profound change in the logic of Canadian economic policy, which has always been outward looking and supportive of foreign trade, even at the expense of domestic growth. As pointed out by Albo (1997), however, such a strategy would ultimately be successful only if other countries abandon similar neomercantilist "beggar-thy-neighbour" policies and espouse an "international Keynesian" perspective in which all countries would be committed to a domestic growth strategy. Without such international coordination it would be very difficult to pursue a Keynesian growth strategy in one country (because of the obvious leakages through the foreign sector). Notwithstanding the challenge that this pro-growth Keynesian strategy poses in one country, in this age of competitive austerity it becomes ever more imperative that the current policy discourse take a sharp U-turn.

NOTES

With the usual disclaimers, the author would like to thank Marc Lavoie and the editors for their helpful comments.

1 As defined originally by Robert Mundell during the early 1960s, an optimal currency area is simply an economic region in which the benefits of adopting a common currency, especially in terms of lower transactions costs, are strong in relation to the status quo of maintaining separate currencies. Hence, the greater the commercial integration among regions, the greater would be the benefits of introducing a common currency since the introduction of the latter would entail significantly reduced transactions costs.

2 While, unlike "dollarization," "euroization" entails shared seigniorage and symmetric treatment of the member states, in both cases this would imply the loss of important instruments of macroeconomic policy. For further analysis, see Rochon and Rossi (2003).

3 "Somewhere around the first oil shock in 1973 … we entered a period known as the Leaden Age. The Leaden Age has been characterized by low rates of economic growth, low corporate profits, soaring income and wealth inequality, and much higher levels of economic insecurity" (Brenner 2002).

4 As with figure 9.3 below, a trend estimate depicting the underlying historical pattern is also traced in figure 9.2 by using the popular Hodrick-Prescott (H-P) filtering procedure as it is applied to the relevant time series data.

5 One might think that the growing share of non-traditional exports in this period
   is the result of the 1965 Canada-us Auto Pact. This is not the case, since the
   share of motor vehicles and parts remained relatively stable over time (see figure
   9.4).

6 This multiplier demonstrates the relationship between changes in export demand
   and resulting changes in employment.

7 "Unit labour costs" are simply wages divided by average labour productivity –
   that is to say, average labour costs adjusted for changes in the productivity of
   labour.

8 In technical terms, M1 (i.e., currency plus demand, or checkable, deposits).

9 As John Crow himself explains, "zero inflation" was not meant to be taken literally. For him, operationally "price stability" meant inflation "clearly below 2 per
   cent" (Grady 2003). Indeed, when taking into consideration quality changes in
   products entering the Consumer Price Index, it could be argued that a 2 percent
   rate would be much closer to what economists would mean by "price stability"
   than would a zero percent inflation rate.

10 Unless expressed in a foreign currency, in which case exchange rate variations
   would also matter, it should be clear to the reader that there are only two ways to
   reduce unit labour costs: (1) through an increase in average labour productivity
   or (2) through a decrease in wages. Since the late 1980s many economists at the
   Bank of Canada believed that a low inflation environment brought about by a
   tight monetary policy would enhance productivity growth, thereby reducing unit
   labour costs. Unfortunately, these economists did not understand that reducing
   the growth of the economy through a policy of monetary austerity would actually
   slow down (*not* increase) the growth in productivity in accordance with what, in
   the economics literature, has been commonly dubbed Verdoorn's law (which pos-
   tulates a positive correlation between output growth and productivity growth).
   Hence, instead of competing through higher productivity, the high interest rate
   policy of the Bank of Canada (associated with a macroeconomic environment of
   low inflation, low growth, and high unemployment throughout much of the
   1990s) would improve Canada's international competitiveness only by slowing
   wage growth and *not* by increasing productivity. Indeed, it was mainly by capping
   wage growth that Canadian firms were able to compete favourably in the us
   market and, despite the Bank of Canada's rhetoric to the contrary, not primarily
   through higher productivity growth. Hence, as suggested by the stylized facts previously discussed, the shift in favour of higher value-added exports was a result
   of the low wage growth environment and not strong gains in productivity growth
   (which clearly could not have materialized in the low-growth environment of the
   period).

11 Figure 9.7a shows an index that compares employee earnings in Canada with
   those in the United States (the ratio of total hourly compensation of the business
   sector as a whole between Canada and the United States). The top dotted line
   shows that index between 1975 and 2001 on the basis of the actual nominal
   changes calculated in the respective national currencies. The second heavy line

shows the same index when the Canadian hourly compensation rate was calculated based on a common currency, the US dollar.

12 If we consider that aggregate productivity grew more quickly during most of the 1980s and 1990s in the United States than it did in Canada, we still find essentially the same historical pattern, albeit slightly mitigated. Noting that unit labour costs are simply the ratio of hourly labour compensation divided by average labour productivity (output per person-hour), figure 9.7b shows relative unit labour costs in Canada versus relative unit labour costs in the United States. We can easily observe that Canada's competitiveness position deteriorated somewhat during the 1980s (see the top dotted line of the figure), and it then improved during the last decade, largely because of lower wage growth in Canada. However, as before, when adjusting for exchange rate changes, Canadian unit labour costs witnessed a spectacular fall when calculated in US dollars, especially during the 1990s.

13 The core inflation rate is defined as the percentage rate of change in the CPI excluding the eight most volatile components (fruit, vegetables, gasoline, fuel, natural gas, mortgage interest, intercity transportation, and tobacco products) as well as the effects of changes in indirect taxes on the remaining components.

14 The "actual budget balance" is simply the accounting difference between total expenditures and revenues of all levels of governments. The "primary balance" is determined when interest payments on the public debt are netted out of total expenditures, so that only the difference between program spending and revenues remains. The "cyclically adjusted (or structural) balance" refers to the balances that would have existed during each year if one were controlling for non-discretionary net spending arising endogenously from the ups and downs of the Canadian economy (in other words, the difference between expenditures and revenues if the economy were running at full capacity).

15 In Canada, budget balances are measured in accordance with either the "public accounts" or the "national accounts." In estimating the budget balance, among the major differences the national accounts also include revenues and expenditures relating to government employee pension accounts. It is this latter measure that is regularly used, for instance, when doing international comparisons.

16 A budget surplus means that total expenditures are smaller than total revenues. Since the government is pumping out fewer dollars than it is taking in, it has a contractive effect on the money supply.

17 This is a recession followed by a brief recovery followed by another recession.

18 As has been discussed elsewhere (Seccareccia 2003–04), there exists a whole assortment of exchange rate regimes. All regimes outside of a sovereign floating rate entail some degree of constraint (both direct and indirect) on the conduct of macroeconomic policy. For instance, under the umbrella of fixed exchange rates, one finds a whole array of intermediate regimes going from a "hard fix" to adjustable or "crawling pegs" – all being mere variants of a generic archetype described loosely as a system of fixed exchange rates. Hence, a "hard fix" is a pegged exchange rate usually set by government decree. On the other hand, a

fluctuating exchange rate with bands of the type that we had in Canada between 1962 and 1970 is also often referred to as a "fixed" exchange rate regime.

A currency board arrangement is characterized by two key features: (1) much like "hard fix" exchange rate systems, under a currency board arrangement the exchange rate is set by law (e.g., in the Argentine case it was pegged at a conversion rate of one Argentine peso to the US dollar); and (2) the currency board can only issue its own domestic currency if the latter is backed by foreign currency (e.g., in the case of Argentina and Hong Kong by US dollars) at the conversion rate as set out in (1) above. Hence, in order to issue domestic currency as its liability, the currency board would first have to receive US dollars of an equivalent amount.

Finally, dollarization exists when one country unilaterally adopts the currency of another country either de facto (market dollarization) or de jure (policy dollarization). There are literally dozens of dollarized states in the world today, and the vast majority of them reflect an incapacity on the part of the local authorities to issue a generally accepted currency in which their populations have confidence. This is either because of the very tiny geographical size of the country whose state structure is so weak as to be unable to enforce even the payment of taxes in their own currencies (such as with, say, Liechtenstein, the Republic of San Marino, or, more recently, the Republic of Montenegro) or because of a former, and persistent, colonial relation (as with Panama, Puerto Rico, and the Virgin Islands in relation to the United States).

19 A fall in export demand.

20 This rejection of export growth *en outrance* should not suggest to the reader that, as a country, we should not also pursue industrial policies that would compete for high-skill / high-productivity jobs internationally, especially if they would be the type of jobs characterized by high incomes and more stable employment prospects. It is just that a competitiveness strategy based on low wage growth is, by its very nature, highly inimical to productivity improvement. A low domestic growth strategy of the type witnessed during most of the 1990s in Canada would ensure that we would be competing more and more on the basis of low-wage, low-skill production rather than high-skill, high-tech jobs associated with a dynamic economy. Hence, instead of an economy characterized by a virtuous cycle of strong productivity growth based on solid domestic macroeconomic performance, the Canadian economy would face a vicious cycle of competitive deflation, stagnant productivity, and the proliferation of low-wage jobs.

REFERENCES

Albo, Gregory. 1997. A World Market of Opportunities: Capitalist Obstacles and Left Economic Policy. *Socialist Register 1997: Ruthless Criticism of all that Exists*, ed. Leo Panitch, 5–47. London: Merlin Press.

Arestis, Philip, and Elias Karakitsos. 2003. Asset and Debt Deflation in the United States: How Far Can Equity Prices Fall? In *Public Policy Brief No. 73*. Blithewood: Jerome Levy Economics Institute.

Bougrine, Hassan, and Mario Seccareccia. 2004. Alternative Exchange Rate Arrangements and Effective Demand: An Important Missing Analysis in the Debate over Great North American Monetary Integration. *Journal of Post Keynesian Economics* 26 (Summer): 655–77.

Brenner, Mark. 2002. *Trends in the Economy and Their Relationship with the Construction Industry.* Presentation to the AUD Conference. New York: Association for Union Democracy.

Bryce, Robert B. 1939. The Effects on Canada of Industrial Fluctuations in the United States. *Canadian Journal of Economics and Political Science* 5 (3): 373–86.

Courchene, Thomas J. 1976. *Money, Inflation and the Bank of Canada: An Analysis of Canadian Monetary Policy from 1970 to Early 1975.* Montreal: C.D. Howe Institute.

Courchene, Thomas J., and Richard G. Harris. 1999. From Fixing to Monetary Union: Options for North American Currency Integration. In *C.D. Howe Institute Commentary No. 127.* Toronto: C.D. Howe Institute.

Grady, Patrick. 2003. *Straight, Hardhitting Talk from a Former Governor of the Bank of Canada: A Review of Making Money: An Insider's Perspective on Finance Politics, and Canada's Central Bank by John Crow.* Available at <http://www.global-economics.ca>, cited 12 March 2003.

Grubel, Herbert G. 1999. The Case for the Amero: The Economics and Politics of a North American Monetary Union. In *Critical Issues Bulletin.* Vancouver: The Fraser Institute.

Innis, Harold A. 1930. *The Fur Trade in Canada: An Introduction to Canadian Economic History.* New Haven, CT: Yale University Press.

Keynes, John Maynard. 1933. National Self-Sufficiency. In *The Collected Writings of John Maynard Keynes*, vol. 21, ed. D.E. Moggridge, 233–46, London: Macmillan Press, 1982.

McCraken, Michael C. 1998. Recent Canadian Monetary Policy: Deficit and Debt Implications. In *Hard Money, Hard Times: Why Zero Inflation Hurts Canadians*, ed. L. Osberg and P. Fortin, 74–92. Toronto: Lorimer.

Macdonald Report. 1985. *Report of the Royal Commission on the Economic Union and Development Prospects for Canada.* Ottawa: Minister of Supply and Services.

Parguez, Alain, Mario Seccareccia, and Claude Gnos. 2003. The Theory and Practice of European Monetary Integration: Lessons for North America. In *Dollarization: Lessons from Europe and the Americas*, ed. L.-P. Rochon and M. Seccareccia, 48–69. London and New York: Routledge.

Pettifor, Ann, ed. 2003. *Real World Economic Outlook: The Legacy of Globalization – Debt and Deflation.* London: Palgrave Macmillan.

Rochon, Louis-Philippe, and Sergio Rossi. 2003. Dollarization Out, Euroization In. *International Journal of Political Economy* 33 (Spring): 21–41.

Rose, Andrew. 2000. One Money, One Market: The Effect of Common Currencies on Trade. *Economic Policy: A European Forum* 40 (April): 7–45.

Seccareccia, Mario. 1998. Wicksellian Norm, Central Bank Real Interest Rate Targeting and Macroeconomic Performance. In *The Political Economy of Central Banking*, ed. P. Arestis and M.C. Sawyer, 180–98. Cheltenham: Edward Elgar.

– 2002a. Las bajas tasas de ahorro y el endeudamiento domestico son factores que contraen el crecimiento economico? [Are Low Saving Rates and Growing Household Indebtedness Constraining Factors on Economic Growth?]. *Cuestiones Economicas* 18 (1): 169–90.

– 2002b. *North American Monetary Integration: Should Canada Join the Dollarization Bandwagon?* Ottawa: Canadian Centre for Policy Alternatives.

– 2003–2004. Is Dollarization a Desirable Alternative to the Monetary Status Quo? A Critical Evaluation of Competing Currency Arrangements for Canada. *Studies in Political Economy* 71/72 (Autumn/Winter): 91–108.

Seccareccia, Mario, and Marc Lavoie. 1996. Central Bank Austerity Policy, Zero-Inflation Targets, and Productivity Growth in Canada. *Journal of Economic Issues* 30 (2): 533–55.

Seccareccia, Mario, and Alain Parguez. 1998. Les Politiques d'Inflation Zéro: La Vraie Cause de la Hausse Tendancialle du Chômage dans les Pays Occidentaux. In *Objectif Plein Emploi: Le Marché, la Social-Democratie ou l'Économie Sociale*, ed. D.-G. Tremblay, 183–203. Montréal: Presses de l'Université du Québec.

Smithin, John. 1996. *Macroeconomic Policy and the Future of Capitalism: The Revenge of the Rentiers and the Threat to Prosperity.* Cheltenham: Edward Elgar.

Stanford, Jim. 1999. *Paper Boom: Why Real Prosperity Requires a New Approach to Canada's Economy.* Toronto: James Lorimer/Canadian Centre for Policy Alternatives.

White, Derek A. 1967. *Business Cycles in Canada.* Economic Council of Canada, Staff Study No. 17. Ottawa: Queen's Printer.

Wray, L. Randall. 1998. *Understanding Modern Money: The Key to Full Employment and Price Stability.* Cheltenham: Edward Elgar.

10

All Pain, No Gain:
Canadian Labour in the Integrated North American Economy

DAVID ROBINSON

The increased benefits from the Trade Agreement will start to be realized shortly after the implementation of the Agreement on January 1, 1989. Prices for a wide range of consumer goods will begin to decline, expanding the purchasing power of Canadian households. Investment in plant and equipment will expand as Canadian firms move to take advantage of their enhanced access to the huge US market place. Increased consumer and investment spending will lead to stronger economic growth and more job creation. Department of Finance estimates of the impacts of the Agreement on employment over the government's medium-term fiscal planning horizon indicate that 120,000 net new jobs will be created by 1993, only five years into the agreement.

Department of Finance, Canada, 1988

Economists, being the dismal scientists they are, are not known for their sense of humour. Yet, seen now in the harsh light of the past decade and a half, the positive projections offered by Canada's Department of Finance number crunchers of the gains to be reaped by free trade with the United States could easily be interpreted as one of the cruellest jokes in Canadian history. Following the implementation of the Canada-United States Free Trade Agreement (CUFTA) in 1989, the economy defied the boosters of trade liberalization by abruptly sliding into the most protracted recession since the Great Depression of the 1930s. Real economic growth stagnated, unemployment rates soared, consumer spending flat-lined, and household incomes dropped sharply. Just five years into the agreement, as illustrated below, the 120,000 net new jobs so confidently predicted in 1988 turned into a net loss of more than 350,000, with the national unemployment rate skyrocketing from 7.5 percent to 11.4 percent.

This chapter analyzes the fallout of Canada's deepening economic integration with the United States from the perspective of working people, paying particular attention to the impact on employment, wages, workers' rights, and labour market policies. It highlights the dismal performance of the Canadian labour market in the wake of trade liberalization over the past decade and considers the potential impact of further economic integration. A variety of factors were to blame for the deterioration of the labour market in the 1990s, including quite centrally the negative impact of high interest rates and fiscal retrenchment on the Canadian economy in the early part of the last decade. However, while restrictive monetary and fiscal policies were clearly the key drivers of the great slump of the 1990s, there are nevertheless strong links between these policies and Canada's deepening economic integration with the United States. As argued below, trade liberalization has been a central part of a broader package of initiatives aimed at radically restructuring and readjusting the Canadian economy in a way that has hurt working people. In short, economic integration with the United States is closely connected with other institutional changes in the Canadian economy that have adversely affected the labour market.

THE LOST DECADE: THE LABOUR MARKET IN THE 1990S

Neoclassical economic theory suggests that increased trade liberalization and economic integration may have limited short-term negative impacts on certain sectors of the economy and certain groups of workers but that it eventually produces long-term gains in productivity and growth that, in turn, fuel strength in the labour market. The elimination of tariffs and other barriers to the free flow of goods and services, it is argued, opens up access to new markets and promotes new investment as firms seek to take advantage of new growth opportunities. Increased competition from foreign producers encourages domestic firms, now no longer protected by tariff barriers, to become more competitive and efficient. This, in turn, promotes the reallocation of capital to more productive industries and the specialization and division of labour that will, it is argued, result in stronger productivity gains, increased employment, and higher incomes. Such gains for working people, the theory suggests, will be achieved even in the case of deeper economic integration between higher wage economies with stronger labour standards (like Canada) and lower wage nations with weaker labour market regulations.

This neoclassical theory of the mutual gains to be achieved from trade liberalization rests on a number of questionable assumptions, however. Critically, it is assumed that an economy enjoys full employment so that workers displaced from one job can easily move to another job in a now more productive and efficient sector. In the context of high unemployment and a scarcity of jobs, however, the mobility of workers displaced as a result of trade liberalization is highly curtailed.

Similarly, the theory also assumes that capital investment will automatically flow from less efficient to more productive sectors that will, in turn, generate new jobs in expanding firms to offset those jobs lost due to an increase in imports. The problem is that trade agreements like CUFTA and NAFTA are about more than tariff reductions. One of the most troubling aspects of these agreements is the degree to which they facilitate capital mobility and empower capital over labour. It is no mistake that investment provisions lie literally at the heart of NAFTA. Neoclassical theorists ignore the fact that trade agreements free up capital to more easily cross borders, thereby providing no guarantee that new investment in the domestic economy will balance out declining investment in industries being displaced by imports. The real possibility of capital flight unleashed by trade and investment agreements means that capital may not necessarily be reallocated from declining sectors of the economy but may, instead, flow to foreign sources (Jackson 1999).

The claims that early proponents of free trade with the United States made about the positive outcomes of deeper economic integration were so unabashedly confident precisely because they relied heavily on neoclassical economic logic and largely ignored its theoretical flaws. The Economic Council of Canada, for instance, predicted that the "most likely outcome" of the free trade agreement would be a real increase of 2.5 percent of GDP by 1998 and a 1.8 percent boost in employment, or a net gain of 251,000 jobs (ECC 1988, 18). The council did anticipate some job losses in heavily protected industries but concluded that these declines would be very small and easily offset by growth in other industries. Similarly, the federal Department of Finance claimed that the agreement would raise real incomes by 2.5 percent, with a whopping 10.6 percent increase in manufacturing employment to be realized (Canada 1988, 22–3, 108). Both studies concluded that the gains from trade liberalization would be distributed evenly across the country.

The record of Canada's labour market performance could not be more different than that predicted by the proponents of free trade. The projected jobs windfall never materialized, and Canada's labour market posted one of the weakest performances on record over the decade following the implementation of CUFTA. The national unemployment rate soared from 7.5 percent in 1989 to 11.4 percent in 1993 and remained over 9 percent through 1997 (see table 10.1). Overall, it was not until the end of the decade that the unemployment rate finally returned to its pre-recession level, although as of 2005 the unemployment rate for youth remained higher than it had been in 1989.

Table 10.1   Canada's unemployment rate, 1989 to 2005 (%)

	1989	1991	1993	1995	1997	1999	2003	2005
Total	7.5	10.3	11.4	9.4	9.1	7.6	7.6	6.8
Men	7.4	10.9	12.0	9.8	9.3	7.8	8.1	7.0
Women	7.8	9.7	10.6	9.0	8.9	7.3	7.1	6.5
15–24 years old	11.0	15.8	17.1	14.7	16.2	14.0	13.6	12.4

Source: Statistics Canada, Labour Force Survey.

Table 10.2   Manufacturing employment, Canada, 1988 and 1993 (000s)

	1988	1993	% change
Total	1,992	1,719	–13.7
Food	208	180	–13.5
Clothing	121	85	–29.8
Primary metals	103	80	–38.5
Fabricated metal products	174	135	–22.4
Machinery (non-electrical)	85	65	–23.5
Electrical and electrical products	157	116	–26.1
Transportation equipment	224	197	–12.1

Source: Statistics Canada, Employment Earnings and Hours.

Interestingly, the unemployment rate was lower for men in 1989 than it was for women, but it rose more rapidly following the implementation of CUFTA than did the rate for women. This largely reflects the heavy job losses in the male-dominated manufacturing sector that followed deeper economic integration with the United Sates. Between 1988 and 1995 nearly one in five manufacturing plants in Canada disappeared as firms closed or relocated, with the steepest declines recorded in clothing, furniture, and printing and publishing (Jackson 1999). In just the first four years of the deal, employment plummeted between 22 percent and 39 percent in key industries like steel and primary metals, clothing, electrical products, machinery, and fabricated metal products (see table 10.2).

The severe hit taken by the manufacturing sector meant that job losses were heavily concentrated in the country's industrial heartland. Ontario experienced an unprecedented wave of plant closures and layoffs in the early 1990s, and the provincial unemployment rate more than doubled between 1989 and 1992 (see table 10.3). Quebec also suffered from a large loss of manufacturing jobs, with the unemployment rate rising from 9.3 percent to nearly 13 percent. In Atlantic Canada, already high unemployment rates rose even further, while the resource-based economies of the Western provinces experienced more moderate changes.

Table 10.3   Provincial unemployment rates, 1989–2005 (%)

	1989	1992	1995	1999	2003	2005
Newfoundland	15.7	20.2	18.1	16.9	16.7	15.2
PEI	14.0	17.9	15.0	14.4	11.1	10.8
Nova Scotia	9.9	13.1	12.1	9.6	9.3	8.4
New Brunswick	12.4	12.8	11.2	10.2	10.6	9.7
Quebec	9.3	12.8	11.4	9.3	9.1	8.3
Ontario	5.1	10.9	8.7	6.3	7.0	6.6
Manitoba	7.6	9.7	7.2	5.6	5.0	4.8
Saskatchewan	7.5	8.2	6.6	6.1	5.6	5.1
Alberta	7.3	9.5	6.9	5.7	5.1	3.9
British Columbia	9.1	10.5	8.7	8.3	8.1	5.9

Source: Statistics Canada, Labour Force Survey.

Table 10.4   Labour force participation rates, Canada, 1989–2005 (%)

	1989	1992	1995	1997	1999	2003	2005
National	67.5	65.9	64.9	64.8	65.6	67.5	67.2
Men	77.1	74.0	72.5	72.5	72.5	73.6	72.8
Women	58.3	58.0	57.5	57.4	58.9	61.6	61.8
15-24 years old	70.6	65.3	63.2	61.2	63.5	67.0	65.9
Adults	66.7	66.0	65.3	65.5	66.0	67.6	67.5

Source: Statistics Canada, Labour Force Survey.

As the labour market soured, the participation rate – the proportion of the working-age population working or looking for work – also declined sharply. Table 10.4 illustrates trends in the participation rate over the 1990s. The rate fell steadily from 1989 to 1997, reflecting the weakness of the job market over this period. Over the entire period of recession and slow growth between 1989 and 1999, the share of the working-age population in the labour force fell from 67.5 percent to 65.6 percent. Put another way, if the labour force participation rate in 1999 had been the same as in 1989, there would have been an additional 299,000 unemployed workers, and the unemployment rate would have been 9.5 percent instead of 7.6 percent.[1] It was not until 2003 that the participation rate finally recovered to its 1989 level.

Further evidence of the severe downturn in the labour market at this time can be seen in the rapid rise in the average duration of unemployment. As illustrated in table 10.5, the average number of weeks unemployed Canadians remained without a job jumped sharply in the downturn of the early 1990s, from 17.8 weeks in 1989 to 22.6 weeks in 1992. Strikingly, it was

Table 10.5   Average duration of unemployment (weeks), selected years*

	1976	1989	1992	1998	2002	2005
All	13.9	17.8	22.6	20.4	16.2	15.5
Men	14.1	18.9	23.8	21.6	16.9	15.9
Women	13.7	16.5	20.8	18.9	15.3	14.9

*calculated with an upper limit of ninety-nine weeks
Source: Statistics Canada, Labour Force Survey.

Table 10.6   Employment by class of worker, 1989 and 1998 (000s)

	1989	1992	1997	1998	% change 1989–98
Total employment	13,086	12,842	13,941	14,326	9.5
Self-employment	1,809	1,936	2,488	2,525	39.6
Full-time paid employment	9,449	8,937	9,349	9,679	2.4
Part-time paid employment	1,828	1,969	2,103	2,122	16.1

Source: Statistics Canada, Labour Force Survey.

well over a decade before the average time unemployed Canadians spent before finding work returned to pre-recession levels, indicating just how difficult it was to secure a job over the course of the 1990s.

One key reason for the increase in the duration of unemployment was that the number of permanent layoffs in the manufacturing sector rose dramatically in the 1990s as a result of plant closings and relocations. The permanent layoff rate among Canadian men rose from 6.9 percent in 1978 to 8.6 percent in 1994 (Sunter and Bowlby 1998). The experience of Canadians laid off during the recession of the 1990s contrasted markedly with those who lost their jobs a decade earlier. During the recession of 1981–82, most unemployed workers were eventually rehired by the company that laid them off. Just 22 percent of workers lost their job because of plant closings during this time, compared with 65 percent following the implementation of CUFTA (Merrett 1996, 156).

The result was that the labour market of the 1990s was also characterized by a rapid rise in precarious employment. Table 10.6 illustrates changes in employment from 1989 to 1998 by class of worker. What is striking is that the number of full-time paid jobs in Canada did not return to its 1989 level until 1998, meaning that nearly all the job growth in this period came in the form of self-employment and part-time jobs. Self-employment rose an unprecedented 40 percent. Most of this growth was not due to individuals setting up successful businesses but, rather, as a result of an increase in low-wage "own account" employment – individuals who work just for themselves and have no employees. The average annual salary of those self-employed on their own account was just $22,000 in 1995, with own-account female workers earning just $14,800. Overall, nearly three-quarters of the 716,000 self-employed "jobs" created between 1989 and 1998 were own account jobs, compared to just one-third of all self-employed jobs created in the 1980s (Hughes 1999; Jackson and Robinson 2000). Clearly, the massive growth in self-employment in the 1990s reflected the lack of full-time paid jobs and not, as some claimed, the blossoming of a new entrepreneurial spirit in the country.

Weakness in the labour market following CUFTA meant that wage growth remained anaemic over the course of the 1990s. Average hourly earnings rose less than 2 percent in real terms. Median annual earnings of working people, adjusted for inflation, fell nearly 3 percent between 1989 and 1998. Lower-income families bore the brunt of this decline in wages as earning inequalities widened. Excluding government transfers, the market income received by the bottom 10 percent of families fell 31 percent between 1990 and 1996 (Yalnizyan 1998). Overall, the bottom 40 percent of all households in Canada saw their total inflation-adjusted income fall by close to 5 percent between 1989 and 1998. The next 40 percent saw virtually no change in income (Robinson 2001). It is striking that even those workers in sectors that have been "winners" under free trade have seen virtually no wage growth (Jackson 1999).

By the late 1990s trade liberalization, sold to a sceptical public on the promise of rising employment and incomes, had clearly failed to deliver the goods for working people in Canada. Job growth stalled for nearly an entire decade and wages and incomes stagnated. That the 1990s was one of the worst decades on record for working people is not in dispute. What remains at issue is to what extent deepening economic integration is to blame for the disastrous economic performance of the 1990s.

EXPLAINING THE GREAT CANADIAN SLUMP OF THE 1990S

Determining what the precise impact CUFTA and NAFTA have had on Canada's poor labour market performance and slow wage growth of the 1990s is no simple matter. Proponents of trade liberalization have been at pains to point to other factors that might explain the downturn, including everything from an alleged skills mismatch to purportedly high levels of taxation. It is certainly true that a range of factors, including quite centrally monetary and fiscal policy, can influence employment in a variety of ways. Nevertheless, recent research into the employment impact of the trade agreements has generally supported the concern of critics that deeper economic integration with the United States would produce negative labour market outcomes, particularly in those industries in the manufacturing sector previously protected by tariffs. The debates that remain centre largely on the extent of job losses that can be attributed to CUFTA and NAFTA, and whether the initial steep decline in employment has been offset by longer-run gains in productivity and renewed job growth.

Supporters of deeper economic integration with the United States promised strong job gains once CUFTA was in place. As the economy slipped into recession and unemployment rates skyrocketed in the early 1990s, they were quickly put on the defensive. The federal government initially blamed the rise in joblessness on the global recession, but that alone failed to explain why Canada's rate of per capita economic growth in the 1990s was the slowest of any industrial country. Later, it was argued that the job shortage was really a "skills shortage" as unemployed workers simply lacked the skills demanded by employers in the emerging "knowledge-based" economy. However, as Osberg and Lin (2000) have detailed, only 1 percentage point of unemployment in the 1990s can be attributed to a skills mismatch.

Recent research into the employment effects of increasing economic integration with the United States does point to a negative impact on particular sectors of the Canadian economy and certain segments of the workforce. Beaulieu (2000), for instance, identifies a link between CUFTA and job losses among less-skilled production workers, a significant finding given that the government's promised job retraining program for workers displaced as a result of the trade agreement never materialized. Schwanen (2001) concludes that, in liberalized sectors of industry facing an import surge, employment was already weakening throughout the 1980s but dropped markedly after CUFTA came in effect in 1989. Similarly, Trefler (2000) estimates that roughly a quarter of the drop in manufacturing employment between 1989 and 1996 was directly related to the fallout of CUFTA. Merrett (1996, 281–6) calculates that, in the first few years of CUFTA and NAFTA, more than 42,000 manufacturing jobs were moved from Canada to the United States and Mexico.

In a detailed analysis of the labour market between 1989 and 1997, Dungan and Murphy (1999) show that, while exports grew quickly after the implementation of CUFTA, the domestic content of exports actually fell. Overall, imports expanded sharply in this period and adversely affected the labour market in Canada. They conclude that trade liberalization has meant that "imports are displacing 'relatively' more jobs than exports are adding" (Dungan and Murphy 1999, iv). Based on this research, Campbell (2000) calculates that, as of 1997, the FTA and NAFTA had cost the Canadian economy nearly 300,000 jobs.

Other research, while concluding trade liberalization has had a negative impact on employment, nevertheless suggests that the number of jobs lost as a result of CUFTA and NAFTA has been relatively modest. Osberg, Wien, and Grude (1995) argue that free trade has been a critical factor in explaining job losses in some sectors but, overall, played only a minor role in the rise in total unemployment in the early half of the 1990s. They note that over 70 percent of the labour force is employed in the service sector where, they claim, the impact of the CUFTA and NAFTA has been relatively small. In addition, they argue, many manufacturing industries remained unaffected by the deal as they either always exported most of their products or because, like the automobile and aerospace sector, they had operated with low or no tariffs to begin with.

Overall, then, while debates remain about the full extent of job losses under trade liberalization, even many supporters of CUFTA and NAFTA do not dispute the fact that there has been a negative impact on employment in Canada. However, proponents tend to stick to the belief that these job losses were only a temporary dose of pain needed to secure more permanent gains in productivity and employment. Trefler (2000) and Dungan and Murphy (1999) suggest, echoing neoclassical theory, that CUFTA forced firms previously protected by tariff barriers to become more productive, while resources in the economy as a whole were reallocated from nonefficient to more competitive sectors. This, in turn, is making the economy more productive and will drive new job growth. At first blush, the rapid rise in employment at the end of the 1990s and the beginning of the new millennium would seem to lend credence to this view.

The evidence in support of this contention, however, is sorely lacking. On the productivity front, it is clearly the case that the sharp gains predicted after the implementation of CUFTA have simply not materialized. Put plainly, Canadian firms are barely more efficient than they were before CUFTA was put in place. Even the very slow growth in productivity in the post-CUFTA era did not come as a result of firms improving their efficiency. As Gu, Sawchuck, and Whewell (2003) have shown, the small gains that have been recorded are chiefly the result of less competitive firms closing down rather than surviving firms becoming more efficient. Essentially, productivity increases have come as a result of inefficient plants going out of business and remaining firms reducing their payrolls. By this measure, as Andrew Jackson argues in chapter 8 (this volume), free trade has been a complete bust.

Suggestions that the rebound in employment by the late 1990s proves that free trade has finally generated the long anticipated payoff ignore the centrality of monetary and fiscal policies at play. The most compelling explanation for Canada's great economic slump of the 1990s and the subsequent turnaround is that monetary and fiscal policies were the key factors (Fortin 1999; Seccareccia, chapter 9, this volume). An aggressive and misguided stance on the part of the Bank of Canada in the early 1990s

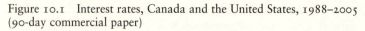

Figure 10.1   Interest rates, Canada and the United States, 1988–2005
(90-day commercial paper)

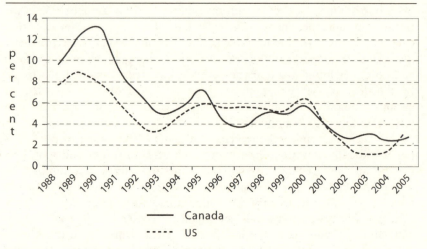

Source: Bank of Canada; US Federal Reserve.

to wipe out inflation led to high interest rates that choked off private investment and consumer spending, pushed up unemployment, and drove the economy deep into recession. As illustrated in figure 10.1, short-term interest rates in Canada jumped to over 13 percent in 1990 and were 5 percentage points higher than those in the United States. This fuelled a sharp rise in the Canadian dollar at the same time – not coincidentally, some would suggest – that CUFTA came into force in 1989.[2]

This steep appreciation in the dollar had serious consequences for Canada's manufacturing sector. As is shown in figure 10.2, employment in manufacturing dropped sharply as the dollar rose in value in the early 1990s, and it increased only when the dollar fell below seventy-five cents. The result of a high currency in the early 1990s was that exports became less competitive, Canada's merchandise trade surplus with the United States fell, firms scaled back on employment and new investments, consumer spending contracted, and the economy was dragged into a deep recession.

High interest rates also put pressure on public finances as governments in Canada suddenly faced huge increases in their debt-servicing costs. This occurred at the same time as the recession was cutting government revenues, while skyrocketing unemployment rates were increasing demand for income support programs. Thus, a vicious cycle of debt accumulation was unleashed that eventually paved the way for a wave of severe fiscal retrenchment that prolonged the recession.

Figure 10.2   Manufacturing employment and exchange rates, 1987–2005

Source: Bank of Canada; US Federal Reserve.

That said, it is critical to recognize that there is more to this story than just a series of gross errors in monetary and fiscal policy judgment. While critics have rightly condemned the Bank of Canada for its single-minded determination to not just reduce but also completely eliminate inflation, they have often failed to recognize the link between monetary tightening and the onset of CUFTA. It is, after all, difficult to justify the bank's high interest rate policy in the early 1990s solely on the basis of a perceived inflationary threat. Inflation in 1989 was 5 percent, only a fraction above the level recorded in the United States. This alone hardly justified the more extreme interest rate hikes in Canada. In the United States inflation was tamed with a much more modest dose of monetary discipline, and the recovery began much quicker than it did here. At the same time, while wage increases in Canada were rising somewhat faster than productivity growth, these increases still showed little sign of fuelling serious inflationary pressures. The tight money policy adopted was clearly motivated by more than just an anti-inflation crusade. As Campbell (2000), Jackson (1999), and Seccareccia (chapter 9, this volume) convincingly argue, monetary policy that fuelled high unemployment also had the effect of disciplining labour in the new post-CUFTA era.

Seen in this light, monetary policy was an important instrument being wielded to increase Canadian industry's competitiveness in relation to the United States. It is worth recalling that the latter half of the 1980s

Figure 10.3   Manufacturing unit labour cost index, Canada and the United States, 1977–2004 (national currency basis)

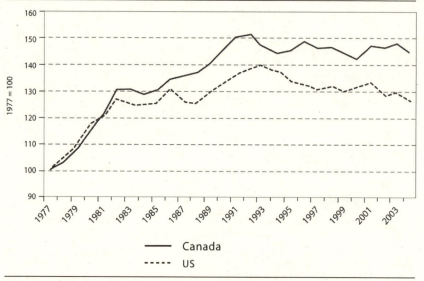

Source: Calculations based on us Bureau of Labor Statistics.

witnessed a steady increase in unit labour costs and the erosion of Canada's competitive position vis-à-vis the us manufacturing sector.[3] Figure 10.3 plots changes in manufacturing unit labour costs (in national currencies) in Canada and the United States. As illustrated, unit labour costs grew at about the same pace in Canada and the United States from 1977 to the early 1980s. After that, however, costs rose more rapidly in Canada in the 1980s than they did in the United States. Over this period, productivity was rising more slowly in Canada, but wages, even though barely increasing in real terms, were nevertheless climbing faster than they were in the less unionized us manufacturing sector.

The increase in unit labour costs in Canada, however, was partly offset by differences in the exchange rate and a weaker Canadian dollar. As is illustrated in figure 10.4, when measured against a rising us dollar, Canada's unit labour costs actually fell in the mid-1980s. As the Canadian dollar gained strength towards the latter half of the decade, however, unit labour costs in relative terms increased again. By the late 1980s Canadian manufacturers were becoming less cost competitive than their us counterparts just when they were about to become more integrated into the us economy through CUFTA. Not surprisingly, then, many business groups in Canada were loudly bemoaning their loss of competitiveness in the late 1980s.

Figure 10.4   Manufacturing unit labour cost index, 1977–2004 (US dollar basis)

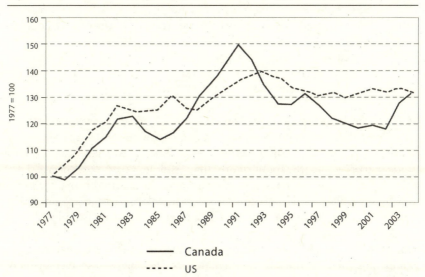

Legend:
——— Canada
----- US

Source: Calculations based on US Bureau of Labor Statistics.

Set against this backcloth, the monetary tightening of the early 1990s served the purpose of imposing a kind of shock therapy on the Canadian economy that had serious consequences for labour. While extraordinarily high interest rates led to a drastic but short-term deterioration in Canada's cost-competitive position as a result of an overvalued dollar, they also produced a long-term decline in unit labour costs as the economy slowed, unemployment rose, and wage growth stalled. As monetary policy finally began to ease somewhat in the mid 1990s, the value of the dollar began falling in relation to the US currency. This, in turn, sharply lowered relative manufacturing unit labour costs and helped fuel an export boom. By 2003, however, the Bank of Canada once again began raising interest rates, driving up the value of the dollar and slowing growth.

The key point is that both the severity of the recession and the long-delayed economic rebound were driven primarily by monetary policy. However, the Bank of Canada's obsession with fighting inflation was also linked to deeper economic integration with the United States. Adopting high interest rates to slow wage growth was a key strategy in boosting Canada's competitiveness with the United States. In the end, while unit labour costs did remain fairly steady during the 1990s, they actually fell in the United States, where wage growth was slower and productivity increases higher. Only an additional depreciation in the Canadian dollar in the late 1990s restored Canada's competitiveness. However, as the currency

began rising above seventy-five cents again in 2003, many Canadian manufacturing exporters were once again being priced out of the US market,
although overall trade volumes rose on the strength of the export boom of
oil and gas.

THE IMPACT OF ECONOMIC INTEGRATION
ON LABOUR STANDARDS

Aside from the negative impact on jobs and wages, there is some evidence
to suggest that deepening economic integration with the United States has
worked to undermine labour standards in Canada. At their heart, today's
trade agreements are about more than simple tariff reductions. They
encompass a range of measures on investment, intellectual property, subsidies, monopolies, and state enterprises that, taken together, dramatically
shift enormous power to capital. The elimination of tariffs coupled with
strict rules protecting private investors means firms are more able to relocate production and jobs. Jurisdictions thus find themselves increasingly
competing for investment, while employers are able to use the threat of
relocation to head off union drives and to check labour demands. As one
of Canada's leading industrial relations experts has concluded, the upshot
of these developments is that economic integration forces Canadian governments to be more aware of the competitive consequences of labour policies: "the forces of globalization and trade liberalization are creating powerful pressures *towards* harmonization of labour laws and policies, and
that pressure is likely to lead to harmonization *towards* the lowest common
denominator in the sense of reducing costly policies" (Gunderson 1998,
22).

It is certainly the case that business lobby groups and governments of
various political stripes in Canada have pushed for a weakening of labour
standards on the grounds of the need to be competitive with jurisdictions
in the United States and Mexico. The Grocery Products Manufacturers of
Canada, for instance, argued during the first free trade debate that deeper
economic integration with the United States would require "fundamental
realignments in legislated benefits, income expectations, programs and
labour union organizations," (cited in Lynk 1988, 72). Similarly, a report
produced by the federal Privy Council Office in 1996 warned that "the
basic affordability of the [social safety net] system and the benefits payment
regime has a direct consequence on competitiveness ... By raising the cost
of labour as a productive input, such programs can either drive jobs south
or encourage further substitution of capital for labour" (cited in Campbell
2000, 28).

Such concerns reflect the fact that Canada as a whole has traditionally
maintained more union-friendly legislation and higher labour standards

Table 10.7   Union density,* Canada and the United States, 1984–2005 (%)

	1984	1988	1997	2003	2005
Canada	41.8	39.5	33.7	30.4	30.7
United States	19.1	17.0	14.2	12.9	12.4

*Union density is the number of unionized workers as a percentage of non-agricultural paid employment.
Source: Jackson and Schetagne (2003); Statistics Canada; US Bureau of Labor Statistics.

than have most jurisdictions in the United States.[4] This is reflected, for instance, in the higher rates of unionization in Canada. As illustrated in table 10.7, rates of unionization in Canada, while falling sharply since the late 1980s, have remained significantly higher than have those in the United States. While this difference can, in part, be explained by higher rates of unionization in a comparatively larger Canadian public sector, private-sector union density has also remained at more than twice the rate of that in the United States.

The decline in unionization rates in Canada, while a long-term trend, has clearly accelerated following the implementation of CUFTA and NAFTA. One reason for this no doubt lies with the decline in unionized manufacturing jobs and the growth of contract and part-time work in the wake of the con-tinental corporate restructuring over the past fifteen years. In addition, CUFTA and NAFTA have given employers a powerful new stick to wield over their workforce – the credible threat of plant relocation. Such threats can be used to win concessions at the bargaining table and, critically, to prevent new union drives.

In a detailed study of the impact of CUFTA and NAFTA on union certifi-cation drives at US plants, Brofenbrenner (1996) found that employers' threats to relocate plants and to outsource portions of their operations have had a serious impact on union organizing in the United States. Between 1993 and 1995 more than half of all employers facing a union organizing drive used the threat of relocating all or some part of their oper-ations. In an update of this study for the years 1998–99, Brofenbrenner (2000) found that the incidence of such threats had risen to nearly 70 percent in the manufacturing sector. The "win rate" for organizing drives during which an employer threatened to move jobs was just 38 percent, compared to 51 percent in cases where no overt threats were made. While no equivalent survey of the use of such threats during union organizing drives in Canada has been made, there is a good deal of anecdotal evidence to suggest that employers are using the threat of job relocation to prevent unionization and to win concessions at the bargaining table (Merrett 1996, 181–3).

More broadly, employers and governments in Canada have used trade

Table 10.8   Percentage of unemployed receiving UI/EI benefits, 1990–2001*

	1990	1993	1996	1999	2001
Total	74	57	42	38	39
Men	78	59	45	43	44
Women	69	53	39	32	33
15–24 years old	52	34	22	15	16

*without earnings
Source: Canadian Labour Congress (CLC 2003).

liberalization to justify a weakening of labour standards and union protections. While such standards still remain higher in Canada as a whole, the dominant trend over the past decade, as Klassen and Schneider (2002) have shown, is towards labour market deregulation. Increasingly, several provinces have justified a weakening of labour and employment protections by raising the need to compete with jurisdictions in the United States and Mexico for new investment. The Province of Ontario, under the former Conservative government, changed labour laws to lift the ban on so-called "replacement workers," make it more difficult for workers to join a union, and allow employers to more easily decertify a union. The minimum wage was also frozen, and the maximum number of hours of work allowed under employment standards rules was raised.

In addition, benefits for workers have also been eroded. In the 1980s about twice the share of unemployed workers in Canada qualified for unemployment insurance (UI) benefits compared to their counterparts in the United States. Beginning in the first half of the 1990s, however, Canada's UI program was incrementally rolled back in response to claims that it was undermining work incentives and that its cost was hurting the competitiveness of Canadian businesses. Three successive rounds of changes meant that eligibility requirements were tightened, benefits were cut, and the duration of payments lowered. In 1996 the entire UI system was replaced with the Orwellian-sounding Employment Insurance (EI) Program. EI more than tripled the minimum number of hours worked required to qualify and reduced the maximum number of weeks of entitlement from fifty to forty-five. In constant dollars, the average amount of benefits an unemployed person received fell from $9,350 in 1990 to just $5,907 in 1997 (Haddow 2000).

One other consequence of these changes was that the share of unemployed Canadians eligible for benefits plummeted. As is illustrated in table 10.8, the decline in the total coverage fell from about 74 percent in 1990 to just 38 percent in 1999. Strikingly, only one in three unemployed women received benefits in 1999 and just 15 percent of young people.

CONCLUSION:
WHICH WAY FOR LABOUR?

The above analysis of the impact of economic integration on Canadian labour suggests that the major fallout has been on the bargaining power and benefits of working people. The direct employment impacts, while significant in some sectors, were overall relatively limited. Restrictive monetary policy adopted by the Bank of Canada, and not the elimination of tariffs, was the key driver of joblessness in the 1990s. However, the key conclusion reached here is that the high interest rates adopted in the early 1990s were themselves directly related to the implementation of CUFTA. A restrictive monetary stance could not be justified on the basis of taming inflation alone but was also employed as a dose of shock therapy to check wage growth and to improve Canada's long-run competitiveness with the United States. This policy appears to have failed given that Canada's emerging competitive advantage, which fuelled the export boom in the later half of the decade, was entirely the result of depreciation in the dollar rather than any real gains in productivity. In fact, as the dollar gained in value against the US currency in 2002–03, exports of manufactured products plummeted and the Canadian economy slowed.

Given this, a further deepening of economic integration with the United States poses serious challenges for organized labour on several fronts. While there remains significant manoeuvring room for governments in Canada to maintain higher labour and social standards, deepening integration will nevertheless intensify the downward pressures to harmonize such standards. Deeper economic integration with the United States will further erode labour's bargaining power, with the trend towards declining rates of unionization accelerating. This, in turn, will continue to put downward pressure on wages, benefits, and employment standards. The key policy challenge facing the labour movement is how to ensure that these trends can be stalled and eventually reversed. Two key initiatives are critical in this regard.

First, a priority of the labour movement in both Canada and the United States must be to increase the level of unionization in order to help restore a more equitable balance of power between capital and labour. Simply put, more resources need to be put into serious organizing campaigns, particularly among sectors that have low rates of unionization and among the growing ranks of part-time and contingent labour. To be successful, such a campaign should give serious consideration to continental and sectoral coordination among unions rather than the narrow turf battles that have plagued the labour movement in recent years. To be sure, the challenges here are enormous, particularly south of the border where organizing drives can be extremely difficult to win given the extreme anti-union bias of many state laws. Nevertheless, a coordinated and determined effort to organize

more working people is the best bulwark to head off the increasing concentration of power in the hands of capital.

Second, organized labour will need to rethink its strategies around how
best to respond to deepening economic integration. To date, unions have
pressed for social clauses and core labour rights to be included in trade and
investment agreements. Such pressure did lead to the creation of the so-
called labour side agreements to NAFTA and the creation of the North
American Commission for Labour Cooperation. However, many in the
labour movement now recognize that the side agreement is deeply flawed.
It only requires NAFTA members to respect their existing labour laws,
however inadequate they may be. Nor does the accord prohibit members
from weakening current legislation. In truth, within the rubric of current
trade agreements, labour rights and social clauses will only ever be mere
side accords with little meaning. Such trade liberalizing agreements, by
their very nature, will always privilege capital at the expense of labour and
social rights. Pressing for the inclusion of core labour rights in such agreements may be a useful strategy in exposing the flaws in CUFTA and NAFTA.
However, it must not be seen as an end itself. Even if core labour rights
were adopted in such agreements, it would ultimately offer little security to
working people when the overriding goal of deeper economic integration is
the locking-in and intensification of a neoliberal economic agenda.

A more appropriate course of action lies in developing an alternative
agreement in which labour rights and standards take precedence over trade
agreements. Such a project would involve generating new continental regulatory instruments and institutions that raise labour standards upward
rather than promote harmonization downward, as do CUFTA and NAFTA.
At the heart of such a new agreement would be enforceable labour and
human rights protections that would prevent the erosion of the living standards of working people across the continent. Of course, this is clearly a
long-term project that, given the political realities that hold in the NAFTA
countries, would require a dramatic shift in public policy. Nevertheless, the
way forward for labour in this era of increasing economic integration
cannot be one of simply trying to modify what are deeply flawed agreements; rather, the future lies in developing new transnational institutions
and agreements that work for all the continent's working people.[5]

NOTES

1 There has been some debate over whether calculating "hidden unemployment"
   in this way is legitimate. Sunter and Bowlby (1998) argue that the decline in
   participation rates may also be driven by other factors, such as increased school
   enrolment and earlier retirement. Of course, early retirement and increased

participation in school may also be the result of a poor labour market. However, the return to the 1989 participation rate in 2002 suggests that the decline over the 1990s was primarily driven by a lack of jobs rather than by any longer-term structural change.

2   During the CUFTA negotiations, the US National Manufacturers Association aggressively lobbied Washington to use the trade agreement to eliminate the exchange rate advantage they felt Canadian companies were unfairly enjoying (Foster and Dillon 2003, 90). Sinclair Stevens, a former Progressive Conservative cabinet minister, later publicly alleged there was a secret deal reached between Canadian and American officials negotiating a trade deal that Canada would raise the value of its dollar after the implementation of CUFTA. See Barlow and Campbell (1993, 11).

3   Unit labour costs are an important element in determining the price competitiveness of manufactured products. Briefly, unit labour costs are a measure of total worker compensation costs, including wages and benefits, per unit of manufactured output. Unit labour costs rise when total compensation costs rise faster than productivity, and they fall when productivity increases faster than wages and benefits. When comparing unit labour costs between different nations, changes in relative compensation levels over time are also affected by changes in relative currency exchange values. A drop in the value of the Canadian dollar relative to the US currency, for example, lowers the unit labour costs of Canadian manufacturers exporting to the United States relative to US manufacturers. For this reason, comparative unit labour costs are presented in two ways: on a national currency basis and on a fixed, usually US dollar, basis. The former presents unit labour costs in the national currency of manufacturers; the latter converts those costs to US dollars and thus provides a better measure of international competitiveness as it takes into account differences and fluctuations in currency exchange values.

4   It should be noted, however, that there are significant variations in labour laws and standards between states. States such as California have comparatively strong protections for unions as opposed to the notorious "right-to-work" states such as North Carolina.

5   In this regard, see the proposals for an alternative hemispheric agreement developed by the People's Summit of the Americas (CCPA 1999).

REFERENCES

Barlow, Maude, and Bruce Campbell. 1993. *Take Back the Nation 2: Meeting the Threat of NAFTA*. Toronto: Key Porter Books.

Beaulieu, Eugene. 2000. The Canada-US Free Trade Agreement and labour market adjustment in Canada. *Canadian Journal of Economics* 33 (2): 540–63.

Brofenbrenner, Kate. 1996. The Effects of Plant Closings or the Threat of Plan

Closings on the Right of Workers to Organize. Washington, DC: North American Commission for Labour Cooperation.

Brofenbrenner, Kate. 2000. *Uneasy Terrain: The Impact of Capital Mobility on Workers, Wages, and Union Organizing*. Washington: US Trade Deficit Review Commission.

Campbell, Bruce. 2000. False Promise: Canada in the Free Trade Era. Washington, DC: Economic Policy Institute.

Canada. 1988. The Canada-US Free Trade Agreement: An Economic Assessment. Ottawa: Department of Finance.

CCPA. 1999. Alternatives for the Americas: Building a People's Hemispheric Agreement. Ottawa: Canadian Centre for Policy Alternatives.

CLC. 2003. Falling Unemployment Insurance Protection for Canada's Unemployed. Ottawa: Canadian Labour Congress.

Dungan, Peter, and Steven Murphy. 1999. The Changing Industry and Skill Mix of Canada's International Trade: Perspectives on North American Free Trade. Paper No. 4, Industry Canada, Ottawa.

ECC. 1988. *Venturing Forth: An Assessment of the Canada-US Free Trade Agreement*. Ottawa: Economic Council of Canada.

Fortin, Pierre. 1999. *The Canadian Standard of Living: Is There a Way Up?* Toronto: C.D. Howe Institute.

Foster, John W., and John Dillon. 2003. NAFTA in Canada: The Era of a Super-Constitution. In *Lessons from NAFTA: The High Cost of Free Trade*, ed. K. Hansen-Kuhn and S. Hellinger. Ottawa: Canadian Centre for Policy Alternatives.

Gu, Wulong, Gary Swachuk, and Lori Whewell. 2003. *The Effect of Tariff Reductions on Firm Size and Firm Turnover in Canadian Manufacturing*. Ottawa: Statistics Canada.

Gunderson, Morley. 1998. Harmonization of Labour Policies under Trade Liberalization. *Industrial Relations* 53 (1): 1–33.

Haddow, Rodney. 2000. The Political and Institutional Landscape of Canadian Labour Market Policy-Making. In *Federalism, Democracy and Labour Market Policy*, ed. T. McIntosh, 29–64. Kingston: Institute of Intergovernmental Relations, Queen's University.

Hughes, Karen G. 1999. Gender and Self-Employment in Canada. Ottawa: Canadian Policy Network.

Jackson, Andrew. 1999. *Impact of the FTA and NAFTA on the Canadian Labour Markets*. Ottawa: Canadian Labour Congress.

Jackson, Andrew, and David Robinson. 2000. *Falling Behind: The State of Working Canada, 2000*. Ottawa: Canadian Centre for Policy Alternatives.

Jackson, Andrew, and Sylvain Schetagne. 2003. Solidarity Forever? An Analysis of Changes in Union Density, Research Paper No. 25, Canadian Labour Congress, Ottawa.

Klassen, Thomas R., and Steffen Schneider. 2002. Similar Challenges, Different Solutions: Reforming Labour Market Policies in Germany and Canada during the 1990s. *Canadian Public Policy* 28 (1): 51–69.

Lynk, Michael. 1988. Labour Law Erosion: Our Labour Relations System Faces Americanization. *The Facts* 10 (11): 72–7.

Merrett, Christopher D. 1996. *Free Trade: Neither Free nor about Trade*. Montreal: Black Rose Books.

Osberg, Lars, and Zhengxi Lin. 2000. How Much of Canada's Unemployment Rate is Structural? *Canadian Public Policy* 26 (supplement 1): S141–S157.

Osberg, Lars, Fred Wien, and Jan Grude. 1995. *Vanishing Jobs: Canada's Changing Workplace*. Toronto: James Lorimer and Company.

Robinson, David. 2001. *State of the Economy*. Ottawa: Canadian Centre for Policy Alternatives.

Schwanen, Daniel. 2001. Trade Liberalization and Inequality in Canada in the 1990s. In *The Review of Economic Performance and Social Progress*, edited by Keith Banting, Andrew Sharpe and France St-Hilaire, 161–82. Montreal: Institute for Research on Public Policy.

Sunter, Deborah, and Geoff Bowlby. 1998. Labour Force Participation in the 1990s. *Canadian Economic Observer* 11 (10): 3.1–3.11.

Trefler, Daniel. 2000. *The Long and Short of the Canada-US Free Trade Agreement*. Ottawa: Industry Canada.

Yalnizyan, Armine. 1998. *The Growing Gap*. Toronto: Centre for Social Justice.

11

The Costs and Benefits of a Canada-US Customs Union

MARC LEE

Pressures for deeper integration between Canada and the United States appear across a number of policy dimensions, including border security, defence policy, and immigration, as other chapters in this volume have pointed out. However, economic issues, in particular Canada's trade and investment relationship with the United States, carry a great deal of weight for Canada's proponents of deeper integration. To the extent that Canada might agree to common policies of a more political nature, these would likely be the outcome of a negotiation in which Canada's principal aim is to keep the border open to bilateral trade.

While the North American Free Trade Agreement (NAFTA) has already achieved a high level of economic integration, it can be viewed as one large step towards deeper integration encompassing both economic and non-economic factors. In terms of economic integration, the next step beyond NAFTA is a customs union. For supporters of free trade, a customs union is a natural extension of the same liberalization logic. As a result, there are many supporters of the customs union concept among Canada's business elite, politicians, and senior bureaucrats. But there are many prominent dissenters as well.

The divisions among Canada's elite were evident in the hearings of two parliamentary committees. The House of Commons Standing Committee on Foreign Affairs and International Trade released a report in December 2002 that noted the differences of opinion on a customs union and recommended that the government undertake "a detailed review of the advantages and disadvantages of the concept in the North American context" (SCFAIT 2002, 194). The second report, from the Standing Senate Committee on Foreign Affairs, recommended Canada not enter into discussions with the United States on a customs union. The senate committee stated that, "after seriously examining both sides of the issue, the Committee has concluded that upgrading NAFTA to a customs union would not be in

Canada's best interests. We are not prepared to make the sacrifices in Canadian sovereignty that would be required to realize the economic benefits of a customs union" (SSCFA 2003, 69).

Despite being the subject of internal debate within elite policy circles, the idea of a customs union has had comparably little public debate, perhaps because of its potential to polarize. This chapter aims to address this lack of debate by setting out the arguments made in favour of a customs union and subjecting them to critical scrutiny. It proceeds on the presumption that there are both costs and benefits associated with a customs union. We need to carefully assess not only whether the benefits outweigh the costs but also who the winners and losers would be.

In fact, the likely benefits of a customs union are quite small and are frequently overstated by promoters of the idea. On the other hand, there are non-trivial economic and political costs associated with a customs union, plus risks entailed in an actual negotiation. Expanding the scope of a negotiation could offer greater gains – such as exemption from US trade remedy laws – but would entail higher costs and bigger risks that Canadians are unlikely to support.

What precisely is being proposed under the banner of a "customs union" is not necessarily clear and consistent – proposals typically include more economic integration than the standard economic definition. The next section pins down the debate by looking in more detail at the differing degrees of economic integration, from free trade areas to customs unions to single markets, and how these relate to the proposals seen to date. The third section looks at the case for a customs union – namely, the elimination of rules of origin – and critically assesses its potential benefits. The fourth section considers the implications for Canada of having a common trade policy with the United States. The fifth section looks at the issue of trade remedy measures, a major irritant for Canada with regard to US trade. The sixth section brings costs and benefits together with an overall assessment of political feasibility and negotiation realpolitik to assess whether a strategic bargain would be in Canada's interest.

CUSTOMS UNION
AND ECONOMIC INTEGRATION

Terminology is important in this debate. There is a fairly clear economic meaning to the term "customs union" that differs from the specific proposals being made for a Canada-US "customs union." This section looks first at traditional economic definitions of a customs union and other economic integration arrangements, and then it turns to Canadian proposals in favour of a customs union.

Conceptually, it is best to think of integration as a process that occurs and is formalized in stages. The 1989 Canada-US Free Trade Agreement (CUFTA) was such a stage, as was the move to the 1994 North American Free Trade Agreement (NAFTA). NAFTA not only extended the trade bloc to Mexico, it deepened the liberalization measures of CUFTA. Hence, the question is not so much whether we want a customs union to clean up the "unfinished business arising out of NAFTA," as former trade minister (and Canada's ambassador to the United States at the time of writing) Michael Wilson put it (2003), but whether we want a customs union as another step towards ever-increasing integration.

Defining Terms

To begin, it is worth distinguishing among types of economic integration arrangements. In increasing order of integration they are: free trade area, customs union, common market, and single market (or economic union).[1] All of these arrangements are considered preferential agreements that exist within the bounds of the multilateral trading system of the World Trade Organization (WTO). The WTO allows preferential trading agreements as set out in Article XXIV of GATT 1947, so long as they do not raise barriers to trade with other parties.

In a *free trade area*, strictly defined, tariffs are eliminated on imports of goods and services among participating nations, although each country may maintain differing external tariffs that apply to other countries. In practice, free trade agreements can go far beyond this definition. NAFTA, for example, encompasses policies regarding investment, intellectual property rights, government procurement, standards, and competition policy – elements typically associated with a common market.

A *customs union* is the next step past a free trade area towards deeper economic integration. The key features of a customs union are the creation of a *common external tariff* that applies to all nations not part of the free trade area and the establishment of a common trade policy. It also involves the elimination of *rules of origin*. Rules of origin appear in free trade agreements to ensure that exports from country A to country B originate in A or at least have substantial value–added to them in A. This is to ensure that country C, which is not party to the free trade agreement, does not export only to the country with the lowest tariffs on its product as a means of serving the entire trade bloc.

In NAFTA, for example, rules of origin stipulate that exported goods within the free trade area should have at least 60 percent North American content (62.5 percent for automobiles) in order to benefit from tariff-free access. NAFTA also sets up a process to determine that exported goods within the NAFTA region containing non-North American content are substantially transformed in order to qualify for tariff-free status. The rules vary slightly from sector to sector, although for autos and textiles there are some additional specific requirements.

A stage beyond customs union is the establishment of a *common market*. At a theoretical level, this means allowing the free movement of all factors of production – capital, labour, and technology – across borders. In practice, it also includes harmonization of regulations, standards, and other economic and social policies across the area. A full common market would eliminate trade actions against partners and subsume trade remedy measures (such as antidumping and countervailing duties) to a common competition policy.[2] New supranational institutions would need to be created to oversee the common market.

The end-point of economic integration is a *single market*, or *economic union*, within which producers and consumers are governed by the same overarching rules, with highly harmonized fiscal and monetary policies. The European Union (EU) is the most significant modern example of a single market, where a common currency has been established (though not applicable to all EU members) and rules govern the ability of individual countries to run deficits (though recently broken by Germany and France). The EU has evolved joint supranational political institutions and has eliminated internal border checkpoints. The EU recently expanded its membership and has contemplated (unsuccessfully) an EU constitution – another illustration of the dynamic process of deepening integration.[3]

What Do Canadian Proponents Want?

Just as NAFTA should be viewed as an economic integration agreement that goes beyond a free trade deal, so should customs union proposals. The term "customs union" is occasionally used in a broad sense to include some of the policy terrain of a common market. Ultimately, any negotiation between Canada and the United States for deeper integration will be driven by perceived problems and issues in relation to the border and Canada-US relations, not by theoretical stages of integration.

Among customs union supporters is David Dodge, the governor of the Bank of Canada and former deputy minister of finance. Dodge views a common external tariff (a traditional customs union) as a step towards an extensive economic integration agenda, including harmonization of commercial policies and regulation, ending the application of trade remedy measures within North America, and uniform rules on subsidies (Dodge 2003). Dodge has also advocated labour market integration and even delicately supported the idea of a currency union "once we have made more progress towards establishing a single market for goods and services, capital, and labour" (ibid.).

Former Canadian trade officials Michael Hart and William Dymond argue that "if the bilateral CUFTA and trilateral NAFTA have benefited both Canada and the United States, more effort along the same lines should be even better" (2001, 6). They call for an initiative that is broad in scope leading to a formal agreement. This includes custom union proposals, plus a new deal on trade remedies, national treatment for government procurement, elimination of other border restrictions, cooperative enforcement of competition policy, and harmonized standards and regulations.

In a series called *The Border Papers*, the C.D. Howe Institute is championing more economic integration with the United States. Wendy Dobson calls for a "strategic bargain" that would be a "pragmatic mix of customs union-like and common market-like proposals plus Canadian initiatives in areas of strength that are of particular interest to the Americans" (Dobson 2002, 20) in exchange for market access guarantees to the US market. This would include greater cross-border labour mobility, harmonization of corporate income tax bases, and dispute settlement procedures around the application of trade remedy laws.

A C.D. Howe study by Danielle Goldfarb (2003) considers three stylized variants of the customs union idea.[4] She distinguishes between a "basic" customs union consisting only of a common external tariff, a "deep" customs union that includes a common external tariff plus common trade and commercial policies, and a "sectoral" customs union with common external tariffs in only some sectors. Interestingly, due to political and logistical challenges and concerns over the loss of policy space, Goldfarb ultimately recommends a sectoral approach as a practical option to improve the status quo.

Another key contributor to the proponents' side is the Canadian Council of Chief Executives (or CCCE, the lobby group formerly known as the Business Council on National Issues). CCCE president Tom d'Aquino (2003) argues for "a *customs initiative* designed to reduce differences in Canadian and United States treatment of third country trade and eliminate the need for rules of origin and other burdensome customs requirements on most goods." However, this is but one small point in an expansive "new partnership agenda" that includes: harmonization of standards, regulations, inspection, and certification procedures (the "tested-once" principle); more integrated resource sectors; and common security measures for the external border. He does not call for new supranational institutions and, thus, argues that the CCCE is not seeking a common market.

Hence, it is not always obvious precisely what is on the table when the term "customs union" is invoked. Much has to do with the perceived issues on the part of Canada and, thus, which Canadians are the *demandeurs*. Most are seeking an integration package that goes further than a customs union. Calling for a common market, however, is likely beyond what Canadians would be prepared to accept, whereas the administrative-sounding term "customs union" could have greater saleability to a sceptical public.

At the political level, the Security and Prosperity Partnership (SPP), proposed by NAFTA ministers in June 2005, does not mention customs union specifically, but does set a timetable to liberalize, but not eliminate, rules of origin.[5] The SPP report (2005) states this initiative will affect $30 billion of trilateral trade. Thus, it would appear that elements of a customs union are being considered in a new liberalization package.

ELIMINATING RULES OF ORIGIN[6]

There are no real economic benefits to having a common external tariff per se. In fact, Canadian and US tariff structures are already quite close on a high percentage of goods, as Goldfarb (2003) points out. Rather, the benefit stems from eliminating rules of origin that, it is argued, pose administrative costs to exporters and distort trade patterns. It is worth taking such arguments with a healthy dose of scepticism, however, since these are theoretical costs and benefits in the economics literature. They do not seem to be a major irritant to exporters.

Rules of origin do pose some costs to businesses. There are administrative and legal requirements that must be accounted for by exporters. As a result, there are benefits for exporters in eliminating rules of origin. But it is not obvious that these costs really are that large. In the seventeen years since the 1989 CUFTA, there have been no public complaints from Canadian business groups about allegedly large costs attributable to rules of origin, nor did these "barriers" impede the expansion of exports from Canada to the United States in the 1990s. Were these costs so large, the two countries had an opportunity to set things right a few years later when NAFTA was being negotiated. In actual fact, however, rules of origin were made more stringent.

Much has been made of the alleged complexity of rules of origin – several commentators note that some 200 pages of NAFTA text are devoted to spelling out rules of origin – and the administrative burden this poses. While this number of pages may seem daunting, it misrepresents rules of origin in practice. The vast bulk of these 200 pages is an annex containing a long list of the specific rules on a product-by-product basis. Not every exporter must understand every rule for every product, only those for the specific products they are exporting.

The main legal text on rules of origin in NAFTA (Chapter 4) is twenty-six pages in length: six of these are devoted to definitions, and another three refer specifically to the auto industry. Thus, the legal aspect of rules of origin is no greater than it is anywhere else in the NAFTA text. Even counting the entire twenty-six pages, this is shorter than the chapters on Investment (Chapter 11) and Intellectual Property Rights (Chapter 17), neither of which seems to be under attack for being overly complex, despite being quite prescriptive.

To the extent that rules of origin mean additional paperwork for exporters, much of this is a one-time cost in terms of getting the paperwork right and ensuring that the product supply conforms to specifications. In practice, the NAFTA certificate of origin that accompanies exports across the border is a one-page document (Mirus 2003). There may be some legal and accounting costs that go along with this, but it is unlikely that they are any greater than any of the other legal and accounting work that companies must comply with as part of doing business. Compared to the resource requirements dedicated to payroll, general administration, tax filing, applying for permits, and so on, the costs of rules of origin are a drop in the bucket.

Moreover, the rules of origin were put in place for a reason as part of the negotiation of CUFTA and NAFTA. Presumably, this situation is better for exporters than the tariffs that prevailed before CUFTA. While precise numbers are not available, rules of origin likely support economic activity in Canada and North America, specifically because of the incentives created to source inputs on a continental basis, even if deemed "inefficient" by some economists. Eliminating rules of origin would likely pose economic and social losses in vulnerable sectors, and these costs would have to be considered alongside any benefits.

This analysis that rules of origin are not very costly is at odds with an estimate that rules of origin cost 2 percent to 3 percent of North American GDP, cited in Goldfarb (2003).[7] This estimate derives from an unpublished PhD thesis by Alex Appiah (1999) at Simon Fraser University under the supervision of Richard Harris, the professor who estimated massive gains from CUFTA fifteen years before. Most estimates of economic gains from CUFTA as a whole were much less than the 2 percent to 3 percent attributed to rules of origin.[8] The outlier was Harris and Cox (1984), which produced the astounding prediction that the gains would be 8 percent to 10 percent of GDP.[9]

Appiah uses a computable general equilibrium (CGE) model to generate his results, a quasi-empirical approach with a number of shortcomings that tend to bias results in favour of free trade. This is in part due to its grounding in the assumptions of neoclassical economics and in part due to data and modelling issues.[10] Appiah also uses a particular methodology that is prone to producing unrealistically large estimates. His estimates of economic gain range from 0.3 percent to 2.8 percent for Canada. Citing 2 percent to 3 percent GDP gains (the top end) from eliminating rules of origin as a plausible estimate is problematic, however, without reference to the nuanced findings in the thesis.

Appiah essentially assumes rules of origin pose huge costs to exporters that undercut the gains from tariff reductions. In his model, eliminating these costs would induce structural change in the Canadian economy similar to that predicted for CUFTA: they would reduce input costs, increase productivity, enable exporters to capture previously unexploited economies of scale, boost investment, and so forth.

In sum, there is no reason to expect major economic benefits from the elimination of rules of origin because they are not really that costly. Businesses would save some money by not having rules of origin in place. But this would do little to ease congestion and delays at the border, as some have argued. Indeed, the rules of origin process as applied at the border is extremely straightforward, whereas the concerns of US authorities about immigration, drugs, arms, security, and smuggling that consume most border resources would not go away if rules of origin were eliminated.

Finally, rules of origin may actually generate some benefits to the Canadian economy that are not being considered. As a result, any incremental gains as a result of moving from NAFTA to a customs union are likely to be extremely small, if there are positive gains at all. Moreover, there are likely to be costs as well as benefits, as we will see in the next section, and to the extent that we would want to eliminate rules of origin, there will be negotiating trade-offs that will have to occur for the United States to accept such a change.

THE DOWNSIDE OF "COMMON" TRADE POLICY

A crucial aspect of a customs union and the implementation of a common external tariff is the need for a common trade policy with the rest of the world. In practical terms, this would mean surrendering Canada's trade policy to the US trade representative. Such a move would have sweeping implications for Canadian institutions and how we manage our place in the world.

Consider even the most basic implications of having a common external tariff with the United States. Both countries would need to set common tariffs by harmonizing tariff schedules, establishing uniform customs procedures, and determining how to share tariff revenues. It is hard to imagine that the United States would enter into a negotiation with Canada to jointly set common tariffs; rather, given the highly asymmetric differences in economic size and power, Canada would adopt US tariff rates, convert to US customs procedures, and take whatever share of tariff revenues the United States would deem appropriate.

The history of the South African Customs Union (SACU) gives pause for thought. Founded in 1910, SACU is the longest-standing customs union in the world, consisting of South Africa, Botswana, Lesotho, and Swaziland. It is one of highly asymmetric economic and political power – perhaps as asymmetric as Canada and the United States – dominated by South Africa. The result, according to McDonald and Walmsley (2001), is that "historically the RSA [Republic of South Africa] enjoyed carte blanche over the setting of tariff and excise duty rates for SACU, and used implicit threats, not least over transit rights, to reinforce its control. Consequently the development of trade policies within the SACU was determined by the 'development' agenda of the RSA."

In many areas where Canadian and US most favoured nation (MFN) tariffs are very close (less than two percentage points apart), a move to a customs union would not be too difficult. However, in both countries there are politically sensitive sectors that have been protected from the full force of international trade agreements. In Canada, these include public services, Crown corporations, agricultural marketing boards in eggs and dairy (protected by 200 percent to 300 percent tariffs), the Canadian Wheat Board, cultural industries, telecommunications, and banking. Many of these have been targeted for dismantling by Washington, so it is hard to believe that if these sectors survived a customs union negotiation that they would be given preferential treatment by a future US-set trade policy. Moreover, the threat to these industries – cultural industries in particular – comes from south of the border. Even if the United States were to give preferential treatment in these areas with respect to countries *outside* the customs union, this is of little consolation.

For its part, the United States also has key sectors that have been protected. These include tobacco, peanuts and peanut butter, footwear, porcelain and glassware, tuna, brooms, dates, sugar, bovine meat cuts and carcasses, trucks, sweet corn, and dried onions (Goldfarb 2003). Given the US Congress's tendency to protect these areas in the first place, Canada could be asked to substantially raise its tariffs to US levels to meet the common external tariff.[11] Moreover, in certain areas, Washington has pressured trading partners like Japan to accept voluntary export restraints (VERs), effectively quotas, for its domestic market. Would these VERs be extended to Canada under a customs union? If not, Japan could route its exports to the United States via Canada to end-run the VERs, something Washington would likely contest.

It is also unclear how far such arrangements would go given the vast scope of trade policy today. The concept of a customs union leading to a joint trade policy was obvious when most trade discussions focused on goods sectors and the principal barriers to trade were border measures like tariffs. This alone – the loss of capacity to set external tariffs or at least to negotiate their levels in international negotiations – constitutes a huge loss of autonomy in trade policy.

The current scope of "trade" policy includes a wide variety of measures taken by governments inside their borders. Services negotiations are explicitly about removing perceived barriers in the form of domestic regulations and standards, temporary work arrangements, access to network infrastructure, public services, and so on. Trade agreements also cover investment, competition policy, intellectual property rights, and food safety standards.

Another consideration is that, over the course of history, Canada and the United States have developed different trade ties and political relationships with other countries. Reconciling these within the context of a customs union could prove to be difficult. The United States has embargoed trade relations with some countries while Canada continues to maintain trade relations (often in spite of US pressures to follow its lead). Washington also restricts the trade of certain products (defence industries, satellite, nuclear, encryption technology), particularly with specific countries. Canada may be unwilling to sign on to such restrictions on our trade.[12]

Cuba stands out as an example in the Americas. In the years following the Cuban revolution the United States restricted trade with Cuba, and over the 1960s it tightened its embargo. Washington prevents its citizens from travelling to Cuba and has sought to rope in other countries in support of its embargo through extraterritorial means, such as the Helms-Burton Act, 1996, and its predecessors. The United States has also balked at including Cuba in the now stalled negotiations towards a Free Trade Area of the Americas (FTAA). Canada, on the other hand, maintains trade ties with Cuba. Canadian companies invest in Cuba, and thousands of Canadians travel to Cuba each year. Two-way trade (imports and exports) between Canada and Cuba was $753 million in 2001 (with a peak of $815 million in 1998) (DFAIT 2004b).

Another example is Iran. The United States prohibits most trade with Iran, as commercial relations are restricted by US sanctions (US Department of State 2003). In contrast, two-way Canada-Iran trade was about $700 million in 2000, and Iran is one of Canada's major export markets for wheat (DFAIT 2004a).

In the event that economic sanctions were imposed on other countries by future US administrations, under a common trade policy Canada would have to join the US trade action independently of the will of Canadian citizens and federal and provincial governments. Thus, even though a common trade policy is ostensibly limited to trade, it would likely creep into foreign policy as a whole. This would have a significant impact on Canada's trade relations with other nations.

Even when embargoes are not involved, Canada and the United States have differing relationships with other countries. Canada has a different set of trade agreements than does the United States, and it grants different trade preferences to developing countries. Reconciling these differences would be complicated and difficult.

A common trade policy with Washington would also foreclose the possibility on all kinds of independent policy initiatives for Canada. For example, what if Canada wants to move ahead with the generic production of AIDS medication for poor countries in Africa that do not have domestic manufacturing capacity? After a long fight at the WTO, this could become practice in Canada, but under a common trade policy with the United States it would likely never happen due to the powerful influence of brand-name American pharmaceutical companies. On a similar note, Canada extended duty-free and quota-free access to forty-eight less-developed countries as of 1 January 2003. This kind of international development policy could not be implemented unilaterally under a common trade policy with the United States.

Parties to a customs union must present a united front on trade policy when negotiating in forums like the WTO. It is far from clear how this would work in practice, given the asymmetrical balance of power between Canada and the United States. But it would likely involve the devolution of substantial power at the negotiating table to Washington. This, of course, raises a number of questions. What role would Canada have in setting trade policy and priorities? What capacity would Canada have to defend significant interests to which US negotiators might be indifferent? Would all final negotiating decisions affecting Canada be made in Washington?

Canada could probably negotiate some form of process by which its views would be heard, but the likely outcome would still be living with whatever US negotiators decided was in their best interests. This could result in all kinds of decisions with which Canada would have to adhere – decisions with which, internally, we would disagree.

Thus, the expansion of Canada-US trade to a customs union has major implications for Canadian trade and foreign policy. If anything, Canada needs a more multilateral trade policy: the gains from more trade are not with the United States but with the rest of the world (Helliwell 2003). Yet, a customs union would not only shift Canada away from a multilateral approach but would also give away the very tools needed to pursue a future multilateral trade diversification strategy.

US TRADE REMEDY LAWS, RETALIATION AND HARASSMENT

Most proponents of a customs union would like Canada to negotiate some form of exclusion from the application of US trade remedy laws (including countervailing and antidumping duties, safeguard measures, and other means, such as Super 301 actions related to perceived non-compliance with intellectual property treaties). More broadly, some suggest replacing these mechanisms with a common competition policy regime. These proposals go beyond the definition of a traditional customs union but are clearly of policy significance to Canada. The major stumbling block is in the US political arena.

The desire for an exemption from US trade remedy laws has a long history in Canada. It was one of Canada's main objectives, and a key selling point to the public, in entering CUFTA negotiations. Canada put trade remedies on the table early on, but Washington deferred the issue until the very end of the negotiations, when Canada was already so committed to securing an agreement that the perceived costs of failure were high. The result was an agreement to establish a non-binding binational panel that would assess whether trade remedies were appropriately applied in accordance with the laws in that country (Ritchie 1997).

From Canada's viewpoint, the failure to secure exemptions from US trade remedy laws has proved to be a major weakness of CUFTA. It is most visible in recent trade harassment over softwood lumber, wheat, tomatoes, and potatoes. Often the US Congress will set down sweeping duties that apply to all countries, including Canada, and Canada must grovel for an exemption. This is much the same as was the case prior to CUFTA. In the specific case of softwood lumber, Canada and the United States came to a tentative agreement in April 2006 after five years of duties being imposed by the latter. The resulting agreement is a return to "managed trade," which penalizes Canadian exporters when the price of softwood lumber falls. In addition, Canada was able to secure a return of $4 billion out of $5 billion in antidumping duties collected during the dispute (BC Government 2006).

Certainly, there could be benefits for Canada in achieving some sort of agreement on trade remedies. For example, negotiating clearly defined rules on what constitutes a subsidy (this was supposed to happen as a result of CUFTA but was dropped by the United States once the deal was in place) would cut to the heart of the dispute over softwood lumber. Dealing with anti-competitive practices under competition policy rather than antidumping policy would raise the bar in a way that would likely make most antidumping cases against Canada go away.

This is all in the realm of theory, however, because barring a sea change in attitude in the US Congress, changing trade remedy laws or even negotiating an exemption is essentially a non-starter. In other words, this potentially huge source of gain for Canada is, for all intents and purposes, off-limits. Even if such political will existed south of the border, Canada would probably have to pay a very high price to get a deal.

ASSESSING THE BARGAIN

While the prospect of a customs union is problematic, this should not rule out space for some pragmatic initiatives. Under NAFTA, for example, there is already an agreement to waive rules of origin for most computers and parts. If it is in the interests of companies on both sides of the border, there seems to be little problem in negotiating sectoral agreements. There are a large number of sectors in which MFN tariff rates are already identical or close enough that they could be harmonized on a sectoral basis. Autos and steel, for example, represent sectors in which Canada and the United States could gain from a common trade policy. As long as costs to Canadian industry and workers are taken into account, such an approach could harvest the "low-hanging fruit," reaping most of the benefits but without the dramatic loss of sovereignty.

This may indeed be the approach to this issue taken by the Security and Prosperity Partnership process, which focuses on rules of origin but does not set common external tariffs or establish a common trade policy. Time will tell. The SPP contains other, more sweeping, elements that pose challenges to Canadian sovereignty, however.

Ultimately, the issue before Canadians is whether this is the correct road to be on in the first place. As Helliwell argues, there are diminishing returns to further integration with the United States and attempts to increase north-south trade flows. The gains for Canada from trade are more likely to be found in enhancing trade with Europe or the global South, which suggests a multilateral approach to trade policy rather than a narrow bilateral one. And Canada's concerns would be better addressed via multilateral institutions and international cooperation with other countries that share those concerns. This is the only way to get the leverage necessary with Washington to make changes on issues of real substance, such as its punishing trade remedy laws.

One of the key reasons why, for Canada, the costs of economic integration will likely exceed the benefits is that there are a number of institutional differences that underpin our levels of well-being, which are higher than are those in the United States. Our quality of life, and improving that quality of life, is about much more than GDP per capita. Helliwell's (2002) research points out that beyond per capita incomes of about US$15,000 per year, there is little gain in measures of subjective well-being (how people personally rate their quality of life). Further increases in well-being are more closely linked to levels of health and education, quality of communities, and participation in public life. Deeper integration would undermine these institutions and, thus, our standard of living and quality of life.

When benefits and costs are laid out, the case for entering into a new negotiation with the United States over a customs union is weak, and the risks entailed in a broader negotiation that would include a customs union as one component are great. Closer economic ties to the United States via a customs union would likely lower Canadians' standard of living, not raise it.

NOTES

The author would like to thank the following people for their comments: Andrew Jackson, Seth Klein, Danielle Goldfarb, Ricardo Grinspun, Stephen McBride, Mario Seccareccia, Yasmine Shamsie, and Jim Stanford. Any errors are the responsibility of the author. This chapter is updated and adapted from Lee (2004).

1 I follow the taxonomy used by Krueger (1995).
2 International trade rules permit the application of *antidumping duties* in cases of dumping, when a good is sold for export at a price lower than cost of production and/or the price of sale in the domestic market. When a good is deemed to be subsidized by a foreign government, a country is allowed to impose *countervailing duties* to offset the impact of the subsidy. Trade rules also permit temporary tariffs to be put in place as *safeguards* against import surges or for balance of trade purposes. In practice, rich countries often use these trade remedy measures to protect domestic industries. The United States is generally considered to be one of the worst offenders. The prolonged Canada-us dispute over softwood lumber is a case in point.
3 A layer down, the nineteenth-century German Zollverein began as a customs union (like the EU) and evolved a few decades later into the German nation-state.
4 These stylized variants follow Dobson (2002) and are not consistent with the standard economic definition of customs union.
5 In the remainder of this chapter, Mexico as a potential third party to the customs union is left out of the analysis in order to focus more directly on Canada-us relations. This presumes that a new bilateral arrangement between Canada and the United States can be made independently of Mexico and that it would not involve renegotiating NAFTA in a way that would require Mexican approval.
6 This section is an abridged version of a more detailed and technical text published by the Canadian Centre for Policy Alternatives (Lee 2004).
7 Goldfarb notes that there are no studies that specifically address a move to a Canada-us customs union, only a North American one. In addition to Appiah (1999), Goldfarb also cites Brown, Deardorff, and Stern (2001), which models a move to a common external tariff, finding minimal long-run changes, but not elimination of rules of origin.
8 These CUFTA estimates did not consider rules of origin as offsetting costs, a point made by Appiah in the thesis.
9 See Hazeldine (1990) for a review of the alternative specifications used by modellers that come to such a wide range of forecasts about the impact of Canada-us free trade as well as for a methodological critique of Harris and Cox (1984). He finds that "only a model with an extreme combination of non-competitive product market and free entry (as well as unexploited scale economies) can generate substantial gains from free trade" (Hazeldine 1990, 791). Other

forecasts ranged from net losses to gains of 0.7 percent and 1.2 percent of GDP.

10 CGE modelling is just a tool that, under standard assumptions, leads to biases. Stanford (1993) develops a CGE model of the impacts of NAFTA using "real-world" assumptions and finds a negative impact on GDP and employment.

11 This would be an ironic outcome. However, WTO rules would frown on one or both countries raising tariffs to form a customs union. To the extent that this was possible, compensation would be required for WTO members experiencing adverse effects.

12 I am not arguing here that Canada should be an arms dealer of last resort, only that decisions about who we trade with and what we trade should be made by Canadians not by our neighbours to the south.

REFERENCES

Appiah, Alex. 1999. Applied General Equilibrium Model of North American Integration with Rules of Origin. PhD diss., Simon Fraser University, Vancouver.

BC Government. 2006. *Basic Terms of a Canada-United States Agreement on Softwood Lumber.* 27 April. Victoria: Ministry of Forests and Range, Government of British Columbia.

Brown, Drusilla, Alan Deardorff, and Robert Stern. 2001. Impacts on NAFTA Members of Multilateral and Regional Trading Arrangements and Initiatives and Harmonization of NAFTA's External Tariffs. In *Working Paper 471. Research Seminar in International Economics.* School of Public Policy, Department of Economics, University of Michigan.

d'Aquino, Thomas. 2003. Security and Prosperity: The Dynamics of a New Canada-United States Partnership in North America, Presentation to the Annual General Meeting of the Canadian Council of Chief Executives, 14 January, Toronto.

DFAIT. 2004a. *Canada-Iran Relations.* Department of Foreign Affairs and International Trade. Available at <http://www.dfait-maeci.gc.ca/middle_east/ iran_relations-en.asp>, cited 9 April 2004.

– 2004b. *Cuba: Canada-Cuba Trade and Investment.* Department of Foreign Affairs and International Trade. Available at <http://www.dfait-maeci.gc.ca/latinamerica/cubarelations-en.asp>, cited 9 April 2004.

Dobson, Wendy. 2002. Shaping the Future of the North American Space: A Framework for Action, Commentary no. 162, C.D. Howe Institute, Toronto.

Dodge, David. 2003. Remarks by David Dodge Governor of the Bank of Canada to the Couchiching Institute on Public Affairs, Geneva Park, 7 August 2003, Ottawa, Bank of Canada.

Goldfarb, Danielle. 2003. The Road to a Canada-US Customs Union: Step-by-Step or in a Single Bound? C.D. Howe Institute Commentary No. 184, C.D. Howe Institute, Toronto.

Harris, Richard G., and David Cox. 1984. *Trade, Industrial Policy and Canadian Manufacturing*. Toronto: Ontario Economic Council.

Hart, Michael, and William Dymond. 2001. *Common Borders, Shared Destinies: Canada, the United States and Deepening Integration*. Ottawa: Centre for Trade Policy and Law.

Hazeldine, Tim. 1990. Why Do the Free Trade Gain Numbers Differ so Much? The Role of Industrial Organization in General Equilibrium. *Canadian Journal of Economics* 23 (4): 791–806.

Helliwell, John. 2002. *Globalization and Well-Being*. Vancouver: UBC Press.

– 2003. Border Effects: Assessing Their Implications for Canadian Policy in a North American Context. Revised version of paper presented at Industry Canada/Human Resources Development Canada workshop entitled Social and Labour Market Aspects of North American Linkages, Montreal, 20–22 November. Available at <http://strategis.ic.gc.ca/pics/ra/helliwell.pdf>.

Krueger, Anne. 1995. Free Trade Agreements versus Customs Unions, Working Paper No. 5084, National Bureau of Economic Research, Cambridge.

Lee, Marc. 2004. *Indecent Proposal: The Case against a Canada-US Customs Union*. Ottawa: Canadian Centre for Policy Alternatives.

McDonald, Scott, and Terrie Walmsley. 2001. Bilateral Free Trade Agreements and Customs Unions: The Impact of the EU Republic of South Africa Free Trade Agreement on Botswana. Paper presented at the 2001 ESRC Development Economics Study Group Annual Conference, 5–7 April, Nottingham, UK.

Mirus, Rolf. 2003. *After September 11: A Canada-US Customs Union*. Edmonton: Western Centre for Economic Research.

Ritchie, Gordon. 1997. *Wrestling with the Elephant: The Inside Story of the Canada-US Trade Wars*. Toronto: MacFarlane, Walter and Ross.

SCFAIT. 2002. *Partners in North America: Advancing Canada's Relations with the United States and Mexico*. Ottawa: Standing Committee on Foreign Affairs and International Trade, House of Commons, Canada.

SPP. 2005. *Security and Prosperity Partnership of North America: Report to Leaders*. 27 June. Washington: US Department of Commerce.

SSCFA. 2003. *Uncertain Access: The Consequences of US Security and Trade Actions for Canadian Trade Policy*. Ottawa: Standing Senate Committee on Foreign Affairs, Senate of Canada.

Stanford, Jim. 1993. *Estimating the Effects of North American Free Trade: A Three Country General Equilibrium Model with "Real-World" Assumptions*. Ottawa: Canadian Centre for Policy Alternatives.

US Department of State. 2003. *Background Note: Iran*. Washington, DC: Bureau of Near Eastern Affairs.

Wilson, Michael. 2003. What's Next for NAFTA? Paper presented at 72nd Annual Summer Conference, 7–10 August 2003, Couchiching Institute of Public Affairs, Geneva Park.

PART FOUR

Free Trade:
Impacts on Public Policy and Culture

12

An International Bill of Rights for Foreign Investors

STEVEN SHRYBMAN

During the past decade or so, international trade agreements have been dramatically expanded to encompass areas of law, public policy, and government services that had previously been matters of strictly domestic concern. Today, international trade agreements contemplate and rule upon such wide-ranging matters as investment, procurement, public services, intellectual property, and domestic regulation, including environmental protection. Indeed, so broad is the reach of these new regimes that virtually every sphere of domestic economic and social policy is now potentially subject to their rules, no matter how tenuously those policies relate to international trade in any conventional sense. Moreover, unlike the treaties they superseded, the new generation of trade agreements is binding and enforceable.

The result has embedded a framework of international rules in the agreements of the World Trade Organization (WTO), and regional agreements such as the North American Free Trade Agreement (NAFTA), that reflect a single-minded preoccupation with the interests of commerce and trade, in accordance with a neoliberal model that seeks to reduce the role of government through deregulation and privatization. Together, these regimes impose upon governments at all levels broad constraints that can be ignored only at the risk of retaliatory trade sanctions or damage awards by international arbitral tribunals. Indeed, developments in international trade regulation are so far-reaching that, according to Renato Ruggiero (1998), the first director general of the WTO, neither governments nor industries appreciate the full scope or value of the guarantees being provided to foreign investors and services providers.

THE SPECIAL CASE OF FOREIGN INVESTMENT TREATIES

Because of the breadth of their application and the fact that they may be unilaterally enforced by countless foreign investors, international agreements concerning foreign investment arguably represent the most pernicious feature of the entire free trade edifice, and they warrant particular attention. The investment provisions of NAFTA – set out in Chapter 11 of that trade deal – empower foreign investors (read: transnational corporations) to sue Canada and its NAFTA partners to enforce the largely exclusive rights the treaty accords them. In many cases these broad investor "rights" have no domestic analogue and could not be enforced before national courts. Moreover, when a claim is made under Chapter 11, it is determined by a secretive international tribunal, operating entirely outside the framework of domestic law and constitutional guarantees of fairness, fundamental justice, and equality.

Notwithstanding the disturbing implications of such developments for a democratic society, until efforts by Organization for Economic Co-operation and Development (OECD) countries to establish the Multilateral Agreement on Investment (MAI) in 1998 drew public attention to NAFTA and similar investment treaties, few outside of an inner cadre of trade officials and corporate lawyers had any understanding of these international regimes. The potential impact of the MAI on the sovereignty, independence, and regulatory role of governments, particularly in the areas of cultural policy, the environment, and labour rights, were the most prominent issues in the public debate that arose in Canada, the United States, and other OECD countries concerning this proposed investment treaty. While efforts to establish the MAI were turned back by public opposition, the prototype for the MAI remains firmly entrenched in NAFTA and in literally hundreds of bilateral investment treaties (BITs) that have been quietly negotiated between developed and developing nations over the past decade or so (Trebilcock and Howse 1999, 362–5; UNCTAD 1999). In addition, Canada and the United States continue to promote the entrenchment of hemispheric foreign investor rights as part of the Free Trade Area of the Americas (FTAA) agenda.

A REVOLUTIONARY EXPANSION OF INVESTOR RIGHTS

The most remarkable feature of investment regimes is the right of private enforcement they accord foreign corporations. Under NAFTA's Chapter 11, for example, foreign investors are granted a virtually unqualified right to enforce the constraints imposed by the agreement upon government policy and regulation by submitting damage claims for alleged interference with foreign investor rights. By allowing countless foreign investors to invoke binding arbitration processes to enforce expansive investment rights, NAFTA and other investment treaties represent a dramatic departure from the norms of international law in two important ways.

First, these regimes give foreign investors the right to enforce directly an international treaty to which they are neither party nor under which do they have any obligations. Formerly, only nation-states were accorded access to the powerful dispute procedures of international trade law, and nation-states were often reluctant to seek the strict enforcement of trade disciplines they must also observe. However, unlike state-to-state trade disputes, there is no reciprocity between the parties to a foreign investor claim under NAFTA because the foreign investor has no obligations whatsoever under the treaty it may now enforce. As a result, the powerful enforcement mechanisms of these international treaties have been freed from the diplomatic, strategic, and practical constraints that often limit state-to-state dispute resolution.

Second, Chapter 11 accords foreign investors the right to invoke private and secretive international commercial arbitration processes to determine claims that involve important issues of public policy and law. Such arbitration procedures, however, were designed for the purpose of resolving private disputes, typically arising between two parties under a commercial contract rather than for resolving disputes involving areas of public policy and law that have broad societal and economic implications.

Under the rules of international commercial arbitration, no party other than the disputing investor and the NAFTA signatories has any right to notice of a foreign investor claim, access to the pleadings or evidence, or opportunity to observe let alone participate in the proceedings. The rights of those who may be directly or indirectly affected by such claims are entirely ignored by the NAFTA regime. Even the publication of the final award is not guaranteed under NAFTA rules. In other words, investor-state procedures allow foreign corporations to put Canadian policies, programs, and laws on trial without giving those citizens affected any right to know about or participate in the process. Not surprisingly, Canadian trade unions and civil society groups have roundly condemned the regime for fundamentally undermining basic constitutional guarantees of fairness and fundamental justice.

NAFTA investment rules have therefore placed a coercive international enforcement regime at the disposal of countless foreign investors who may now use it to challenge freely any public policies and/or laws that they happen to oppose. Not surprisingly, a growing number of foreign corporations are taking advantage of this opportunity to claim substantial damages from governments that have allegedly failed to respect the constraints imposed on their authority by NAFTA rules.[1] The targets of these claims have included water export controls, fuel additive regulations, hazardous waste export controls, and, most recently, public services. Even more ominously, just the threat of litigation is now often sufficient to warn off government regulatory initiatives, such as requiring cigarettes to be sold in plain packaging or sustaining a ban on the use of a neurotoxic fuel additive.[2]

Summing up these developments, one informed commentator on matters relating to international investment law described NAFTA in the following manner: "By allowing direct recourse by private complainants with respect to [such] a wide range of issues, these treaties create a dramatic extension of arbitral jurisdiction in the international realm" (Paulsson 1995, 233).

DEPLOYING INVESTOR RIGHTS

As noted, corporations are now taking up the opportunity provided by investment treaties to attack government efforts to provide for public health care, environmental protection, and other societal goals.[3] Take, for example, one particularly important area of public policy and law – that concerning water. Several investor claims have been made over the past few years under NAFTA and various BITs relating to government efforts to protect and conserve this vital resource, or to provide domestic water services to their constituents, including the following:

- by Canadian-based Methanex Corporation against the United States for US$970 million in damages because of a ban by California and other states on the fuel additive the company manufactures, which has become a major groundwater contaminant. Among other claims, Methanex is arguing that the ban was unnecessary because less trade-restrictive measures were available;
- by US-based Sun Belt Water Inc. against Canada for US$10 billion because a Canadian province interfered with its plans to export water to California. Even though Sun Belt had never actually exported water, it claims that the ban expropriated its future profits;
- by Compañía de Aguas del Aconquija (CAA), an affiliate of Compagnie Générale des Eaux (a subsidiary of Vivendi), against Argentina for US$300 million, arising from a water and waste-water privatization deal gone sour (ICSID 2000). The claim alleges that public-health orders, mandatory service obligations, and rate regulations all offended its investor rights;
- by Aguas del Tunari, an affiliate of US-based Bechtel, against Bolivia for more than US$25 million for breach of its contract to provide water services to the City of Cochabamba. When public anger erupted over rate increases too steep for many residents to afford, Bolivia cancelled its privatization deal with the company;[4]
- by US Metalclad Corporation against Mexico for more than US$15 million because an impoverished rural municipality refused to grant it a

building permit for a 650,000-ton per annum hazardous waste facility on land already so contaminated by toxic wastes that local groundwater was compromised.

In particular, two NAFTA cases recently decided in favour of disputing investors illustrate how pernicious NAFTA investment disciplines can be when interpreted by tribunals entirely ill-equipped, if not simply indifferent, to the broader public interest that routinely arises in this context.

Metalclad v. Mexico and S.D. Myers v. Canada

In the case of *Metalclad v. Mexico*, the arbitral tribunal ruled that a local municipality had no right to deny the US-based waste company a permit to build a hazardous waste facility either because of environmental and public health concerns or because the company had built much of its project before applying for a local construction permit. The tribunal concluded that, by refusing Metalclad's permit application on public interest and environmental grounds, the local government had expropriated[5] the company's investment in the waste facility, notwithstanding the fact that it had never operated. The tribunal similarly objected to a decision by the state government to establish an ecological preserve that included the company's site. In its view, this also represented an unlawful expropriation of Metalclad's property.

In October 2000 Mexico asked the Supreme Court of British Columbia to overturn the tribunal's ruling that it pay Metalclad US$18 million for interfering with its rights under NAFTA. The case was the first to consider a tribunal decision made under NAFTA investment rules. The Supreme Court essentially upheld the damage award against Mexico, concluding that it had little authority to interfere with the tribunal's decision. This is what the court had to say about the tribunal's views of NAFTA's expropriation provision:

The Tribunal gave an extremely broad definition of expropriation ... In addition to the more conventional notion of expropriation involving a taking of property, the Tribunal held *that expropriation under the NAFTA includes covert or incidental interference with the use of property* which has the effect of depriving the owner, in whole or in significant part, of the use of reasonably to be expected economic benefit of property. This definition is sufficiently broad to include a legitimate rezoning by a municipality or other zoning authority. However, *the definition of expropriation is a question of law with which this Court is not entitled to interfere under the International Commercial Arbitration Act.* (*United Mexican States v. Metalclad* 2001, para. 99, emphasis added)

The Metalclad case is important for two reasons. First, it demonstrates the enormous breadth of NAFTA's expropriation rule, which effectively entrenches private property rights in a manner that Canada and Canadian courts have firmly rejected as a feature of our constitutional framework. Second, it shows the wide latitude international arbitral tribunals will be allowed to interpret NAFTA investment disciplines as they see fit. As the law now stands, Canadian governments at all levels are vulnerable to foreign investor claims for implementing measures that are entirely lawful under Canadian law.

This point is illustrated by the outcome of a NAFTA claim against Canada by another US-based hazardous waste company. In the S.D. Myers case, the tribunal found that Canada was in breach of its obligations under NAFTA because it temporarily banned the export of PCBs to the United States for a brief period during the mid-1990s. S.D. Myers argued that by doing so Canada had interfered with its ambition to treat Canadian waste at its US facility. Like Metalclad, S.D. Myers did not have an ongoing business in managing Canadian wastes but merely a corporate plan to do so.

Astonishingly, the fact that the importation of hazardous waste was illegal under US law didn't deter the tribunal from ruling that Canada had nevertheless offended the rights of the US hazardous waste company. Nor did the fact that in banning PCB exports to the United States, Canada was seeking only to comply with its obligations under the Basel Convention on the Transboundary Movement of Hazardous Waste, an important international environmental treaty to which more than 100 other nations are signatory. Canada ultimately paid S.D. Myers more than US$8 million in damages pursuant to the tribunal's order.

What the Metalclad and S.D. Myers cases illustrate is how corrosive NAFTA investment rules are to the sovereign prerogatives of governments to regulate in the public interest. But the constraints of NAFTA investment rules are even broader in scope and extend to imposing constraints on the authority of governments to provide public services.

INVESTOR RIGHTS AND PUBLIC SERVICES

Since the advent of Chapter 11, the presence of significant private or foreign investment interests in a particular sector may create a formidable impediment to establishing new social services. This is true because, as we have seen, NAFTA investment rules effectively entrench private property rights, as Canada's Constitution does not, allowing foreign investors to claim compensation when their businesses are adversely affected by public policy initiatives such as efforts to expand the framework of Canada's

Medicare system to include homecare or pharmacare.[6] This new and sober-ing reality was pointed out by one of Canada's most senior international trade lawyers in a report prepared for the Romanow Commission on the future of health care in Canada (Johnson 2002). The chilling effect of NAFTA investment rules can further be observed in New Brunswick's retreat from plans to establish a public auto insurance scheme in the face of threats by the insurance industry to claim compensation under NAFTA if it did so (NUPGE 2004).

UPS v. Canada[7]

Indeed, NAFTA investment rules have now provided a mechanism for transnational corporations to assail a wide variety of public services, as is evidenced by a NAFTA claim against Canada by the United Parcel Service of America Inc. (UPS), which describes itself as the world's largest express carrier and package-delivery company. The gist of the UPS claim for US$250 million is that Canada Post has taken advantage of its monopoly position in delivering letter-mail to underwrite the costs of its competitive parcel and courier-delivery services. But in an era when many Crown cor-porations and public agencies deliver at least some services in competition with the private sector, that argument could apply to virtually all public sector services – from water supply to health care. Moreover, the integra-tion of competitive (courier) and non-competitive services (letter-mail) is often essential not only to provide comprehensive services to all Canadians but also to keep public-sector services current and relevant to consumer needs.

A decision is expected in late 2006 or early 2007, and if UPS succeeds, Canadian governments will be under enormous pressure to re-examine the model for delivering all social services, from child and health care to public libraries. The result could well erode a fundamental building block of our society: the notion that basic services should be available to all Canadians regardless of their ability to pay.

P3S, PRIVATIZATION, AND INVESTOR RIGHTS

Efforts to privatize public services are most often promoted under the rubric of establishing public-private partnerships (P3s) between govern-ments and private investors under which the latter finance, build, and operate water treatment plants, public hospitals, highways, and other public institutions and infrastructure while formal ownership, but not control, remains with the government. In effect, P3 schemes privatize public services in all but name. However, since the advent of international investment treaties, the potentially wide scope of foreign investor rights has emerged as an important concern for governments and public institutions contemplating P3 schemes.

Much of the rationale for public-private partnerships depends upon claims made about the value of transferring risk from the public to the private sector, and proponents of P3 initiatives acknowledge the need for rigorous analysis of risk identification and allocation for a particular project. Yet to date, these risk equations have typically ignored the risks associated with P3 relationships in light of international trade disciplines concerning foreign investment and services. The typical private partner to a P3 contract is a consortium, often headed by a transnational corporation that can claim the exclusive rights accorded by international trade, investment, and services agreements. When considered in light of these binding international obligations, P3 projects engender significant risks that need to be carefully assessed and taken into account, including:

- that a contractual dispute, including a decision by government to terminate the P3 contract, will be characterized as expropriation for the purposes of founding an investor-state claim that will then be resolved according to secretive norms of commercial arbitration and in accordance with international, not Canadian, law and procedures;
- that the right to insist on purchasing preferences or other local economic benefits as the quid pro quo of being awarded a P3 contract be eliminated because such requirements are prohibited "performance requirements" under investment and procurement rules;
- that environmental and public-health measures – from safe drinking-water standards and water pollution controls to the remedial orders of local health officials – would be exposed to trade challenges and foreign investor claims;
- that contractual provisions seeking to limit the sale of the private partner or its interest in the P3 contract would be negated;
- that a new precedent, according to the standard of national treatment, would be created, compelling governments to follow suit in like circumstances, even where the P3 initiative is undertaken as a pilot project; and
- that the claim that such public services be regarded as social services, or otherwise be exempt from the full application of NAFTA investment rules, would be undermined.

In fact, foreign investors are now turning to the extraordinary rights they now enjoy under foreign investment treaties to expand their rights in the cases of privatization schemes gone sour. Such cases further underscore the very real risks posed by the new investment regimes for would-be public-sector partners looking to privatize public services.

Générale des Eaux v. Argentine Republic

In a case involving a P3 agreement for water and sewer services (Fortier, Crawford, and Fernandez 2002) the *Compagnie Générale des Eaux* (CGE), an affiliate or subsidiary of Vivendi, together with its Argentinian affiliate *Compañía de Aguas del Aconquija* (CAA), brought a claim for over US$300 million against Argentina pursuant to the provisions of a BIT with features similar to those in NAFTA. The dispute arose from a concession contract that CAA had entered into with the provincial government of Tucumán in 1995, which itself grew out of a 1993 decision by the same government to privatize its water and sewage facilities.

However, disagreements soon arose between CGE and the province concerning the concession contract and became the subject of extensive public scrutiny and controversy. The intractable nature of the disagreements ultimately drew the governments of France and Argentina into the dispute. When efforts to settle the dispute failed, the French-based conglomerate sued under the investment provisions of the BIT. The company cited a long list of grievances, predominantly directed at the provincial government and its officials, including complaints that one can readily imagine arising in a Canadian context:

- health authorities had improperly issued orders and imposed fines concerning the company's alleged failure to install proper water-testing equipment or to conduct and provide proper water testing;
- an Ombudsman had improperly deprived CGE of the right to cut off service to non-paying customers; and
- the province had failed to allow "proper" rate increases.

The first issue addressed by the tribunal was its jurisdiction to consider the complaint in light of the concession contract's explicit assignment of such disputes to the exclusive jurisdiction of local administrative tribunals. Article 16.4 of the contract provided that "the resolution of contract disputes, concerning both its interpretation and application, ... be submitted to the exclusive jurisdiction of the contentious administrative courts of Tucumán" (Fortier, Crawford, and Fernandez 2002, 95). Rejecting the argument and the contract notwithstanding, the tribunal found that it had jurisdiction to hear the CGE claim that Argentina had violated its obligations under the investment treaty: "Neither the forum-selection provision of the Concession Contract nor the provisions of the ICSID Convention and the BIT on which the Argentine Republic relies preclude CGE's recourse to this Tribunal on the facts presented" (Fortier, Crawford, and Fernandez 2002, 96).

Having found that it had authority to consider the complaint, the tribunal

also ruled that, given the complexity of the 111-page single-spaced concession contract, it was impossible to distinguish or separate violations of the
investment treaty from breaches of the contract without first interpreting and
applying the detailed contract provisions. The tribunal also found that,
absent a clear and independent breach of the investment treaty by Argentina,
the claimants had a duty to pursue their rights before the domestic tribunals
referred to by the concession contract before seeking recourse to international arbitration.

Unhappy with this result, the company successfully appealed to the International Centre for Settlement of Investment Disputes (ICSID) for an annulment of the tribunal's ruling. It is noteworthy that the president of that
tribunal was a Canadian, L. Yves Fortier. In deciding that Vivendi was entitled to have its claim under the BIT determined, whatever the provisions of
the concession contract, the tribunal concluded:

In the Committee's view, it is not open to an ICSID tribunal having jurisdiction
under a BIT in respect of a claim based upon a substantive provision of that BIT,
to dismiss the claim on the ground that it could or should have been dealt with
by a national court. In such a case, the inquiry which the ICSID tribunal is required
to undertake is one governed by the ICSID Convention, by the BIT, and by applicable international law. Such an inquiry is neither in principle determined, nor precluded, by any issue of municipal law, including any municipal agreement of the
parties.

Moreover the Committee does not understand how, if there had been a breach
of the BIT in the present case (a question of international law), the existence of
Article 16(4) of the Concession Contract could have prevented its characterization
as such. A state cannot rely on an exclusive jurisdiction clause in a contract to avoid
the characterisation of its conduct as internationally unlawful under a treaty.
(Fortier, Crawford, and Fernandez 2002, para. 102–3)

As for distinguishing between claims arising from a P3 contract within
the context of an international treaty according the private partner certain
and often exclusive rights, the tribunal had this to say:

In accordance with the general principle ... whether there has been a breach of the
BIT and whether there has been a breach of contract are different questions. Each
of these claims will be determined by reference to its own proper and applicable law
– in the case of the BIT, by international law; in the case of the Concession Contract, by the proper law of the contract. (Fortier, Crawford, and Fernandez 2002,
para. 96)

The tribunal went on to quote from leading cases on the question:

Compliance with municipal law and compliance with the provisions of a treaty are different questions. What is a breach of treaty may be lawful in the municipal law and what is unlawful in the municipal law may be wholly innocent of violation of a treaty provision. (Fortier, Crawford, and Fernandez 2002, para. 97)

To the degree that there was ever any doubt about whether a government could contain or restrict the rights of foreign investors under NAFTA, other than by renegotiating the treaty itself, the Vivendi annulment decision conclusively answers the question: "no." Nevertheless, such pro-privatization groups as the Canadian Council for Public-Private Partnerships continue to claim that this is possible.

Bechtel vs. Bolivia

In 1999, under pressure from the World Bank, the Bolivian government sold off Cochabamba's public water system to a pool of investors, including a Bechtel subsidiary, *Aguas del Tunari*. Promises were made to pour millions into expansion and improvement. But when the consortium raised prices, sometimes by more than 100 percent, public anger erupted. Many Bolivian families living in and around Cochabamba earn as little as $100 a month. For them, a twenty-dollar water bill can be a catastrophe.

Protests and a general strike that brought the city to a halt for four days followed. Ultimately, the Bolivian government was persuaded to cancel its privatization deal with the Bechtel subsidiary. The company protested, claiming that factors other than increased water rates were responsible for the civil unrest, and swiftly reaffirmed its commitment to meeting the area's water service needs. However, according to newspaper accounts *Aguas del Tunari* has now invoked a bilateral investment treaty between Bolivia and the Netherlands to claim more than US$25 million in damages for breach of its contract to supply water to the City of Cochabamba. None of the pleadings or other material relating to this claim is available publicly.

CONTRACTING OUT OF NAFTA?

A legal opinion prepared for the Canadian Council for Public Private Partnerships takes the position that "a properly drafted contract *would eliminate the possibility* that any public health or regulatory measure could be challenged as an expropriation, and that such a contract could avoid any claim for expropriation under NAFTA" (Kirby and Doubilet 2001, 10, emphasis added). Simply put, this view entirely misapprehends one of the most fundamental principles of international law. There are few things that are certain about NAFTA investment rules, but one of them is that it is simply not possible for governments through contractual, or any other means, either to deny private-sector partners recourse to NAFTA dispute procedures or to alter in any way the rights foreign investors have been accorded by this treaty. Nor, absent an amendment to NAFTA or GATS, is it possible for any Canadian government through contractual or legislative means to suspend, circumvent, or otherwise alter the binding obligations engendered by these trade agreements.

In fact, Canada has declared only one exception to the invocation of NAFTA enforcement procedures.[8] In every other case, it has extended its prior and unilateral consent to be bound by the investor-state suit procedures.[9] Indeed, the federal government acknowledged the unconstrained access accorded foreign investors to these dispute procedures when it amended the International Boundary Waters Treaty Act to address the problem of water exports. The government conceded: "Canada cannot prevent other countries, or, in the case of Chapter 11 of NAFTA, private investors, from challenging its laws and regulations before dispute settlement or arbitration panels" (DFAIT 2001). Of course the right to invoke these procedures is no guarantee of success, but the assurances of P3 promoters that governments can *eliminate* the possibility of foreign investor claims concerning P3 investments is plainly wrong.

INVESTOR RIGHTS IN SEARCH OF A RATIONALE

In a speech delivered to the Conference Board of Canada in 2002, Canada's then minister of international trade Pierre Pettigrew described the Canadian international investment agenda as based on two key assumptions: (1) that foreign direct investment (FDI) benefits both recipient and capital exporting nations and (2) that international investment treaties foster FDI (Pettigrew 2002). The minister's remarks offered a number of declaratory statements about the putative benefits of FDI but did not present or point to any evidence that might support them.

In general, there has been scant effort to substantiate the loose claims made in support of international investment regimes, and the limited research available in fact undermines their validity. A recent report published by the World Bank (Hallward-Driemeier 2003), for example, indicates that, far from always being beneficial, there is a real possibility that FDI can have net negative impacts, especially when it displaces domestic investment, appropriates domestic research and development capabilities, or overwhelms domestic and democratic policy processes. In a similar vein, a recent empirical study by the United Nations Conference on Trade and Development (UNCTAD) concluded that it is only the more selective and interventionist Asian countries who have been able to derive significant and demonstrable net benefits from their FDI flows (Agosin and Mayer 2000). In other words, developing nations that embrace strong foreign investment controls have fared far better than have those that have abandoned them.

However, even putting aside the question of whether it is sound policy to indiscriminately embrace both inward and outward FDI flows, there is little if any evidence to support the claim that binding international investment rules are necessary either to attract foreign investment to this country or to protect the interests of Canadian investors abroad. In fact, the same World Bank study previously noted describes the relative disconnect between FDI and bilateral investment treaties as follows:

Clearly, a BIT is not a necessary condition to receive FDI. There are many source-host pairs with substantial FDI that do not have a BIT. Japan, the second largest source of FDI has only concluded 4 BITs. The US does not have a BIT with China, its largest developing country destination. Brazil, one of the top receivers of FDI has not ratified a single BIT. In addition, there are also numerous examples of countries that have concluded many BITs and yet have received only moderate inflows. Sub-Saharan Africa, for instance, has had difficulties in attracting FDI, though it has tried to improve the environment for FDI by entering into various agreements to protect the interests of investors. There are also examples such as Cuba, where it does not have a BIT with either Canada or Mexico, its two biggest foreign investors. On the contrary, almost 60% of the countries it does have a BIT with actually have no foreign investment in Cuba. (Hallward-Driemeier 2003, 13–4)

The overwhelming majority of Canadian direct investment abroad goes to the United States and Europe. Moreover, the majority of developing country recipients, including the largest such recipients, are countries with which Canada has no bilateral investment treaty in force, such as Brazil. The same is true for other countries outside the EU, such as Hungary.

Not only does the available evidence refute the optimistic assumptions that Canada promotes to justify its foreign investment agenda, but it also points to some potential negative consequences. As we have seen, the rights given to foreign investors under NAFTA and many BITs expose policy makers to potentially large-scale liabilities and seriously restrict the development of public policy. More problematic is the corrosive effects of these regimes on the integrity of domestic parliamentary and judicial institutions – the very institutions that are so fundamental to creating the stable social and political environments that are truly conducive to foreign investment. In other words, by undermining sovereignty and the rule of law, foreign investment treaties actually destabilize the very democratic institutions that their advocates argue are necessary to attract foreign investment.

THE UNCERTAIN FUTURE
OF FOREIGN INVESTOR RIGHTS

Despite the significant adverse impacts of NAFTA investment rules and the absence of any demonstrable benefits to Canada, federal trade officials remain wedded to promoting foreign investor rights as part of their trade agenda. However, there have recently been a number of encouraging signs that they are unlikely to succeed with this project.

To begin, the theoretical and policy arguments offered to support the need for international investment treaties have been exposed as dubious at best (Dezalay and Garth 1996; Sornarajah 2002). For example, the establishment of powerful international enforcement mechanisms, such as those of the NAFTA investor-state provisions, has often been promoted as serving the interests of developing nations. It is argued that these procedures bring the rule of law into previously unequal relationships and foster foreign direct investment in poorer nations. Yet there is little, if any, evidence to support the claim that developing countries are the beneficiaries of these developments (Sornarajah 1994, 235–6). Indeed, notwithstanding the rise of international foreign investment regimes, the bulk of foreign direct investment still flows to the wealthiest of nations, and the gap between rich and poor nations has grown.[10] Moreover, the lack of accountability that attends investor-state procedures fundamentally undermines, rather than fosters, the institutions that are central to democratic governance.

Second, developing countries are now more or less united in resisting the inclusion of NAFTA-like investment rules as part of the WTO framework. Thus, the trade negotiations that ultimately led to the establishment of the WTO failed to yield a comprehensive set of investment rules along the lines of those engendered by NAFTA, notwithstanding the persistent efforts of the United States to achieve that objective (Trebilcock and Howse 1999, 351–2). In addition, and as noted, subsequent efforts by OECD nations to revive their multilateral investment agenda also foundered (358).

The issue of foreign investment once again arose within the context of a new round of WTO trade negotiations initiated at the meeting of the WTO Ministerial Council in Doha, Qatar. However, efforts by Canada and a few other developed nations to push this agenda forward have been firmly rebuffed by an increasingly determined and cohesive group of developing countries.

As we have seen, the advent of international treaties according foreign investors the unilateral right to invoke binding arbitration and to assert claims against nation-states represented a dramatic departure from the norms of both international and domestic law. It is only very recently that the broader implications of these developments have come to light and attracted any significant degree of informed discussion and debate. And with that debate has come growing scepticism about and opposition to the establishment of international investor-state arbitral regimes, such as the one established by Chapter 11 of NAFTA.

HUMAN RIGHTS NOT CORPORATE RIGHTS

Aided by this growing understanding and international resistance, the time is opportune to challenge the preoccupation of federal trade officials with protecting the interests of powerful foreign corporations to the exclusion of virtually all other priorities. Towards this end, successive Canadian governments have shown little reluctance to trade away sovereignty and even the independence of our courts. But when it comes to protecting human rights, the environment, biodiversity, or the rights of workers, these same governments have repeatedly raised concerns about sovereignty to frustrate the establishment of meaningful international protection for basic human, environmental, and social rights. In fact human rights, environmental, and other organizations have assailed international investor rights regimes for not just ignoring these goals but for actively frustrating their realization.

This systematic discrimination in favour of wealthy and influential corporate elites not only offends Canadian constitutional guarantees but also violates the solemn commitments Canada has made in becoming party to international human rights, environmental, and labour conventions. It is time for Canadians to insist that their elected officials dramatically realign their priorities to place greater emphasis on human rights, environmental sustainability, and social development – before NAFTA-like investment rules do any more damage to these non-commercial policy goals.

NOTES

1 Information about other Chapter 11 claims can also be found on the DFAIT website: <www.dfait-maeci.gc.ca/tna-nac/gov-en.asp>. As of 12 June 2006 the website listed thirteen arbitration claims brought against Canada (including active, previous, notices received, and notices withdrawn), twelve against the United States, and fifteen against Mexico. As of the same date, a site maintained by a professor of law at the University of Windsor identified thirteen claims against Canada, sixteen against the United States, and fifteen against Mexico: <www.naftaclaims.com>. While the NAFTA Commission is required to keep a public record of all Chapter 11 Notices of Claim (Article 1126), as of the same date these claims were not recorded on its website: <www.nafta-sec-alena.org/english/ index.htm>.

2 See discussion of *Ethyl Corp. v. Canada* and the broader discussion of the chilling effect of these regimes in Howard Mann (2001) and David Schneiderman (2000).

3 A good description of several NAFTA investment claims is presented in Mann (2001).

4 This and several other investor-state claims arising under NAFTA or other investment treaties can be found at <www.worldbank.org/icsid>, a website maintained by the International Centre for the Settlement of Investment Disputes, which operates under the auspices of the World Bank Group.

5 NAFTA's expropriation rule is set out by Article 1110, which provides:

> 1. No Party may directly or indirectly nationalize or expropriate an investment of an investor of another Party in its territory or take a measure tantamount to nationalization or expropriation of such an investment ("expropriation"), except:
> (a) for a public purpose;
> (b) on a non-discriminatory basis;
> (c) in accordance with due process of law and Article 1105(1); and
> (d) on payment of compensation in accordance with paragraphs 2 through 6.
> 2. Compensation shall be equivalent to the fair market value of the expropriated investment immediately before the expropriation took place ("date of expropriation"), and shall not reflect any change in value occurring because the intended expropriation had become known earlier. Valuation criteria shall include going concern value, asset value including declared tax value of tangible property, and other criteria, as appropriate, to determine fair market value.
> 3. Compensation shall be paid without delay and be fully realizable.

6 See Schneiderman (1996, 521–3; 2000). See also Greider (2001, 6) quoting Ron Price, now in private practice but then a key US negotiator, on NAFTA investment rules.

7 Various documents relating to this claim can be viewed through a website maintained by DFAIT; see note 1.

8 Annex 1138:3 refers to decisions by Canada following a review under the Investment Canada Act.

9 Article 1122:1.

10 See Schneiderman (2000, 764) and the UNCTAD studies cited therein.

REFERENCES

Agosin, Manuel R, and Ricardo Mayer. 2000. *Foreign Investment in Developing Countries: Does It Crowd in Domestic Investment?* Geneva: United Nations Conference on Trade and Development.

Dezalay, Yves, and Bryant Garth. 1996. *Dealing in Virtue: International Commercial Arbitration and the Construction of a Transnational Legal Order*. Chicago: University of Chicago Press.

DFAIT. 2001. *Questions and Answers (in Relation to a Bill to Amend the International Boundary Waters Treaty Act)*. Ottawa: Department of Foreign Affairs and International Trade. Available at <http://www.dfait-maeci. gc.ca/can-am/washington/shared_env/q_a-en.asp>

Fortier, L. Yves, James R. Crawford, and José Carlos Fernandez. 2002. Decision on Annulment. In the Matter of Annulment Proceeding in the Arbitration between *Compañía de Aguas Aconquija S.A. and Vivendi Universal v. Argentine Republic*. ICSID Case No. ARB/97/3. Washington: International Centre for Settlement of Investment Disputes.

Greider, William. 2001. The Right and US Trade Law: Invalidating the 20th Century. *The Nation*, 15 October, Available at <http://www.thenation.com/doc/20011015/greider>.

Hallward-Driemeier, Mary. 2003. *Do Bilateral Investment Treaties Attract FDI? Only a Bit ... and They Could Bite*. Washington: World Bank.

ICSID. 2000. *Compañía de Aguas del Aconquija S.A. and Vivendi Universal v. Argentine Republic* – ICSID Case ARB/97/3. Washington: International Centre for Settlement of Investment Disputes.

Johnson, Jon. 2002. *How Will International Trade Agreements Affect Canadian Health Care?* Ottawa: Commission on the Future of Health Care in Canada.

Kirby, Peter, and David Doubilet. 2001. *Comments of Fasken Martineau DuMoulin LLP on the Shrybman Opinion*. Toronto: The Canadian Council for Public-Private Partnerships.

Mann, Howard. 2001. *Private Rights and Public Problems: A Guide to NAFTA's Controversial Chapter on Investor Rights*. Winnipeg: International Institute for Sustainable Development.

NUPGE. 2004. Free Trade Threat Killed N.B. Public Auto Insurance. July 14 News. Nepean: National Union of Public and General Employees.

Paulsson, Jan. 1995. Arbitration without Privity. *ICSID Review – Foreign Investment Law Journal* 10 (2): 232–56.

Pettigrew, Pierre. 2002. Address to the Conference Board of Canada on Canada's Plan for Foreign Investment Promotion. Ottawa: Department of Foreign Affairs and International Trade.

Ruggiero, Renato. 1998. Towards GATT 2000: A European Strategy. Paper presented to the Conference on Trade and Services. 2 June, Brussels, European Commission.

Schneiderman, David. 1996. NAFTA's Takings Rule: American Constitutionalism comes to Canada. *University of Toronto Law Journal* 46 (4): 499–537.

– 2000. Investment Rules and New Constitutionalism. *Law and Social Inquiry* 25 (3): 757–88.

Sornarajah, M. 1994. *The International Law of Foreign Investment*. Cambridge: Cambridge University Press.

– 2002. A Developing Country Perspective on International Economic Law in the
    Context of Dispute Settlement. In *Perspectives in International Economic Law*,
    ed. A.H. Qureshi, 83–110. London: Kluwer Law International.
Trebilcock, Michael J., and Robert Howse. 1999. *The Regulation of International
    Trade*. 2nd ed. London/New York: Routledge.
UNCTAD. 1999. Lessons from the MAI. UNCTAD/ITE/IIT/MISC 22. New York:
    UNCTAD.
United Mexican States v. Metalclad Corporation. 2001. Supreme Court of British
    Columbia. BCSC 664.

13

Impact of Trade Agreements on Subnational Governments

KATHY CORRIGAN

This chapter considers the impact of trade agreements on provincial and local government policy, with a focus on educational and municipal services. These impacts operate within the context of many forces: the principles and the provisions of the trade agreements themselves, the agreement negotiating process, economic globalization and US hegemony, Canada-US relations, and political and power relationships within Canada. Most important, however, trade agreements and their impacts are shaped by the ever more insistent, cohesive, and powerful corporate forces demanding the increased free flow of trade and the privatization of services.

TRADE AGREEMENTS: CUFTA, NAFTA, WTO AND AIT

Canada has a long, sometimes uneasy, but generally beneficial trade relationship with the United States. The attitude of each country towards either trade liberalization or protectionism has varied over time and according to the prevailing economic and political circumstances. Over the past twenty years, however, there has been a decided shift in favour of trade liberalization, with Canada negotiating and signing far-reaching trade agreements with the United States (the Canada-US Free Trade Agreement [CUFTA]) and with the United States and Mexico (the North American Free Trade Agreement [NAFTA]).

Canada is also a signatory to the multilateral agreements administered by the World Trade Organization (WTO), including the General Agreement on Trade in Services (GATS). Governments regulate or deliver a vast variety of services, including health, education, social, transportation, environmental, security, and municipal services. The framework of rules that makes up GATS, however, proscribes government policies, laws, or regulations that are inconsistent with the trade liberalization provisions of the

agreement, thus threatening a wide range of government statutes and services. Moreover, GATS is being renegotiated to submit an expanding number
of the services governments provide to its most forceful provisions and to
create new obligations regarding domestic regulations, procurement, and
subsidies.

At about the same time as NAFTA and GATS were being negotiated, Canadian provinces were negotiating the Agreement on Internal Trade (AIT),
which entered into force on 1 July 1995. While NAFTA and the various WTO
agreements, including GATS, deal with external trade, the AIT applies many
NAFTA-style rules to trade within and between provinces.

While few would disagree with the need for trade, the dizzying evolution
of the world economy and the rapid expansion of commitments under
these new trade agreements have raised serious concerns about national
sovereignty and democracy. These new treaties are far more than mere
trade agreements. On the contrary, they reach to the very core of the ability
of governments to regulate activities within their respective territories.
Uncertainty about the implications of trade liberalization has been further
heightened by the reliance upon unaccountable dispute resolution panels to
interpret the intricacies and ambiguities of these complex treaties. While
interpretation may vary from case to case, the undemocratic compromises
embedded in these agreements are very clear: they create rules that bind
present and future governments, are administered by non-elected bureaucrats, and are arbitrated by foreign tribunals behind closed doors, without
representation from the subnational governments directly affected by the
decisions.

Despite supporting the trade objective of unfettered access to foreign
markets, countries still wish to protect their economy, institutions, and
values. The Canadian public remains particularly concerned about the public
delivery of a variety of services that it feels are crucial to its national security
and identity. From that perspective, according to former New Democratic
Party (NDP) trade critic Bill Blaikie (2003), Canadians have more to lose than
perhaps any country in the world. Canadians remain proud of, and committed to, our public health, education, and social assistance programs. Canadians also feel a strong need to protect their identity on a continent dominated
by the United States.

Free Trade: Fair Play, or Stacking the Corporate Deck

Although the advocates of free trade agreements argue that they are necessary in order to ensure a fair international trading system and Canadian
access to the US market, Canadians do not trust the United States to "play
fair" when it comes to either trade or trade agreements. The perception
that Washington will utilize the agreements when it is to its benefit and

ignore them at any sign of disadvantage is commonplace. Joseph Stiglitz – former chief economist of the World Bank, chairman of Bill Clinton's Council of Economic Advisors and Nobel Prize winner in economics – argues that such perceptions are validated by the activities of the US government, which do little to build confidence in a fair international trading system:

The US Trade Representative or the Department of Commerce, often prodded by special interests within the United States, brings an accusation against a foreign country; there is a review process – involving only the US government – with a decision made by the United States, after which sanctions are brought against the offending country. The United States sets itself up as prosecutor, judge and jury. The rhetoric the United States uses to push its position adds to the image of a superpower willing to throw its weight around for its own special interests. (Stiglitz 2003, 62)

The softwood lumber disputes provide a telling Canadian example. According to Roger Simmons, then consul general of Canada in Seattle, the rationale for US tariffs against Canadian forestry products does not stand up to scrutiny: "The people who fabricate their arguments don't believe it either. Their own Commerce Department has found them wrong three times." But they continue to impose the tariffs because "the launch of the investigation disrupts the Canadian industry" (Simmons 2003).

Rather than secure a fair playing field for international traders, free trade agreements are in reality a key disciplinary mechanism for a much wider neoliberal agenda. Indeed, Brian Mulroney was surprisingly candid about the new policy directions represented by the trade agreements:

If you believe in free trade, then you have to believe in open investment, you have to believe in deregulation and privatization. And so these are the changes that we made because it all went together. It was a package of attitudes: free trade, getting rid of FIRA, getting rid of the National Energy Program, privatizing Air Canada, privatizing Canadair, privatizing Petro-Canada and so on. Deregulation and all those things ... And so what began as a free trade agreement has wound up shaping attitudes, not only of my government and my party and people on the right, but it has forced the Liberals into a completely new set of policies which they adopted from us. (Watson 2000, 38)

As Michael Hart (2000, 25) points out, "the debate in Canada on the merits of the CUFTA was in many ways a debate on the merits of deepening integration."

Thomas Barrett, director of the European Investment Bank, recently offered a concise, if sterile, exposition of the corporate free trade position:

"What is needed is a standard commoditized approach that works for all countries and all sectors." We must "reform the processes of government so we can meet the challenge of privatization." The key, he said, "is identifying and eliminating legal and institutional bottlenecks" (Barrett 2002). Although Barrett did not elaborate upon what might constitute such legal and institutional "bottlenecks," they would certainly include any restriction on capital movement as well as any public policy measure that could be interpreted as imposing an "unnecessary" regulatory burden upon investors.

Broadly put, the ultimate aim of trade agreements is not to enhance trade per se but, rather, to provide corporations with unfettered access to global markets and resources. At the extreme, every law that government makes (every tax, every public subsidy, every regulation, including zoning, standards, requirements, and prohibitions) represents a potential impediment to unrestricted trade. Only those that can be shown to be not "unnecessarily burdensome" to business, according to the standards set by negotiated agreements and unaccountable tribunals, will be free from challenge.

Yet while Mulroney may be correct in assessing the reasons for a change of attitude in the Liberal Party, opinion polls repeatedly indicate that Canadians want public services to stay in public hands (Ipsos 2004). Widespread public opposition has forced the cancellation of numerous proposed privatization schemes, frustrating the advocates of privatization. At the 10th Annual Conference of the Canadian Council for Public-Private Partnerships the frustration was widespread and palpable: "While some excellent public private partnerships have been put in place, to be frank, progress has been disappointingly slow and one might say there has been more talk than action" (Fell 2002).

In the face of public opposition from unions, community organizations, and even some politicians, the Canadian government is under considerable pressure from the corporate community to expand and to entrench privatization within trade agreements. Powerful, well organized and very well funded lobbyists drive and dominate the negotiating process. These include organizations like the US Coalition of Service Industries, whose foremost goal is "To open foreign markets to US business and allow them to compete abroad. Most broadly stated, our goal is to use every available opportunity to achieve the greatest liberalization of trade in services that we can obtain" (Vastine 2002). Its members encompass information technology and computer services, insurance and other financial services, express delivery, energy services, professional services, consulting and accountancy, travel and tourism, telecommunications and retailing, with affiliate relationships with health, education, and other service organizations.

The companies that comprise the US Coalition of Service Industries "meet regularly with government representatives to consult on US positions on a wide range of issues ... [and] travel abroad to meet with foreign governments and business leaders." They also "lobby in our Congress for liberal trade legislation" and "work particularly well with the WTO, where we have close ties with the current Director General." The Coalition's president, Robert Vastine, noted that "recently, we took a group of US Congress staff members to the WTO for an intensive familiarization with its goals, methods, and leaders as we prepare to build support in Congress" (Vastine 2002).

The WTO argues that "Decisions in the WTO are generally by consensus. In principle, that's even more democratic than majority rule because no decision is taken until everyone agrees" (WTO 2003, 10). However, the reality remains that the process of "getting everyone to agree" means getting everyone to agree with the corporate agenda. Indeed, so dominant has the corporate-driven trade liberalization perspective become within governmental and negotiating circles that it resembles not public policy but religious creed. As Bill Blaikie (2003), NDP member of Parliament, explains:

DFAIT spend their whole lives living and breathing trade liberalization. It's a quasi-religion. I was in Qatar, in Singapore, in Geneva, and in Seattle. And I will be in Cancun. I'm a minister by profession, and when you listen to people talk trade liberalization, it's evangelical ... And there's this quasi-religious conviction about everything that ... if there's a problem, even if it's created by trade liberalization, it can only be solved by more trade liberalization.

The comments of Blaikie are further supported by the observations of George Puil, former chair of the Greater Vancouver Regional District and chair of the Federation of Canadian Municipalities Finance Committee, who met several times with officials from the Department of Foreign Affairs and International Trade (DFAIT) to discuss the impact of trade agreements on municipalities. According to Puil (2003),

Their whole interest was increasing trade, almost as if they had blinders on. They didn't realize that if they did that, it could have some implications for every municipality in Canada. I don't know if they were being evasive so much as they just had their blinders on, and they were interested in one thing only. And they couldn't understand why a lower level of government would be questioning the good of the nation, so to speak, as far as increasing world trade and that was their goal.

But if the only interest of the Canadian government during negotiations is the extension of trade liberalization, the question for Canadians becomes, who is representing the interests and values of the Canadian public?

The corporate determination to open up markets, including services like water, health, and education, coupled with a Canadian mandate directed

solely towards the improvement of investment and export opportunities for
Canadian businesses, severely compromises public services and government regulatory authority. The potential impacts of these trade agreements
reach into virtually all government activities, affecting every level of government. The balance of this chapter considers more specifically the impact
of trade treaties upon Canadian provinces and municipalities, with a particular focus on educational and municipal services.

Trade Agreements and the Provinces

It is clear that the obligations assumed by the Canadian government in
international trade agreements extend to subnational governments, including the provinces. Article 105 of NAFTA ("Extent of Obligations") provides
that: "The Parties shall ensure that all necessary measures are taken in
order to give effect to the provisions of this Agreement, including their
observance, except as otherwise provided in this Agreement, by state and
provincial governments."

Similarly, Article 1.3 (a) ("Scope and Definitions") of GATS requires that:
"In fulfilling its obligations and commitments under the Agreement, each
Member shall take such reasonable measures as may be available to it to
ensure their observance by regional and local governments and authorities
and non-governmental bodies within its territories" (WTO 1994).

While there is no provision for other countries or investors to sue subnational governments directly (the cases are taken against Canada), the
threat of lawsuits against the federal government could easily transform
into federal measures to coerce the provinces into compliance with trade
agreements, such as the refusal to fund provincial programs or the removal
of subsidies. For example, in the NAFTA Chapter 11 case involving Metalclad and the Mexican government, a US company was awarded US$16.7
million in compensation for the fact that it was prevented from operating
a federally approved toxic waste disposal facility in Mexico, when the local
government would not issue a permit. The lawsuit against the federal government is now being turned into political and financial pressure on subnational governments as the Mexican government seeks to recover the
award from the state government (*United States v. Metalclad* 2001).

Despite the applicability of trade agreements to subnational governments, there has been surprisingly little in the way of public debate at the
provincial level. Some provinces (Alberta, for example) embrace free trade.
Most have been surprisingly quiet. The most active and articulate provincial government opposition came from British Columbia in the mid-1990s.
Glen Clark (2003), the premier at the time, opposed the trade agreements
because, as he explains, "the internal trade agreement and the free trade
agreement both restrict the government's ability to act in the public inter-

est, or in whatever way that elected governments feel is appropriate. They fetter government's power, and they subordinate government's power to act."

There was also recognition that the removal of barriers and the harmonization of standards could be interpreted in such a way as to enforce provincial compliance with international trade agreements signed by the federal government. Certainly, a 1990 General Agreement on Tariffs and Trade (GATT) Policy Review identified the area of provincial services as a key concern of the GATT Council:

Members of the Council identified several areas of concern. Among these ... [was] how the Canadian Government could ensure the implementation of international commitments in trade-related areas where provincial governments had jurisdiction. It was noted that this issue could become of special importance as multilateral rules were extended to new areas such as services. (GATT 1990, 177)

Canada's response during that review included the comment that:

trade policy power was held by the Federal Government, which worked actively with the provinces in the trade policy area ... Current efforts included discussions on a range of trade policy matters such as services, agricultural support and procurement. Canada would be in a position to implement any agreements that it undertook. (GATT 1990, 340)

According to Glen Clark, British Columbia pushed hard for the protections afforded to Crown corporations under the Agreement on Internal Trade, but ultimately the NDP government decided to sign the agreement, excluding the so-called MASSH sector (municipalities, academic institutions, social services and health).[1]

One of the difficulties in monitoring and encouraging discussion about the effects of these agreements on public policy is that, once an agreement is in place, provinces, municipalities, school boards, or other agencies must devote their resources towards compliance rather than continuing the public policy debate or tracking the effects of the new deal. The public thus remains largely unaware of ongoing policy changes as governments rewrite legislation to comply with trade agreements. For example, the provisions of the Agreement on Internal Trade impose non-discriminatory processes for procurement, which negatively affect local businesses. As Glen Clark (2003) points out:

Traditionally there was what was called a 5 percent preference. If you were bidding on building a bridge, there was a 5 percent preference given to local firms over foreign firms. BC's Crown corporations and government procurement policy always had a bias towards local providers. That's illegal in Canada today. Procurement is all done electronically, and there is absolutely no preference.

According to Clark, both British Columbia and Ontario considered challenging the constitutionality of NAFTA. As late as October 1993 then Ontario premier Bob Rae notified the legislature that the Ontario government would challenge NAFTA through a legal reference to the Ontario Court of Appeal. However, it did not go ahead with the challenge:

We [the Ontario Provincial government] considered it very carefully. We spent a lot of time talking to lawyers about it and studying it. We eventually concluded that it probably wouldn't succeed and that the implication would be that it would strengthen [NAFTA], because the court would reject our claim. It would clarify the law, if you like, in a way that we didn't really want to see happen. (Rae 2003)

Moreover, while Rae (2003) asserts that CUFTA was not the decisive factor in the Ontario government's decision not to proceed with public auto insurance, he did remark that had the NAFTA Chapter 11 expropriation provisions been in place, trade issues would have played a more decisive role: "CUFTA was not the decisive factor with respect to car insurance. However, NAFTA would be, because there is a significant legal difference between NAFTA and the Free Trade Agreement [CUFTA] with respect to the protection of property rights."

Provincial governments, moreover, are not monolithic: debate also occurs within individual provincial departments and cabinets. The province of Ontario, for example, is a massive institution, and while some in the government certainly wanted to oppose and challenge the trade agreements, others were quite enthusiastic about them. Different provinces also approach issues within the context of their diverse relationships with the federal government. Governments of "have-not" provinces that might be expected to vocally oppose the treaties may not do so for fear of jeopardizing their share of federal disbursements – joint funding of projects, for example. Clark (2003) noted that, when the federal government was driving the agenda for internal trade, it was "pretty close to impossible for those provinces who rely on the federal government for major sources of their funding to stand up to them. So, even if they agree with you, and they might even argue the case (as in the case of Newfoundland, which was very helpful in arguing my case), when it comes down to votes, they would always vote with the federal government."

How trade treaties are affecting provincial public policy today varies. One of the most insidious effects – and this applies to local as well as provincial governments – is their role in narrowing the scope of public policy options available in the future. While all provincial governments may not have exercised their powers (for example, to set conditions on investment that would spur local economic jobs or development), they retained the power to do so in the future. The non-discriminatory procurement policies of trade agreements, however, mean that such policy options are no longer available to governments. With the stroke of a pen, trade treaties therefore proscribe a vital range of local, provincial, and national development policies.

As a practical matter, it is clear that provinces are increasingly vetting proposed legislation to ensure compliance with the provisions of federally adopted trade agreements. In Manitoba, for example, Ministry of Industry, Trade and Mines policy analysts acknowledge having raised trade agreement issues with lawyers in the Department of Justice. In Newfoundland and Labrador, while there is no formal process for vetting legislation, Manager of Trade Policy Tom Fleming discusses trade issues with solicitors in the Department of Justice. He notes that:

To date, several pieces of legislation have had to be amended due to trade agreements. In one case, amendments were made to change local residency requirements for professionals and in another case amendments were made to delete a local preference policy. Our government's position on trade agreements is that we generally support them. There are certain areas in ongoing negotiations where we are monitoring them very closely. The areas we are concerned about include, but are not limited to, fish, energy, shipbuilding, education and social services. (Fleming 2003)

Alberta is similarly supportive of trade agreements and trade liberalization and has a well established group of officials from almost every governmental department that meet regularly to discuss trade policy issues. Issues concerning provincial compliance with trade treaties are dealt with early in the legislative process. According to Daryl Hanak (2003), of the Ministry of International and Intergovernmental Relations,

Legislative proposals that are significantly inconsistent with our trade obligations are usually identified by officials involved in the legislative drafting process. We have had very few instances where any proposed legislation is inconsistent with our trade obligations. In the few cases where inconsistencies have been identified, we were able to devise an approach that achieves the same policy objective, but in a manner that respects our trade obligations.

The NDP government of British Columbia devoted significant resources to analyzing trade treaty issues throughout the second half of the 1990s. In a significant departure from traditional government approaches, both the Harcourt and Clark governments produced reports on the proposed Multilateral Agreement on Investment (MAI) forged from their close working

relationship with the broad community on a wide variety of trade policy
issues (British Columbia 1998, 1999).

Subnational governments can also use trade agreements to advance their
legislative agenda. In July 2004, for example, the BC government decided
to outsource management of the Medical Services Plan (MSP) and Pharma-
Care information to a US corporation. When resistance to the idea
emerged, the government raised the spectre of trade sanctions as an argument against limiting an outsourcing contract to Canadian bidders. Moreover, when the BC Information and Privacy Commissioner held hearings on
the implications of the US Privacy Act for personal information, the provincial government argued that "a fair and rational person would not consider
it reasonable to expect public bodies to exclude companies with US connections from bidding on contracts where to do so would violate international treaty obligations" (British Columbia 2004, 42). The submission
then list-ed various NAFTA and WTO obligations, without analysis, implying
that any number of these provisions could force the government to offer
the contract to US as well as Canadian companies. Interestingly, the submission appears inconsistent with the written advice received several weeks
earlier from a provincial trade official that the agreements do not apply:

The Ministry of Health Services has announced the culmination of a process
whereby the Ministry selected a private sector partner – Maximus Inc. – for the
delivery of the MSP and PharmaCare programs. The Provincial Government's procurement policy is for fair and open competition for government purchase of goods,
services and construction contracts. Provincial Government procurement is not
subject to the procurement provisions of the WTO or NAFTA.[2]

Why is this example important? It plainly demonstrates that the ambi-
guity and complexity of the agreements can also be used to the advantage
of governments, depending on the context. How often is legislation
amended, or killed, or policy changed internally because of these agreements? And what kind of policies tend to get scrapped? The very disturbing bottom line for those who favour government intervention in the interests of social justice is that no one knows for certain how the agreements
will be interpreted, which provides neoliberal administrations with a ready-
made justification for their agenda of economic liberalization, privatization, and deregulation.

It is also interesting that there has been a shift away from advancing
public policy positions in trade negotiations. Instead of focusing on how to
protect public policy room in those negotiations, policy analysts and politicians are now forced to spend more and more time on furthering compliance with the growing number and scope of existing trade agreements.
Manitoba, for example, is particularly concerned about US requests for

electrical energy deregulation under GATS. The province has a surplus of hydro-generated power for export. According to Alan Barber (2003), director of policy planning and coordination, Department of Industry, Trade and Mines: "the government has every intention of maintaining the utility that generates the power as a public utility. That's an area where we've carefully engaged the federal government to ensure that there is no Canadian offer that would in any way jeopardize that."

The pressure to conform to the stipulations of trade agreements is compounded by the fact that provincial governments are playing catch-up in developing trade policy expertise. Even today, there is a dearth of such expertise at the provincial level. By comparison, there are hundreds of trade policy analysts or lawyers at the federal level.

EDUCATION AND PRIVATIZATION

Canada's education system is overwhelmingly public. The vast majority of Canadian children attend schools that are publicly built, operated, financed, and managed. But the escalating privatization and globalization of educational services are blurring the edges of the universal public delivery of educational services. The private sector is making incursions into the public education system in a variety of ways, and public funding is finding its way to private educational institutions.

Judy Darcy (2006), former president of the Canadian Union of Public Employees (CUPE), which represents public school and postsecondary staff across Canada, notes that school boards as well as provincial governments "are turning increasingly to private corporations to provide portions of our primary and postsecondary education system, whether that's P3 schools,[3] whether that's contracting out of school maintenance, whether it's private language training."

While the numbers may be low at present, an increasing number of students are attending private schools. In 1998/99, 5.6 percent of all children in elementary and secondary schools in Canada were enrolled in private schools, up from 4.6 percent in 1987/88 (Statistics Canada 2001). In some provinces, new students are enrolling in private schools in droves. According to Gerard Kennedy, then Ontario Liberal education critic, one in four new students is enrolling in a private school (Sokoloff 2003). In that province private school growth over the last seven years has been staggering, with "26 per cent of the 140,000 new students enrolling in Ontario education facilities choosing privately funded institutions over the public school system between 1995 and 2002" (ibid.).

Government policies and programs often encourage enrolment in private schools, including tax credits that subsidize tuition costs (Ontario), funding formulas that deplete the public system of resources, and the public funding of private education (in British Columbia, private schools receive 50 percent of the per pupil allocation). Alberta premier Ralph Klein, in advocating a US-style voucher or credit system, commented that private school vouchers would be worth only 60 percent of public school vouchers. According to leading educator and writer Henry Giroux (1998), such policies are closely and strategically linked to privatization: "A different, but no less important and dangerous, strategy of the corporate dismantling and take-over of public education is the right wing promotion of educational choice, vouchers, and charters as a way of both opening public schools to private contractors and using public tax monies to finance the creation of private forms of education."

Dexter Whitfield (2001, 74) speaks of the process of privatization of education services through "commodification":

Education is being commodified by the separation of training, courses, supplementary activities from core teaching, i.e. the segmentation of teaching into particular products which can be specified and thus delivered by other contractors, organizations or individuals; the separation of school buildings and their maintenance from the core service provided within them, and thus between core and non-core staff; and schools are being established as individual entities, separate from the Local Education Authority (LEA) and collective educational planning. Individual school performance has become a key factor determining the school's "attractiveness" and "market position."

Key initiatives to realize privatization include channelling funds directly to schools, inviting the intervention of management consultants and education service contractors, and piloting procurement brokerage schemes. While various elements of Whitfield's pattern are recognizable in several provinces, the delivery model and attitude of provincial education ministries towards privatization nevertheless vary. It is also dangerous to assume that, when a government embraces a corporate governance model or one or more of the initiatives mentioned by Whitfield, it necessarily intends to privatize its educational services. Nevertheless, while a board or government following such a policy direction may not intend to privatize, there are companies directly or indirectly influencing policy that are fully aware of the long-term implications.

Whitfield notes that privatization is usually preceded by savage criticism of local school authorities for delivering substandard educational services. Government then "solves" the problem by privatizing, centralizing, threatening abolition of the local school authority, and using management consultants to justify those decisions. In Ontario, Tory education minister John Snobelen created a furor in 1995 after he was caught telling a private audience of his plan to "create a crisis" in education to pave the way for drastic restructuring (Ontario 2001, 2020). The reality, however, is that it is very difficult to attack the quality of educational services in Canada. Canadian students continually rank very highly in international assessments (PISA 2000), and the public generally has faith in, and is supportive of, publicly funded education. In Ontario the 2002 OISE/UT Survey found that public support for spending on elementary and secondary schools is near its highest level since monitoring of spending preferences began in 1980. Further, since 1998 there has been little change in opinion on what schools should be supported. In 2002, 29 percent supported funding only for public schools, 36 percent supported the status quo funding of the public and separate Roman Catholic school system, 7 percent supported funding of Roman Catholic and private religious schools, while 27 percent supported funding of all public and private schools (Livingstone, Hart, and Davie 2002, 17). Support for the Ontario private school tax credit, on the other hand, declined significantly after implementation. In 2000, for example, 42 percent of those surveyed agreed with the tax credit, while 46 percent disagreed. Yet by 2002 only 37 percent agreed with the program, while 52 percent disagreed (18). The tax credit was cancelled in late 2003.

Nevertheless, teachers and boards continue to be attacked on various fronts, and this includes replacing school boards who refused to submit balanced budgets – as was the case in Hamilton, Ottawa, and Toronto – with supervisors.[4] Governments have also aggressively undermined the autonomy and independence of teachers and school boards. In British Columbia, for example, cabinet can appoint trustees to conduct the affairs of a district if, in its opinion, there is a risk to student achievement in the district and it is in the public interest to do so. In addition, the College of Teachers was restructured so that teacher representatives on the board were in the minority (a decision that was subsequently revisited). In other provinces, boards have been amalgamated or eliminated altogether in favour of more centralized provincial control.

With regard to the "channelling of funds directly to schools," Edmonton has operated on a school-based budgeting model since the early 1980s. In British Columbia, where private school funding, "school choice," and "accountability" are all high on the provincial agenda, the government directed school boards in September 2003 to prepare "notional funding" reports for school districts and individual schools. These reports will indicate per capita funding after district administrative expenses. While the funding is not going directly to the schools (yet), the recently created School Planning Councils are to be involved in resource allocation decisions at the school level. In Saskatchewan a consultant's report recommended that the Saskatoon district move towards a corporate governance structure, with increased decentralization and the adoption of site-based management within the Saskatoon Public School Division. The affected union locals were concerned that the proposed structure moved away from a "democratic, publicly accountable governance model" and that, if the role of school principals is changed to take on a more administrative, budgetary, and supervisory role, then the "important role that principals play as educators" would be lost (CUPE 2002).

In Ontario the Tories encouraged what Whitfield (2001, 74) called the "separation of school building and their maintenance from the core service provided within them, and thus between core and non-core staff" through a funding formula that created an artificial distinction between "classroom" and "non-classroom" expenditures. As funding was reduced, boards began to look for ways to cut costs on the non-classroom side, including hiring contractors to clean or maintain buildings. Few, however, followed through.

A key priority of the Liberal government of British Columbia has likewise been the identification of "core" and "non-core" services. In the health sector the government centralized health care into five large regional authorities and then contracted out "ancillary" health services, such as cleaning, food preparation, and laundry services. While there has so far been no move in the education sector to privatize maintenance and other services presently in the hands of local school boards, the provincial government recently passed astonishing legislation empowering it to override all constraints to any project deemed "provincially significant." It is conceivable that the government could regionalize at least some aspects of education, then hand out large contracts for regional delivery of "non-core" functions, such as maintenance and janitorial functions. Such a move would have particular significance not only with regard to the trade union movement but also with regard to free trade agreements (see below).

According to Giroux (1998), underlying the call for privatization "is a reform movement in which public education is seen as a local industry that over time will become a global business." In Canada, as in the United States, public education represents a huge market. The right-wing assault, says Giroux, has been quite successful at the policy level: in the United States "more than 28 states have drafted legislation supporting vouchers, choice programs, and contracting with for-profit management companies, such as the Edison Project and Sabis International Schools" (ibid.). However, it is not clear whether Canadian provinces will buy into the US model of wholesale privatization of education in the near future; the quality of public education and the public willingness to continue to finance and invest in public education diminishes the attractiveness and feasibility of extensive privatization.

Education and the General Agreement on Trade in Services (GATS)

Charles Ungerleider (2003, 219), deputy minister of education for British Columbia from 1998 to 2001, is deeply concerned about the potential impact of trade agreements on public education: "Provincial governments and school boards may not continue to be the jurisdictions that govern the content and provision. While it is too soon to determine the impact of the WTO on the governance of public schooling, there is good reason for Canadians to be concerned and vigilant."

Of particular concern is the ambiguous definition of services in GATS, which exempts services that are "supplied in the exercise of government authority" (GATS, Part 1, Article 1, section 3[b]). However, section 3(c) subsequently defines a service supplied in the exercise of government authority as "any service which is supplied neither on a commercial basis, nor in competition with one or more service suppliers."

School boards across the country are increasingly undertaking business enterprises to augment insufficient levels of funding. At what point are their services being supplied on a commercial basis or in competition with one or more service suppliers? Perhaps the greatest vulnerability is in the marketing of education services, either directly by boards or by separately created school foundations or corporations. This is touted as being necessary and, often, is encouraged by provincial governments.

The Nanaimo school board, for instance, facing significant service cuts as a result of a three-year funding freeze, formed the School District 68 Business Corporation to raise revenues. The *Nanaimo Daily News* reported that:

Last year, the Ministry of Education provided school boards with greater financial flexibility that enabled boards to be more entrepreneurial in raising revenue, including forming companies to conduct business activities. At Wednesday's meeting, the board asked senior staff to prepare business plans for the offering and marketing of such services as carpentry products, information systems services, vehicle maintenance services, print shop services, facilities and bus rentals. (Barron 2003)

While the purpose is to provide funds for public education, the services offered are clearly intended to be supplied on a commercial basis in competition with one or more suppliers.

And districts are marketing not only ancillary services such as vehicle maintenance and bus rentals but also services that are clearly educational. As Ungerleider (2003, 219) points out, "a number of school boards throughout Canada provide education to international students in exchange for tuition payment. British Columbia and Ontario operate schools offshore that offer students the opportunity to study the provincial curriculum and earn diplomas issued by the sponsor province." BC school boards also sell their curriculum overseas. In addition, several school boards are raising revenue by attracting international students to their schools. The fees charged are usually about double ($10,000 to $12,000) the per capita funding for Canadian students.

While Canadian provinces, according to Ungerleider, are in agreement that public schooling should not be included as a service under the provisions of GATS, they are at the same time seeking export opportunities for Canadian health and education providers in other countries. Further, even if Canada continues to protect "public education" one has to ask what that term will come to mean. Are the operation, maintenance, and even administration of our schools, necessary components of "public education"? What if, for example, education authorities, either boards or provinces, choose to enter into a private-public partnership for the operation of their schools? What if, as discussed above, a provincial government chooses to regionalize any number of ancillary services related to the operation of districts? It is certainly arguable that such services are not core to public education and, therefore, do not qualify for the GATS education exemption.

Finally, the GATS Working Party on Domestic Regulation[5] continues to negotiate provisions to ensure that "qualification requirements and procedures, technical standards and licensing requirements" do not constitute unnecessary barriers to trade. The working party created a list of potentially unnecessary barriers, some of which may be of interest to educators: "overly burdensome licensing requirements," "different sub-federal regulations for recognition of qualifications," "qualification procedures," "need for in-country experience before sitting for examinations," "a non-transparent regulatory environment" (education services are particularly mentioned in this regard), "subsidies for higher and adult education," and "national technical standards which diverge from international standards." Teachers unions in particular should be concerned that one of the barriers in the working group list is the requirement that "to be licensed as a professional, there is a requirement or pre-requirement to be a member of an affiliate organization. This organization has no regulatory authority over the profession (i.e., union, country club, etcetera)" (WTO 2002, 1–3).

It is perplexing that provincial education ministries are not providing more guidance and information to school boards about potential GATS challenges, as they certainly must be aware of the possibilities. Discussions within the Council of Ministers of Education in Canada (CMEC)[6] have included "the possible consequences for education of the General Agreement on Trade in Services (GATS)." Further, the CMEC working group on GATS, led by Ontario and Quebec, has been instructed by the ministers to "follow this issue closely from the education sector perspective" (CMEC 2002).

It is ironic that our public education system has developed so successfully as to be a temptingly marketable commodity. However, if pieces of it are going to be sold here or abroad, educators, politicians, and the public must first be fully aware of the policy implications of free trade agreements. Unfortunately, local school boards do not appear to share Ungerleider's concerns. The author is unaware of any instance where concern about trade agreement impacts has materially influenced school board policy. CUPE has raised concerns about trade agreements, for example, in relation to the P3 school experiment in Nova Scotia, but there is no evidence that the argument has ever been the decisive factor in any school board decision to reject privatization.

TRADE AGREEMENTS AND MUNICIPALITIES

Municipalities are not a separate order of government: they are creatures of provincial statutes. Motivated by fiscal constraints at the provincial level, these statutes are increasingly extending municipal powers to enable the privatization of public services, particularly through the mechanism of public-private partnerships. When it comes to municipal services, the line between the public sector and the private sector is becoming, as in education, increasingly blurred.

Generally, municipal politicians do not get involved in trade issues. As Jack Layton (2003), leader of the federal New Democratic Party (NDP), observes: "Your typical city council meeting where a trade issue is raised will begin with the Chair or the Mayor ruling it out of order, because it doesn't relate to municipal business. At least, that will be the opening position." Yet in 2000 and 2001 dozens of municipalities across Canada passed resolutions expressing concern about the impact of the trade agreements on municipalities. For example, a resolution by the City of London, Ontario, included a request that "the government of Canada be requested to consult extensively with the people of Canada, especially and including municipal councils, before taking any further action with respect to the GATS" (London 2001, 1). Moreover, many municipalities have asked for exemptions from the provisions of the trade agreements. The City of Vancouver unanimously agreed that Canada should get a "permanent and explicit exemption in the GATS that would limit its application to areas of federal jurisdiction" (Vancouver 2000, 14).

While the resolutions passed varied, they often indicated thoughtful and diligent concern about the issues. For example, the City of Coquitlam, British Columbia, made substantial and detailed reference to the Metalclad case when it resolved

to petition the Federal Government to use its intervenor status in the BC Supreme Court review of the Metalclad case, to defend the ability of local government to act in the interest of citizens and the environment and to ensure that measures taken by local governments are not subject to challenge under NAFTA's investor-state provisions. (Coquitlam 2001, 15)

On the occasions when trade agreements are raised and councils seek guidance, they often receive a wide and contradictory range of advice, partly because of the lack of jurisprudence concerning novel treaty provisions and partly because decisions by trade tribunals cannot be predicted with confidence. Where hard knowledge is lacking, ideology can easily fill the gaps.

Concern about trade agreements was a central factor in a decision not to enter into a proposed public-private partnership in one prominent BC case. By early 2001 the Greater Vancouver Regional District (GVRD) was well on its way to contracting out operation of the proposed Seymour Water Filtration Plant to a private company. The candidates had been short-listed to four. Provincial CUPE president Barry O'Neill, the Council of Canadians, and a few directors of the GVRD (most notably then Councillor, now Mayor, Derek Corrigan of Burnaby), however, started raising concerns about proceeding by way of a P3, and the public agreed. Hundreds of citizens from all walks of life turned up at several raucous meetings across the Lower Mainland. In Vancouver, at least, the public did make the connection that, under trade agreements, the public risks losing control of public services. While there were many concerns, it is fair to say that the most important concern, and certainly the one that changed the mind of many directors, was the concern about loss of control of the water system.

CUPE commissioned a legal opinion from international trade lawyer Steven Shrybman. The opinion was lengthy, but the following short excerpt is representative: "we believe that the risks posed by Canada's commitments under NAFTA and the WTO, as these obligations affect the Seymour project, are both substantial and real" (Shrybman 2001, 7).

Some members of the GVRD Board were sceptical of an opinion produced by CUPE, so they sought out a second legal opinion from lawyer Donald Lidstone. Lidstone's opinion, which has not been made public, rang alarm bells for George Puil (2003), then chair of the GVRD: "To me, even with the shadow of a doubt, I felt we couldn't take a chance ... if there was any possibility we could lose control over water." He expressed similar doubts as a panellist at the Canadian Council for Public-Private Partnerships 10th Annual Conference: "There are uncertainties in trade treaties. Some action is needed from the Canadian government to correct that or to indemnify local governments from the possible unintended consequences of trade treaties. Without that, P3s will need to be looked upon with great caution by local governments when considering areas as sensitive to the public as water" (Puil 2002).

It is worth noting that, for the most part, municipalities and the provincial-level local government associations have relied heavily on the Federation of Canadian Municipalities to represent their interests with regard to the trade agreements. The City of London, for example, has looked to the

Federation of Canadian Municipalities to monitor "WTO discussions and the activities of the Government of Canada for the purpose of alerting local governments of any potential encroachments onto local government jurisdictions and authorities resulting from trade agreements, so that local government can respond accordingly" (London 2003, 1). Similarly, the Union of Nova Scotia Municipalities commented that: "This [trade agreements] is not an issue which we are actively involved in, and we have not heard of any major concerns from our members ... the Federation of Canadian Municipalities has paid significant attention to this issue and has been bringing to the Federal Government, municipal concerns (UNSM 2003, 1).

The Union of BC Municipalities is a notable exception and has been very active on the trade front, producing several excellent papers on the trade agreements to guide its members.

The Working Group on International Trade

The concern over trade agreements raised in the proposed P3 of the Seymour Water filtration plant set in motion a train of events at the Federation of Canadian Municipalities (FCM). First, DFAIT officials were invited to the FCM Finance Committee, and, according to George Puil, chair of both the GVRD and the Federation of Canadian Municipalities Finance Committee, they were confrontational and provided few concrete answers. A joint FCM Finance Committee-DFAIT working group on international trade was then created and met several times through late 2001 and early 2002, including one meeting with Foreign Affairs Minister Pierre Pettigrew. In November 2001 the FCM presented a series of detailed questions to DFAIT regarding: market access, national treatment, domestic regulation, the scope of the agreements (coverage of services), public-private partnerships, traditional public services in general, water supply, procurement, and subsidies. The meetings, however, were less than satisfying and were certainly not reassuring.

The DFAIT responses to FCM's questions, received in April 2002, were similarly unsatisfying. The following is just one of many examples. The FCM requested that the Canadian government provide "written confirmation that ... [it] would not sue or otherwise claim compensation from ... any municipality whose actions or decisions result in an international trade tribunal decision that goes against the Government of Canada, so long as the municipality's conduct would have been valid under domestic law" (DFAIT 2002, 4). The response from DFAIT (2002, 4–5) was as follows:

This request approaches trade agreements from the wrong direction. Surely our objective should be to agree on what obligations Canada should take in trade

negotiations and a shared undertaking to respect those obligations ... your request
seeks licence from Canada not to respect international obligations.

and

In the case of financial awards under investment agreements, it is the Government
of Canada that is liable ... certainly there have been no circumstances to date in
which compensation from another level of government has been contemplated. This
having been said, we do not believe that federal governments, both present and
future, should waive their rights in respect of all possible circumstances in the future.

The FCM also wanted DFAIT to ensure that: "future NAFTA dispute tribunals confine themselves to ruling on whether the parties have complied
with international law, and that it be explicitly reinforced that, unless given
specific authority, these tribunals cannot overrule the decisions of domestic
courts or act as if they were an appellate body from domestic courts"
(DFAIT 2002, 3).

DFAIT responded that "NAFTA tribunals only have authority to interpret
the NAFTA. They cannot overrule domestic law nor act as an appeal process
for domestic law" (DFAIT 2002, 4). Yet in the case of Canada's Landing
Requirement for Pacific Salmon and Herring (Arbitrar Panel 1989),
decided under CUFTA, the tribunal determined that, although each state has
the sovereign right to determine conservation measures, the preamble to
GATT Article XX, which expressly prohibits disguised restrictions on international trade "is an acknowledgement by the Parties that they will submit
trade-restricting conservation measures to third-party scrutiny. By directing
the application of this provision, the Panel's terms of reference required the
Panel to make its own independent evaluation of the conservation justification in question" (Arbitrar Panel 1989, 25).

Further, the Metalclad decision, referred to earlier, specifically states that
a legitimate municipal rezoning that results in economic loss for an investor
could be considered actionable under the NAFTA Chapter 11 "expropriation" clause (*United States v. Metalclad* 2001, 35).

With this concern in mind, the FCM also asked DFAIT to clarify the provisions of the investment chapter of NAFTA and, more specifically, that the
federal government ensure that "the promised review of NAFTA Chapter 11
takes place, with the objective of narrowing the investment protections and
ensuring that expropriation is defined to mean the explicit taking of property and does not also include incidental interference with the use of property which may deprive an owner of economic benefit" (DFAIT 2002, 3).

Again, the DFAIT response was worrisome. Although it vaguely commented that "the scope of the expropriation discipline is one of the possible issues for discussion with our NAFTA partners," DFAIT repeated its com-

mitment to the expropriation provisions of Chapter 11 and its intention not to retreat from those principles. Clearly, the federal government promotes trade treaties with little apparent knowledge of, or concern for, how their provisions will affect subnational governments. The FCM's dealings with DFAIT simply confirmed this.

This lack of concern for the interests of subnational governments was also very clear to the Canadian Library Association (CLA). In a letter to DFAIT, the association expressed concern that Canadian libraries *already* offend GATS sections 3(a) and 3(b):

Libraries in CLA's reading of section 3 of Article 1 of the GATS, can be defined as non-governmental bodies exercising powers delegated by central, regional or local government or authorities. The services provided by these bodies come under the terms of the Agreement unless it can be shown that they are supplied "neither on a commercial basis, nor in competition with one or more commercial services suppliers." As not-for-profits, libraries meet the first condition for exemption; they do not, however, necessarily meet the second condition. (CLA 2002)

According to Paul Whitney, director of the Vancouver Public Library, the Department of Foreign Affairs characterized the governmental authority exception as "Undefined, ambiguous and contentious. Their advice is to not seek clarity." They advised the CLA not to seek a definition, particularly for libraries, because in Whitney's (2003) characterization of their advice, "they don't think we are on the radar screen." This admission by DFAIT is unsettling and inconsistent with its response to a number of Federation of Canadian Municipalities questions:

The GATS excludes "services supplied in the exercise of governmental authority" ... This exclusion covers many services provided directly by municipal governments, such as library services or water services. It is important to note that the GATS does not attempt to define the notion of "public services", as this is for each country to decide in the context of its own domestic environment (DFAIT 2002, 6–7).

In the letter of query to DFAIT, the CLA also specified which library services they were concerned about, raising the question as to whether subnational governments or non-profits invite and inadvertently provide evidence for a potential WTO challenge when they seek clarity as to whether particular public policies or measures offend trade agreement provisions.

WHAT HAPPENS NEXT?

It is difficult to predict the precise future impacts that trade agreements and deepening integration will have on Canadian public services. Thus far, specific impacts have been scattered and uneven, and there is little reason to believe the political and economic dynamics will grow simpler over time.

An increasing number of academics and lawyers are focusing on specific sectoral analyses that could broaden the understanding of the links between the provisions of trade agreements and the day-to-day operations of governments. For example, despite earlier clashes, the Federation of Canadian Municipalities and the Government of Canada have cooperatively launched *International Trade Agreements and Local Government: A Guide for Canadian Municipalities*.[7] Although the guide does not address some of the most troubling interpretive questions (such as the definition of services in GATS), it may stimulate local politicians and citizens to apply political pressure on federal politicians to give greater consideration to subnational interests in future negotiations.

While one may hope that political pressure will influence senior government behaviour, it is more likely that, at least in the foreseeable future, public policy adaptations will remain largely aimed towards agreement compliance. There may, however, be a specific tribunal decision that shocks Canadians into action. Certainly events like the invocation of potential trade challenges as a justification for exposing Canadian medical services to the provisions of the US Patriot Act, or the threat of trade retaliation over the Ontario government's promise to prevent toll increases on Highway 407, have all raised public concern. Also, it is worth noting that the Canadian Union of Postal Workers, together with the Council of Canadians, has launched a lawsuit challenging the constitutionality of NAFTA. Success would obviously have a profound effect on future negotiations and the politics around trade agreements.

Future negotiations will also be shaped by Conservative prime minister Stephen Harper, who, like Paul Martin before him, supports trade liberalization and deeper integration with the United States. Much will also depend on the speed with which countries and corporations embrace trade agreement challenges as a way to pry open much sought after access to Canadian public services. The process is expensive and time-consuming, but we may find that, increasingly, the corporate world may decide that the prize is well worth the effort. In the face of the continued push by governments and corporations to advance the free trade agenda, it will fall to federal opposition politicians, subnational governments, governments from the global South, and civil society groups to develop a sustained and coherent stand against the expansion of trade liberalization agreements.

The collapse of the WTO's fifth ministerial meeting in Cancun in September 2003 and the unanimous agreement in August 2004 to end export subsidies on farm products and cut import duties around the world suggest the emergence of a new dynamic at the international level. Nevertheless,

Canada continues actively to push for a comprehensive Free Trade Agreement of the Americas (FTAA). In the United States, moreover, there is tremendous corporate pressure to include investor-state provisions in the FTAA. In fact, dozens of the largest corporations have demanded, in a letter to then US trade representative Robert Zoellick, provisions that ensure "protection of assets from direct or indirect expropriation to include protection from regulations that diminish the value of investors' assets" (PBS 2002). And the stakes will only be increased if the process of deepening integration is hastened by new trade agreements related to a customs union, monetary integration, or harmonization of standards. Nevertheless, civil society interests in the United States can very successfully leverage their position. As Colin Campbell (2004) points out: "All you have to do is get twenty Congressmen to write a letter to the President and it brings things to a screeching halt."

One cannot end the discussion without returning to the recurring theme of this chapter. It is impossible to be definitive in predicting future impacts of trade agreements because the provisions themselves are ambiguous and tribunal decisions are unpredictable. One of the few predictable future trends, however, is that tribunals will continue to interpret trade agreements in ways that generally favour trade liberalization because that is the ultimate goal of both the agreements and the tribunal panellists. It is also clear that trade treaties will continue to constrain the actions of elected governments and democratic institutions, even if in unpredictable ways.

Ultimately, the future in Canada depends on the Canadian public. International trade rules will only be as effective as the Canadian public allows them to be. So far, the Canadian public has not faced the litmus test of a direct clash between fundamental Canadian values and a trade agreement challenge.

NOTES

1 The Campbell government removed the MASSH sector exclusion in March 2002, despite a motion passed unanimously by the Greater Vancouver Regional District requesting it not to proceed.
2 E-mail response from Glen Scobie, Economic Services Branch, Ministry of Small Business and Economic Development, sent as provincial government response to questions of various hearing attendees (Scobie 2004).
3 P3s (public-private partnerships) refer to projects that include private involvement in their operation, financing, or ownership.
4 This decision was reversed when the Conservatives lost power to the Liberals.
5 The GATS Working Party on Domestic Regulation (WPDR) is a WTO committee established in 1999.

6 CMEC is an intergovernmental body made up of the ministers responsible for
   elementary, secondary, and advanced education for the provinces and territories.
7 This on-line guide is available on the DFAIT website at
   <http://www.dfait-maeci.gc.ca/tna-nac/fcm/module-en.asp>.

REFERENCES

Arbitrar Panel. 1989. Final Report of the Panel under Chapter 18 of the Canada-
   United States Free Trade Agreement in the Matter of Canada's Landing Requirement for Pacific Coast Salmon and Herring. CDA-89-1807–01.

Barber, Alan. 2003. Interview, 3 September.

Barrett, Thomas. 2002. PPP's and the transformation of the European Union. Paper
   presented at the Canadian Council for Public Partnership's 10th Annual Conference, 25 November, Toronto.

Barron, Robert. 2003. Union Keeping Close Watch on School Board Revenue Initiative. *Nanaimo Daily News*, 28 March, A-1.

Blaikie, Bill. 2003. Interview, 23 August.

British Columbia. 1998. *First Report of the Special Committee on the Multilateral
   Agreement on Investment*. Victoria: Legislative Assembly of British Columbia.

– 1999. *Second Report of the Special Committee on the Multilateral Agreement on
   Investment*. Victoria: Legislative Assembly of British Columbia.

– 2004. *Examination of USA Patriot Act Implications for Personal Information of
   British Columbia Residents Involved in Outsourcing of Government Services to
   US-Linked Service Providers: A Submission on the USA Patriot Act to the Infor-
   mation and Privacy Commissioner for British Columbia*. Victoria: Province of
   British Columbia.

Campbell, Colin. 2004. Address to the Institute of Public Administrators Annual
   General Meeting, September 1, by Colin Campbell, Canada Research Chair in US
   Studies, University of British Columbia. Toronto, Institute of Public Administra-
   tors.

CLA. 2002. Letter to Paul Robertson of Department of Foreign Affairs and International Trade, October 23. Ottawa, Canadian Library Association.

Clark, Glen. 2003. Interview, 29 August.

CMEC. 2002. Education Ministers Discuss Pan-Canadian Education Priorities. Press
   Release, 10 April. Toronto: Council of Ministers of Education, Canada.

Coquitlam. 2001. Minutes of Regular Council Meeting for February 19. Coquitlam, BC: Coquitlam City Hall.

CUPE 2002. Brief to the Saskatoon Public School Board on the Administrative
   Review Report, Presented by CUPE Locals 34, 1948 and 4436. 22 May. Saskatoon: Saskatoon Public School Board.

Darcy, Judy. 2006. Interview, 12 July.

DFAIT. 2002. Reply to the Federation of Canadian Municipalities Questions on

International Trade Agreements. 11 April. Ottawa: Department of Foreign Affairs and International Trade.

Fell, Tony. 2002. Canada: Capital Rich, Project Poor. Address to the Canadian Council for Public-Private Partnerships, 25 November, Toronto.

Fleming, Tony. 2003. Private correspondence, 12 August.

GATT. 1990. *Trade Policy Review of Canada*. Geneva: General Agreement on Tariffs and Trade.

Giroux, Henry A. 1998. The Business of Public Education. *Z Magazine* (July-August), 15–17.

Hanak, Daryl. 2003. Private correspondence, 28 August.

Hart, Michael. 2000. The Road to Free Trade. In *Free Trade: Risks and Rewards*, ed. L.I. MacDonald, 3–34. Montreal: McGill-Queen's University Press.

Ipsos. 2004. *Canadians' Views on Public-Private Partnerships*. 8 April. Available at <http://www.ipsos-na.com/news/pressrelease.cfm?id=2116>

Layton, Jack. 2003. Interview, 18 August.

Livingstone, D.W., D. Hart, and L.E. Davie. 2002. *Public Attitudes towards Education in Ontario*. Toronto: Ontario Institute for Studies in Education.

London. 2001. Minutes of Council Proceedings for Twelfth Meeting. 22 May, London, ON, City of London.

– 2003. Letter to the author, 29 August, London, ON.

Ontario. 2001. Official Report of Debates (Hansard), 30 May. Toronto: Legislative Assembly of Ontario.

PBS. 2002. Trading Democracy: A Bill Moyers Special. Transcript, 1 February. Alexandria, VA: Public Broadcasting Service Online.

PISA. 2000. *Knowledge and Skills for Life: First Results from Programme for International Student Assessment* (PISA). Paris: Organization for Economic Co-Operation and Development.

Puil, George. 2002. Paper presented at session entitled Public Private Partnerships: Natural Allies and Natural Opponents at the Canadian Council for Public-Private Partnerships' 10th Annual Conference, 25–26 November. Toronto.

– 2003. Interview, 25 August.

Rae, Bob. 2003. Interview, 17 October.

Scobie, Glen. 2004. E-mail communication from the Ministry of Small Business and Economic Development, Economic Services Branch, British Columbia, Victoria.

Shrybman, Steven. 2001. *A Legal Opinion Concerning the Potential Impact of International Trade Disciplines on Proposals to Establish a Public-Private Partnership to Design, Build and Operate a Water Filtration Plant in the Seymour Reservoir*. Ottawa: Canadian Union of Public Employees. Available at: <http://www.sgmlaw.com/AssetFactory.aspx?did=53>.

Simmons, Roger. 2003. Intervention by the Canadian Consul General in Seattle, Washington, panel discussion on softwood lumber, British Columbia Municipal Finance Authority Annual General Meeting, 27 March, Vancouver.

Sokoloff, Heather. 2003. Private Enrolment Shoots up, Data Show. *National Post*, 24 June, A6.

Statistics Canada. 2001. Trends in the Use of Private Education. *The Daily*, 4 July. Available at: <http://www.statcan.ca/english/dai-quo/>.

Stiglitz, Joseph E. 2003. *Globalization and Its Discontents*. New York: W.W. Norton and Company.

Ungerleider, Charles. 2003. *Failing Our Kids: How We Are Ruining Our Public Schools*. Toronto: McClelland and Stewart.

United States v. Metalclad. 2001. Supreme Court of British Columbia. BCSC 664.

UNSM. 2003. Written communication to the author, 14 August. Halifax, NS: Union of Nova Scotia Municipalities.

Vancouver. 2000. Regular Council Meeting Minutes, 2 May. Vancouver: Council of the City of Vancouver. Available at: <http://www.city.vancouver.bc.ca/CTY-CLERK/CCLERK/000502/regmin.htm>.

Vastine, Robert. 2002. Outline of Remarks of Robert Vastine, President, US Coalition of Service Industries, to the Bogotá Chamber of Commerce, Bogotá, Colombia, 27 June. NJ: US Coalition of Service Industries. Available at: <http://www.uscsi.org/publications/papers/Colombia.pdf>.

Watson, William. 2000. Interviews with Brian Mulroney and John Turner. In *Free Trade: Risks and Rewards*, ed. L.I. MacDonald, 35–47. Montreal: McGill-Queen's University Press.

Whitfield, Dexter. 2001. *Public Services or Corporate Welfare: Rethinking the Nation State in the Global Economy*. London: Pluto Press.

Whitney, Paul. 2003. Interview. Vancouver, 10 October.

WTO. 1994. *The Uruguay Round Agreements: Annex 1B – General Agreement on Trade in Services (GATS)*. Geneva: World Trade Organization.

– 2002. Examples of Measures to Be Addressed by Disciplines Under GATS Article VI:4. Informal Note by the Secretariat. JOB (02)/20/Rev.2, 18 October. Geneva: Working Party on Domestic Regulation, World Trade Organization.

– 2003. *10 Common Misunderstandings*. Geneva: World Trade Organization.

14

Trade Treaties, Privatization, and Health Care Reform in Canada

JIM GRIESHABER-OTTO, SCOTT SINCLAIR,
AND RICARDO GRINSPUN

The Canadian health care system is at a crossroads. Although it is a defining feature of modern Canadian life and our most valued social program, its condition could soon become unstable as it is eroded through steady, incremental commercialization. This chapter argues further that Canada's trade treaty obligations risk making such incremental changes effectively permanent by foreclosing important options for future reform. These trade treaty risks are not the only challenge facing the Canadian health care system, but no serious proposal to reform Canadian Medicare can afford to ignore them. They are a potentially corrosive and destabilizing influence that must be confronted and contained in order to secure the future of Canada's Medicare system.

The concern over the future of our health system has generated much debate in recent years. In particular, 2002 was a year when the terms of the debate were clearly delineated. Three major government-sponsored commissions proposed blueprints for health care reform, including the Mazankowski Report (PACH 2002), the Kirby Report (SCSAST 2002), and the Romanow Report (2002). These reports contained frequently opposing recommendations about the Canadian health care system's financial sustainability, the values upon which the system is and should be based, and how the health care system should be reformed. In effect, the three reports prescribed conflicting courses of treatment for an underfunded system already stressed by increasing doses of commercialization. Apart from the Romanow Report, which gave the issue some attention, the destabilizing interactions between trade treaty obligations and the growing trend towards commercialization in the Canadian health care system were almost entirely neglected.

This chapter aims to remedy this potentially dangerous oversight. When Canada's trade treaty obligations are considered, the possibility exists that ongoing efforts to decentralize health care delivery, to outsource services to private, for-profit corporations, and to expand the use of public-private partnerships (P3s) – practices that are recommended in the Mazankowski and Kirby Reports – could set in motion a dynamic that would make halting or reversing the privatization process increasingly difficult. This is due to a complex of overlapping provisions within both the North America Free Trade Agreement (NAFTA) and the General Agreement on Trade in Services (GATS), which are designed to reduce the regulatory powers of government and to pry open new economic spheres for private investment. The existing safeguards within NAFTA and GATS, which the Canadian government claims exempt public services such as health care from these provisions, are inadequate as they are loosely framed and designed to wither away. New trade agreements, such as the proposed Free Trade Area of the Americas (FTAA) or the bilateral Canada-Korea Free Trade Agreement, could aggravate the privatization thrust of NAFTA and GATS. Proposals put forward by Canadian business lobby groups for "deep integration" with the United Sates pose another set of challenges for the health care system. Frustrated in their attempts so far to privatize Medicare, Canada's elites may also use either new trade agreements or deep integration initiatives to put pressure on the public system.

Preserving the public nature of the Canadian health care system thus requires not only that the beginning forays into private, for-profit delivery and payment be reversed but also that the federal government change its approach to international trade treaties and continental integration. Developments since 2002 have not followed this prescription. The two health accords signed in 2003 and in 2004 promised significant transfers of resources to the provinces and territories without any concomitant mechanisms for lessening the growth of private, for-profit health care. Neither accord gave priority to enforcing the Canada Health Act (CHA) – the foundation stone of our publicly funded and administered health care system. The Supreme Court gave a major boost to the advocates of for-profit care with their 2005 ruling on the prominent *Chaoulli* case. And the 2006 election of Stephen Harper – a long-time opponent of the CHA – as prime minister in a minority government was another sign that the most prominent social program in Canada is in peril.

UNSAFE PRACTICES: UNDERFUNDING, COMMERCIALIZATION, AND DECENTRALIZATION

Both federal and certain provincial governments have pursued policies that are slowly transforming the nature and effectiveness of Canada's health care system. Chronic underfunding over many years undermined the public's confidence in the system, and a growing apprehension at the resulting declining quality of care was met with government measures of increasing commercialization, privatization, and the promotion of market-based decentralization. A host of new practices at the provincial level, including P3s, were put in place that, at minimum, violated the spirit of the CHA but that various Liberal federal governments and the current Conservative government have not opposed.

Unacceptably long waiting lists for health care became the most visible and politically damaging symptom of a faltering service, and politicians felt pressure to act. Two health care agreements thrashed out among federal, provincial, and territorial first ministers purported to address this and other major health care challenges. The September 2003 Accord on Health Care Renewal, led by Prime Minister Jean Chrétien, and the September 2004 Ten Year Plan to Strengthen Health Care, led by Prime Minister Paul Martin, achieved secure stable federal funding for health over the next decade as federal cash transfers and the cost escalator were both restored. Because it was signed and contains more specifics, the 2004 agreement was a better deal than was the 2003 accord (and better than an earlier one, signed in 2000). However, according to the Canadian Health Coalition, they all have the same weaknesses: poor accountability, reporting, and enforcement. And they perpetuate a Medicare that is still on life support – this time not from lack of money but from weak controls on where and how the money will be spent (CHC 2004).

These agreements do not mention, let alone address, the most serious threat to the integrity and sustainability of public health care in Canada: the tide of privatization and commercialization. The ten-year plan does *not* signal the expectation that public dollars will only be used for the public, non-profit delivery of health care. Furthermore, it does *not* require the minister of health to actively enforce the criteria and conditions of the CHA so that all Canadians receive insured health services on uniform terms and conditions. Thus the plan fails to provide accountability – the real thing, not a decoy – and the federal guardianship that are essential to ensuring that public funds are used to protect and strengthen Medicare (CHC 2004).

Not surprisingly, the health accords opened the door for an expansion of P3 activity. Public-private partnerships have become a central vehicle for incremental private involvement in the health care system. A P3 can be defined as an arrangement between the public and private sector for the purpose of delivering a project or a service that is traditionally provided by the public sector. There are many models of P3s, and the degree of private-sector involvement may vary widely. At one end of the spectrum, for example, public assets may be privatized or turned over to the private sector. Similarly, services traditionally delivered by public employees may be contracted out for delivery by private, for-profit corporations. Other

arrangements involve the private sector in operating and maintaining publicly owned facilities; designing, building, financing, and operating new
facilities under long-term leases; or financing, building, owning, and operating a facility or providing a service for a specified time or in perpetuity.
All of these arrangements involve differing degrees of accountability, control,
and financial risk.

There has been a significant increase in P3 activity in health care at both
the federal and provincial levels. Former prime minister Paul Martin
appointed a parliamentary secretary for P3s, created a P3 office that is part
of Industry Canada, and created an office for "alternative service delivery"
– the new code word for P3s. In British Columbia, Alberta, New Brunswick, and Quebec, governments have requested that proposals be tendered
by the private sector for privately financed and operated hospitals. In
Ontario, the previous Conservative government called for the establishment of two new private hospitals in Brampton and Ottawa that would
provide "non-clinical" services. While Dalton McGuinty campaigned
against P3s, his current Ontario government has taken up where the
provincial Tories left off, announcing a scheme that pushes private financing and P3s for enhancing the province's services and infrastructure, including hospitals (CUPE 2005a). Under the new name of "alternative financing
and procurement," the government announced the construction of five new
hospitals, in addition to the two under way, and there are plans in the
works for many more (CUPE 2005b).

Furthermore, public hospitals in Ontario and British Columbia are also
outsourcing certain services, such as MRI scans, certain surgical procedures,
administration, and cleaning and food services. Prominent companies
involved in supplying or bidding for these services include Sodexho Canada, whose parent company is one of the three largest outsourcing service
corporations in North America (Walker 2002), and Aramark Canada Ltd.,
a us-based corporation with operations in eighteen countries, supplying
prison, food, housekeeping and daycare services, along with media
management, human resources, and information technology (Walker
2003).

P3s raise important health policy concerns. Four prominent economists
and a former director of audit operations with Canada's auditor general
characterized P3 hospitals as "a serious threat to the public health care
system" (CCPA 2003). In their crisp analysis, the authors criticize P3 hospitals on the basis of increased cost, diminished public accountability, and a
deterioration of the quality and extent of universal service. They conclude
that, "when properly accounted for, it is clear that public ownership and
not-for-profit administration will cost provincial taxpayers less, and result
in hospitals that more clearly operate in the interests of patients and in
accordance with the requirements and criteria of the *Canada Health Act*"

(Auerbach et al. 2003, 4). The involvement (including through various forms of P3s) of private, for-profit corporations in health care administration and information management raises other important concerns about privacy and democratic accountability.[1] Despite these concerns, contracting out in specific areas, such as health information systems, is increasingly common, and many for-profit corporations anticipate hefty profits.

The creeping privatization of health care enjoys the support of the federal government in a variety of ways. A crucial point of contention is the government's failure either to enforce the Canada Health Act with regard to transgressing provinces and territories or to recognize the limitations of the CHA and apply additional policy tools to safeguard a vibrant public health care system. Although the federal government does have the ability to withhold federal transfers to any province that violates the CHA, it does not make effective use of that power (CHC 2006a; Derfel 2006). While the federal auditor general has criticized the federal government for not living up to its obligations (Kennedy 2004), and public health advocates have mounted a legal challenge against Ottawa for failing to monitor provincial delivery of health services (Bueckert 2004), Liberal governments and the current Conservative government have not altered their approach. That approach was also evident in the 2003 and 2004 health accords, which failed to include provisions to enforce the CHA.

A major limitation of the CHA is that it does not prevent for-profit companies from delivering publicly funded health services. Neither the 2003 nor the 2004 health accords included conditionality that new health funding should be used exclusively for not-for-profit delivery, despite the mounting evidence that for-profit care is less desirable in terms of financial and health outcomes (Sandborn 2006).[2] Furthermore, the new Health Council of Canada established under the 2003 accord to keep track of health care reforms was not mandated to distinguish, in its data collection, between for-profit and not-for-profit delivery. Overall, governments have consistently failed to recognize any of the concerns about for-profit delivery, including their implications for trade treaty obligations.

The question of wait-times continues to be at the centre of the health care debate. The two major federal parties consistently ignore accumulating evidence that solutions should be sought within the public system, not within the private for-profit sector (Rachlis 2006). During the 2006 federal election campaign, both the Conservatives and the Liberals made "care guarantees" central to their health platforms (Picard 2006). Both promised to adopt benchmarks for the treatment of specific conditions and to provide funding for patients to travel to other jurisdictions for treatment if they were not treated within a predetermined time frame. The major distinction between the two was that Paul Martin stressed that federal money could be spent only in Canadian public institutions, while Stephen Harper set no such conditions, implying care could be provided in for-profit clinics in Canada or even in the United States, Europe, and elsewhere. Although the notion of health-care guarantees – such as promising to treat patients promptly and close to home or to pay for them to be treated in another jurisdiction – may seem attractive on the surface, critics argue it will undermine Medicare. The concern is that, in their bid to meet care guarantees, provinces will open the door to more privately delivered care (Picard 2006). In June 2006 Prime Minister Harper indicated his intent to fulfill his promise by negotiating a patient wait-times guarantee with the provinces, establishing benchmarks for timely care (Sands 2006).

RECENT GOVERNMENT REPORTS ON HEALTH CARE REFORM

As tentative steps towards commercialization were being made in the health care system, three major government-sponsored commissions were asked early in the decade to provide blueprints for more structural reforms. These blueprints were the Mazankowski Report (the Report of the Alberta Premier's Advisory Council on Health, chaired by former deputy prime minister Don Mazankowski) (PACH 2002); the Kirby Report (the recommendations of the Standing Senate Committee on Social Affairs, Science and Technology, chaired by Senator Michael Kirby) (SCSAST 2002); and the Romanow Report (the report of the Commission on the Future of Health Care in Canada, chaired by former Saskatchewan premier Roy Romanow) (Romanow 2002). These reports helped define the intellectual framework for the current debate over the future of Medicare.

All three reports take strong positions on the appropriate role of private financing and for-profit delivery of health care services. Both Mazankowski and Kirby regard Canadians' substantial investment in health care as a rich commercial opportunity for the private sector. Both assert that subjecting the health care sector to entrepreneurial values and market "discipline" is necessary in order to modernize it. Mazankowski envisages a significantly expanded role for both private financing and for-profit delivery, while Kirby generally adheres to the principle of public financing (even envisioning expanding the Medicare insurance monopoly to new services) while embracing market-based mechanisms and an expanded private-sector role in delivery.

Romanow, by contrast, vigorously supports renewing Medicare around the key principles of public financing and not-for-profit delivery. The Romanow Report advocates a significant expansion of the public insurance monopoly to cover new services, strongly rejects a for-profit role in the delivery of core health services, and suggests that the inroads already made by for-profit providers in key areas such as diagnostic services be rolled back. Yet even Romanow, in a concession to the forceful privatization lobby, leaves the door open to an expanded private-sector role in the delivery of so-called ancillary health services, which could include food services, cleaning services, maintenance services, computer and data management services, administration, and many other services that are critical to the health care system.

Commercializing health care is a key theme of the Mazankowski and Kirby reports, and implementing their recommendations would entail a significant expansion of private, for-profit health care delivery. Curiously, neither report dwells on the expansion of P3s. No concerns are raised about these types of arrangements, and both reports provide implicit support for the concept. For example, the Mazankowski discussion of regional "care groups," while not advocating public-private partnerships specifically, could readily conform to, and is strongly suggestive of, a joint public-private arrangement for facilities and an intermingling of public and private, for-profit service delivery. So too is that report's proposal for the various aspects of the health care system to be "unbundled" – that is, separated according to different functions within the system – a controversial practice that splits apart integrated public entities and is generally accompanied by deregulation and privatization. Similarly, Kirby promotes devolving authority to regional authorities and increasing competition in health care – both of which imply a supportive environment for public-private arrangements. The Romanow Report does raise important concerns about public-private partnerships. He notes that they "often cost more in the longer term" – due to higher rental costs, higher cost of borrowing, and higher administration costs – and have been criticized for providing lower-quality services. He concludes that P3s "are no panacea and their use and value need to be carefully considered" (Romanow 2002, 30).

The Romanow Report appears to offer support for public-private partnerships in health information systems, but this support is limited and the reference somewhat oblique. The Mazankowski Report is more explicit, recommending that governments and health authorities consider P3s as one of the alternatives to developing or purchasing the information technology that would be necessary for electronic health care cards. Kirby clearly supports a public-private partnership in information technology, which in the report is considered a key aspect of health care infrastructure. In particular, the Kirby Report focuses on developing a national system of electronic health records. This proposal has been advanced by a private, not-for-profit corporation known as Canada Health Infoway, whose corporate members are deputy ministers of health and whose board of directors have diverse (often private health industry or information technology) backgrounds (Infoway 2006). The Kirby committee underlines its enthusiasm for the corporation's work and recommends that the federal government provide it with additional financial support. In addition to this increased federal funding, Kirby asserts that an electronic health record system would "require … partnerships with the private sector" (scsast 2002, chap. 10).

An equally contentious aspect of the health care debate involves the scope of public insurance. The Mazankowski approach would almost certainly lead to the expansion of private health care insurance and a retrenchment of the existing public insurance system. Under the Mazankowski recommendations, the list of publicly insured health care services would either be frozen at its current level or reduced. An expert panel would determine what services should be removed from the public insurance system. Moreover, the Mazankowski approach to public insurance coverage for most new treatments, services, or drugs would preclude an expansion of the public insurance system. New services would be covered only if there were sufficient existing revenues to cover the costs or if other services were removed from the list of publicly covered services. The report explicitly envisions the removal of services and treatments from the list of publicly insured services, noting that citizens would pay for these privately, in part through private supplementary insurance.

For the Mazankowski commission, contracting public insurance coverage would be only the first step in restructuring the Canadian health care system. Mazankowski also proposes sharp increases in private delivery of those health care services that remain within the public insurance system. Instead of providing health services, governments' primary role would be reduced to setting health policy and allocating funding. Regional health authorities would deliver or contract with private, for-profit and private, non-profit corporations and agencies for the delivery of a full range of publicly insured services. The Mazankowski approach would open the door to for-profit foreign companies or their affiliates to become directly involved in most or all publicly insured health care services.

The Kirby Report also proposes reducing the government's role to system governance, policy setting, and funding, with a new focus on market-based devolution of authority. The report recommends funding be service-based largely because this would allow the government, as financier, to be neutral on the issue of whether health care institutions are publicly owned or owned by private not-for-profit or for-profit organizations. Though the report does not emphasize the point, it is significant that service-based funding would also be neutral on the issue of whether services are publicly delivered or contracted out to private – including foreign – service suppliers. Kirby explicitly promotes increased private delivery of some publicly insured services, including day surgery and long-term care, on the basis that this would enhance competition with public service providers. In accordance with the report's theme of increased competition, it is noteworthy that Kirby's proposal to expand public insurance to include home care envisions private delivery. The expansion of the scope of public insurance coverage would thus come at the cost of consolidating and facilitating private, for-profit delivery – including by foreign affiliated suppliers – in the new publicly insured services.

The Romanow Report advocates strongly for public, non-profit delivery of core health care services and expresses concerns about increases in the private delivery of publicly insured services, including certain diagnostic and surgical services. Romanow's position is based on his underlying vision of the health care system providing timely access to quality health care services as a right of citizenship. However, the report also notes that public, non-profit delivery has the added benefit of reducing the risks of successful trade treaty challenges. Unfortunately, the Romanow Report draws a distinction between "direct" and "ancillary" health care services. In doing so, it lends tacit approval to increased privatization, commercialization, and for-profit delivery – presumably including by foreign suppliers – of a significant range of important health care services.

Taken together, these proposed steps away from a public-payer, public-provider health care system are worrisome. But it is disingenuous for governments to argue that these policy innovations should be seen as simply "experiments" that can later be reversed if they prove unsatisfactory. Canada's trade treaty commitments could make health care commercialization a one-way street. Foreign-service corporations operating along the margins or in the very heart of the Canadian health care system can use trade treaty rules to consolidate their commercial position. Under the shadow of international trade treaties, the health care commercialization illustrated in the aforementioned examples can no longer be characterized as easily-reversible policy experiments. Increasing commercialization now threatens to ensnare Canadian health policy in a complex web of binding international rules designed specifically to facilitate international business. Regrettably, most local health authorities and governments at all levels that are engaged in this commercialization – and Canadian citizens generally – have little, if any, appreciation of the power of these trade treaty rules to "lock-in" health care commercialization.

HAZARDOUS MIXTURE:
EXISTING TRADE TREATIES AND
HEALTH CARE REFORM

Few would deny that the principles that underlie Canada's Medicare system are at odds with the principles of so-called free trade treaties. By establishing a public-sector health insurance monopoly, and by regulating who can provide health care services and on what terms, the Canada Health Act and the Medicare system cut against the grain of trade and investment liberalization. While Canadians have repeatedly been assured that the health care system is beyond the reach of free trade treaties, Canada's health care system is in fact only partially shielded from their ambit. While the treaties provide some critical protection, the safeguards fall short of the full "ironclad" exemptions for health repeatedly promised to Canadians. These exemptions, as we explain below, will become even less effective as commercialization of the system proceeds. The implementation of P3s and the move towards delisting services and encouraging private insurance in particular are reforms that represent possible flashpoints – instances in which commercialization combines with trade treaty obligations to curtail the ability of governments to pursue health policies in the public interest. And, as we will see, the dangers embedded in these treaty obligations were brought sharply to the forefront by the *Chaoulli* Supreme Court decision.

Commercialization and the NAFTA and GATS Exemptions

Both NAFTA and GATS contain features that partially shield health services from the treaties' force, but in neither case can these be relied upon to provide full protection. NAFTA Annex I general reservation permits provincial, territorial, and local governments to maintain existing (as of 1 January 1994) health care measures that do not conform to certain NAFTA rules. The reservation is subject to a legal ratchet: it only permits changes to measures that increase their conformity with NAFTA rules. Once such a provincial non-conforming measure – ensuring non-profit delivery of diagnostic lab services or cataract operations, for example – is changed so as to be more NAFTA-consistent, protection for the original measure is lost forever. Increased commercialization thus permanently reduces the number and types of existing health measures that remain protected from the full force of the treaty.

NAFTA Annex II-C-9 provides protection for future government measures against certain NAFTA obligations. This annex protects otherwise NAFTA-inconsistent health measures that are deemed to be "social services established or maintained for a public purpose." Some Canadian analysts maintain that this safeguard is sufficiently broad to protect services that are publicly funded, even if they are delivered privately. Others assert that the annex protects only health services that are insured under the Canada Health Act. Still others have expressed concerns that this crucial reservation may be interpreted even more narrowly, exposing health care measures that disadvantage foreign private interests to successful challenge under NAFTA rules. Ominously, the United States Trade Representative takes an extremely narrow view of the scope of this exemption, asserting that, if social services "similar to those provided by government ... are supplied by

a private firm, on a profit or not-for profit basis" then the "NAFTA investment and services rules apply" (CCPA 2002, 12–14).

Despite the wide range of views about the efficacy of the protective
annex, several observations can be made with confidence. It is clear that
the scope of this protective provision remains undefined, untested, and controversial. Also, critically, increasing private delivery of publicly insured
services shifts the character of such services along the spectrum from those
provided for a "public purpose" towards those provided for a "private
purpose," the latter being fully subject to applicable NAFTA rules. Finally, it
must be acknowledged that in the event of a dispute, the scope of the annex
in any particular case will ultimately be determined not by governments
but by appointed NAFTA arbitral panellists.

Increasing private delivery of publicly insured services could also reduce
the effectiveness of parallel protections in GATS. The key GATS "governmental authority" exclusion purportedly protects measures pertaining to services
"supplied in the exercise of governmental authority." But this protection
applies only to services that are provided neither on a commercial nor a competitive basis (GATS 1994, Article I:3.c). Increasing private delivery of publicly insured services, arguably opening the services to commercialism or
competition, would thus make it far more difficult, if not impossible, for governments to satisfy these criteria. Specifically, even services that continue to
be provided publicly on a non-commercial basis may be deemed to be "in
competition with" a newly commercialized "like" service. In this indirect
way, commercialization could lead to the loss by publicly delivered services
of any protection the "governmental authority" would otherwise have
afforded. The proliferation of private health care delivery could thus greatly
increase the number and types of health care services falling within the scope
of GATS.

Increasing for-profit health care would increase foreign corporations' stake
and influence in the Canadian health care system and trade policy making.
As the number of for-profit health service suppliers increases, so too would
foreign, for-profit service providers, of which most would be large transnational corporations. Many of these new entrants into the Canadian system
would likely be US-based and have longer experience in for-profit health care,
deeper pockets, and other "comparative advantages" over their Canadian
for-profit counterparts and, especially, over Canadian not-for-profit health
service providers. They would also gain influence as "stakeholders" in Canadian health policy making and, of direct relevance to this analysis, in health-
related trade policy.

The increased involvement of foreign corporations in the health care sector
would, in turn, make reversing increases in for-profit health care delivery
much more difficult and expensive. Under NAFTA, US investors and service
suppliers would acquire certain investment rights that are not enjoyed by

Canadian investors or service suppliers. In particular, if future Canadian governments took steps to reverse health care commercialization by returning services to the public or not-for-profit sector, us investors could mount investor-to-state challenges, claiming financial compensation for what they would assert, using the NAFTA definition, to be expropriation (see Shrybman, chapter 12, this volume). Even if the Canadian measures were non-discriminatory, treating Canadian and American firms alike, the Canadian government would still face an increased risk of compensation claims. The increased complexity and financial liability caused by NAFTA investment rules would thus make it far more difficult and expensive to reverse health care commercialization.

Similarly, under GATS, any health-related services that a future Canadian government decided to subject to the treaty's national treatment and market access rules would entitle foreign providers to receive the same subsidies as their Canadian counterparts. Subsequently retracting such a benefit from foreign firms could cause the companies' home governments to mount GATS challenges to such discriminatory treatment. To reiterate, the more involved foreign investors and service providers become in the health care system the more difficult and costly it will become to limit or reverse the trend towards commercialization – no matter how pressing or legitimate the underlying public policy purpose.

Trade Treaty Implications of P3s

Since public-private partnerships are a specific form of health care commercialization, and because they can span almost the entire range of health care services, P3s open the door for foreign corporations to use trade policy rules to distort key aspects of Canadian health care policy. Under domestic laws, governments must satisfy rigorous legal requirements that protect the rights of both parties whenever they cancel contracts with private service providers for inadequate service or other legitimate public reasons. Trade treaty rules, particularly NAFTA investment provisions, however, are biased towards the rights of the foreign investor, requiring governments to provide affected foreign corporations financial compensation for measures that are broadly defined as expropriation. P3s could encompass most health sectors, including information systems, hospital construction, hospital ownership and investment, the ownership and investment of other health care facilities and other infrastructure, and even the management and day-to-day operation of health care facilities and entire systems. In each of these areas, to the extent that P3s would entail increased involvement by foreign corporations, trade rules make cancelling or revising these arrangements more expensive and difficult than would otherwise be the case. Trade treaties therefore shift much of the risk of failed P3s to governments, in effect insuring the private partners at taxpayer expense.

P3s in areas covered by trade treaty rules would also constrain governments' ability to maximize local, regional, or national benefits or to achieve other social goals, for example, by favouring domestic non-profit providers, negotiating performance requirements, or enforcing quantity-based quotas and restrictions. All of these conditions, which in theory can be written into P3 agreements to make them more palatable, are unenforceable under trade and investment treaty rules.

Finally, where governments choose to contract for services (rather than providing them directly), they will gain the greatest clarity and protection under trade treaties by adopting a traditional procurement model (where governments purchase and pay for the required services directly). For example, Canadian provincial and local government procurement is not covered under NAFTA or the WTO Agreement on Government Procurement. Structuring a service contract as procurement therefore minimizes trade treaty entanglement. But most P3s do not follow a standard procurement model. Consequently, there are strong arguments that they are subject to the investment and services rules rather than the procurement rules of NAFTA and GATS. This greatly increases the risk of trade treaty challenge and of governments facing fines or trade sanctions for the breach of trade treaties with regard to the operation, management, or termination of a P3.

Under trade treaties P3s thus have the potential to diminish governments' regulatory ability in vital areas of health care policy, to shift risk from the investor or service provider to the public, and to increase costs through trade fines or sanctions.

Trade Treaty Implications of Reduced Public Insurance

Any move away from the current single-payer system would have a number of trade treaty implications. First, any reductions in public health insurance coverage would be difficult and expensive for future governments to reverse. The Government of Canada has listed health insurance as one of its GATS specific commitments, and GATS National Treatment and Market Access rules therefore apply in this sector.[3] As a result, bringing delisted services back within the universe of publicly insured services could cause foreign-service providers whose commercial opportunities are adversely affected to pressure their home government to mount trade challenges against Canada.

Individual foreign investors could also be expected to use NAFTA's controversial investor-to-state dispute settlement process to mount direct challenges against reinsuring health care services under the public insurance system after they had been delisted. These investors could seek financial payments as compensation for what under NAFTA rules is broadly considered expropriation of their for-profit insurance business.

Second, delisting health care services from the universe of publicly insured services would make it more difficult to regulate aspects of privately insured services within Canada. Canada's existing GATS commitments in Market Access mean that Canadian governments are precluded from limiting the numbers of insurance suppliers for these services, for example, or the number of offices a foreign supplier is permitted to have in any region, or limits on the involvement of foreign investors. Canada's National Treatment commitments, which apply to subsidies, would also prevent the possibility of targeting subsidies to domestic insurance cooperatives, non-profit insurers, or domestic for-profit insurance suppliers of the delisted services.

Third, shrinking the universe of publicly insured services would reduce the effectiveness of existing protections against certain trade treaty rules. For example, NAFTA's social services exclusion (Annex II-C-9) provides only limited protection. It allows Canadian governments to adopt or maintain otherwise inconsistent health care measures only to the extent that they are "social services established or maintained for a public purpose." As discussed previously,[4] there is sharp disagreement about the scope and efficacy of this safeguard. However, while the protection that the II-C-9 exclusion now affords remains unclear, its ability to shield Canadian health care measures from NAFTA rules would certainly be diminished by the Mazankowski proposals. Reductions in the number and scope of publicly insured services would shrink the universe of those health care services that are protected by virtue of them being "established or maintained for a public purpose."

Finally, it should be noted that Canada's GATS commitments undeniably apply to private health insurance. Canada has listed "life, accident and health insurance services" as covered services in its GATS schedule. This means that foreign health insurers are guaranteed full access to the Canadian private insurance market and to any advantages, including subsidies, provided to Canadian private insurers. It also means that if Canada expands its public health insurance system, then it is required by GATS to compensate other WTO members for their lost market access. This compensation takes the form of "adjustments" in Canada's schedule (not monetary compensation as under the NAFTA investor-state dispute system), but if adjustments cannot be successfully negotiated, then Canada could face trade sanctions from other WTO member governments. Obviously, the greater the degree of foreign penetration of the Canadian health insurance market, the higher the level of compensation or sanctions that Canadians could ultimately face (CCPA 2002, 25; Sanger 2001, 77–89).

Supreme Court Health Ruling
Oblivious to Trade Treaty Threats[5]

The danger that trade treaty commitments present for Canada's health care system became obvious when the Supreme Court made public its stunning decision on the *Chaoulli* case (SCC 2005). Dr Jacques Chaoulli is the Quebec physician whose complaint led the Supreme Court to strike down Quebec's ban on private health insurance. In a four-three decision, the court said banning private insurance for a list of services ranging from diagnostic tests to cataract surgery was unconstitutional under the Quebec Charter of Rights, given that the public system had failed to guarantee patients access to those services in a timely manner (CBC 2005).

The majority view in the Court somehow failed to grasp what was immediately obvious to Chaoulli and right-wing lobbyists in the United States: overturning the ban on private health insurance will open the gates for multinational insurance corporations and for-profit heath care companies to enter and proliferate within the Canadian health care system. The decision ignored the fact that trade treaties pose serious risks and that these need to be considered before any major health care reforms are undertaken. Just as Canada's public health care system has been built around the public monopoly over health insurance, the limited protections that Canada negotiated in NAFTA and GATS are based on the existing separation between private and public health insurance "markets." The Supreme Court ruling could destroy this basic separation by permitting private insurers, including foreign companies, to cover the full range of health services. This would neuter the trade treaty exemptions for Canadian health care.

In their scathing dissent, the minority on the Court stated that "the proposed constitutional right to a two-tier health system for those who can afford private medical insurance would precipitate a seismic shift in health policy" (SCC 2005, 94). The ruling emboldened those who have staked their interest in privatization, while Medicare advocates found it disturbing for a slim majority of judges to trigger such a fundamental change in our country's public health care system and, furthermore, to do so without considering the long-term consequences under Canada's trade treaties (Sinclair 2005).

It is to be hoped that the impact of this ruling will be limited and that the strong surge of support for Medicare it evoked will prevail. At the moment, the ruling applies only to Quebec, and the Supreme Court has suspended its judgment for twelve months in response to a request from the Quebec and federal governments (CP 2005). Both federal and provincial governments are taking measures to address waiting lists and are reinvesting in the public system, which helps resolve the issue. In an ominous sign, the government of Quebec's proposed response has been to establish wait time guarantees for cataract, knee, and hip surgeries and to allow elective surgeries for those three to be covered by private insurance and performed by a limited number of affiliated private clinics. Still, the advocates of for-profit care are disappointed that, so far, the ruling has had less effect than they had wished (Kondro 2006). Finally, the arrival of two new justices on the Supreme Court bench may lead to a different outcome in future cases.

LOOMING CHALLENGES:
NEW TRADE TREATY NEGOCIATIONS

The more intrusive and potent trade treaties become, the more hazardous they can be to Medicare and other public services systems. The most significant new risks are now posed by ongoing, previously mandated negotiations on GATS, by negotiations (currently stalled) to conclude a Free Trade Area of the Americas (FTAA), and by proposals for continental integration extending beyond NAFTA. Each successive set of multilateral, regional, and bilateral trade and investment negotiations along the lines of GATS and the FTAA makes the task of protecting Canada's health care system from erosion more difficult. Each agreement sets precedents for more intrusive provisions in the next. These cascading negotiations subject Canada to continuous pressure to weaken or even remove vital exceptions and reservations for health care.

Ongoing Negotiations
on the General Agreement on Trade and Services

GATS contains a feature that is especially relevant to future health care reform. It has built into its structure an overarching commitment to repeated renegotiations to increase the treaty's coverage. Canada and other GATS members have already agreed to this open-ended, ratchet-like commitment to ever-higher levels of liberalization. While few members have so far specifically agreed to list health measures, over the long term, pressure to apply GATS rules more extensively in the health sector poses a grave threat to health care development and reform both in Canada and elsewhere.

Ongoing GATS negotiations to expand the treaty threaten health care reform in several general ways (Grieshaber-Otto and Sanger 2002, 106–20; Sanger 2001, 77–89). First, basic misunderstandings about the complex treaty increase the risk that some governments may inadvertently apply GATS rules to health care services. For example, WTO officials and developed country negotiators have made reassuring but misleading statements that could encourage unwary governments to believe, wrongly, that public services are fully excluded from the treaty. This uncertainty could cause governments to make new or more expansive specific commitments that unintentionally expose important aspects of the health care system to successful GATS challenge. Second, secretive treaty negotiations can provide political cover for governments making unpopular regulatory changes in the sensitive health care sector. As the WTO secretariat has candidly acknowledged, they can also facilitate governments' efforts in "overcoming domestic resistance to change" (WTO 1998, 57). And finally, the treaty contains important provisions that are unclear, about which members disagree, and that will ultimately be clarified by unelected WTO dispute panellists. The treaty grants these individuals the ability to rule on such key issues even though most pan-ellists have little expertise in health care policy and have no legitimate authority for balancing oft-competing public policy priorities.

In the current and future rounds of GATS renegotiations governments will face intense pressure to make new, more extensive specific commitments. In the long term, this pressure will almost certainly extend to health-related services. For example, firms seeking expanded markets overseas often apply pressure on their governments to use the GATS negotiations to obtain market-opening concessions in other countries. Also, foreign firms apply similar pressure on their governments to extract equivalent concessions in Canada. Such pressure can be strong and hard to resist. Canadian representatives have repeatedly stated that Canada will make no GATS commitments cover-ing health care in this round of negotiations. However, as one of the strongest proponents of GATS expansion, Canada is likely to come under increasing pressure, both in the current round and in future rounds of renegotiations, to make GATS requests and offers affecting services that are integral to the Canadian health care system. This pressure will become even more pro-nounced as, in future rounds, health becomes one of the few remaining sectors in which Canada has not taken commitments. As unfavourable trade rulings involving Canadian cultural policy have shown, such constant pres-sure can be difficult to resist successfully over long periods of time, even in areas that, like health, are particularly politically sensitive and important to the public. Moreover, once any single future Canadian federal government yields to this pressure, GATS makes it very difficult for subsequent govern-ments to reverse course. In this way, the treaty interferes unacceptably with the normal ebb and flow of decision making in a democratic system of gov-ernment (Sinclair and Grieshaber-Otto 2002).

GATS renegotiations that are now under way entail other threats to Canada's health care system. The most important of these is the proposed "disciplines" on governments' domestic regulation. These proposed rules have a number of features that could give them extraordinary power.[6] The proposed rules would comprise a new, distinct class of GATS rules. They would be intended to act like a fine-meshed drift net – capturing government measures not caught by other GATS constraints. For example, even govern-ment measures that are consistent both with the tough non-discrimination rules contained in GATS and the treaty's market access provisions could still be found to violate the new domestic regulation restrictions.

The proposed new rules would also cover subject matter that is very broad and highly relevant to health care services. They would extend to "measures relating to qualification requirements and procedures, technical standards and licensing procedures" (GATS 1994, Article VI:4). While these terms are not defined precisely in the treaty, they can be expected to include, for example, the accreditation of doctors and other professionals, and the licensing and certification of hospitals and clinics. The provision's reach could be lengthened further by a broad interpretation of the term "technical standards." According to the WTO Secretariat, the term refers not just to the "technical characteristics of the service itself" but also to "the rules according to which the service must be performed" (Sinclair and Grieshaber-Otto 2002, 31).

Significantly, the proposed restrictions are intended to apply a test of "necessity" to measures covered by this broad provision. That is, governments would face the difficult onus of demonstrating that their regulations affecting the health care system were "necessary" to achieve a legitimate objective. Governments would also have to prove that no alternative measure was available that was less commercially restrictive. While the precise application of these concepts is now under negotiation, there can be little doubt that the intent is for their application to capture a very wide range of government regulations.[7]

Also, though it is a matter for negotiation, it is possible that the proposed GATS domestic regulation rules will apply across-the-board to all measures, even to those for which members have made no specific commitments.[8] And finally, whatever domestic regulation rules are agreed to during negotiations, they are likely to apply without exception since the article does not allow for any country-specific exceptions or limitations (Sinclair and Grieshaber-Otto 2002). While the rules will not themselves establish global standards, they would subject domestic health care standards and practices to GATS restrictions – a worrisome and anti-democratic development.

Together, these features indicate that the GATS domestic regulation negotiations could soon bring public health care systems even further within the purview of the WTO. If the negotiations proceed as expected, the resulting rules would allow dispute panels to oversee an extraordinarily broad range of domestic procedures and standards to ensure they meet GATS rules. These panels could second-guess policies concerning many important aspects of Medicare. The GATS negotiations on domestic regulation, which are now well under way, thus pose a serious threat to the regulatory underpinnings of Canada's public health care system.

The Proposed Free Trade Area of the Americas Agreement

At the FTAA ministerial meeting held in Miami in late November 2003, trade ministers from the thirty-four countries negotiating a hemispheric free trade agreement scaled back their plans for the final stage of negotiations. At the insistence of Brazil, the other Mercosur countries, and Venezuela, ministers agreed to work towards a so-called "two-tier" agreement. According to the Ministerial Declaration, the FTAA negotiating committee will "develop a common and balanced set of rights and obligations applicable to all countries" that will include provisions in each of the following areas: "market access; agriculture; services; investment; government procurement; intellectual property; competition policy; subsidies, antidumping, and countervailing duties; and dispute settlement." And "on a plurilateral basis, interested parties may choose to develop additional liberalization and disciplines" (FTAA Secretariat 2003, para. 10). Consequently, the main focus on negotiations became defining "what core obligations will constitute the 'balance of rights and obligations' and what 'additional obligations and benefits' will be optional" (SELA 2003, 5).

The advance in the negotiations came to a halt in the November 2005 Summit of the Americas held in Mar del Plata, Argentina. While thousands protested in the streets against US president George Bush, the leaders failed to reach a consensus on renewed negotiations due to the firm resistance of the four nations of the Mercosur (Brazil, Argentina, Paraguay, and Uruguay) and Venezuela. Led by Venezuelan president Hugo Chávez, they argued that the necessary conditions are not yet in place to achieve a balanced and equitable free trade agreement (Carlsen 2005). Despite the setback for Bush policies, many analysts believe a postmortem for the FTAA is premature, and they cite the advance of bilateral free trade agreements as evidence that US free trade strategy is still alive and kicking in Latin America (Ibid.).

Given the likelihood of renewed future negotiations either in an FTAA forum or in other similar forums, the Canadian position on the FTAA remains highly relevant for the future of Medicare. The Canadian government has continued all along to strongly support a comprehensive FTAA with NAFTA-type, or "NAFTA-plus," obligations covering all sectors, including services, investment, intellectual property, and government procurement. Obligations in these sectors pose the greatest risks to Canada's health care system. Even if the FTAA ultimately contains certain optional obligations in these key areas, it is very likely that the Canadian government will agree to be bound by them. In fact, Canada has already made an offer to cover services and investment in the FTAA, and this offer remains on the table. This initial offer, together with drafts of the services and investment chapters, indicates that the Canadian government pursued an FTAA that combines the most intrusive features of the NAFTA investment chapter and the GATS services provisions.[9]

The Canadian government continues to support incorporating many of the most controversial features of the NAFTA investment chapter into the FTAA, including investor-state dispute settlement, broad expropriation-compensation provisions, minimum standard of treatment rules, and performance requirements prohibitions. Moreover, the draft FTAA services chapter also includes some significant "NAFTA-plus" provisions drawn from GATS. Article 7 of the services chapter, on market access, would prohibit monopolies in all covered sectors, and Article 5 would apply national treatment to subsidies (by contrast, subsidies are exempted from NAFTA's national treatment rule).

The impacts of these NAFTA-plus features drawn from GATS would be compounded by the approach, again strongly supported by Canada, that the FTAA services chapter be "top-down." Combining these tough NAFTA-plus provisions with a top-down approach obviously dictates that Canadian negotiators take a fresh, serious look at the potential for challenges to the Canadian health care measures and to develop new, more strongly worded, reservations to protect the Canadian health care system. Yet Canada's proposed FTAA reservation for health and social services is exactly the same as its flawed 1994 NAFTA reservation. Canada's proposed reservation does not even, for example, provide any protection against the controversial expropriation claims, which many trade experts and the Romanow Commission agree pose a serious threat to the reform and renewal of the Canadian health care system.

Proposals to Deepen North American Integration

While proponents for greater economic integration within North America commonly focus primarily on border and security issues, their aims are far more ambitious, and their proposals, if acted upon, would place Canada's health care system squarely on the negotiating table.

Ardent NAFTA-supporters and former federal trade officials Michael Hart and William Dymond have proposed a comprehensive "NAFTA-plus" agreement with the United States "to achieve a seamless market governed by a single set of rules" (Hart and Dymond 2001, 45) throughout North America. They believe that "geography and history suggest that Canada's economic destiny lies with the US market" (16) and that "deeper Canada-US integration is the only realistic option for progress in developing significant market access" (ibid.) for Canadian products. In order to sufficiently engage US interests, they argue that a new bilateral initiative must be "bold, broad, and deep" (21), requiring "serious commitments by Canada" (20). While they advise against using "the energy card" for fear of creating a "political backlash" (37), and although they avoid mention of health care, Hart and Dymond propose fundamental changes in traditionally highly sensitive areas. For example, they suggest deal-sweetening changes to "the current system of supply management and the state-trading practices of the Canadian Wheat Board" and "Canadian cultural protection programs" (20). They propose a "formal" bilateral treaty with the United States, though short of a European-style customs union, to address a broad range of issues, including: "cumbersome rules of origin; discriminatory government procurement restrictions ... burdensome regulatory requirements ... and other restrictive measures ..." (3). "Proceeding in this direction," they acknowledge, "... will have implications that go beyond trade and commercial considerations" (44).

From the Canadian side, in March 2005 former deputy prime minister

John Manley and head of the Canadian Council of Chief Executives Thomas d'Aquino led the Independent Task Force on the Future of North America, which also included us and Mexican partners. Their chairmen's statement, entitled *Creating a North American Community*, proposes the "creation of a single economic space" – a "community" with a "common security perimeter" and a "common external tariff" that would eliminate rules of origin. The task force also asserts that "regulatory differences among the three countries" raise costs and are thus problematic; it proposes a "trinational approach" to address "regulatory policy" and other "concerns." The proponents note that "trade in ... key areas ... remains far from free." They recommend that Canada, Mexico and the United States "enter into negotiations ... to find a joint approach to unfair trade practices and anti-competitive behaviour" (Manley, Aspe, and Weld 2005, 7–11).

Former prime minister Paul Martin, President George Bush, and President Vicente Fox of Mexico appear to have been guided by these recommendations when they launched the trinational Security and Prosperity Partnership of North America (SPP) in their summit in Waco, Texas, in March 2005. They created ten working groups to advance an ambitious continental agenda, including sectoral and regional competitiveness, business facilitation, e-commerce and information and communications technologies, and financial services (SPP 2005a). In detailing their "Prosperity Agenda," they stated that one of their main goals is "regulatory cooperation to generate growth," which would include:

- Lower costs for North American businesses, producers, and consumers and maximize trade in goods and services across our borders by striving to ensure compatibility of regulations and standards and eliminating redundant testing and certification requirements.
- Strengthen regulatory cooperation, including at the onset of the regulatory process, to minimize barriers. (SPP 2005b)

Prime Minister Stephen Harper embraced these recommendations and committed to move them forward in his SPP summit with presidents Bush and Fox in Cancun, Mexico, in March 2006. One of their first steps was to establish the North American Competitiveness Council in order to ensure "private sector engagement in the SPP by adding high-level business input" (SPP 2006).

The logic of these types of integration proposals conflicts with the fundamental principles of Medicare. Like the recent trade treaties upon which they are based, they promote the freer flow of goods, services, and investments by constraining and redirecting the regulatory ability of governments. Conversely, Canada's health care system deliberately constrains and, in certain circumstances, prohibits the operation of market forces in order to provide health care services to all citizens on the basis of need rather than the ability to pay. The Canadian health care system, despite its need for rejuvenation, far surpasses its inferior US counterpart. Maintaining it intact would thus stand in the way of a key aim of these proposals – eliminating "regulatory differences" between the countries to create a "seamless market" or "single economic space." Moreover, because Canada's public insurance system precludes entry by US-based insurance firms, it is by its very nature, according to the logic of integration, "discriminatory" and "anti-competitive." Indeed, a fundamental aspect of the Canadian system's continued success is that trade in health care services and insurance "remains far from free." In sum, while integration proponents rarely mention health care specifically, embarking on a new round of comprehensive NAFTA-style negotiations with the United States and Mexico would inevitably place fundamental aspects of Canada's health care system at greater risk.

CONCLUSION:
TOWARDS *HEALTHY* HEALTH CARE REFORM

Examination of Canada's trade and investment treaty obligations and the scope of the exemptions for health care under those treaties add a crucial dimension to the debate on health care reform. It reveals that Canada's trade treaty commitments threaten to make commercializing reforms difficult and costly to reverse (Evans et al. 2000). But despite the significant threats that these treaty provisions pose, it is our view that Canadian health care reform can navigate these risks. To do so successfully will require new initiatives on a range of policy fronts. It will require careful planning of future health care reforms to avoid trade treaty problems; fundamental changes in Canadian trade policy strategies and negotiating objectives; and new thinking and creative diplomacy to achieve a better balance in the international system between promoting health as a public good and protecting commercial and trading interests.

The risk of the trade challenges enumerated above also needs to be kept in perspective. Canada's exposure to foreign investors' and service-provider treaty claims is, in most instances, not yet that extreme. This is because, while health care commercialization in Canada is clearly proliferating, its scale is still limited, and the level of foreign involvement is smaller still.[10] Only foreign interests have enforceable rights under trade treaties. As the Romanow Report observes:

Rather than conclude … that Canada is hemmed in to the current system and cannot change, the more reasonable conclusion is that if we want to expand the range of services in the public system, it is better to do it now while there still is very little foreign presence in health care in Canada and the potential costs of [trade] compensation are low. (Romanow 2002, 238)

While real, the risks of trade treaty litigation should not be used as a pretext to thwart progressive health care reform. Canada has a window of opportunity to expand its public health insurance system, but unless action is taken soon that window could close.

Avoiding commercialization of health services – and taking prompt action to contain or reverse existing commercialization – is good public policy. But it also has the benefit of reducing the risk of future trade treaty challenges. As a crucial first step, governments at all levels should not proceed with so-called public-private partnerships in health care and should avoid P3 arrangements in the future. Strictly avoiding commercialization maximizes the protection afforded by the existing trade treaty exemptions. It also curbs the stake of all for-profit providers and investors in the Canadian health care system, and it minimizes the stake of foreign for-profit providers and investors. As discussed, there is an inherent tension between the public policy objectives of Medicare – that is, providing care to all on the basis of need rather than ability to pay – and the commercializing imperatives of modern trade and investment treaties. The Canadian health care system is a mixed public-private system. With regard to trade and investment treaties, the goal must be to preserve the ability of governments to closely regulate Canada's entire mixed health care system. Governments' ability to shift this mix – without fear of becoming entangled in trade disputes and threat of sanctions – should be fully protected.

Canada's current exemptions in NAFTA and GATS, while they do provide some protection, are flawed and inadequate. Concerted changes in Canada's existing trade policy commitments and its objectives in ongoing negotiations will be necessary to secure strong, fully effective protection for health care and to relieve the distorting pressure that trade treaties exert on the Canadian health care system and its future reform.

Several concurrent shifts are desirable. Those existing commitments that already pose a threat to health care reform need to be changed. In order to achieve more effective safeguards for health in ongoing and future negotiations, Canada's negotiating goals and strategies should be overhauled. Finally, Canada should champion longer-term changes in the international system to assure that health protection and promotion no longer takes a back seat to the protection and promotion of commercial rights.

Despite setbacks in Cancun, Miami, and Mar del Plata, the Canadian government remains an enthusiastic and relatively uncritical supporter of further trade and investment treaty expansion. Canada supports the revival of negotiations to create a Free Trade Area of the Americas (FTAA), is involved in other bilateral and regional free trade agreements, and is actively engaged in the Doha Round of WTO negotiations. Each of these agreements touches upon health issues, such as health-related services, investment, and intellectual property. And, as mentioned, the minority Conservative government of Prime Minister Stephen Harper is advancing a number of parallel agendas for greater continental economic integration, several of them directly affecting the regulation of services, in the Security and Prosperity Partnership with the United States and Mexico.

Canada should adopt a precautionary approach to prevent further exposure of our health care system to increased pressure and possible challenge. Although the Canadian government continues to insist that health care is "off the table" and "non-negotiable" in all these arenas, the very breadth and complexity of the new trade and investment treaty agenda, combined with shortcomings in Canada's approach to exempting health policy measures, makes the validity of such assurances highly questionable.

The FTAA services and investment negotiations provide a lesson on this point. The 2002 draft services text contained NAFTA-plus features – supported by Canada – that would pose even more formidable problems for Canada's health care system. Despite this looming threat and rising concern about flaws in the NAFTA reservations, the Canadian government in its opening offer on services and investment simply recycled an exact carbon copy of the flawed NAFTA reservations for health and social services. When it came to safeguarding health, Canadian negotiators' actions during the various Liberal governments spoke louder than their words. In the context of the current Conservative government under Prime Minister Stephen Harper, which leans heavily towards Bush-type policies, these concerns are compounded.

Wherever conflicts between health and commercial policy persist, what Canada should be doing is not to rely exclusively on country-specific exceptions for social services, which have significant shortcomings and should be regarded only as stopgap measures. Instead, Canada should pursue generally agreed upon exceptions or safeguards – permanent features of treaties that are far more likely to endure over time. To this end, Canadian negotiators should be directed to pursue a self-defining exemption for health polices in all its international trade and investment agreements. Furthermore, Canada should lodge a new exception in its GATS schedule (a "horizontal limitation") making clear that no commitment in any sector affects the Canadian health care system or Canada's ability to protect the health of Canadians. In ongoing negotiations on GATS, the proposed FTAA, other bilateral or subregional forums, or continental economic integration negotiations, Canada should not make commitments covering any aspect of the health care system (e.g., telehealth, health information systems, or hospital management) or that affect its ability to regulate for health purposes (e.g., distribution of prescription drugs, tobacco, or alcohol). Finally, to be a good global citizen and to minimize future pressure on Canada to cover health, Canada should make no requests of other countries to cover any health-related services or services that affect their ability to regulate for health purposes.[11]

In short, the federal government must change its current approach to trade treaties – whether NAFTA, FTAA, or GATS – which promotes unbalanced treaties and increases commercializing pressure on Canada's health care system. The federal government should begin by acknowledging the existing threats to public service systems and public interest regulation, and changing its trade negotiating objectives and existing treaty commitments to secure the strong, fully effective protection for Medicare that Canadians were promised but not given. In holding elected representatives to account in international trade negotiations affecting Canadians' cherished health care system, citizens should demand that their governments begin to put health first.

NOTES

This chapter was adapted and updated from a book published by the Canadian Centre for Policy Alternatives (Grieshaber-Otto and Sinclair 2004). We gratefully acknowledge the editorial contribution of Ian T. MacDonald.

1 Some of these concerns have been raised by the BC Government and Service Employees' Union in connection with the BC government's privatization of its Medical Services Plan and Pharmacare systems.
2 The Canadian Health Coalition has compiled peer-reviewed evidence that for-profit health care facilities have many disadvantages over not-for-profit ones (e.g., they have higher death rates, cost more, and provide lower quality of care) (CHC 2006b).
3 GATS national treatment and market access provisions apply only to those sectors that each government has listed in its country schedule. These listed commitments are referred to as specific commitments.
4 This is discussed at greater length in a report prepared by the Canadian Centre for Policy Alternatives and the Consortium on Globalization and Health for the Romanow Commission (CCPA 2002, 13–14).
5 This section was adapted from Sinclair (2005).
6 This section draws heavily upon Sinclair (2000), Sinclair and Grieshaber-Otto (2002), and Grieshaber-Otto and Sanger (2002).
7 In a paper prepared for a OECD/US forum on trade in educational services, GATS proponent Pierre Sauvé (2002, 28) emphasizes the importance of the GATS domestic regulation provisions:
   The GATS could play a useful role ... in ensuring that regulatory measures in this area ... even while non-discriminatory in character, are not unduly burdensome or indeed disguised restrictions to trade and investment in the sector. The adoption of possible disciplines on domestic regulation ... and in particular the adoption of a necessity test ... could be important in this regard, though one cannot underestimate the political sensitivities that lie ahead in this area.

8 In sharp contrast to other clauses in Article VI, subsection 4 does not contain language that would limit its application to "sectors in which a Member has undertaken specific commitments."

9 The 1 November 2002 drafts of the FTAA services and investment chapters are available at <http://www.dfait-maeci.gc.ca/tna-nac/ftaa_neg-en.asp>.

10 For example, only two major US health insurers are active in the Canadian private health insurance market: Liberty Health, a Canadian unit of Liberty Mutual Insurance Co. of Boston, and Maritime Life Assurance Co, a subsidiary of John Hancock Financial Services, also of Boston. US insurers estimate their share of the Canadian private insurance market at less than 10 percent. This market share, however, could increase rapidly through competition or a possible takeover of a Canadian insurer. See Knox (2002).

11 Canada's current position is that it will make no GATS requests of others to cover direct health services, but Canada continues to press other countries to cover health insurance and other health-related services where it has already made GATS commitments.

REFERENCES

Auerbach, Lewis, Arthur Donner, Douglas D. Peters, Monica Townson, and Armine Yalnizyan. 2003. *Funding Hospital Infrastructure: Why P3s Don't Work and What Will.* Ottawa: Canadian Centre for Policy Alternatives.

Bueckert, Dennis. 2004. Federal Government Fights Judicial Review of Its Record Defending Medicare. *Canadian Press*, 10 May.

Carlsen, Laura. 2005. Timely Demise for Free Trade Area of the Americas. 23 November. Silver City, NM: International Relations Center.

CBC. 2005. Top Court Strikes down Quebec Private Health-Care Ban. CBC.ca, 9 June. Available at <http://www.cbc.ca/story/canada/national/2005/06/09/newscoc-health050609.html>.

CCPA. 2002. *Putting Health First: Canadian Health Care Reform, Trade Treaties and Foreign Policy.* Ottawa: Canadian Centre for Policy Alternatives and Consortium on Globalization and Health.

– 2003. *Cancel Private Hospitals.* News release. Ottawa: Canadian Centre for Policy Alternatives.

CHC. 2004. Found: Federal Funding; Missing: A Plan to Stem Privatization – Canadian Health Coalition's Analysis of the First Ministers' Health Care Agreement. Ottawa: Canadian Health Coalition.

– 2006a. Canada Health Act Annual Report: Missing Information and Secret Tabling. May 11. Ottawa: Canadian Health Coalition.

– 2006b. The Debate Is Over! Ottawa: Canadian Health Coalition. Available at <http://www.healthcoalition.ca/micro.html>, cited 17 July.

CP. 2005. Supreme Court suspends judgment on private health services for 12 months. *Canadian Press*, August 4.

CUPE. 2005a. Ontario Budget Takes P3 Page from Tories. 1 June. Ottawa: Canadian Union of Public Employees.

– 2005b. P3s Spreading in Ontario Hospitals. 31 August. Ottawa: Canadian Union of Public Employees.

Derfel, Aaron. 2006. Quebec Escapes Fines: Three other Provinces Dinged for Violations. *Montreal Gazette*, 11 May, A1.

Evans, Robert G., Morris L. Barer, Steven Lewis, Michael Rachlis, and Greg L. Stoddart. 2000. *Private Highway, One-Way Street: The De-Klein and Fall of Medicare?* Vancouver: Centre for Health Services and Policy Research.

FTAA Secretariat. 2003. Free Trade Area of the Americas Eighth Ministerial Meeting, 20 November, Miami. Ministerial declaration. Mexico City: FTAA Secretariat.

GATS. 1994. General Agreement on Trade in Services (GATS). Uruguay Round Agreement, Annex 1B. Geneva: World Trade Organization.

Grieshaber-Otto, Jim, and Matthew Sanger. 2002. *Perilous Lessons: The Impact of the WTO Services Agreements (GATS) on Canada's Public Education System.* Ottawa: Canadian Centre for Policy Alternatives.

Grieshaber-Otto, Jim, and Scott Sinclair. 2004. *Bad Medicine: Trade Treaties, Privatization and Health Care Reform in Canada.* Ottawa: Canadian Centre for Policy Alternatives.

Hart, Michael, and William Dymond. 2001. *Common Borders, Shared Destinies: Canada, the United States and Deepening Integration.* Ottawa: Centre for Trade Policy and Law.

Infoway. 2006. Our People. Montreal: Canada Health Infoway. Available at <http://www.infoway-inforoute.ca/en/WhoWeAre/OurPeople.aspx>, cited 17 July.

Kennedy, Mark. 2004. Liberals Softening Stance on Medicare Rules: Critics. *Ottawa Citizen*, 27 April, A8.

Knox, Paul. 2002. Do International Trade Agreements Threaten System of Medicare? *Globe and Mail*, 6 December, A14.

Kondro, Wayne. 2006. *Chaoulli* Decision Resonates One Year Later. 9 June. *Canadian Medical Association Journal Online.* Available at <http://www.cmaj.ca/news/09_06_06.shtml>.

Manley, John P., Pedro Aspe, and William F. Weld. 2005. *Creating a North American Community: Chairman's Statement.* Washington: Independent Task Force on the Future of North America, Council on Foreign Relations.

PACH. 2002. *A Framework for Reform: The Report of the Premier's Advisory Council on Health.* The Mazankowski Report. Edmonton: Premier's Advisory Council on Health, Government of Alberta.

Picard, André. 2006. Medicare Advocates Criticize Wait-Time Pledges. *Globe and Mail*, 17 January, A13.

Rachlis, Michael. 2006. Shortening the Health-Care Queues: Better Public Than Private Solutions to Medicare Wait Problem. *CCPA Monitor* 13, (1): 34.

Romanow, Roy J. 2002. *Building on Values: The Future of Health Care in Canada.* Ottawa: Royal Commission on the Future of Health Care in Canada.

Sandborn, Tom. 2006. Voters in Sweden Reject Market Medicine and Privatization. *CCPA Monitor* 13 (1): 30–1.

Sands, Andrea. 2006. Wait-Time Guarantees Called Benefit for Private Clinics. *Edmonton Journal*, 12 June, A12.

Sanger, Matthew. 2001. *Reckless Abandon: Canada, the GATS, and the Future of Health Care.* Ottawa: Canadian Centre for Policy Alternatives.

Sauvé, Pierre. 2002. *Trade, Education, and the GATS: What's In, What's Out, and What's All the Fuss About?* Paris: Trade Directorate, Organization for Economic Co-operation and Development.

SCC. 2005. *Chaoulli v. Quebec (Attorney General).* SCC 35. Ottawa: Supreme Court of Canada.

SCSAST. 2002. *The Health of Canadians: The Federal Role.* The Kirby Report. Ottawa: Standing Senate Committee on Social Affairs, Science and Technology.

SELA. 2003. Free Trade in the Americas. In *SELA Antenna, N. 68, 3rd Quarter.* Caracas: Latin American and Caribbean Economic System.

Sinclair, Scott. 2000. *GATS: How the World Trade Organization's New "Services" Negotiations Threaten Democracy.* Ottawa: Canadian Centre for Policy Alternatives.

– 2005. Supreme Court Health Ruling Oblivious to Trade Treaty Threats. Ottawa: Canadian Centre for Policy Alternatives.

Sinclair, Scott, and Jim Grieshaber-Otto. 2002. *Facing the Facts: A Guide to the GATS Debate.* Ottawa: Canadian Centre for Policy Alternatives.

SPP. 2005a. SPP Prosperity Working Groups. Washington: White House, US Government. Available at <http://www.spp.gov/prosperity_working/index.asp?dName=prosperity_work ing>.

– 2005b. Security and Prosperity Partnership of North America: Prosperity Agenda. Washington: White House, US Government. Available at <http://www.whitehouse.gov/news/releases/2005/03/20050323-1.html>.

– 2006. The Security and Prosperity Partnership of North America: Next Steps. 31 March. Washington: White House, US Government. Available at <http://www.spp.gov/factsheet.asp?dName=fact_sheets>.

Walker, Tom. 2002. *Privateer Watch: Who Is Sodexho?* Ottawa: Canadian Union of Public Employees.

– 2003. *BC Housekeeping Bad News for Workers, Patients.* Ottawa: Canadian Union of Public Employees.

WTO. 1998. *Services: GATS, Training Package.* Geneva: World Trade Organization.

15

Free Trade and Deep Integration in North America: Saving Canadian Culture

GARRY NEIL

Twenty years ago, a blue ribbon panel of US industry representatives chaired by Thomas H. Wyman, chairman and CEO of CBS Inc., conducted a survey of leading executives and trade associations that sought to identify "the major problems the motion picture and television, pre-recorded entertainment, publishing and advertising industries incurred in exporting their products and services." The final report, tabled with the office of the United States Trade Representative (USTR) in September 1984, is important because it explains to a great extent the negotiating posture of the United States in subsequent trade talks and in bilateral relationships. The various measures that Canada had developed to support its cultural industries, which were targeted by the panel, serve as a checklist against which we can judge subsequent Canadian actions in the cultural field. Successive governments have buckled to US pressure, and the slow erosion of Canadian cultural sovereignty can be traced directly to September 1984, when we found ourselves in the sights of this powerful panel.

The report entitled *Trade Barriers to US Motion Picture, Pre-recorded Entertainment, Publishing and Advertising Industries* (Wyman 1984) was designed initially to inform the position of the US government heading into the next meeting of the General Agreement on Tariffs and Trade (GATT). The survey results highlighted copyright infringement, particularly piracy of content, as the most significant problem facing the US industry. Thus, the first recommendation to the USTR was "that the US work toward the inclusion of intellectual property issues, including copyright, within the GATT trading rules" (Wyman 1984, 2). The US government embraced this recommendation, and the outcome of that round of GATT negotiations included the new Agreement on Trade Related Aspects of Intellectual Property Rights (TRIPS). While contemporary debates around TRIPS focus on pandemics, medicines, and the abuse of the patent system, it is clear that, in large part, the United States pushed hard for TRIPS in order to promote the interests of its entertainment industry.

Canada featured heavily in the Wyman Report, with Canadian cultural policy measures front-and-centre in virtually every area. Before we examine the measures the US industry executives targeted, let us first look at the history of Canadian cultural policies and the reasons Canada has been a world leader in using public policy tools to support its artists and cultural producers.

THE CANADIAN CULTURAL DILEMMA

Canada is a nation of only thirty-two million people, spread over the second largest landmass in the world. An "undefended" 5,500-kilometre border is all that separates us from the world's largest producer of cultural materials, and twenty-four million of us share a language and idiom with our southern neighbour. Canada is also an open market for cultural products. We value the free movement of cultural expressions, ideas, and information in all media as well as our access to arts, culture, and popular entertainment from abroad.

But other cultural producers have a competitive advantage over our own. For some, the advantage arises because they have a substantially larger domestic market, others are protected by language, and still others by physical distance. Cultural producers in some countries have enjoyed all three of these advantages and, like France and India, have capitalized on them and built strong domestic cultural industries.

In contrast, English Canadian cultural producers have a small domestic market, are right next door to the world's largest exporter of cultural materials, and are working in the same language as are their competitors. Several practical examples highlight the problems they face, particularly given the smaller market they serve. An independent television producer can expect to receive a licence fee of perhaps 20 percent to 30 percent of the overall budget from the primary client, a Canadian conventional broadcaster such as CTV, CanWest Global, or the Canadian Broadcasting Corporation (CBC). This producer must acquire the additional resources from specialized and smaller Canadian broadcasters, foreign sales, and supplemental markets. For an independent television producer in the United States, the situation is far different. A licence fee equal to 70 percent to 80 percent of the budget is generated from the conventional broadcaster (CCAU 2003). After one or two additional pre-sales, the US producer will be in a profit-generating position, which can be lucrative if the program does well in the syndication market. The reason for the substantially different licence fees is that the US broadcaster has larger audiences in the home market and can thus easily recoup the investment from advertising revenues. Even the biggest Canadian conventional broadcaster has a market only a fraction of the size and thus does not have an equivalent number of viewers to offer to the advertisers.

In addition, the US producer's budget will be far higher than that of the Canadian counterpart – three times or more – and this will translate into a production that will appear more sophisticated and attractive. In her 2003 report on the desperate state of Canadian television drama, broadcast executive Trina McQueen outlined what this means for a fictional Canadian series she called PMO (Prime Minister's Office), which she compared to the popular US show, *West Wing*. The budget for each hour of PMO would be perhaps $1.0 million compared to over $3.5 million for each hour of *West Wing*.

Here's what [the Canadian producer] can't buy that the Americans can:

1. Stars. The producer might see the Prime Minister's press secretary as the lead role in the series; and might believe that Kiefer Sutherland would be excellent in a Jim Munson-like role. The very lowest probable cost, if Kiefer felt very patriotic: $500,000 per episode ...
2. Writers. A series like *West Wing* will use between six and 12 writers in a season. PMO will be lucky to afford four.
3. Extras. In *West Wing* the press conference room will be filled with 30 actors playing reporters, even for a scene which lasts only a couple of minutes. On screen, the full room will generate a sense of excitement and tension. In PMO the press encounter might include two or three reporters in a mini-scrum.
4. Sets. The *West Wing* sets on the Warner's lot cover thousands of square feet, fully dressed. A camera can follow C.J. for five minutes through the sets as she leaves her office, walks down the hall to talk with Toby; walks down another hall towards the President's ante-room, enters the Oval Office and finds the President on the Patio. During her walk, an assistant director will have directed another 30 actors in background activities. The viewer will have a complete illusion of being in a busy White House. In PMO the press secretary will leave his office and walk across an empty hall to see the Prime Minister.

The list goes on, through shooting days, second units, extra locations, hit music and all the production values that Canadians see every evening. The expensive grammar of American television is the lingua franca for our viewers. Canadian producers must compete with talent, cunning and stories that are intensely relevant to their viewers. They do well. On a program budget cost per viewer, Canadian shows do as well or better than American shows. Unfortunately, this is no one's measure of success.

Moreover, before *West Wing* was picked up by NBC, the network had commissioned about 100 different scripts; and funded 10 to 20 pilots at a cost per hour of anywhere between US$2 and $4 million each. And hundreds of thousands of dollars will have been spent on audience research.

Here in Canada, the network that chooses to produce PMO will have commissioned, perhaps, five other scripts. There will be no pilots and no audience research. (McQueen 2003, 4–5)

Another challenge facing the Canadian industry is the cut-rate price of the works imported from the United States. The cost to the broadcaster for Canadian rights to *West Wing* might be $200,000 to $250,000 per hour, much less than the cost of the original one-hour Canadian television drama series. At the same time, the broadcaster will obtain far greater advertising revenues from *West Wing* than from the Canadian drama because it attracts a larger Canadian audience, which is drawn to it by the production values and the ubiquitous promotional system of the US entertainment industry.

The Canadian book publishing industry experiences similar disadvantages. The average Canadian print-run for a fictional work from a promising new author is 1,500 copies, while a US publisher's print-run will be 10,000 copies. The US publisher thus has a lower unit cost for each book. Since Canada does not have tariffs on the importation of the US-published works, the consumer price has been set by the cost of the cheaper imported work.

During my tenure in the 1990s as executive director of the Association of Canadian Publishers, the trade association of the Canadian-owned book publishing companies, a senior executive of a major Canadian publishing house told me what, in practice, this means for his bilingual firm. Since the price of an English-language Canadian trade paperback is set by the value of the imported book, he works backwards to determine whether or not a particular title can be published. Working from this artificial price-point, he subtracts the costs of distribution, marketing, and promotion. Next, he looks at his production costs, then his editorial expenses. Finally, he factors in some fee for the author and some profit for the firm. But when he publishes that same book in French, he approaches the finances in a more traditional business manner, by starting with the author's fee and editorial expenses, adding production costs and expenses to get the work to the bookstore. The final calculation is a mark-up that will provide a profit to the house and income for the bookseller. He can do that because the consumer price for the French-language book will be 30 percent higher than the English-language book. This is the case because, historically, the cost of books from his primary foreign competitors in France has been elevated by the high costs of the physical transportation of the books; thus, the higher consumer price is accepted as normal.

To counterbalance these inherent cost disadvantages, Canada must rely on public policies and programs that attempt to level the playing field for the independent television producer, book and magazine publisher, music company, and other producers of Canadian artistic expressions. Most Canadians accept that this approach is one of the costs of maintaining our national identity. Politicians of all political stripes have implemented a series of measures, at both the federal and provincial levels, designed to allow our artists and cultural industries to emerge and develop. While we are happy to share our creative expressions with others, the primary objective of these programs and measures is to ensure we have choice in our own country.

The very first Canadian cultural policy was the 1849 postal subsidy, which allowed newspapers and journals to be mailed at a reduced rate and thus helped publishers to overcome the challenge of widely dispersed readers. The Canadian Radio Broadcasting Corporation, forerunner of the CBC, was established in 1932 to provide a Canadian alternative to the rapidly developing US radio broadcasters. The National Film Board was created in 1939. Most of the support measures and programs were introduced after the 1951 report of the Massey-Lévesque Royal Commission on National Development of the Arts, Letters and Sciences (Massey and Lévesque 1951). The report recommended aggressive public support measures, including the formation of the Canada Council. It is therefore not surprising that it is in this same period that Canadians began to have access to Canadian artists and that some of our writers, actors, and singers became significant international stars.

Canada has developed and maintained a wide range of sophisticated cultural policy tools, including:

- limits on foreign ownership of cultural industry firms in publishing, film distribution, broadcasting, and the music industry;
- financial subsidies for domestic artists and cultural producers in all media;
- content regulations that guarantee shelf space for Canadian materials, especially in radio and television;
- preferential treatment of domestic films and television shows, broadcasters, books and CDs, including regulations implemented by the Canadian Radio-Television and Telecommunications Commission (CRTC);
- preferential treatment of domestic rights holders in copyright laws;
- government agencies, like public service broadcasters, film institutes, heritage institutions, and a host of others;
- rules requiring commercial interests to direct resources to the production and promotion of domestic material; and
- special taxes or tax concessions that support production.

CANADA-UNITED STATES FREE TRADE AGREEMENT: THE SELL-OUT BEGINS

Prior to the Canada-United States Free Trade Agreement (CUFTA), there were virtually no external limits on our ability to develop our cultural programs and measures in a way that made sense for Canada. The only significant multilateral trade agreement, the 1947 GATT, contains a specific exception for cinema screen quotas, and most believe that this exception would sustain television and radio content quotas as well, in the unlikely event of another nation challenging them. To succeed, any challenge would first have to demonstrate that a television show or film is a good and, thus, that the rules of GATT apply. However, if the challenge did succeed, there would be a downside for the Hollywood studios. US films and television shows would then be susceptible to an action on the grounds they are "dumped" into foreign markets as they are sold substantially below the normal price set in the US market.

Although there was considerable debate over the cultural implications of CUFTA during its negotiation, Canadians were assured that their culture would never be traded away. When the terms of the agreement were released the "Cultural Exemption" was trumpeted as the solution since, theoretically, it meant that all of the cultural industries we knew at the time were outside the terms of the agreement and that Canada retained all of its rights to regulate, promote, and encourage these industries. But what did the deal really mean for culture?

When Wyman compiled his survey of industry executives for his September 1984 report, his respondents were vigorous in their condemnation of Canada. US industry executives regarded copyright infringement issues as the most serious barrier, and Canada made the list as a "problem area." Of primary concern was the fact that the signals of US television stations were taken by Canadian cable television companies and redistributed to consumers outside the normal range of the broadcast signal without any compensation. As part of the CUFTA settlement, Canada agreed to introduce a "retransmission right" in the Copyright Act with regard to distant signals. Canadian cable and satellite companies now pay royalties for the television and radio signals they pick up and redistribute to consumers beyond the range of the terrestrial microwave broadcast facility. This right was provided to both Canadian and US copyright owners, although the bulk of the royalty flows to US rights holders since their signals are more likely to be retransmitted to a "distant" market. The measure became effective with CUFTA in 1989.

In a section entitled "Restriction on Earnings, Discriminatory Taxation or Limitations on Rental Terms and Royalties," Wyman's report singled out Canada and France for placing the most serious limitations on US operations. While there is no discussion in the main report about what specific Canadian tax measures concerned US industry executives – and Canada certainly has no measures that restrict the flow of capital from a subsidiary to the foreign parent company – it is likely to have been the provisions of Section 19.1 of the Income Tax Act. Since 1976 Canada had maintained certain restrictions on advertising expenditures, directed at ensuring maximum support for Canadian content material and cultural producers. In particular, under Section 19.1 Canadian taxpayers could not deduct as a business expense the costs of advertising in certain non-Canadian media. These included US border television and radio stations whose signals were received in Canada and US magazines, including their split-run derivatives. To qualify as a Canadian magazine, a periodical had to be Canadian-owned and controlled, had to contain 80 percent Canadian editorial content, and had to be typeset and printed in Canada. This last requirement was eliminated as part of the CUFTA settlement.

Wyman's report also covered the advertising industry, alleging that Canada maintained limits on the importation of foreign television commercials. While the CRTC had at one time in the 1970s considered imposing Canadian content requirements on television and radio commercials, it decided not to do so, since it was told that roughly 80 percent of all commercials broadcast on Canadian television were produced domestically at that time (AATC 2001). It also determined that content regulations would be too difficult to implement since broadcasters do not control which commercials are placed on their station. Instead, the CRTC accepted an informal industry agreement to maintain the existing level of Canadian content commercial production. That did not stop the Wyman Report from objecting to Canadian limitations on the US advertising industry. The third cultural issue in CUFTA was a specific agreement to include the advertising industry as a covered economic sector.

The effects of CUFTA, combined with global economic integration in the advertising industry, have brought profound changes to Canada's advertising industry over the past twenty years. Prior to CUFTA, five of the top ten advertising agencies in Canada were Canadian-owned; today, only one firm in the top ten is Canadian-owned. More important, we have witnessed a dramatic decline in the production of Canadian television commercials. According to a 2002 submission by an ad hoc industry coalition to the House of Commons Standing Committee on Canadian Heritage: "In 1997, the last year for which the detailed analysis was undertaken, fewer than 50 percent of the commercials broadcast by Canadian television services were created in Canada ... If the study were repeated today, the industry believes the results would be similar or worse" (AATC 2001, 2). The submission argued that the decline is more than an economic concern about the overall health of the television production industry and the earnings of creative talent. It noted that "the issue also has a cultural dimension. Commercials are a powerful cultural medium, a means of transmitting the mores, values, traditions, and lifestyle of a society to future generations and new citizens" (AATC 2001, 2).

Wyman and his committee also complained about the fact that it was not possible for foreign owned advertising firms to bid on Canadian government contracts, the most lucrative part of the business. Starting with several provinces in the 1990s, government business has been gradually opened to the giant foreign firms, most with their headquarters in the United States. In March 2003 the federal government announced its new policy for the procurement of advertising services, which included opening the process to foreign firms.

When it released the proposed CUFTA to the public, the government proudly pointed to Article 2005, which purported to "exempt" culture from the terms of the agreement. Government officials argued that the "minor" cultural measures in the agreement were good public policy for Canada. They said that the "notwithstanding" clause, which authorized commercial retaliation against any future cultural program "that would have been inconsistent with the terms of this agreement" save for the exemption, was merely a confirmation of existing US law and practice.

It is now clear that our sovereign and unfettered right to develop and implement cultural policies came to end with CUFTA. For the first time, we agreed to put certain policies in place primarily because a foreign government wanted them, not because they made sense for Canada. We also agreed to put limits on the kinds of policies and programs we would implement in the future. This US pressure on Canadian cultural policies has continued since the Wyman Report, and with each successive trade agreement and each bilateral squabble over a Canadian measure the scope for implementing public policy solutions to cultural challenges has narrowed.

In a 1986 article Canadian media commentator Joyce Nelson (1992) argued that the concept of the free trade agreement was essentially a US idea driven by unhappiness with the lack of "progress" in the multilateral trading forum and that, far from being an ancillary issue, the interests of the US entertainment industry were a primary motivating factor for the negotiations. While the free trade talks were getting under way, the government of Quebec was in the process of implementing a Cinema Act that, in its initial incarnation, would have been an aggressive move against Hollywood's domination of the Quebec cinema system. At the same time, the federal government was beginning to make similar noises about addressing the fact that Canadian movies received less than 3 percent of the available time in Canadian cinemas. Under the ownership rules then in effect, the government was also threatening to force Gulf and Western (the parent company of Paramount Pictures) to divest itself of the Canadian book publishing interests of Prentice-Hall, which it had indirectly acquired when it took over the US parent company.

In 1985 the federal government tabled the *Film Industry Task Force Report*, a comprehensive study of our inability to develop a Canadian film industry (Raymond and Roth 1985). According to the report, the principal problem was that Canada's distribution sector is foreign-owned and that

Canada, along with Mexico, is considered part of the US domestic market by the US film business. This is reflected, for example, in the fact that the collective bargaining agreements between the US industry and its unions stipulate that fees for "foreign" uses are not made until the films are distributed outside North America. The task force argued that Canada could begin to break this monopoly by first tackling the insistence of the US distributors that they acquire North American rights when they contract with a foreign or independent producer to distribute a film. If Canadian distributors could negotiate for Canadian-only rights to such films, the profits they would earn from the release could be used to increase their investment in Canadian movies. This would improve their audience appeal.

The president and CEO of the Motion Picture Association of America (MPAA), Jack Valenti, railed against these proposals. He threatened that his companies would boycott Quebec's theatres and might take similar action throughout Canada. US president Ronald Reagan, a strong supporter of Hollywood interests, raised this issue with Canadian prime minister Brian Mulroney at the infamous March 1985 Shamrock Summit held in Quebec City. Canada and Quebec both backed down. Quebec's Cinema Act was effectively gutted through regulations. The initial, very tentative steps announced with great fanfare by Canada's communication minister Flora Macdonald in 1987, including a watered-down Film Products Importation Bill, were also gutted, and the bill died on the Order Paper when the federal election was called in 1988. These cinema measures were thus also victims of the free trade negotiations.

As a result, Canadians are still denied an opportunity to watch Canadian movies in their own cinemas. In 2001 English-language Canadian movies – that is, films that are created, written, produced, directed, and performed primarily by Canadians – achieved a paltry 0.2 percent of domestic market share according to the industry press. During the past twenty years, Canada has become an important location for shooting Hollywood movies, but we make fewer movies that are Canadian in character and that use Canadian artists. In hindsight, Nelson's thesis about the central role of the US entertainment industry in the genesis of CUFTA appears profound, although it might be taking somewhat longer for the US industry to achieve its objectives than Wyman and his colleagues had originally expected.

PRESSURE ON
CANADIAN CULTURAL POLICIES CONTINUES

It is not surprising that the United States aggressively pursues the interests of its entertainment industry. A recent study reported that the US copyright industries rule the nation's economic roost. In 1999, creative industries, including movies, television programs, software, books, and music, accounted for nearly 5 percent of the US gross domestic product and employed 4.3 million people in the United States. Foreign sales and exports reached US$79.65 billion, and the positive balance of trade is greater here than for any other US economic sector. "The study confirms that the American copyright industries form the bedrock of the US economic landscape and are this nation's greatest trade assets," said the MPAA's Jack Valenti. "No other sector in this new millennium can claim to play as pivotal a role in the new economy" (Hollywood Reporter 2000). Or, one might add, claim as much attention from USTR.

By 2001 foreign sales and exports had reached more than US$89 billion. Movies alone accounted for US$10.85 billion of this amount, and foreign sales (not including Canada and Mexico) represented 53 percent of total box office receipts (Kilday 2004).

CUFTA was only the beginning of the erosion of Canada's cultural sovereignty. The Wyman Report argued that "cultural restrictions," including content rules and discriminatory regulations, were another serious problem for the US industry, and once again Canada topped the list of offenders. Pressure on Canada continued to grow throughout the 1990s and the capitulation continued.

When the CRTC licensed Canadian specialty television services in 1994, including New Country Network (NCN), it removed Country Music Television (CMT), a competitive US specialty channel, from the list of services that Canadian cable companies are permitted to carry. This change was made under a policy in place when CMT was initially authorized for Canadian carriage. The CRTC decision was challenged both by the US government and the company involved, and for the first time Washington threatened retaliation under the terms of CUFTA's "notwithstanding" clause. These actions were halted when CMT effectively entered Canada in partnership with NCN under a commercial deal. This settlement brought Canadians a channel that is simply a derivative of its US cousin and, in 1997, without any warnings or opportunity for public debate, the CRTC quietly announced that it would no longer enforce its policy that a competitive service would be removed when a similar Canadian service is licensed.

Other important content rules in broadcasting have been eroded as well. In a shift in television policy announced in 1999, the CRTC decided to deemphasize drama production and to remove from Canadian broadcasters the obligations to spend fixed minimum percentages of their revenues on "priority programming," the programs that are the most culturally significant (CTRC 1999). The effects of this policy have been profound, and the number of original Canadian television drama series available on our airwaves has declined from twelve to four in only three years, according to the media performers' union (the Alliance of Canadian Cinema, Television, and Radio Artists) and the scriptwriters' union (the Writers Guild of

Canada), both of which call Canadian drama "an endangered species" (CCAU 2003, 37).

The next battle was in 1999 when the United States challenged Canada's magazine support measures at the World Trade Organization (WTO). A split-run magazine is one that recycles US editorial content, inserts a so-called Canadian section, and then presents itself to advertisers as Canadian. To help level the playing field for Canadian magazines against this unfair practice, importation of US split-runs was prohibited by a long-standing tariff that was further supported by an excise tax introduced when technology allowed split-runs to circumvent the tariff border measure. The Canadian government also subsidized Canada Post so that it could provide a preferential postal rate to Canadian magazines that were being shipped across the country, and Section 19.1 of the Income Tax Act continued to discourage advertising in US magazines directed at the Canadian market. Canada argued that these measures were directed at the advertising content of magazines – a service – and thus should be judged against Canada's obligations under the WTO's General Agreement on Trade in Services (GATS). Under GATS rules, Canada has not committed its advertising sector. The United States argued successfully that the measures were directed at magazines, which are goods, and thus that the measures should be judged against GATT provisions. The WTO panel and the subsequent appellate body agreed. They found that Canadian and US magazines were "directly competitive and substitutable" and struck down the Canadian programs. The postal subsidy was lost on a technicality. While it is permissible to subsidize a domestic producer, the appellate body found that the postal subsidy was a subsidy to Canada Post and not to the individual magazine publishers. Canada was given a year to remove all of the measures.

Canada responded to the decision by eliminating the offending policies. It reorganized the postal subsidy so that financial support would be credited to individual magazine accounts, and it introduced a new law that prohibited split-run magazines from selling advertising in Canada. These changes should have satisfied Washington because this finally brought an end to Section 19.1 of the Income Tax Act, the magazine component of the act that Wyman had identified fifteen years earlier as a "barrier." Overall, however, the United States was not satisfied with the prohibition against selling advertising and threatened retaliation under CUFTA. Canada responded by effectively acquiescing to US demands and gutting the provisions of the new law. It is likely someone in government recognized that, since Canada had included its advertising industry under CUFTA, any discriminatory policy would have been susceptible to challenge under that agreement or under the North American Free Trade Agreement (NAFTA). As a consequence of these decisions, Canada can now support Canadian magazine publishers only by providing direct grants. It cannot use any of the other cultural policy tools it has historically relied upon. The problem with the grant-only approach was highlighted in the 2003 federal budget, when the government announced a reduction of more than 20 percent in the resources available to the magazine support program as part of a cost-cutting exercise (Canadian Heritage 2003).

Another item on the Wyman hit list was government-owned or government-subsidized distribution or production systems. The CBC, the National Film Board of Canada, and the provincial educational broadcasting services all fall under this heading. The report signalled the importance of this area when it stated that these subsidized agencies were "not just a problem with the USSR and China but with some major trading partners such as Canada" (Wyman 1984, 21). In addition, governments at all levels have various programs that provide financial support to film and television producers, new media developers, the music industry, book and magazine publishers, and individual artists that enable them to practise their craft and make their work available to audiences and cultural producers.

It is difficult to analyze how Canadian public policy has developed over the past twenty years in the area of direct public expenditures because there is a constant flux in funding various aspects of cultural activities. Over the years there have been winners and losers. But there has been a clear decline in several critical areas. For example, the total federal grant to the CBC (operating, capital, and working capital) calculated in 2001 dollars declined from $1,280.9 million in 1990–91 to $901.1 million a decade later. This represents a decrease of almost 30 percent in the decade ending 2000/01 (FRIENDS 2001). Overall, federal spending on culture totalled $2.7 billion in 1997–98, almost 8 percent lower than in 1990–91, according to Statistics Canada. Funding of the performing arts by all levels of government in Canada declined through the 1990s by 12.9 percent (Statistics Canada 2002). While Prime Minister Jean Chrétien's and Heritage Minister Sheila Copps's 2001 announcement of additional resources for the cultural sector was welcomed by the community, the additional resources were not sufficient to replace the monies lost in the 1990s to a succession of slash-and-burn budgets and are only guaranteed through 2006. These developments highlight the reason most cultural activists prefer legislative and regulatory measures to public subsidies (i.e., because they are less prone to shifting political whims).

Each year, the USTR publishes a foreign trade barriers report that outlines its continuing concerns about measures maintained in other countries. Canadian cultural policy measures continue to be listed as irritants, and the report continues to have an impact. For example, the 2003 report noted that the CBC was prohibited from showing popular non-Canadian feature films during peak viewing hours, and this was viewed as a barrier to Hollywood sales (USTR 2003). In August 2003 the CRTC eliminated this CBC licence condition.

EROSION OF FOREIGN OWNERSHIP LIMITS

The next series of measures targeted by Wyman were the restrictions on foreign ownership, where Canada was cited as being a "particularly troublesome area" and was placed close to the top of the hit list. Wyman's report argued that "successful distribution of their product depends on a well-orchestrated pattern and timing of release" that could only be achieved through direct subsidiaries, not partnership arrangements (Wyman 1984, 22). Perhaps the greatest erosion of Canadian policies since the negotiation of CUFTA has been in this field.

An important belief underlying Canada's cultural policies since the early days has been that Canadian ownership will bring more Canadian presence and that Canadians are more likely than are non-Canadians to tell our stories and to reflect our worldview. Statistics Canada reports from all of the cultural industries bear this out: Canadian-owned firms are responsible for the overwhelming preponderance of production by Canadian artists. For example, over 80 percent of Canadian books and virtually all movies and television programs that are Canadian in content and character are produced by Canadian-owned firms (Canadian Heritage 2001).

In 1985 Communications Minister Marcel Masse responded to critics who warned that the proposed CUFTA would have dire consequences for Canadian cultural industries by convincing cabinet to implement the Baie Comeau foreign ownership policy, which prohibited the sale of a Canadian-owned publisher to a non-Canadian and stipulated that, if a foreign firm indirectly acquired a Canadian subsidiary as part of a takeover of another foreign firm, then it would have to divest its interest in the Canadian subsidiary. The policy was expanded later to cover record producers and film and video distributors. In the case of distributors, it prevented the establishment of any new foreign firm in Canada except where the sole activity is to distribute proprietary products (these are products in which they had invested at least 50 percent of the production costs or held worldwide release rights).

As a result of this policy, Gulf and Western was required to sell Ginn Publishing, the Canadian publishing interests of Prentice-Hall. Because there was no successful Canadian bidder for the company, it was purchased in 1988 by the Canadian Development and Investment Corporation (CDIC). In a move that received a great deal of publicity at the time, the firm was sold back to the new US parent of Prentice-Hall in 1994. At the time, it was revealed that CDIC had paid three times more than the highest private-sector offer for the company in 1988 and had sold it back for the same amount six years later.

The resolve of the federal government to maintain Canadian ownership in the cultural industries has weakened significantly over the years. Soon after it was implemented, the Baie Comeau policy was amended to provide that a foreign firm could acquire a Canadian subsidiary if the transaction was "of net benefit to Canada." Instead of forced divestment, the Foreign Investment Review Agency (FIRA) began to approve the acquisitions when the foreign firms offered benefits, such as job guarantees. This approach generated some troubling consequences for Canadian cultural industries. Most troubling was the requirement that foreign firms working in Canada publish Canadian authors and record Canadian musicians. This obligation increased the value of leading Canadian artists as they became sought after by the large multinational firms. Although this benefited some artists, who signed lucrative deals, the policy hurt Canadian firms as they were generally too small to compete with these lucrative contracts and could not offer the foreign distribution. As a result, Canadian firms lost an important revenue stream that, previously, they had used to reinvest in the development of up-and-coming Canadian talent.

More recent examples of the erosion of Canadian ownership rules include the decision in 2002 to permit the sale of Distican, one of Canada's largest book distribution companies, to US giant Simon and Schuster, and the permission given to Amazon.ca to enter the Canadian market, thus weakening independent booksellers. The government also allowed the effective disposition of McClelland and Stewart (M&S) to the German conglomerate Bertlesmann AG and to the University of Toronto Press. It also allowed the sale of 49 percent of CDG Books/Macmillan to IDG Books – a sale that led to the recent complete absorption of Macmillan by Wiley Publishing Inc., another of the world's big publishers. With the bankruptcy of Stoddard Publishing, the three largest Canadian book publishing firms of the 1980s and 1990s (including Canada Publishing Corporation and M&S) have either ceased to operate or been radically transformed. These firms were a critical part of the global success of Canadian literature, and these developments do not bode well for a positive future for Canadian publishing or literature.

In the recorded media, the ownership rules governing telecommunications companies, cable television firms, and broadcasters were standardized in 1996 as part of the federal government's *Convergence Policy Statement*, which recognized that there would be increasing competition between them (Industry Canada 1996). At the same time, the foreign ownership limits in the broadcasting and cable sectors were increased. As of 2004 foreign interests were limited to no more than a 20 percent direct interest and up to one-third of a holding company, effectively permitting foreign ownership of up to 46.7 percent (Canadian Heritage 2004). But even that is not enough for some, and, in 2003, the House of Commons Industry Committee recommended that the rules be relaxed even further (SCIST 2003). In the same year, the House of Commons Standing Committee on Canadian Heritage recommended that the restrictions be retained (SCCH 2003).

Following the election of the Conservative Party government in 2006, there has been a new push to permit greater foreign ownership of Canada's telecommunications, broadcasting, and cable companies. The report of the federal Telecommunications Policy Review Panel released in March 2006 recommends that the government relax the ownership rules for these sectors and appoint a panel to review Canada's broadcasting policy in order to look at how Canadian content regulations can be maintained if ownership rules are relaxed (TPRP 2006). In early 2006, Canada joined nine other WTO members in a plurilateral request to twenty-three other member countries that seeks the removal of all limits on foreign investment in the domestic telecommunications sector (Sinclair 2006).

DEFENDING AGAINST CULTURAL ASSIMILATION

Given the weakening of Canadian cultural policies since the implementation of CUFTA, it is no wonder that Canadians are concerned about cultural survival. According to a 2002 Leger Marketing Poll, "six out of 10 Canadians feel the prevalence of US culture in the country was a threat to our own culture's survival" (CP 2002). Statistics Canada reports that, despite Canadian cultural exports rising to a record $2.3 billion in 2002, Canada also imported a record $3.6 billion worth of foreign cultural goods, from films, magazines, and CDs to art, sheet music, and architectural plans. The StatsCan report doesn't include cultural services such as performances or broadcasts. The United States dominated cross-border trade, accounting for 96 percent of Canadian cultural exports and 80 percent of imports. Imports from the United States rose 1.5 percent to $2.8 billion after three years of decline (Statistics Canada 2003). The figures are misleading though since Canada's cultural "exports" include the value of US movies and television programs that are produced in Canada. These on-location shoots account for more than half of the total export volume.

Since Thomas Wyman tabled his report, Canadian culture has been on the defensive, and a succession of governments has whittled away important policies in the face of relentless US pressure. CUFTA's cultural "exemption" is clearly inadequate, and extending it to the North American Free Trade Agreement only made the situation worse since NAFTA covers more sectors of economic activity than does CUFTA. The agreement repeats the CUFTA cultural exemption and its definition of cultural industries. This is significant because it fails to cover important aspects of culture such as the performing arts, visual arts, heritage, and crafts, which were outside the provisions of CUFTA but are now captured by NAFTA. Furthermore, there is no dynamic element to the definition of cultural industries: it includes only those sectors known at the time and not those that will appear in the future. Thus, the new media industry is not covered despite the fact that it is likely to be the most culturally significant in this century. In addition, we cannot imagine what economic sectors will become culturally important in the decades ahead. There is also no cultural exemption in the WTO agreements, and the proposed Free Trade Area of the Americas (FTAA) would simply continue NAFTA's exemption for Canada.

Two trade lawyers who have studied this issue argue that, however inclusive one makes the definition, the "cultural exemption" is effectively meaningless or worse. Barry Appleton (1994, 191) has written that, "while the NAFTA contains a cultural industries exception, its effect may be seen to be more diplomatic in nature than legal. Since the exemption does not protect a Party from retaliation for relying upon it, it provides little actual protection for a Party's cultural industries." Steven Shrybman has an even harsher interpretation: "In fact, Article 2005 is merely an exercise in sophistry that offers no effective protection for Canadian culture." He argues that the article "may actually expose Canadian cultural support programs ... to even harsher treatment than would be visited upon other measures that offend free trade constraints." This is so because it allows for automatic retaliation "without going through the consultation and negotiations provisions of NAFTA." In other words, in the absence of Article 2005 the United States would have to go through the normal NAFTA dispute settlement procedures if it found a Canadian cultural policy to be offensive. With this article, it can skip the dispute settlement process and automatically apply sanctions (Shrybman 2001, 32–3).

CONVENTION ON CULTURAL DIVERSITY

In 1998, when he was appearing before a BC legislative committee considering the potential cultural implications of the Multilateral Agreement on Investment, Canadian actor R.H. Thomson argued that what Canada needs is a global charter of cultural rights. The charter would be specific to culture, would permit countries to support their own artists and cultural producers, and would require the huge multinational media conglomerates to support local and diverse cultures. At the same time, the cultural industries Sectoral Advisory Group on International Trade (SAGIT), a government advisory board, was developing its concept for a new instrument on cultural diversity, which it presented in its February 1999 report (SAGIT 1999). In the SAGIT vision, the new instrument would:

• acknowledge the importance of cultural diversity;
• establish rules on what kinds of measures countries could use to protect that diversity; and
• establish how trade disciplines and measures adopted in conformity with these rules would co-exist.

The concept of a legally binding convention to promote cultural diversity has been the primary catalyst for the launch of significant global cultural diversity movements both among governments and within civil society. The world's culture ministers are organized in the International Network on Cultural Policy, and the parallel civil society group – the International Network for Cultural Diversity (INCD) – brings together non-governmental organizations working to counter the adverse effects of globalization on the world's cultures.[1] Initially, the work of both the ministers' network and the INCD was directed at building a consensus on the need for a new convention on cultural diversity.

The concept was quickly embraced in other developed countries, which had come to share the Canadian concern over increasing pressures to subject cultural goods and services to the disciplines of the trade and investment treaties. The competitive advantages that cultural producers from some of these countries have enjoyed are breaking down as technology eliminates the protection of physical distance and English-language production dominates world markets. Governments and civil society groups in the developing world embraced it for complementary reasons. While these governments generally lack sophisticated cultural policies and have few resources to support local artists and cultural producers, they saw that, if it was to achieve its objectives, the convention would need to be a vehicle to promote cultural development.

The network of culture ministers decided that UNESCO, the UN's cultural arm, was the appropriate agency through which to develop the convention, and it agreed to take on this task in October 2003. Within a remarkably short time frame for such a controversial proposal, UNESCO succeeded in drafting, negotiating, and finalizing the terms of the Convention on the Protection and Promotion of the Diversity of Cultural Expressions within two years (UNESCO 2005). At the October 2005 meeting of the General Conference, UNESCO's governing body, the convention was adopted overwhelmingly, with 148 states voting in favour and only two, the United States and Israel, voting against. Four states abstained.

The new UNESCO convention is an important political tool that confirms the right of states to take actions in support of their own artists and cultural producers as well as in favour of cultural diversity. It confirms in international law the dual nature of cultural activities, goods, and services as having both economic and cultural value. The convention defines the issues in a way that clarifies the challenges and gives states the scope to respond to the changing technological and political environment. While civil society activists failed in their efforts to ensure the convention has equivalent status to the trade and investment agreements, at least in the short term, it does provide a focus and a forum for states to continue to work together and with civil society to achieve, in the long term, the objective of carving out cultural goods and services from the trade and investment agreements.

The convention is also an important political tool for cultural development. By outlining the range of measures that states can take to promote their domestic cultural capacity, it can act as a model for countries that do not yet have developed cultural policies. Civil society groups can use it in their advocacy work. By enunciating detailed measures that developed countries should use to support the development of cultural capacity and creative industries in countries of the global South, it has established benchmarks for the former to meet. It may well exercise moral suasion on these states to take the actions contemplated.

The convention is now open for ratification, and it will come into effect once thirty states have acceded to it. Since the European Commission has endorsed and will become a party to the convention, all members of the EU are obliged to ratify it as well. Thus, it should not be difficult to obtain the minimum number of ratifications. However, there is much work to be done to ensure that the convention is implemented as effectively as possible. Article 21 requires parties to work together to promote the convention's principles in other international forums. To have any real impact in the WTO, there will need to be sixty to seventy-five or more signatory states, with an appropriate geopolitical and economic balance, working together to promote cultural diversity principles. UNESCO will need to improve its statistics in order to track the global exchange of cultural contents and the international movement of artists from the South. States will need to provide adequate resources to the new International Fund for Cultural Diversity created by the convention.

While key civil society participants in the UNESCO process believe the convention fell short of the objectives, its adoption represents a watershed moment for the cultural diversity movement and for Canada. When it comes into effect, Canada will regain some measure of the cultural sovereignty it has lost since negotiations for CUFTA were launched. While Wyman and his colleagues would be disappointed to see the first reversal of their fortunes, Canadians will benefit from having access to far more diverse cultural contents in all media, including a wide range of high-quality and popular Canadian choices.

NOTES

1 Their websites are < http://incp-ripc.org> and < http://www.incd.net>, respectively.

REFERENCES

AATC. 2001. Submission to the Standing Committee on Canadian Heritage, House of Commons. Ottawa: Alliance for Advertising Tax Credits.

Appleton, Barry. 1994. *Navigating NAFTA: A Concise User's Guide to the North American Free Trade Agreement.* Toronto: Carswell.

Canadian Heritage. 2001. *Canadian Arts and Culture: Tomorrow Starts Today.* Ottawa: Canadian Heritage, Government of Canada.

– 2003. *Government of Canada Modifies Its Support Programs for Canadian Magazines and Periodicals.* News release, 8 July. Ottawa: Office of the Minister of Canadian Heritage.

– 2004. *Annex 2: Canadian Heritage Review of Foreign Investments.* Ottawa: Canadian Heritage, Government of Canada.

CCAU. 2003. *The Crisis in English-Language Drama: A Report Prepared by the Canadian Coalition of Audio-Visual Unions.* March. Toronto: Coalition of Canadian Audio-visual Unions.

CP. 2002. Sixty Per Cent of Canadians Feel Culture Is Threatened by US: Poll. *Canadian Press,* 30 June.

CTRC. 1999. *Building on Success: A Policy Framework for Canadian Television.* CTRC PN 1999-91. Ottawa: Canadian Radio-Television and Telecommunications Commission.

FRIENDS. 2001. *Follow the Money: Who Paid for Canadian Television, 1990–2000?* Toronto: Friends of Canadian Broadcasting.

Hollywood Reporter. 2000. Creative Industries Top Trade Assets for US. *Hollywood Reporter,* 13 December. Available at <http://www.lexisnexis.com/>

Industry Canada. 1996. *Convergence Policy Statement.* Ottawa: Spectrum Management and Telecommunications, Industry Canada.

Kilday, Greg. 2004. Piracy, Recorded B.O. Hot Topics at ShoWest Opener. *Variety,* 23 March. Available at <http://www.variety.com/>.

Massey, Vincent, and Father Georges-Henri Lévesque. 1951. *Report of the Royal Commission on National Development in the Arts, Letters, and Sciences, 1949–1951.* Ottawa: King's Printer.

McQueen, Trina. 2003. *Dramatic Choices.* Ottawa: Canadian Radio-Television and Telecommunications Commission (CRTC).

Nelson, Joyce. 1992. Losing It in the Lobby: Entertainment and Free Trade. In *Sign Crimes/Road Kill: From Mediascape to Landscape,* 71–90. Toronto: Between the Lines Press.

Raymond, Marie-José, and Stephen E. Roth. 1985. *Canadian Cinema: A Solid Base – Report of the Film Industry Task Force.* Ottawa: Film Industry Task Force, Queen's Printer.

SAGIT. 1999. *Canadian Culture in a Global World, New Strategies for Culture and Trade, the Cultural Industries Sectoral Advisory Group on International Trade.* Ottawa: Queen's Printer.

SCCH. 2003. *Our Cultural Sovereignty: The Second Century of Canadian Broadcasting.* June. Ottawa: Standing Committee on Canadian Heritage, House of Commons.

SCIST. 2003. *Opening Canadian Communications to the World.* April. Ottawa: Standing Committee on Industry, Science and Technology, House of Commons.

Shrybman, Steven. 2001. *World Trade Organization.* 2nd ed. Toronto: Lorimer.

Sinclair, Scott. 2006. The GATS Negotiations and Canadian Telecommunications Foreign Ownership Limits. CCPA *Trade and Investment Briefing Paper,* March 27, 7(1).

Statistics Canada. 2002. Facing the Challenge: Performing Arts in the 1990s. *Focus on Culture* 14 (1): 1–8.

– 2003. Culture Trade and Investment Project: Data Tables. Available at <http://www.statcan.ca/english/freepub/87-007-XIE/data.htm>.

TPRP. 2006. Telecommunications Policy Review Panel: Final Report. Ottawa: Telecommunications Policy Review Panel, Industry Canada.

UNESCO. 2005. *Convention on the Protection and Promotion of the Diversity of Cultural Expressions.* Paris: United Nations Educational, Scientific and Cultural Organization.

USTR. 2003. *National Trade Estimate: Report on Foreign Trade Barriers.* Washington, DC: United States Trade Representative.

Wyman, Thomas. 1984. *Trade Barriers to US Motion Picture, Pre-recorded Entertainment, Publishing and Advertising Industries.* New York: CBS Broadcasting Inc.

16

Free Trade
and Quebec Models of Development

DORVAL BRUNELLE AND BENOÎT LÉVESQUE

In this chapter we bring to light the effects of free trade on the two models of development implemented in Quebec since 1960. First, we establish the influence of endogenous and exogenous factors on the first-generation model, that of the "Quiet Revolution"; second, we examine the free trade option in relation to a second-generation model perfected and implemented since the 1980s by Quebec Liberal Party (QLP) and Parti Québécois (PQ) governments (up until the elections of spring 2003). We argue that the free trade option has led to two interrelated sets of social practices: one that led to collaboration between social and economic actors in the establishment of a model of development in Quebec itself, and one that led the social actors to question the liberalization of trade instigated by the governments of Quebec and Canada.

We briefly describe the Quiet Revolution model before examining how and why social actors challenged it. We work with the hypothesis that Quebec is currently at a crossroads. On the one hand there is the prospect for deepening free trade and neoliberal policies (which appears to be the preference of the Jean Charest government); on the other hand, there is the emergence of a new paradigm of development that could lead to the establishment of a "second-generation" Quebec model – a model that would adapt the economy and its institutions to an open market while, at the same time, supporting efforts to temper the rigors of that market.

THE QUIET REVOLUTION

In 1960 the newly elected government of Jean Lesage engaged in a profound reform of the provincial administration and provincial institutions. Both internal and external factors played a role. Among the internal factors one can count the obsolescence of Quebec's institutions and bureaucratic apparatus, the electoral commitments made by the Quebec Liberal Party, and the restructuring of alliances among social actors (Brunelle 1978). The external factors had federal, provincial, and, most crucially, continental dimensions: at the continental level, what was crucial was, without question, the consolidation of an industrial axis around the Great Lakes area. Partly induced by a process of spatial expansion proper to North America, this movement took on new geo-political functions during the Cold War as development policies in the United States as well as in Canada favoured industries in the heart of the continent to the detriment of those on the East Coast (as well as Montreal and its harbour). The continental option led the federal government to encourage the industrialization of Ontario throughout the postwar period and, thus, separated the two large central provinces of the country – the former Lower and Upper Canadas – which had been the main beneficiaries of the previous phase of industrialization.[1] Finally, at the provincial level, the continental option consolidated relations between Queen's Park and Ottawa, and it pushed the provincial government to adopt a protectionist policy towards goods and services coming from other provinces. As a result of this evolution, Quebec found it increasingly difficult to gain access to outside markets, and its provincial budgetary deficit increased exponentially.

In the meantime, the Quiet Revolution was carried forward through a dialogue between the government and its three main socioeconomic partners: the business community, the unions, and the cooperative movement. All three partners understood that, from now on, economic and social development must have common and interrelated goals. The idea was to apply the ideas of John Maynard Keynes and those of William Beveridge, the founder of the British welfare state, to the provincial level. This project of modernization was one dear to the hearts of many French-Canadians, and for some it became tied to nationalist aspirations. The model was driven by economic growth sustained by planning and technical progress and by the values of universal access to collective and basic services – health care and education in particular – and even mass consumption.

This approach to development took for granted that the market should not be the only integrating force in society – a lesson that had been learned during the Great Depression and had been confirmed by the recession that followed the cessation of hostilities in Korea in 1953. For the unions and the cooperative movement, the Quebec state appeared to be the only possible entity that could negotiate with the business community and shape market forces to advance national development goals. One example of its ability to do this was the confrontation with the electricity cartel during the nationalization of Hydro-Québec in 1962; another was its takeover of collective services, which, up until then, had been provided by religious and charitable organizations.

The government became an entrepreneur in order to promote industrial diversification. Public spending in industry and manufacturing (excluding other levels of government) increased from 8.5 percent in 1961 to 26.8 percent of GDP in 1985 (Bourque 2000, 52). Several large state-owned enterprises were put in place in the wake of the nationalization of Hydro-Quebec, the main issue of the 1962 electoral campaign.[2] The percentage of companies under French-Canadian control in Quebec grew from 47.1 percent in 1961 to 61.6 percent in 1987. In the crucial sector of finance, it grew from 25.8 percent to 58.3 percent during the same period.[3] In the social sector, the Quiet Revolution of the 1960s and the Castonguay Reform of the 1970s favoured modernization, accessibility, and universality in education, social services, and health. However, the organization of these services was highly bureaucratic and hierarchical (Bélanger and Lévesque 1992). Social and health services were offered more and more in hospitals and social service centres rather than in local neighbourhoods (Vaillancourt and Jette 1999). Home care services remained underdeveloped, and the Local Centres for Community Services (*Centres locaux de services communautaires*, or CLSC) were underused until the end of the 1970s. Consequently, at that time, public authorities neglected community networks, prevention, and social determinants of health and well-being.

Meanwhile, in most OECD countries, the implementation of the Keynes-Beveridge development model was experiencing a number of important setbacks towards the end of the 1960s. This was amply confirmed by the magnitude of the international social protests and student movements during the course of 1968.[4] In Quebec, social movements explicitly questioned the model of the Quiet Revolution, its hierarchical approach, and its fake democratism. In the beginning of the 1970s social tensions reached their peak with the radicalization of the unions and the formation of small parties of the extreme left (Desy et al. 1980).

Carried to power in November 1976 within a highly charged social context,[5] the Parti Québécois (PQ) government published *Building Quebec* (*Bâtir le Québec*) in 1979 and *The Technological Turn* (*Le virage technologique*) in 1982 in order to adapt the Quiet Revolution model to changing times (Québec 1979, 1982). These two reports defended an option based on comparative advantage, industrial specialization, and international competition. They reflected a growing consensus that the first-generation model had become outdated, with some studies even concluding that Quebec's economy was poised to become deindustrialized (Canada 1982, 55).[6] Under the new "ride-the-winner" strategy, industrial policies would no longer assist companies in difficulty; rather, they would favour those that were innovative and capable of reaching foreign markets. This change of policy was important since the model of the Quiet Revolution had aimed at the establishment of a relatively self-sufficient economy and banked on diversification in order to support non-profitable sectors.

Henceforth, a new set of objectives was laid out: (1) the implementation of big industrial projects and the maximization of their economic effects on Quebec; (2) the development of a dynamic tertiary sector comprised mostly of specialized services for industries and consulting engineering; and (3) the development and exploitation of electronic technologies (Canada 1982).

In order to garner support for its strategy, the PQ government convened a series of socioeconomic summits to which the business community, the unions, and the cooperative movement were invited. Three national summits were held (1977, 1979, and 1982), along with close to thirty regional and sectoral summits. During the 1982 summit the Quebec Federation of Labour (*Fédération des travailleurs et travailleuses du Québec*, FTQ) presented a proposal to set up an FTQ Solidarity Fund (*Fonds de solidarité des travailleurs du Québec*), which was approved by the Quebec government and, soon after, by the federal government.[7] However, after the defeat of its sovereignty-association project in the referendum of May 1980, and in the wake of the budgetary crisis and unpopular measures taken during the short but severe recession of 1980–82,[8] the PQ government's economic policies lost popular support.[9]

In January 1985 the PQ held an extraordinary congress against the backdrop of a profound crisis, during which revisionist and orthodox positions clashed over the question of an alliance with the federal government. But if Premier René Lévesque's proposition to put the issue of sovereignty on the back-burner met with the approval of the delegates, it came at a high cost. Denis Vaugeois and Camille Laurin, ministers belonging to the orthodox wing, tendered their resignations, closely followed by Gilbert Paquette.[10] In February the protest gained momentum, and in June the premier announced that he was quitting political life.

The recourse to economic nationalism during the Quiet Revolution caused the economy to lag behind significantly both in external and Canadian markets. Even though Quebec exports to the United States had increased by 25 percent in 1984, in the rest of the country exports had grown by 33 percent, resulting in the continued decline of Quebec's share of Canadian exports to 16 percent by 1985 (Black 1985, 11). Throughout this period the most striking (and most widely publicized) indication of this decline was the exodus from Quebec of the headquarters of large Canadian and US corporations.[11] Moreover, the supporting role that the provincial government had played ended up costing it dearly: in 1986 the Quebec public debt had reached $60 billion, which was the equivalent of 56.6 percent of provincial GDP.[12]

FREE TRADE IN CONTEXT

The strategy implemented by Brian Mulroney's Progressive Conservative federal government relied on the reform of federal-provincial relations as well as on the negotiation of a free trade agreement with the United States. This had profound consequences for Canada's commercial policies and, as a result, on the Quebec model of development.[13] First, the federal government proposed to implement a "New Federalism" in order to gain the support of the provinces during the economic Summit of Regina convened in mid-February 1985.[14] Henceforth, commercial negotiations and constitutional reform were pursued in parallel, an important strategic move when one recalls that the premier of Quebec, Robert Bourassa, was, along with the premier of Alberta, most favourable to free trade with the United States. However, some economic sectors, notably small business, were opposed to free trade, which largely explains why negotiations were conducted very discretely.[15] The federal government's market-oriented and free trade strategy had important implications at the domestic level, as is evidenced by the creation, in the days following the federal elections, of a working group headed by Deputy Prime Minister Erik Nielsen and responsible for scrutinizing public programs. The group's mandate was to "examine the government's programs in order to simplify them and make them more understandable and accessible to their clientele" (Nielsen 1985, 11). The group surveyed 989 programs run by 126 ministries and government departments, which totalled spending costs of about $92 billion in the form of benefits allocated to individuals, companies, and provincial governments. All these programs were examined by mixed study groups composed of specialists from both private and public sectors which, "given the imperious necessity to reduce spending and the deficit, will attempt where possible to economize in all sectors" (Nielsen 1985, 11). Thus, it was made clear to all that the Conservative government was planning a profound reform of programs and institutions. Henceforth, the emphasis would be on the market, entrepreneurship, and regional dynamism rather than on large projects or a national plan. The Quebec Liberal Party government subscribed completely to this new vision.

THE EMERGENCE OF
A SECOND-GENERATION DEVELOPMENT MODEL

Upon winning the December 1985 elections, Robert Bourassa's government set up three working groups to develop its economic policy: one on privatization (Rapport Fortier 1986), one on governmental reorganization (Rapport Gobeil 1986), and one on deregulation (Rapport Scowen 1986). The content of these three reports was inspired by the neoliberalism prevalent in the United States and the United Kingdom at the time, and it was also in line with the recommendations of the Macdonald Report (1985). Key ministers within the Bourassa cabinet were actively involved in incorporating the Macdonald Report's recommendations into Quebec's development strategy.[16] But, paradoxically, in doing so, the Bourassa government was no longer aligning itself with the federal Liberals, who had established the commission, but with the Mulroney Conservatives, who had decided to make the commission's recommendations their own.

During the following eight years, the Quebec Liberal Party's economic policies pursued the following three goals: (1) the promotion of industry in key sectors such as aerospace, communications, public transit equipment, electrochemistry, engineering, and food and agriculture; (2) the preservation of key industries, such as petro-chemistry and pharmaceuticals; and (3) the promotion of exports (Canada 1982, 56–61). That being said, the Bourassa government did apply at least one recommendation coming out of *The Technological Turn* (*Le virage technologique*) concerning the implementation of megaprojects, and it proceeded with the building of hydro-electric power dams – a strategy denounced by its critics as "hydroelectric pharaonism."

The transition from a Quebec development strategy that emphasized self-sufficiency[17] to one based on openness and the promotion of exports had major consequences in many areas. Among the public enterprises and programs that were put into question by the Bourassa government were the Industrial Development Society (*Société de développement industriel, or sDI*) and the preferential policy known as the "buy at home policy" (*politique d'achat chez nous*). This policy had required the government and state-run companies to purchase from Quebec companies as long as their prices did not exceed those of their competition by more than 10 percent. The government hoped that this policy reversal would encourage the other provinces, which accounted for 40 percent of Quebec's small businesses exports, to further open their markets to Quebec products. The realignment of its economic policy also had considerable fallout in the social policy arena. For instance, in 1989 Minister of Labour Pierre Paradis piloted a profound reform of the social insurance regime by establishing the Positive Action Program for Work and Employment. This program was aimed at reducing the levels of social assistance received by those who were still able to work.

In his critical analysis of the Fortier, Gobeil, and Scowen Reports, the former minister of finance in the Lévesque cabinet, Jacques Parizeau, warned the Bourassa government against what he called the *virage majeur* (significant change of direction) it was about to make by entrusting Quebec's development to the private sector and market forces. He emphasized that, in a marketplace where the "mastodons" rule, it is important to preserve the pivotal role of the state in the creation, support, and expansion of private enterprise in Quebec. To make his point he highlighted the following cases: the role of the Quebec Deposit and Investment Fund (*Caisse de dépôts*) in the creation of Provigo (which was subsequently bought by Loblaws in 1998); the role of the General Financing Society (*la*

Société générale de financement [SGF]) in the development of the petro-chemical sector and the rescue of Domtar and Rexfor; the role of Hydro-Quebec during the expansion of subcontracting; and the role of the Quebec Stock Saving Plan (*Régime Épargne-Actions* [REA]) during the expansion of Cascades, a firm involved in paper making. Parizeau concluded his analysis by arguing that, if indeed the time had come to review and evaluate existing government programs, as well as to examine questions of "procurement, priorizing, and management," then "it would be ridiculously optimistic to imagine that the [role of the state in the] construction of the Quebec economy had come to an end" (Parizeau 1986). The message was no doubt received because the economic policies applied and sanctioned by the provincial liberals did at least try to temper the perverse effects of their liberalizing policies by lending timid support to the development of social and community initiatives – support that would be taken up and increased with the PQ's return to power in 1994. It is to this other dimension, which supports the idea of a second-generation model of development for Quebec, that we now turn.

Parallel to, and supporting, the market liberalization agenda, we saw the emergence of a new model of development. This model was a synthesis of the lessons learned from past experiences in Quebec and elsewhere, notably in the European Community. It was reflected, at the beginning of the 1990s, in a number of civil society-sponsored initiatives and in certain social and economic government measures. These experiments, financed in part with the support of the provincial and federal governments (Bélanger, Brunelle, and Deblock 1996, 341),[18] fell within the framework of a pluralist economy in which civil society, the state, and the market assumed important functions (Favreau and Lévesque 1996).

Thus, in certain specific sectors, the government shifted its role, no longer intervening as a planner but, rather, as a partner of private socioeconomic sectors. Within this context, increased competition placed a premium on innovation and encouraged the emergence of the "knowledge economy." Some companies responded by adopting new modes of governance, which sought to mobilize social dynamism and to obtain economic benefits in the form of social capital, confidence-building, learning communities, and the creation of an innovative milieu. Government was called upon to play the role of catalyst, facilitating synergies between economic and non-economic partners. Public intervention in the economy did not disappear but was transformed as industrial policies came to be articulated around a strategy of "integrated offers" (Matzner and Streeck 1991). Consequently, industrial policies were not goals in themselves but, rather, served to support policies in areas such as education, training, and research. They emphasized specialization in certain strategic sectors and encouraged the formation of industrial groups or local production systems

(Porter 1990). The idea was that, through dialogue and partnership, a new mixed economy that banked on the collaboration between the capitalist, public, and social sectors could emerge. This economy would be as different from the earlier administrated economy (which was based on government control) as it would be from the old mixed economy (in which the private and public sectors were separate from each other). The new mixed economy offered different challenges as it required striking a balance between dynamic market forces and public interest, between accountability and citizen participation, and between regulation and deregulation at the national and local levels (Monnier and Thiry 1997).

The fact that civil society played a central role in economic development was the result of demands formulated by a number of social actors such as unions, community and women's groups, local collectivities, cultural communities, and ecological groups. The PQ's return to power in 1994 confirmed this. During the economic summit of 1996 both community and women's groups were called upon to support the unions and the business community in their struggle against unemployment, poverty, and other social needs. Likewise, several intermediary authorities (such as the regional councils of development, sectoral discussion tables, and local partners) represented new areas where civil society organizations worked with government representatives to define and implement development strategies. Thus the role of the state was transformed from one of intervention to one of cooperation. This partnership was still timid, however, and social and economic actors did not participate to the same extent. The new model also tended to cause tensions within large unions, pitting partisans and opponents of these partnerships against each other.

At the same time, changes in the workplace were affecting participation (Lapointe et al. 2002). Even though Taylorist organization prevailed, it was put to the test by increased competition as well as by new technologies that required flexibility and further integrating the workforce to market requirements (the just-in-time model). These new approaches led to a reconsideration of the traditional labour organization that was manifested, for example, in a transition to teamwork and a review of areas of competence. They also led to a redefinition of the division of power between management and unionized labour, as is illustrated by the creation of joint committees and continuous negotiations (Bélanger, Grant, and Lévesque 1994; Grant, Bélanger, and Lévesque 1997). Since the beginning of the 1980s, workers' participation in the ownership of their companies as well as in profit-sharing schemes had, thanks to the establishment of workers' funds and worker-shareholder cooperatives, become a reality (Comeau and Lévesque 1993).

In the social domain the participation of civil society became unavoidable, given the in-depth reorganization of the welfare state (Giddens 1999).

Faced with persistently high levels of unemployment, social exclusion, and public debt, proponents of a "third way" looked to equity rather than to equality, targeted interventions rather than integral protection, and opted for active rather than passive measures. In short, the emphasis was on responsibility rather than on dependence. Welfare-state reform became polarized between two alternative forms: the first anchored social protection to the market and, in so doing, left the disadvantaged at the mercy of the charitable initiatives of civil society; the second favoured empowering individuals and collectives by developing a new relationship between social organizations and the state (Noêl 1996; Vaillancourt and Laville 1998). Accordingly, it became necessary to substitute a so-called "negative" approach to welfare, in which the welfare state reacts and repairs, with a "positive" approach, in which citizens are empowered or rehabilitated.

It was in this way that community organizations adopted a vision of development in which the boundaries separating the social and the economic were called into question. This was evidenced by the fact that the new social economy emphasized not only social and health services but also services related to local development (Favreau and Lévesque 1996). Under the Côté-Rochon reform, in social and health sectors, community organizations were accepted and recognized as partners. In socio-sanitation in particular, the reconfiguration of the welfare state was not accomplished through privatization and the commodification of collective services (Vaillancourt 1996, 1999). In short, the politics of openness and the advent of free trade and market liberalization mobilized social actors and unions, leading them to develop actions and strategies on two fronts: internally (against the perverse effects of liberalization) and externally (against free trade policies). On the internal front the unions and their allied social actors supported the more socially progressive initiatives of the PQ government, while on the external front, and particularly on the question of free trade, their stance was critical of the government.

For various reasons it is not easy to evaluate the impact that these social movements (and the inevitable tensions between strategies of participation and strategies of opposition) had on the second-generation Quebec model of development. The difficulty stems from the large number of mobilizations and the numerous battlegrounds in the areas of health, education, poverty, housing, the environment, and free trade. Another difficulty is that the social actors, be they from the women's, student, or union movements (to name only a few), were each engaged on several fronts at once, thus making it difficult to measure the effectiveness of each struggle in transforming the overall socioeconomic model. Finally, evaluating their overall impact is rendered all the more complex by the fact that, as noted earlier, cooperation at the top created enormous tensions within the organizations that were involved in the construction and establishment of a second-

generation model. In spite of these difficulties, it is clear that the mobilization against free trade, in particular, contributed to reinforcing the position
of these social actors as they looked for alternatives to the extreme liberalization of the market.

CONCLUSION

On the social front, the most important repercussion of the free trade
policies was the Lucien Bouchard government's decision to apply the zero-
deficit policy adopted by the G-8 during the 1995 Halifax summit. Moreover, by associating the main economic and social actors with its deficit-
reduction policy during the Summit on Employment and the Economy in
1996, the Bouchard government gave itself free reign to make deep cuts
in health and education while, at the same time, promoting their involvement in the social economy at the grassroots level in the dispensation of
social services. One of the first results of the summit was a focus on deregulation and on eliminating "red tape" through the creation of the Advisory
Group on Regulatory Streamlining under Bernard Lemaire, president of
Cascades.[19]

As for economic development, the government shifted away from its traditional approach of "picking the winners" (i.e., providing direct support
to preferred companies) to a strategy that provided subsidies to entire
sectors of production, as was the case with the policy that allotted 1
percent of the government budget to research and development (R&D)
training. However, in most areas, the government continued to rely on a
top-down model of development that was characteristic of the Quiet Revolution era. This was particularly evident when it came to municipal
mergers and regional development. In fact, the inflexible manner in which
the government handled these two issues played a significant role in its
defeat in 2003, despite its implementation of other initiatives that had a
social democratic content, such as the law against poverty and the creation
of new daycare centres.

Just as the first-generation Quiet Revolution model of development
involved political options, so did the so-called second-generation model of
development. To highlight this we must evaluate the latter's performance
and compare it to those of other national development models. To the
extent that its objectives included sustainability, quality of life, and social
cohesion based on equity rather than on equality, its choice of objectives
had a profound impact on the model itself. This was evident in the debates
over its respective virtues and defects. One side argued that it had contributed to a decrease in poverty levels and unemployment as well as to the
reduction of disparities in income and regional development, while the
other side denounced its bureaucratic rigidity and the resultant high levels

of taxation.[20] Furthermore, the second-generation model drew criticism as much from within the government as from without, and this dissension foretold a difficult future (Brunelle and Drouilly 2002).

This brings us back to social actors and the tension between their two types of response to the second-generation model of development: one response favoured collaboration between social and economic actors in the hope of creating a new model of development, and the other favoured confrontation in order to forestall the implementation of neoliberal policies that would harm public programs. The tension between these two responses goes a long way towards explaining the PQ's electoral defeat. More fundamentally, we could go further and ask if the approaches, techniques, and strategies applied by successive Liberal and PQ governments between 1985 and 2003 really constituted a single model of development or whether they were, in fact, an eclectic mix of models. The latter view is supported by the fact that the governments had a difficult time manoeuvring between the imperatives of market liberalization on the one hand, and social, community, and cooperative imperatives pushed by important socioeconomic actors on the other.

In the meantime, the Charest government, which came to power in April 2003, appears to be clearly in favour of revising whole sections of the second-generation Quebec model and securing Canadian federalism. In so doing, it places itself directly in line with the previous Bourassa governments. Besides, by immediately taking on the unions, the government's strategy called into question the alliances that had been woven between important socioeconomic actors during the 1996 Economic Summit. After more than three years in power, and despite persistent opposition coming out of civil society organizations, the government was able to further its own agenda and to liberalize the Quebec economy to a certain degree.

However, the general hypothesis upon which the Quebec model of development had been built was that it was impossible to pursue both a better economic integration within Canada and a profitable integration with the US economy. Indeed, the strengthening of the Quebec model is intimately tied to the constraints of the continentalization of the Canadian economy, where north-south trade patterns prevail over east-west commercial ties. In order to fully implement its own model, a nationalist and social-democratic Quebec government must maximize the possibilities and prerogatives offered by a fully decentralized federalism. This was the basic idea behind the promotion of a type of sovereignty tied to economic association with Canada. However, from a Canadian perspective, the constraints of economic continentalization led the federal government to infringe on provincial fields of jurisdiction, notably in education and social services, in order to strengthen Canadian solidarity and to promote Canadian values. At times in the recent past, the two approaches have proven incompatible, as the federal-provincial negotiations surrounding the Social Union Framework Agreement (SUFA) of February 2002 showed all too well, where, once again, Quebec found itself at odds with the other provinces and refused to sign on.

The option defended by the Charest government does not question the reality of economic continentalization but, rather, seeks to promote an individualistic approach to integration by loosening the existing ties between social actors and their membership. This strategy rests on the belief that the weakening of the unions, and other social actors such as those involved in the women's and student movements, could pave the way for further federal intrusions into fields of provincial jurisdiction, which, in turn, should lead to an improvement of relations within the federal system. But this strategy could prove short-sighted indeed if the next phase of continental integration should force the federal government to liberalize precisely those sectors (e.g., education, health, and other social services) that had been shielded from privatization and deregulation while they were under provincial jurisdiction. Over the past years, union and social mobilization have shown that the Charest government's option is a difficult one to sustain, and only the next provincial election will show to what degree these social oppositions can be translated into a political stance of consequence.

NOTES

This article was translated from French by Daphné Brunelle.

1 Both sectoral free trade agreements signed by the federal government at the time, the Defence Production Sharing Agreement of 1956 and the Auto Pact of 1965, reinforced the implementation of heavy industry in Ontario.

2 Among these initiatives we can mention: the General Financing Society (*la Société générale de financement*) (1962); the steel state enterprise SIDBEC (1964); the Society for Mining Exploration (*la Société d'exploration minière*) (1965); the Deposit and Investment Fund (*la Caisse de dépôt et placements*) (1965); the Society for Industrial Development (*la Société de développement industriel*) (1971); the James Bay Energy Society (*la Société d'énergie de la Baie James*) (1971); the Housing Development Society (*la Société de développement immobilier*) (1971); the Quebec Society for Agricultural Initiatives (*la Société québécoise d'initiatives agro-alimentaires*) (1975), and the National Asbestos Society (*la Société nationale de l'amiante*) (1978).

3 Data are from Vaillancourt and Leblanc (1993), as cited in Bourque (2000, 63).

4 These mobilizations and protests were stirred up in no small part by the Vietnam War.

5 Two famous conflicts, the strike at United Aircraft and the strike of the *Gens de l'Air*, had a profound impact on the electoral campaign.

6 The document also recognized that "coordination should prevail between the federal and Quebec programs."

7 The *Fonds* was created in 1983. Its assets reached $4.4 billion on 31 December 2002 The fund's mission is to invest in Quebec firms and to provide them with services in order to promote their development and to create or maintain jobs (FTQ 2003).

8 In 1982 Quebec lost around 140,000 jobs, 50,000 of which were in the manufacturing sector, and unemployment rose to 15 percent (Bourque 2000, 64).

9 The PQ government established the Ministry of Employment and Concertation in 1984.

10 In addition to the names cited, this crisis led to the departure of Jacques Parizeau, Jacques Léonard, Denise Leblanc-Bantey, and Louise Harel, ministers who were all prominent members of the PQ government.

11 Here is a partial list: Northern Telecom moves to Nashville, Seagram to New York, *Ciment Lafarge* to Dallas, AMCA de C.P. (previously Dominion Bridge) to Hanover. Moreover, other large Canadian companies (like Canadian Pacific, Molson, and Bell Canada) and entire sectors (like banks and insurance companies) that maintained their headquarters in Montreal had, in fact, moved operations and personnel to Toronto (Black 1985).

12 The debt breakdown was as follows: government debt was equal to $22 billion, that of state-run societies was $23.2 billion, and that of the municipalities was $15.2 billion (Comeau 1986).

13 Important milestones were the election of the federal Progressive Conservative Party in September 1984, Premier Lévesque and his minister of justice P-M. Johnson's constitutional accord proposal in May 1985 (known as the "beautiful risk"), and the failed 1987 Meech Lake Accord. It was the return to power of Robert Bourassa's Quebec Liberal Party in December 1985 that renewed collaboration between Quebec and its partners within the Confederation. The free trade negotiations between Canada and the United States were launched in Quebec City in March 1985 during the "Shamrock Summit," which brought together the two "Irishmen," President Reagan and Prime Minister Mulroney.

14 The four major subjects on the agenda were investment, international commerce, regional economic development, and the training of labour.

15 In January 1986 the Bourassa government named Jack H. Warren as president of the Consulting Committee of the Quebec Government on issues related to free trade, and it formed a ministerial subcommittee presided over by Minister of Foreign Trade Pierre MacDonald, which also included Minister of Trade and Industry Daniel Johnson, Minister of Small Businesses André Vallerand, and Minister of International Relations and Intergovernmental Affairs Gil Rémillard. However, precious little came out of this.

16 The content of these reports provoked a very negative outcry. Apart from Jacques

Parizeau's intervention, which we examine later, we can cite, for example, L'Allier (1986).

17 As an example, we can point out that one of the effects of the agricultural policy of the Quiet Revolution was to increase Quebec's self-sufficiency from 55 percent to 77 percent of total consumption between 1977 and 1985 (Hamann 2004).

18 Such double financing can lead to duplications, not to mention tensions, at the grassroots level.

19 Cascades is a Quebec-based multinational that specializes in packaging and paper.

20 See, for example, Lisée (2003), in response to Wolfson and Murphy (2000) and Migué (1999).

REFERENCES

Bélanger, Paul R., Michel Grant, and Benoît Lévesque. 1994. *La Modernisation sociale des enterprises*. Montréal: Les Presses de l'Université de Montréal.

Bélanger, Paul R., and Benoît Lévesque. 1992. Le Mouvement populaire et communautaire: de la revendication au partenariat. In *Québec en Jeu*, ed. G. Daigle and G. Rocher, 713–47. Montréal: Les Presses de l'Université de Montréal.

Bélanger, Yves, Dorval Brunelle, and Christian Deblock. 1996. *Éléments de stratégie pour une relance indusrielle dans la région de Sorel-Tracy*. Montréal: Université du Québec à Montréal.

Black, Larry. 1985. La position du Québec apparaît incertaine dans un contexte de libre échange avec les Etats-Unis. *Le Devoir*, 12 March, 11.

Bourque, Gilles L. 2000. *Le Modèle québécois de développement: de l'émergence au renouvellement*. Québec: Presses de l'Université du Québec.

Brunelle, Dorval. 1978. *La Désillusion tranquille*. Montréal: Hurtubise HMH.

Brunelle, Dorval, and P. Drouilly. 2002. Le Parti québécois à bout de souffle. *Le Monde diplomatique*, Novembre, 22.

Canada. 1982. *Perspectives de développement économique au Québec*. Québec: Gouvernement du Canada, Département d'État au Développement économique, Bureau du coordonnateur fédéral du développement économique (Québec).

Comeau, P. 1986. Bloc-notes: le débat sur le néo-libéralisme. *Le Devoir*, 17 July, 11.

Comeau, Yvan, and Benoît Lévesque. 1993. Workers' Financial Participation in the Property of Enterprises in Québec. *Economic and Industrial Democracy* 14 (2): 233–50.

Désy, M., M. Ferland, B. Lévesque, and Y. Vaillancourt. 1980. *La Conjoncture au début des années 1980: Enjeux pour le mouvement ouvrier et populaire*. Rimouski: Librairie Socialiste.

Favreau, Louis, and Benoît Lévesque. 1996. *Développement économique communautaire. Économie Sociale et Intervention*. Québec: Presses de l'Université du Québec.

FTQ. 2003. Rapport annuel 2002. Montréal: Fonds de solidarité FTQ.

Giddens, Anthony. 1999. *The Third Way: The Renewal of Social Democracy*. Cambridge: Polity Press.

Grant, Michel, Paul R. Bélanger, and Benoît Lévesque. 1997. *Nouvelles formes d'organisation du travail: études de cas et analyses comparatives*. Paris and Montréal: L'Harmattan.

Hamann, Jean. 2004. Etre agriculteur aujourd'hui. Interview of economist and author Michel Morisset, director of the Research Group on Economy and Agriculture [Groupe de recherche en économie et politique agricole]. In *Contact. Magazine des diplômés et des partenaires de l'Université Laval* (Spring). Available at <http://www.contact.ulaval.ca/articles/etre-agriculteur-aujourd-hui-104.html>.

L'Allier, Jean-Paul. 1986. La démolition tranquille. *Le Devoir*, 19 July, A7.

Lapointe, Paul-André, Paul R. Bélanger, Guy Cucumel, and Benoît Lévesque. 2002. *Innovations en milieu de travail dans le secteur manufacturier au Québec*. Montréal: Cahier du Crises.

Lisée, Jean-François. 2003. Un mauvais procès au modèle québécois. *Le Devoir*, 11 February, 9.

Macdonald Report. 1985. *Report of the Royal Commission on the Economic Union and Development Prospects for Canada*. Vol. 1. Ottawa: Minister of Supply and Services.

Matzner, Egon, and Wolfgang Streeck. 1991. *Beyond Keynesianism: The Socio-Economics of Production and Full Employment*. Northampton: Elgar Publishing Ltd.

Migué, Jean-Luc. 1999. *Étatisme et déclin du Québec: bilan de la Révolution tranquille*. Montréal: Les Éditions Varia.

Monnier, Lionnel, and Bernard Thiry. 1997. *Mutations structurelles et intérêt général*. Brussels: De Boeck Université.

Nielsen, Erik. 1985. The Conservative Government Examines Old Programs (excerpts from a speech to the Canadian Club in Toronto). *Le Devoir*, 20 February, 11.

Noël, A. 1996. Vers un nouvel État-providence? En jeux démocratiques. *Politique et sociétés* 28 (2): 1–22.

Parizeau, Jacques. 1986. Ne jetons pas le bébé avec l'eau du bain! *La Presse*, 19 July, 5.

Porter, Michael E. 1990. *The Competitive Advantage of Nations*. New York: The Free Press.

Québec. 1979. *Bâtir le Québec: énoncé de politique économique*. Québec: Gouvernement du Québec, Ministre d'Etat au développement économique.

– 1982. *Le virage technologique: Bâtir le Québec, phase 2: programme d'action économique 1982–1986*. Québec: Gouvernement du Québec, Ministre d'Etat au développement économique.

Rapport Fortier. 1986. *Report of the Working Group on the Privatization of Government Corporations*. Québec: Gouvernement du Québec.

Rapport Gobeil. 1986. *Report of the Working Group on the Revision of Functions and Governmental Organizations.* Quebec: Government of Quebec.

Rapport Scowen. 1986. *Final Report on Deregulation, Working Group on Deregulation.* Québec: Les Publications du Québec.

Vaillancourt, Yves. 1996. Sortir de l'alternative entre privatisation et étatisation dans la santé et les services sociaux. In *Société civile, État et Économie plurielle,* ed. B. Eme, J.L. Laville, L. Favreau and Y. Vaillancourt, 148–224. Montréal, Hull, et Paris: CRISES, Université du Québec et CNRS.

– 1999. Tiers secteur et reconfiguration des politiques sociales. *Nouvelles Pratiques Sociales* 11 (2): 21–39.

Vaillancourt, Yves, and C. Jetté. 1999. *L'Aide à domicile au Québec: Relecture de l'historie et pistes d'action.* Montréal: UQAM.

Vaillancourt, Yves, and Jean Louis Laville. 1998. Les rapports entre associations et Etat: Un enjeu politique? Socio-Économie du fait associatif. *Revue du MAUSS semestrielle* 11: 119–35.

Vaillancourt, François, and Michel Leblanc. 1993. La propriété de l'économie du Québec en 1991 selon le groupe d'appartenance linguistique. Québec: Office de la langue française.

Wolfson, Michael, and Brian Murphy. 2000. Inégalités de revenu en Amérique du Nord: Le 49e parallèle a-t-il encore de l'importance? In *Observateur économique canadien,* ed. Michael Wolfson and Brian Murphy, 13 (8): 3.1–3.24. Ottawa: Statistique Canada.

PART FIVE

Deep Integration: Impacts on Environment, Energy, and Patent Law

17

Breaking the Free Trade Addiction: An Intervention on Environmental Grounds

ELIZABETH MAY AND SARAH DOVER

Imagine that it's Friday afternoon, around four o'clock. You are getting ready to leave for the weekend when the lights in your office go out. You peak out your office door and see that the entire floor is dark and heads are gophering up inquisitively from cubicles. You make your way out of the building, head down the stairs, and emerge into the chaotic and confused streets of downtown Toronto. More than the building, more than the block or the city, entire grids have gone down, and all is dark. All around you is chaos: people trapped in elevators and subways, hospitals and nursing homes scrambling, car accidents and furious motorists, scurrying 9-1-1 services, and cell phone circuits down.

On 14 August 2003 there occurred the largest blackout in North American history, affecting more than fifty million people in eastern Canada and the northeastern United States (Ontario 2003). In the confusion that followed, the Prime Minister's Office blamed the blackout on a lightning strike near Niagara Falls, New York, while one of Canada's federal ministers, John McCallum, told the media the blackout had been caused by a fire in a US nuclear power plant (World Net Daily 2003). Where and how he was served up that imaginative and wholly false explanation is anyone's guess. Officials from the Pennsylvania Emergency Management Agency shot back: "That is absolutely not true. We have a direct line to each of our five [nuclear] plants and they are all running at 100 percent. There's not even a trash can fire; we would know" (World Net Daily 2003). The urban myth in the United States to this day is that the problem originated "somewhere in Canada." The truth is even more unbelievable, given its sheer triviality: fifty million people lost their power because of a tree branch in Ohio.[1]

If anyone needed more evidence that Canada and the United States have become "hard-wired," 14 August 2003 should have provided them with it.

The pro-corporate policies of the Bush administration that led to the Enron debacle and contrived the California power "shortage" also contributed to the rogue tree branch in Ohio. The privatized utility, in a cost-saving measure, had reduced such routine maintenance as tree trimming. The failure of US authorities to create or enforce legal standards has spawned the suggestion that Canada needs to unplug from the integrated scheme in order to avoid further consequences of US regulatory failure (Ontario 2003). In the end, privatization and deregulation in the United States were crucial factors in the blackout (CUPE 2003).

The right-wing in Canada thinks we need more integration. One author argues: "From a Canadian perspective, the most important policy issue today is managing the Canada–US relationship in light of the changed US role in the world ... Canadians see NAFTA as having outlived its usefulness. Deeper integration is required" (Dobson 2002a, 1). Wrong. The most important policy issue today is "the environment" – our bodies, our neighbourhoods, our schools and hospitals, our great green spaces and blue waters. Who cares how many brands of US bubble gum sit on store shelves when we don't have clean air to breathe? Who cares if George W. Bush likes Mexico more than Canada when we are in the throes of one of the worst extinction crises in the history of life on Earth?[2]

The problem with today's environmental crisis is that, on a human time scale, it is occurring too slowly. Yet, on a geological time scale, the rate of change visited on the Earth by our species in the last century is of unprecedented speed. If the 3.8-billion-year lifespan of planet Earth were placed on a timeline one kilometre long, humanity would not make its appearance until the last two centimetres. The Industrial Revolution is a mere one eight-thousandth of a centimetre from that end point. Yet now, other than insect life, we are the most populous species on the planet, plundering more resources than any other and unleashing more pollution than the Earth has experienced since the toxic gases subsided and the earliest signs of life began (Millennium Ecosystem Assessment 2005, 2).

Nevertheless, each of us experiences time within the context of our own brief lifespan; consequently, the worsening condition of our environment is muted by a lack of sudden cataclysmic events. True, we have a few *Exxon Valdez* moments that grab the world's attention. Yet the same amount of oil spilled on Alaska's coastline in that incident kills 300,000 seabirds off Newfoundland's shores every single year as the result of "chronic oil pollution" – the illegal discharge of bilge oil by ships seeking to cut corners and to expand profits (Canada 2003c). Routine environmental devastation is often worse than the dramatic events that catch the news. Like a lake undergoing acidification, this devastation occurs incrementally. If the various environmental crises – endangered species, climate change, food insecurity, and so on – suddenly occurred on one Friday afternoon at 4:00

PM, the outrageous inadequacy of Canadian policies would be obvious, even to decision makers.

The Great Blackout of 2003 will stand as a symbol that "economic integration" is about more than dollars and cents, trucks and trains crossing borders, and cold trade statistics: it's about the lights staying on; it's about safe food, clean air, and access to public transportation, schools, and health services. It's also about wild spaces and species – and our ability to protect them. Perhaps the most potent symbol emerging from the Great Blackout is that of the one unconsidered tree branch that reached out and ripped down a massive electrical grid, as though nature itself had reached out, demanding consideration.

This chapter takes aim at the Canada-US Free Trade Agreement (CUFTA) and the North American Free Trade Agreement (NAFTA) for their role in setting the stage for the vast experiment in economic integration that has taken place over the last decade and a half. NAFTA has entrenched economic patterns that are environmentally unsustainable and has made it more difficult for governments to respond to the growing environmental crisis. We join the growing chorus of voices concerned about the next steps being proposed in what is now being framed as the "post-NAFTA" era. We argue that any "next step" must not simply be informed by environmental considerations but driven by them.

WHAT WE ARE LOSING:
THE STATE OF CANADA'S ENVIRONMENT

Canada is the trustee of an enormous environmental responsibility. We boast the world's longest coastline, 20 percent of the world's remaining natural areas, 25 percent of all wetlands, 20 percent of the fresh water, and more than 10 percent of the remaining forests (WWF 2003). Yet our natural wealth is in decline. We are not living in a sustainable way. Economist Herman Daly, among others, has argued that we should only live off the "interest" provided by "natural capital," and not eat into the capital itself. As he put it, we cannot treat the Earth "like a business in liquidation" (Daly 2004). For example, the Gross Domestic Product (GDP) is a false measure of economic success because it does not respond to the idea that environmental exploitation is deficit spending;[3] instead, it measures as wealth creation the very devastation of the environment that leads to ecological – and attendant economic – collapse. Here are a few examples of the "liquidation" of the Canadian environment:

- As of May 2005 there are 500 species on the list of Canadian species at risk (COSEWIC 2005), but the actual number is likely far higher (Lawton 2000). Of the species put on this list since 1978 and that have been re-evaluated, twice as many are now more imperilled than before (Canada 2003b, 11).

- Canada's greenhouse gas emissions (GHGs) have increased by a dramatic 20 percent over the last decade, outpacing the 11 percent rise in population and even the 17 percent rise in domestic energy consumption (Canada 2003b, 6).
- The average temperature in Canada is increasing; in 2001 it was 1.7 degrees Celsius above normal. The rate of warming is two times faster in Canada's north; the ten warmest years since 1860 have all been in the last fifteen (Canada 2003b, 7).
- Acid rain continues to fall on parts of Canada in concentrations that are twice as high as ecosystems can tolerate (Canada 2003b, 8).
- Fish species in all of Canada's oceans have experienced decline; one of the most dramatic examples is the collapse of the Northern cod, which is now only 3 percent of its historical average biomass (Lien 2002). On the Pacific side, the value of British Columbia's salmon fisheries has more than halved since 1989 (Canada 2003a).
- Pesticides can pose threats to human health and the environment; yet over half of the pesticides registered by the federal Pest Management Regulatory Agency (PMRA) have been approved despite gaps in the information on their effects (Canada 2003d, Chapter 1).
- Communities in all regions of Canada have struggled with boil-water advisories (including half of all communities in Newfoundland). On any given day, there are between 300 and 350 boil water advisories in British Columbia alone (FCM Undated; Sierra Legal 2003).
- Air pollution levels are now so high that the Ontario Medical Association has signalled a "public health crisis." It estimates there are 5,800 premature deaths in Ontario alone from this cause. (OMA 2005, 1-2).

The term "ecological footprint," coined by Dr William Rees of Simon Fraser University, accounts for the totality of the ecological damage for which each one of us is responsible (Wackernagel and Rees 1996). Our ecological footprint is a measure of how much water we use, how much energy we consume and from where, how much solid waste we produce, and how many tropical mangrove forests were clear-cut for ponds to give us grocery shelves stocked with cheap Tiger shrimp. In contrast, all such economic activities are included as positive additions to GDP, including all the oil that is sold or spilled into the ocean and the associated clean-up efforts, while failing to discount the crushing results of environmental devastation to local communities, natural resources, wildlife, and future generations. The ecological footprint measures what our lifestyle (and GDP) costs the Earth.

The United Nations Environment Programme (UNEP) World Conservation Monitoring Centre, along with its partners, releases their annual

Living Planet Report, which calculates the ecological footprint of humanity globally and by country. A country's ecological footprint is measured as "the total area required to produce the food and fiber that it consumes, and provide space for its infrastructure" (Loh and Wackernagel 2004, 10). In 2001 humanity exceeded "global bio-capacity" by 21 percent. Not surprisingly, North America has the highest ecological footprint of any region in the world (Loh and Wackernagel 2004).

How do the countries rank within the NAFTA region? Many may have the impression that Canada performs well in terms of environmental protection in comparison with the United States. After all, in Canada, we have blue boxes and green bins, we put images of nature on our currency and our flag, and we take pride in our national parks and our large open spaces. However, in ecological terms, the two economies rank among the most unsustainable in the world. The United States has the second highest ecological footprint per person in the world (behind the oil-producing United Arab Emirates), while Canada is not far behind in eighth place (Loh and Wackernagel 2004, 10).[4] Mexico, however, is much farther down the list, behind at least 50 other countries, even ranking ahead of Chile, Argentina, and Jamaica. The high cost of the "North American lifestyle" is not the fault of Mexico: it is the fault of the wildly unsustainable economies of Canada and the United States. There is little difference in ecological terms between a "Canadian lifestyle" and an "American lifestyle" – both are synonymous for "wildly unsustainable."

The global economy is built around false and dangerous signals that equate destruction of our life-support systems with economic growth. International trade laws, such as NAFTA, work to authorize, describe, facilitate, and even promote the global unsustainable economy. At the time NAFTA was established, some argued it would *improve* environmental quality. For example, an economic theory called the environmental Kuznets Curve postulated that free trade would result in reduced levels of pollution. It argued that, following an initial transition period, environmental improvements would occur in correlation with rising income levels (Bradford et al. 2005,1). Research in the ensuing years has indicated, however, that the theory was too ambitious as a general description of the environmental outcomes of free trade. Studies have shown that environmental effects vary when disaggregated by sector, geography, or environmental indicator. For example, a rise in pollution and invasion of alien species are two measured effects of the increased transportation resulting from NAFTA (Bradford et al. 2005, 3). Further, research has shown an increase in GHGs and habitat loss as GDP per capita increases (Vaughan and Block 2002, 1–2).

However, it cannot be said that the full impact of NAFTA on the environment is known. There is a massive research lag on the question of the environmental effects of trade agreements.[5] Further research is also needed in order to understand the environmental crisis that is under way. But let us not continue to use the need for further research as an excuse to continue entrenching highly unsustainable existing economic patterns through international trade laws.

WHO KNEW?
LOOKING BACK ON THE ESTABLISHMENT OF NAFTA

On 14 September 1993 US president Bill Clinton announced: "In a few moments, I will sign three agreements that will complete our negotiations with Mexico and Canada to create a North American Free Trade Agreement." In addition to claiming that NAFTA would create American jobs, he claimed that environmental concerns had been central to the negotiations and pointed to the endorsement offered by the US-based Audubon Society and the Natural Resources Defence Council (United States 1993). However, most environmental voices were unconvinced, remaining concerned that such international trade rules would further entrench unsustainable economic activities.

Environmental concerns were also raised during the negotiations of CUFTA in the late 1980s and NAFTA in the 1990s. Concerns focused on the impacts of increased trade on the environment and on whether, in an effort to attract investment, governments would be rationally motivated not to implement environmental laws.[6] If we knew then what we know now, we would also have raised the flag over NAFTA provisions that not only support unsustainable economic activities but that also actually impair governments from responding to the environmental crisis.

Debate during the NAFTA negotiations focused on the "race to the bottom," or the concern that Canadian environmental standards would be lowered to US (or Mexican) standards. Canadians worried about the threat of our laws being "weakened" to US levels as our economies became further integrated through NAFTA. The irony is that, while US environmental laws have failed to prevent the United States from being a world leader in unsustainability, they are generally more protective of the environment than are Canadian laws. President Richard Nixon, for example, brought in a suite of environmental laws that has yet to be matched by Canadian equivalents: the Clean Water Act, the Clean Air Act, the National Environmental Protection Act, and the Endangered Species Act. The point is not that US environmental standards ought to be applied to protect Canada's environment, or that they ought to be the standard for harmonization across NAFTA markets. The point is that the job of governing includes setting locally appropriate standards, such as environmental standards, that apply to economic activities and that the Canadian government is far behind numerous developed nations in setting Canadian standards to protect many areas of the environment.

To further illustrate this point, the Environmental Protection Agency (EPA) in the United States is arguably a far better model than is Environment Canada. While the EPA is responsible for protecting human health and the environment, Environment Canada's jurisdiction stops at the water and the fish. It does not include the people who eat the fish: that is Health Canada's turf. Historically, turf wars between these departments have contributed to failures in environmental protection.[7] US regulation of pesticides under the Federal Insecticide, Fungicide, Rodenticide Act (FIFRA) is also superior to Canada's. The United States banned the phenoxy herbicide 2,4,5-T (half of Agent Orange) in the early 1980s. Canada, on the other hand, never took regulatory action against 2,4,5-T, with regulators insisting that the herbicide was safe until it was no longer possible to import it due to restrictions elsewhere: once banned in the United States, the EPA and the manufacturer, Dow Chemical, reached an agreement to cease its exportation (May 2005).

Of course, the recent rollbacks of the Bush administration have done serious damage to US environmental performance. Nevertheless, Canada's environmental laws and regulations still lag behind those of its neighbour. Even in the area of climate change, combined state and federal actions in the United States are more advanced than are combined Canadian efforts (Bramley 2002). Once again, the point is not that US laws ought to have application in Canada. Developing, passing, and implementing environmental standards are processes that take place among citizens, affected parties, and governments. Local and national law-making initiatives may culminate in regulatory diversity without resulting in lower environmental standards (e.g., different communities may place different priorities among protective mechanisms as a result of unique regulatory histories or relationships to the environment). Canadian governments, in comparison with US governments, have failed to ensure that these processes give rise to high environmental standards appropriate to Canadian contexts.

The concern with differing regulatory standards is that economic actors may be rationally motivated to migrate to places with lower compliance costs. One of the most dramatic environmental effects directly associated with NAFTA, for example, is the 400 percent increase in hazardous waste imports from the United States since its implementation. The dramatic rise is considered to be a result of the differing regulatory environments (Jacott, Reed, and Winfield 2002). The "pollution haven hypothesis" speculates that efficiency gains from lower environmental standards will cause a migration of corporations to regions of lower environmental protection (and associated pressure on governments to lower or not enforce environmental laws). Whether NAFTA has caused much migration of dirty business to areas of lax environmental regulation is still up for debate. Some research has indicated that businesses, rely on a number of factors when deciding where to invest, not just the compliance costs associated with environmental regulations (Johnson 1996, 45). However, some evidence, such as the spike in imports of hazardous wastes to Canada, suggests circumstances in which the pollution haven hypothesis is correct.

In order for a country to avoid being a pollution haven, it may need to raise its environmental standards. However, if a NAFTA country, such as Canada, wanted to raise its environmental standards to the level of another NAFTA country, such as the United States, then it could face legal barriers. NAFTA, in its legal operation, is indifferent to comparative standards of environmental protection – that is, it provides no special allowances to the country wishing to raise standards. So if Canada undertook measures that are not NAFTA compliant, under Chapter 11 it would be fully liable for a foreign investor's claims of "expropriation without compensation" in relation to lost existing or future profits.

Steven Shrybman's chapter 12 (this volume) deals with what, to date, is one of the most shocking impacts of NAFTA: foreign corporations launching secret lawsuits against governments for passing laws to protect the environment. Chapter 11's "investor protection" regime was not widely perceived as a threat to democracy and sovereignty during the NAFTA debates. But today there is broader recognition that Chapter 11 is a supra-constitutional corporate bill of rights (Clarkson 2002) that has been most often used to challenge environmental laws. Chapter 11 has proven an effective enforcement mechanism against national governments, a powerful international mechanism for the advancement of the neoliberal agenda that underpins NAFTA and other trade liberalizing agreements. Chapter 11, in the hands of foreign investors driven solely by the bottom line, has been devastating to domestic environmental regulation – and a stunning blow to Canadian democracy.

Even the Canadian government has recognized that Chapter 11 needs to be "patched." The problem is that reopening NAFTA is a political non-starter: renegotiation would be a too-public admission that NAFTA has serious problems, even though the problems lamented by environmentalists and others are more than apparent to some government officials: "As you know, there is a real danger of the NAFTA being dragged down by ambiguous provisions pertaining to investor-state disputes ... Ambiguities in the drafting and uneven interpretation of Chapter 11 have brought about unanticipated consequences with cases being heard that should have been rejected" (Canada 2000b). The potential extent of the liability of the Canadian government from environmental laws that violate NAFTA rules is difficult to estimate but easy to imagine, given that legal experts claim "most existing and many future measures would not survive trade law challenges" (Mann 2000, 232).

It is worth noting that the European Union took a very different approach to regional trade liberalization than did North America. Arguably, international law involves states accepting a reduced level of sovereignty for the sake of international order. The issue with international trade rules such as NAFTA is that democratic values, such as accountability, are indirectly affected in unacceptable ways. These impacts are compounded by the fact that there are no mechanisms within NAFTA, such as a supranational democratic body, capable of matching the power of trade rules and their associated institutions. In the case of the EU a European parliament was created, with its members directly elected. The commissioner of the environment for the EU is an important champion for action on climate change. Moreover, the terms of membership in the EU trading block include all states meeting the toughest environmental standards. This has meant that Spain had to upgrade its environmental regulations to meet those established by Germany. Funds were provided within the EU from the wealthiest (generally also the same countries with the most stringent environmental laws) to the poorest (generally those whose regulation was lax). The EU example makes it clear that trade rules need not ignore or depress environmental regulation, as is the case in NAFTA. With a different orientation, such agreements can engineer a significant improvement in environmental protection without the corrosive loss of democracy implicit in the agreements to which Canada has subscribed.

ON THE SIDELINE: NAFTA'S ENVIRONMENTAL INSTITUTIONS

In 1992, during the last days of NAFTA gestation, environmental and labour concerns dominated public consciousness. Environmental concerns concentrated, inter alia, on mitigating the impacts of NAFTA on the environment and a citizen's mechanism to monitor trade impacts on the environment. In 1992 and 1993 candidates Bill Clinton and Jean Chrétien both pledged to their respective electorates to block NAFTA if it did not protect the environment and labour standards (Pastor 1997). The Liberal Party platform could not have been more clear in its commitment to "renegotiate both the [CU]FTA and NAFTA" (Liberal Party of Canada 1993, 24). Instead, once they were elected, both politicians approved an unaltered NAFTA text and two side agreements. The objectives of the environmental side agreement, the North American Agreement on Environmental Cooperation (NAAEC), included fostering and improving environmental protection and promoting sustainable development (NAAEC 1993). The cornerstone of NAAEC was the establishment of the North American Commission for Environmental Cooperation (CEC).

The CEC was established and based in Montreal while Sheila Copps was environment minister in the early days of Jean Chrétien's first mandate.

The first executive director of the CEC, Victor Lichtenger, was from Mexico and would later become that nation's environment minister. Copps recruited committed environmentalist Janine Ferretti of Pollution Probe to be the top-ranking Canadian in the CEC. Later, Ferretti would replace Lichtenger as the second head of the institution. Both must be credited with making something of a silk purse from a sow's ear. Governments had not actually wanted the CEC to do anything. In spite of near constant interference from the bureaucracy of the three member governments, the CEC managed to publish annual reports and the *National Pollution Release Inventory*, launch regional programs (such as those protecting the Monarch butterfly), assist Mexico in the elimination of DDTs, and produce periodic reports pointing to the dark side of enhanced trade (such as the 2004 report that showed increased diesel traffic on the US-Mexican border was resulting in children in border communities dying from air pollution).[8] Citizen and environmental group advisory bodies were established and open hearings set up in tandem with the annual meeting of the nations' three environment ministers.

An important mechanism for environmental protection in the NAAEC is the citizen-complaint process. The objective of the NAAEC to promote compliance with and enforcement of environmental laws relies heavily on citizen involvement since citizen interests are more strongly correlated with domestic environmental objectives than with those of foreign countries. Articles 14 and 15 of the NAAEC provide that the secretariat of the CEC "may consider a submission from any non-governmental organization or person asserting that a Party is failing to effectively enforce its environmental law" (NAAEC 1993). While the idea of citizens having recourse to international oversight bodies is not unusual in international law (in the area of human rights law, for example), the NAAEC mechanism is seen as novel since it applies in the environmental realm. However, despite its promise, the mechanism has proven to be onerous for citizens who are attempting to launch a complaint as well as ineffective since governments can truncate the process before there is any effective conclusion. For instance, if a citizen satisfies the criteria for investigation, the secretariat may only proceed with developing a factual record if it gets the consent of two-thirds of the council – that is, if the ministers of the environment from the two other NAFTA countries who are not the subject of the complaint agree. The same threshold must also be met to make any factual record that might eventually be made available to the public (NAAEC 1993, Article 15, 7).

At best, the citizen submission process has proven to be a means of occasionally prompting a party to discuss a particular environmental issue. It has not proven capable of forcing governments to act. These conclusions were succinctly stated by the council-appointed Joint Public Advisory Committee (JPAC) in correspondence to the council:

Bold as this experiment has been, however, putting the Article 14/15 process into practice has been neither easy nor obvious. As this process has evolved and unfolded, the Commission for Environmental Cooperation (CEC) Council has struggled to interpret this part of the Agreement, the Secretariat has tested the boundaries of independence in their legitimate role in the process, and the public has found that the high expectations they had at the outset may have been unrealistic in relation to what the citizen submission process is actually able to deliver. It is clear that the process has not yet reached maturity. Although 50 submissions have been received by the Secretariat since the signing of the Agreement, only 30 have advanced past the Secretariat's initial review stage and only 10 factual records have been completed and published to date. (JPAC 2004, 2)

The CEC has managed to resist the political pressures from three governments to report on levels of toxic pollution, facilitate a discourse on the impacts of the NAFTA regime on the environment, and maintain a limited "watch dog" role. Despite successes, however, it has been an unmitigated failure at moderating the impact of NAFTA on the environment and at being a mechanism for ensuring the enforcement of domestic environmental laws.

Therefore, the precedent of the NAAEC, in terms of considering future trade and economic agreements and environmental concerns, is extremely limited. The NAAEC is not a model to be replicated in the future to address concerns relating to the negative impacts of trade on the environment. While the ability of the CEC to foster environmental cooperation among the NAFTA parties is important, it is the subject of a separate analysis regarding international cooperation and environmental outcomes. The NAAEC has not succeeded in mitigating, or even identifying, the negative impacts of trade on land, water, air, ecosystems, human health, and so on. Further, the impression that the NAAEC ensures that NAFTA parties are enforcing environmental laws and promoting democracy through citizen engagement may have distracted attention from the forums within which trade-policy decisions are actually being made.

THE FAILURE OF STRATEGIC ENVIRONMENTAL ASSESSMENT OF TRADE AGREEMENTS

Generally speaking, there is a disconnect between environmental considerations, democracy concerns, and trade policy (and promotion). This divide is chiefly responsible for Canadian officials' neglect of the environment in the realm of trade policy. In other words, the environment is not a priority in the development of trade policy, nor is it considered in meaningful or effective ways.

Evidence of this disconnect may be observed in the government's failure to consider alternatives through effective environmental assessment. Environmental considerations respecting trade policy are mainly deferred to a process of strategic environmental assessment (SEA). SEAS have been conducted on a number of trade agreements, including the Free Trade Area of the Americas (FTAA) and the World Trade Organization (WTO) agreements. The SEAS are conducted by International Trade Canada (ITCan) under the auspices of *The Cabinet Directive on the Environmental Assessment of Policy, Plan and Program Proposals* (Canada 2004a). To date, the SEAS fall far shy of the promise of a "systematic and comprehensive process of evaluating the environmental effects of a policy, plan or program and its alternatives" (ibid.). Many Canadians, including these authors, would applaud an evaluation of the alternatives to NAFTA.

It is difficult to take the SEA process conducted by ITCan seriously because it lacks the specificity and candour needed to attract and sustain effective public participation. The WTO and FTAA negotiations, for example, together touch upon virtually every aspect of Canadian trade, including agriculture, chemicals, fishing, forest products, tourism, transportation, manufacturing, and so on. However, the initial SEAS of the FTAA and the WTO, despite covering a myriad of different trade issues and geographies, conclude with the exact same sentence. The template conclusion is that negotiations will not directly translate into increased trade flows and, therefore, have no appreciable environmental impact (DFAIT 2002, 2003).

The November 2002 Initial Environmental Assessment (IEA) of the economic activity and trade policy changes resulting from the WTO negotiations concluded as follows:

The analysis performed for this Initial EA suggests that in the aggregate, any effects the new WTO negotiations may have on the Canadian environment are likely to be minimal on account of one or a combination of three reasons: (1) further trade liberalization affects only a small proportion of Canada's trade (the bulk already being subject to NAFTA and other Free Trade Agreements); (2) federal and provincial environmental legislation that can mitigate negative effects is, or will soon be in place; (3) some negotiations that seek clarification in procedures or establish a system of negotiation and registration will not directly translate into increased production or trade. (DFAIT 2002, 4)

In May 2003 the government released the IEA of the proposed hemispheric expansion of NAFTA, specifically considering all nine of the FTAA negotiating groups: market access, agriculture, services, government procurement, investment, competition policy, dispute settlement, intellectual property rights, and subsidies, anti-dumping, and countervailing duties. Despite the obvious differences between the FTAA negotiations and the WTO negotiations in scope of issues and geographic areas, the IEA once again concluded as follows (words differing from those in the WTO IEA are highlighted in italics):

The analysis performed for this Initial EA suggests that, in the aggregate, any effects the *FTAA* negotiations may have on the Canadian environment are likely to be minimal on account of one or a combination of *the following* reasons: (1) further trade liberalization affects only a small proportion of Canada's trade (the bulk already being subject to NAFTA and other Free Trade Agreements); (2) federal and provincial environmental legislation that can mitigate negative effects is, or will soon be in place; (3) some negotiations seek *to create a rules-based trading system, which will facilitate trade by creating a consistent international framework in which to conduct trade, but may* not directly translate into increased production or trade. (DFAIT 2003, 5)

In May 2004 the government published the IEA for the Canada-Singapore Free Trade Agreement negotiations, and it concluded with the same paragraph (Canada 2004b). The use of template conclusions by ITCan reveals a failure to effectively consider the environmental implications of each agreement and to genuinely consider alternatives.

The failure to properly conduct SEA does not distinguish ITCan from other government departments. The government commitment to strategic environmental assessment came in for harsh criticism in the 2004 report of the Commissioner for Environment and Sustainable Development, within the Office of the Auditor General. The commissioner found "major gaps" in the application of the cabinet directive and concluded that the "overall application of the directive does not provide assurance that environmental issues are assessed systematically, so ministers and the Cabinet can receive sufficient information to make informed decisions on proposed policies, programs, and plans" (Canada 2004c, Chapter 4). This would indicate that the failure to systematically consider environmental impacts is generalized practice in government. Thus it is not surprising that Canadian trade policy would follow the same pattern.

NAFTA AND THE (IN)ABILITY TO RESPOND TO THE ENVIRONMENTAL CRISIS

While the government has failed to look forward to the environmental consequences of trade negotiations, it has also failed to look back. After fifteen years of free trade there has been no comprehensive effort by the government to assess its impact on the Canadian environment or on democratic institutions. Such an assessment, had it occurred, should have included recognition of the environmental impacts experienced by natural resource-dependent industries and communities. For example, as a consequence of

NAFTA, Prairie farmers lost the subsidized Crow rate for shipping grain by rail. As a result, the shipping of grain shifted to trucks and transportation costs rose. The high costs of shipping grain created local surpluses and the economic preconditions that have led to a boom in mega-hog factories. Because NAFTA led to the loss of the Crow rate, it opened the door to an increase in intensive livestock operations and problems of nutrient (manure) management and water pollution.

In addition to these types of direct impacts, NAFTA has affected Canadian laws and law-making institutions. While attempts to predict the environmental implications of new trade agreements are, of necessity, problematic, the failure to examine post facto the impact of CUFTA and NAFTA is harder to forgive. This is especially true where the institutions of law making in Canada have been shaped by trade agreements.

One of the most striking evolutions within the federal regulatory process is the burgeoning authority of ITCan. The advancement of trade policy goals and the day-to-day implementation of agreements like NAFTA have invited ITCan into environmental files in such a manner that, in effect, it operates more like a central coordinating agency and less like a "line department." This role is structurally supported through the 1999 Regulatory Policy, which guides the federal regulatory process (PCO 1999). Appendix A to this policy binds regulatory officials to take account of international agreements like NAFTA and the WTO and officially charges ITCan with coordinating the implementation of these agreements across all departments (PCO 1999, Appendix A).[9]

The result is that ITCan's scope of influence has grown proportionally with the scope and depth of international trade commitments. As the trade regime grows through negotiation and interpretation, so then does ITCan's role within the Canadian regulatory process. ITCan may exercise effective oversight of any governmental "measure" by providing expert legal opinion respecting the risks that such measures would be challenged under international trade laws.

Further institutional impacts of NAFTA have taken place as a result of Chapter 11. Foreign corporations have successfully used the investor lawsuit provision to quash Canadian environmental laws. It has also been successfully used within the context of "strategic litigation," forcing the government to yield environmental measures in the face of expensive and burdensome litigation.

Strategic litigation launched by US-based Ethyl Corporation successfully used Chapter 11, in combination with other legal approaches, to force the Canadian government to withdraw the ban on the neuro-toxic gasoline additive MMT. Not only was the ban on trade of MMT across borders withdrawn but the government also issued a public apology to Ethyl Corporation and awarded the company US$13 million from the core budget of

Environment Canada. Important lessons can be learned from the approach of Ethyl Corporation to its "market access" problem caused by the ban of MMT. The intent of corporations in filing Chapter 11 claims is not to win the court case: it is to win their market back. The design of Chapter 11 as a dispute settlement mechanism is awkward, unwieldy, and expensive. It allows foreign corporations to raise the price of regulation and *the process* heavily burdens governments faced with Chapter 11 claims. Thus the negative impacts of Chapter 11 on the process of government occur long before any Chapter 11 panel issues a decision on the dispute in question.

The experience under Chapter 11 has been so bad, even in the opinion of governments, that the United States has not included one in its bilateral free trade agreement with Australia (Baker and Hostetler LLP 2004). Some of the key defects of Chapter 11 include:

- lack of definitions for key terms such as "expropriation";
- clear exemptions for environmental regulations;
- a mechanism to dismiss frivolous and vexatious claims; and
- the express inclusion of provincial or state governments in all aspects of disputes when their measures are at issue.

The problem of how to "fix" Chapter 11 is a subject of debate within the Canadian government. Efforts to repair the mechanism within the NAFTA process, for example through the negotiation of an interpretive note to clarify the issues, are limited since the scope of the problem is so big and political sensitivities among the parties so high. In the words of one Canadian official:

Due to continuing litigation, the threat of new cases, the range of legal, policy and procedural issues being challenged in these cases, the scope of the current clarification initiative will not be sufficient to address all the issues raised in the current Chapter 11 investor-state arbitrations. For example, the recent Notice of Intent filed by UPS against Canada raises a new set of sensitive public and strategic issues as it relates to a government reserved activity as the operation of Canada Post mail service and the privatization of government services ... [T]rilateral progress on this initiative has been difficult due to Mexico's reluctance to engage in serious negotiations as it prefers clarifications to take place through decisions of the arbitration tribunals. (Canada 2000a, 3–4)

Following from this logic, it would fall on subsequent negotiations over new agreements, such as the FTAA and "deep integration" proposals, to fix this situation. Indeed, there are some within government who seek to overlay NAFTA with a new set of rules that would prevail over Chapter 11. However, to try to "repair" Chapter 11, directly or indirectly, through

Canadian negotiation positions in larger, broader trade agreements is evidence of a bad gambling habit on the part of the government. It is clear that all parties to NAFTA gambled and lost when they agreed to the overly expansive and ambiguous text of Chapter 11. The solution is to come clean with the Canadian people and to work to directly limit or remove the operation of the investor lawsuit provisions and not, once again, to gamble with Canadian sovereignty at international trade negotiations.

NAFTA, CLIMATE CHANGE, AND THE APPETITE FOR OIL

Continental energy integration, already well under way through NAFTA, will inevitably court a showdown with Canadian measures to address climate change. Corporations may seek to use trade rules to protect their interests, and the conditions of dwindling supply, environmental stresses, and divergent policy and regulatory paths threaten a clash between NAFTA and environmental governance of unprecedented proportions.

Canada and US Energy Policy:
Behind Deep Integration and Climate Change

Canada now supplies more oil and gas to the United States than does Saudi Arabia. As a recent report of the Sierra Club of Canada and the Natural Resources Defence Council puts it, Canada has become "America's Gas Tank" (Price and Bennett 2002, 2). The George W. Bush White House needs deeper integration to feed the US fossil fuel addiction.

By far the most dangerous element of the policies of George W. Bush – and the agenda for deeper integration of Canada-US policies – lies in the US president's efforts to sabotage global action to reduce greenhouse gas emissions while, simultaneously, aggressively seeking to exploit the remaining deposits of coal, oil, and gas. Whether it is opening up the pristine Arctic National Wildlife Refuge, invading Iraq, or importing crude from Canada's tar sands, Bush's energy strategy can be summed up in one word: "MORE." In a speech on energy policy, Vice-President Dick Cheney (2001) remarked: "Conservation may be a sign of personal virtue, but it is not a sufficient basis for a sound, comprehensive energy policy." The evolution of the US energy strategy is a case history in corporate control of democratic institutions. The Bush White House, operating as a wholly owned subsidiary of Big Carbon, has brought corporate CEOs into the inner circle to draft policy. Ken Lay of Enron exercised particular power. So great has the corporate influence over government energy policy become that the Sierra Club in the United States has gone to court to force the release of the names of companies on Cheney's Energy Taskforce (*Sierra Club v. Cheney* 2004).

To meet its unsustainable demand for energy, the United States will need an ever-increasing amount of energy. Linda McQuaig (2004) makes a convincing case that the United States has occupied Iraq and its oil fields largely to meet its fossil fuel addiction. The homeland security agenda has the United States preoccupied with continental energy "self-sufficiency" and looking to the Athabasca Tar Sands and its vast amount of Canadian hydrocarbons in order to reach this goal. NAFTA's energy provisions ensure that, in the event that Canada wishes to moderate its energy flows to the US, it can only to do so while maintaining proportionality. It is not possible for Canada to reduce the proportion of energy it shares with the United States in comparison with its domestic markets without being in violation of NAFTA Article 605.

Concerns regarding the integration of Canadian and US energy markets and the energy clauses of NAFTA are magnified by the fact of global climate change. Climate change is not a distant or hypothetical danger. Human activity, primarily through burning fossil fuels, has already changed the chemistry of our atmosphere, and we have dramatically increased the concentration of warming gases. Thanks to sophisticated science, which measures air pockets in Antarctic ice cores, we can directly measure how much carbon dioxide has been in our atmosphere going back 800,000 years. Through proxy measurements (of things like pollen and fossilized snail shells) we know how much carbon dioxide has been in the atmosphere going back 20 million years. Indicators show that, within the last three decades, we have broken all the records.

The CO_2 concentrations prior to the Industrial Revolution were 280 ± 10 parts per million (ppm) for several thousand years. Current levels – due to the increased emissions of greenhouse gases, primarily from burning fossil fuels – have now reached 367 ppm (IPPCC 2001, 185). This concentration, unprecedented over the last 20 million years of Earth history, is irreversible, at least in human time frames. This means that increased severe-weather events, a melting Arctic, more droughts, forest fires, and floods are now inevitable.

To avoid even more catastrophic levels of climatic disruption, to which we may well not be able to adapt, such as a doubling of CO_2 to 550 ppm (IPPCC 2001, 186), the global scientific consensus is that we need reductions of 60 percent below 1990 levels. The first step taken by the international community to address this threat was the 1992 UN Framework Convention on Climate Change (FCCC). The FCCC got a rough ride from George H.W. Bush, which was made clear by his memorable statement that the "American lifestyle is not on trial" (*Toronto Star* 2000). Bush would refuse to sign any convention that included timelines and targets for carbon dioxide reductions. Despite the lack of specifics, the FCCC did set out that all parties accept that the threat of climate change is real and that enough is known to act to avoid "dangerous levels" of CO_2 concentrations in our atmosphere. Virtually every nation on Earth, including the United States, has signed and ratified the FCCC.

Through the process of Conferences of the Parties (COPS) to the FCCC, a meaningful set of targets was negotiated that included the United States. In December 1997, at the Third Conference of the Parties in Kyoto, Japan, a binding protocol was signed. The Kyoto Protocol includes commitments by Canada to a 6 percent reduction of greenhouse gases below 1990 levels and by the United States to a 7 percent reduction.

In spring 2001 President George W. Bush surprised even his own environmental protection chief by pulling the United States out of the Kyoto Protocol. As revealed in former secretary of treasury Paul O'Neill's memoir of his time in the Bush administration, Bush never even took the issue to full cabinet. EPA head Christine Todd-Whitman and O'Neill had been tasked with preparing Bush's Kyoto plan. Neither of them was consulted. On the other hand, the coal lobby and Exxon were fully engaged.

As of 31 August 2005 the Kyoto Protocol, a modest first step in addressing global climate change, had been ratified by 155 states. Canada and most of the industrialized world has ratified Kyoto. The formula for entry into force of the Protocol as a binding treaty requires two things: that a minimum of 55 nations ratify (that was the easy part) and that those nations represent the equivalent of 55 percent of global GHG emissions in 1990. When Bush repudiated the US commitment to Kyoto, he not only pulled one vote away for the first half of the formula, he also made meeting the second half extremely difficult.

The United States, with only 4 percent of the world's population, produced 25 percent of GHGs in 1990. To reach the 55 percent threshold without the United States meant that virtually every other industrialized country had to ratify. The Bush administration applied pressure on Russia to reject the treaty. It also twisted arms in the developing world, pressuring India, for example, to reject binding targets when the next round of post-Kyoto negotiations commence. This effort is particularly hypocritical as the US fossil fuel industry has mounted a very successful public relations effort to persuade US citizens that Kyoto is "unfair" to the United States because it leaves India out. The fact that Canada has ratified Kyoto, in and of itself, should be celebrated. It was not easy to withstand the combined pressure of the US administration, Alberta, and a powerful lobby of self-interested and irresponsible corporations (it should be noted that many Canadian business leaders supported ratification).

In terms of implementation, Canada has faltered. In fact, Canadian measures to address climate change lag behind combined US state and federal efforts. Many dissenters of the Kyoto Protocol argued that the NAFTA context requires Canada to "keep pace" with the United States on climate change efforts. If that basic premise is true, then Canada "keeping pace" means Canada catching up. One study that examines and compares the totality of government action in the United States and Canada concludes as follows: "State actions, while still far from sufficient to reverse the rising trend in total US emissions, are having real impacts now and are gathering pace ... The argument that, since the US isn't acting, Canada similarly can't afford to – or that the US isn't acting so it's fine for Canada to also sit back – is faulty logic" (Bramley 2002, 1). The Liberal governments released at least three separate versions of plans to meet the Kyoto commitment. It is not clear whether any of these would lead us to achieve the reduction target of 6 percent below 1990 levels between 2008 and 2012 (translating to a reduction of 270 million tons, or megatons, of GHG emissions). In the meantime, Canada's GHGs are rising by a larger percentage than are those in the United States: US emissions are up 16 percent above 1990 levels while Canada's are over 20 percent (Canada 2003b, 6; Worldwatch 2005).

With the election of the minority Conservative government of Stephen Harper, the situation took a radical turn for the worse. Rather than having a Liberal government that lacked political will, we now have a full-blown anti-Kyoto government. The Conservative Party is a new political animal, being the result of an Alliance Party take-over of the Progressive Conservative Party. The Alliance Party had vociferously opposed the ratification of the Kyoto Protocol. As of mid-2006, the Harper Conservatives are attempting to confuse the public with claims that Kyoto targets set out in the first commitment period cannot be met. At the same time, the government insists it is not withdrawing formally from Kyoto – a complex legal procedure, in which legal notice cannot be served prior to 2008. The Harper government is thus taking a position that is likely to create enormous damage to Canada's international standing and to the ecological health of our planet. It is, on the one side, openly thwarting legally binding targets and attempting to sabotage global progress for the post-2012 period, while, on the other, claiming to be acting within the Kyoto Protocol.

The biggest cause of Canada's rapid growth in emissions is the energy-intensive operation of producing crude from the Athabasca Tar Sands. The tar sands alone will, by 2015, be responsible for emitting an incredible 57 to 97 megatons of carbon (depending on several scenarios) – as against a national emission reduction target of 270 (Woynillowicz, Severson-Baker, and Raynolds 2005, 20). This figure does not include the carbon released when the oil is burned in the engines of US SUVs: it is solely the amount of carbon released in the production of oil from bitumen muck and in the combustion of the natural gas required for the extraction process. The Athabasca Tar Sands are the world's biggest strip mine, with gargantuan vehicles stripping away thousands of hectares of forest, bogs, wetlands, and streams. For each barrel of oil produced as much as ten barrels of water are needed (Price and Bennett 2002, 15). Huge amounts of energy are needed to squeeze oil from the tarry mud. If oil prices were not going through the roof, no one would consider trying to get at the oil embedded in the tar sands. In fact, until recently, the Athabasca Tar Sands were not counted in world oil reserves. Now, the tar sands are listed as having as much oil as Saudi Arabia. Canada's tar sands may get over C$60 billion of investment by 2015, according to publicly announced development plans (NEB 2004, xiv).

Getting the oil from the muck requires prodigious amounts of energy. The Mackenzie Valley Gas Project is being touted as the solution to the Athabasca energy crunch. In fact, Premier Ralph Klein boasted, in a recent speech at Harvard University, that the Mackenzie gas will flow to the tar sands (Thomas 2005), although more recently he has denied this (Canadian Press 2005). It is one of the most staggering megaprojects anywhere on the planet. Three gas production facilities are proposed along the Beaufort Sea at the Mackenzie Delta. The natural gas will be conducted through 1,300 kilometres of buried pipeline through intermittent permafrost (which will also be melting due to climate change impacts in the north). The pipeline will lead to the industrialization of the Mackenzie Valley, including a watershed that is one-fifth the size of Canada. The whole region will cease to be intact wilderness and will be fragmented and industrialized. The most outrageous aspect is that a relatively clean-burning fossil fuel – natural gas – will be consumed in order to produce a heavy carbon fuel for export to the United States.

Feeding the US addiction to fossil fuels while it refuses to accept any responsibility for arresting climate change is, quite simply, suicidal. Fundamentally, we must reframe the climate debate into one about the massive security threat represented by climate change. In 2003 the Pentagon commissioned a study to examine the national security dimensions of climate change. Its conclusions included the following:

It is quite plausible that within a decade the evidence of an imminent abrupt climate shift may become clear and reliable ... In short, while the US itself will be relatively better off and with more adaptive capacity, it will find itself in a world where Europe will be struggling internally, large number so [sic] refugees washing up on its shores and Asia in serious crisis over food and water. Disruption and conflict will be endemic features of life. (Schwartz and Randall 2003, 22)

The study concluded, as did Hans Blix, UN weapons inspector, and Sir David King, science advisor to UK prime minister Tony Blair, that climate change is a bigger threat to security around the world than is terrorism.

If the George W. Bush administration and its supporters are really worried about security, they would be moving heaven and earth to reduce the burning of fossil fuels around the world. It is the security of oil, coal, and gas profits that is their priority. Global security is gravely imperilled by the reckless policies of the fossil fuel industry and its captive politicians.

Economic integration with the United States makes Canada more than complicit in this act of global irresponsibility – it makes us a participant.

Kyoto Implementation versus NAFTA

Canadian implementation of its commitment to the Kyoto Protocol, if and when it happens, will potentially be the largest environmental policy shift in the NAFTA era. The issue for Canada becomes one of dual compliance: obeying the strictures of both NAFTA and the Kyoto Protocol. The implementation of Kyoto, including emissions trading, marketing of alternatives and new technologies, and environmental regulation, will raise many trade issues relating, for example, to dispute settlement, investment, market access, subsidies, and countervailing duties.

Will Kyoto implementation invite disputes under NAFTA? Put another way, could NAFTA undermine the Canadian implementation of the Kyoto Protocol? The short answer is likely "yes." The following legal opinion considers the risk of trade challenges to Kyoto implementation as low: "Assuming that the emissions reduction targets selected by the Government are not so draconian as to oblige a virtual or actual cessation of operation, it is difficult to view the proposed Kyoto implementation measures as creating a viable expropriation claim" (Forcese 2004, 419). However, consider the phrase "actual cessation," for example, within the context of the Ontario government's commitment to close its five coal-fired electricity generation facilities. This will include Nanticoke, a long-time target of environmentalists, which is Canada's top industrial source of pollution, emitting GHGs equivalent to 3.5 million cars. The issue, in terms of NAFTA, is that the coal for these plants is supplied by US companies and the Ontario government plans to replace the loss of supply with locally produced renewables. Toronto trade lawyer Barry Appleton, the lawyer to numerous NAFTA litigants, has labelled this a "clear violation of NAFTA" (Leahy 2005). The closing of Ontario coal-fired generation facilities may be Canada's first stand in the NAFTA arena in defence of its commitment to Kyoto.

Whether a dispute panel will find in favour of US coal suppliers is not the immediate concern. Given the problems with Chapter 11 as a mechanism for dispute settlement, how expensive can foreign companies make Kyoto implementation for Canadian governments? How plausible is it that a provincial government, such as Alberta, would team up with foreign corporations, as they did with Ethyl Corporation, and together pursue a strategy to bury Kyoto implementation under a mountain of litigation? In the event that Canadian governments are forced to buy off foreign investors in order to allow for climate change measures (either to avoid litigation or in damages resulting from litigation) this will not be an additional cost of implementing Kyoto but, rather, a further cost to implementing NAFTA.

Canadian governments cannot afford to be impeded in their efforts to address climate change. Rapid, comprehensive action is needed now to avoid a catastrophic future. We may or may not be forgiven by future generations. It rather depends on whether we curb the climate change threat at a point that will allow future generations to exist.

TAKING BAD TO WORSE: "THE BIG, STUPID IDEA"

"Deep integration" represents a variety of proposals respecting the furtherance of Canada-US economic interdependence. While there are a host of environmental concerns that could be raised within the context of deep integration, we focus on three:

- further entrenchment of environmental problems created under the NAFTA regime;
- the specific proposal to establish a natural resources common market; and
- the impact of expanded fossil fuel production in Canada to meet US energy demands within the context of climate change.

Deep integration, as a progression on the NAFTA trajectory, is an opportunity to take trade policy from bad to worse. The proposals to date concentrate on increasing economic interdependence with the United States in a way that risks making NAFTA look like the environmental high-water mark. Deep integration is scrubbed clean of environmental garnishes, rhetorical mentions of sustainable development, and the establishment of lacklustre institutional provisions.

"The Big Idea," one deep integration proposal, offers four pillars of further integration: security, defence, natural resources, and economic efficiency. The author, Wendy Dobson (2002b), argues that energy markets require further integration to satisfy US interests for continental energy self-sufficiency in the wake of the 9-11 disaster.

There is a certain irony to the continental integration of natural resources, such as oil and gas, within the NAFTA-plus context because, at the insistence of Mexico, NAFTA recognizes the heightened importance of sovereignty with regard to natural resources exploitation. The North American Agreement on Environmental Cooperation (NAAEC) preamble affirms "the sovereign right of States to exploit their own resources pursuant to their own environmental and development policies" (NAAEC 1993, 2). This statement, however, is rhetorical as natural resources have not even had the bantam benefit afforded to "the environment" through the NAAEC. Natural resources are actually carved out of the environmental side agreement in order to prevent disputes over non-enforcement of domestic laws in the area of natural resources. The NAAEC (1993, 30) states: "the term 'environmental law' does not include any statute or regulation, or provision thereof, the primary purpose of which is managing the commercial harvest or exploitation ... of natural resources." If the environmental side agreement can be said to have provided any benefits of oversight, they have not been afforded to natural resources.

The NAFTA foundation from which deep integration would build towards the further integration of natural resources is largely encapsulated in Chapter 6 of NAFTA.[10] What warrants further comment here is the means proposed to further integration and the scope of this integration. Proponents of the integration of continental energy markets acknowledge that it will require the federal government to negotiate international protocols in an area that is the primary constitutional jurisdiction of the provinces. The inconvenience of federalism is to be mitigated, so says Wendy Dobson (2002b, 26), through "quiet discussion with provinces one at a time"; this and other measures are designed to create a "fund of credibility and goodwill" that Canada may "spend" in order to get what it wants.

The suggestion is that the federal government achieve deep integration through utilizing divide and conquer tactics with the provinces, who, understandably, may want a say in how their constitutional mandates are affected by international protocols. The suggestion that the federal government should proceed with deep integration without express consultation with, and the cooperation of, the provinces and territories is disrespectful, in addition to undermining the Constitution.

Sneaky diplomacy is also recommended as a tactic to broaden the scope of deep integration to include water. Dobson (2002b, 26) writes: "Such an approach could also provide a model for dealing with demand pressures on other politically sensitive natural resources, such as water. Because of these sensitivities, neither Canada nor the United States has addressed the pricing of this resource in a serious way."

The problem is that NAFTA does not expressly exempt all forms of water commercialization. Efforts by the parties to assure people that water is not a commodity under NAFTA consistently contain qualifiers that imply that "some water resources" may fall under NAFTA strictures. For example, a 1993 water accord signed by the NAFTA parties states: "The NAFTA creates no rights to the natural water resources of any Party to this Agreement; unless water, in any form, has entered into commerce and become a good or product, it is not covered by the provisions of any trade agreement, including the NAFTA" (Governments 1993). There have already been efforts to utilize NAFTA to advance some forms of water commercialization. For example, California water transportation company Sun Belt Water Inc. filed a notice of claim under Chapter 11 in 1999 against Canada to challenge a British Columbia ban on bulk water exports. It has not been acted upon.

Trade and the environment are likely to continue to clash as the commercialization of water provides a powerful incentive to use trade rules to gain economic advantage while international environmental protocols provide protection to natural ecosystems. For example, the proposed 2004 Great Lakes Annex would have allowed interbasin diversions of Great Lakes water, and its development was largely driven by trade concerns. The Council of Great Lakes Governors received a single legal opinion advising that it was impossible to stop out-of-basin transfers. This legal opinion warned of the effect of interstate trade laws and WTO rules on the current Water Resources Development Act of the US Congress. Thankfully, environmental groups persuaded the Ontario government to lead a charge in the Great Lakes Council against diversions. The new agreement was signed in December 2005, committing all ten Great Lakes jurisdictions (eight states and two provinces) to the Prohibition of Diversions principle. The victory to protect bulk water from export through environmental protocols, should it be achieved, could be nullified if the proposals for deep integration involving fresh water come into effect.

Deep integration of natural resources also acknowledges the tricky and meddling business of environmental regulatory regimes. The suggestion is to "harmonize where necessary, but not necessarily harmonize." It is important to note here the important distinction between cooperation (such as it occurs through the Organization for Economic Co-operation and Development or the CEC) and harmonization that uses a "one size fits all" approach to environmental standards. To suggest that Canadian environmental laws (i.e., endangered species, protected areas, toxics, pesticides, and environmental assessment) might have, through harmonization, a transboundary legal effect is to formally invite the powerful US lobby interests to Ottawa. Lobbyists and lawyers will both stand in the shadow of formalized integration wherever it extends. If an agreement were struck to harmonize environmental regulations with respect to natural resources, the outcome would either be to relocate the site of Canadian environmental decision making to Washington or to attract a hurricane of US lobby interests to Ottawa. The proposal for greater integration of natural resources is an attempt to decouple a wide range of Canadian resources, including water, from the minimal protections provided by existing or future domestic regulatory regimes. Any purported benefit from this integration would be a Trojan horse that would leave Canadian environmental law unguarded against motivated US corporate lobby interests.

In evaluating proposals for regulatory harmonization, one should consider that Canada's natural resource and environmental regulatory regimes are neither comprehensive nor effective with regard to protecting domestic environmental values. Many of these regimes are underfunded, in need of reform, or are too new to be judged. Consider the effort to meet the Kyoto targets, which will require the introduction of a number of new measures. This will be challenging enough for the Canadian government to accomplish, but it will be impossible if Canada's regulatory regime has to be harmonized with that of the United States.

The effect of NAFTA has been to fortify and further economic forces that are causing a global environmental crisis. The agreement has been utterly ineffective as a tool to identify or mitigate environmental impacts and, instead, has hamstrung governments' abilities to respond to urgent environmental issues. Proposals for deeper integration are premised on a NAFTA foundation and represent more of the same approach that got us into this mess in the first place.

CONCLUSION

All too often, proponents of "free trade" place the burden for proving significant effects on those expressing environmental concerns. The usual response from these proponents, as witnessed in the SEAs of trade agreements, is that environmental concerns are not sufficient to provoke a change of direction. "Insufficiency" as justification for the avoidance of environmental consideration is predicated on a misunderstanding of the basic link between trade and the environment. Environmental concern does not begin where scientific certainties prove a negative effect on the environment. Where trade rules touch on an industry or commodity, they also touch on the environmental aspects of that sector or activity. For example, agricultural trade policy affects beneficial insects because one-third of Canada's food supply depends on pollinating insects (WWF 2003, 47). Trade policy on forestry affects protected areas because the exploitation of Canada's forests is foreclosing on conservation opportunities. Trade policy that encourages urbanization affects endangered species because Canada's cities are generally in sensitive southern habitats.

The message is not that some trade policy may have negative environmental impacts but, rather, that all trade policy has environmental relevance. And in an age of environmental crisis, this relevance should be of paramount and guiding concern. Specifically, the ten-year review of NAFTA, progress towards and negotiation positions respecting new trade agreements, and contemplation of "deep integration," must all be driven by their relevance to environmental values.

After a decade of NAFTA, Canadian environmentalists have a strong case that the trade deal and deeper integration with the United States has been achieved at a heavy environmental price. The urgency of addressing the crisis of climate change requires that the assumptions implicit in the energy chapter of NAFTA be re-examined. Selling an ever-growing quantity of fossil fuels to the United States from our off-shore and from the Athabasca Tar

Sands is fuelling global suicide. The hard-wiring of our economy and energy infrastructure made evident in that 2003 summer blackout needs to be reconsidered. The response to bigger and deeper integration lies in strengthening the local and decentralized: "sustainable and local" are the antidote to "rapacious and global."

NOTES

This chapter draws on Dover (2004) and a presentation made at the conference that initiated this volume.

1 The tree branch was not the only cause of the blackout. In the words of the US-Canada Power System Outage Task Force, "long-standing institutional failures and weaknesses" were behind the blackout (Task Force 2004). This report cites four groups of causes behind the blackout, including Group 3, a "failure to manage adequately tree growth."

2 See Office of Public Affairs (2002), which cites the work of Dr Donald A. Levin (University of Texas at Austin) and Phillip S. Levin (National Marine Fisheries Service): "Half of all living bird and mammal species will be gone within 200 or 300 years; the rate of extinction is 100 to 1,000 times greater than normal; a distinct species of plant or animal becomes extinct every 20 minutes; the present period of extinction is one of the six great periods of mass extinction in the history of Earth."

3 Stated eloquently in a speech by Robert F. Kennedy Jr. (2004):

We could do what they're encouraging us to do in Washington, which is to treat the planet as if it were a business liquidation. Convert our natural resources to cash as quickly as possible. Have a few years of pollution-based prosperity. We can generate an instantaneous cash flow and the illusion of a prosperous economy, but our children are going to pay for our joyride, and they're going to pay for it with the noosed landscape, and poor health and huge cleanup costs that they're going to have to fight over time, and they're never going to be able to pay. Environmental injury is deficit spending.

4 The Canadian ecological footprint in 2001 was 6.4 global hectares per person while the US figure was 9.5 global hectares. The higher US footprint is owing to the higher energy footprint: 6.1 global hectares per person compared to the Canadian 3.3 global hectares (Loh and Wackernagel 2004, 28). Despite this difference, Canada ranks eleventh highest globally in energy footprint and joins other high-income countries that, together, have energy footprints fourteen-fold higher than those of low-income countries (Loh and Wackernagel 2004, 14).

5 These paragraphs are not intended to be a comprehensive presentation of the environmental effects of NAFTA but merely a sampling of the information.

6 For a historical overview of some the environmental concerns raised, especially during US ratification, see Johnson (1996, chap. 1).

7 Examples drawn from the experiences of both authors include the implementation and legislative reviews of the Pest Control Products Act and the Canadian Environmental Protection Act (CEPA).

8 These reports and others published are available at the Commission for Environmental Cooperation website: <http://www.cec.org>.

9 The text reads:

When developing or changing technical regulations, federal regulatory authorities must

1. ensure that regulatory officials are aware of and take account of obligations agreed to by the Government of Canada, such as the provisions of the World Trade Organization (WTO) Agreement, the North American Free Trade Agreement (NAFTA), and other multilateral, regional and bilateral Agreements. (PCO 1999, Appendix A)

Appendix A (under the subheading "Responsibilities") also relates to the role of (then) DFAIT in the coordination of WTO and NAFTA commitments.

10 A good review of the operation of this section of NAFTA in relation to deep integration is contained in Jackson (2003).

REFERENCES

Baker and Hostetler LLP. 2004. *Protecting Investors: Can Governments Stop the Music? NAFTA Chapter Eleven Background Paper.* Washington: The Canadian American Business Council and the Center for Strategic and International Studies.

Bradford, David F., Rebecca A. Fender, Stephen H. Shore, and Martin Wagner. 2005. The Environmental Kuznets Curve: Exploring a Fresh Specification. *Contributions to Economic Analysis and Policy* 4 (1): 1073–101.

Bramley, Matthew. 2002. *A Comparison of Current Government Action on Climate Change in the US and Canada.* Drayton Valley, AL: Pembina Institute.

Canada. 2000a. *Aide-Memoire: NAFTA Chapter 11 Investor-State Arbitration.* Ottawa: Trade Law Bureau (JLT), Department of Foreign Affairs and International Trade. (Document obtained through Access to Information Act.)

– 2000b. Clarifications, Transparency and Participation Issues Related to NAFTA Chapter 11 (Investor-State). Speaking Notes, Ottawa, 2 October. (Document obtained through Access to Information Act.)

– 2003a. *Canada's Troubled Fisheries.* Ottawa: Statistics Canada.

– 2003b. *Environmental Signals: Headline Indicators 2003.* Ottawa: Environment Canada.

- 2003c. *Oil Pollution and Birds.* Ottawa: Hinterland Who's Who website, Canadian Wildlife Service.
- 2003d. *Report of the Commissioner of the Environment and Sustainable Development.* Ottawa: Office of the Auditor General.
- 2004a. *The Cabinet Directive on the Environmental Assessment of Policy, Plan and Program Proposals.* Ottawa: Canadian Environmental Assessment Agency.
- 2004b. *Initial Environmental Assessment Report of the Proposed Canada-Singapore Free Trade Agreement.* Ottawa: International Trade Canada.
- 2004c. *Report of the Commissioner of the Environment and Sustainable Development Report to the House of Commons.* Ottawa: Office of the Auditor General.
Canadian Press. 2005. Alberta Premier Says Nuclear Energy Is Not a Good Option for His Province. *Canadian Press NewsWire,* 18 October.
Cheney, Dick. 2001. *The Vice President's Remarks to the Annual Meeting of the Associated Press.* Ottawa: The United States Embassy in Canada.
Clarkson, Stephen. 2002. *Canada's Secret Constitution: NAFTA, WTO and the End of Sovereignty.* Ottawa: Canadian Centre for Policy Alternatives.
COSEWIC. 2005. 500 Species Now Considered to Be at Risk. Press release. Ottawa: Committee on the Status of Endangered Wildlife in Canada.
CUPE. 2003. *Deregulation, Privatization and the Ontario Power Failure.* Ottawa: Canadian Union of Public Employees.
Daly, Herman E. 2004. *Ecological Economics: Principles and Applications.* Washington: Island Press.
DFAIT. 2002. *Initial Environmental Assessment: Trade Negotiations in the World Trade Organization.* Ottawa: Department of Foreign Affairs and International Trade.
- 2003. *Initial Strategic Environmental Assessment Report of the Free Trade of the Americas Negotiations.* Ottawa: Department of Foreign Affairs and International Trade.
Dobson, Wendy. 2002a. *North American Integration in an Integrating World: Remarks to the Asia-Pacific Summit.* Vancouver: Asia-Pacific Summit.
- 2002b. Shaping the Future of the North American Economic Space: A Framework for Action. In *The Border Papers.* Toronto: C.D. Howe Institute.
Dover, Sarah. 2004. Canada's Commitments to Kyoto and NAFTA: Risk Management and Political Smarts. Unpublished paper. Toronto: Osgoode Hall Law School.
FCM. Undated. *Water Infrastructure: Why Investment Is Needed – Budget Backgrounder Series.* Ottawa: Federation of Canadian Municipalities.
Forcese, Craig. 2004. The Kyoto Rift: Trade Law Implications of Canada's Kyoto Implementation Strategy in an Era of Canadian-US Environmental Divergence. In *The First Decade of NAFTA; The Future of Free Trade in North America,* ed. P. Kennedy, 393–421. Ardsley, NY: Transnational Publishers.
Governments. 1993. Statement by the Governments of Canada, Mexico and the United States, 2 December, Ottawa.
IPPCC. 2001. *Climate Change 2001: The Scientific Basis – Contribution of Working Group I to the Third Assessment Report of the Intergovernmental Panel on Climate Change.* Cambridge, UK: Cambridge University Press.

Jackson, Andrew. 2003. *Why the "Big Idea" Is a Bad Idea: A Critical Perspective on Deeper Economic Integration with the United States.* Ottawa: Canadian Centre for Policy Alternatives.

Jacott, Marisa, Cyrus Reed, and Mark Winfield. 2002. *The Generation and Management of Hazardous Wastes and Transboundary Hazardous Waste Shipments between Mexico, Canada and the United States.* Montreal: Commission on Environmental Cooperation of North America.

Johnson, Pierre-Marc. 1996. *The Environment and NAFTA: Understanding and Implementing the New Continental Law.* Washington: Island Press.

JPAC. 2004. *Review of Council 00–09, which allows any Party, the Secretariat, or members of the public through the JPAC, or the JPAC itself, to raise issues concerning Articles 14 and 15 of the North American Agreement for Environmental Cooperation: Council's views on Council Resolution 00–09 and Report on the Council Review of the Operation of Council Resolution 00–09.* Montreal: Joint Public Advisory Committee, Commission for Environmental Cooperation.

Kennedy, Robert F. 2004. Speech for the Max Pickerill Lecture Series, 11 March. Colby, KS: Colby Community College.

Lawton, Valerie. 2000. Caribou, Badger Now Endangered: 14 Animals and Plants Join Canada's "Tragedy" List. *Toronto Star*, 6 May, A16.

Leahy, Stephen. 2005. Kyoto vs. NAFTA. *Inter Press Service*, February 18.

Liberal Party of Canada. 1993. *Creating Opportunity: The Liberal Plan for Canada.* Ottawa: Liberal Party of Canada.

Lien, Jon. 2002. Health of Our Oceans: A Food and Health Issue. *The Food Security Network of Newfoundland and Labrador Newsletter*, April-December.

Loh, Jonathan, and Mathis Wackernagel. 2004. *Living Planet Report 2004.* Washington: World Wildlife Fund for Nature.

McQuaig, Linda. 2004. *It's the Crude, Dude: War, Big Oil and the Fight for the Planet.* Toronto: Doubleday.

Mann, Howard. 2000. Assessing the Impact of NAFTA on Environmental Law and Management Processes. Paper presented at the First North American Symposium on Understanding the Linkages between Trade and Environment, North American Commission for Environmental Cooperation, 11–12 October, Washington.

May, Elizabeth. 2005. *At the Cutting Edge: The Crisis in Canada's Forests.* Toronto: Key Porter Books.

Millennium Ecosystem Assessment. 2005. *Ecosystems and Human Well-Being Synthesis.* Washington: Island Press.

NAAEC. 1993. North American Agreement on Environmental Cooperation. Montreal: Secretariat of the Commission for Environmental Cooperation.

NEB. 2004. *Canada's Oil Sands: Opportunities and Challenges to 2015.* Calgary: National Energy Board.

Office of Public Affairs. 2002. UT Research: Global Extinction Rate Reaches Historical Proportions. *On Campus*, an online publication of the University of Texas at Austin. 29 January, 28 (14). Available at <http://www.utexas. edu/opa/pubs/ oncampus/020c_issues/0c020129/0c_extin ction.html>.

OMA. 2005. *The Illness Costs of Air Pollution: 2005–2006 Health and Economic Damage Estimates.* Toronto: Ontario Medical Association.

Ontario. 2003. *Report on August 14, 2003 Outage.* Toronto: Ministry of Energy, Government of Ontario.

Pastor, Robert A. 1997. The Clinton Administration and the Americas: The Postwar Rhythm and Blues. *Journal of Interamerican Studies and World Affairs* 38 (4): 99–128.

PCO. 1999. *Government of Canada Regulatory Policy.* Ottawa: Privy Council Office.

Price, Matt, and John Bennett. 2002. *America's Gas Tank: The High Cost of Canada's Oil and Gas Export Strategy.* New York: Natural Resource Defense Council.

Schwartz, Peter, and Doug Randall. 2003. *An Abrupt Climate Change Scenario and Its Implications for United States National Security.* Washington: Pentagon.

Sierra Club v. Cheney, et al. (No. 03-475). 2004. US Supreme Court.

Sierra Legal. 2003. BC Drinking Water Protection: Riskiest in Canada. Press release. Vancouver, 10 October.

Task Force. 2004. *Final Report on the August 14, 2003 Blackout in the United States and Canada: Causes and Recommendations.* Ottawa: Canada-US Power System Outage Task Force, Natural Resources Canada.

Thomas, Graham. 2005. Klein Fails to Impress Harvard Crowd. *Edmonton Journal,* 25 March, A1.

Toronto Star. 2000. "Godfather of Environmental Movement" Strong in His Passions. 4 July, F1.

United States. 1993. *Remarks by President Clinton, President Bush, President Carter, President Ford, and Vice President Gore in Signing of NAFTA Side Agreements.* Washington: The White House.

Vaughan, Scott, and Greg Block. 2002. *Free Trade and the Environment: The Picture Becomes Clearer.* Montreal: Commission for Economic Cooperation of North America.

Wackernagel, Mathis, and William E. Rees. 1996. *Our Ecological Footprint: Reducing Human Impact on the Earth.* Philadelphia, PA: New Society Publishers.

World Net Daily. 2003. Lights out! Record Blackout Strikes Northeast; Power Gradually Returning to New York, New Jersey, Detroit, Toronto, Cleveland. *World Net Daily,* 15 August. Available online at <http://www.worldnetdaily. com/>.

Worldwatch. 2005. *Climate Change: Reducing the Threat of Climate Change in the US: A Survey of Activities.* Worldwatch Institute 2005. Available at <www.worldwatch.org>, cited 27 December 2005.

Woynillowicz, Dan, Chris Severson-Baker, and Marlo Raynolds. 2005. *Oil Sands Fever: The Environmental Implications of Canada's Oil Sands Rush.* Drayton Valley, AL: Pembina Institute.

WWF. 2003. *The Nature Audit: Setting Canada's Conservation Agenda for the 21st Century.* Report No.1 2003. Toronto: World Wildlife Fund.

18

Imperialist Regulation: US Electricity Market Designs and Their Problems for Canada and Mexico

MARJORIE GRIFFIN COHEN

On 14 August 2003 the worst blackout in Canadian and US history knocked out power to over 50 million people, closed down main financial and industrial centres, and shut down more than 100 power-generating facilities. This massive power failure in the US northeast and Ontario demonstrated the unreliability of the US grid system and ramped up calls within the United States to further integrate the North American electricity market under the control of the US regulator, the Federal Energy Regulatory Commission (FERC). Security of the system is the justification for increased integration, but a significant impact of such integration would be to further facilitate the privatization of electricity not only in the United States but also in Mexico and Canada. It would also encourage the greater use of Canadian- and Mexican-generated electricity to both meet increased US electricity demand and help ease the price surge that accompanies electricity market restructuring.

A "North American Energy Market" was first proposed by George W. Bush during his 2000 election campaign. This vision of a seamless energy market throughout the continent was reiterated in the *National Energy Policy*, the document produced by Vice-President Dick Cheney, Secretary of State Colin Powell, and other members of the National Energy Policy Development Group (NDPD) in May 2001 (Cheney et al. 2001). Canada and Mexico feature prominently as energy sources for a country stressed by energy shortages, botched deregulation attempts, and electricity system unreliability.

The inability of the United States to meet its own future electricity needs can be blamed on the nature of the electricity sector redesign and, more specifically, on the shift to a market-driven system. Despite this, not only does the United States continue to embrace the same approach, but it would like its neighbours to adopt it as well. However, Washington's plans for an integrated continental market will have serious consequences for both Canada and Mexico – consequences that will change the entire nature of the public systems within these nations. In the case of Canada, it seems that the problems within the US system are driving Canadian governments' positions more firmly into the US orbit of deregulation, with relatively little public debate. In the case of Mexico, the debate on privatization has shifted public sentiment even more firmly away from the Mexican government's privatization plan. But even in Mexico the pieces that have been put into place so far by private independent power producers (IPPS), coupled with the imperialist nature of the US regulatory design, may have the effect of introducing Mexico to the electricity nightmares of a US-styled system.

Neither Mexico nor Canada need follow this US regulatory imperialism. The North American Free Trade Agreement (NAFTA) guarantees the ability to trade without adopting an identical system. But Canada, strangely, does not exercise this right, primarily because Canada's federal regulatory body, the National Energy Board (NEB), does not assert itself with the same kind of vigour as does FERC. In the absence of a strong federal regulatory body in Canada, FERC is setting the rules for both industry restructuring and reliability standards (McKenna 2004). Mexico, on the other hand, has constitutional provisions protecting electricity that place it in a much stronger regulatory position than Canada. This chapter analyzes FERC's attempts to move towards a fully integrated North American electricity market. It describes how the Mexican and Canadian governments are responding to this US imperialism, and it explores the options that both countries have for dealing with FERC's initiatives.

THE FEDERAL ENERGY REGULATORY COMMISSION (FERC)

FERC is an independent federal government agency in the United States that is part of the Department of Energy. It is responsible for regulating the interstate transmission of natural gas, oil, and electricity and regulates the wholesale electricity market, although it has no jurisdiction over retail sales. While the agency has jurisdiction over the activities of private utilities, it cannot control public ones.[1] FERC's mission became more aggressive and imperialist with the George W. Bush administration's determination to develop private electricity production and to shift the industry from a planned system, based on long-term projections (through regulation of both public and private utilities), to one that relies on market responses to prices in order to meet electricity needs.

Soon after Bush appointed Pat Wood as chair of FERC, Wood issued a detailed plan for a "seamless" marketplace throughout North America (NWEC 2001). This was to be accomplished through the construction of a standard market design (SMD) for the entire continent. The SMD initiatives intend to restructure the North American industry by shifting it from a reg-ulated utilities-based model for providing electricity to a competitive market-based model.[2] As FERC (2003) noted with regard to electricity in the United States, "the industry has been evolving toward a market-based approach for well over a decade." But what the agency was proposing through SMD was far from an evolutionary approach: as a well known US business rating firm noted, imposing a standard design for the electricity system "is profound, amounting to a thorough redesign of the entire US electricity market" (Lapson, Santoro, and Smyth 2002).

The point of SMD is to build on previous significant FERC orders to encourage competition in electricity generation. In 1996 Order No. 888 opened up the transmission grid through offering open access transmission tariffs. Then in 1999, through order No. 2000, FERC called for the volun-tary creation of Regional Transmission Organizations (RTOS), the infra-structure that will permit the integration of the North American system. The intention of SMD is to strengthen these earlier directives and to re-reg-ulate the industry so that wholesale markets are designed with a "level playing field" between the new private electricity providers and the exist-ing public and private utilities (FERC 2003).

Since the late 1990s about half the states in the United States have moved towards a competitive electricity system. Still, a considerable amount of electricity remains either in the public sector or is produced by monopolis-tic but highly regulated private utilities. Electricity in both Canada and Mexico is primarily in the public sector, although some provinces in Canada have initiated competitive markets and limited changes have occurred to allow some private production of electricity in Mexico.[3]

By moving towards an SMD and instituting one of the SMD's major fea-tures – RTOS – FERC is invading the regulatory territory of US state govern-ments as well as the sovereignty of Canada and Mexico. Interestingly, Washington's plans for the North American market have encountered con-siderable resistance from state governments within its own borders but rel-atively little from any governments in Canada or Mexico. Opposition in the United States has come from consumer groups, public utilities, and state officials of various kinds, including representatives from both houses of Congress (FERC 2002a; US Department of Energy 2002; Western Gover-nor's Association 2002). The main objection is to the imposition of a com-petitive market model of electricity supply that would force even integrated public utilities to break up their systems and surrender control over trans-mission in order to encourage and accommodate private electricity pro-ducers. US public utilities are incensed about losing control over their trans-mission systems and argue that FERC does not have the authority to implement such sweeping changes. The Western Governors' Association objects to FERC's imperialism because the governors feel the agency's action is unwarranted and because they do not trust its ability to understand the complexity of the issues involved. This scepticism with regard to FERC's competence stems from the agency's cavalier approach to electricity changes and its failure to take adequate consideration of the consequences of change. In reference to FERC's handling of electricity in California, the Western Governors' Association has stated that "experience in the West over the past two years has shown the immense personal and economic hardship resulting from FERC not fully understanding the implications of changes in electricity policy."[4] The governors point out that the proposed huge Western Interconnection would span three nations rather than parts of the same country (as was the case in the eastern United States) (Western Governor's Association 2002).[5] They are concerned that grafting onto the western regions of three countries a solution (SMD and an RTO) that was originally intended to meet reliability problems in the eastern part of the country could lead to unintended, and seriously negative, consequences.

The issue of SMD has been so controversial that in its April 2003 White Paper FERC backed down somewhat with regard to some features, and the timing, of its original proposal. But this was not sufficient to satisfy its critics in the United States and, during negotiations over the US Energy Bill, various attempts at compromise language failed. The result was that FERC's chairman, Joseph Kelliher, formally ended the proposal in July 2005 (FERC 2005). FERC, however, is still proceeding in its attempt to exert control over North America's transmission systems, and it is doing this by establishing three very large RTOs and revisiting and strengthening Order No. 888 to ensure private access to transmission. Ultimately FERC feels that the voluntary development of RTOs and independent systems operators (ISOs) will bring about a SMD without eliciting the political controversy of a formal SMD. An integrated North American grid would entail both creating a much larger integrated transmission system in each region and taking control of transmission away from the utilities that now own and operate them. Once again, FERC's main objective is to ensure access to markets for private producers of electricity and to shift the industry to respond to market signals. In this sense, setting up transmission as separate from existing utilities is the core of the electricity industry's restructuring exercise.[6]

REGIONAL TRANSMISSION ORGANIZATIONS (RTOS)

At the heart of FERC's standard market design is the establishment of an independent transmission provider in each megaregion. This involves separating the transmission system of each integrated utility (such as Hydro-Québec, BC Hydro, or Manitoba Hydro) from its generation and distribution capacity so that private energy producers can use the lines that are owned by public or private monopolies. The goal is to create competition in electricity generation using the model established by the telecommunications industry in its deregulation exercise.[7]

Various FERC directives in the late 1990s required that each investor-owned utility open up its transmission system to competing power providers on a non-discriminatory basis.[8] While these orders did not directly apply to public utilities and certainly had no legal implications outside the United States, they did end up having considerable significance for Canada as well as for US public utilities. Each utility exporting to the United States understood that, unless it made plans for assuring IPPs' access on its transmission lines, it would find it difficult to engage in power trading or sales within the United States. In order to assure FERC that third-party access was non-discriminatory, public utilities in Canada began establishing procedures to ensure the internal separation of transmission from generation. But even with internal "firewalls" to guarantee access, FERC was not satisfied. It therefore put considerable pressure on utilities to completely sever their transmission lines of business from generation and distribution.

All four major exporting provinces in Canada have complied in some measure with FERC orders, although some have been more proactive in encouraging the privatization of electricity generation than have others. Ontario passed the Energy Competition Act in 1998, which separated Ontario Hydro into five distinct corporations and created Hydro One Incorporated as a separate transmission corporation so that transmission assets could be privatized.[9] In British Columbia the government broke up BC Hydro early in 2003 and established BC Transmission Corporation as a separate, private company.[10] While in both cases the governments of the day had a predilection for privatization, their motivations were certainly bolstered, and frequently justified to the public, by the anticipated requirements of the establishment of a North American SMD and the development of regional RTOs. Both Manitoba Hydro and Hydro-Québec have kept their corporations intact, although they have created separate transmission divisions within their companies to ensure private-sector access. According to Hydro-Québec it was necessary to create Hydro-Québec TransÉnergie in order to ensure its power marketer status in US markets. "Hydro-Québec had to offer credible, reliable and reciprocal conditions to other producers and marketers ... the utility cannot allow itself to derive any unfair commercial benefit from its integrated structure at the expense of other market players. If it did, it would put itself in a conflict of interest situation and would not be able to benefit from reciprocal advantages" (Hydro-Québec 2004).

While the provincial governments in Canada seem to realize that FERC, with its demands for the creation of RTOs, is encroaching on their regulatory authority, they appear to be cooperating with the agency to a much greater extent than are many of their US counterparts and are handing over control of their transmission systems to RTOs. For example, BC Hydro's Annual Report stated that, "while BC Hydro doesn't fall under FERC jurisdiction, we proactively participated to ensure that the same open, non-discriminatory transmission access which exists in BC is available for wholesale market participants throughout the region" (BC Hydro 2002a, 70).

The creation of any RTO requires that all participants give up the operation and control of their transmission systems to the new organization. The RTO will be controlled and operated privately and no utility will have a voice in its governance structures.[11] This is a very radical change for public utilities and will have particular significance for Canadian utilities because it will transfer the control of a public electricity system to a foreign entity. RTOs will have the authority to set prices, enact all interchange schedules, maintain system reliability and security, and plan for future expansion of the system. While the original companies may still own the assets – that is, the transmission lines and control centres – the RTO will be able to determine the extent and nature of new investment. This would radically change the nature of the transmission system within any province since the RTO could potentially direct the owners of a transmission line to invest specifically in transmission lines that focus on exporting power to the United States. This could, then, affect the way investment decisions in generation are made and greatly encourage private-sector generation specifically for export.

The RTOs will have governing bodies that will develop their own rules and regulations over the way the transmission network will work, and if this diverges significantly from the original design, there will be little recourse for a dissenting position. Basically, any utility entering into an RTO must take it on faith that its interests will be met into the future.

Exactly how new investment in transmission facilities will be undertaken within the area of each participating transmission owner (PTO) is not certain. But FERC does have objectives in place that make it clear what the priorities for expansion will be. Expansion will occur for projects that (1) expand trading opportunities, (2) better integrate the grid, and (3) alleviate congestion that may enhance generator market power.[12] These expansion priorities, coupled with the primary objectives of an RTO, indicate that the objectives of existing transmission systems could shift their focus away from the needs of people within a jurisdiction to the objectives of export expansion, increased integration with the US grid system, and greater private access to the US market.

When some utilities in the Pacific Northwest attempted to restrict RTO West's investment role to a right to review the transmission companies' investment decisions, FERC's ruling was very clear. It stated specifically that this type of modification to its original proposal would diminish the authority of RTO West. FERC decided that the RTO would have "primary responsibility and *final decision making* authority for transmission planning and expansion of transmission facilities" (FERC 2002d, 70, emphasis in original). More recently, however, after considerable pressure from state (not Canadian) governments, FERC was a little more equivocal. In its White Paper it recognized that final authority would rest with state governments and that its FERC requirement that RTOs produce technical assessments and plans for states should be viewed as a way for RTOs to "assist" states in their decisions (FERC 2003). But, according to FERC, the Final Rule (yet to be established) would require RTOs "to have a regional planning process in place as soon as practicable" (ibid.). It seems fairly clear that, for all intents and purposes, the RTOs will be in charge of system planning.

New investments in cross-border transmission lines could well turn out to be very expensive for Canada's provincial governments. This is mainly because of the existing technical problems that ensue from the relatively small proportion of electricity that can be handled on the existing transnational transmission lines. The desire for the private sector to export into the more expensive US electricity market will almost certainly result in greater demands for greater transmission access to the United States. Since, for the most part, the wires will remain in the public sector in Canada, it is likely that the public will pay for the expansion of a system that will serve American rather than Canadian customers. The implications of having RTOs controlling future investment decisions in both countries are enormous. Canada's transmission systems have been geared to serving domestic customers, with only a relatively small proportion of the electricity generated being exported. The priorities for grid expansion through the RTO system of planning may well not include the needs of various domestic customers who require transmission expansion. At the very least it will leave the final authority regarding what areas get served in the hands of a foreign entity.

One of the major implications for both Canada and Mexico in the new design for the transmission market is that it will encourage both exports and imports of power and cause an escalation of domestic prices. If increased access to US markets occurs, as is the intention of the RTOs, all new private-sector energy generation in both countries will have the option of selling electricity within the province or to the United States. This will result in domestic consumers competing with US consumers for power produced within their own countries.[13] As FERC notes, cost-shifting can occur – that is, cheap power can leave one region to be sold in another, higher-priced, region – when generation is not already under contract for purchase (as is the case in most regulated monopolies). The only remedy for this cost-shifting, according to FERC, would be for domestic utilities to contract for all private-sector power to ensure that future generation "stays at home." Under these circumstances, any domestic utility will need to pay a premium in order to buy the private power produced within the country. It is clear that the anticipated expansion of trade with the United States as a result of the RTO would result in a progressive ratcheting up of prices.

CREATING LARGER MARKETS

The notion that the "market" is a natural phenomenon that automatically coordinates demand and supply is very far off the mark when it comes to an electricity market. Unlike the housing market, where buyers and sellers meet at some point, the electricity market has to be coordinated so that electricity sellers can get the electricity to the buyers. This requires two sets of coordinators – one that oversees the actual buying and selling (normally an electricity pool of some sort, like NordPool in Norway or an independent systems operator [ISO]) and one that coordinates the transmission. An electricity market is considerably more complex than are other markets because one of its absolutely critical aspects – the transmission system – has limited capacity, and this makes it necessary for a third party to sort out who is going to get to use it at various points in time.[14]

Several important changes in North American electricity markets have given rise to serious problems. One is related to the relentless increase in the sheer size of the electricity markets and the distances over which electricity is transported. The electricity grids between Canada and the United States serve two main purposes: to ensure the reliability of the system and to permit the trading of electricity. Reliability is a very important aspect of the interconnections that need to be maintained through some integration of the grid. This works extremely well if various independent jurisdictions are able to depend on other electricity providers when their systems need support. This occurs constantly at present. The trading that occurs is also important, both for the efficiencies it can create and for the income it brings to exporting jurisdictions. But the main concern with the creation of continent-wide markets is the extent to which the objectives of trade may override other important social objectives associated with the delivery of electricity, such as equity, low costs, regional development, Aboriginal rights, reliability, and conservation. As trading areas extend thousands of miles across the continent, efficiencies are lost, the reliability of the system is compromised, and meeting local needs can be superseded by the lure of large incomes from exports.

A second problem created by the restructuring of the electricity sector is the startling increase in electricity trading by corporations that do not produce electricity but, rather, buy and sell it in order to take advantage of price differences across the continent. The redesign of the system is occurring to facilitate the increase in trading by private traders, such as Duke Energy, and public utilities like Hydro-Québec and British Columbia's Powerex. While Enron's trading needs sparked the system's redesign and a new set of rules to facilitate traders, these initiatives have taken on a life of their own, long after Enron's activities have been discredited.

A third problem related to restructuring comes from the attempts to deregulate some parts of the electricity business (generation), while retaining the monopoly aspects of other aspects (transmission and distribution). The literal disintegration process of electricity deregulation involves the separation of generation from transmission and privatizing and deregulating the generation sector. This separation of two previously interconnected aspects of electricity production proceeds on the notion that, while once the electricity industry in general was a natural monopoly, electricity generation can now be open to competition. New technology, mainly the rise of combined cycle gas turbines (CCGS), allows generation facilities to be built more cheaply and, therefore, does not require monopoly conditions to succeed. The planning and public investment of funds, which occur with hydro and nuclear facilities, are not necessary with newer generation technologies and, therefore, make electricity generation more attractive to the private sector (Rothwell and Gomas 2003).

The technology of transmission, however, has not changed its characteristic as a natural monopoly; this is mainly because the construction of a transmission system is complex, expensive, and does not efficiently allow for competing transmission lines. The result is a hybrid system with a competitive market in electricity generation that encourages increased supply coupled with a limited and monopolistic transmission system. The bottlenecks that are created, then, tend to limit the expansion of the generation market and have a tendency to increase the unreliability of the system itself. It is this problem that is most crucial in overcoming the barriers that now exist to a continent-wide electricity market.

The big advantage of a system operated as an integrated utility (whether in the public sector or a regulated private utility) is that planning for supply, transmission, and distribution is undertaken simultaneously. As long as electricity was considered a natural monopoly, it remained bound by specific geographical limits and relatively little competition occurred between utilities. The system, if properly regulated to ensure that special interests did not capture the planning of the utility, worked well, was efficient, and generally produced electricity at low prices. But the separation of transmission from generation has torqued the system in ways that distort both reliability and efficiency.

THE ELECTRICITY DEBATE IN MEXICO

Attempts to privatize any aspect of energy resources in Mexico are watched very closely and elicit strong resistance from opposition political parties and the public. Every major and overt privatization initiative has been defeated, including President Ernesto Zedillo's 1999 attempted outright sale of the state's electricity assets.[15] This does not mean that private interests are absent from the electricity sector, however. Private power producers and private production from self-generation or co-generation account for about 12 percent of capacity in Mexico. By the time the new generation facilities under construction are in operation, about 20 percent of electricity generation capacity will be in private hands.[16] It is anticipated that by 2010 more than half the electricity generated will come from independent power producers (IPPs) and self-producers (Breceda-Lapeyre 2002).

This incremental, or concealed, privatization is rooted in the 1992 Public Electricity Service Act (*Ley del Servicio Público de Energía Eléctrica*), which attempted to modify constitutional prohibitions against private electricity production (Alvarez-Garvin 2001). The law was adopted in order to justify Mexico's NAFTA commitments to private investment and trade – commitments that appeared to contradict the explicit prohibitions against private electricity production in the Constitution. The 1992 law has subsequently been challenged as unconstitutional, putting Mexico's electricity commitments under NAFTA into question. While these issues are as yet unresolved, the debate over the privatization of electricity remains very public. As the following will show, the very strong wording in the Mexican Constitution, while highly unusual in its protection against privatization, is the basis for resisting privatization attempts.

Electricity was nationalized in 1960 and, at the same time, constitutional prohibitions were made against private electricity. Mexico's Constitution establishes that the generation, transmission, distribution, and supply of electricity to be used as a "public service" remain the exclusive responsibility of the federal government. Article 27 of the Constitution states that: "the nation will have exclusive responsibility to generate, deliver, transform, distribute and supply electric energy that is directed to provide service to the public. In this area, concessions will not be authorized to private companies and the nation will make use of the assets and natural resources that are required to meet this end."[17]

Two government-owned companies have the sole legal responsibility for carrying out these tasks – the Federal Electricity Commission (*Comisión Federal de Electricidad*), which supplies most of the electricity to the entire country, and Central Light and Power (*Luz y Fuerza Centro*), which provides electricity to Mexico City and other municipalities. These two companies comprise the National Electricity System (*Sistema Eléctrico*

Nacional). In December 1992 the first step towards privatization was taken with the Public Electricity Service Act. This act sidestepped the Mexican Constitution by declaring that certain kinds of activities do not constitute providing electricity as a public service and, therefore, could be provided by the private sector.[18] These reforms were made possible by redefining the concepts of public service and public utility. The act also excludes some types of private production from the concept of public utility. Article 3 of the new law reads:

The following are not considered to be elements of public utility:

I. Power generation for self-sufficiency, cogeneration or small-scale production;
II. Power generation by producers for sale to the Federal Electricity Commission;
III. Power generation deriving from cogeneration, independent production, and small-scale production for purposes of export;
IV. Importation of electrical power by natural or legal persons exclusively for their own use; and
V. Electrical power generation for use in emergencies arising from interruptions in public electricity service.[19]

Independent power producers and small-scale generators (covering all forms of electricity generation) must sell exclusively to Mexico's Federal Electricity Commission (CFE), unless they export their supply. CFE may purchase up to 20 megawatts of capacity from any private producer.[20] This redefinition of what constitutes electricity production as a public service was crucial because it brought Mexican law in line with NAFTA. The NAFTA language that had been negotiated did not reflect the wording of the Constitution and was clearly not as restrictive as was the Constitution itself.

The following is the wording in NAFTA (NAFTA Secretariat 1994, Chapter 6, Annex 602.3):

Reservations:
1. The Mexican State reserves to itself the following strategic activities, including investment in such activities and the provision of services in such activities:
(c) the supply of electricity as a public service in Mexico, including, except as provided in paragraph 5, the generation, transmission, transformation, distribution and sale of electricity.

Paragraph 5 shows the exceptions, which include (1) production for own use, (2) co-generation, and (c) independent power production.

The change in the meaning of public service in NAFTA creates an opening for a variety of actions that would benefit either trade or investment in electricity. The change allows private producers within Mexico to sell electricity to the United States; it encourages an increase in private electricity production for sale to the CFE; and it permits an increase in both co-generation and self-generation of electricity by private companies. While the initial impact of this change was relatively small, in terms of stimulating private production, it did pave the way for increased private production in the future.

Since private power producers are allowed to import and export electricity, the conditions have been established for the development of a private electricity industry for export to the United States. Under the Foreign Investment Act foreign corporations are allowed to participate in all activities that are not categorized as public service. Thus, these changes have added significance for foreign producers who want to produce electricity for the Mexican market or for trade.[21] The result is that this modest opening of the electricity market to allow private power production will have significant repercussions. This is evident in the plans for extensive inter-ties[22] between Mexico and the United States, including four lines from Baja California, two from the Northwest, and two from the North (NAEWG 2002).

Within Mexico the major constraints on private electricity production relate to the underdeveloped nature of gas explorations. But should this sector also become more liberalized, exports of electricity to the United States would increase considerably. Currently, Mexico is exporting very little, although the amount of imports from the United States will likely be substantial once the new transmission lines are completed.

Within Mexico the major controversy over electricity privatization centres on the discrepancies between NAFTA and the Constitution. If the Public Electricity Service Act is unconstitutional, then so too will be the NAFTA commitment. In any case, overt privatization is so unpopular with people that this is unlikely to be brought to the public in the same manner as it was by President Zedillo. A more likely scenario is that the relatively rapid growth of private production, coupled with increased inter-ties with the United States, could bring increased privatization to Mexico through incremental means. The major difference between Canada and the United States, however, is that Mexico does not at present have a significant export market. This means that US regulatory changes will not affect existing regulations in Mexico. However, as Mexico develops greater inter-ties with its northern neighbour, US regulatory changes will come into direct conflict with the limits to privatization established in the Mexican Constitution.

CANADA'S REGULATORY SYSTEM

Canada's electricity system is gradually shifting from a planned, regulated, public system to an unplanned system that relies increasingly on the private sector to provide electricity based on North American market rates.[23]

However, the bulk of Canada's electricity is still provided by public, provincially based utilities. Regulation of electricity is very different in Canada from what it is in the United States. The Canadian Constitution gives the provinces authority over generation, transmission, and distribution of electricity within their borders, and national oversight over electricity is minimal. The provinces also have jurisdiction over intraprovincial transmission grids. The National Energy Board's (NEB) mandate is restricted, under the National Energy Board Act, to the regulation of exports and the construction of facilities related to international trade (NEB 1992). The act does not regulate energy within provincial boundaries, interprovincial electricity trade, or energy emissions.

In recent years NEB's close monitoring of exports, which, in the past, included public hearings on each application for an export permit, has been replaced by blanket export permits that last for up to ten years. This change occurred in response to the increase in trading activities of the provincial utilities – activities that relied on being able to sell electricity on the spot market. The result of this change in oversight is that frequently export permits are given to companies before they have any electricity generating capacity. For example, Duke Energy, headquartered in Charlotte, North Carolina, was given a ten-year blanket export permit to export electricity from British Columbia, yet to date it has no generation facilities in that province. This indicates that many companies are involved, or hope to be involved, in electricity trading alone, leaving aside the generation aspect of the industry. While, officially, the federal government has jurisdiction over all interprovincial trade, it has chosen not to exercise its powers with regard to electricity. Nor has the federal government attempted to impose a national transmission grid system – or even regional grid systems – in order to encourage trade among the provinces. The underdeveloped nature of the grid system within Canada is directly attributable to the absence of effective federal authority in this area. Two important consequences flow from this: first, very little trade in electricity occurs between Canadian provinces; second, the major electricity-producing provinces have stronger ties with US markets than they do with neighbouring provinces.

Canada's willingness to give up the benefits of effective electricity systems in the face of FERC demands does not make sense. It is strange, given the overwhelming public presence in the Canadian electricity sector, that discussions of electricity restructuring have been so heavily dominated by private-sector needs. For example, private-sector interests have captured the Canadian Electrical Association (CEA), the professional association of electrical producers. The CEA, during a crucial period of restructuring, was chaired by David McD. Mann, the president and CEO of one of the smallest electricity companies in Canada – Emera. Emera is an investor-owned utility located in Nova Scotia, and while it exports little electricity to the

United States at the moment, it would clearly like to be part of a bigger picture. Since Emera has a share in the natural gas pipeline that exports to the northeastern United States, and also owns a utility in Maine, it supports "integrated US and Canadian energy markets" (Mann 2003). In a speech delivered in Washington, DC, in June 2003 Mann called for SMD and RTOS as a way to address the problems that have caused uncertainty in the industry (ibid.).

The absence of a strong Canadian regulator of electricity becomes glaringly evident in negotiations between the two countries over SMD and RTOS. Each province is basically on its own with regard to determining its relationship with the United States. This is unfortunate, given FERC's drive to control the entire North American electricity industry. In particular, FERC is giving the impression that Canadian electricity systems will have to mirror developments in the United States in order to gain access to the US market.

The major electricity trading provinces seem to have accepted this FERC dictum without question. In British Columbia, for example, the energy minister has stated that separating its transmission system from BC Hydro and handing it over to the US-based RTO West is necessary in order "to satisfy the US Federal Energy Regulatory Commission, which has been pressing utilities in North America to separate the transmission from the generation components of their businesses" (Kennedy 2002).

With a strong federal presence in the negotiations, Canadian provinces *could* maintain the main features of integrated public systems and still have access to the US market. This is because there is no requirement in international law that compels any government in Canada to change its system in order to export to the United States. This is a fundamental protection that has been retained under NAFTA. According to the NAFTA Commission for Environmental Cooperation, in its assessment of the cross-border electricity trade, provincial decisions to acquiesce to FERC demands are voluntary, at least under NAFTA legal requirements:

The demand for reciprocity from US producers has already become a prominent issue relating to cross-border trade. Under NAFTA, a Party is not required to provide reciprocity, but only national treatment for the goods of another Party. *Market participants in Canada, such as BC Hydro, have for the time being chosen to agree to reciprocity voluntarily rather than insist on their rights.* (CEC 1999, emphasis added)

What this means is that, as long as a province treats domestic and foreign firms in the same way (which is a requirement under "national treatment" provisions), it is not contravening NAFTA. This would mean, then, that if domestic firms have any access to transmission infrastructure, foreign firms are entitled to the same kind of access under the same conditions. Under the conventional treatment of independent power producers (IPPS), within a system dominated by a public utility IPPS sell their power directly to the utility, or, if wholesale competition has been introduced, they must have access to the utility's wires in order to sell to another distributor. This access is already granted to both domestic and foreign IPPS in all provinces in Canada.

In short, NAFTA is not driving electricity-sector deregulation and privatization, as is frequently the case in other public-sector industries. NAFTA could be used to maintain and protect the distinct nature of Canada's electricity industries, although up until now these powers have been assiduously ignored. The political reason why Canada does not invoke NAFTA's protection seems to be related to the commitment to neoliberal ideology. Governments appear determined to shift as much of the electricity industry as possible to the private sector. IPPS recognize the tremendous export potential that would be available if the system were designed to allow greater access to transmission lines to the United States: they want to be in on the ground floor of the expansion of the private electricity market in North America. If they can convince governments, as they seem to have done in Ontario, Alberta, and British Columbia, that provincial treasuries will also benefit from the private export of energy, then following the US example is not only the path of least resistance but will also ensure that all new electricity production will be firmly in private hands.

While the notion that increased exports will generate huge financial gains for the provinces can backfire, as occurred with British Columbia Powerex's involvement with market manipulation in California, no government seems ready to rethink the project of fully integrating Canada's electricity with the United States. The federal government, through the NEB, seems to support these initiatives. Certainly the shift of the NEB's offices from Ottawa to Calgary, where it became even more heavily influenced by the private sector's campaign for energy deregulation in all sectors, may explain the agency's reluctance to confront FERC and cross-border issues more generally.

CONCLUSION

For the most part electricity privatization in Canada and Mexico is not taking Britain's route of selling-off electricity assets to the private sector; rather, privatization is occurring incrementally through regulatory change. The external regulatory change that is likely to have the most profound impact on both countries, regardless of whether privatization is sought, will be the attempt to establish a North American market with a standard market design that demands competition in generation and privately controlled transmission systems.

Electricity production, transmission, and distribution have unique characteristics that require long-term planning. Long-term, coordinated, strategic planning is not a feature of a privatized system within which generation
is deregulated. FERC's directives to the market are an explicit attempt to fix
problems faced in some US electricity markets. The solutions to these US
"problems" also benefit the large private electricity producers who are carrying on the Enron objective of privatizing and deregulating electricity
throughout the continent. None of the changes that have occurred and are
proposed by Washington provides solutions to the energy problems that
confront Canada and Mexico.

With Washington in charge of North American electricity through FERC,
Mexico and Canada face a "lose-lose" future. If the attempt to restructure
North American electricity fails, the consequences will be disastrous: blackouts, brownouts, and whiteouts will become as commonplace as they are
in some developing countries.[24] But even if restructuring succeeds, prices
will skyrocket, particularly for people in hard-to-serve areas. Governments
that want to remain in office will respond by shelling out money to angry
consumers – at least for a while. When ensuring an adequate supply
becomes a driving force in the market deregulation initiative, governments
inevitably end up massively subsidizing private production.

The main issue before both Canada and Mexico is whether electricity
systems should remain independent and controlled by their own public
systems or be subsumed within the US system. Integrating the American,
Canadian, and Mexican electricity markets, which is FERC's goal, will result
in prices that are established by US markets and regulations that further the
energy objectives of both Washington and private companies. Canada and
Mexico are free to make their own decisions and need not adopt the US
strategy for continental electricity integration. NAFTA allows both trading
and investment across borders without having to establish standard market
designs. But in order to pursue this route, at the very least, the Canadian
National Energy Board and the federal government would have to become
proactive in protecting the country's interests.

NOTES

The author would like to thank Bruce Laxdal, Robert Shaw-Wood, Leticia
Campos Aragón, and Steve Thomas for their help in understanding the Mexican
electricity market.

1 The Department of Energy (DOE) has exclusive jurisdiction over the construction
   of cross-border electric transmission lines and the export of electricity.
2 The initial filing on this issue is in FERC (2002b). This and various other FERC
   filings on this issue can be found at <www.ferc.gov>.

3 For a discussion of electricity systems in each province in Canada see Marjorie Griffin Cohen (2001). For a discussion of changes in the electricity system in Mexico see Leticia Campos Aragón (2003).

4 During California's energy crisis of 2000–01 many utilities in the Pacific Northwest were forced into expensive purchase contracts in order to avoid relying on spot market prices. They locked into high prices largely because FERC would not impose regional wholesale market price caps. For more on this, see Ellen Lapson, Lina Santoro, and Philip Smyth (2002).

5 The Western Interconnection would ultimately link three large RTOs and include the entire western regions of the United States, Canada, and Mexico.

6 At a US Senate hearing on electricity deregulation FERC chairman James Hoecker elaborated on the significance of an independent and integrated transmission system: "it is the strategic asset, the integrated network platform, upon which any competitive and transparent wholesale power market must be built" (BC Hydro 2002b, 2).

7 For a discussion of the deregulation of the telecommunications industry, see Sam Peltzman and Clifford Winston (2000).

8 These were FERC orders 888 and 889.

9 For a variety of reasons this sale did not occur, but privatization was the aim when Hydro One was created as a distinct and separate company.

10 This is a wholly government-owned private corporation, but the rules for private corporations are distinct from those of a Crown Corporation. In particular, a private corporation does not have the public scrutiny that a Crown Corporation has, and its shares are more easily sold.

11 For a discussion of the proposed governance structure of RTO West, the most advanced RTO to date, see Marjorie Griffin Cohen (2003).

12 These were the priorities for expansion listed in FERC's filing for RTO West (FERC 2002c).

13 In Canada the major constraint at the moment is the limits to the transmission system into the United States. The major constraint in Mexico is the constitutional limit to gas exploration, which, in turn, limits electricity production possibilities.

14 The transmission constraints are compounded by the technical necessity to coordinate production and distribution because electricity needs to be used as it is generated.

15 Zedillo proposed a model similar to the British model, which included selling electrical assets and moving towards a power pool. See Leticia Campos Aragón (2003) and Steve Thomas (1999).

16 These figures represent very rapid increases in private electricity capacity in recent years. According to the 2001 Annual Report of Mexico's Federal Electricity Commission, IPPs accounted for 3.4 percent of electricity capacity and co/self-generation for 4.3 percent for a total of 7.7 percent of generation capacity in the private sector. Within the following two years an additional 2,300 megawatts of capacity was added, bringing the total capacity in the private sector to 12 percent.

The 20 percent figure includes capacity under construction in 2002 (Shaw-Wood 2003).

17 Translation by Bruce T. Laxdal.

18 This act says: "*It is the exclusive competence of the Nation to generate, conduct, transform, distribute* and supply electrical power for purposes of public utility, pursuant to Article 27 of the Constitution. No concessions will be awarded to private interests, and the Nation, through the Federal Electricity Commission, will use the natural goods and resources required for such purposes" (Mexico 1992, Article 1), quoted in Breceda-Lapeyre (2000, 24, emphasis added).

19 Mexico (1992, Article 3), quoted in Breceda-Lapeyre (2000, 33).

20 President Fox's attempt to increase this to 50 percent of an IPP's capacity was overturned by the Supreme Court but was the catalyst for an examination of the contradiction between the Public Service Electricity Law and the Constitution (Souccar and Newman 2003).

21 Currently, there is considerable foreign building for electricity production in Mexico. See Breceda-Lapeyre (2000).

22 "Inter-ties" is a commonly used term in the industry: it denotes the connections between regional grids.

23 The largest electricity systems in Canada are public systems. Some provincial systems are private but, until recently, have operated as highly regulated monopolies.

24 Blackouts occur when whole areas lose power for a specific length of time. Typically, this is short-term (such as a result of a storm or generation failure) and can be rectified by fixing the power lines or importing power from elsewhere on the grid. Brownouts refer to periodic, and often expected, times when electricity is not available for some users, such as occurs frequently in Third World countries. This is primarily a problem of capacity on the system. Whiteouts refer to the failure of whole networks or grids, such as occurred in the US Northeast in August 2003, with the result that networks that must "cold-start" an entire system.

REFERENCES

Alvarez-Garvin, R. 2001. Objeciones a la Privatización del Sector Eléctrico Mexicano. Paper presented at I Foro Electrico Nacional, Universidad Obrera de México, Mexico City, 26 September.

Aragón, Leticia Campos. 2003. *El Modelo Británico en la Industria Eléctrica Mexicana*. Coyocan: Siglo Veintiuno Editores.

BC Hydro. 2002a. *Annual Report*. Vancouver: BC Hydro.

– 2002b. A Briefing on BC Hydro's Transmission Capacity Requirements, 002/09/26.v2, BC Hydro Executive Operations, Vancouver.

Breceda-Lapeyre, Miguel G. 2000. *Debate on Reform of the Electricity Sector in*

Mexico: Report on its Background, Current Status and Outlook. Montreal: North American Commission for Environmental Cooperation.

– 2002. *Private Investment in Mexico's Electricity Sector.* Montreal: North American Commission for Environmental Cooperation, Environment, Economy and Trade Program.

CEC. 1999. *Electricity in North America: Some Environmental Implications of the North American Free Trade Agreement (NAFTA).* Montreal: Commission for Environmental Cooperation.

Cheney, Dick, Colin L. Powell, Paul O'Neill, Gale Norton, Ann M.Veneman, Donald L. Evans, Norman Y. Mineta, Spencer Abraham, Joe M. Allbaugh, Christine Todd Whitman, Joshua B. Bolton, Mitchell E. Daniels, Lawrence B. Lindsay, Ruben Barrales, and Andrew D. Lundquist. 2001. *National Energy Policy: Report of the National Energy Policy Development Group.* Washington, DC: US Government Printing Office.

Cohen, Marjorie G. 2001. From Public Good to Private Exploitation: GATS and the Restructuring of Canadian Electrical Utilities. *Canadian-American Public Policy* 48 (December): 1–79.

– 2003. *High Tension: BC Hydro's Deep Integration with the US through RTO West.* Vancouver: BC Citizens for Public Power.

FERC. 2002a. Initial Comments of the Consumer Federation of America and Consumers Union, Docket No. RM01-12-000, Federal Energy Regulatory Commission, Washington, DC.

– 2002b. Remedying Undue Discrimination through Open Access Transmission Service and Standard Electricity Market Design, Docket No. RM01-12-000, Federal Energy Regulatory Commission, Washington, DC.

– 2002c. *RTO West, Stage 2 Filing, RTO1-35.* Washington, DC: Federal Energy Regulatory Commission, 29 March.

– 2002d. Declaratory Order on Regional Transmission Organization Proposal, Docket No. RTO1-35-006 and RTO1-35-007, 18 September, Federal Energy Regulatory Commission, Washington, DC.

– 2003. *White Paper: Wholesale Power Market Platform.* Washington, DC: Federal Energy Regulatory Commission.

– 2005. Order Terminating Proceeding. Docket No. RM01-12-000. Washington DC: Federal Energy Regulatory Commission.

Hydro-Québec. 2004. *Profile.* Available at <www.hydroquebec.com/transenergie>, cited 19 May 2004.

Kennedy, Peter. 2002. BC to Reform Electricity Sector, Lift Rate Freeze. *Globe and Mail*, 13 November, B6..

Lapson, Ellen, Lina Santoro, and Phylip Smyth. 2002. *FERC Standard Market Design: Credit Implications.* New York: Fitch Ratings. Available at <www.fitchratings.com>.

McKenna, Barrie. 2004. Energy Rules Could Freeze Out Canada. *Globe and Mail: Report on Business*, 14 January, B3.

Mann, David McD. 2003. Remarks to Embassy of Canada Energy Trade Show, 12 June, Washington, DC.

Mexico. 1992. *Public Electricity Utility Law* [Ley del Servicio Público de Energía Eléctrica]. Mexico City: Official Gazette of the Federation.

NAEWG. 2002. *North America: The Energy Picture*. Washington, DC: North American Energy Working Group.

NAFTA Secretariat. 1994. *North American Free Trade Agreement (NAFTA): Legal Text*. Ottawa, Mexico City, and Washington: NAFTA Secretariat.

NEB. 1992. *Inter-Utility Trade Review: Inter-Utility Cooperation*. Ottawa: National Energy Board.

NWEC. 2001. *New FERC Chair Threatens Shake-Up of Power Industry*. Oregon: NW Energy Coalition.

Peltzman, Sam, and Clifford Winston. 2000. Deregulation of Network Industries: What's Next. AEI-Brookings Joint Center for Regulatory Studies, Washington DC.

Rothwell, Geoffrey, and Thomas Gomas. 2003. *Electricity Economics: Regulation and Deregulation*. Piscataway, NJ: IEEE Press.

Shaw-Wood, Robert. 2003. Personal communication with Robert Shaw-Wood, Commercial Counsellor. Mexico, February.

Souccar, David, and Gray Newman. 2003. *Electric Utilities: Power to Converge*. New York: Morgan Stanley, 27 January, 1–30.

Thomas, Steve. 1999. Comentarios a la 'Propuesta de reforma estructural de la industria eléctrica mexicana,' publicado por el Secretario de Energía, Dr. Luis Téllez K. *Problemas del Desarrollo* (July/September).

US Department of Energy. 2002. Senators Criticize SMD during Energy and Natural Resources Committee Hearing. *Electricity Restructuring Weekly Update* (20 September).

Western Governor's Association. 2002. Governors Cite Concerns over FERC's Proposal for Electricity Grids. Washington, DC, 22 August.

19

Pipelines and Pipe Dreams:
Energy and Continental Security

LARRY PRATT

All that foreign oil, controlling American soil.
> Bob Dylan, "Slow Train Coming"

For America, buying oil from Canada should be akin to buying a used pick-up truck from your brother-in-law. He might be cutting you a deal, and maybe you don't like the fact that he thinks the Edmonton Oilers are better than the New York Rangers, but you need the truck, he needs the money, and you are pretty sure that the other is not seeking your total annihilation.
> Washington energy analyst Frederick Cedoz

The idea of a Fortress North America in energy is not a recent one. It occurred, in the first instance, as a solution to a problem in social engineering. Beginning in the 1920s and 1930s a variety of individuals and organizations advocated the pooling of the resources of the North American continent, giving American resource consumers unlimited access to Canadian supplies of energy in return for guaranteed access to the vast American market. To some, it was simply a matter of engineers reorganizing the physical and social assets of North America. The idea that the continent's resources – notably its water and energy – ought to be "operated as a self-contained functional unit under technological control" without borders was proposed by Technocracy Inc. as a way of ameliorating the Depression in the 1930s (Technocracy Inc. 2004), and this supposedly scientific and apolitical approach won the support of some prominent American intellectuals – such as Thorstein Veblen, L. King Hubbert, and Charles Steinmetz. Technocracy went so far as to propose the elimination of money in favour of energy credits for all North Americans.

Later, at the end of the 1960s, the idea of a "continental energy deal" was raised in the context of the discovery of oil and gas resources in Alaska and the High Canadian Arctic. Under this scheme, Canadian exporters of energy would gain unfettered access to the US market, while the Americans would be given complete freedom to develop Alaskan and Canadian northern oil and gas resources, and to bring them in large pipelines to the lower forty-eight states. No such "deal" was ever struck, in part because of nationalistic objections in Canada but also because of the high cost of developing frontier resources.

The notion of a Fortress North America in energy was raised again during the first Organization of Petroleum Exporting Countries (OPEC) energy crisis of 1973–74, though at that time the emphasis was on the rapid exploitation of the vast bituminous oil sands of northern Alberta. Canada and the Province of Alberta were urged to bring on new production from the oil sands for the US market, at a production cost then reckoned at US$20 per barrel, in order to reduce American import dependence on unstable Middle East oil. But, once again, the costs and technical obstacles involved in bringing the oil sands into large-scale production prevented the realization of a Fortress North America in energy supply.[1]

It was a pipe dream. Costs and timing of the huge projects rather than political disagreements prevented any early deep integration of the US and Canadian energy markets, though US investment and access to the American export market via a network of pipelines did play important roles in the exploitation of western Canada's oil and natural gas in the 1950s and after. The rationale for a much deeper integration of the two markets was made by the Macdonald Royal Commission (1985): free trade in energy and other goods and services would enhance productivity and allocate resources most efficiently, but the Royal Commission had no answer to the fundamental problem of high costs and energy trade.

This chapter argues that the Canada–US Free Trade Agreement (CUFTA) and the subsequent North American Free Trade Agreement (NAFTA), with their special energy provisions, mark the true beginning of the deeper integration of the oil and gas industries of North America. NAFTA made feasible the financing of new takeaway export pipelines from the Maritimes and western Canada, which encouraged consolidation and made it possible to export far more gas at much higher prices than was hitherto possible. Since NAFTA, the integration process has been advanced, in part, by continental security concerns over depletion of US reserves and growing reliance on Middle East oil. Since the terrorist attacks of 11 September 2001 some American energy companies have sought insurance from supply disruption by buying up Canadian resources and corporations, while Canadian politicians and energy companies have played the security card by offering to build new pipelines and develop new sources of oil and natural gas supply for the US consumer. Canada's dominant oil pipeline system has embraced a "continental strategy" aimed at bringing oil from the oil sands of Alberta to southern markets (Enbridge. n.d.; *Financial Post* 2003a). The idea of building east-west pipelines and of exploiting Canadian resources for the Canadian market has been dropped. Self-reliance, Canadianization, a national energy strategy – these policies have been abandoned in favour of a deregulated energy structure dependent for its growth on the US market.

At the same time, the US government, worried about excessive dependence on oil and gas exporters from the Middle East, has been sponsoring import diversification, the growth of liquefied natural gas import facilities, and the development of new energy supplies in areas such as West Africa and South America – a strategy that is likely to limit the penetration of Canadian exports of oil and natural gas over the long run. American energy security policy stresses the advantages of globalization and the investment in many potential suppliers rather than a reliance on one supplier or group of suppliers, however neighbourly and eager to sell they might be. Fostering competition among a broad range of suppliers helps hold prices down and also enhances energy security. US national energy strategy, as reflected in a bill proposed by Congressional Republicans in November 2003, provides billions of dollars in tax breaks for power producers and the oil and gas industry but no incentives for activities in the NAFTA bloc (Hulse 2003). As the old Congressional saying goes, foreigners don't vote.

Canada's real (though not stated) energy policy is to be the principal and most secure supplier to the world's largest market for oil, gas, and electricity. As of fall 2003,[2] Canada was the number one supplier of oil and refined products to the United States, shipping about two million barrels a day, ahead of Saudi Arabia, Venezuela, and Mexico; Canada also accounts for more than 90 percent of all US imports of natural gas, shipping by pipelines 9.6 billion cubic feet per day (*Financial Post* 2003d). Imports from Canada now account for close to one-fifth of the total American consumption of natural gas, the fastest-growing fuel in both countries. The oil sands of Athabasca and the natural gas reserves of northern Alberta, British Columbia, and the Nova Scotian offshore are being developed for the US market. What drives this deepening integration of the oil and gas industries of the United States and Canada is a mixture of US demand, high prices, the low value of the Canadian dollar, NAFTA rules, new export pipelines and other infrastructure, and – since 9/11 – security concerns.

Security is often regarded as a public-sector issue – a matter for the state. However, it is not difficult to show that major private-sector investments in North American energy markets are being shaped by security interests as well as by commercial goals – though in some cases security provides a selling point for energy ventures whose true motive is commercial. Insecurity is prompting a rather predatory continentalism, and there is little evidence that Canadians involved in the lucrative energy trade see any serious risks or long-term costs in this.

It used to be taken for granted that Canadians had first call on their own energy resources, with only the "surplus" being available for export. Security used to mean *national* security of supply. We had the National Oil Policy for many years. In the fall of 1973, with the Arab oil embargo and OPEC's quadrupling of the world price, Canada responded with a series of nationalistic interventions, such as price control, an export tax on oil, and the creation of Petro-Canada, a national oil company. In 1979–80, at the time of the second oil crisis, following the Iranian revolution, Ottawa responded to international insecurity with the National Energy Program (NEP), a deeply interventionist and centralizing package of price controls, production taxes, exploration incentives, and public investment. Canadianization of the energy sector was a major object of NEP, and the program was highly unpopular with Washington and the major foreign-owned oil companies.

The point to emphasize is that, in both oil crises, security concerns drove the Canadian government in an interventionist and nationalistic, not a continental, direction. Security meant *security of energy supply for Canadian consumers*, not the security of North American energy users. But since the 1994 NAFTA, and especially since September 11, security has come to mean North American security or, what amounts to the same thing, US security of supply and how Canada can advance it. It has meant a steady trek of Canadian politicians, federal as well as provincial, to Washington, offering Canadian resources to support the war on terrorism. Deregulation and NAFTA, as we shall see, virtually rule out government interventions to secure a national energy supply.

A MATCH MADE IN HEAVEN

In this section I provide examples of actual and potential investments that seem to have been shaped by security concerns post-September 11. This will be followed by a discussion of US energy security policy and the economic, technological, and political-legal forces that have prompted – and limited – the deeper continental integration of Canada's oil and gas industries.

Burlington's Takeover of Canadian Hunter Exploration

On Friday, 14 September 2001, three days after the terrorist attacks on the World Trade Center and the Pentagon, the board of Burlington Resources of Houston, Texas, met to consider its future strategy and growth. Burlington, known as one of Texas's "super-independent" energy firms,[3] is a direct descendant of the old Burlington Railroad and the legendary Atchison, Topeka, and Santa Fe railway empire, but now it is heavily oriented towards the natural gas industry, with 90 percent of its business in North America. Depletion rates in the US gas industry are high – in some cases 75 percent per year. With September 11 and its implications obviously in mind, the board of Burlington boldly decided to reinforce its position within North America by buying up one of western Canada's most valuable corporate empires – Canadian Hunter Exploration, a major player in the Canadian industry since the 1970s and the owner of some 1.2 trillion cubic feet of gas reserves and 2 million undeveloped acres of land, mostly in the Deep Basin of northwest Alberta.

Bobby Shackouls, the chairman and chief executive officer of Burlington, was willing to pay a rich price for Hunter: C$53 per share (a total of C$3.3 billion), which was almost 40 percent above the market price for Hunter's shares in the fall of 2001 (CBC 2001). "You can't buy a Mercedes for Ford prices," Shackouls said. He added that this "match made in heaven" was long-range investing, not a venture in cost-savings (Condon 2002). Did he pay too much? Was the security premium excessive? Or had the stock market undervalued Hunter? Burlington was faced with declining production from its own properties in New Mexico and the Gulf of Mexico; like many producers, it was stagnating, not replacing the reserves it was using up, and this was affecting its stock price.

Security concerns aside, there were solid commercial reasons for the Hunter takeover. Prompted by the low Canadian dollar, cash-flush US corporations had already invested some C$40 billion in equity and debt in takeovers of independent Canadian gas firms (Howes 2001; NGI 2001). Still, the timing and dollar amount of Burlington's offer were evidence of a Fortress North America approach. In an insecure world, Canadian reserves and production were at least as attractive as were domestic resources. Moreover, relative to US petroleum and natural gas basins, Canada was still seen as underexplored and underdeveloped, and finding costs were low relative to those in the United States. Depletion was not as far advanced as it was in US gas fields. Moreover, there were no security concerns. "They see Canada as, effectively, another state," said one analyst. "To a Burlington, buying production in Wyoming, Texas or Alberta – there's really no difference."[4]

Devon Energy Acquires Anderson Exploration

Immediately following Burlington's takeover of Canadian Hunter, another large US oil and gas independent, Devon Energy, acquired Anderson Exploration, one of Alberta's more dynamic producers and a holder of large properties in the Beaufort Sea. Devon first moved into Canada in 1998, bringing with it a strong commitment to the concept of North American integration. Since 2001 Devon has pursued a continental corporate strategy, calling itself "definitely a dominant North American player, combining Canada and the

US, which is really one natural gas market. 98% of our production is North American and our assets are focused in the Gulf of Mexico, the Gulf Coast, the Permian/Mid-Continent area, the Rocky Mountains, and the Western Canadian Sedimentary Basin" (TWST 2002). Devon's acquisitions and pattern of investment are shaped by a strategic vision of Fortress North America, a continental energy market. The Canadian oil executive, John Richels, who headed up Devon Canada, was promoted in January 2004 to the post of president of the parent firm, Oklahoma City-based Devon Energy Corp (*Financial Post* 2004).

The Expansion of the Alberta Oil Sands

Fortress North America is also the vision behind the expansion of the Alberta Oil Sands, whose recoverable reserves have been estimated at 175 to 320 billion barrels. Proponents of this multi-billion dollar resource are seeking to use American security fears to displace oil imports from the Middle East and Latin America with synthetic crude from Alberta. Chamber of Commerce projections have the oil sands supplying 5 million barrels per day by 2025, most of it to be exported to the US market. Investments in new oil sands ventures are predicated on Canadian pipelines penetrating the American market, displacing oil from Venezuela and Mexico.

Enbridge Inc., Canada's main oil pipeline system, has unveiled plans for two new oil pipelines to carry upgraded crude from the oil sands to American markets. One line would connect its Superior terminal in Wisconsin to Wood River, Illinois; a second, known as Gateway, would transport synthetic crude oil from Fort McMurray to a terminal on the BC coast, where it would be loaded onto tankers and shipped to California. "Security of supply is a huge issue in the US, and this plan goes a long way to meeting some of those concerns," said an Enbridge executive. "What we want to do is move a lot more Canadian crude into the US market than anybody has ever seen before" (Jang 2003, B1).

This is an example of Canadian ambition being driven by American fears. Enbridge has purchased pipelines in the United States as part of its long-range plan to penetrate the US market. Whether the economics of oil sands production and transportation justify the plan is an open question. The question is, would synthetic crude oil shipped from west coast terminals to California be competitive with conventional crude from, say, Mexico or Venezuela? Much would depend on the relative costs of production and transportation, but it will be a challenge for non-conventional Canadian oil to compete with much less costly supplies from a myriad of sources. About ninety countries today produce oil, so the United States has a great deal of choice in its imports (gas is much less flexible). Moreover, because US importers will buy the cheapest barrel available, there will be a relentless pressure on oil sands producers to lower their operating costs in order to stay competitive. Distance, labour shortages, high gas prices, limits on water supply and environmental concerns will constrain the producers' options.

Oil and Gas Investment Trusts

An alternative approach to continental security of supply has been the creation of Canadian oil and gas investment trusts by US power companies seeking to acquire capital for the exploitation of a reliable base of reserves. For example, Calpine Corporation, of San Jose, California, is one of North America's largest power producers and a massive user of natural gas supplies. Rather than rely upon third parties to supply its gas needs, Calpine has pursued a strategy of direct control over its resource base. In the fall of 2003 Calpine Corp., which holds oil and gas properties in the Sylvan Lake region of Alberta, spun off part of its production into Calpine Natural Gas Trust. It was structured so Calpine retains a 25 percent stake in the trust, investors get direct exposure to the energy market, and – crucially – Calpine Corp. has the right to purchase 100 percent of the ongoing production for its power needs (Calpine 2003). There are other energy and royalty trusts, but Calpine's is worth noting for its emphasis on security of supply.

US Energy Security Policy

The security scare over September 11 has definitely reinforced the consolidation of the North American oil and gas industries, though other corporate interests – such as the low value of the Canadian dollar and the need to acquire new reserves, land, and better stock values – have been at work as well. (In fact, much of the takeover of Canadian oil and gas firms since 2000 would have occurred even if September 11 had not happened.) Washington's security of supply dilemma has been seen as an opportunity by the Province of Alberta, Canadian exporters, and pipeline companies. But the growing reliance on Canadian energy, especially on high-priced gas imports, which, as noted, have accounted for nearly one-fifth of US consumption in recent years, has not been welcomed by all policy makers in Washington. Some argue that North America is a "mature" supplier, and a declining one relative to many alternate sources of oil and gas. Canada's National Energy Board has warned that production from the Western Canadian Sedimentary Basin "is levelling off. Consequently the producing industry will need to drill more wells and spend more on exploration just to maintain production" (NEB 2004).

The United States is, if anything, deeper in decline.[5] Alan Greenspan, chairman of the Federal Reserve Board, pointed out in testimony to the Senate Committee on Energy and Natural Resources in July 2003 that the long-term equilibrium price of natural gas had risen, in spite of improving technologies, from US$2 per million British thermal units (BTU) to more than $4.50, while depletion rates of US reservoirs had reached an annual rate of 27 percent. "The updrift and volatility of the spot price for gas have put significant segments of the North American gas-using industry in a weakened competitive position" (Fed 2003). So too has environmental opposition to drilling on many federal lands.

Greenspan's solution was to dampen prices and to increase flexibility by expanding gas imports via the accelerated development of an American liquefied natural gas (LNG) industry, thereby giving American gas-users access to a much wider range of global suppliers.[6] "If North American natural gas markets are to function with the flexibility exhibited by oil, unlimited access to the vast world reserves of gas is required" (Fed 2003). He wanted to create a "price-pressure safety valve through larger import capacity of LNG." This internationalist/global position is in direct opposition to the idea of a Fortress North America in energy. Greenspan, then the top US economic policy maker, argued against further reliance on Canada and on declining North American gas reserves and production. Gas, like other commodities, was becoming a globalized industry. The tight market in gas was creating competitive weakness in the US economy, and Canada, he implied, was part of the problem. Canada, said Greenspan, had little capacity to "significantly expand its exports, in part because of the role that Canadian gas plays in supporting growing oil production from tar sands" (ibid.). Thus, he concluded that there is need for gas from overseas and for the rapid approval for LNG terminals.

I argue below that the growth of LNG as a major supply source to the North American market will weaken the market position of Canadian pipelines and producers. LNG could be a source of future surplus capacity and the disintegration of the North American gas market (Cattaneo 2003a).[7] Alternatively, Canada might choose to become an LNG exporter, competing for markets in Asia and the United States.

DEREGULATION, NAFTA,
AND THE PROMOTION OF EXPORTS

In order to understand the reorganization of the oil and gas industries since deregulation and free trade, it is necessary to explain why the prior system of "regulated stability" of government control was abandoned, especially in the case of natural gas. In brief, Canada was following US precedent and bowing to pressures from the industry in western Canada. Canada began to decontrol oil and deregulate the oil and gas industries in 1985, with the Western Accord. The Mulroney Conservative government, then strongly backed in the west, was fulfilling its pledge to the producing provinces and its supporters in the petroleum industry to roll back the National Energy Program and shift to market prices for oil and gas. The 1985 accord clearly anticipated a wide open continental market. At the same time, Petro-Canada was partially privatized and foreign ownership restrictions in the industry were abandoned. The gutting of NEP was Mulroney's biggest concession to the west, and he was repaid with the founding of the western-based Reform Party two years after the signing of the Western Accord.

In 1986 Canada marketed 2.9 trillion cubic feet (TCF) of gas, 75 percent to Canadian users and 25 percent to US consumers. In sharp contrast Canada produced 5.7 TCF of gas in 1998 and exported 54 percent (3.3 TCF) to the US, leaving 46 percent for consumers in western and eastern Canada. With deregulation the numbers show a large increase in production and prices and a shift to the export market. But how did the Canadian gas producers and pipeline companies strengthen north-south trade in such a brief period of time?

Going to world oil prices was simple but painful: deregulation of oil occurred just at the moment when the world price skidded below ten dollars per barrel; the industry was fully exposed when the price of oil collapsed in 1986. The deregulation of the natural gas industry was a more complex, less bloody affair. It was already being deregulated in the United States, and much of the risk and instability in the US industry was shifted upstream to Canadian exporters. The long-term supply contracts and insurance, such as "take or pay" provisions favouring gas producers, was a fortress under attack by energy-consuming interests. The big interstate pipelines, formerly carriers of their own gas, were now required to act as "common carriers" transporting other people's gas, and the Federal Energy Regulatory Commission (FERC) issued sweeping orders promoting competition up the supply chain to the producers. FERC's actions opened up the pipelines and forced them to disaggregate their services, so buyers and producers could deal directly with one another in the market. FERC intended to keep American capitalism competitive by opening up the gas market.

The rules of the game were changing in the United States, and Canadian gas exporters now had to adapt and move to market structures or be shut out by US competitors. Canada's exporters were price-takers and had little influence on the US market at this point. Canadian pipelines were moving towards deregulation in the mid-1980s at a time when producers had a large "deliverability surplus" on hand: it was referred to as trapped gas – gas that had no place on the exporters' pipelines. The trapped gas situation weakened the bargaining power of producers until 1998, when new export pipelines went into operation. Until then, Canada's National Energy Board kept offering the Americans more and more gas at declining real prices. Leaving gas in the ground for future generations was unthinkable. "We've got too much gas!" was the rallying cry of Canadian negotiators, leaving some Americans with the impression that Canada had limitless reserves of inexpensive natural gas – "energy to burn," as the premier of Alberta called it. For a seller, this was a curious approach to negotiation.

It was NAFTA that administered the coup de grâce to the old system of regulated national stability. NAFTA opened the way to new pipelines and a much deeper integration of the American and Canadian energy sectors. The energy provisions of CUFTA and NAFTA are roughly similar and cover many of the same issues; though NAFTA extended coverage to basic petrochemicals and expanded the free trade area to Mexico (Mexico, however, proclaimed exemptions for its energy sector). NAFTA applied the principles of "non-discrimination" and "national treatment" to energy regulatory bodies, including subnational agencies, forcing them to treat producers, pipelines, and investors in the NAFTA trade area no less favourably than they treated domestic ones. It is interesting that this anti-discriminatory language was inserted into Chapter 6 of NAFTA as Canada had experienced trouble from the California Public Utilities Commission (CPUC) in the early 1990s. The CPUC tried unilaterally to nullify existing sales contracts in favour of short-term contracts, but it was forced to back down when Alberta threatened to withhold gas supplies. NAFTA, then, does offer Canadian energy exporters some relief from the more petty types of US protectionism.

NAFTA creates a continental market in energy services as well as goods, and transforms electricity into a good rather than – as under the General Agreement on Tariffs and Trade (GATT) – a service. It bans export taxes on energy and basic feedstocks, and prohibits floor prices or ceilings on both imports and exports. In the controversial Article 605 of Chapter 6, the governments are restricted from limiting the volume of exports of any energy or basic petrochemical good under the usual justifications. NAFTA has a "proportional access requirement" (only between the United States and Canada) that can be triggered when energy imports are cut by a government citing one of several GATT-era rationales: conservation of exhaustible resources, the need to supply domestic processors such as petrochemicals, and relief of domestic shortages. If Canada were to reduce its energy exports to the United States under one of these headings, then it could be obliged to provide a proportion of the existing supply to both export customers and domestic users. The proportion would be calculated on the basis of the average share purchased during the previous thirty-six-month period. So, if the Canadian government tried to cut back gas exports by, say, 20 percent to conserve resources, it would be obliged to treat American consumers as it treated Canadian consumers. If – as is roughly the case with natural gas – it had been exporting 60 percent of the resource and allocating 40 percent to the domestic market over the past three years, then proportionality would favour the United States on a 6:4 basis, and the Americans would be allotted 60 percent of the available Canadian supply. In an energy crisis, Canadian consumers would quickly learn the meaning of Article 605.

It is not obvious why Canadian producers would have lobbied for this "proportional access" article of NAFTA, but they did. It was inserted at their insistence as it effectively ties the hands of the federal government of Canada in a supply crisis. It has the effect of discouraging consumer-oriented federal policies that would restrict supply and interfere with North American integration. Its true underlying function is to deter Ottawa's intervention. The ghost of the 1980 National Energy Program kept sending shivers through the Canadian architects of NAFTA as they lunched at the free trade banquet. This ghost, who may have resembled former Prime Minister Pierre Trudeau or his energy minister, Marc Lalonde, was one that many western Canadians, particularly oil and gas producers, wanted to exorcise by restricting Ottawa's choices in advance.

NAFTA's Chapter 6 is particularly strong on growth and trade but very weak on the conservation of scarce North American energy resources. It makes it politically impossible for any Canadian government of the future to restrict production and exports to the United States without inflicting shortages on its own citizens. One can envision a number of scenarios in which Washington could use this article to gain "proportional access" to Canadian gas, oil, or electricity or to prevent limits from being applied to our exports of energy. The higher our exports relative to domestic consumption, the greater the Americans' access would be.

NAFTA, however, does provide a stronger legal and, perhaps, financial basis for the development of new infrastructure, such as takeaway export pipelines and the elimination of the surplus capacity that had challenged producers since the mid-1980s. With the NAFTA accord in place, Canadian shippers could go to their banks looking to finance new pipelines, and long-term investments in resources such as the oil sands could be made. These new market arrangements were "banked" by the end of 1998, and that is precisely when Canadian gas prices equalized with those in the United States. Following that, US energy independents, attracted by the low Canadian dollar, began to move into Alberta in a new wave of consolidation.

Finally, Chapter 11 of NAFTA, on investment, reinforces the energy provisions by placing a very broad ban on conditions, standards of treatment, and performance requirements demanded of foreign investors. Consistent with the neoliberal investment regimes promoted by multinationals in return for capital all over the globe, Chapter 11 prohibits the state from fixing levels of equity in multinational enterprises; or from imposing levels of goods, employment, or services; or from implementing domestic content provisions; or from restricting technology transfers.

Basically, Chapter 11 nullifies the past option, utilized by many provincial and federal governments, of using Crown-owned resources for purposes of economic development. As an example, Alberta has, since the 1970s, tried to foster a petrochemical complex based on chemicals extracted from natural gas prior to its export from the province. But NAFTA (and the Canadian Constitution)[8] render illegitimate such provincial interference with interprovincial and international trade. Thus, when the big Alliance gas pipeline was built from British Columbia to Chicago, going into production in 2000, Alberta was unable to capture the industrial benefits, which went to the Chicago hub, instead. If big Arctic gas pipelines from Alaska or the Mackenzie Valley link up with southbound pipelines in Alberta, or simply traverse the province without offering benefits to the petrochemical interests of Alberta, the province's impotence will be plain for all to see. Where are the feedstocks going to come from to support value-added industry such as petrochemicals?

CORPORATE STRATEGIES:
PRESSURES TO EXPORT

The push to export more Canadian oil and gas and to build new north-south pipelines was led by a group of Calgary-based upstream independents who wanted to raise prices and profits by ridding themselves of the so-called trapped gas, or chronic deliverability surplus, that they had been sitting on for over a decade. Companies such as the Alberta Energy Company and Pan Canadian – these two big independents would later merge under the name EnCana – as well as Renaissance, Canadian Hunter, Norcen, Poco, Chauvco, Alberta Natural Resources, Canadian 88, Ranger, Talisman, Precision Drilling, First Energy, and others had campaigned for free trade and for new transportation for their gas reserves.

The owners and executives of these Alberta independents were successors to the major[9] oil companies, most of which were in the process of writing off Alberta and the whole western Canadian Sedimentary Basin as mature, unproductive, and geologically uninteresting. Thousands of new gas pools were being discovered, but, in comparison with the giant pools of the early prewar years, the new pools were insignificant in size. The majors had been discovering conventional oil and gas fields in Alberta from the late 1940s until the 1960s, but these fields were now experiencing high rates of depletion, and the big companies all believed that the next big fields would be discovered off the East Coast or in the Arctic or outside North America. They were packing their bags for an early exit.

The drive for a deeper integration of the Canadian and American markets came from the upstream operators – the independents – who were active on both sides of the forty-ninth parallel. Cost-conscious, highly focused on a few opportunities, and keeping high working interests (and control) over their projects, the new breed emerging in Calgary sought to be free of the majors and resilient to low prices. They were a remarkably tight-knit group, a number of them survivors of the bloodbath of 1986 (and thus labelled the "generation of '86"), when so many of Calgary's best engineers, technicians, geoscientists, and geologists were tossed out on the street – albeit with good buy-out packages – after oil prices plunged below ten dollars per barrel.

That was a seminal moment for Alberta's oil and gas industries because many of these talented people decided to stay in Calgary and began to set up their own companies. They would only work for themselves; their loyalty was to the local community. They were committed to lowering supply costs while increasing the volume of production and exports, building a resilience to the world oil cycle, exploiting the newest geophysical and drilling technologies, and "doing it right together," as Allan Markin, one of the most successful of them, stated.[10] They wanted low overheads and few employees, only the best and those with the right philosophy. The belief was that "the low-hanging apples might be gone" but that there were opportunities galore a little higher up the tree.

The major oil companies, having plucked the low-hanging apples, had packed it in 1986. Some of the majors retained interests in the oil sands and gas-bearing lands, but in general they were moving on to the East Coast or overseas. Petro-Canada made a staged exit from Alberta's conventional oil industry, though it kept interests in the Athabasca Oil Sands. BP dumped its Canadian affiliate and a new oil independent, Talisman, was born. Suncor, the pioneer of oil sands mining, was cut loose by its US parent. Alberta Natural Resources bought up Ranger Oil, with its North Sea interests. Some of the larger independents saw growth and autonomy overseas – in West Africa, the Caspian Sea, Ecuador, Argentina, and Indonesia. By 1999 they were producing around 500,000 barrels a day of crude oil overseas. The expansion of the Calgary independents was a direct outgrowth of the 1986 oil crisis. It restructured the industry, and this, as much as NAFTA, deepened the integration of oil and gas.

If there was a single problem that dogged independent producers in the late 1980s and early 1990s, it was the surplus capacity of "trapped" gas resources. The deliverability surplus kept growing, field prices were very low, and the producers were dependent on a couple of large pipelines – Nova and TransCanada – to reach the bigger markets. The effect was monopsony, or buyer's monopoly. Like Prairie farmers who saw the Canadian Pacific Railroad as a barrier to their growth, the generation of '86 focused their hostility on the dominant pipelines to whom they sold their gas. To address the deliverability issue, there would need to be new export lines, more competition for Alberta's gas. Gas prices in New England were three times higher than they were in western Canada: that was a market they wanted.

The push for expanded exports and deeper integration was resolved between 1995 and 1998. Against the objections of the existing pipeline interests, the independent producers reached a consensus on the need for a new all-export pipeline – Alliance – to carry 1.325 billion cubic feet per day from northern British Columbia and Alberta to the Chicago hub – a non-stop "bullet" into the energy-guzzling heart of the American heartland. Alliance was positioned to receive and transport future gas from the north, and it was controlled by a group of American and Canadian pipeline companies. Fort Chicago, formed to sponsor Alliance, also controlled the Aux Sable extraction facilities in the Chicago hub area. Nova and TransCanada fought these plans to the bitter end but lost and were eventually merged. Alliance and its downstream supply outlet, Vector, which moves gas from Illinois to Ontario, went into production in December 2000, just as US gas prices began to rise dramatically. The Alliance/Aux Sable complex represented a major deepening of the integration of the natural gas industry in North America. Further deepening of the integration of the gas markets came from the inception of the Maritimes & Northeast pipeline, carrying Nova Scotia offshore gas into New England. Gas exports rose to 3.3 trillion cubic feet by 2001. (By 2003, the United States was importing over four trillion cubic feet, all but a fraction of which came from pipelines from Canada. Total US demand was about twenty-two trillion cubic feet in 2003) (EIA 2003, table 8).

The independent gas producers, the generation of '86, were remarkably successful in their challenge to the dominance of TransCanada Pipelines and Nova (Pratt 2001). The Canadian producers found allies among the American pipeliners – Coastal, Williams, El Paso – and from Enbridge, the Canadian oil pipeliner. Threatened by price stagnation and by buyer's monopoly, they seized the opportunities created by NAFTA and deregulation to increase exports and gas prices through increased competition in key regions of the United States. US demand for gas – and therefore the price – was sharply rising for a host or reasons, including declining reserves, the requirements of the new gas-fired power generators, and a preference for gas over coal and oil for environmental reasons.

But this export-oriented energy strategy, though successful in the short term, was vulnerable for two basic reasons: first, it did not take into account changing technologies and the United States' ability to diversify its supplies; and, second, the policy of accelerating the development of Canadian energy for the export market ignored the issue of greenhouse gas emissions and the likely impact of the Kyoto Protocol. In the long term, new technologies and climate change seem likely to weaken Canada's role as a supplier to the American energy market. This is not a conspiracy by conservation groups; rather, it is a problem of common property resources. Quite simply, as "low-hanging" fossil fuels are depleted and we move out to exploit marginal resources, the impact on clean air, water, and climate change is multiplied. To develop the oil sands, for instance, we are forced to use up great quantities of natural gas and water. These are indicators of real resource scarcity, and technology can mitigate but not eliminate these constraints.

Under free trade and new pipelines, it became attractive for US companies with weak stock prices to buy up Canadian firms and then export their reserves back south of the border. A group of feisty US independents, led by Burlington Resources, Devon Energy, Apache, and Anadarko, moved into Alberta and British Columbia between 1999 and 2001, acquiring Canadian firms and reserves of gas with the clear intention of exporting gas back to the United States. Indeed, the logic of acquiring upstream properties in western Canada in an integrated continental market and with a favourable exchange rate was unassailable. In the US oil and gas industry, wells are being developed in smaller fields and with much faster decline rates. Western Canada, though mature and subject to the same inexorable depletion, was still more sustainable and attractive to many US explorers, who spent $40 billion in 2000–01 acquiring Canadian firms, such as Poco, Renaissance, Hunter, Anderson and many others – this, in a context within which there are no limits on the degree of foreign ownership. As prices escalated, the generation of '86 was mostly eaten by the bigger, predatory American fish. Calgary has quickly become a mere outpost of Houston – a very *rich* outpost, to be sure – and the few remaining large Canadian-owned oil companies are increasingly investing overseas rather than in a mature Alberta oil patch.

LIMITS TO INTEGRATION

The Canadian oil and gas industries are already deeply integrated with those of the United States, but there are countervailing forces that should limit further integration in the future. The United States consumes about a quarter of all the oil produced worldwide and relies on imports for close to 60 percent of its supplies. No single oil-producing state can satisfy the American appetite for petroleum. Canada will remain an important energy supplier to its neighbour while it has resources, but Washington does not seek a Fortress North America in energy. It prefers to supplement domestic supplies and government-owned reserves with a global strategy in which oil and LNG imports would be widely diversified over a range of relatively secure non-OPEC sources. American oil companies – independents as well as majors – are tending to invest outside North America, and this has reduced the capital available for investment in Canada.

As the Americans view the future (Larson 2002), Canada would be only one of ten to fifteen oil exporters serving the US market. Diversifying supply would have the effect of lessening dependence on an unstable Middle East and weakening the market power of the OPEC group as a whole. West Africa and parts of Latin America are favoured. Further limiting North American integration, as the United States sees it, are steep technical barriers and economic costs that will slow the exploitation of Canadian gas and the development of the Athabasca Oil Sands for the US market. It seems plausible to state that the pinnacle of Canadian integration into the US energy market has already been reached. The days of easy integration are over. Indeed, the higher Canadian dollar in 2003–04 has clearly discouraged some of the US firms that bought into the Canadian oil patch a few years earlier.

According to US officials, the United States has experienced six serious interruptions of oil supply in the past thirty years: the Arab oil embargo of 1973–74; the Iranian revolution of 1979; the Iran-Iraq war of the late 1980s; the Iraqi invasion of Kuwait and the Gulf War, 1990–91; the general strike in Venezuela, winter of 2002–03; and the war in Iraq, 2003. In addition, high natural gas prices are blamed for the loss of some two million US manufacturing jobs from June 2000 to late 2003. Industrial energy users have lobbied for the development of new supply to force down prices (OGJ 2003). In December 2003 the US Department of Energy's Energy Information Administration (EIA) estimated, in a twenty-five-year forecast, that Canadian gas exports will decline from recent levels of about 3.6 TCF per year to 2.6 TCF in 2025, forcing the Americans to import much more of their gas from LNG suppliers (Edmonton Journal 2003a).

The United States has relied on market forces, overseas investments in new supplies, and the diversification of existing oil suppliers – with the Strategic Petroleum Reserve, the Naval Oil Reserves, and the military (the number one consumer of energy in the United States) as back-up – to deal with these disruptions. Washington believes that future interruptions of supply are less likely to come from the decisions of sovereign states than from domestic conflicts in some of the leading oil-producing states: ethnic and religious tensions; fights over the use of petroleum rents; prolonged labour actions, poverty, and the distribution of income; and political instability (Brodman 2003). The several-months disruption in 2003 caused by the strike in Venezuela seriously interfered with traditional oil supplies, and it seems to be a model of the type of conflict challenging US energy security. These events persuaded the Bush administration that an exporter nation's being in the Western Hemisphere is no guarantee of its reliability as a supplier of oil.

Washington's focusing its energy options exclusively on NAFTA, drawing down its imports from just Canada and Mexico, would mean risking supply shortages and foregoing the economic benefits of a globalized energy market. In part for environmental reasons, the United States has embraced the new gas-fired technology to generate electricity. Its use of natural gas in power production has increased by 40 percent since 1990, and much more growth is expected. Over 200,000 megawatts of new power-plant capacity has been constructed recently or will soon begin production (Yergin and Stoppard 2003). But traditional sources of gas supply are not adequate to prevent shortages and high prices: the overall decline rate from the Western Canada Sedimentary Basin is estimated at 25 percent, or three billion cubic feet per day each year (NEB 2002). The supply situation in the United States is even more dire. Thus, many commentators have agreed with Federal Reserve Chairman Greenspan that the United States ought to assist the globalization of the gas industry by becoming a major importer of LNG. If it does so, it would supplement its gas imports from Canada with a pipeline transporting LNG imported from suppliers such as Nigeria, Qatar, Abu Dhabi, Indonesia, Malaysia, and others. In a globalized gas market, American reliance on Canadian energy would diminish. Canada would become one of several gas exporters serving the American market. It would require a price of US$3 to 3.50 per million BTU – well below recent values – to build the infrastructure for LNG imports, according to the National Petroleum Council[11] and other industry sources.

It is even less likely that Canadian oil supplies will be able to hold their share of the American market over the long run (the United States imports about 60 percent of the oil it consumes, and about half of its imports come from the Western Hemisphere). We are a mature producer facing a rising cost curve on oil production. Our conventional oil reserves have declined to four billion barrels and reserve additions have tended to lag behind production. Though Canada is the leading net exporter of oil to the Americans, competition for the US oil market has heated up. There are ninety countries now in a position to produce oil, and the share of the top ten producers has fallen to 60 percent of total supply. Russia and China will have an immense impact on the world market. Import diversity in oil supply is the security strategy of the United States. For example, the Americans are fostering oil developments and import supplies in West Africa, where production could rise to seven million barrels a day by 2010. US multinational oil companies and the US Department of Energy are active in Angola, Gabon, Equatorial Guinea, the Congo, and Cameroon. Other current prospective Africa oil-producing countries include Gambia, Liberia, Sierra Leone, and Togo. West Africa will never be able to compete with the Middle East, but it could be the source of several million barrels per day in the next decade, and those barrels could be decisive in holding down prices. African oil exports to the United States seem sure to increase, given the dominant position of the US oil majors in these states. Washington is also looking to develop new supplies in Latin America: Argentina, Uruguay, Brazil, Colombia, and Bolivia are thought to be promising targets for energy development. The emphasis on generating new sources of non-OPEC exports from Africa and South America is much in keeping with the overall supply-side energy strategy of the Bush administration. US agencies like the Department of Energy and USAID have been active in assisting these potential exporters in developing (neoliberal) national energy strategies (Ballem 1991).

In recent years Canada has been producing over two million barrels a day of crude oil and equivalent, but less and less of it comes from the few conventional light oil fields discovered from the late 1940s to the 1960s. Like a bottle of soda that is effervescent at the top but loses its fizz as it is emptied, these older oil fields require more and more effort and energy simply to slow their depletion. Although there have been significant oil discoveries off the East Coast since 1979, the outlook for light conventional oil on the Prairies is poor. By far the greatest amount of drilling on the plains has been for gas, and most of the gas drilling has been developmental rather than exploratory. By 2025 the Western Canadian Sedimentary Basin will be depleted of all but heavy oils and bitumen. Given the gloomy outlook for conventional oil, it is curious that in recent years we have been exporting 1.7 million barrels a day to American refiners. Technological improvements can slow but not stop the rate of depletion over the long run. Canada has little choice but to shift to its high-cost petroleum resources, and here the fundamental debates have to do with technology, future oil prices, and the costs of extracting and upgrading bitumen from heavy oils and oil sands. The production processes used to extract and upgrade these resources consume massive amounts of water and natural gas, and they also contribute significantly to atmospheric pollution (see May and Dover's chapter). Operating costs vary, but bitumen is expensive relative to all conventional oils, and there is a history of state subsidization. Is there a place for this very costly resource in a globalized world energy market?[12]

The Athabasca, Cold Lake, and Peace River deposits of crude bitumen or oil sands contain an ultimate volume of 2.5 trillion barrels: between 175 billion and 370 million barrels are thought to be recoverable under current prices and technology. About 15 percent can be recovered via surface mining, while the remaining 85 percent must be extracted through in situ production processes. Among the three oil sands mining ventures – Suncor, Syncrude Canada Ltd., and Shell (with partners Chevron/Texaco and Western Oilsands) – there are wide variations in operating costs and the price required to stay in production. Suncor is the most profitable, with operating costs below $10/barrel; Syncrude's operating costs are close to $20 per barrel, and Shell, which is not in full commercial production, is estimating costs in the area of $12 to $14 per barrel, depending on the price of natural gas (of which these operations are huge consumers). In situ oil sands production, using steam assisted gravity drainage (SAGD) technology, can produce 1,000 barrels a day of bitumen, and new technologies have reduced the break-even price to half that of the massive mining projects. Optimistically, production in the oil sands is estimated to reach 1.9 million barrels a day by 2010 and 3.3 million by 2025.[13]

The oil sands are what the economic historian Harold Innis used to call "hard frontier" staples. There is a pessimistic school of thought, associated with Petro-Canada (*Financial Post* 2003c), which argues that capital cost overruns at Syncrude and at its own in situ facility have permanently undermined the attractiveness of investment in the oil sands. Petro-Canada believes that it will be fortunate to recover its capital costs (10 percent) in the oil sands (Jang 2003). Accordingly, it has cut back domestic capital spending in the oil sands in favour of spending overseas. Other large Canadian-owned oil companies, such as EnCana, Talisman, and Canadian Natural Resources, have also gone multinational and shifted investment out of Canada; it is estimated that these companies will soon be generating a million barrels a day of overseas production. Opportunities overseas are more attractive than are the oil sands – finding costs are lower and net returns higher overseas (*Edmonton Journal* 2003b). For companies like Petro-Canada, which are sceptical about the costs of recovering and refining oil sands and heavy oils, going multinational is an excellent alternative to developing the oil sands.

It is vital to see that the oil sands and heavy oils projects of western Canada are competing, not with one another, but worldwide with conventional oil sources that can be produced for far less effort and money. To repeat, US energy security policy emphasizes the need for a diversity of imports in order to reduce dependence on Mideast oil and OPEC: it does not envisage a costly Fortress North America based on high-cost frontier resources like the oil sands. A plunge in the world oil price like the one in 1985–86 would probably put the oil sands out of business.[14]

CONCLUSION

As some Canadian oil companies have already discovered, the future of the Canadian petroleum industry lies in globalization, not in the backwaters of continentalism. Leaving aside the oil sands, North America has about 2 percent of the world's recoverable oil reserves. Further internationalization seems inevitable because the best prospects are overseas.

The deeper integration of the Canadian and American oil and gas industries began with CUFTA and NAFTA, which facilitated the building of new export pipelines to the United States. Particularly in the case of gas, the "generation of '86" was able to overcome resistance from traditional pipelines, and Canada secured almost one-fifth of the US market.

In the case of oil, Canada is for now the number one source of US imports. But exports of Canadian gas will decline, and the United States has many sources for its oil imports. It has the potential to become an LNG buyer on a large scale; and, above all, it has global interests that rule out a Fortress North America energy security strategy. It is important for Canadians to be aware of the countervailing forces and costs that work against the deeper continental integration they may be anticipating. The future may look more like disintegration. Future terrorist actions in the United States might prompt the Americans to take over more Canadian resources, as Burlington and Devon did after September 11. But history does not move on a single, preordained path. Canadians need to remember that the United States is a world power that will pursue its own interests. It would be ironic – and expensive – if Canadians overbuilt their energy supply infrastructure and, too late, found the American consumer buying oil from Norway, LNG from Trinidad, and reducing demand through increased energy efficiency.

NOTES

The author is grateful to the Alberta Foundation for the Arts and the Canada Council for its support for this work. Parts of this chapter draw on an earlier publication (Pratt 2001).

1 See *An Analysis of Technocracy* (Technocracy Inc. 1960). The continental energy deal received critical treatment in Laxer (1971), and a similar critique of the oil sands proposals is found in Pratt (1976).
2 This article was written in February 2004.
3 A producer is "independent" when it produces for the market and has no pipeline or refining capacity (lexicon of terms, Maverick Energy Inc., <http://www.maverickenergy.com>). "Super-independents" are the largest firms in that category. In contrast, the "majors" are the dominant firms and have both pipeline and refining capacity.
4 The initial tentative offer was made on 14 September; Hunter's board met on Sunday, 16 September, and agreed to accept Burlington's offer. All of this was done in the midst of the turmoil and panic that followed on the terrorist attacks of 11 September 2001.
5 In 2001 the United States had an estimated 21.8 billion barrels of oil reserves, equivalent to 2 percent of global reserves or 9.5 years at current rates of production (Aljazeera 2003).
6 LNG involves the cooling of gas to minus 260 degrees Fahrenheit in the liquefaction stage, and the transport of the LNG in LNG tankers to special marine terminals, where the fuel is degasified (Yergin and Stoppard 2003).
7 Though the United States imports only 1 percent of its gas via LNG, and there are just four US LNG terminals, costs have declined and gas prices have sharply climbed, making the LNG option attractive to larger producers (Yergin and Stoppard 2003).

8 For a commentary on pipelines and federal power, see Ballem (1991), who concludes that all of the big pipelines, including Nova, the gas-gathering system in
   Alberta, are under federal jurisdiction.
9 See note 3 for definitions of "independent" and "major."
10 The "generation of '86" is developed in Pratt (2001).
11 The National Petroleum Council advises the Office of Fossil Energy and the US
   Secretary of Energy. Its views on future LNG supplies can be studied at
   <http://www.fossil.energy.gov> .
12 On costs and delays owing to labour shortages in the oil sands and heavy oils, see
   Financial Post (2003b).
13 Information on costs and production draws from interviews with industry officials in the fall of 2003.
14 On variable costs, see Cattaneo (2003b).

REFERENCES

Aljazeera. 2003. Increasing Dependence on Oil Imports. *Aljazeera.net English*, 10
    August. Available at <http://english.aljazeera.net/NR/exeres/2CDA8F31-A5D7-
    4071-B12D-1B804E1C15EE.htm>.
Ballem, John Bishop. 1991. Pipelines and the Federal Transportation Power.
    Alberta Law Review 29 (3): 617–32.
Brodman, John. 2003. US *Energy Official Testifies on US Oil and Gas Imports*.
    United States Congress 2003. Available at <http://allafrica.com/stories/
    200310280098.html>, cited 27 October 2003.
Calpine. 2003. Calpine Natural Gas Trust Announces October and November
    Distribution. Press release. 19 November. Alberta: Calpine Natural Gas
    Trust.
Cattaneo, Claudia. 2003a. LNG Could Be World's Next Big Energy Prize. *National
    Post*, FP3.
– 2003b. Why Operating Costs Are Different. *National Post*, 3 November, FP03.
CBC. 2001. Canadian Hunter Bought by Burlington Resources for $3.3 billion.
    CBC.ca, 9 October.
Condon, Bernard. 2002. Collect Now, Deliver Later. *Forbes.com*, 13 May.
Dylan, Bob. 1981. *Slow Train Coming*. Special Rider Music.
Edmonton Journal. 2003a. End of the Line for Low-Cost Gas. *Edmonton Journal*,
    26 December, E1.
– 2003b. Rising Costs, High Taxes Sending Oil Companies Overseas for New
    Drilling. *Edmonton Journal*, 2 December, A1.
EIA. 2003. *Short-Term Energy Outlook: September 2003*. Washington, DC: US
    Energy Information Administration.
Enbridge. N.d. *Southern Access Pipeline*. Calgary: Enbridge Inc. Available at
    <http://www.enbridge.com/pipelines/about/plannedSystemGrowth/system-
    growth-southernAccess.php>.
Fed. 2003. Testimony of Chairman Alan Greenspan before the Committee on

Energy and Natural Resources, US Senate. 10 July. Washington, DC: Federal
    Reserve Board.

Financial Post. 2003a. Can a Pipeline Lead to "Next Great City?" *National Post*,
    4 December, FP01.

– 2003b. Labour Shortage May Slow Project. *National Post*, 15 October, FP06.

– 2003c. Petro-Canada Severely Cuts Oilsands Plan. *National Post*, 12 December,
    FP03.

– 2003d. US Turns to Canada for Secure Energy. *National Post*, 14 October, FP01.

– 2004. Canadian Now in Line for Top Job at Devon Energy. *National Post*, 9
    January, FP01.

Howes, Carol. 2001. Americanization a Concern in Calgary. *National Post*, 11
    October, FP5.

Hulse, Carl. 2003. Accord Reached by Republicans for Energy Bill. *New York
    Times*, 15 November, 1.

Jang, Brent. 2003. Enbridge Reveals Plan to Expand Pipeline. *Globe and Mail*, 7
    October, B1.

Larson, Alan P. 2002. The International Aspects of US Energy Security: Testimony
    of the Under-Secretary for Economic, Business, and Agricultural Affairs, House
    International Relations Committee, Washington, DC.

Laxer, James. 1971. *The Energy Poker Game: The Politics of the Continental
    Resource Deal*. Toronto: New Press.

Macdonald Report. 1985. *Report of the Royal Commission on the Economic Union
    and Development Prospects for Canada*. Ottawa: Minister of Supply and Services.

NEB. 2002. *Short-term Natural Gas Deliverability from the Western Canadian Sed-
    imentary Basin, 2002–2004*. Calgary: National Energy Board.

– 2004. *RRP 2003–2004 Estimates*. Calgary: National Energy Board. Available at
    <http://www.tbs-sct.gc.ca/est-pre/20032004/NEB-ONE/NEB-ONEr34_e.asp>.

NGI. 2001. US Producers Continue Quest for Canadian Reserves. *Natural Gas Intel-
    ligence*, 15 October. Available at <http://intelligencepress.com/>.

OGJ. 2003. Industrial Trade Organization Reports 41-Month "Natural Gas Crisis"
    in US. *Oil and Gas Journal Online*, 17 December. Available at <http://www.ogj.
    com/currentissue/index.cfm?p=7&v=101&i=49>.

Pratt, Larry. 1976. *The Tar Sands*. Edmonton: Hurtig.

– 2001. Energy: Free Trade and the Price We Paid. Parkland Institute, University of
    Alberta, Edmonton.

Technocracy Inc. 2004. *An Analysis of Technocracy: Information Brief # 50 –
    1960*. Technocracy Inc. 1960. Available at <http://www.technocracyinc.org/>, cited
    28 November 2004.

TWST. 2002. Interview with Vincent W. White, Devon Energy Corporation.
    TWST.com, 7 May.

Yergin, Daniel, and Michael Stoppard. 2003. The Next Prize. *Foreign Affairs* 82
    (6): 103–14.

20

Of Harvard Mice and Prairie Farmers: Canadian Patents on Life

MICHELLE SWENARCHUK

This chapter deals with the theme of Canada-US integration from a particular vantage point: that of changes that have been made to the Canadian
legal regime to bring it into conformity with trends established in the
United States. I show that many Canadian laws that relate to the patenting
of life forms have been brought into conformity with US legal norms and
trends and that only determined resistance by Canadians has held back
change in some important cases. As with the other chapters in this volume,
the protagonists are governments, transnational corporations, social forces,
and private citizens, and once again the public interest is at stake. However,
in contrast to other chapters, the focus here is on the Canadian judicial and
patent systems.

I argue that, over the past twenty-five years, patent law has diverged substantially from its original purpose and design, and has been manipulated to
serve the monopolistic interests of transnational corporations. Further, I
argue that, behind the scenes, Canadian patent officials have followed the
US precedent of granting patents on life forms, without consulting the Canadian legislature or public, and even though Canadian law does not require
these officials to look south for legal precedent. Finally, after exploring the
worldwide debate in the scientific and legal communities on the patenting
of life forms, I argue that life patents are harming the public interest in
health care, the advancement of science, and the equitable distribution of
the benefits derived from genetic resources.

On 5 December 2002 the Supreme Court of Canada released its decision
that a higher life form, a genetically engineered mouse developed at
Harvard University for use in cancer research, was not patentable (SCC
2002, 356). The case was covered extensively in the media, bringing to
public attention the little known practice of granting patents on living
things. Harvard had argued that Canada needed to follow the patent

practice in the United States, where the mouse and other animals are considered patentable. Although the Canadian Patent Office had long granted patents on single-cell life forms, the court declined to follow the US precedent regarding patents on higher life forms.

In the 2004 *Schmeiser* case, however, the same court ruled that a patent on a gene in a genetically modified canola seed effectively confers patent rights to the entire seed – a higher life form (SCC 2004). The court decided that Saskatchewan farmer Percy Schmeiser therefore infringed upon the rights of the patent holder, Monsanto Canada Inc., by planting canola seeds derived from genetically modified canola plants that had blown onto his land and adjacent road allowances. On the unique and contested facts of the case the court decided that patent infringement had occurred, but it relieved Schmeiser of the burden of paying damages and Monsanto's legal costs. The two Supreme Court decisions confront Canadian patent law with contradictory directions on the important question of whether patent rights should be granted on complex life forms. These contradictions underscore the need for legislative action in Parliament to resolve the matter definitively.

WHAT IS A PATENT?

A patent is a form of intellectual property, a "category of intangible rights protecting commercially valuable products of the human intellect," which includes trademarks, copyrights, and trade-secret rights (*Black's Law Dictionary* 1999, 813). These forms of property essentially compensate thinkers for their work and contribution to society. In contemporary law, patents are available to those who create new inventions, defined as "any new and useful art, process, machine, manufacture or composition of matter, or any new and useful improvement in any art, process, machine, manufacture or composition of matter" (Canada 1985, s. 2). Patentability requires that something be new, inventive (not obvious), and useful. Historically, patents were available for objects and processes (e.g., widgets and chemical reactions) that were invented by humans, but they were not available for something that occurred in nature (e.g., an element on the periodic table). Patent law represents a social contract: an inventor receives an exclusionary right to use and control an invention for twenty years in return for disclosure – a description of how he/she made the invention – so that someone else "skilled in the art" can eventually do the same thing. This bargain was intended to provide public benefits by encouraging inventors to disclose information rather than to assert other forms of property rights, such as trade secrets, which precludes the dissemination of new ideas.

Life Patents

In 1980, in a 5–4 decision, the US Supreme Court granted a patent on a micro-organism, a bacteria used in treating oil pollution, thus opening the door to the patenting of living things *(Diamond v. Chakrabarty* 1980). Since then, thousands of patents on micro-organisms, plants, animals, genes, and cells have been granted in the United States, Europe, and Japan. The US standard for patentability was expressed by the court in *Chakrabarty* as "anything under the sun made by the hand of man." The World Trade Organization (WTO) Agreement on Trade-Related Intellectual Property (TRIPs), concluded in 1994, has extended the controversy to developing countries by requiring its 150 members to adopt patent regimes consistent with those of the OECD countries.

The Canadian Intellectual Property Office (CIPO) grants patents on single-celled life forms. According to spokesman Michael Gillen, senior biotechnology examiner, "We're not questioning whether genes should be patented because US courts have ruled that they can" (Hurst 2001). Canada now patents proteins, genes, and cells from plants, animals, and humans as well as on human and animal diagnostics performed on the human or animal body but not outside the body. Patents are not granted on plant varieties, human and animal organs, or human and animal therapies (including gene therapies) performed on the human or animal body (Canada 2002).

The Harvard Oncomouse in Canada

In 1985 Harvard University applied for a Canadian patent on a transgenic mouse. Scientists developed the mouse by inserting a foreign gene into the animal, disposing it to develop tumours for use in cancer research. This was the precedent claim on a "higher life form" – a multicellular, complex mammal. The commissioner of patents refused the claim, which included "all [similar transgenic] non-human mammals," and the decision went to the Supreme Court of Canada. Justice Bastarache, writing for the majority of the court, held that "the unique concerns and issues raised by the patentability of plants and animals necessitate a parliamentary response. Only Parliament has the institutional competence to extend patent rights or another form of intellectual property protection to plants and animals and to attach appropriate conditions to the right that is granted" (SCC 2002, 49).

THE LIFE PATENTS DEBATE

Harvard University advanced several arguments in favour of patents on life. First, it argued that patents are necessary to enable biotechnology companies to raise money from investors for research and innovation. Further, since every cell in the body is changed, transgenic animals are human inventions. And, finally, if Canada does not grant life patents, as do the United States and Europe, it will lose significant amounts of private investment in one of the world's fastest-growing industries (Smart and Biggar 2002).

The Question of Invention

Patents are available by law for inventions. A fundamental dispute related to patents on life forms is whether humans can be considered to have invented them or whether they are phenomena of nature, which humans are only able to discover. Dr John Sulston (2002), winner of the 2002 Nobel Prize in Physiology or Medicine, argues that

the genome sequence is a discovery, not an invention. Like a mountain or a river, the genome is a natural phenomenon ... Inventing human genes is impossible. So every discovery relating to genes – their sequence, functions and everything else – should be placed in the pre-competitive arena ... We should not be patenting whole life forms, such as transgenic mice or cotton plants ... we did not invent these organisms, only the specific modification that made the mice susceptible to cancer or the cotton resistant to pests.

Nor does he accept the rationale commonly advanced by patent officials for granting patents on genes if they can be isolated or replicated outside the body: "This argument has always seemed absurd to me. The essence of a gene is the information it provides – the sequence. Copying it into another format makes no difference. It is like taking a hardback book written by someone else, publishing it in paperback and then claiming authorship because the binding is different" (Sulston 2002).

An animal such as a transgenic mouse, into which a novel gene has been introduced, with its complexity and myriad natural qualities, remains a product of nature. Scientists are entitled to obtain patents on the processes by which the mouse is modified, as Harvard did, enabling them to obtain economic returns from that work. But it is difficult to see how isolating a gene or replicating it transforms it from being a natural phenomenon into a human invention; rather, it is illogical and contrary to human and evolutionary history to hold that the cells and genes whose evolution over millennia made humanoids into homo sapiens were invented in the past three decades by humans. The distinction between discoveries of nature and human invention has been largely erased in patent law, leaving an edifice of life patents whose foundation is a legal fiction.

Patents reward inventors for the application of knowledge to practical uses. However, as Dr Sulston argues, the essence of genes is in the information, or the knowledge, that they contain. Hence, to patent genes is to patent knowledge itself, depriving society as a whole of the time needed to disseminate and explore a new type of knowledge in order to maximize its social benefits (Franklin 2003). "We no longer have a patent system that rewards inventors for their creativity but one that essentially rewards investors for their investment," argues Deryck Beyleveld, director of the Sheffield Institute of Biotechnological Law and Ethics in the United Kingdom (Adam 2002, 356).

Equitable Access to the Benefits of Biodiversity

The patenting of life forms also impedes equitable access to the benefits of biodiversity as patents on the genes of crops and livestock concentrate economic power in large agricultural businesses and facilitate their appropriation of genetic resources and knowledge developed over millennia by indigenous and local communities in developing countries. This exploitation of indigenous peoples' knowledge is a growing global concern. Applicants for patents need identify neither the geographic origin of genetic materials claimed nor whether the purported invention was developed using the knowledge of indigenous peoples. This results in a clear risk of the misappropriation of indigenous knowledge through patenting, without the consent of the peoples whose knowledge has been used and without providing them with appropriate compensation (CELA 2001). Indeed, the United Kingdom Commission on Intellectual Property Rights concluded that an expansion of intellectual property rights is unlikely to benefit developing countries and, on the contrary, is likely to lead to higher-priced medicines and seeds, making poverty reduction more difficult (Mayer 2002).

Impacts of Patents on the Advancement of Science

Many contributions to the scientific and legal literature demonstrate the harmful effects that the patenting of life forms is having on the advancement of science. Patenting is making research tools (transgenic animals, markers, assays, laboratory reagents) expensive or unavailable; preventing "downstream" research on genes; preventing development of new drugs and diagnostic tests; reducing or delaying the publication of research results; and reducing the information that would otherwise be freely available to scientists. According to one expert, the proliferation of patenting has

changed the conduct of biomedical research in some ways that are not always consistent with the best interests of science ... It has encouraged some companies to make protected materials and methods available to investigators under terms that seem unduly onerous. In a few well-publicized cases, and likely in many more undocumented ones, it has fostered policies that have inhibited the use of new scientific findings, even in the not-for-profit sectors, and has reduced open exchange of ideas and materials among academic scientists. (Varmus 2000)

Transgenic Mice as Research Tools:
The US Experience with the Harvard Mouse

The patenting of life forms has resulted in the inaccessibility and high cost of research tools, including transgenic mice. Approximately twenty five million mice were used worldwide for research in 2000, constituting 90 percent of all animals used. Since the patenting of the Harvard mammals, however, scores of mice have been patented in the United States (Malakoff 2000), leading to a well publicized controversy. Harvard granted DuPont Corporation an exclusive licence to distribute the mice, but some scientists objected to the terms of DuPont's distribution licences. Dupont placed limits on the breeding or redistribution of the animals, and it imposed a "reach through" clause requiring anyone who developed a product from her or his work with the mouse, or any of its derivative strains, to pay royalties to DuPont.

Dr Harold Varmus, then director of the US National Institute of Health (NIH), initiated a four-year process of negotiation with DuPont to make the mice broadly available to non-profit researchers. Ultimately, NIH and Dupont signed a Memorandum of Understanding providing that the Public Health Service and its grantees (non-profit academic researchers) may use the patented mice without cost for biomedical research purposes. NIH has subsequently contributed funding to a mouse breeding facility to make unpatented mice available to academic researchers (Smaglik 2000b). It is difficult, in this case, to see how the patent was intended to facilitate the innovation and dissemination of medical knowledge and materials, as patents, in theory, are supposed to do. On the contrary, the Dupont patent so threatened the non-profit medical research that the Public Health Service was forced to intervene to reverse the impacts of the patents on transgenic mice.

Human Cells and Genes

The patenting of single-cell life forms, cells, and genes holds widespread impacts for medical science and health care as the number of gene patents continues to rise at an alarming rate. In 2001 the US Patent Office granted over 5,000 DNA patents. Of the 9,456 patents claiming "nucleic acid" granted as of 2002, 8,334 of them had been granted since 1996. In addition, the European Patent Office has granted several thousand patents on genetic inventions, while in Japan the number is over 5,000 (OECD 2002).

One growing controversy created by the patenting of single-cell life forms concerns the patenting by Human Genome Sciences Inc. (HGS) of a protein, CCR5, required for HIV infection. The patent application covered the gene, its protein, fragments of DNA used to locate the gene, details related to the chemical components of the gene, and any potential applications of this knowledge. Despite the fact that independent researchers at the NIH in the United States had subsequently discovered that the gene facilitates the entry of HIV into the human body, the patent was granted to Human Genome Sciences. Because the patent covered use of the gene for any purpose, it allowed HGS to profit from the later discovery. The patent thus conferred considerable commercial control over the development of a new class of HIV/AIDS drugs, even though HGS did not know of the role of CCR5 in HIV infection when it filed for its original patent (Marshall 2000; Smaglik 2000a).

Myriad Claims

Genetics is a factor in approximately 5 percent to 10 percent of breast cancers, and mutations on genes called BRCA1 and BRCA2 cause 80 percent of these cancers. They are common but not exclusive to Jews of Ashkenazi descent. By the age of seventy, most women carrying these genes will have breast cancer. Women who have the BRCA2 gene are also at high risk for ovarian cancer. In 2001, 1,200 Ontario women were tested for these genes, and almost 4,000 people received counselling to help them cope with the possibility of carrying the disease (Hurst 2001; Macdonald 2002).

Myriad Genetics Inc. of Utah has obtained a series of patents in Canada, the United States, and Europe on the BRCA1 and BRCA2 genes, giving it control over both the genes and the specific test the company developed for the gene. Myriad essentially claims a monopoly on the entire gene set, any information relating to or derived from it, and all methods developed to diagnose and treat hereditary breast cancer and ovarian cancer, including therapies for cancers from genetic mutation, screening of drugs for cancer therapy, and screening for the genes in women. Myriad also claims that its patents give it the right to store all new information about these genes in its own labs (thus building up the only source of this genetic data in the world) and, through the DNA samples in its labs, control over the "raw material" of this gene worldwide. In Europe, the Myriad claims have been described as "a monopoly on all genetic work associated with the breast and ovarian cancer predisposition gene brca1" (Lecubrier 2002) and as "an unwarranted and novel restriction on medical practice" (Wadman 2001).

CANADIAN REACTIONS TO THE PATENTS

In July 2001 Myriad told Canadian provincial governments to stop using any tests other than its own to detect BRCA1 and BRCA2 or face legal proceedings. Whereas tests of equal reliability developed in Canada cost only $1,300, the Myriad test costs about $3,850. Counselling is also an important part of the testing procedure since tests may lead to difficult medical and ethical decisions, including prophylactic mastectomies or drugs, questions about whether to inform family members, and the risk of discrimination from employers and insurers. The government of British Columbia stopped funding the testing after the Myriad threats. As a result, BC women must now pay Myriad out of pocket and do not benefit from the counselling services that accompanied the test under the provincial health program.

The governments of Ontario, Manitoba, Quebec, and Alberta decided to contest the Myriad claims and continue using the Canadian test. Tony Clement (2001), the Ontario minister of health and long-term care, explained:

How can publicly-funded healthcare and equitable coverage be sustained when we add to the existing financial pressures on our health system the potential monopoly pricing of a whole new category of diagnostics over which Ontario – and indeed Canada's other provincial and territorial jurisdictions – have little or no control over approval or pricing ... We are therefore forced to ask ourselves the much larger question: Is the entire fruit of human genome project research and the mapping of the human gene going to come down to a series of monopolies setting exclusive prices for tests which most of Canada – indeed most of the world, especially the poorer countries – cannot afford?

Patent claims on a gene sequence that cover uses for all diagnostic innovations in the future are not in the public interest or in the interests of the promotion of a competitive market in diagnostic testing.

In January 2003 Clement, joined by then BC minister of health Colin Hansen, described the patenting of genes as "abhorrent" and again called on the federal government to prohibit the practice. Toronto geneticist Dr Josef Penninger noted that a Myriad legal victory in Canada "could ruin the health care system ... [since] in 10 years, we will probably know 50 genetic defects that predispose us to strokes, heart disease, cancer, diabetes, etc., and of course people will want to know. But no health care system in the world will have enough money to do this if profit is involved and only a few people will have the money to afford it" (Schmidt 2003). The Canadian Cancer Society also expressed concern at the breadth of the patents and called on the federal government to take action to ensure that the patents do not interfere with Canadian women's access to testing, accompanied by appropriate counselling and the timely development of knowledge of the relationship of genes to health. The society further advocated that provincial governments continue to challenge the breadth of claims and Myriad's administration of them (Canadian Cancer Society 2003).

REACTION TO THE MYRIAD PATENTS IN EUROPE
Despite the granting of patents to Myriad in Europe, seventeen European laboratories do diagnostic tests on the BRCA1 using other tests. Officials of the *Institut Curie* in France believe that the direct sequencing technology used by Myriad, and its focus on the detection of point, or small-sized, genetic abnormalities, fails to detect 10 percent to 20 percent of expected mutations. Europeans also expressed concern that a Myriad monopoly on this technology would cause them to lose expertise in the field, prevent their improving or developing diagnostic tests, and increase the costs of screening. Further, concerns were expressed that the Myriad requirements conflict with a holistic approach to public health by separating biological research and clinical investigation from patient care.

In 2001 a challenge to the Myriad patents was launched in the European Patent Office by the *Institut Curie*, almost all European genetics societies, many scientific institutions, the governments of Holland and Austria, and the Swiss Social Democratic Party. The opponents argued that, since the gene sequences were available in databases, the patents should be revoked on the grounds of lack of priority, novelty, and inventiveness as well as insufficient description of future therapeutic uses. The institutions began by challenging two patents but subsequently added a third. The challenge is necessary, in the view of Gert Matthijs of the Belgian Centre for Human Genetics, as "it is not only about breast cancer but about hundreds of gene patent applications. If nothing is done, it will be almost impossible to practice genetic analyses properly in the future" (Lecubrier 2002).

CURRENT STATUS
Myriad did not sue the Canadian provinces for their continuing use of Canadian tests for BRCA1 and 2. The European Patent Office revoked one Myriad patent and restricted the scope of several others. Myriad appealed these decisions, and the appeal processes will continue until 2007 (Kelly 2006). Patents have been granted in many countries on genes implicated in numerous diseases, including Alzheimer's, HIV/AIDS, and cancer, but the Myriad cancer gene patents are the most notorious in the literature, having provoked opposition from governments and scientists across Canada and Europe. Whether or not Myriad is ultimately successful in maintaining these patents will, therefore, be indicative of the effectiveness of public interest arguments in limiting the negative impacts of life patents.

Stem Cell Patents

Human stem cells have the potential to develop into many types of tissues and organs and have an extraordinarily wide range of revolutionary health care applications. Not surprisingly, stem cell research has become a hotly contested field as companies race to obtain exclusive patent rights over this potentially highly lucrative area. For example, the Geron Corporation signed a licensing agreement with the Wisconsin Alumni Research Foundation, which holds patents on five of the seventy-two stem cell lines used in US federally funded research, granting it exclusive rights to develop products from stem cells derived from nerve, heart, and pancreas cells as well as non-exclusive rights to the use of blood, cartilage, and bone cells. Geron has also developed heart, nerve, pancreas, bone, liver, and blood cells from the stem cells and has filed for patents on the methods used. Patents on stem cells, however, may restrict access to stem cell materials and may mean that royalty fees will have to be paid for the future development of replacement human organs and tissues (Ontario 2002; WARF 2002).

Diagnostic Tools and Tests

Over 400 clinical genetic tests were available by 2001, and hundreds more are being developed (OECD 2002). Biomedical patents, however, have been criticized for restricting the availability of diagnostic tools and tests. Haematochromatosis, a progressive iron-overload disease, is a case in point. A survey of US laboratories showed that some labs have refrained from offering genetic testing services because of patents granted on tests for the disease. Moreover, 30 percent of those surveyed reported discontinuing or not developing genetic testing after the granting of the exclusive patent, in spite of the fact that limited clinical testing will inhibit further discoveries regarding the gene that causes the disease. The study also showed a delay in publication of data regarding cloning the gene linked to haematochromatosis (called HFE) for a year after the patent application was filed (Merz et al. 2002).

Impacts of Patents on the Dissemination of Scientific Results

Other studies have shown more generally how the commercialization of science, including through biomedical patents, has contributed to delay in the publication of scientific results. For example, a survey of life scientists found that 19.8 percent of those questioned had had their publication results delayed by more than six months at least once, considerably longer than the sixty days considered acceptable by the NIH. Of those, 46 percent reported delays to allow time for patent applications; 33 percent to protect the proprietary value of research results by means other than patent applications; 26 percent to allow time to negotiate licence agreements; and 17 percent to resolve disputes over intellectual property. Further, 34 percent of faculty had been denied access to research results, suggesting that data withholding has affected many life-science faculty (Blumenthal et al. 1997). Unfettered and timely sharing of research results, however, is a fundamental requirement for scientific advance:

Openness in the sharing of research results is a powerful ideal in modern science ... communalism, the shared ownership and free exchange of research results and approaches, is a fundamental norm underlying the social structure of science. Such sharing is critical to the advancement of science ... External pressures (for breaching the ideal of openness) include ... processes and procedures related to the commercialization of university research. (Blumenthal et al. 1997, 1224)

The commercialization of science, including through patenting of results, may be undermining the very integrity of scientific publications: "Commercial considerations may also lead to a culture of secrecy, including delays in publication while patents are filed ... The most serious concern, however ... is that conflicts of interest may affect what gets published (Editors 2000, 299). The editors of the journal went on to cite studies showing that drug and cancer treatment studies supported by manufacturers are more likely to find results favourable to the companies' products than studies not funded by commercial interests.

In August 2001 the journal *Nature* instituted a new editorial policy. This was due to "suggestive evidence" that publication practices in biomedical research have been influenced by the commercial interests of writers and as well as to general concern among researchers and others that the integrity of scientific research was being undermined by increasing commercial links between researchers and private interests. Authors are now "invited" to disclose competing financial interests, including funding, employment, personal financial interests, and "patents or patent applications whose value may be affected by publication." Those authors who decline to provide the information may still publish, but their refusal to provide disclosure is reported (Campbell 2001).

Role of Patents in Promoting Market-Focused Research

Patents on genes, an aspect of the commercialization of research, may contribute to companies disproportionately focusing on discoveries that maximize profits to the private sector by targeting large, potentially lucrative markets rather than those that would most benefit public health. This exacerbates disparities of treatment between rich and poor populations and between industrialized and developing countries. It also shifts research away from major public health concerns that are not caused by genetic problems, such as obesity, smoking, and inactivity (Willison and MacLead 2002).

Summary of Life Patent Impacts

In summary, patents on life forms provoke numerous concerns regarding the advancement of science and the provision of medical diagnosis and treatment, including:

- Patent holders being allowed to patent a part of nature, a basic constituent of life.
- The costs of patented research data impeding the development of diagnostics and therapeutics.
- Patent stacking (several different ways of patenting a genomic sequence) discouraging product development due to the high royalty costs payable to all patent owners.
- Unexpected licensing costs and patent infringement penalties becoming common due to the secrecy of patent applications. This secrecy results in scientists discovering, after the fact, that patents related to the work they are doing have already been granted.
- Private biotechnology patent holders monopolizing certain gene test markets.
- Patent filings replacing journal articles as places for public disclosure, thus reducing the body of knowledge in the literature.
- Patents contributing to a focus on research that leads to lucrative market gains rather than to public health benefits.
- The limits placed on the types of tests that can be performed with patented genes harming clinical practice (HGP 2002; Ontario 2002).

The failure to address these concerns about life patents threatens to bring the entire system of patents into conflict with its three fundamental purposes: rewarding invention, enhancing disclosure, and fostering invention. Rather than rewarding human invention, life patents allow the private appropriation of natural phenomena, which are not human inventions; rather than encouraging disclosure of new scientific discoveries, life patents reduce the disclosure that would otherwise occur through the venues of scientific discussion and debate; and rather than fostering innovation, life patents in fact deter it by raising the cost of research and reducing the accessibility of knowledge and scientific methods.

LIFE PATENT REFORM PROPOSALS

The confluence of international concern over the potential impacts of TRIPS and the observed impacts of patenting on science and medicine in OECD countries has generated a spectrum of patent reform proposals. Internationally, numerous governments and citizens organizations have expressed opposition to patents on all life forms (Africa Group 2003; Greenpeace 1999). On 14 March 2000 US president Bill Clinton and British prime minister Tony Blair issued a joint statement to applaud the scientists working on the Human Genome Project for publishing their data for all scientists to use and for keeping "raw fundamental data on the human genome, including the human DNA sequence and its variations ... freely available to scientists everywhere" (Clinton and Blair 2000). In Canada, the federal Standing Committee on Health of the House of Commons recommended in 2001 that humans and "any human materials" not be patentable (Canada 2001, recommendation 34).

No Patents that Conflict with "Ordre Public or Morality"

The WTO's TRIPS agreement and European law permit an exception to patentability for inventions whose commercial exploitation must be prevented in order "to protect *ordre public* or morality including to protect human, animal or plant life or health or to avoid serious prejudice to the environment, provided that such exclusion is not made merely because the exploitation is prohibited by law" (WTO 1994, art. 27, s. 2). Canada and the United States, however, do not include this limitation to patenting. The Province of Ontario recommended the inclusion of *ordre public* in Canadian law. However, the Ontario recommendations failed to specify criteria for its application and included it only as a basis for challenging a patent, not as a basis for the refusal of a patent application. Interveners in the *Harvard Oncomouse* case, on the other hand, did propose an assessment of the environmental and human health risks as an element of decision making regarding applications to patent plant and animal life forms (CELA 2001).

Tighten Utility Requirements
and Limit the Scope of Patents on Genetic Materials

Numerous governmental and scientific bodies have proposed changes to patent laws and administration in order to limit the negative impacts of life patents, particularly for genes and stem cells. Recent proposals for change relate to the application of the basic patent requirements of inventiveness and utility as well as to limits on the scope of patent claims. The Ontario government recommended changes to Canadian patent law and administration that include using the utility requirements to restrict patents on fundamental genomic concepts and genetic research tools so that patents are only granted for specified uses and narrow applications. Further, Ontario called for amendments to the Patent Act to limit the scope of gene patents so that use of the information in a gene is not restricted.

Protection from Patent Infringement Lawsuits for Scientists and Health Professionals

Most countries allow use of patented inventions for research and experimentation, but legally the "research exemption" is narrow: "to be precise, the research exemption holds that a product or process covered by a patent may be freely made, or used to test whether the patent description is sufficient to enable one to replicate what the inventor has done and whether the product or process performs as stated in the patent" (OECD 2002, 58). In Canada, the Patent Act permits making, using, and selling a patented invention for research to satisfy regulatory requirements for the sale of a product (Canada 1985, s. 55.2), and a judge-made exemption permits non-commercial research on patented subject matter. However, it is unclear whether research using a patented invention with a long-term potential for commercialization constitutes infringement of the rights of the patent-holder. For policy makers studying the impacts of life patents, an exception for researchers must be a priority. The Ontario government is calling for clarification of the current Canadian law and for broadening the exceptions in order to ensure that researchers will not be sued for research that may ultimately lead to commercial products, including genetic diagnostic and screening tests.

Licensing Strategies

The US National Institute of Health has developed a "strategic licensing policy" on patents "to promote public health and dissemination of research results while encouraging market competition and attempting to obtain appropriate financial returns" (OECD 2002, 56). It grants mostly non-exclusive licences and retains the right to use inventions for non-commercial research and to ensure the broad dissemination of research results. Canada's Patent Act permits the Canadian government to use a patented invention, upon approval by the commissioner of patents, with payment of compensation to the patent holder, or without the commissioner's consent in "cases of national emergency or extreme urgency ... [or for] a public non-commercial use" (Canada 1985, s. 19). In October 2001, for instance, the Canadian federal government was prepared to override Bayer's patent on Cipro should it become necessary to use that product to treat Canadian victims of anthrax attacks.

Opposition Procedure

It is possible to request a re-examination of a patent in Canada (on narrow grounds) or to apply to the Federal Court to challenge a patent, which is an expensive and slow process. In Europe, any person opposed to the grant of a patent may request an administrative review of that patent, on any ground, within nine months of its issuance. The Ontario government has proposed that a similar process be made available in Canada so as to provide greater transparency, rigour, and public confidence in the patent process.

Using Canadian Medicare Listing of Covered Services to Promote Ethical Patenting

It is worth noting that the public Medicare system of Canada may provide an innovative opportunity to influence patent applications. Medical necessity is the standard for the current listing of services, including test and drug coverage under Medicare. Richard Gold (2000, 432) proposes, however, that a broader test based on the use of biomedical materials be used regarding services, medications, and tests – namely, that they "only be listed if the person having patent rights ... to the biomedical material demonstrates that ethical concerns have been appropriately dealt with." This would include research leading to the product, availability of the patented materials to other researchers on an equitable basis, and ethical marketing and distribution of the product. Use of the broad policy umbrella provided by Medicare would mean that a wider range of ethical concerns could be addressed than is the case under the patent law system alone.

CONCLUSION

The decisions leading to the proliferation of single-cell life patents in Canada occurred without public scrutiny or involvement. Few Canadians are aware of the *Chakrabarty* case in the us Supreme Court or the uncritical thinking in the Canadian patent office that led to its bureaucratic emulation in Canada. The *Harvard Mouse* case was the first life patent case to attract wide media coverage, and anecdotal evidence suggests that most Canadians are shocked to learn that a private company may have effective ownership rights to the genes and cells that exist in their bodies. The

Schmeiser decision has created further uncertainty in the law regarding how patent rights apply to higher life forms. The terms "repugnant," used by the Canadian Federal Health Committee, and "abhorrent," used by former Ontario health minister Tony Clement, in reference to these developments suggest that at least some Canadian legislators would support restraints on life patents.

Canada now urgently needs what should have occurred before life patents were approved twenty years ago: a full public debate, not only among governments and legal, scientific, and ethical experts but also among all Canadians. This debate should include a credible examination of the totality of impacts of life patents and it should result in legal reforms that rebalance patent law to ensure that it reflects not only the original social purpose of the patent system but also contemporary Canadian values. As it stands, the law is aptly described by a sixteenth-century English proverb:

> The law doth punish man or woman
> Who steals the goose from off the commons,
> But lets the greater felon loose
> Who steals the commons from the goose.

REFERENCES

Abbott, Alison. 2004. Clinicians Win Fight to Overturn Patent for Breast-Cancer Gene. *Nature* 429 (6990): 329.

Adam, David. 2002. Bioethics Council Demands Tighter Rules on Gene Patents. *Nature* 418 (6896): 356.

Africa Group. 2003. *Taking Forward the Review of Article 27.3B of the TRIPS Agreement*. World Trade Organization. Available at <http://docsonline.wto. org>, cited 7 August 2003.

Black's Law Dictionary. 1999. 7th ed. St. Paul: West Group.

Blumenthal, David, E.G. Campbell, M.S. Anderson, N. Causino, and K.S. Louis. 1997. Withholding Research Results in Academic Life Science, Evidence from a National Survey of Faculty. *Journal of the American Medical Association* 277 (15): 1224–8.

Campbell, Phillip. 2001. Declaration of Financial Interests. *Nature* 412 (6859): 751.

Canada. 1985. *Patent Act, R.S., c. P-4: An Act Respecting Patents of Invention*. Ottawa: Ministry of Justice.

– 2001. *Assisted Human Reproduction: Building Families*. Ottawa: Standing Committee on Health, House of Commons.

– 2002. *Patenting of Higher Life Forms and Related Issues*. Ottawa: Government of Canada Biotechnology Ministerial Coordinating Committee, Canadian Biotechnology Advisory Committee.

Canadian Cancer Society. 2003. *The Patenting of BRCA1 and 2 Genes*. Canadian Cancer Society. Available at <http://www.cancer.ca/ccs/internet/standard/0,3182,3172_31282995_32777 862_langId-en,00.html>, cited 3 April 2003.

CELA. 2001. *Intervenor's Memorandum of Fact and Law, Commissioner of Patents v. Harvard College*. Toronto: Canadian Environmental Law Association.

Clement, Tony. 2001. *Myriad Gene Patent Issue*. Toronto: Ontario Ministry of Health and Long-Term Care.

Clinton, Bill, and Tony Blair. 2000. *Joint Statement by President Clinton and Prime Minister Tony Blair of the UK*. 14 March. Washington: Office of the Press Secretary, White House.

Diamond v. Chakrabarty. 1980. 447 US 303.

Editors. 2000. Financial Conflicts in Biomedical Research. *Nature Neuroscience* 3 (4): 299.

Franklin, Ursula. 2003. Personal communication, 17 January.

Gold, E. Richard. 2000. Biomedical Patents and Ethics: A Canadian Solution. *McGill Law Journal/Revue de droit de McGill* 45 (2): 413–55.

Greenpeace. 1999. *No Patents on Life: Greenpeace Protests at the European Patent Office in Munich*. Greenpeace International. Available at <http://archive.greenpeace.org/geneng/highlights/gmo/99_08_31.htm>, cited 31 August 1999.

HGP. 2002. *Genetics and Patenting*. Human Genome Project Information Online. Available at <www.ornl.gov/hgmis/elsi/patents.html>, cited 9 April 2004.

Hurst, Lynda. 2001. *Utah Patent-Holder Claims Exclusive Right to Diagnose Cancer Gene*. Democratic Underground 2001. Available at <http://www.democraticunderground.com>, cited 11 August 2001.

Kelly. 2006. Owning the genetic code. Dublin and Belfast: F.R. Kelly and Co. Available at <www.frkelly.com/html/body_biotech.html>, cited 26 June 2006.

Lecubrier, Ande. 2002. Patents and Public Health. EMBO *Reports* 3 (12): 1120–22.

Macdonald, Lynn. 2002. Gene Patenting: Is It Too Late to Stop It? *Canadian Breast Cancer Network – Network News* 7 (1): 12-13.

Malakoff, David. 2000. Suppliers: The Rise of the Mouse, Biomedicine's Model Mammal. *Science* 288 (5464): 248–53.

Marshall, Eliot. 2000. Gene Patents: Patent on HIV Receptor Provokes an Outcry. *Science* 287 (5457): 1375-7.

Mayer, Sue. 2002. *Are Gene Patents in the Public Interest?* Bio-IT World, 12 November. Available at <www.bio-itworld.com/archive/111202/insights_public.html>.

Merz, J.F., A.G. Kriss, D.G.B. Leonard, and K.C. Mildred. 2002. Diagnostic Testing Fails the Test. *Nature* 415 (6872): 577–9.

OECD. 2002. *Genetic Inventions, Intellectual Property Rights and Licensing Practices: Evidence and Practices*. Paris: Organization of Economic Cooperation and Development.

Ontario. 2002. *Genetics, Testing and Gene Patenting: Charting New Territory in Healthcare.* Toronto: Ontario Ministry of Health and Long Term Care.

SCC. 2002. *Commissioner of Patents v. President and Fellow of Harvard College.* SCC 76. Ottawa: Supreme Court of Canada.

– 2004. *Percy Schmeiser and Schmeiser Enterprises Ltd. v. Monsanto Canada Inc.* SCC 34. Ottawa: Supreme Court of Canada.

Schmidt, Sarah. 2003. Ottawa Pressured to Outlaw Gene Patents: Myriad Genetics Case – Provinces Back Ontario in Defying Firm's Threats. *National Post,* 8 January, A12.

Smaglik, Paul. 2000a. Could AIDS Treatments Slip through Patents Loophole? *Nature* 404 (6776): 322.

– 2000b. NIH Cancer Researchers to Get Free Access to "OncoMouse." *Nature* 403 (6768): 350.

Smart and Biggar. 2002. *Commissioner of Patents v. Harvard College, Respondent's Factum.* Ottawa: Smart and Biggar, Barristers and Solicitors.

Sulston, John. 2002. Heritage of Humanity. *Le Monde Diplomatique – English edition,* December, available at <http://mondediplo.com/>.

Varmus, Harold. 2000. *Testimony of Harold Varmus, Hearing on Gene Patents and Other Genomic Inventions.* The House Judiciary Subcommittee on Courts and Intellectual Property, 13 July.

Wadman, Meredith. 2001. Testing Time for Gene Patent as Europe Rebels. *Nature* 413 (6855): 443.

WARF, Geron Reach Agreement on Stem Cells. 2002. *Milwaukee Business Journal,* 9 January. Available at <http://milwaukee.bizjournals.com/milwaukee/stories/2002/01/07/daily22 .html>.

Willison, D., and S. MacLead. 2002. Patenting of Genetic Material: Are the Benefits to Society Being Realised? *Canadian Medical Association Journal* 167 (3): 259–62.

WTO. 1994. *Agreement on Trade-Related Aspects of Intellectual Property Rights.* Geneva: World Trade Organization.

PART SIX

The Way Forward:
Building a Movement,
Developing Alternatives

21

Challenging the Forces
of Deep Integration

MURRAY DOBBIN

Sensibly discussing a strategy for democratic resistance to "deep integration" in Canada is really no different – except for strategic and tactical
details – than discussing resistance to the broad neoliberal agenda, the
Washington Consensus model, and the "facts" on the ground that this
agenda and consensus have helped establish. For the most part this is an
exercise in coming to grips with the material and ideological context that
we are facing. In other words, we need to examine the material social,
political, and economic reality of Canada after twenty years of structural
adjustment by both Tory and Liberal (and provincial) governments, and
the dominance of the ideology that supports that reality. Deep integration
itself is simply the latest stage in a process that involves Canada's own economic and political elites applying the Washington Consensus to their own
country.

While following a set of policies that would essentially see Canada
assimilated into the United States may seem to contradict some aspects of
this consensus, it is clear that it is completely consistent with the nature of
Canada's ruling elites: a comprador class[1] – both economic and political –
that has always had limited loyalty to the idea of the Canadian nation,
grudgingly accepting nation-building policies only when it suited its
narrow economic interests.

The ideological context that progressive forces face is, at first glance, bleak,
and it is difficult not to be pessimistic. Due to both the power of the elites and
their almost total unity in this project, we face the hegemony of neoliberal
ideas within the formal public discourse. The right has moved with exceptional effectiveness to seize control of, or exert dominance over, almost all the
key institutions of democracy in Canada. They not only own the media, but
they also have consciously and strategically used it as a tool to establish ideological hegemony, in part, by marginalizing the ideas and organizations that
challenge it. While the Canadian Broadcasting Corporation (CBC) still stands

out as a critical alternative to the commercial media, even it is often cowed by the critics of public broadcasting and its budget is regularly cut. Corporate interests are gaining significant control over our universities, corrupting their long-standing connection to community and public interest (Dobbin 2003, 106–9).

The federal government bureaucracy is now in the advanced stages of being infected by neoliberal ideology, and Canada faces a rather bizarre situation in which many senior policy makers and departmental managers are actually committed, often openly, to dismantling the nation they are paid to serve. The only remaining institutions critical to a functioning democracy that have not been corrupted are what we now collectively refer to as civil society – social movement organizations, labour unions, NGOs, service organizations, churches, and so on – that have been engaged in battle with the elites since the new consensus emerged decisively in the mid-1980s.

In 1976 the Trilateral Commission published a book, *The Crisis of Democracy*, in which its principal author declared that the crisis could be traced to "an excess of democracy" (Huntington, Crozier, and Watanuki 1975, 113). There can be little doubt that the elites have largely dealt with this crisis – at least temporarily. Huntington described it as one of rising expectations of democratic government among "previously marginalized" groups in society (113). It is now the left that decries the crisis of democracy – as manifested by its severe shortage. That shortage of, or decline in, democracy can be seen precisely as a reversal of those rising expectations, as a grudging acceptance of an eroding social democratic role for government.

The bright spot in the ideological battle is progressive Canadian social and cultural values – in contrast to actual expectations – that have not only persisted with the vast majority of citizens but have actually been strengthened during the past decade. Several studies – prominent among them the 2003 *Citizens' Dialogue on Canada's Future* by Canadian Policy Research Networks – demonstrate that increasing numbers of Canadians support a return to so-called "activist" government (MacKinnon et al. 2003). Extensive yearly polling by Ekos reveals a continuing and dramatic gap between Canadian elites and ordinary citizens regarding the appropriate role of government (Graves 2001). This fact has been obscured by voting patterns and stated intentions for almost fifteen years. The political configuration in national politics and in the provinces is a reflection of the principal success of the right-wing ideological project: a counter-revolution of lowered expectations. It is this major change in the political culture in Canada that must be addressed and countered if systemic Americanization (a more accurate term than "deep integration") and its consequences are to be challenged.

There were positive signs in this regard emanating from the 2004 federal election, which demonstrated a closing of the gap between values and expectations. Paul Martin's Liberals had to abandon their early strategy of running on a right-wing platform and move to the left to counter a resurgent New Democratic Party (NDP). The victory of Stephen Harper's Conservatives in 2006 was driven by the Liberal implosion in the wake of the Quebec sponsorship scandal as well as by a very disciplined Conservative campaign that managed to soft-pedal their extreme right-wing agenda.

THE FACTS ON THE GROUND: THE MATERIALIST AND POLITICAL REALITY OF ASSIMILATION

The deep integration project can be seen as the final stage of the assimilation of the Canadian economy into that of the United States, and if we are to come to grips with this final stage, it is critical that we have a clear idea of the context of its introduction. The policies and actions of the Brian Mulroney (1984–93) and Jean Chrétien (1993–03, with Paul Martin as finance minister) governments prepared the ground for this final stage by systematically dismantling or weakening those aspects of the Canadian state that were key to the nation-building initiatives of the postwar period. The Canada-US Free Trade Agreement (CUFTA) was the single most significant policy initiative in this regard.

For Canada to exist at all in the context of living next to the most powerful economy in the world, policies resisting that north-south pull were and are critical. Eliminate or weaken those policies and you automatically unleash the "natural" direction of unregulated market forces. While Mulroney was responsible for the key foundational policy shift respecting the dismantling of the Canadian nation-state, Paul Martin got down to the detailed work of ending two generations of nation building. In his 1995 budget Martin took very deliberate steps to reverse the role of the federal government with respect to this long-time imperative. That budget is most famous for its 40 percent reduction in the federal contribution to social programs in Canada (Barlow and Campbell 1995, 127).

But more significant was the new Canada Health and Social Transfer (CHST) legislation.[2] The CHST replaced the two most important pieces of social and nation-building legislation in postwar Canadian history – Established Program Funding (EPF) and the Canada Assistance Plan (CAP). The EPF, in particular, targeted spending through Ottawa's superior revenue base to a national medicare program and also created, in effect, a national network of public universities and colleges. Overcoming the barrier to nation building contained in the constitutional division of powers – provincial jurisdiction over health, education, and social welfare – the federal government had in effect made the provinces financial offers they could not refuse.

The significance of the funding was such that it overcame all obstacles before it – narrow regionalism, political parochialism, ideological resistance, Quebec nationalism – to create national programs in the most important areas of nation building and social equality. With the stroke of a pen, Paul Martin's CHST balkanized the Canadian nation in these critical areas by handing authority back to the provinces and deliberately undermining the principle of universality. The importance of this latter principle is difficult to overstate as it gave enormous substance to what it meant to be a Canadian citizen. It was the most important repository of citizen entitlement. The same analysis applies to CAP.

Less well known than the CHST and its implications were the targeted cuts of what I have referred to as nation-building departments in the federal government. Martin's cuts were very strategic, belying the notion that deficit cutting was his principle concern. The "core" activities of the state, as defined by the Fraser Institute and other neoliberal agencies, suffered by far the smallest cuts – from 10 percent to 15 percent. Those critical to maintaining a viable nation were cut by between 40 percent and 60 percent (Martin 1995). Transportation, the environment, regional and industrial development, fisheries, and agriculture were slashed so badly that large swaths of their mandates were simply eliminated.

In his 1995 budget speech Martin made it clear that there was one single economic development policy at the federal level: trade promotion. In effect, Martin was declaring that policies focusing on our economic relationship with the United States were more important than were those nurturing the domestic Canadian economy.

There are many aspects of state intervention in the economy that testify to the federal government's efforts at structural adjustment. Other initiatives take the normal structural adjustment imperative even further, harnessing state agencies ever more explicitly to the interests of corporate advancement and trade enhancement. Taken as a whole, this restructuring process is gradually transforming the Canadian nation-state into a homogeneous and increasingly deregulated economic unit of the US economy.

The election of a minority Stephen Harper government in early 2006 was an ominous sign in this regard, particularly if Harper manages eventually to win a majority government. Harper has embraced the Security and Prosperity Partnership of North America signed by Paul Martin, George Bush and Vicente Fox in March 2005 in Waco, Texas. At their meeting in Cancun, Mexico, in March 2006, Harper, Bush, and Fox announced the creation of a "North American Competitiveness Council" composed of corporate leaders from the three countries, clearly signalling whose interests will guide the Partnership. On the domestic front, Harper has promised to derail the incipient national childcare program – started by the Liberals in response to public demand – and to fix the "fiscal imbalance," which appears to be an effort to further deregulate the Canadian federation and align it along a north-south axis.

THE RECORD OF THE LEFT
IN CHALLENGING THE RIGHT'S HEGEMONY

The history of the fight against the right, beginning with the fight against CUFTA, suggests that, while we started out well, actually winning the hearts and minds of a majority of Canadians, we did not fair as well when facing the subsequent assaults on democracy and equality, especially those with the most significant ideological importance. The most important political assaults by the elite were substantially ideological, while progressive forces focused more on the particular public policies targeted by those assaults: medicare, education, the environment, poverty, workers rights, corporate regulation, and other discrete issues within the constellation of social and political life in Canada.

The results of the fifteen years of political struggle that ensued after CUFTA came into effect are not easy to sort out. Compared to other English-speaking countries experiencing the neoliberal counter-revolution, progressive forces have dedicated enormous resources and much effective organizing into the fight for democracy and sovereignty. The fact that Canadians' progressive, communitarian values remain essentially intact is in no small measure due to this fight-back. But how much of that maintenance of values is due to our campaigns and how much simply to Canadians' resilience is difficult to determine. Certainly values have been at the core of what issues we chose to fight on and why we fought. It is less clear just how explicitly and effectively we used the idea of values in our propaganda and political language. What is clear is that values aside – and our resistance aside – Canadians succumbed to the neoliberal assault on their expectations with respect to the activist role of government.

I would argue that the reason for this can be found, at least in part, in our failure to consistently and effectively fight the neoliberal assault as a counter-hegemonic struggle. This was especially true at the national level, where, for most of the past fifteen years, there has not been a coherent, national response to the corporatization of the federal state. This is the case simply because there has been no formal national coalition of forces that could provide that coherence. Examining this period from the perspective of the right's ideological battle to achieve hegemony, the left – with some important but haphazard exceptions – did not engage the right with a clear counter-hegemonic strategy.

As detailed in the next section, the right's twenty-year effort to lower people's expectations consisted of five key campaigns: (1) the idea of the inevitability of corporate globalization, (2) deficit "terrorism," (3) the assault on public employees and government in general, (4) the promotion of the private sector as the repository of the public interest, and (5) the drive to cut taxes for the wealthy and corporations. More recently, taking advantage of the attacks on 11 September 2001, we have seen legislation undermining human rights and civil liberties, although this legislation has not yet been extensively used. I am not arguing that progressive forces were blind to the growing hegemony of neoliberalism – just that this conscious-ness of the ideological nature of the fight did not consistently or effectively find its way into the organized resistance. More specifically, while much of the left's analysis of this period was conceived within a counter-hegemonic framework, the resistance itself was not. In other words, the intellectual framing of the struggle was lost in operationalizing the public fight against neoliberalism.

While the ideological project of the right actually began in the mid-1970s, with the formation of groups like the Business Council on National Issues (BCNI), the Fraser Institute, and the National Citizens Coalition, the first pitched battle utilizing right-wing ideology was the fight over CUFTA. The left took up the challenge with exceptional effectiveness and with com-pletely new organizational forms. The Pro Canada (later the Action Canada) Network was formed on the initiative of the Council of Canadi-ans, the Canadian Labour Congress (CLC), and the churches. Provincial coalitions of similar make-up formed in almost every province. A consen-sus on the nature of the struggle developed quickly: free trade was an assault on sovereignty and democracy.

Our victory in the "free trade" propaganda war was, in part, due to the context within which it was fought. The Washington Consensus model for the state and the global economy was still relatively new. Canadian politi-cal culture was still characterized by the widely held assumptions of the postwar social contract. Expectations of government and people's values still, more or less, coincided. The notion that a trade agreement would have the power to undermine the fruits of democracy and dilute our sovereignty struck many Canadians as a radical departure from the consensus that had included all three political parties for over a generation.

In effect, progressive forces took on the first serious right-wing campaign for cultural hegemony and, even though we lost the election, we won people's hearts and minds. That victory was one of the last times we were able to decisively accomplish that political feat – the goods and services tax (GST) fight being perhaps the last clear victory and, again, a Pyrrhic one. And like the free trade fight, it, too, was largely defensive, with progressive tax alternatives playing only a minor role. Within three years of that fight, progressive forces would be on a more or less permanent defensive footing. The loss of the free trade fight had enormous implications. Once that political battle was lost, neoliberal forces had a tremendous political and ideological advantage and began the process of actually restructuring the nation-state and further promoting the ideas of neoliberalism.

Free trade was a form of insurance against any advance of social democracy. The task for the right was now to move forward on both fronts – on the ground through retrenchment with respect to social program spending, public ownership, and regulation; and ideologically through what I have referred to as the "revolution of lowered expectations" (Dobbin 1998). As soon as the 1988 election was over, the BCNI and other business groups and their ideological shock troops in the media and thinks tanks began lobbying for cuts to social programs – using the federal government's large deficits as a "useful crisis." Arguing that free trade and its attendant imperatives were "inevitable" was now much easier: it was in place and was changing the country. From that juncture forward the posture of progressive forces was more narrowly defensive, in large part because it was fractured among many players.

THE RIGHT'S HEGEMONIC CAMPAIGNS

When the corporate elite and their political parties looked at the problem of democracy, one of the goals they identified was the lowering of popular expectations. At the root of the strong democratic movements in the postwar era was the increasing recognition of the idea of social and economic rights (often derided by the right as "entitlements") and the growing expectation that governments existed for the benefit of citizens. It was this high level of expectation that drove people's demands for better social programs and better wages. From the perspective of big business in the mid-1970s, democracy needed a cold shower.

This campaign to lower people's expectation was absolutely deliberate and carefully thought out. It followed a pattern that was virtually identical to those in other English-speaking developed countries such as Australia, Britain, and New Zealand. The first, overarching campaign was the restructuring of the political dialogue in favour of radical change: the "there is no alternative" (TINA) campaign. First used by Margaret Thatcher, it was highly successful, entering popular political culture as a result of its relentless repetition over many years. As Susan George (1997, 4) expresses it: "Defining, sustaining and controlling culture is crucial: get into people's heads and you will acquire their hearts, their hands and their destinies."

The second ideological assault on Canadians' expectations of the state, following the TINA campaign, was what I called the "deficit terror" campaign. It was relentless and continuous over a period of almost five years. The debt and annual deficits were a national "crisis": if we did not solve it we would hit the "debt wall." This campaign was especially brilliant because it actually appealed to citizens' better instincts – sacrificing to solve a national crisis. It is a technique that has been used by the right on many occasions – and was once described by Ontario Tory education minister John Snobelen as "creating a useful crisis."[3] The argument was simple: people won't accept radical changes to government services unless there is a crisis. Create a "useful crisis" and people will feel duty-bound to make sacrifices to resolve it.

The third phase of the counter-revolution was the assault on the public service. In story after story public employees were referred to as "bureaucrats," even if those in the story were rank and file government workers. People who worked for government were repeatedly portrayed as overpaid, underworked, lazy, inefficient, self-serving, and over-privileged – basking in the luxury of high-paid, secure jobs while everyone else faced economic insecurity – the new "normal." The goal here was to drive a wedge between citizens and those who provided them with the services they needed. Again, the purpose was to establish in the political culture hostility towards service providers so that when governments, both federal and provincial, began their massive layoffs, public sympathy would be minimized. It was largely successful.

The fourth phase of this campaign to lower expectations involves the genuine crisis that comes from making huge cuts to public services. If you cut billions of dollars from health care and education and municipal services, those services will inevitably erode, despite the heroic efforts of public employees. People begin to have less faith in the public services they use. And even though they may make the connection between eroded services and funding cuts, at the psychological level (which is where the propaganda is directed), they become vulnerable to the message that everything connected with government is somehow bad: unresponsive, inefficient, just not working, and probably corrupt.

Coming hard on the heels of this erosion of public confidence in public services is the white knight of the market – private service providers. The marketplace is portrayed in the media and by pro-business politicians as the paragon of efficiency, effectiveness, and cost-saving. They are ready and willing to move in where public services have failed. They will argue that competition is good for everyone: competition from private schools or hospitals will force public institutions to become more efficient. Privatization and public-private-partnerships (P3s) hold out the promise of improved services.

The fifth and final ideological assault on high public expectations involves tax cuts, and this campaign is still under way even though the tax base has already been radically reduced from what it was twenty years ago. The message is multifaceted: the product – government – is no good, so we will give the "customers" their money back. We have to reduce corporate and personal taxes in order to be competitive. The tax cutters have a single goal: permanently financially handcuff governments so as to curtail their ability to govern on behalf of ordinary citizens, and write in stone the massive cuts to services already implemented.

These five elements of the right's hegemonic project constitute its nearly complete domination of the political discourse in Canada. And if we examine the response by progressive forces, the picture is not encouraging. There was an effective and coordinated left response to CUFTA, the GST, and, to a lesser extent, NAFTA, and the current organized resistance to the proliferation of P3s has been very successful. In all these cases there was either a coalition whose specific task was to respond to the threat or there was an existing organization whose governing mandate included taking on the threat.

The lessons regarding the importance of coalitions are found in other political victories: the blocking of bank mergers; the role Canadian groups played in defeating the MAI; the victory against Monsanto's growth hormone for dairy cows, and, more recently, its GMO wheat; the blocking of Paul Martin's plan to gut Old Age Security and to join Bush's missile defence; the organizing around support for the Romanow Report on medicare; the campaign for Canada to ratify the Kyoto Protocol on climate change, and the decisive role played by a rejuvenated peace movement in Chrétien's decision to stay out of the Iraq war. All of these were important victories, and all involved coalitions with the capacity and resources to develop a consensus position and effective mobilizing. Yet, in sum, they did not seriously challenge the right's hegemonic project. In effect, the left has forced a series of tactical retreats on the right, while their ideological dominance continues. That dominance results from an inadequate challenge by the collective left to specific elements of the right's hegemonic strategy.

The failure to respond to the deficit hysteria campaign was especially damaging to the future of progressive politics and underlies the current weakness of progressive forces in facing the new threat of systemic Americanization. The dominance of right-wing ideas is built largely on the foundation established by the deficit hysteria campaign of the early to mid-1990s. The notion that deficits are bad, a threat to good government, and a "mistake" that we dare not repeat again is so rooted in the public consciousness that it is difficult to imagine what would reverse it. It was the most important victory of the right, and it was achieved largely by default.

Our response to the deficit campaign was essentially to declare that it was a red herring. By ignoring the campaign we appeared irresponsible because clearly the deficit was a problem: it just wasn't *the* problem. While Canadians of their own accord resisted the deficit issue for a long time, they could not resist it forever in the absence of any counter-hegemonic campaign. The left allowed the Canadian public to be a punching bag on the issue: with a few minor exceptions, mostly on the part of individuals, we said nothing. The Canadian Centre for Policy Alternatives (CCPA) put out two excellent popular pieces – *The Deficit Made Me Do It* (Finn 1992) and *Ten Deficit Myths* (Cameron and Finn 1995). But no social movement or labour organization took responsibility for mounting a public campaign using their arguments.

An effective counter-campaign on the deficit would not have been easy, given the resources that a panoply of right-wing agencies devoted to the hysteria campaign. But the political conditions at the time were not wholly to our disadvantage. The CCPA's work on the issue, the availability of many good left economists who could have been mobilized, a strong public resistance (reflected in polling throughout the period) to seeing the deficit issue as important compared to other issues, excellent studies showing that the debt was increasing due to falling revenue and high interest charges rather than to "over-spending," and powerful arguments about how we should deal with the deficit – economic growth rather than massive cuts – were all available as elements of an effective counter-campaign. In the 1993 election the Liberal Red Book in fact attacked spending cuts as a solution to the deficit and promoted economic growth as the way forward. The early 1990s, up to and including the Liberal election victory, was still a period during which the political culture largely reflected the assumptions of the old social contract.

Organizationally, progressive forces were ill-prepared and ill-equipped at the national level to take on the fight. A major strategy meeting of the Action Canada Network (ACN) in the summer of 1992 rejected the need to mount a campaign against deficit hysteria. There was no recognition among most of the key organizational players in the ACN that we were facing a fundamental shift in political culture that would affect all our fight-back campaigns. No other organization was capable of coalescing labour and civil society groups into such a project. Once we failed to engage the enemy on the most crucial political battle of the early 1990s, we effectively created barriers for every other single-issue fight. Defending and promoting social spending and an activist state was now much more difficult since all roads led to the now-demonized deficit. Keynesian economics was the foundation of the social contract, and critical to Keynesianism was its reliance on strategic deficit spending. Demonize deficits and you strike a critical blow to activist government.

Similarly, there was no coordinated approach to three other ideological assaults on the culture of the postwar social contract. The concerted attack on public employees has proceeded for years, and yet organized labour has not devised a comprehensive, centralized strategy aimed specifically at countering the intent of this campaign – that is, to drive a wedge between the public and the workers who provide the public with the services it actually supports. Again, labour in general tended to behave as though the political context had not changed, employing the same strategy and tactics despite the sea change in political culture regarding public employees' rights.

Three campaigns of the five identified are ongoing, and the deficit campaign has morphed into a less intense, but equally dangerous, campaign to rapidly pay down the debt so that surpluses need not be used for enhanced or revived social programs. The effort to sell the private sector as the white knight that will save us from inefficient and scandal-plagued government goes on apace and is now pitched primarily through P3s. The advent of P3s is even more alarming in some ways than is outright privatization as P3s provide the advantage to capital of reducing its investment and risk costs, guaranteeing a set rate of return, and putting contractual restrictions on changes to regulation.

The progressive community across the country is still facing the campaign for tax cuts, though this one appeared for some time to have run its course. The enormous cuts implemented by Martin during his tenure as finance minister made it difficult for this piece of the agenda to go much further, but in the 2006 federal election Harper's Conservatives promised to reduce the Goods and Services Tax as well as other taxes. But again, the right's tax cut agenda was implemented with no serious challenge from a broad-based counter-campaign on the part of a progressive constellation. This is a great pity because the propaganda campaign for tax cuts was actually a failure. For example, tax cuts are never the first choice when Canadians are polled about what to do with federal surpluses. This is shown by a survey conducted by the Centre for Research and Information on Canada in October 2003, which revealed that 63 percent favoured using the surplus for social spending, 24 percent for debt reduction, and just 12 percent for tax cuts.

The lack of a left counter-attack on this issue can be traced to two weaknesses: (1) the failure to see the tax cut issue as an important part of the right's hegemonic project and, thus, demanding a collective response, and (2) the lack of a national organization on the left capable of debating the need for such a response and carrying it out.

There is evidence that such a national campaign would be fruitful. The Ontario Liberals actually ran successfully in the last provincial election on a promise to halt and even reverse some of Harris's tax cuts. It is no coincidence that it was only in Ontario that a concerted and well funded campaign against tax cuts – a campaign that explicitly linked cuts to social programs with tax cuts for the privileged – was carried out. It is difficult to assess the influence of that campaign, which was conducted by the Centre for Social Justice, but Ontario was the only province in which progressive forces took on the issue, and it was the only province in which a mainstream political party felt comfortable running on a campaign of reversing tax cuts.

FIGHTING DEEP INTEGRATION
AS A COUNTER-HEGEMONIC STRUGGLE

The prospect of deep integration itself and, more important, the implications of dealing with a comprador ruling elite, presents us with very specific ideological and political problems. Over the past fifteen years progressive forces have tended to fight each new defensive battle as a discrete engagement, unrelated to and uninformed by the previous battle. In other words, instead of fighting a war with a clear strategy for its entire duration, we tended to fight each engagement as though it were unique. This speaks to the importance not only of understanding the context for each of these battles – free trade, the GST, the CHST, cuts to medicare, deficit hysteria – but also of incorporating the larger picture into our political strategy in each of these fights.

We still fight our battles against an increasingly corporate state as though it were the old social contract state of the 1970s. It is not that we actually believe this to be the case: it is just that we define our fights, strategy, and tactics without sufficiently making this knowledge our constant reference point and our framing imperative. Ursula Franklin's description of our government as a "government of occupation" is an increasingly accurate assessment of our political and social reality, but we fail to act on this reality (Franklin 1997–98).[4]

This peculiar disconnect between our own understanding of reality and our predominant political response to it is reflected in our political stance against the Canadian state. We fight defensive battles: "defending" education; "defending" environmental laws; "defending" public ownership, workers rights, democracy, government itself. Integral to this strategy is a form of strategic defeatism that is instantly recognizable by the people we are trying to engage. By employing this defensive mode and language (or issue framing), we are effectively saying that we know that all we can do is slow down the juggernaut and contain the damage. It is a tacit acceptance that the state will continue to downsize its social democratic role. We tend, as part of this strategy, to spend our resources convincing working people that things are bad and about to get worse. Yet who, other than working families, have a better knowledge of how bad things are? They experience the erosion of equality and quality of life on a daily basis. What they want to hear is not how bad things are but some clear expression of how things can get better.

The two areas of public policy in which progressive forces have to some extent broken the defensive mould are childcare and health care. As a result of the 2004 election campaign, a national childcare program was put on the national agenda, soon to be derailed by the Conservative victory in the 2006 election. And with regard to health care, no other area of public policy has received as much attention from the left. This, in part, is because we know that health care is the most popular public program in Canada and that it is the place where Canadians are willing to draw the line in terms of cutbacks. While the "defend medicare" imperative is still dominant, the success of this campaign in recent years has emboldened key organizations and activists to go on the offensive and to demand that governments enhance medicare through the addition of publicly funded and administered pharmacare, homecare, and primary health care. The fact that Paul Martin and the Liberals, and even the Conservatives under Stephen Harper (who has opposed public medicare for his entire political life), promised more money for medicare and made promises pertaining to pharmacare during both the 2004 and the 2006 election campaigns demonstrates that, if we can escape our defensive posture, then we can redefine the landscape upon which the ideological fight is engaged. By demanding that medicare be enhanced, and not just maintained, the left effectively bridged the gap between Canadians' stated values and their expectations – and forced neoliberal forces onto the defensive. In effect, health care activists reframed the health care issue and, by so doing, redesigned the political landscape upon which the fight was taking place. Thus they forced the right to fight on their terms. The same is true of childcare. While these fights are a long way from being over, they prove that the left, far from being unable to defeat the right, can achieve significant victories if it fights with strategic intelligence.

While much of the ideology and its attendant propaganda around free trade and other Washington Consensus goals – trade liberalization, privatization, deregulation, tax cuts, decentralization, and so on – were cast in terms of responding to the inevitability of globalization, deep integration more or less abandons that rationale. The clear objective is not to make Canada "competitive" in the new global economy so much as it is to admit that corporate Canada has failed to compete with its predominant trade "partner/competitor" and that the only way out is to be effectively subsumed into the American Empire as a quasi-fifty-first state.

But having said that, the corporate elite and its political expressions in the Liberal and Conservative parties are still aggressively committed to the key elements of the Washington Consensus. With the deep integration initiative, the corporate elite is essentially shifting its political strategy while maintaining all of its neoliberal economic imperatives in the service of assimilating Canada into the United States. While the corporate sector has been lobbying for twenty years to get private market access to medicare, education, and a vast array of government social and municipal services, that access will now be cast in terms of integration with the United States. According to press reports cited by Mel Hurtig (2002, 385), former foreign affairs minister Bill Graham revealed this new twist in January 2002: "Mr. Graham said he is personally interested in expanding North American integration beyond trade and tariffs into social policy... NAFTA could be expanded to cover social, environmental, justice and other issues, Mr. Graham said." In their March 2006 communiqué Harper, Bush, and Fox announced that the new corporate-driven North American Competitiveness Council (NACC) "will provide us recommendations on North American competitiveness, including, among others, areas such as ... services." The three leaders furthered their "commitment to strengthen regulatory cooperation among the three countries," signalling that public services and programs will be targeted (Bush, Fox, and Harper 2006).

Progressive forces – labour, environmental, social justice groups, and the NDP – fighting their particular battles on this broad terrain need to have, so far as is possible, a common analysis that incorporates this very specific reality. It is here that, as a broad social and political movement, we face the greatest challenge. The terrain upon which we now fight is still characterized by a contradiction that, so far, has worked to our disadvantage: dramatically lowered expectations among citizens with regard to what is possible from government on the one hand and the fact that the actual values of those citizens are undergoing an unmistakable progressive shift on the other. In other words, we have yet to effectively realize the advantage that the public's progressive values should offer us.

What do we need to do differently in order to address this political dilemma and to actually construct and carry out a counter-hegemonic project? First, of course, leading organizations, labour and social movement leaders, and left-wing researchers and research institutions have to explicitly accept such an analysis. In other words, there needs to be a debate and dialogue about what the political moment is and how to deal with it in a much more systematic way than we have done to date. Such debates do not launch themselves: there has to be an initiative on the part of a respected player or players in the progressive constellation of organizations.

If such a consensus were to be achieved, an important part of the task of systematically developing a counter-hegemonic project would fall to left researchers in general but, more specifically, to research institutions such as the Canadian Centre for Policy Alternatives, the Centre for Social Justice, the Parkland Institute, and others. Such an explicit focus would not only mean that these institutions would have to consciously put their research decisions and research approach through a "counter-hegemonic" filter but also that they would have to cooperate with each other and coordinate their research efforts so that resources could be used efficiently and effectively. Also, they would have to work more closely with the social movement, labour, and political party sectors of the progressive community in order to ensure that the research conducted – and the formats within which it is produced – is actually useful to the carrying out of the project.

At its core, the counter-hegemonic project is a systematic and strategic effort to address the key success of the right: the dramatically lowered expectations of Canadians. It was the rising expectations of the 1970s that was the explicit target of the right – the infamous "excess of democracy" declaration of the Trilateral Commission – and the right has been brilliantly successful in carrying out its campaign. Only by integrating into our research choices, propaganda strategies, and political language an explicit counter-force to this new reality of lowered expectations can we begin to change – in the words of the Fraser Institute's Michael Walker – the "ideological fabric" of society and return it to a place where reclaiming the commons may be seen not only as desirable but also as possible.

An examination of the research projects and publications of left research centres for most of the past fifteen years reveals that the majority of them focused on critiquing the situation we face – revealing the neoliberal agenda, raising the alarm about privatization and P3s, exposing the threat of trade liberalization to social programs, decrying the vicious attacks on the poor, the erosion of environmental protection, tax cuts for the rich, and so on. This approach reflects the defensive posture that the left has taken ever since the free trade fight. And again, it reveals the same sense that we are fighting discrete battles – as though each one of these outrages is somehow an aberration, a departure from the social contract, from democratic governance that we are "demanding" be corrected.

While all of this research was, and still is, necessary and critical in the fight against the right, it also plays into the right's hegemonic strategy, if only indirectly. What is implied by this continuing defensive posture is that our position on these issues is actually marginal – portrayed as "old" while the right's ideas (dragged from the eighteenth century) are put forward as "new." We even refer to our solutions – usually in short declarations appended onto the longer negative critiques – as "alternatives." Yet, ironically, our putative marginal position, far from being marginal, radical, or unrealistic, reflects the values and aspirations of the large majority of Canadians. Our positions are only marginal within the context of lowered expectations and the neoliberal domination of political discourse. In recent years this defensive posture has begun to change, with more papers and studies taking a positive stance and, thus, promoting the expansion of the activist state.

This, it is to be hoped, represents a critical shift in thinking on the left because what has been missing from almost every progressive organization's fight-back strategy is the one element that has been at the core of every successful campaign for social progress in Canadian history: the offer of hope. Our relentlessly negative campaigns do just the opposite of giving hope. We are telling people who experience the ravages of neoliberalism every day of their lives that things are bad. We act as though what is needed are more and more messages that things are bad and about to get worse, when what people need to hear is that, in the slogan of the World Social Forum, "another world is possible." It was a message of hope driven by an ability to imagine a better world that mobilized millions in the "dirty thirties" and, in conjunction with the threat of the Soviet Union and the "spread" of communism, forced on a reluctant ruling class the historic compromise of the postwar period.

In the 1930s working-class organizations and parties rallied people to attack the corporations and the rich for their selfishness and greed, and they argued persuasively that the country was rich enough to provide a decent life for everyone if only wealth were to be distributed more equitably. It was on the basis of that hope that the so-called "golden age" of liberal democratic capitalism was ushered in. That selfishness and greed are just as great today (and our GDP per capita has doubled since Medicare came in 1967), yet our message is no longer one of hope.

That lack of hope is what maintains the right's victory. Even when the population supports, for example, strong publicly funded and operated social programs, when we present that position we somehow end up being on the defensive. Much of this has to do with political language. The right, which controls the media and, therefore, the dissemination of language, has managed to discredit our language as well as to insert many of their themes into popular culture: "There is no alternative," "We have been spending like there's no tomorrow," "We are going to hit the debt wall," "We have to get our fiscal house in order." These were just a few of the easy phrases the right carefully crafted and then deliberately repeated tens of thousands of times in dozens of different forums and contexts. That virtually all the purveyors of right-wing ideology use the same phrases reveals a brilliant strategy, effectively executed. Yet I am not aware of a single institutional response from the left to this core hegemonic victory of the right.

The lack of a systematic response is rooted in our defensive posture. If we were to begin to change that posture, to actually put forward a vision of the future that went beyond defending what we have already lost, the issue of political language would necessarily be addressed. So long as we continue to fight on a terrain defined by our adversaries, so long will we continue to lose. This is because, as it now stands, we are simply waiting in the trenches for their next assault.

A key and obvious aspect of the right's hegemony is not simply the great attention it has played to developing its own language but also its determination to denigrate and neutralize the political language of the social contract political culture – that is, the language of the left. They have largely succeeded in this project as words such as "reform" have been hijacked for their purposes; the terms "deficit financing" and "welfare state" are now epithets; the terms "left" and "right" have been discarded as no longer useful or relevant; and terms such as "equality" and "rights" have simply been devalued.

At the ideological level left writers and thinkers need to address the question of hegemony and to commit to defining and undertaking a serious counter-hegemonic project. The core element of this strategic repositioning is the need for a new language of social change and political resistance that takes into account the damage that the right has done to public discourse. This strategic imperative takes on even greater urgency in the context of the new corporate initiative of deep integration. And this is not just because deep integration is the final challenge to Canadian democracy and sovereignty: it is also because the political moment is so propitious. We have a Canadian citizenry that would be extremely receptive to a genuinely new democratic discourse – one that highlights the differences between the United States and Canada and provides hope for the future. While there is no single project in Canada that has addressed the critical question of issue framing, in the United States there have been real advances on this front. For example, the Rockridge Institute (2005) in Berkeley, California, works to "Reframe the public debate to make a progressive moral vision more persuasive and resonant."

THE LEFT'S ORGANIZATIONAL DILEMMA

All of the problems faced by progressive forces in Canada can be seen as ultimately organizational. The fight against a coherent, well organized, well funded, and often coordinated right wing is carried out by a myriad of underresourced and uncoordinated (or undercoordinated) organizations. This, at least in part, accounts for the fact that we have not defined our fight-back in terms of a counter-hegemonic project. Such a definition can only be carried out by a collective expression that somehow incorporates all, or most of, the elements of the struggle under one roof. A single organization – even a national one – fighting for the preservation of medicare can hardly implement such an analysis by itself. The dilemma is straightforward: the kind of coordinated social justice movement that is needed to resist neoliberal hegemony and the neoliberal project of "deep integration" does not yet exist. Instead, we have issue-based coalitions – some permanent, some ad hoc – designed to fight particular battles or public policy issues. We also have a myriad of individual organizations, all of which are fighting discrete battles that, no matter how well-organized, do not add up to a response to the right's comprehensive declaration of class war.

In spring of 2004 there was an attempt to replicate the effort made to fight the free trade agreement. The coalition was to be called the Our Canada Project (OCP), and it was variously seen by those who came together as a temporary alliance focused on the election, a coalition that would take on deep integration, and/or a broad coalition that would provide long-term coherence to the fight against neoliberalism (CAW/TCA 2004). Partly due to these different interpretations of what was being asked of member organizations, the OCP never really gelled. The confusion over its ultimate purpose reflects just how different the situation is now than it was in the period in which the Action Canada Network was formed. Less formal efforts to form a coalition continued to be made in 2005 and 2006, with similarly disappointing results.

The success of the ACN can be partly traced to the fact that, at that time, the right was in the early stages of its hegemonic project. Not only was our appeal to Canadians rooted in their values but it also still corresponded with their expectations. Fifteen years of mostly defensive resistance by progressive forces, and the infection of virtually every agency and institution of democracy by neoliberal ideas, means that recreating the kind of energy that launched the ACN will require extraordinary leadership and political will. Every sector is now in its bunker, required by its mandate to defend against a myriad of assaults that could exhaust even well resourced organizations. The OCP cast its net very broadly, and for good reason: every aspect of Canada is threatened by deep integration and every corresponding sector organization needs to be at the table. But with an even broader base of organizations, achieving a common analysis of the situation and a consensus on how to proceed is an enormous challenge, both ideologically and politically.

Beyond the need for a systematic coordination effort – that is, the creation of a permanent, broad-based coalition – we need to address what is arguably the Canadian left's single most critical failure of the past thirty years: the huge gap between electoral politics on the one hand and social movement/labour politics on the other. These two solitudes of progressive politics in Canada have meant that there has not even been an ongoing conversation between the two branches of social change politics. For their part, NDP governments were hostile to social movements, seeing them as loose cannons firing random shots at them and making their job of governing more difficult. For their part, social movement organizations seemed to believe that they had the moral high ground simply because they existed and that they had no responsibility for the NDP's dismal popularity in the 1990s. This historic disconnect manifested itself in two ways: (1) an NDP that retreated into strictly electoral machine politics, with no will or capacity to engage in social justice politics between elections; and (2) social movement organizations that virtually sat out elections, almost as though they were observers of a process that had nothing to do with them.

Since 2004 there have been some positive signs on both these fronts. The NDP under Jack Layton has tried to address this historic weakness by attempting to engage social movement organizations on the question of electoral politics. Layton also reorganized and redefined the role of the elected NDP caucus by creating a number of advocacy task forces whose role is to engage in the daily struggles of communities against the neoliberal onslaught. Yet this promising start in bridging the gap is, in 2006, clearly on the wane. The task forces are not functioning and the party no longer has a senior staff position responsible for liasing with social movement organizations. In part, this is due to the slowness of social movement groups to respond to the opening, allowing advocates of the traditional political model to prevail within the NDP leadership. If this opening is really lost, it represents a serious setback indeed.

THE STRUGGLE AGAINST DEEP INTEGRATION: THE AMERICANIZATION OF CANADA

This chapter is intended to address how to fight back against the corporate plan to assimilate Canada into the American Empire. I admit to not yet having dealt with the specifics of such a fight-back campaign. However, without first explicating the context within which such a campaign must be conceived and executed, we would once again end up putting together a solid defence against yet another neoliberal offence. What is needed, rather, is a good offence – a visionary response that posits a coherent strategy for rebuilding and reconceiving the Canadian nation within the context of a socially just and economically equitable hemisphere and that presents a challenge to corporate globalization. Ultimately, such a vision can only come out of a progressive community that has built a consensus around certain key elements.

Having a coherent vision of the kind of country we want does not mean that we do not respond to the deep integration (DI) initiative. But it does change the way we respond. Assuming that progressive forces can move towards establishing the kind of broad coalition described above, the first step in developing a counter-hegemonic strategy to oppose DI involves identifying the initiative's weakest points with respect to the values of Canadian political culture. Then, we should exploit those weaknesses by developing a counter-vision that reflects and builds on those values – and that does so with social and cultural imagination, and with hope rather than despair.

Fighting DI as a single state/corporate initiative is much more problematic than was fighting the free trade agreement in the mid-1980s. That fight gave us the advantage of a single initiative containing a multitude of threats to cherished Canadian institutions and social programs, and it came with a clearly defined implementation date, which galvanized opposition. DI, however, consists of multiple initiatives likely to be pursued with an incremental strategy determined by what its promoters believe is achievable at any given point in the evolving political situation. While DI requires that we expose the overall initiative and its corporate backers, much of our opposition will find expression in multiple battlefields, where DI will be exposed as neoliberalism's comprehensive strategy for dismantling the Canadian nation. I now turn to a discussion of some key areas upon which progressive forces in Canada should focus.

Sovereignty and Democracy

The umbrella issue under which all other individual and strategic issues find themselves is that of sovereignty and democracy. These are not two separate themes, and they should not be separated when considering the development of a counter-hegemonic response to neoliberalism. As mentioned, one of the first publications of the Trilateral Commission – the breeding ground of the Washington Consensus – identified an "excess of democracy" as the key crisis in the developed Western world.

Contrary to the common assumption that only issues that reflect immediate self-interest can mobilize citizens, in recent polls Canadians have demonstrated enormous interest and concern over issues of Canadian sovereignty and democracy. They have indicated an overwhelming support for these goals, at levels comparable to those demonstrated during the historic struggle against free trade. An expression of this sentiment appeared in a March 2004 Ipsos-Reid poll commissioned by the Council of Canadians and the Polaris Institute. It demonstrated that, even if it implied a threat to economic prosperity, Canada must defend its ability to makes its own laws: "a majority of Canadians (91 percent) agree with the statement 'Canada should maintain the ability to set its own independent environmental, health and safety standards and regulations, even if this might reduce cross-border trade opportunities with the United States'" (Ipsos-Reid 2004). We need to imagine a broad campaign of rebuilding the state by imagining how we would put neoliberals on the defensive. We cannot do that by harkening back to the "good old days." Rather than undoing the propaganda victories of the right vis-à-vis the nation-state, we have to take the offensive by appealing to citizens on the basis of what has been referred to as a "different kind of state" – a genuinely democratic state, rooted in community, advocating for the poor and legislating the disempowerment of corporations (Albo, Langille, and Panitch 1993).

Fiscal Policy

A campaign on the issue of sovereignty and democracy entails a strong campaign on the fiscal issues that, collectively, the left has for the most part ignored for fifteen years. We have lost an enormous amount of ground, and the demonization of government deficits is a prime example of this. But it is not too late to mount a counter-attack on the issue of tax cuts with a call for fair taxes and increased taxes on the wealthy, and on the corollary issue of how quickly to pay down the debt. All signs suggest that we would have an extremely receptive audience for a well formulated campaign. Polling again suggests that a majority of people are prepared to pay more taxes to secure robust social programs (Ipsos-Reid 2003). In the 2003 provincial election the Ontario Liberals campaigned successfully on rolling back tax cuts and reinvesting in social programs, and, in the 2004 election, even the Paul Martin Liberals campaigned against the Conservative tax cut program. Yet the issue is not dead. In the late fall of 2004 the finance committee, dominated by Liberals, launched a trial balloon calling for deep tax cuts. In the 2006 federal election both the Liberals and the Conservatives ran an agenda that included tax cuts, although each tried to emphasize that it would favour large demographics as opposed to only the wealthy.

Canada's International Role

We need to formulate, with international development and anti-war organizations, a progressive international role for Canada within the context of aggressive US imperialism. Few areas of public policy offer a greater potential for connecting with the values of the Canadian public. A strong campaign focusing on rebuilding Canada's positive, multilateral role in the world, with respect to a whole range of issues (environment, health, culture, economic development, literacy, infrastructure, arms control) would permit us to put forward a positive vision of the future role for the country without having to focus primarily on the negative. A positive campaign would have the potential for putting the Liberal and Conservative governments, and the corporate backers of DI, on the defensive – something that is the litmus test for a counter-hegemonic campaign. The shift in Canada's military role in Afghanistan from peacekeeping to counter-insurgency warfare under US command – a move initiated by Paul Martin and embraced by Stephen Harper – is one issue that galvanizes a majority of Canadians.

Part of the resistance to US imperialism must be a specific focus on the issues of terrorism and security and on how these are used to undermine democracy, curtail human rights and civil liberties, and cut social spending to free up funding for the military and security apparatuses. As with so many other issues, the right has found in September 11 another "useful crisis" with which to persuade people that the situation is so grave that we must sacrifice elements of our democratic rights in order to confront it. Though the propaganda machine of the right has not had enormous success on this front in Canada, we are entering a period of Canadian politics in which both major national parties are far to the right of what preceded them. The June 2006 arrest of seventeen Muslim youth and men in Toronto on terrorism allegations was given huge media profile by the rightwing and corporate media, signalling a renewed effort to advance this ideological front.

Focusing on the Domestic Economy

The foundational assumption upon which the deep integration initiative is constructed is that trade with the United States and access to its market are so important that we have no alternative but to sacrifice much of our sovereignty and democracy in order to ensure this access and the economic benefits it brings. The conventional wisdom about the Canadian economy suggests that exports account for 40 percent of our GDP. The fact that 85 percent of our export trade is with the United States provides the right with a powerful argument for restructuring the country to ensure this trade relationship.

But, as Andrew Jackson argues in chapter 8 (this volume), that basic assumption is false and is rooted in how you count value added. If we import a widget that is three-quarters complete, contribute the final quarter of value-added, and then export it, some economists count 100 percent of the widget's value in our exports instead of just 25 percent. This is the source of the 40 percent figure, and it is unsupportable. The actual percentage of the GDP accounted for by exports is, according to Canadian Auto Workers economist Jim Stanford (2001), about 20 percent. And if gas and oil are taken out of the picture (because we are not competing with anyone in the energy market) it is closer to 18 percent. According to StatsCan, in 2002 82 percent of exports were attributable to just 4 percent of all Canadian businesses (StatsCan 2004). In other words, we can demonstrate that this whole deep integration agenda is designed to benefit just a handful of powerful corporations.

The positive side of this issue has tremendous possibilities. We could develop and promote an economic policy that focuses on strengthening the domestic economy, while criticizing the obsession with trade, particularly trade with the United States. This focus on the domestic economy gives us the opportunity to appeal to the vast majority of working- and middle-class people whose livelihoods depend upon it. Rather than simply decrying the "race to the bottom" with no viable solution, we should do what the economic facts enable us to do: attack the impoverishment of Canadian working families as immoral and, equally important, point out that labour flexibility policies have done severe damage to the domestic economy, whose health depends on good, high-paying jobs.

The issue of the domestic economy versus the trade economy opens the door to an appeal to non-exporting small and medium businesses that have been abandoned by federal policy makers. While engaging this traditionally reactionary group in any kind of political dialogue is something the left rarely considers, in the context of deep integration and the potential loss of an effective nation-state, it may well be time to consider building an alliance that is much broader – at least in certain temporary and tactical situations – than that to which we have become accustomed.

The last time Canada was threatened with such grave consequences was in the 1930s, and the threat was global fascism. This threat had the effect of bringing together formerly disparate groups and competing political parties – from liberals, and social democrats, to communists – in defence of democracy. The current rapid corporatization of government and its threat to democracy is more than enough reason to explore a similar strategy to that employed in the 1930s. We must also ask whether the left should make explicit efforts to find tactical allies among the Canadian political and economic elite who have not completely written off the Canadian nation.

Class

The issue of class is never easy to inject into Canadian politics, but there has never been a better or more appropriate time to do so. As I argued in detail in my book *Paul Martin: CEO for Canada?* (Dobbin 2003), the federal government, both Tory and Liberal versions, have waged a class war against Canadian workers for over fifteen years. That policy has been euphemistically referred to as "labour flexibility," and it stands as one of the most successful neoliberal assaults on democracy and equality. The program – a combination of radical changes to the Unemployment Insurance Plan, the elimination of the Canada Assistance Plan, and the devastating application of an extremist low inflation policy – has devastated Canadian workers and their families, reducing their bargaining power to levels not seen since the 1930s. At the same time, the income (and the wealth) of the top echelon has skyrocketed. This policy is clearly a part of the corporate elite's determination to "level the playing field" regarding the cost of Canadian labour in preparation for deeper integration.

Medicare

While medicare is rarely mentioned directly in DI strategy documents as a specific objective, it is clearly targeted in the broad initiative calling for a harmonization of social programs. DI promoters would prefer to leave this social program out of the discussion because of its sacrosanct status among the vast majority of Canadians. This is precisely why the fight against the systemic Americanization of Canada should use the medicare issue as a strategic focus in exposing the DI agenda. First, more than any other issue save foreign policy, medicare is the defining difference between Canadian and US political culture and focusing on it highlights the reasons why integration with the United States would be a disaster for ordinary Canadians. Second, as mentioned earlier, it is a social struggle in which, by going beyond its own traditional defensive stance and demanding the expansion of public health care to include drugs and homecare, the left has managed to put neoliberalism on the defensive. Indeed, medicare could be seen as the primary wedge issue in the counter-hegemonic strategy vis-à-vis social policy – a starting point, if you will, for a change in posture for other issues (e.g., public education, the environment, childcare, etc.) where the left needs to redefine the terrain in the fight against neoliberal hegemony.

Energy

If we examine the deep integration initiative from the perspective of our greatest opportunities as well as its greatest threats, it is clear that focusing on the plans for a North American energy accord is an absolutely key issue for the left. No aspect of NAFTA was more egregious than the energy chapter and its proportionality clause. It is an enormous issue, but once again it is one that falls through the cracks of a progressive political response because no single organization has a mandate to respond to it.

The potential of this issue to gain a foothold in the Canadian public is enormous as it combines a real threat to Canada's energy security with a powerful imperative towards alternative and renewable energy strategy. It combines the negative and positive aspects of a campaign in such a way that, if it were to be developed with a counter-hegemonic approach in mind, the strong public support for energy security, energy conservation, and issues such as the Kyoto Protocol could easily force the right and the promoters of DI onto the ideological defensive.

The Ipsos-Reid poll referred to earlier showed overwhelming public support for this issue – so overwhelming that it clearly takes in a significant portion of the country's elite. According to Ipsos-Reid (2004): "nine in ten (90%) of Canadians believe that 'Canada should establish an energy policy that provides reliable supplies of oil, gas and electricity at stable prices and protection of the environment, even if this means placing restrictions on exports and foreign ownership of Canadian supplies.'"

Indeed, the increasingly isolationist United States and its determination to ignore both NAFTA and WTO rulings that favour Canada raises the possibility of a carefully crafted campaign to call for the abrogation of NAFTA. The energy question, combined with the new US isolationism, provides an ideal moment to put the free trade and DI promoters decisively on the defensive. While the right and the media would portray abrogating NAFTA as a radical and dangerous initiative, the call for such a move would be designed to put deep integration advocates on the defensive.

The Struggle against Deep Integration

I argue that deep integration is the final stage of the corporate agenda for Canada. In summary, the fight against deep integration must address two weaknesses of the progressive forces: (1) the lack not only of an explicit and comprehensive counter-hegemonic analysis but also of the political consensus necessary to formulate one, and (2) the lack of a strong national coalition to implement such a strategy in the fight against neoliberal forces. If these two weaknesses are addressed, then the prognosis for success is quite positive. When opposition to any one of the neoliberal initiatives falls within the political mandate of a progressive Canadian organization with sufficient strength and mobilizing capacity, the results can be impressive.

Two examples in addition to medicare come to mind. The first is trade liberalization. The Council of Canadians provided much of the leadership in the fight against the most dangerous and far-reaching investment agreement ever initiated – the Multilateral Agreement on Investment. It not only mobilized public opinion in Canada against this deal – including scores of municipal councils – but it also played an international role in alerting social movements in other countries to the dangers of the agreement. Clearly, this was not just a victory for the Council – labour and other social movements formed parts of ongoing coalitions – but without an organization whose explicit mandate was fighting trade liberalization, it is unlikely that the resistance would have been as effective as it was.

The second example is the ongoing resistance to the aggressive push by governments and corporations for public-private-partnerships (P3s). Here the lead organization has been the Canadian Union of Public Employees

(CUPE), which has been joined by other public-sector unions and, at the local level, by the Council of Canadians and other civil society groups. CUPE has put enormous resources and organizing efforts into fighting this pernicious form of privatization and, along with its other partners, has had real success in exposing P3s and actually stopping several projects. The corporate front group for P3s, the Canadian Council on Public Private Partnerships, which includes the largest corporations in the country in explicit alliance with the federal government, has been put on the defensive.

The notion that the corporate agenda is "inevitable" or that elements of this agenda cannot be defeated because corporate power is too pervasive has been effectively disproven many times. But the circumstances of those popular victories are clearly defined by the presence of a lead organization or a coalition whose mandate identifies that particular struggle. In cases where that mandate is not clearly defined, or the organization is too weak, the results are not encouraging.

At this juncture in the struggle against DI, progressive forces have two advantages. First, the US elites show no interest in negotiating comprehensive agreements with anyone, especially agreements that would imply a sacrifice of US sovereignty, and particularly not with a relatively weak country such as Canada from whom they already get what they most need: secure access to energy. Second, this puts the DI promoters in the risky position of having to make extravagant offers of Canadian assets, sovereignty, and social programs just to get Washington interested. That is the weak ground upon which Canadian participation in the North American Security and Prosperity Partnership stands. This creates a political opening for the left to address its historical weaknesses, to engage broad sectors of the public that profoundly dislike the Bush – and thus Harper – agenda, and to effectively challenge the deep integration initiative.

NOTES

1 The term "comprador class" refers to any national economic elite that enriches substantially itself through selling out its own country's assets and wealth to foreigners. The term, actually Portuguese for "trader," has its origins in China, where high Chinese officials, for a fee, introduced European traders to the Chinese war lords to whom they otherwise had to "kow-tow."
2 Parts of this chapter draw on Dobbin (2003).
3 This quotation comes from a video recording of Snobelen's speech to senior government officials, 6 July 1995. Author's copy. See also (Ontario 2001, 2020).
4 The quotation reads as follows:
We are being occupied by the marketers just as the French and Norwegians were occupied by the Germans. We have, as they did, puppet governments

who run the country for the benefits of the occupiers. We have, as they did, collaborators. We, like the French and Norwegians of the time, have to protect our families and on many occasions have to work with the occupiers ... We are, as they were, threatened by deliberate wilfulness, by people who have only contempt for those they occupy and who see their mission to turn over our territory to their masters. (Franklin 1997–98, 7)

REFERENCES

Albo, Gregory, David Langille, and Leo Panitch. 1993. *A Different Kind of State? Popular Power and Democratic Administration*. Toronto: Oxford University Press.

Barlow, Maude, and Bruce Campbell. 1995. *Straight through the Heart: How the Liberals Abandoned the Just Society*. Toronto: HarperCollins Publishers.

Bush, George, Vicente Fox, and Stephen Harper. 2006. *Leaders' Joint Statement: Leaders Note Progress on the Security and Prosperity Partnership of North America* (31 March, Cancun, Mexico). Ottawa: Office of the Prime Minister.

Cameron, Duncan, and Ed Finn. 1995. *Ten Deficit Myths*. Ottawa: Canadian Centre for Policy Alternatives.

CAW/TCA. 2004. *Statement of the "Our Canada Project" Signed by 25 Organizations*. Canadian Labour Congress 2004. Available at <http://www.caw. ca/campaigns&issues/ongoingcampaigns/our_canada.asp>, cited 18 December 2004.

Dobbin, Murray. 1998. *The Myth of the Good Corporate Citizen: Democracy under the Rule of Big Business*. Toronto: Stoddart.

– 2003. *Paul Martin: CEO for Canada*. Toronto: James Lorimer.

Finn, Ed. 1992. *The Deficit Made Me Do It*. Ottawa: Canadian Centre for Policy Alternatives.

Franklin, Ursula. 1997–98. Global Justice Chez Nous. *Monetary Reform Magazine* (Winter): 7.

George, Susan. 1997. How to Win the War of Ideas: Lessons from the Gramscian Right. *Dissent* 44 (3): 47–53.

Graves, Frank L. 2001. *The Economy through a Public Lens: Shifting Canadian Views of the Economy*. Toronto: EKOS.

Huntington, Samuel, Michel Crozier, and Joji Watanuki. 1975. *The Crisis of Democracy: Report on the Governability of Democracies to the Trilateral Commission*. New York: New York University Press.

Hurtig, Mel. 2002. *The Vanishing Country: Is It Too Late to Save Canada?* Toronto: McClelland and Stewart.

Ipsos-Reid. 2003. *Federal Budget 2003: After Healthcare, Where Should We Go?* Toronto: Ipsos News Center.

– 2004. *Canadians' Views on Future Canada-US Relations: Canadians Support Policy Independence from US*. Toronto: Ipsos-Reid.

MacKinnon, Mary Pat , Judith Maxwell, Steven Rosell, and Nandini Saxena. 2003. *Citizens' Dialogue on Canada's Future: A 21st Century Social Contract.* Ottawa: Canadian Policy Research Networks.

Martin, Paul. 1995. The Canadian Experience in Reducing Budget Deficits and Debt. Notes for an address by the Honourable Paul Martin, Minister of Finance, presented to the Federal Reserve Bank of Kansas City Symposium on Budget Deficits and Debt, Jackson Hole, Wyoming, 1 September. Ottawa: Department of Finance.

Ontario. 2001 (30 May). Official Report of Debates (Hansard). Toronto: Legislative Assembly of Ontario.

Rockridge Institute. 2005. *About Us.* Rockridge Institute 2005. Available at <http://www.rockridgeinstitute.org/aboutus/>, cited 14 April 2005.

Stanford, Jim. 2001. The Global Cheesecake. *Facts from the Fringe:* CAW 37. Available at: <http://www.caw.ca/news/factsfromthefringe/issue37.asp>.

StatsCan. 2004. Profile of Canadian Exporters, 1993–2001. *The Daily*, 22 March. Available at <http://www.statcan.ca/english/dai-quo/>.

22

Managing Canada-US Relations:
An Alternative to Deep Integration

BRUCE CAMPBELL

The end of the Cold War and, more recently, the attacks of 11 September 2001 changed the way US policy makers view the world and the way the world views the United States. For the Bush administration, aggressive unilateralism and coalitions of convenience take precedence over multilateralism and international law, except when US interests deem otherwise. Military and economic agendas are two sides of the same coin: removing threats to US access to the world's energy supplies and other resources, if necessary through pre-emptive wars; prying open markets and entrenching free-market rules and investor rights for US multinationals in trade agreements; and protecting domestic markets for national producers where required. With Canada bound tighter than ever to the United States through an external economic constitution (the North American Free Trade Agreement [NAFTA]), not marching in lockstep with the hyperpower raises the spectre of economic retaliation. It is against this backdrop that discussions over deepening Canada-US integration are playing out.

Canadian business leaders and business-funded think tanks have been beating the drums for broad new economic and security integration arrangements with the United States. As documented extensively in this volume, they are warning once again that the status quo is not acceptable, that the costs of not taking these steps could be catastrophic for the economy – specifically, if another terrorist attack results in a lengthy border disruption.

Have we no choice but to acquiesce and encourage this slow-motion slide into the US orbit? Is that where our destiny lies, as annexationists on both sides of the forty-ninth parallel have argued since the American Revolution? Can we move indefinitely along this path of deepening economic integration without major spillover into the political realm? Or, can we as a nation on the inner rim of the US empire continue to manoeuvre in the intricate dance with our superpower neighbour so as to preserve enough economic and political space to give real weight to our claims of sovereignty? Is it possible for a federal government to chart an alternative to the current deep integration path, and, if so, how? How can a federal government slow down, reshape, or reverse the deep integration juggernaut? What choice will the current government make? Will it resist the pull or will it go with the flow?

I argue that federal policy should resist, reshape, or, where feasible, reverse further integration. Where necessary, integration agreements should be of limited scope and negotiated on terms that minimize the loss of policy flexibility. Core national interests of identity and autonomy must take precedence over arguments of market efficiency. Nor should they be held hostage to potential threats of economic retaliation. Canada should conduct its economic relations with the United States in a spirit of cooperation and mutual respect, as befits neighbours with deep interlocking interests and an unparalleled history of friendly co-existence. The key word is "cooperation," not "capitulation." Canada should act like a proud sovereign nation, not like a colonial supplicant. Below I outline a strategy to halt the further erosion of sovereignty through deep integration agreements and suggest how to reclaim national policy freedom.

I define "integration" as a process in which two or more entities come together to form a single entity. Implied in this definition are the equality of the separate entities and the creation of a new entity that combines roughly equal elements of the pre-existing entities. By contrast, a process of coming together in which one entity is dominant and the resulting combination resembles the dominant entity is defined as "assimilation." The distinction is important. What is being referred to here as "deep integration" is either a series of incremental measures or a series of major bilateral (or trilateral) agreements, ranging from common security to common trade policy and common currency, to common energy and water policies. The results of these policies are, in most cases, more akin to assimilation than they are to integration. Similarly, the term "harmonization," as applied to regulations or policies, almost always means Canada bending to, or adopting, US regulations and policies rather than vice versa.

The manipulation of language extends to opinion polling, and public opinion responses vary with the choice of words. For example, many Canadians currently support the idea of economic integration with the United States, but most Canadians would also prefer to see Canada-US differences maintained or widened. They do not want assimilation. Most support the idea that free trade is good, but they are divided on the benefits of NAFTA (SCFAIT 2002). As public opinion analyst Andrew Parkin told a House of Commons Committee in 2002, although Canadians favour close *cooperation* on economic and security matters, this, they believe, should not compromise Canadian uniqueness or sovereignty (SCFAIT 2002). It is ironic that, as the divergence in values between our two societies is becoming more pronounced (Adams 2003), the policy tools and institutions that enable our governments to give expression to these different values are weakening.

LIVING WITH NAFTA: CONSTRAINTS ON POLICY FREEDOM

The Canada-US Free Trade Agreement (CUFTA) and NAFTA together established a new policy framework, or continental constitution, that set off a major acceleration of the economic integration process. Two-way trade and investment flows, intracorporate trade, the continental restructuring of production, and concentration of exports have grown dramatically over the last fifteen years (see Jackson, chapter 8, this volume; Seccareccia, chapter 9, this volume). This corporate-driven process, short of a major policy shock, will undoubtedly continue.

Integration is also occurring at the policy level through an array of NAFTA bodies engaged in harmonizing everything from labour mobility provisions to standards for pollutants. Harmonization is also taking place outside the NAFTA apparatus. Included here are the post-11 September Smart Border accord measures to increase security, improve the border infrastructure, and expedite the cross-border movement of goods and people (Canada 2001) as well as measures to expand the sharing of intelligence information and harmonize immigration and refugee policies. Integration is also advancing in the transportation, communication, and energy sectors. Recently, these initiatives have been folded under the umbrella of the Security and Prosperity Partnership of North America (SPP). Finally, integration is beginning to move indirectly into the harmonization of social and fiscal policy. While NAFTA did not mandate this kind of harmonization, it did create additional market pressures to align these policies more closely.

NAFTA imposed a long list of constraints on government policy freedom, including: restrictions on the ability to manage and regulate energy and other resources (notably through export taxes and proportional-sharing provisions); limitations on the capacity to regulate foreign investment and other active industrial policy measures as well as on the capacity to privilege home-grown companies over foreign multinationals; restrictions on the ability of public enterprises to operate in the economy; and limitations on the government's ability to control drug prices. And while NAFTA hampered the ability of the government to regulate in the public interest, the protections provided to key social services like health care were weak and left the door open to encroachment by for-profit health care. And though negotiations are currently in a state of indefinite suspension, the Free Trade

Area of the Americas (FTAA) would, if Canada and the United States had their way, go well beyond NAFTA, encroaching on new areas of domestic regulation and creating new constraints on government action.

As NAFTA removed restrictions on the capacity of government to intervene in the public interest, it conferred rights upon transnational corporations to move freely within the continental space, playing governments, communities, and workers off against each other and challenging or blocking legislation and regulations at every turn. Not surprisingly, the NAFTA balance sheet has not been favourable for workers and citizens (see Clarke, chapter 3, this volume; Robinson, chapter 10, this volume). Yet NAFTA proponents, thanks to their stranglehold on the mainstream media, have been very effective in obscuring the memory of NAFTA's failed promises and adverse impacts, rendering an honest public debate on the merits of future integration virtually impossible.

The US superpower basically set the rules of NAFTA to conform to its own model (with Canadian and Mexican concurrence), shifting power from the state to the transnational corporations that dominate the market. Yet whenever an important US corporate interest was at stake, the tremendous power asymmetries between the parties allowed the US government to ignore the rules. The smaller partners have no such luxury – a reality that has become painfully evident in a post-11 September world. But corporate success in driving forward continental integration has always depended on sympathetic governments in power. Social erosion was not inevitable, and it is not irreversible.

CAN THE CURRENT COURSE BE ALTERED?

In an ideal world, three enlightened North American governments would renegotiate NAFTA, transforming it into a trade and development accord in which citizens' rights prevail over those of corporations and where the market is subordinate to the public good (HSA 2002). This is a noble if unrealistic aspiration, except perhaps in the long term, when all things are possible.

Another scenario would be for a Canadian government to abrogate NAFTA and conduct the bilateral economic relationship within the World Trade Organization (WTO) framework as well as through sectoral and functional bilateral mechanisms. Changes in the multilateral trade architecture mean that, by abrogating NAFTA, Canada would, with few exceptions, sacrifice little in terms of market access and would also regain some important policy tools. Tariffs have largely disappeared. Anti-dumping and countervail disputes would be dealt with more effectively under the WTO dispute resolution system.[1] The NAFTA social services and cultural exemptions, though far from adequate, exist in different forms in the WTO. And the pernicious investor-state mechanism would be eliminated.

This scenario, while legal, is a political non-starter at the moment. It would cause an uproar within the powerful business community, among the policy and media elite, and among neoconservative provincial governments. It might also trigger retaliation from the US government. Two conditions would have to be met before a government could consider the abrogation option: the government would have to build a strong popular consensus (1) that NAFTA has been bad and impedes our ability to pursue vital national interests and (2) that the costs of abrogation in terms of the transitional disruption and instability would be manageable. This is, to say the least, no small challenge.

On the assumption that the above scenarios are not feasible in the near future, how should a progressive Canadian government manage its economic relationship with the United States, inside and outside the NAFTA framework, in such a way as to slow down, reshape, or reverse the integration process?

The Mulroney government represented a major break in Canadian foreign policy. Previous governments acknowledged the pressure for continental integration as a force of nature. For them, however, the role of policy was to control and discipline that force, not to encourage it. The purpose of bilateral agreements was, as John Holmes (1981) observed, to reduce conflict and not necessarily to bring us closer together. Mitchell Sharp, an ardent free trader, talked about leaning against US influences through the pursuit of multilateralism. Mulroney had no such reservations, however. He actively embraced integration with the United States, and his policies sought to encourage and accelerate the integration process. My view is that the correct and still valid role of policy is to lean against the forces of continental integration (not to reinforce them), to negotiate multilateral counterweights where possible and, where necessary, to reach bilateral arrangements in areas where the power differential is mitigated and the loss of autonomy is minimized.

Building on the foreign policy tradition that preceded the Mulroney aberration (including, to some extent, the late Chrétien era), my approach might be termed the deliberate pursuit of small steps – but with a coherent vision of reclaiming national policy flexibility – whose cumulative effect may, over time, be transformative. Specifically, as the government reclaims sovereignty it would gain the confidence to push the NAFTA envelope where core national interests are concerned, and it would be prepared to take the consequences of its actions.

I do not advocate maintaining and reclaiming sovereignty for its own sake but, rather, because it enables us to flourish as a separate country on the North American continent – a country with a unique social contract, cultural identity, and political tradition. It enables us to prevail as a society that values "peace, order, and good government," and it balances individual and community rights and obligations. Sovereignty – the capacity to control basic economic, cultural, and social policy levers – is thus a primordial interest, essential to shaping our national destiny.

It cannot be overemphasized that trade is a means and not an end. It should not drive policy. The policy establishment, however, is fixated on liberalization and commercialization, seeing trade as an end in-and-of-itself. The free trade canon seems inviolate. Trade and investment are assumed to be unconditionally good, and more is automatically better. Accordingly, free trade is always viewed as a win-win situation, with the benefits far outweighing the costs in lost production and jobs.[2] Policies and regulations that impede the flow of commerce are viewed (with few exceptions) as inherently bad and to be weakened or eliminated.

Trade and investment may bring benefits, but they may also be harmful. It depends on the nature of the products, on the market power of the corporations involved in their production and distribution, and on the terms and conditions of the exchange. It depends on the domestic institutions in place to appropriate the benefits and to ensure their equitable distribution. Regulation in the public interest and the provision of public goods like health care should always trump market considerations. Proper controls are necessary to limit downward pressure on taxes, wages, and standards. If not properly regulated, foreign investment can cause the loss of employment; the transfer abroad of home-grown technology; the displacement of local suppliers; and, in key, areas such as banking, broadcasting, and resources, the loss of control over public policy.

In some cases, such as toxic waste, trade should be banned outright. In others, it should be restricted to ensure stability and equity in key food sectors (dairy and poultry). In others, it should be tightly controlled (tobacco products). In still others, it should be managed to ensure minimum levels of production and employment (the now defunct Auto Pact). Vital public services, moreover, have no place in international commercial agreements. Trade and investment policy must always be subordinated to national priorities of economic and social well-being.

ELEMENTS OF AN ACTION PLAN

This section lays out some suggestions for a progressive Canadian government committed to the twin goals of resisting the pull of deeper integration and reclaiming policy flexibility.

Strengthen the National Economy

First, the government must reassert and rebuild its capacity to actively manage the economy. It should focus on strengthening the *national* economy through a variety of macroeconomic, labour market, and industrial policy and public investment tools. And it should be more active and aggressive in regulating foreign investment and resources, strengthening the cultural sector, and rebuilding public infrastructure. Though constrained, there is still substantial national policy space remaining under NAFTA (and the WTO). The government must therefore identify and maximize that space and, where appropriate, test the limits (Sinclair 2004). The following is merely an illustrative list of specific measures:

- Assert forcefully that trade agreements will not be allowed to constrain domestic policy in social services. More specifically, follow the Romanow Commission's recommendation regarding the halting of the privatization of health care and other basic public services. This would help to shore up the NAFTA social services exemption and reduce the threat of challenges by foreign investors.
- Assert forcefully that trade agreements – including NAFTA proportional sharing provisions – will not be allowed to trump policies to ensure national energy security and promote energy conservation.
- Rebuild the environmental regulatory capacity that has been gutted over the last fifteen years. It was neither mandated by NAFTA, nor does NAFTA prevent the reinstatement of effective environmental regulations.
- Implement a ban on bulk water exports.
- Trim back the monopoly protection provisions for large pharmaceutical corporations and bring back compulsory licensing (still legal under NAFTA and the WTO) to help rein in the ballooning drug prices that have strained our Medicare system.
- Use public ownership of resources as leverage to ensure local procurement, value-added processing, job creation, the achievement of Kyoto targets, and so on.
- Make aggressive use of remaining industrial policy tools – such as tax incentives, subsidies infrastructure, R&D, procurement, Crown corporations, and public sector investment funds – to meet national economic and environmental objectives, including regional and community development.
- Ensure that foreign restrictions in key sectors such as culture, banking, and telecommunications are maintained and strengthened.

Mitigate Bilateral Power Asymmetries

Second, the government should attempt to maintain cordial relations with the United States, even in the face of disagreements on major policy issues and when leader-to-leader relations are cool. Getting along with Canada is also in Washington's interest, as it is an indicator of its reputation as an effective world leader. The government should deal with Canada-US issues and irritants as they arise and, where possible, develop ways of dealing with them before they reach crisis proportions. It should deal in areas where the impact of the size and power imbalance is minimized. Canada has hundreds of bilateral treaties, protocols, forums, and institutions currently in effect with the United States.

Bilateral agreements that mitigate the asymmetric power relationship and minimize the loss of policy autonomy usually emerge from a border problem identified by *both* countries and where *both* countries have a strong motivation to find a solution. These conditions do not hold in the proposed deep integration agreements. For example, in the case of a monetary union, it is difficult to imagine a compelling reason that would cause Washington to give up even a modicum of monetary policy sovereignty. In such a negotiation, low motivation on the part of the more powerful partner would only accentuate the size and power disadvantage of the smaller country, requiring huge concessions for little in return.

Where bilateral agreements are not necessary, Canada should favour multilateral forums. The emphasis should be on mutual cooperation to solve problems without fundamentally compromising policy flexibility. Where political space is threatened, Canada should not capitulate and should be prepared to take the consequences. For example, Ottawa should resist the harmonization of security regulations and police powers that violate charter rights.

In general, because of the power imbalance, the government should avoid linking issues when negotiating bilateral agreements. Most agreements are, as they should be, compartmentalized and of limited scope. As Stéphane Roussel (2004, 6) argues: "The principle of compartmentalization means that progress or benefits in one area should never be linked to obtaining concessions or results in another." For example, using security concessions as bargaining chips on trade is, according to Roussel, "both counterproductive and dangerous: counterproductive because it is unlikely to work and because of its disregard for the national identity issue risks arousing the distrust of the Canadian population, and dangerous because it breaks the principle of the 'compartmentalization of spheres of activity,' and because it is not based on an analysis of the real needs of Canada and the United States" (5).

The same applies to retaliating against US actions. Should Canada use linkage to retaliate in response to US actions against our forest or farm exports, say by cutting back our energy exports? This is a dangerous game when played outside the framework of international agreements and, ultimately, one that we cannot win given the power asymmetries. However, there are provisions in NAFTA, for example, that would permit Canada to legally retaliate against US violations. Keep in mind that the complex interlocking interests at play in the bilateral relationship do place limits on the extent to which the United States can punish us without experiencing its own blowback. Trade is a two-way street. Canadian business, in its post-11 September panic, underestimated the US interest in keeping the border open. Its economy would have also been hurt by border closure, whether in the integrated auto and other manufacturing sectors or in petroleum and other vital resource sectors. "It is hard to exaggerate the implications of imposing trade restrictions for the two countries. And it is not an over-statement to assert that even an implied threat by the United States to take such steps is madness," wrote US trade expert Sidney Weintraub (2003, 2).

It is important to ensure that goods and people flow smoothly across our borders but that terrorists and weapons do not. Although the United States places primary importance on physical security and Canada on economic security, both are in our mutual interest. The Smart Border accord signed in December 2001 is an example of both countries having a vital interest in keeping the border open and increasing security (Waddell 2003). Unfortunately, in its zeal to please the US administration, Canada has seriously compromised civil liberties and policy autonomy.

It is important for the Canadian government to acknowledge that secure market access is unattainable. There is no permanent solution short of political union. Congress will never surrender power over its trade protection laws. US harassment of our resource exports, like Canadian winters, is a fact of life. Canada must lower its expectations and exercise patience. It must allow existing dispute resolution structures – trilateral and multilateral – to play themselves out.

Strengthen Multilateral Institutions

Third, Canada must work to maintain and strengthen multilateral institutions, especially the UN system, under which counterweights to US adventurism can be forged and the exercise of raw power can be mitigated, however imperfectly. That the Bush administration jettisons these institutions when they conflict with its interests makes commitment to their improvement all the more important. Multilateralism, besides being our best hope as a vehicle for achieving peace, security, social justice, and the prosperity of the planet, serves to amplify our influence in the world through constructive diplomacy and, most important, to advance our interests with the United States.[3]

Canada must work in multilateral forums to forge agreements in the area of human rights, the environment, health, culture, and taxation that are enforceable and that supersede and circumscribe trade agreements like the WTO and NAFTA. Examples of treaties that attempt to attain these goals include the Framework on Tobacco Control and the Cultural Diversity Instrument initiative,[4] where the Canadian government took the lead.

Diversify Relationships

Fourth, we should revisit measures to expand and diversify economic, security, and development cooperation, as well as cultural relationships, with other countries, including the European Union, India, Japan, Korea, China, Brazil, Russia, and others. In order to determine what is needed for successful breakthroughs, we need to analyze why past initiatives did not work. Commercial treaties may be helpful but diversification can be pursued without new trade agreements. John Ralston Saul (2002) makes the point that, while 85 percent of Canada's goods exports now go the United States, only between 20 percent and 25 percent of our cultural exports go there. In other words, we have been very successful in exporting the image of Canada globally. He adds that cultural exports are uniquely important in that image recognition can be a trailblazer for enhanced activity in other sectors – a fact that Canadian business does not seem to have grasped.

The European Union is particularly important to managing our relationship with the United States and bolstering our foreign policy interests. In many areas – such as the environment, social policy, culture, human rights, peacekeeping, multilateral institutions, and voting patterns in the United Nations – our views are closer to those of the European governments than they are to those of Washington. One sees evidence of this in recent agreements: the Kyoto Protocol, the Land Mines Treaty, the International Criminal Court, the Cultural Diversity Instrument, to name just a few. Canada and the European Union can be important partners in advancing a shared global vision. In fact, in March 2004 Canada and the European Union signed a "partnership agenda" agreement to work together on a range of issues, notably strengthening multilateral institutions and the UN system in order to maintain world peace and support the international rule of law.

The parties also announced that negotiations would begin on a trade and investment enhancement agreement. Although Canada-EU trade has been shrinking as a share of total trade for a long time, the investment relationship is significant: 28 percent of Canadian-owned foreign direct investment (FDI) is located in the European Union, and 29 percent of inward FDI in Canada is European. The value of sales of European affiliates of Canadian companies within the European Union are currently over four times greater than the value of Canadian exports to the EU. This is an important base upon which to build effective counterweights to the continentalist drift. The European Union is preoccupied with its own expansion these days, which makes it difficult for Canada to get its attention, but there is a clear willingness on both sides to expand relations.

DEEP INTEGRATION
UNDER THE MARTIN LIBERALS

In the months following September 11 business lobbies and think tanks intensified their push for deeper integration between the two countries (see in this volume the chapters by Cameron, Clarke, and Clarkson and Banda). The C.D. Howe Institute launched its Border Papers series calling for deeper integration agreements across a range of areas, from a common energy and resource policy to a customs union and common trade policy, a common security perimeter, and a common currency. The series began with a paper by Wendy Dobson (2002) advocating a "big bang" negotiation with Washington, with everything on the table – the idea being to trade off economic security (Canada) for homeland security (United States).

Meanwhile, the Canadian Council of Chief Executives (CCCE), led by Tom d'Aquino, pushed its North American Security and Prosperity Initiative (CCCE 2003). The plan called for action on five fronts (CCCE 2003). The first is the reinvention of a border that is a "shared checkpoint" (4). This North American security perimeter would involve developing "shared approaches to commercial processing, infrastructure, intelligence and policing, a North American identity document and a shared institution to provide oversight" (4). The second front is the harmonization of regulations, such as standards, inspection, and certification procedures. It also involves trade remedy, access, ownership, and labour mobility issues. The third priority area is the creation of a common resource-security pact. The fourth front is the creation of a North American defence alliance to defend against missile attacks and other threats from the air, land, and sea. This implies a major increase in military spending to enhance "Canadian homeland security capability within North America" (5) The final front is the creation of binational commissions to manage the continental integration process.

Key Martin economic advisors – notably Bank of Canada governor David Dodge – urged active measures to more deeply integrate the two economies. Dodge gave a speech at the 2003 Couchiching Conference in which he linked security integration and economic integration and outlined several desirable steps to reduce what he called "border risk" for Canada: a common external tariff (customs union), harmonization of trade and commercial policies and regulations, an end to trade remedies in North America, and a uniform policy on federal and state / provincial subsidies (Dodge 2003, 8). He further recommended removing barriers to trade in cultural, legal, financial, and communications services and extending NAFTA coverage to agricultural products. Dodge also advocated moving to a single continental market. In his view, achieving "maximum economic benefits, harmonization of regulatory standards and practices, particularly with respect to capital and labour markets, should be a priority as we move forward" (6). Monetary union, he said, should be considered once significant progress towards a single market has been achieved.

The government's policy-research arm, Policy Research Initiatives, until recently a branch of the Privy Council Office, is also devoting a lot of attention to the integration of the North American market, notably in the areas of regulatory and tariff harmonization. According to Andre Downs, director of its North American Linkages project, their focus is on policies that maximize access to the US market, thereby providing a necessary springboard for Canadian companies to become competitive in world markets (Downs 2004). A 2003 conference of the Ottawa policy establishment hosted by the Public Policy Forum produced a consensus that continental economic integration can safely proceed without compromising policy autonomy (Hulley and Poisson 2003). Thus, at the bureaucratic level, consideration of the risks to policy autonomy appear to have been greatly downplayed if not ruled out, and market efficiency considerations are the overriding priority of the deep integration research agenda.

A 2002 internal government report obtained by then *Globe and Mail* Ottawa bureau chief Drew Fagan (2003, 45) suggested that "more effort must be made to coordinate regulatory oversight with Washington." It went on, according to Fagan, to indicate that Canada must counter the false presumption that regulations must be made in Canada rather than arising out of joint oversight. A common approach, it went on, could involve "harmonized standards" or, preferably, joint recognition of standards.

It should be noted, however, that even incremental – seemingly technical – measures may have major implications for policy freedom. Consider drug approvals, for example. It is claimed that accepting US Food and Drug Administration-approved drugs would reduce costs for Health Canada and increase regulatory and trade efficiency. However, relinquishing independence over drug approvals to a US agency that is controlled by Congress and vulnerable to corporate lobbying, could have huge health and safety implications

On the matter of security, Paul Martin moved quickly to show that Canada could be trusted to take this matter seriously (see Staples, this volume). Indeed, this is the litmus test for Washington, which expected significant increases in security and military spending. Martin took great pains to emphasize that the national security agenda was not being developed to satisfy Washington but, rather, to advance Canada's national interests. For Martin, security and economic issues were inseparable because security is a necessary precondition for ensuring the stability of the now highly integrated and vulnerable Canadian economy. Among the early security measures taken by the Martin government were the following:

- The creation of a new federal department of public safety and emergency preparedness to coordinate security with the US Department of Homeland Security;
- The appointment of a "national security advisor" who reports directly to the prime minister;
- A foreign policy and defence review to flesh out the new national security policy;
- A cabinet committee (and secretariat) on Canada-US relations chaired by the prime minister;
- A cabinet committee on security, public health, and emergencies; and
- A House of Commons national security standing committee.

The Martin government played the lead role in creating the *North American Security and Prosperity Partnership* agreement signed by the three NAFTA leaders in March 2005. The SPP has now replaced NAFTA as the framework under which the deep integration agenda is moving forward. The SPP established nine ministerial working groups with concrete implementation targets. Three months later, the first SPP implementation report released work plans for nearly one hundred initiatives covering a wide range of economic and security issues – to be implemented by trilateral working groups on an ongoing basis with regular progress updates.

The handprints of Tom d'Aquino and his big business colleagues are all over the SPP. The Canadian Council of Chief Executives (CCE) spearheaded a trinational business task force on North American integration (co-chaired by John Manley and with members that included d'Aquino and Michael Wilson, subsequently ambassador to the US). It released its final report, *Building a North American Community,* in May 2005, less than two months after the NAFTA leaders accord (CFR 2005).

Deepening the integration of the two economies was probably Martin's most important economic priority. To improve relations with Washington, Martin expanded consular missions in the United States, improved the border infrastructure, and implemented the Smart Border Accord. Martin moved in small steps, below the radar wherever possible, focusing on short-term practicalities. His agenda included measures to harmonize regulations, tariffs, and standards, as well as measures to enhance the cross border movement of goods, services, and people. He also considered harmonization initiatives in trade, resource, and competition policy.

Martin moved carefully, given public sensitivities about the potential loss of sovereignty associated with closer political ties to the United States.

There was never any serious consideration of a "big idea" negotiation that would risk a replay of the 1980s free trade debate.

CONCLUSION

In March 2006, the NAFTA leaders met to assess progress under the Security and Prosperity Partnership, now with Stephen Harper as Canadian prime minister. Accompanied this time by big business representatives, the leaders announced the creation of a North American Competitiveness Council (NACC). The council, comprised of chief executive officers from major transnational corporations, has already begun meeting to prepare a list of suggestions for the politicians to be delivered in fall 2006. Among the other profiled items were a North American Energy Security Initiative (to assure the flow of oil and gas from Canada and Mexico to meet US demand) and a Framework Agreement on Regulatory Cooperation, to be finalized in 2007. Thus, under the mantle of the SPP, the deep integration agenda continues to move forward.

Though it is early days in the life of the Harper minority Conservative government, there is every indication not only that this government will continue the deep integration initiatives started by the Liberals but that it will push them more aggressively and more openly.

Several prominent Mulroney-era free trade warriors have prominent positions in the new government, including Michael Wilson, who has been appointed ambassador to the United States. Harper has acted quickly on the security front: expanding the scope of NORAD to include maritime approaches to North America and announcing a huge increase in military spending to facilitate collaboration of Canadian forces with US global military actions. His government renounced Canada's Kyoto Treaty commitment to reduce greenhouse gas emissions and aligned itself with George Bush's made-in-North America approach, as urged by big business. It buckled under a US refusal to abide by NAFTA rules and negotiated a controversial settlement to the long-standing softwood lumber dispute – this despite the fact that Canada had won all the NAFTA dispute panel decisions.

Since CUFTA was implemented in 1989, the debate over its economic, social, environmental, cultural, and political impacts continues to be divisive. As I have shown, the loss of policy space that resulted from CUFTA and NAFTA is very serious. Elsewhere, I have argued that, although certain groups and sectors have benefited, the impact of CUFTA and NAFTA – interacting with its neoliberal policy siblings – have adversely affected the well-being of the large majority of Canadians (and, indeed, of Mexican and US citizens)(Campbell 2006).

I believe it is time to undertake a comprehensive review of NAFTA's costs and benefits; time to stand back and ask: is NAFTA working for us? Do the costs outweigh the benefits? Is it serving our needs? Is NAFTA, in its current form, outdated and contrary to the national interest as the overarching framework for managing Canada-US economic relations?

In the meantime – a point I have emphasized in this chapter – the loss of policy space should not be overstated. The room for political manoeuvring remains considerable for a government willing to use it creatively and aggressively.

If the big business integration wish list were to be fully realized, the additional loss of sovereignty would make that which has occurred under NAFTA seem modest by comparison. Canadian business as a whole has yet to coalesce around a new mega-deal with the United States, although the big business consensus, as indicated in the May 2005 trinational report (CFR 2005), is urging a number of ambitious initiatives, notably in the areas of security energy and regulatory harmonization.

And, needless to say, plans for a mega-deal are not currently on the US political radar. However, this could change should something compel the United States to switch its focus from global to "neighbourhood" security and economic interests. There is a dedicated group of business leaders, bureaucrats, politicians, and ex-politicians on both sides of the border who are pushing hard for these deep integration measures. These ideas could, as they did with CUFTA, bubble under the surface for some time among a relatively small but influential group, waiting for the opportunity to spring into action.

There has already been considerable social and fiscal harmonization downward (to US levels) since the implementation of CUFTA and NAFTA, especially in the areas of taxation, income inequality, and social program spending. Nevertheless, Canada-US social and fiscal differences remain substantial, and they are reversible.

North-south economic integration has weakened east-west economic ties. Exports to the United States have doubled as a percentage of GDP since 1989, from 18.6 percent to 37.6 percent, while interprovincial exports have fallen from 22.5 percent of GDP to 19.7 percent (Chen and Curtis 2004, 64). However, as Helliwell's (2002) research shows, the border is a much greater barrier to trade than is commonly thought. For example, trade among Canadian provinces (internal trade) is ten times greater than that between Canadian provinces and US states of equal size and distance.

Deep differences exist between Canadian and American attitudes and values, and they have been growing wider over the last fifteen years, even as economic integration has accelerated (Adams 2003). This should come as no surprise, given that the founding mythologies, historical experiences, and political institutions of our two countries are very different and that these have a much stronger influence on shaping our identity and values than do the forces of economic integration.

Deeper integration, though focused on economic and security policies, involves the harmonization of an ever-widening swath of policies – social, environmental, immigration, cultural, and so on. It is worth noting that such policy uniformity, even without common decision-making institutions, in fact constitutes *political* integration.

It is a slippery slope. As we move further down this deep integration road, how much more difficult is it to slow down, halt, and restore the pre-existing balance? Is there a tipping point beyond which it is irreversible? The bonds of Canadian nationhood have been created primarily in the public sphere, by public policies and institutions. How far down the road will we go before the connection between our national identity and the policy glue that binds us and gives expression to that identity starts to dissolve?

NOTES

1 Former deputy GATT negotiator Mel Clark made the point in conversation with the author that the Chapter 19 dispute system is so flawed that abrogation would actually enhance access to the US market. For example, by reverting to the WTO rules, disputes would be judged according to international law not, as is the case under NAFTA, according to US law and to whether the US is enforcing its own law. It would remove what amounts to an additional layer of trade law – a protectionist tool that makes it easier for US producers to bring a case against Canadian exporters and allows for lengthier obfuscation and delay.
2 Nobel laureate, Paul Samuelson, the dean of modern neoclassical economics, challenged the theoretical underpinnings of the free trade doctrine in an article in the fall 2004 issue of the *Journal of Economic Perspectives*. Under certain circumstances, he argued, free trade may be a net loser for one country. Coming from where it does, this crack in the foundation has unnerved free trade zealots (Samuelson 2004).
3 It is worth noting that even the Bush administration feels compelled from time to time to rein in its rampant unilateralism. For example, under threat of WTO-sanctioned retaliation by twelve nations with regard to illegal US steel tariffs, the Bush administration backed down and removed these tariffs.
4 On cultural diversity, see Neil (chapter 15, this volume).

REFERENCES

Adams, Michael. 2003. *Fire and Ice: The United States, Canada and the Myth of Converging Values*. Toronto: Penguin Canada.
Campbell, Bruce. 2006. Backsliding: The Impact of NAFTA on Canadian Workers. In *Revisiting NAFTA: Still Not Working for North America's Workers*, ed. R.E. Scott, C. Salas and B. Campbell, 53–60. Washington, Economic Policy Institute.

Canada. 2001. *Canada and the United States Sign a Smart Border Declaration.* Ottawa: Department of Foreign Affairs and International Trade.

CCCE. 2003. *Security and Prosperity: Toward a New Canada-United States Partnership in North America.* Ottawa: Canadian Council of Chief Executives.

CFR. 2005. *Building a North American Community.* Washington: Council on Foreign Relations Press.

Chen, Shenjie, and John M. Curtis. 2004. How Does International Trade Affect Business Cycle Synchronization? *Horizons: Policy Research Initiative* 7 (1): 64–68.

Dobson, Wendy. 2002. Shaping the Future of the North American Economic Space: A Framework for Action. In *The Border Papers.* Toronto: C.D. Howe Institute.

Dodge, David. 2003. Economic Integration in North America, Couchiching Institute of Public Affairs, Geneva Park, ON.

Downs, Andre. 2004. North American Integration: Challenges and Potential Policy Responses. *Horizons: Policy Research Initiative* 7 (1): 4–8.

Fagan, Drew. 2003. Beyond NAFTA. In *Canada among Nations: Coping with the Colossus*, ed. D. Carment, F. Hampson, and N. Hillmer, 32–53. Ottawa: Oxford University Press.

Gordon, Walter. 1977. *A Political Memoire.* Toronto: McClelland and Stewart.

Helliwell, John. 2002. *Globalization and Well-Being.* Vancouver: UBC Press.

Holmes, John W. 1981. *Life with Uncle.* Toronto: University of Toronto Press.

HSA. 2002. *Alternatives for the Americas.* Mexico City: Hemispheric Social Alliance.

Hulley, Crystal, and Yves Poisson. 2003. *Rethinking North American Integration.* Ottawa: Public Policy Forum.

Roussel, Stéphane. 2004. Canada-US Security and Defence Relations: A Continentalist-Institutionalist Perspective. Paper presented at Canada and the New American Empire, 26–28 November, Victoria.

Samuelson, Paul. 2004. Where Ricardo and Mill Rebut and Confirm the Arguments of Mainstream Economists Supporting Globalization. *Journal of Economic Perspectives* 18 (3): 135–46.

Saul, John Ralston. 2002. Presentation to the "The Deputy Ministers Present …" Lecture Series. 13 November. Ottawa: Department of Foreign Affairs and International Trade, Government of Canada.

SCFAIT. 2002. *Partners in North America: Advancing Canada's Relations with the United States and Mexico.* Ottawa: Standing Committee on Foreign Affairs and International Trade, House of Commons, Canada.

Sinclair, Scott. 2004. *Thinking Outside the Trade Treaty Box.* Ottawa: Canadian Centre for Policy Alternatives.

Waddell, Christopher. 2003. Erasing the Line: Rebuilding Economic and Trade Relations after 11 September. In *Canada among Nations 2003: Coping with the American Colossus*, ed. D. Carment, F.O. Hampson and N. Hillmer, 54–76. Toronto: Oxford.

Weintraub, Sidney. 2003. Strains in the Canada-US Relationship. In *Issues in International Political Economy*, 15 April. Washington, DC: Center for Strategic and International Studies.

About the Contributors

SHARRYN AIKEN is an assistant professor in the Faculty of Law at Queen's University, Kingston, Ontario. In 2006 she represented a coalition of public interest groups in a constitutional challenge of immigration security certificate procedures at the Supreme Court of Canada. She is a past president of the Canadian Council for Refugees and editor of *Refuge*, an interdisciplinary journal on forced migration.

MARIA BANDA is a graduate of Trinity College at the University of Toronto and of the International Relations Program (as a Rhodes Scholar) at Oxford University in the United Kingdom, where she focused on the interaction of international human rights law and national security imperatives within the context of the global war on terrorism. She is currently doing research at the World Trade Organization in Geneva.

MAUDE BARLOW is the national chairperson of the Council of Canadians, Canada's largest citizens' advocacy organization. She is a director with the International Forum on Globalization and co-founder of the Blue Planet Project, an international civil society movement to stop the commodification of water. She is the bestselling author of fifteen books, including *Too Close for Comfort: Canada's Future within Fortress North America*. In 2005, she was awarded the Lannan Cultural Freedom Fellowship and the Right Livelihood Award, the distinguished "alternative Nobel prize."

DORVAL BRUNELLE is a professor of sociology and current director of the Observatory of the Americas (Observatoire des Amériques) at the Université du Québec à Montréal (UQAM). He has published extensively on the political economy of Quebec and Canada as well as on the economic, political, and social dimensions of hemispheric integration. His most recent book, *Dérive globale*, has been translated into English and will be published in 2007 by UBC Press under the title *From World Order to Global Disorder: States, Markets, and Dissent*.

DUNCAN CAMERON is research associate (and past president) at the Canadian Centre for Policy Alternatives. He writes weekly on politics at *rabble.ca*. Author, co-author, and editor of eleven books, he graduated from the University of Alberta and the University of Paris. He is visiting professor in Canadian Studies and fellow of the Centre for Global Political Economy at Simon Fraser University. He was editor of *Canadian Forum* and is a former president of the Quebec Political Science Association.

BRUCE CAMPBELL is executive director of the Canadian Centre for Policy Alternatives. He has written widely on public policy issues, including on Canada-US relations. He is author or editor of several books, including (with Maude Barlow) *Straight through the Heart: How the Liberals Abandoned the Just Society* (Harpercollins, 1995). His latest, an edited volume entitled *Living with Uncle: Canada-US Relations in an Age of Empire*, was published by Lorimer in the fall of 2006.

TONY CLARKE is the director of the Polaris Institute, which addresses the role of corporations in public policy making. He is the author of *Silent Coup: Confronting the Big Business Takeover of Canada* and formerly chaired the committee on corporations for the International Forum on Globalization. He holds a doctorate from the University of Chicago and is the co-author (with Maude Barlow) of *Blue Gold: the Battle against Corporate Theft of the World's Water*. In 2005, he was awarded the Right Livelihood Award, the distinguished "alternative Nobel prize."

STEPHEN CLARKSON teaches political economy at the University of Toronto, where he focuses on Canada's relationship with the United States and on North American governance. His major books include *Canada and the Reagan Challenge* (1982), the co-authored *Trudeau and Our Times* (Vol. 1, *The Magnificent Obsession* [1990]; Vol. 2, *The Heroic Delusion* [1994]), *Uncle Sam and Us: Globalization, Neoconservatism, and the Canadian State* (2002), and *The Big Red Machine: How the Liberal Party Dominates Canadian Politics* (2005).

MARJORIE GRIFFIN COHEN is a professor of political science and women's studies at Simon Fraser University in British Columbia. Her research areas deal with public policy and economics, with special emphasis on issues concerning women, international trade agreements, the Canadian economy, energy, and labour. Recent books include *Training the Excluded for Work: Access and Equity for Women, Immigrants, First Nations, Youth and People with Low Income* (2003) and *Governing under Stress: Middle Powers and the Challenge of Globalization* (2004).

KATHY CORRIGAN is a researcher with the Canadian Union of Public Employees (CUPE), BC Region, in the municipal and health sector, specializing in privatization and international trade. She has served as a trustee of the Burnaby School Board since 1999 and is currently its vice-chair. Formerly she practised family law and edited a legal journal.

MURRAY DOBBIN has been a journalist, author, broadcaster, and media analyst for more than thirty years. His books include *Preston Manning and the Reform Party*, *The Politics of Kim Campbell*, *The Myth of the Good Corporate Citizen*, and *Paul Martin: CEO for Canada?* He is a research associate and board member of the Canadian Centre for Policy Alternatives and is a past executive board member of the Council of Canadians. He authored the council's "Ziplocking North America: Can Canada Survive Continental Integration?"

SARAH DOVER is a lawyer based in Toronto, Ontario, specializing in environmental, aboriginal and criminal law. She has worked with the Trade and Environment Programme at the Sierra Club of Canada, was a policy advisor to the International and Marine Programs at World Wildlife Fund – Canada, and was the director of the Canadian Endangered Species Campaign.

JIM GRIESHABER-OTTO is a trade policy consultant based near Vancouver. He is a research associate with the Canadian Centre for Policy Alternatives and has written extensively on the impacts of international trade treaties on public services and public interest regulation. His publications include *Facing the Facts: A Guide to the GATS Debate* (with Scott Sinclair) and *Perilous Lessons: the Impact of the WTO Services Agreement (GATS) on Canada's Public Education System* (with Matthew Sanger).

RICARDO GRINSPUN teaches economics at York University in Toronto. Through his work with York's Centre for Research on Latin America and the Caribbean he has directed several international development projects on issues such as Central American integration and sustainable rural development. He is responsible for four books and numerous other publications on questions of development and international trade, hemispheric integration, and globalization in the Americas.

ANDREW JACKSON is national director of social and economic policy with the Canadian Labour Congress. He is also a research professor in the Institute of Political Economy at Carleton University, a research associate with the Canadian Centre for Policy Alternatives, and a fellow with the School of Policy Studies at Queen's University. During a leave of absence from the CLC in 2000–02, he was director of research with the Canadian

Council on Social Development. He is the author of *Work and Labour in Canada: Critical Issues*, which was published by Canadian Scholars Press in 2005.

MARC LEE is a senior economist in the BC office of the Canadian Centre for Policy Alternatives. He is the author of numerous CCPA publications, including *Competition Policy in the WTO and FTAA: A Trojan Horse for International Trade Negotiations*, *Inside the Fortress: What's Going on at the FTAA Negotiations*, and *The Future of Industrial Policy in a Globalizing World: What Are the Options?* He is also a frequent media commentator on economic policy issues. He has a master's in economics from Simon Fraser University and a bachelor's in economics from the University of Western Ontario.

BENOÎT LÉVESQUE is co-founder (with Paul R. Bélanger) and former director (1986–2001) of a research group on the social economy, the Centre de recherche sur les innovations sociales (CRISES), an interuniversity and multidisciplinary research centre that brings together some sixty researchers affiliated with seven universities. The main offices of CRISES are located on the Université du Québec à Montréal campus.

ELIZABETH MAY is an environmentalist, writer, activist, and lawyer. She was the executive director of the Sierra Club of Canada between 1989 and 2006. She was a member of the Board of the International Institute of Sustainable Development and is former vice-chair of the National Round Table on the Environment and the Economy. She is an officer of the Order of Canada and the author of five books. In August 2006 she was elected leader of the Green Party of Canada.

GARRY NEIL has worked since 2000 as the executive director of the International Network for Cultural Diversity, a global network of NGOs, artists, cultural producers, and others working to counter the adverse effects of economic globalization on world cultures. As president of Neil Craig Associates, he brings close to thirty years experience in Canada's cultural sector to clients in the arts and cultural industries. He has written extensively on the impact of trade agreements on cultural sovereignty.

LARRY PRATT is an Edmonton writer and a retired professor from the University of Alberta. He has a doctorate from the London School of Economics and is the author/co-author or editor of eight books of non-fiction, including *The Tar Sands*, *Prairie Capitalism*, and *The Last Great Forest*.

DAVID ROBINSON is associate executive director (research and advocacy) with the Canadian Association of University Teachers in Ottawa. He is also a research associate with the Canadian Centre for Policy Alternatives and a trade consultant for Education International, the global federation of teachers' unions.

MARIO SECCARECCIA is a professor of economics at the University of Ottawa and instructor at the Labour College of Canada. He holds a bachelor's and a doctorate from McGill University. He is the editor of the *International Journal of Political Economy*, and his recent publications include *Dollarization: Lessons from Europe and the Americas* (2003, with L.-P. Rochon) and *Central Banking in the Modern World: Alternative Perspectives* (2004, with M. Lavoie).

YASMINE SHAMSIE is an assistant professor in the Department of Political Science at Wilfrid Laurier University, where she teaches Latin American politics and international relations. Her research has focused on OAS peacebuilding efforts in Haiti and conflict prevention work in Guatemala. She is also a fellow at the Centre for Research on Latin America and the Caribbean (CERLAC) at York University.

STEVEN SHRYBMAN is a partner in the law firm of Sack, Goldblatt and Mitchell and practises international trade and public interest law in Ottawa. He is the former executive director of the West Coast Environmental Law Association. He has written, spoken, and published extensively on international trade and investment law, and his recent publications include *A Citizen's Guide to the World Trade Organization*, which is in its second edition.

SCOTT SINCLAIR is a Canadian trade policy specialist. He has advised several Canadian provincial and territorial governments, spending five years as a senior trade policy advisor to the Government of British Columbia. He is currently a senior research fellow with the Canadian Centre for Policy Alternatives. His numerous publications include *Putting Health First: Canadian Health Care Reform* and *Trade Treaties and Foreign Policy*, a report written with Matthew Sanger for the Romanow Commission on the Future of Health Care in Canada.

STEVEN STAPLES is the former director of Security Programs of the Polaris Institute. He is a long-time peace activist from Vancouver and has dedicated himself to exposing the links between globalization and militarism, and how globalization promotes war. He is the former chair of the International Network on Disarmament and Globalization (INDG). Recently, he has led the struggle against Canada's association with Washington's national missile defence program, and he is the author of *Missile Defence: Round One* (2006, Lorimer).

MICHELLE SWENARCHUK is counsel and executive director of the Canadian Environmental Law Association and a senior public interest lawyer practising environmental, trade, health, and international law. She advises individuals, groups, and governments, and she directs legal education and law reform initiatives in Canadian and international law. In 2004 she received the Medal of the Law Society of Upper Canada for her contributions to public policy law.

Index